T0183481

Lecture Notes in Computer Science 12260

Founding Editors

Gerhard Goos
Karlsruhe Institute of Technology, Karlsruhe, Germany

Juris Hartmanis
Cornell University, Ithaca, NY, USA

Editorial Board Members

Elisa Bertino
Purdue University, West Lafayette, IN, USA

Wen Gao
Peking University, Beijing, China

Bernhard Steffen
TU Dortmund University, Dortmund, Germany

Gerhard Woeginger
RWTH Aachen, Aachen, Germany

Moti Yung
Columbia University, New York, NY, USA

More information about this series at http://www.springer.com/series/7409

Avi Arampatzis · Evangelos Kanoulas ·
Theodora Tsikrika · Stefanos Vrochidis ·
Hideo Joho · Christina Lioma ·
Carsten Eickhoff · Aurélie Névéol ·
Linda Cappellato · Nicola Ferro (Eds.)

Experimental IR Meets Multilinguality, Multimodality, and Interaction

11th International Conference of the CLEF Association, CLEF 2020
Thessaloniki, Greece, September 22–25, 2020
Proceedings

Springer

Editors
Avi Arampatzis (iD)
Department of Electrical
and Computer Engineering
Democritus University of Thrace
Xanthi, Greece

Theodora Tsikrika
Information Technologies Institute
Centre for Research and Technology Hellas
Thessaloniki, Greece

Hideo Joho (iD)
Faculty of Library, Information
and Media Science
University of Tsukuba
Ibaraki, Japan

Carsten Eickhoff (iD)
Brown University
Providence, RI, USA

Linda Cappellato (iD)
Department of Information Engineering
University of Padova
Padua, Italy

Evangelos Kanoulas (iD)
University of Amsterdam
Amsterdam, The Netherlands

Stefanos Vrochidis (iD)
Information Technologies Institute
Centre for Research and Technology Hellas
Thessaloniki, Greece

Christina Lioma (iD)
Department of Computer Science
University of Copenhagen
Copenhagen, Denmark

Aurélie Névéol (iD)
LIMSI-CNRS
Orsay, France

University Paris-Saclay
Saint-Aubin, France

Nicola Ferro (iD)
Department of Information Engineering
University of Padova
Padua, Italy

ISSN 0302-9743   ISSN 1611-3349 (electronic)
Lecture Notes in Computer Science
ISBN 978-3-030-58218-0   ISBN 978-3-030-58219-7 (eBook)
https://doi.org/10.1007/978-3-030-58219-7

LNCS Sublibrary: SL3 – Information Systems and Applications, incl. Internet/Web, and HCI

© Springer Nature Switzerland AG 2020
This work is subject to copyright. All rights are reserved by the Publisher, whether the whole or part of the material is concerned, specifically the rights of translation, reprinting, reuse of illustrations, recitation, broadcasting, reproduction on microfilms or in any other physical way, and transmission or information storage and retrieval, electronic adaptation, computer software, or by similar or dissimilar methodology now known or hereafter developed.
The use of general descriptive names, registered names, trademarks, service marks, etc. in this publication does not imply, even in the absence of a specific statement, that such names are exempt from the relevant protective laws and regulations and therefore free for general use.
The publisher, the authors and the editors are safe to assume that the advice and information in this book are believed to be true and accurate at the date of publication. Neither the publisher nor the authors or the editors give a warranty, expressed or implied, with respect to the material contained herein or for any errors or omissions that may have been made. The publisher remains neutral with regard to jurisdictional claims in published maps and institutional affiliations.

This Springer imprint is published by the registered company Springer Nature Switzerland AG
The registered company address is: Gewerbestrasse 11, 6330 Cham, Switzerland

Preface

Since 2000, the Conference and Labs of the Evaluation Forum (CLEF) has played a leading role in stimulating research and innovation in the domain of multimodal and multilingual information access. Initially founded as the Cross-Language Evaluation Forum and running in conjunction with the European Conference on Digital Libraries (ECDL/TPDL), CLEF became a stand-alone event in 2010 combining a peer-reviewed conference with a multi-track evaluation forum. The combination of the scientific program and the track-based evaluations at the CLEF conference creates a unique platform to explore information access from different perspectives, in any modality and language.

The CLEF conference has a clear focus on experimental information retrieval (IR) as seen in evaluation forums (like CLEF Labs, TREC, NTCIR, FIRE, MediaEval, RomIP, TAC, etc.) with special attention to the challenges of multimodality, multilinguality, and interactive search ranging from unstructured, to semi-structured, and structured data. CLEF invites submissions on new insights demonstrated by the use of innovative IR evaluation tasks or in the analysis of IR test collections and evaluation measures, as well as on concrete proposals to push the boundaries of the Cranfield/TREC/CLEF paradigm.

CLEF 2020[1]. was jointly organized by the Center for Research and Technology Hellas (CERTH), the University of Amsterdam, and the Democritus University of Thrace, and it was expected to be hosted by CERTH, and in particular by the Multimedia Knowledge and Social Media Analytics Laboratory of its Information Technologies Institute, at the premises of CERTH, in Thessaloniki, Greece, during September 22–25, 2020. The outbreak of the COVID-19 pandemic in early 2020 affected the organization of CLEF 2020. The CLEF Steering Committee, along with the organizers of CLEF 2020, after detailed discussions, decided to run the conference fully virtually. The conference format remained the same as in past years, and consisted of keynotes, contributed papers, lab sessions, and poster sessions, including reports from other benchmarking initiatives from around the world. All sessions were organized and run online.

CLEF 2020 continued the initiative introduced in the 2019 edition during which, the European Conference for Information Retrieval (ECIR) and CLEF joined forces: ECIR 2020 hosted a special session dedicated to CLEF labs where lab organizers presented the major outcomes of their labs and their plans for ongoing activities, followed by a poster session to favor discussion during the conference. This was reflected in the ECIR 2020 proceedings, where CLEF lab activities and results were reported as short papers. The goal was not only to engage the ECIR community in CLEF activities but also to disseminate the research results achieved during CLEF evaluation cycles as submission of papers to ECIR.

---

[1] http://clef2020.clef-initiative.eu/

The following scholars were invited to give a keynote talk at CLEF 2020. Ellen Voorhess (NIST, USA) delivered a talk entitled "Building Reusable Test Collections" which focused on reviewing various approaches for building fair, reusable test collections with large documents sets. Yiannis Kompasiaris (CERTH-ITI, Greece) gave a speech on "Social media mining for sensing and responding to real-world trends and events", presenting the unique opportunity social media offer to discover, collect, and extract relevant information that provides useful insights in areas ranging from news to environmental and security topics, while addressing key challenges and issues, such as fighting misinformation and analyzing multimodal and multilingual information.

CLEF 2020 received a total of nine submissions, of which a total of seven papers (five long, two short) were accepted. Each submission was reviewed by three Program Committee members, and the program chairs oversaw the reviewing and follow-up discussions. Seven countries are represented in the accepted papers where many of them were a product of international collaboration. This year, researchers addressed the following important challenges in the community: a large-scale evaluation of translation effects in academic search, advancement of assessor-driven aggregation methods for efficient relevance assessments, development of a new test collection or dataset for 1) missing data detection methods in knowledge-base, 2) Russian reading comprehension, and 3) under-resourced languages such as Amharic (Ethiopia), revisiting the concept of session boundaries with fresh eyes, and development of argumentative document retrieval methods.

Like in previous editions since 2015, CLEF 2020 continued inviting CLEF lab organizers to nominate a "best of the labs" paper that was reviewed as a full paper submission to the CLEF 2020 conference according to the same review criteria and PC. Seven full papers were accepted for this "best of the labs" section.

The conference integrated a series of workshops presenting the results of lab-based comparative evaluations. CLEF 2020 was the 11th year of the CLEF conference and the 21st year of the CLEF initiative as a forum for IR evaluation. 15 lab proposals were received and evaluated in peer review based on their innovation potential and the quality of the resources created. The 12 selected labs represented scientific challenges based on new data sets and real-world problems in multimodal and multilingual information access. These data sets provide unique opportunities for scientists to explore collections, to develop solutions for these problems, to receive feedback on the performance of their solutions, and to discuss the issues with peers at the workshops.

In addition to these workshops, the labs reported results of their year-long activities in overview talks and lab sessions. Overview papers describing each of the labs are provided in this volume. The full details for each lab are contained in a separate publication, the Working Notes[2].

The 12 labs running as part of CLEF 2020 comprised new labs (ARQMath, CheMU, HIPE, Lilas, and Touché) as well as seasoned labs that offered previous editions at CLEF (CheckThat!, CLEF eHealth, eRisk, ImageCLEF, LifeCLEF, and PAN) or in other platforms (BioASQ). The following labs were offered:

---

[2] Cappellato, L., Eickhoff, C., Ferro, N., and Névéol, A., editors (2020). *CLEF 2020 Working Notes*. CEUR Workshop Proceedings (CEUR-WS.org), ISSN 1613-0073.

ARQMath: Answer Retrieval for Mathematical Questions[3] considers the problem of finding answers to new mathematical questions among posted answers on the community question answering site Math Stack Exchange. The goals of the lab are to develop methods for mathematical IR based on both text and formula analysis.

BioASQ[4] challenges researchers with large-scale biomedical semantic indexing and question answering (QA). The challenges include tasks relevant to hierarchical text classification, machine learning, IR, QA from texts and structured data, multi-document summarization, and many other areas. The aim of the BioASQ workshop is to push the research frontier towards systems that use the diverse and voluminous information available online to respond directly to the information needs of biomedical scientists.

ChEMU: Information Extraction from Chemical Patents[5] proposes two key information extraction tasks over chemical reactions from patents. Task 1 aims to identify chemical compounds and their specific types, i.e. to assign the label of a chemical compound according to the role which it plays within a chemical reaction. Task 2 requires identification of event trigger words (e.g. "added" and "stirred") which all have the same type of "EVENT_TRIGGER", and then determination of the chemical entity arguments of these events.

CheckThat!: Identification and Verification of Political Claims[6] aims to foster the development of technology capable of both spotting and verifying check-worthy claims in political debates in English, Arabic, and Italian. The concrete tasks were to assess the check worthiness of a claim in a tweet, check if a (similar) claim has been previously verified, retrieve evidence to fact-check a claim, and verify the factuality of a claim.

CLEF eHealth[7] aims to support the development of techniques to aid laypeople, clinicians, and policy-makers in easily retrieving and making sense of medical content to support their decision making. The goals of the lab are to develop processing methods and resources in a multilingual setting to enrich difficult-to-understand eHealth texts and provide valuable documentation.

eRisk: Early Risk Prediction on the Internet[8] explores challenges of evaluation methodology, effectiveness metrics, and other processes related to early risk detection. Early detection technologies can be employed in different areas, particularly those related to health and safety. The 2020 edition of the lab focused on texts written on social media for the early detection of signs of self-harm and depression.

HIPE: Named Entity Processing on Historical Newspapers[9] aims at fostering named entity recognition on heterogeneous, historical, and noisy inputs. The goals of the lab are to strengthen the robustness of existing approaches on non-standard input; to enable performance comparison of named entity processing on historical texts;

---

[3] https://www.cs.rit.edu/dprl/ARQMath/.

[4] http://www.bioasq.org/workshop2020.

[5] http://chemu.eng.unimelb.edu.au/.

[6] https://sites.google.com/view/clef2020-checkthat.

[7] http://clef-ehealth.org/.

[8] http://erisk.irlab.org/.

[9] https://impresso.github.io/CLEF-HIPE-2020/.

and, in the long run, to foster efficient semantic indexing of historical documents in order to support scholarship on digital cultural heritage collections.

ImageCLEF: Multimedia Retrieval[10] provides an evaluation forum for visual media analysis, indexing, classification/learning, and retrieval in medical, nature, security, and lifelogging applications with a focus on multimodal data, so data from a variety of sources and media.

LifeCLEF: Biodiversity Identification and Prediction[11] aims at boosting research on the identification and prediction of living organisms in order to solve the taxonomic gap and improve our knowledge of biodiversity. Through its biodiversity informatics related challenges, LifeCLEF is intended to push the boundaries of the state of the art in several research directions at the frontier of multimedia IR, machine learning, and knowledge engineering.

Lilas: Living Labs for Academic Search[12] aims to bring together researchers interested in the online evaluation of academic search systems. The long term goal is to foster knowledge on improving the search for academic resources like literature, research data, and the interlinking between these resources in fields from the Life Sciences and the Social Sciences. The immediate goal of this lab is to develop ideas, best practices, and guidelines for a full online evaluation campaign at CLEF 2021.

PAN: Digital Text Forensics and Stylometry[13] is a networking initiative for the digital text forensics, where researchers and practitioners study technologies that analyze texts with regard to originality, authorship, and trustworthiness. PAN provides evaluation resources consisting of large-scale corpora, performance measures, and web services that allow for meaningful evaluations. The main goal is to provide for sustainable and reproducible evaluations, to get a clear view of the capabilities of state-of-the-art algorithms.

Touché: Argument Retrieval[14] is the first shared task on the topic of argument retrieval. Decision-making processes, be it at the societal or at the personal level, eventually come to a point where one side will challenge the other with a why-question, which is a prompt to justify one's stance. Thus, technologies for argument mining and argumentation processing are maturing at a rapid pace, giving rise for the first time to argument retrieval.

As a group, the 71 lab organizers were based in 14 countries, with Germany and France leading the distribution. Despite CLEF's traditionally Europe-based audience, 18 (25.4%) organizers were affiliated with international institutions outside of Europe. The gender distribution was biased towards 81.3% male organizers.

The success of CLEF 2020 would not have been possible without the huge effort of several people and organizations, including the CLEF Association[15], the Program Committee, the Lab Organizing Committee, the reviewers, and the many students and

---

[10] https://www.imageclef.org/2019.

[11] http://www.lifeclef.org/.

[12] https://clef-lilas.github.io/.

[13] http://pan.webis.de/.

[14] https://events.webis.de/touche-20/.

[15] http://www.clef-initiative.eu/association.

volunteers who contributed. Finally, we thank the generous support of ACM SIGIR and BCS IRSG, both of which provided general funding support.

July 2020

Avi Arampatzis
Evangelos Kanoulas
Theodora Tsikrika
Stefanos Vrochidis
Hideo Joho
Christina Lioma
Aurélie Névéol
Carsten Eickhoff
Linda Cappellato
Nicola Ferro

Organization

CLEF 2020, Conference and Labs of the Evaluation Forum – Experimental IR meets Multilingualism, Multimodality, and Interaction, was hosted (online) by the Multimedia Knowledge and Social Media Analytics Laboratory (MKLab) of the Information Technologies Institute (ITI) of the Center for Research and Technology Hellas (CERTH), Thessaloniki, Greece.

General Chairs

Evangelos Kanoulas	University of Amsterdam, The Netherlands
Theodora Tsikrika	Information Technologies Institute, CERTH, Greece
Stefanos Vrochidis	Information Technologies Institute, CERTH, Greece
Avi Arampatzis	Democritus University of Thrace, Greece

Program Chairs

Hideo Joho	University of Tsukuba, Japan
Christina Lioma	University of Copenhagen, Denmark

Lab Chairs

Aurélie Névéol	Université Paris Saclay, CNRS, LIMSI, France
Carsten Eickhoff	Brown University, USA

Lab Mentorship Chair

Lorraine Goeuriot	Université Grenoble Alpes, France

Proceedings Chairs

Linda Cappellato	University of Padua, Italy
Nicola Ferro	University of Padua, Italy

Local Organization

Vivi Ntrigkogia	Information Technologies Institute, CERTH, Greece

CLEF Steering Committee

Steering Committee Chair

Nicola Ferro   University of Padua, Italy

Deputy Steering Committee Chair for the Conference

Paolo Rosso   Universitat Politècnica de València, Spain

Deputy Steering Committee Chair for the Evaluation Labs

Martin Braschler   Zurich University of Applied Sciences, Switzerland

Members

Khalid Choukri   Evaluations and Language resources Distribution
                                Agency (ELDA), France
Paul Clough   University of Sheffield, UK
Fabio Crestani   Università della Svizzera Italiana, Switzerland
Norbert Fuhr   University of Duisburg-Essen, Germany
Lorraine Goeuriot   Université Grenoble Alpes, France
Julio Gonzalo   National Distance Education University (UNED),
                                Spain
Donna Harman   National Institute for Standards and Technology
                                (NIST), USA
Djoerd Hiemstra   University of Twente, The Netherlands
Evangelos Kanoulas   University of Amsterdam, The Netherlands
Birger Larsen   University of Aalborg, Denmark
David E. Losada   Universidade de Santiago de Compostela, Spain
Mihai Lupu   Vienna University of Technology, Austria
Josiane Mothe   IRIT, Université de Toulouse, France
Henning Müller   University of Applied Sciences Western Switzerland
                                (HES-SO), Switzerland
Jian-Yun Nie   Université de Montréal, Canada
Eric SanJuan   University of Avignon, France
Giuseppe Santucci   Sapienza University of Rome, Italy
Jacques Savoy   University of Neuchêtel, Switzerland
Laure Soulier   Pierre and Marie Curie University (Paris 6), France
Christa Womser-Hacker   University of Hildesheim, Germany

Past Members

Jaana Kekäläinen   University of Tampere, Finland
Séamus Lawless   Trinity College Dublin, Ireland
Carol Peters   ISTI, National Council of Research (CNR), Italy
                                (Steering Committee Chair 2000–2009)
Emanuele Pianta   Centre for the Evaluation of Language and
                                Communication Technologies (CELCT), Italy
Maarten de Rijke   University of Amsterdam, The Netherlands
Alan Smeaton   Dublin City University, Ireland

Sponsors

 Information Retrieval
Specialist Group

 Special Interest Group
on Information Retrieval

Contents

CLEF 2020 Lab Overviews

Full Papers

SberQuAD – Russian Reading Comprehension Dataset: Description and Analysis

Pavel Efimov[1], Andrey Chertok[2], Leonid Boytsov[3],
and Pavel Braslavski[4,5](✉) (iD)

[1] St. Petersburg State University, St. Petersburg, Russia
pavel.vl.efimov@gmail.com
[2] Sberbank, Moscow, Russia
achertok@sberbank.ru
[3] Pittsburgh, PA, USA
[4] Ural Federal University, Yekaterinburg, Russia
pbras@yandex.ru
[5] JetBrains Research, St. Petersburg, Russia

Abstract. The paper presents SberQuAD – a large Russian reading comprehension (RC) dataset created similarly to English SQuAD. SberQuAD contains about 50K question-paragraph-answer triples and is seven times larger compared to the next competitor. We provide its description, thorough analysis, and baseline experimental results. We scrutinized various aspects of the dataset that can have impact on the task performance: question/paragraph similarity, misspellings in questions, answer structure, and question types. We applied five popular RC models to SberQuAD and analyzed their performance. We believe our work makes an important contribution to research in multilingual question answering.

Keywords: Reading comprehension · Evaluation · Russian language resources · Multilingual question answering

1 Introduction

Automatic Question Answering (QA) is a long-standing important problem, which can be broadly described as building a system that can answer questions in a natural language. The modern history of QA starts from TREC challenges organized by NIST in 2000s [7] and extended by CLEF to a multilingual setting [10]. Reading comprehension (RC) is a subtask of QA, where the system needs to answer questions for a given document. This task has recently become quite popular with the introduction of an English large-scale Stanford Question Answering Dataset (SQuAD) [17].

P. Efimov—Work done as an intern at JetBrains Research.

© Springer Nature Switzerland AG 2020
A. Arampatzis et al. (Eds.): CLEF 2020, LNCS 12260, pp. 3–15, 2020.
https://doi.org/10.1007/978-3-030-58219-7_1

In this paper, we present a large Russian RC dataset, which was created for a data science competition organized by Sberbank (hence SberQuAD) and is freely available for public.[1] The paper focuses on a post hoc analysis of the dataset properties and reports several baselines results. Given the importance of the RC task and scarcity of non-English resources, we believe it is an important contribution to research and evaluation in multilingual QA.

Table 1. Aggregate statistics of SQuAD and existing Russian RC datasets. LCMS stands for the longest contiguous matching subsequence.

	SberQuAD	SQuAD 1.1 train/dev	XQuAD (ru)	TyDi QA (ru) train/dev
# questions	50,364	87,599/10,570	1,190	6,490/812
# unique paragraphs	9,080	18,896/2,067	240	6,490/812
Number of tokens				
Avg. paragraph length	101.7	116.6/122.8	112.9	79.5/73.1
Avg. question length	8.7	10.1/10.2	8.6	6.4/6.5
Avg. answer length	3.7	3.16/2.9	2.9	3.9/3.9
Avg. answer position	40.5	50.9/52.9	48.4	25.9/25.6
Number of characters				
Avg. paragraph length	753.9	735.8/774.3	850.3	585.4/539.3
Avg. question length	64.4	59.6/60.0	64.9	44.8/47.1
Avg. answer length	25.9	20.2/18.7	21.4	25.7/26.5
Avg. answer position	305.2	319.9/330.5	364.5	190.7/188.9
Question-paragraph LCMS	32.7	19.5/19.8	20.1	12.4/14.9

2   Related Work

SQuAD [17] contains more than 100K questions posed to paragraphs from popular Wikipedia articles. Questions were generated by crowd workers. An answer to each question should be a valid and relevant paragraph span. Wide adoption of SQuAD led to emergence of many RC datasets. TriviaQA [12] consists of 96K trivia game questions and answers found online accompanied by answer-bearing documents. Natural Questions dataset [14] is approximately three times larger than SQuAD. In that, unlike SQuAD, questions are sampled from Google search log rather than generated by crowd workers. MS MARCO [2] contains 1M questions from a Bing search log along with free-form answers. For both MS MARCO and Natural Questions answers are produced by in-house annotators. QuAC [4] and CoQA [18] contain questions and answers in information-seeking dialogues. For a more detailed discussion we address the reader to a recent survey [23].

There are several monolingual non-English RC datasets, e.g. for Chinese [11] and French [9]. Recently, Artetxe et al. experimented with cross-language transfer learning and prepared XQuAD dataset containing 240 paragraphs and 1,190

---

[1] https://github.com/sberbank-ai/data-science-journey-2017.

Q&A pairs from SQuAD v1.1 translated into 10 languages, including Russian [1]. MLQA [15] covers seven languages with over 12K English Q&A instances and 5K in each other languages. Yet, the Russian data is missing. TyDi QA [6] covers 11 typologically diverse languages with over 200K Q&A instances. However, there are only about 7K Russian items. Two latter papers [6,15] provide a good overview of non-English RC resources. Statistics of Russian RC datasets are summarized in Table 1.

P6418 The term "computer science" appears in a <u>1959</u> article in Communications of the ACM, in which <u>Louis Fein</u> argues for the creation of a Graduate School in Computer Science ... Louis Fein's efforts, and those of others such as numerical analyst George Forsythe, were rewarded: universities went on to create such departments, starting with <u>Purdue</u> in 1962.

Q11870 When did the term "computer science" appear?

Q28900 Who was the first to use this term?

Q30330 Starting with <u>wich</u> university were computer science programs created?

Fig. 1. A translated sample SberQuAD entry: answers are underlined and colored. The word **which** in *Q30330* is misspelled on purpose to reflect the fact that the original has a misspelling.

3 Dataset

SberQuAD contains 50,364 paragraph–question–answer triples and was created in a similar fashion to SQuAD. First, Wikipedia pages were selected, split into paragraphs, and paragraphs presented to crowd workers. For each paragraph, a Russian native speaking crowd worker had to come up with questions that can be answered using solely the content of the paragraph. In that, an answer must have been a paragraph span, i.e., a contiguous sequence of paragraph words. The tasks were posted on Toloka crowdsourcing platform.[2] SberQuAD has always only one correct answer span, whereas SQuAD can have multiple answer variants (1.7 *different* answers for each question on the development set).

Examples and Basic Statistics. Figure 1 shows a translated sample SberQuAD paragraph with three questions: Gold-truth answers are underlined in text. Generally, the format of the question and the answers mimics that of SQuAD. Note, however, the following peculiarities: Question *Q30330* contains a spelling error; Question *Q28900* references prior question *Q11870* and cannot, thus, be answered on its own (likely both questions were created by the same crowd worker).

Basic dataset statistics is summarized in Table 1: SberQuAD has about twice as fewer questions compared to SQuAD. However, the number of Russian questions in SberQuAD is substantially higher compared to XQuAD and TyDi QA.

---

[2] https://toloka.yandex.com.

The average lengths of paragraphs, questions, and answers are similar across three datasets – SberQuAD, SQuAD, and XQuAD. TyDi QA stands out due to a different approach to data collection: Annotators generated questions in response to a non-restrictive prompt, then a top-ranked Wikipedia article for each question is retrieved. Finally, annotators were presented with articles split into paragraphs and had to choose a relevant paragraph and an answer within. This annotation scheme led to shorter questions and paragraphs, and more importantly – to a lower question/paragraph overlap. In SberQuAD, there are 275 questions (0.55%) having at least 200 characters and 374 answers (0.74%) that are longer than 100 characters. Anecdotally, very long answers and very short questions are frequently errors. For example, for question *Q61603* the answer field contains a copy of the whole paragraph, while question *Q76754* consists of a single word 'thermodynamics'.

For experiments described in this paper, we used the SberQuAD split into a training and testing sets (45,328 and 5,036 items, respectively) made by DeepPavlov team.[3]

Analysis of Questions. Most questions in the dataset start with either a question word or preposition: ten most common starting words are *что* (*what*), *в* (*in*), *как* (*how*), *кто* (*who*), *какие* (*what*$_{adj}$), *когда* (*when*), *какой* (*what*$_{adj}$), *где* (*where*), *сколько* (*how many*), *на* (*on*). These starting words correspond to 62.4% of all questions. In about 4% of the cases, an interrogative word is not among the first three words of the question, though. Manual inspection showed that in most cases these entries are declarative statements, sometimes followed by a question mark, e.g. *Q15968 'famous Belgian poets?'*, or ungrammatical questions.

While manually examining the dataset, we encountered quite a few misspelled questions. To estimate the proportion of questions with misspellings, we verified all questions using Yandex spellchecking API.[4] The automatic speller identified 2,646 and 287 misspelled questions in training and testing sets, respectively. We also found 385 and 51 questions in training and testing sets, respectively, containing Russian interrogative particle *ли* (*whether/if*). This form implies a yes/no question, which is generally not possible to answer in the RC setting by selecting a valid and relevant paragraph phrase. For this reason, most answers for these yes/no questions are fragments supporting or refuting the question statement. In addition, we found 15 answers in the training set, where the correct answer 'yes' (Russian *да*) can be found as a paragraph word substring, but not as a valid/relevant phrase. Thus, we estimate that in the testing set, 5.7% of the questions have misspellings and 1% of questions cannot be answered using a paragraph.

Analysis of Answers. Following [17], we analyzed answers presented in the dataset by their type. To this end, we employed a NER tool from DeepPavlov

---

[3] http://docs.deeppavlov.ai/en/master/features/models/squad.html.
[4] https://yandex.ru/dev/speller/ (in Russian).

library.[5] In our analysis, we focus on the following NEs: DATE, NUMBER, PERSON, LOCATION, and ORGANIZATION. In total, almost 43% of answers in testing set contain NEs, while about 14% are exact NEs. Obtained information is used to evaluate models' performance on different answer types (see Tables 3 and 4). We complemented our analysis of answers with syntactic parsing. To this end we applied the rule-based constituency parser AOT[6] to answers without detected NEs. AOT parser supports a long list of phrase types (57 in total), we grouped them into conventional high-level types, which are shown in Table 5.[7] Not surprisingly, noun phrases are most frequent answer types (24%), followed by prepositional phrases (10.5%). Verb phrases represent a non-negligible share of answers (7.1%), which is quite different from a traditional QA setting where answers are predominantly noun phrases [16].

Question/Paragraph Similarity. We further estimate similarity between questions and paragraph sentences containing the answer: The more similar is the question to its answer's context, the simpler is the task of locating the answer. In contrast to SQuAD analysis [17] we refrain from syntactic parsing and rely on simpler approaches. First, we compared questions with complete paragraphs. To this end, we calculated the length of the longest contiguous matching subsequence (LCMS) between a question and a paragraph using the `difflib` library.[8] The last row in Table 1 shows that despite similar paragraph and question lengths in both SQuAD and SberQuAD, the SberQuAD questions are more similar to the paragraph text. Second, we estimated similarity between a question and the sentence containing the answer. First, we applied `DeepPavlov` tokenizer[9] to split the dataset into sentences. Subsequently, we lemmatized the data using `mystem`[10] and calculated the Jaccard coefficient between a question and the sentence containing the answer. The mean value of the Jaccard coefficient is 0.28 (median is 0.23). Our analysis shows that there is a substantial lexical overlap between questions and paragraph sentences containing the answer, which may indicate a heavier use of the copy-and-paste approach by crowd workers recruited for SberQuAD creation.[11]

---

[5] The multilingual BERT model is trained on English OntoNotes corpus and transferred to Russian, see http://docs.deeppavlov.ai/en/master/features/models/ner.html.

[6] http://aot.ru.

[7] Table 5 provides data for the testing set, but the distribution for the training set is quite similar.

[8] https://docs.python.org/3/library/difflib.html.

[9] https://github.com/deepmipt/ru_sentence_tokenizer.

[10] https://yandex.ru/dev/mystem/ (in Russian).

[11] Note that in the interface for crowdsourcing SQuAD questions, prompts at each screen reminded the workers to formulate questions in their own words; in addition, the copy-paste functionality for the paragraph was purposefully disabled.

4   Employed Models

We applied the following models to SberQuAD: 1) two baselines provided by the competition organizers; 2) four pre-BERT models that showed good performance on SQuAD and were used in a study similar to ours [21] – BiDAF, DocQA, DrQA, and R-Net; and 3) BERT model provided by the `DeepPavlov` library.

Preprocessing and Training. We tokenized text using `spaCy`.[12] To initialize the embedding layer for BiDAF, DocQA, DrQA, and R-Net we use Russian case-sensitive `fastText` embeddings trained on Common Crawl and Wikipedia.[13] This initialization is used for both questions and paragraphs. For BiDAF and DocQA about 10% of answer strings in both training and testing sets require a correction of positions, which can be nearly always achieved automatically by ignoring punctuation (12 answers required a manual intervention). Models were trained on GPU nVidia Tesla V100 16Gb with default implementation settings.

Baselines. As a part of the competition two baselines were made available.[14] *Simple Baseline:* The model returns a sentence with the maximum word overlap with the question. *ML baseline* generates features for all word spans in the sentence returned by the *simple baseline.* The feature set includes TF-IDF scores, span length, distance to the beginning/end of the sentence, as well as POS tags. The model uses gradient boosting to predict F1 score. At the testing stage the model selects a candidate span with maximum predicted score.

Gated Self-matching Networks (R-Net): This model, proposed by Wang et al. [22], is a multi-layer end-to-end neural network that uses a gated attention mechanism to give different levels of importance to different paragraph parts. It also uses self-matching attention for the context to aggregate evidence from the entire paragraph to refine the query-aware context representation. We use a model implementation by HKUST.[15] To increase efficiency, the implementation adopts scaled multiplicative attention instead of additive attention and uses variational dropout.

Bi-directional Attention Flow (BiDAF): The model proposed by Seo et al. [20] takes inputs of different granularity (character, word and phrase) to obtain a query-aware context representation without previous summarization using memory-less context-to-query (C2Q) and query-to-context (Q2C) attention. We use original implementation by AI2.[16]

Multi-paragraph Reading Comprehension (DocQA): This model, proposed by Clark and Gardner [5], aims to answer questions based on entire documents

---

[12] https://github.com/buriy/spacy-ru.

[13] https://fasttext.cc/docs/en/crawl-vectors.html.

[14] https://github.com/sberbank-ai/data-science-journey-2017/tree/master/problem_B/.

[15] https://github.com/HKUST-KnowComp/R-Net.

[16] https://github.com/allenai/bi-att-flow.

(multiple paragraphs). If considering the given paragraph as the document, it also shows good results on SQuAD. It uses the bi-directional attention mechanism from the BiDAF and a layer of residual self-attention. We also use original implementation by AI2.[17]

Document Reader (DrQA): This model proposed by Chen et al. [3] is part of the system for answering open-domain factoid questions using Wikipedia. The Document Reader component performs well on SQuAD (skipping the document retrieval stage). The model has paragraph and question encoding layers with RNNs and an output layer. The paragraph encoding passes as input to RNN a sequence of feature vectors derived from tokens: word embedding, exact match with question word, POS/NER/TF and aligned question embedding. The implementation is developed by Facebook Research.[18]

Bidirectional Encoder Representations from Transformers (BERT): Pre-trained BERT models achieved superior performance is a variety of downstream NLP tasks, including RC [8]. The Russian QA model is obtained by a transfer from the multilingual BERT (mBERT) with subsequent fine-tuning on the Russian Wikipedia and SberQuAD [13].[19]

Evaluation. Similar to SQuAD, SberQuAD evaluation employs two metrics to assess model performance – 1) the percentage of system's answers that exactly match (EM) any of the gold standard answers and 2) the maximum overlap between the system response and ground truth answer at the token level expressed via F1 (averaged over all questions). Both metrics ignore punctuation and capitalization.

5   Analysis of Model Performance

Main experimental results are shown in Table 2. It can be seen that all the models perform worse on the Russian dataset than on SQuAD. In that, there is a bigger difference in exact matching scores compared to F1. For example, for BERT the F1 score drops from 91.8 to 84.8 whereas the exact match score drops from 85.1 to 66.6. The relative performance of the models is consistent for both datasets, although there is a greater variability among four neural "pre-BERT" models. One explanation for lower scores is that

Table 2. Model performance on SQuAD and SberQuAD; SQuAD part shows single-model scores on test set taken from respective papers.

Model	SberQuAD		SQuAD	
	EM	F1	EM	F1
Simple baseline	0.3	25.0	–	–
ML baseline	3.7	31.5	–	–
BiDAF [20]	51.7	72.2	68.0	77.3
DrQA [3]	54.9	75.0	70.0	79.0
R-Net [22]	58.6	77.8	71.3	79.7
DocQA [5]	59.6	79.5	72.1	81.1
BERT [8]	66.6	84.8	85.1	91.8

[17] https://github.com/allenai/document-qa.
[18] https://github.com/facebookresearch/DrQA.
[19] http://docs.deeppavlov.ai/en/master/features/models/squad.html.

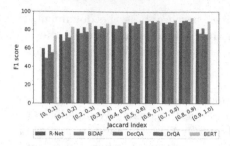

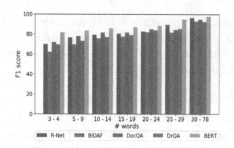

Fig. 2. Model performance depending on Jaccard similarity between a question and the sentence containing an answer.

Fig. 3. Model performance depending on question length (# of words).

SberQuAD has always only one correct answer. Furthermore, SberQuAD contains many fewer answers that are named entities than SQuAD (13.8% vs. 52.4%), which—as we discuss below—maybe another reason for lower scores. Another plausible reason is a poorer quality of annotations: We have found a number of deficiencies including but not limited to misspellings in questions and answers.

Figure 2 shows the relationship between the F1 score and the question-answer similarity expressed as the Jaccard coefficient. Note that 64% of question–sentence pairs fall into first three bins. As expected, a higher value of the Jaccard coefficient corresponds to higher F1 scores (with the exception of 14 questions where Jaccard is above 0.9).[20] Furthermore, in the case of the high similarity there is only a small difference among model performance. These observations support the hypothesis that it is easier to answer questions when there is a substantial lexical overlap between a question and a paragraph sentence containing the answer.

Longer questions are easier to answer too: the F1 score increases nearly monotonically with the question length, see Fig. 3. Presumably, longer questions provide more context for identifying correct answers. In contrast, dependency on the answer length is not monotonic: the F1 score first increases and achieves the maximum for 2–4 words. A one-word ground truth constitutes a harder task: missing a single correct word results in a null F1 score, whereas returning a two-word answer containing the single correct word results in only $F1 = 0.67$. F1 score also decreases substantially for answers above average length. It can be explained by the fact that models are trained on the dataset where shorter answers prevail, see Table 1. Models' average-length answers get low scores in case of longer ground truth. For example, a 4-word answer fully overlapping with a 8-word ground truth answer gets again only $F1 = 0.67$.

---

[20] Among these 14 questions the majority are long sentences from the paragraph with a single word (answer) substituted by a question word; there is an exact copy with just a question mark at the end; one question has the answer erroneously attached after the very question.

Table 3. Model performance (F1) on answers containing named entities.

NE	% test	R-Net	BiDAF	DocQA	DrQA	BERT
Date	12.2%	88.0	86.6	90.0	88.9	91.3
Number	9.6%	73.1	69.1	75.5	72.5	80.4
Person	8.8%	78.3	73.1	81.0	77.7	86.6
Location	7.6%	79.8	75.7	81.1	77.8	85.8
Organization	4.1%	79.0	77.3	82.3	78.3	88.2
Other NE	2.1%	72.7	59.4	73.6	64.7	80.9
Any NE	42.7%	80.3	76.4	82.6	79.7	87.0
Test set		77.8	72.2	79.5	75.0	84.8

Table 4. Model performance (F1) on answers matching NER tags.

NE	% test	R-Net	BiDAF	DocQA	DrQA	BERT
Date	2.2%	87.1	87.3	90.8	87.5	95.0
Number	3.3%	78.2	72.4	80.1	77.7	90.2
Person	4.2%	83.2	74.0	85.1	82.9	91.4
Location	1.7%	78.3	72.8	82.1	77.9	88.6
Organization	1.5%	80.7	76.5	81.6	79.2	91.8
Other NE	0.9%	80.9	54.9	78.1	66.4	88.9
Any NE	13.8%	81.6	74.5	83.6	80.2	91.2
Test set		77.8	72.2	79.5	75.0	84.8

Following our analysis of the dataset, we break down model scores by the answer types. Tables 3 and 4 summarize performance of the models depending on the answers containing named entities of different types. Table 3 represents answers that contain at least one NE, but which are not necessarily NEs themselves (42.7% in the test set). Table 4 represents answers that are NEs (13.8% in test). A common trend for all models is that F1 scores for answers mentioning dates, persons, locations, and organizations are higher than average. NUMBER is an exception in this regard, probably due to a high variability of contexts might contain numerals both as digits and words. Answers containing *other NEs* also show degraded performance – probably, again due to their higher diversity and lower counts. The scores are significantly higher when an answer is exactly a NE. This is in line with previous studies that showed that answers containing NEs are easier to answer, see for example [19].

For about 48% of the answers in the testing set that do not contain NEs we were able to derive their syntactic phrase type, see Table 5. Among them, non-factoid verb phrases stand out as most difficult ones— all models perform worse

Table 5. Model performance (F1) on answers not containing NEs by constituent type (NP – noun phrase, PP – prepositional phrase, VP – verb phrase, ADJP – adjective phrase, ADVP – adverb phrase, non-R – words in non-Russian characters; None – not recognized).

Type	% test	R-Net	BiDAF	DocQA	DrQA	BERT
NP	24.0	77.5	70.3	78.2	73.5	84.5
PP	10.5	83.1	78.6	84.9	81.4	89.1
VP	7.1	61.9	54.0	62.7	55.5	71.6
ADJP	5.9	73.0	65.3	75.5	67.2	80.5
ADVP	0.3	67.9	45.3	70.7	51.2	76.6
non-R	0.3	91.7	88.2	98.2	92.9	95.1
None	9.1	75.7	69.0	77.1	70.1	83.0
Test set		77.8	72.2	79.5	75.0	84.8

Table 6. Model performance (F1) on misspelled (upper part) and yes/no (lower part) questions.

	% test	R-Net	BiDAF	DocQA	DrQA	BERT
w/typos	5.7	74.1	66.7	77.5	67.5	81.1
correct	94.3	77.1	72.5	79.6	75.4	85.0
w/ли	1.0	66.6	53.7	71.0	57.5	73.3
other	99.0	77.9	72.4	79.6	75.2	84.9
Test set		77.8	72.2	79.5	75.0	84.8

on such questions.[21] In contrast, answers expressed as prepositional phrases are easier to answer compared to both noun and verb phrases. Noun phrases—most common syntactic units among answers—are second-easiest structure among others to answer. However, F1 scores for noun phrases are lower than average.

The models behave remarkably differently on questions with and without detected misspellings, see Table 6. DrQA seems to be most sensible to misspellings: The difference in F1 is almost 8% (scores are lower for misspelled questions). DocQA has most stable behavior: The difference in F1 scores is about 2%.

Questions with interrogative ли-particle represent around 1% in the whole dataset. Although score averages for such small sets are not very reliable, the decrease in performance on these questions is quite sharp and consistent for all models: It ranges from 8.5% in F1 points for DocQA to 18.7% for BiDAF, see Table 6. We hypothesize that these questions are substantially different from other questions and are poorly represented in the training set.

---

[21] Adverbial phrases appears to be even harder, but they are too few to make reliable conclusions.

Finally, we sampled 100 questions where all models achieved zero F1 score (i.e., they returned a span with no overlap with a ground truth answer). We manually grouped the sampled questions into the following categories (number of questions in each category in parentheses; questions can be assigned to more than one category):

- An entire paragraph or its significant part can be seen as an answer to a *broad/general question* (12).
- An answer is *incomplete* (29), because it contains only a part of an acceptable longer answer. For example for *Q31929 'Who did notice an enemy airplane?'* only the word *pilots* is marked as ground truth in the context: *On July 15, during a reconnaissance east to Zolotaya Lipa, pilots of the 2nd Siberian Corps Air Squadron Lieutenant Pokrovsky and Cornet Plonsky noticed an enemy airplane.*
- *Vague questions* (19) are related to the corresponding paragraph but seem to be a result of a misinterpretation of the context by a crowd worker. For example, in *Q70465 'What are the disadvantages of TNT comparing to dynamite and other explosives?'* the ground truth answer *'a detonator needs to be used'* is not mentioned as a disadvantage in the paragraph. A couple of these questions use paronyms of concepts mentioned in the paragraph. For example, *Q46229* asks about *'discrete policy'*, while the paragraph mentions *'discretionary policy'*.
- *No answer in the paragraph* (3) and *incorrect answer* (14) constitute more straightforward error cases.
- Some questions require *reasoning* (10) and *co-reference resolution* (12).
- A small fraction of questions uses *synonyms and paraphrases* (3) that are not directly borrowed from the paragraph.
- A relatively large fraction of 'difficult' questions contains *misspellings* (6) and imply *yes/no* (3) answers.

One can see from the list that most potential causes of degraded performance can be attributed to poor data quality: Only 25% of cases can be explained by a need to deal with linguistic phenomena such as co-reference resolution, reasoning, and paraphrase detection.

6   Conclusions

We presented a large Russian reading comprehension dataset SberQuAD, which is nearly seven times larger compared to the next competitor. The SberQuAD was created similarly to SQuAD, but as our analysis shows, SberQuAD has a higher lexical overlap between questions and sentences with answers; not all questions are well-formed. At the same time, SberQuAD has a lower proportion of named entities as answers and a non-negligible share of answers that are verb phrases.

We applied five RC models to SberQuAD. Expectantly, a BERT-based model outperforms its predecessors. All models perform better on questions with higher overlap with paragraph text, on longer questions, on average-length answers, as well as when an answer contains a named entity. Despite the similarities between SQuAD and SberQuAD, all the models perform worse on Russian dataset than on its English counterpart, which can be attributed to smaller training set, having only a single answer variant in SberQuAD (as opposed to SQuAD, which has at least two variants) and fewer answers that are named entities. Furthermore, SberQuAD annotations might have been of poorer quality, but it is hard to quantify. These observations can be used to guide a creation of more difficult RC data sets. We believe that our work constitutes an important contribution to research in multilingual QA and will lead to a wider adoption of SberQuAD by the community.

Acknowledgments. We thank Peter Romov, Vladimir Suvorov, and Ekaterina Artemova (Chernyak) for providing us with details about SberQuAD preparation. We also thank Natasha Murashkina for initial data processing. PB acknowledges support by Ural Mathematical Center under agreement No. 075-02-2020-1537/1 with the Ministry of Science and Higher Education of the Russian Federation.

References

1. Artetxe, M., Ruder, S., Yogatama, D.: On the cross-lingual transferability of monolingual representations. arXiv preprint arXiv:1910.11856 (2019)
2. Bajaj, P., et al.: MS MARCO: a human generated machine reading comprehension dataset. arXiv preprint arXiv:1611.09268 (2016)
3. Chen, D., Fisch, A., Weston, J., Bordes, A.: Reading Wikipedia to answer open-domain questions. arXiv preprint arXiv:1704.00051 (2017)
4. Choi, E., et al.: QuAC: question answering in context. In: EMNLP, pp. 2174–2184 (2018)
5. Clark, C., Gardner, M.: Simple and effective multi-paragraph reading comprehension. arXiv preprint arXiv:1710.10723 (2017)
6. Clark, J.H., et al.: TyDi QA: a benchmark for information-seeking question answering in typologically diverse languages. arXiv preprint arXiv:2003.05002 (2020)
7. Dang, H.T., Kelly, D., Lin, J.J.: Overview of the TREC 2007 question answering track. In: Proceedings of the 16th TREC (2007)
8. Devlin, J., et al.: BERT: pre-training of deep bidirectional transformers for language understanding. arXiv preprint arXiv:1810.04805 (2018)
9. d'Hoffschmidt, M., Vidal, M., Belblidia, W., Brendlé, T.: FQuAD: french question answering dataset. arXiv preprint arXiv:2002.06071 (2020)
10. Giampiccolo, D., et al.: Overview of the CLEF 2007 multilingual question answering track. In: Peters, C., et al. (eds.) CLEF 2007. LNCS, vol. 5152, pp. 200–236. Springer, Heidelberg (2008). https://doi.org/10.1007/978-3-540-85760-0_27
11. He, W., et al.: DuReader: a Chinese machine reading comprehension dataset from real-world applications. arXiv preprint arXiv:1711.05073 (2017)
12. Joshi, M., et al.: TriviaQA: a large scale distantly supervised challenge dataset for reading comprehension. In: ACL, pp. 1601–1611 (2017)
13. Kuratov, Y., Arkhipov, M.: Adaptation of deep bidirectional multilingual transformers for Russian language. arXiv preprint arXiv:1905.07213 (2019)

14. Kwiatkowski, T., et al.: Natural questions: a benchmark for question answering research. TACL **7**, 453–466 (2019)
15. Lewis, P., Oğuz, B., Rinott, R., Riedel, S., Schwenk, H.: MLQA: evaluating cross-lingual extractive question answering. arXiv preprint arXiv:1910.07475 (2019)
16. Prager, J.M.: Open-domain question-answering. Found. Trends Inf. Retrieval **1**(2), 91–231 (2006)
17. Rajpurkar, P., Zhang, J., Lopyrev, K., Liang, P.: SQuAD: 100,000+ questions for machine comprehension of text. arXiv preprint arXiv:1606.05250 (2016)
18. Reddy, S., Chen, D., Manning, C.D.: CoQA: a conversational question answering challenge. TACL **7**, 249–266 (2019)
19. Rondeau, M.A., Hazen, T.J.: Systematic error analysis of the Stanford question answering dataset. In: MRQA Workshop (2018)
20. Seo, M., Kembhavi, A., Farhadi, A., Hajishirzi, H.: Bidirectional attention flow for machine comprehension. arXiv preprint arXiv:1611.01603 (2016)
21. Wadhwa, S., Chandu, K.R., Nyberg, E.: Comparative analysis of neural QA models on SQuAD. arXiv preprint arXiv:1806.06972 (2018)
22. Wang, W., Yang, N., Wei, F., Chang, B., Zhou, M.: Gated self-matching networks for reading comprehension and question answering. In: ACL, pp. 189–198 (2017)
23. Zhang, X., Yang, A., Li, S., Wang, Y.: Machine reading comprehension: a literature review. arXiv preprint arXiv:1907.01686 (2019)

s-AWARE: Supervised Measure-Based Methods for Crowd-Assessors Combination

Marco Ferrante[1], Nicola Ferro[2], and Luca Piazzon[2(✉)]

[1] Department of Mathematics "Tullio Levi-Civita",
University of Padua, Padua, Italy
ferrante@math.unipd.it
[2] Department of Information Engineering, University of Padua, Padua, Italy
{ferro,piazzonl}@dei.unipd.it

Abstract. Ground-truth creation is one of the most demanding activities in terms of time, effort, and resources needed for creating an experimental collection. For this reason, crowdsourcing has emerged as a viable option to reduce the costs and time invested in it.

An effective assessor merging methodology is crucial to guarantee a good ground-truth quality. The classical approach involve the aggregation of labels from multiple assessors using some voting and/or classification methods. Recently, *Assessor-driven Weighted Averages for Retrieval Evaluation (AWARE)* has been proposed as an unsupervised alternative, which optimizes the final evaluation measure, rather than the labels, computed from multiple judgments.

In this paper, we propose s-AWARE, a supervised version of AWARE. We tested s-AWARE against a range of state-of-the-art methods and the unsupervised AWARE on several TREC collections. We analysed how the performance of these methods changes by increasing assessors' judgement sparsity, highlighting that s-AWARE is an effective approach in a real scenario.

Keywords: Crowdsourcing · Ground-truth · Assessor merging · AWARE

1 Introduction

System-oriented evaluation is based on the use of experimental collections consisting of document corpora, topics, and relevance judgements, defining which documents are relevant for which topics. Obtaining relevance judgments and creating the ground-truth is a human-based activity and it is one of the most demanding tasks in preparing an experimental collection. Traditionally, it has been performed by relying on expert assessors [10], being quite onerous in terms of time and costs.

Therefore, a more recent approach to ground-truth creation relies on crowdsourcing [2]. Multiple judgements are collected for each document from many

© Springer Nature Switzerland AG 2020
A. Arampatzis et al. (Eds.): CLEF 2020, LNCS 12260, pp. 16–27, 2020.
https://doi.org/10.1007/978-3-030-58219-7_2

crowd-assessors, possibly less qualified than the experts but cheaper, leveraging on the larger number of assessors to shorten the overall task execution time. The multiple judgments by crowd-assessors are then merged together, with the overall objective to achieve an assessment quality comparable to the one of traditional expert assessors. Several studies, e.g. [3], have shown that crowd-assessors often agree with experts, in particular when it comes to relevant documents [4].

Traditional approaches, like *Majority Vote (MV)* [13] or *Expectation Maximization (EM)* [7], merge multiple labels by the different crowd-assessors into a final label which is used as the relevance judgement to compute performance measures. However, a labelling error at the ground-truth level may have a different impact on different measures. For example, suppose that in the top-five documents one is actually relevant while another one is mislabelled as relevant; precision at five will have the same value, independently of the rank position of the mislabelled document; on the other hand, *Average Precision (AP)* will have different values depending on the rank position of the mislabelled document. Therefore, the same error may have different effects on different measures and also on different runs for the same measure, since different runs may rank the mislabelled document differently. To overcome these issues, Ferrante et al. [5] proposed *Assessor-driven Weighted Averages for Retrieval Evaluation (AWARE)* which, differently from traditional approaches, computes performance measures based on each crowd-assessor judgements and then merges these crowd-measures into a final weighted measure, optimizing the merging process to the considered measures and runs.

While AWARE adopts an unsupervised approach to determine the weights to be used to merge the crowd-measures, in this paper we propose a supervised extension of AWARE, that we call s-AWARE. We evaluate our s-AWARE against unsupervised AWARE and state-of-the-art supervised and unsupervised methods by using the TREC 2012 Crowdsourcing track [11] and the TREC 2017 Common Core track [1] datasets.

The paper is organized as follows: Sect. 2 presents some related work; Sect. 3 explains the s-AWARE methodology; Sect. 4 describes the experiments and the evaluation results; Sect. 5 draws some conclusions and outlooks for future work.

2 Related Works

The most common approach, still very effective, to crowd-assessor merging is *Majority Vote (MV)* [13]: it assigns to each document the most popular judgement among those expressed by crowd-assessors; to deal with variable quality workers, several weighted versions of MV have been proposed, e.g. [13, 14].

Expectation Maximization (EM) [7] addresses the problem in a probabilistic way, by iteratively estimating the probability of relevance of each document and then by assigning it the most probable judgement. Several versions of EM algorithms have been proposed, optimizing whether the document relevance probability in an unsupervised [7] or semi-supervised way [12]. Georgescu and Zhu [6] proposed an EM method for optimizing the assessors' reliability used to dynamically merge crowd judgements. Whiting et al. [17] proposed a network based

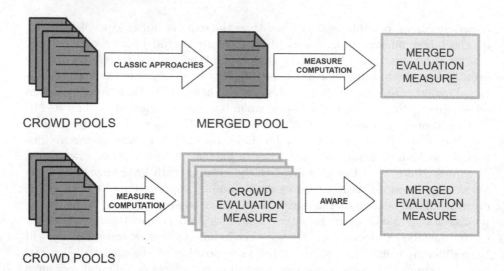

Fig. 1. Traditional vs AWARE approach.

approach to estimate the assessor's trustworthiness, using a modified version of PageRank. Nellapati et al. [9] developed a mixed method, combining expert supervision, machine learning algorithms and automatic error correction.

As shown in Fig. 1, all the above methods end up by selecting an optimal label, according to some criterion, among those assigned by crowd-assessors and producing a single merged pool then used to compute performance measures. However, different evaluation measures can be unfairly affected in by mislabelled documents. Therefore, *Assessor-driven Weighted Averages for Retrieval Evaluation (AWARE)* [5] directly computes the performance of a system on the judgements given by every crowd-assessor and then combine the obtained measures by weighting each assessor on the basis of her/his estimated accuracy:

$$aware\_\mu(r_t) = \sum_{k=1}^{m} \mu\left(\hat{r}_t^k\right) \frac{a_k(t)}{\sum_{h=1}^{m} a_h(t)}$$

where m is the number of crowd-assessors to merge, $\mu\left(\hat{r}_t^k\right)$ is the value of the performance measure computed on run r for topic t according to the k-th crowd-assessor, and a_k is the accuracy of the k-th crowd-assessor.

AWARE adopts an unsupervised approach to compute the a_k accuracy scores: the more a crowd-assessor is "far way" from three random assessors (uniform, over-estimating relevance, under-estimating relevance), the more accurate the crowd-assessor is.

We will refer to this unsupervised version of AWARE as u-AWARE when needed to distinguish it from the supervised version proposed in this paper.

3   s-AWARE Methodology

s-AWARE adopts a supervised approach where the more a crowd-assessor is "close" to the gold standard, the better is her/his accuracy.

Given a set of systems S and a set of topics T, let M_k be the k-th crowd-measure, i.e. the $|T| \times |S|$ matrix containing the performance scores computed on the judgments of the k-th crowd-assessor; let M^* be the performance measure corresponding to the gold standard. We consider two alternatives to quantify the "closeness" C_k to the gold standard[1]:

- *Measure closeness*: we consider the *Root Mean Square Error (RMSE)* between the crowd-measure and the gold standard one

$$C_k = RMSE\left(\overline{M}_k(\cdot, S) - \overline{M}^*(\cdot, S)\right) = \sqrt{\sum_{s=1}^{|S|} \frac{\left(\overline{M}_k(\cdot, s) - \overline{M}^*(\cdot, s)\right)^2}{|S|}}$$

where $\overline{M}(\cdot, s)$ indicates the average measure by topic
- *Ranking of Systems closeness*: we use the Kendall's τ correlation between the ranking of systems using the crowd-measure and the gold standard one

$$C_k = \tau\left(\overline{M}_k(\cdot, S), \overline{M}^*(\cdot, S)\right) = \frac{A - D}{|S|(|S| - 1)/2}$$

where A is the number of system pairs ranked in the same order in $\overline{M}_k(\cdot, S)$ and $\overline{M}^*(\cdot, S)$, and D is the number of discordant pairs.

All the "closenesses" C_k are then normalized in the [0,1] range, setting normalized C_k equal to 1 with gold standard behaviour (RMSE equal to 0 or Kendall's τ equal to 1).

Finally, to further emphasize the "closeness", accuracy scores a_k are computed as: the original normalized C_k, the squared C_k and the cubed C_k. Algorithm 1 summarizes the accuracy computation process.

4   Evaluation

4.1   Experimental Setup

We compared s-AWARE approaches against the following baselines:

---

[1] The original AWARE methodology considered additional ways to quantify "closeness", i.e. Frobenious norm, *Kullback-Leibler Divergence (KLD)*, and *AP Correlation (APC)*. Here, we focus on the two approaches which produced the best and most stable results across different configurations.

Algorithm 1: s-AWARE accuracy computation.

Data: T training topic set; $\hat{r}_t^k$ $\forall t \in T$ ground truth generated by assessor k; $\hat{r}_t$ $\forall t \in T$
      experts ground truth
Result: a_k accuracy score for assessor k

1 $M_k \leftarrow$ compute $\mu(\cdot)$ on $\hat{r}_t^k$;   // assessor measures
2 $M^* \leftarrow$ compute $\mu(\cdot)$ on $\hat{r}_t$;   // gold measures
3 **if** $RMSE$ **then**
4      $C_k = RMSE\left(\overline{M}_k(\cdot, S) - \overline{M}^*(\cdot, S)\right)$;   // Closeness computation
5      $w_k = 1 - C_k$;   // [0,1] normalization
6 **else if** $Kendall\ Tau$ **then**
7      $C_k = \tau\left(\overline{M}_k(\cdot, S), \overline{M}^*(\cdot, S)\right)$;   // Closeness computation
8      $w_k = |\,C_k\,|$;   // [0,1] normalization
9 **end**
10 **if** *squared closeness* **then** $a_k = w_k^2$;
11 **else if** *cubed closeness* **then** $a_k = w_k^3$;
12 **else** $a_k = w_k$;

- unsupervised
  - Majority Vote (mv) [13];
  - Expectation Maximization with MV seeding (emmv) [7];
  - u-AWARE with uniform accuracy scores (uniform);
  - u-AWARE with squared distance from random assessors (unsup_rmse_tpc, unsup_tau_tpc), using RMSE and Kendall's τ, respectively, for "closeness" computation;
- supervised or semi-supervised
  - supervised EM method (hard labels, PN discrimination, no boost version) (emGZ) [6];
  - semi-supervised EM (emsemi) [12], using the same training-test proportion of s-AWARE.

We used *Average Precision (AP)* as performance measure. To evaluate the different approaches, as done in the TREC 2012 Crowdsourcing track, we used the AP Correlation (APC) [18] between the ranking of systems induced by each merging approach and the gold standard.

We used the TREC 2012 Crowdsourcing track [11] data where participating groups submitted 31 pools for 10 topics; these 10 topics were used in TREC 08 Adhoc track (T08) [16], consisting of 129 runs, and TREC 13 Robust track (T13) [15], consisting of 110 runs. We also used a portion of real crowd-sourced data from the TREC 2017 Common Core track dataset (T26) [1], consisting of 75 runs and 50 topics; Inel et al. [8] gathered relevance judgments by 406 crowd-assessors, considering a subcorpus of NYTimes containing short documents ($\leq$1000 words) and providing 7 judgments for each (topic, document) pair. In both cases, we used the original NIST judgments as gold standard.

Since the first aim of crowd-sourcing is to save time and costs, relying on a large expert-assessors training set is not feasible in a real scenario. For this reason, we considered an extremely challenging 30%–70% split between training and test, repeated 100 times, i.e. we used 3 topics as training and 7 topics as test for T08 and T13 and 15 topics as training and 35 topics as test for T26. In

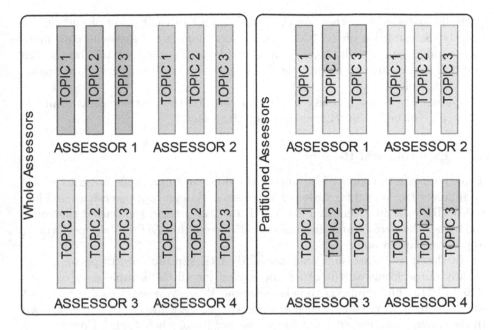

Fig. 2. Crowd-assessors experimental assembling

all the cases, we considered k-tuples from 2 to 7 crowd-assessors and for each k-tuple size we repeated all the computations 100 times, for validation purposes.

Since s-AWARE trains on a set of topics and `emsemi` trains on a partition of the documents for each topic, the evaluation is computed on the intersection of the two test sets (i.e. 70% of the documents from 70% of the topics).

We explore two configurations of crowd-assessors, that we call *Whole Assessors* (Fig. 2 on the left) and *Partitioned Assessors* (Fig. 2 on the right).

In the *Whole Assessors* case, each crowd-assessor judges completely all the topics; this is the ideal and most favourable condition for supervised and semi-supervised approaches because the crowd-assessors we learn from in the training phase exactly match those we are evaluated against in the test phase. This configuration is possible only for the T08 and T13 tracks, since in the TREC Crodwsourcing 2012 track each participating group judged all the topics, but not for the T26 track.

In the *Partitioned Assessors* case, each crowd-assessor judges just some documents of a topic and she/he possibly does not judge all the topics. Therefore, the final set of judgements for each topic is assembled by combining judgements coming from more assessors, in different proportions from topic to topics, and also using different assessors for different topics. This is a more frequent case in real crowd-sourcing scenarios and it is more challenging for supervised and semi-supervised approaches since what they learn from in the training phase only partially matches what they are evaluated against in the testing phase. This is exactly the condition of the T26 tracks, where more crowd-assessors contribute to the judgments of each topic. We also simulated this configuration on the T08 and T13 tracks, by assembling the judgments coming from more participants into each topic.

To ease the reproducibility of the experiments, the source code is available at: https://bitbucket.org/Lucapiaz/clef2020_saware/.

4.2 Experimental Results

Table 1 reports the comparison among the different approaches in terms of AP on different tracks and for various k-tuple sizes. Baseline approaches are in blue, u-AWARE ones in green, and s-AWARE ones in orange; the darker the color, the higher the performance in terms of *AP Correlation (APC)*; best performing approaches are in bold.

In the *Whole Assessors* case, the s-AWARE sup_tau_cubed approach constantly outperforms all the other approaches for all the k-tuple sizes on both T08 and T13. This supports the idea that the *Whole Assessors* case is the most favorable to supervised approaches, since we find the same crowd-assessors both in the training and test sets and crowd-assessor judge whole topics. However, the same does not happen for the supervised and semi-supervised baselines – emGZ and emsemi – which have lower performance than all the s-AWARE approaches and most of the unsupervised approaches, especially emGZ on T13. We hypothesize that this is due to s-AWARE approaches being much more effective at exploiting even a small training set (remember we use 30% data for training and 70% for testing). When it comes to s-AWARE alternatives, we can observe as Kendall's τ performs better than RMSE as "closeness" quantification and that the more sharp cubed weighting typically gains some more performance. We can also note how u-AWARE approaches have good performance too, typically better than state-of-the-art baselines, confirming the previous findings by [5]. Finally, we can observe as the performance of all the approaches tend to increase as the k-tuple size increases.

In the *Partitioned Assessors* case, we can observe that on T08 and T13 u-AWARE performs generally better than s-AWARE and the state-of-the-art baselines. This supports the idea that the *Partitioned Assessors* case is the most favorable to unsupervised approaches, since the training phase reflects less what happens in the test phase; k-tuples size $2, 3, 4$ on T13 are an exception, since s-AWARE outperforms all the other approaches. In general, we can observe that s-AWARE still performs remarkably better than the supervised and semi-supervised baselines – emGZ and emsemi – and better than the other unsupervised baselines. In a sense, this turns out to be a "duel" all internal to the AWARE family, which seems to better adapt to this fragmented case. This is further highlighted by the case of T26, where s-AWARE always outperforms all the other approaches. We hypothesize this is due to the fact that T08 and 13 partitioned assessor are a bit more fragmented, i.e. smaller pieces from more crowd-assessors, than the T26 ones, where there is a bunch of crowd-assessors who judge a large

Table 1. Baseline approaches in blue, u-AWARE ones in green, s-AWARE ones in orange. The darker the color, the higher the performance in terms of *AP Correlation (APC)*. Best performing approaches are in bold.

		sup_rmse	sup_tau	sup_rmse_squared	sup_tau_squared	sup_rmse_cubed	sup_tau_cubed	unsup_rmse_tpc	unsup_tau_tpc	uniform	mv	emmv	emGZ	emsemi
T08-whole	k02	0.6048	0.6184	0.6086	0.6278	0.6120	**0.6326**	0.6075	0.6031	0.6008	0.5326	0.5183	0.5455	0.5470
	k03	0.6317	0.6499	0.6366	0.6659	0.6414	**0.6766**	0.6324	0.6298	0.6265	0.6099	0.6025	0.5413	0.6097
	k04	0.6492	0.6707	0.6546	0.6905	0.6598	**0.7045**	0.6422	0.6501	0.6436	0.6147	0.6154	0.5562	0.6329
	k05	0.6689	0.6958	0.6751	0.7221	0.6812	**0.7409**	0.6808	0.6732	0.6625	0.6569	0.6512	0.5445	0.6535
	k06	0.6555	0.6833	0.6620	0.7120	0.6685	**0.7340**	0.6622	0.6651	0.6492	0.6163	0.5918	0.5095	0.5963
	k07	0.6719	0.6998	0.6782	0.7274	0.6845	**0.7482**	0.6709	0.6834	0.6657	0.6696	0.6396	0.5028	0.6443
T13-whole	k02	0.6111	0.6192	0.6139	0.6238	0.6162	**0.6254**	0.6005	0.6078	0.6079	0.5410	0.4974	0.5012	0.5186
	k03	0.6526	0.6616	0.6562	0.6692	0.6594	**0.6733**	0.6254	0.6548	0.6486	0.6088	0.5926	0.4770	0.6085
	k04	0.6687	0.6825	0.6728	0.6941	0.6765	**0.7008**	0.6250	0.6823	0.6641	0.6214	0.6119	0.4910	0.6241
	k05	0.7061	0.7237	0.7106	0.7387	0.7148	**0.7478**	0.6797	0.7209	0.7011	0.6613	0.6491	0.4478	0.6497
	k06	0.6872	0.7068	0.6923	0.7253	0.6971	**0.7379**	0.6502	0.7151	0.6818	0.6197	0.5913	0.4289	0.5919
	k07	0.7045	0.7232	0.7092	0.7402	0.7135	**0.7515**	0.6552	0.7330	0.6996	0.6708	0.6452	0.4062	0.6476
T08-partitioned	k02	0.5314	0.5390	0.5332	0.5456	0.5350	0.5500	**0.5508**	0.5317	0.5294	0.4919	0.4944	0.5024	0.4913
	k03	0.5466	0.5587	0.5497	0.5700	0.5526	0.5783	**0.5831**	0.5457	0.5436	0.5171	0.5292	0.5050	0.5321
	k04	0.5549	0.5690	0.5584	0.5830	0.5621	0.5935	**0.6037**	0.5553	0.5512	0.5153	0.4967	0.4992	0.5191
	k05	0.5564	0.5725	0.5604	0.5891	0.5645	0.6019	**0.6168**	0.5599	0.5523	0.5368	0.4804	0.4914	0.5118
	k06	0.5683	0.5863	0.5729	0.6064	0.5775	0.6220	**0.6552**	0.5692	0.5638	0.5287	0.4785	0.4782	0.4962
	k07	0.5672	0.5900	0.5737	0.6150	0.5797	0.6333	**0.6872**	0.5696	0.5615	0.5373	0.4774	0.4639	0.4776
T13-partitioned	k02	0.5842	0.5959	0.5862	0.6038	0.5879	**0.6078**	0.5998	0.5767	0.5820	0.5406	0.5052	0.4945	0.4847
	k03	0.6155	0.6299	0.6181	0.6406	0.6206	**0.6474**	0.6412	0.6015	0.6126	0.5728	0.5854	0.4611	0.5742
	k04	0.6372	0.6528	0.6402	0.6647	0.6430	**0.6722**	0.6706	0.6270	0.6340	0.5848	0.5757	0.4157	0.5838
	k05	0.6481	0.6641	0.6515	0.6773	0.6549	0.6862	**0.6929**	0.6508	0.6444	0.6079	0.5619	0.3521	0.6009
	k06	0.6616	0.6776	0.6653	0.6914	0.6691	0.7015	**0.7211**	0.6663	0.6579	0.6165	0.5573	0.3044	0.5840
	k07	0.6560	0.6728	0.6603	0.6884	0.6642	0.7006	**0.7306**	0.6412	0.6512	0.6209	0.5332	0.1963	0.5568
T26-partitioned	k02	0.3817	0.4008	0.3796	0.4084	0.3774	**0.4124**	0.3531	0.3928	0.3837	0.3731	0.3362	0.3506	0.3625
	k03	0.3863	0.4067	0.3839	0.4151	0.3815	**0.4191**	0.3522	0.4028	0.3886	0.3783	0.3512	0.3753	0.3680
	k04	0.3824	0.4072	0.3795	0.4179	0.3767	**0.4236**	0.3421	0.4029	0.3853	0.3791	0.3525	0.3688	0.3625
	k05	0.3832	0.4102	0.3796	0.4228	0.3761	**0.4295**	0.3396	0.4077	0.3866	0.3785	0.3602	0.3648	0.3729
	k06	0.3926	0.4232	0.3896	0.4366	0.3870	**0.4441**	0.3568	0.4207	0.3961	0.3781	0.3584	0.3466	0.3737
	k07	0.4534	0.4787	0.4521	0.4918	0.4507	**0.4980**	0.4171	0.4841	0.4561	0.4400	0.4302	0.3715	0.4239

part of several topics. Therefore, the gap between the training and test phases is slightly smaller in this case and s-AWARE better exploit the additional information available. As in the previous *Whole Assessors* case, cubed and squared s-AWARE approaches achieve, in general, better performance than the basic closeness approach, since they emphasize more sharply the difference between good and bad assessors.

Figure 3 shows the interaction plot between *k*-tuple size and the different approaches. An interaction plot displays the levels of one factor on the X axis, *k*-tuple size in our case, and has a separate line for the means of each level of the other factor on the Y axis, approach effectiveness in terms of APC in our case. This plots allows us to understand whether the effect of one factor depends

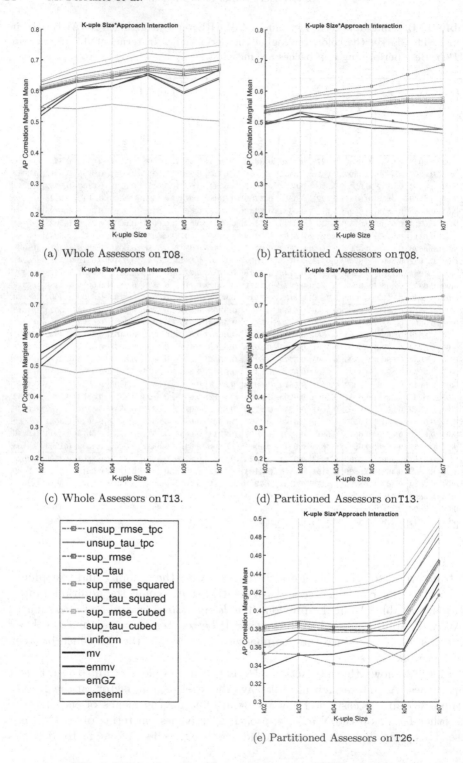

(a) Whole Assessors on T08.

(b) Partitioned Assessors on T08.

(c) Whole Assessors on T13.

(d) Partitioned Assessors on T13.

(e) Partitioned Assessors on T26.

Fig. 3. Interaction plots between approach and k-tuple size.

on the level of the other factor. Two parallel lines indicate that no interaction occurred, whereas nonparallel lines indicate an interaction between factors; the more nonparallel the lines are, the greater the strength of the interaction.

Figure 3a and 3c show the *Whole Assessors* case on T08 and T13. We can observe how all the AWARE approaches, and especially the s-AWARE, better exploit small k-tuple sizes and grow more rapidly than the baselines as the k-tuple size increases. We can also note how the supervised emGZ approach struggles in effectively exploiting the higher k-tuple sizes.

In Fig. 3b and 3d we consider the *Partitioned Assessors* case for T08 and T13. Again, we can observe that AWARE approaches better interact with the k-size, even if in this context u-AWARE approaches dominate the scene, being this case easier for unsupervised approaches. Finally, Fig. 3e highlights the good performance of s-AWARE on the T26 track which is possibly the most realistic dataset.

Overall, Fig. 3 confirms and supports the previous observations about the differences between the various approaches when facing the *Whole Assessors* and *Partitioned Assessors* cases and highlight the strengths of the s-AWARE approaches.

5   Conclusions and Future Work

In this paper, we have faced the problem of effectively merging crowd-assessors and we have extended the AWARE approach to supervised techniques. We conducted an extensive experimental evaluation based on several TREC collections. We have evaluated approaches using few training data – just 30% for training and 70% for testing – since this is the most suitable, yet challenging, case for a real world scenario

We found that s-AWARE approaches outperform all the others in the *Whole Assessors* case and they are still quite robust also in a real scenario under the *Partitioned Assessors* case. Moreover, supervised and unsupervised AWARE approaches perform consistently better than the analyzed state-of-the art approaches and they are especially effective at small k-tuple sizes, i.e. fewer crowd-assessors, making them more attractive for real world settings.

Future work will investigate how to extend AWARE approaches to better deal with sub-assessors, i.e. the *Partitioned Assessors* case, by allowing for multiple a_k scores for a topic, each one corresponding to a different sub-assessor.

References

1. Allan, J., Harman, D.K., Kanoulas, E., Li, D., Van Gysel, C., Voorhees, E.M.: TREC 2017 common core track overview. In: Voorhees, E.M., Ellis, A. (eds.) Proceedings of The Twenty-Sixth Text REtrieval Conference (TREC 2017). National Institute of Standards and Technology (NIST), Special Publication 500-324, Washington, USA (2018)

2. Alonso, O.: The Practice of Crowdsourcing. Morgan & Claypool Publishers, San Rafael (2019)
3. Alonso, O., Mizzaro, S.: Using crowdsourcing for TREC relevance assessment. Inf. Process. Manag. **48**(6), 1053–1066 (2012). https://doi.org/10.1016/j.ipm.2012.01. 004. ISSN 0306-4573
4. Clough, P., Sanderson, M., Tang, J., Gollins, T., Warner, A.: Examining the limits of crowdsourcing for relevance assessment. IEEE Internet Comput. **17**(4), 32–38 (2013). https://doi.org/10.1109/mic.2012.95
5. Ferrante, M., Ferro, N., Maistro, M.: AWARE: exploiting evaluation measures to combine multiple assessors. ACM Trans. Inf. Syst. **36**(2), 1–38 (2017). https://doi. org/10.1145/3110217
6. Georgescu, M., Zhu, X.: Aggregation of crowdsourced labels based on worker history. In: Proceedings of the 4th International Conference on Web Intelligence, Mining and Semantics (WIMS 2014). ACM, New York (2014). https://doi.org/10. 1145/2611040.2611074. ISBN 9781450325387
7. Hosseini, M., Cox, I.J., Milić-Frayling, N., Kazai, G., Vinay, V.: On aggregating labels from multiple crowd workers to infer relevance of documents. In: Baeza-Yates, R., et al. (eds.) ECIR 2012. LNCS, vol. 7224, pp. 182–194. Springer, Heidelberg (2012). https://doi.org/10.1007/978-3-642-28997-2_16
8. Inel, O., et al.: Studying topical relevance with evidence-based crowdsourcing. In: Cuzzocrea, A., et al. (eds.) Proceedings of 27th International Conference on Information and Knowledge Management (CIKM 2018), pp. 1253–1262. ACM Press, New York (2018)
9. Nellapati, R., Peerreddy, S., Singhal, P.: Skierarchy: Extending the power of crowdsourcing using a hierarchy of domain experts, crowd and machine learning. In: Proceedings of the TREC 2012 Crowdsourcing Track, pp. 1–11 (2012)
10. Sanderson, M.: Test collection based evaluation of information retrieval systems. Found. Trends Inf. Retr. (FnTIR) **4**(4), 247–375 (2010)
11. Smucker, M.D., Kazai, G., Lease, M.: Overview of the TREC 2012 crowdsourcing track. In: Voorhees, E.M., Buckland, L.P. (eds.) Proceedings of The Twenty-First Text REtrieval Conference (TREC 2012). National Institute of Standards and Technology (NIST), Special Publication 500-298, Washington, USA (2013)
12. Tang, W., Lease, M.: Semi-supervised consensus labeling for crowdsourcing. In: Proceedings of the SIGIR 2011 Workshop on Crowdsourcing for Information Retrieval (CIR), pp. 36–41. ACM, New York (2011). ISBN 9781450325387
13. Tao, D., Cheng, J., Yu, Z., Yue, K., Wang, L.: Domain-weighted majority voting for crowdsourcing. IEEE Trans. Neural Netw. Learn. Syst. **30**(1), 163–174 (2019). https://doi.org/10.1109/tnnls.2018.2836969
14. Tian, T., Zhu, J., Qiaoben, Y.: Max-margin majority voting for learning from crowds. IEEE Trans. Pattern Anal. Mach. Intell. **41**(10), 2480–2494 (2019). https://doi.org/10.1109/tpami.2018.2860987
15. Voorhees, E.M.: Overview of the TREC 2004 robust track. In: Voorhees, E.M., Buckland, L.P. (eds.) Proceedings of The Thirteenth Text REtrieval Conference (TREC 2004). National Institute of Standards and Technology (NIST), Special Publication 500-261, Washington, USA (2004)
16. Voorhees, E.M., Harman, D.K.: Overview of the eigth Text REtrieval Conference (TREC-8). In: Voorhees, E.M., Harman, D.K. (eds.) Proceedings of The Eighth Text REtrieval Conference (TREC-8), pp. 1–24. National Institute of Standards and Technology (NIST), Special Publication 500-246, Washington, USA (1999)

17. Whiting, S., Perez, J., Zuccon, G., Leelanupab, T., Jose, J.: University of Glasgow (qirdcsuog) at TREC crowdsourcing 2001: TurkRank - network based worker ranking in crowdsourcing. In: Proceedings of The Twentieth Text REtrieval Conference, TREC 2011, Gaithersburg, Maryland, USA, 15–18 November 2011, pp. 1–7, January 2011

18. Yilmaz, E., Aslam, J.A., Robertson, S.E.: A new rank correlation coefficient for information retrieval. In: Chua, T.S., Leong, M.K., Oard, D.W., Sebastiani, F. (eds.) Proceedings of 31st Annual International ACM SIGIR Conference on Research and Development in Information Retrieval (SIGIR 2008), pp. 587–594. ACM Press, New York, USA (2008)

Query or Document Translation for Academic Search – What's the Real Difference?

Vivien Petras[1](✉)[iD], Andreas Lüschow[2][iD], Roland Ramthun[3][iD],
Juliane Stiller[4][iD], Cristina España-Bonet[5,6][iD], and Sophie Henning[6]

[1] Berlin School of Library and Information Science, Humboldt -Universität zu Berlin, Berlin, Germany
vivien.petras@ibi.hu-berlin.de
[2] Göttingen State and University Library, Göttingen, Germany
lueschow@sub.uni-goettingen.de
[3] Leibniz Institute for Psychology Information, Trier, Germany
rr@leibniz-psychology.org
[4] You, We & Digital, Berlin, Germany
julstiller@gmail.com
[5] DFKI GmbH, Saarbrücken, Germany
cristinae@dfki.de
[6] Saarland University, Saarbrücken, Germany
s8sohenn@stud.uni-saarland.de

Abstract. We compare query and document translation from and to English, French, German and Spanish for multilingual retrieval in an academic search portal: PubPsych. Both translation approaches improve the retrieval performance of the system with document translation providing better results. Performance inversely correlates with the amount of available original language documents. The more documents already available in a language, the fewer improvements can be observed. Retrieval performance with English as a source language does not improve with translation as most documents already contained English-language content in our text collection. The large-scale evaluation study is based on a corpus of more than 1M metadata documents and 50 real queries taken from the query log files of the portal.

Keywords: MLIR · PubPsych · Document vs. query translation · IR evaluation

1 Introduction

Multilingual access is a well-known challenge in the information retrieval community: if documents exist in only one language, they are often not retrievable or usable for searchers using a different language [4]. This poses a particular challenge in contexts in which access to all relevant documents concerning a specific knowledge area is a requirement for work. Scientific knowledge production

© Springer Nature Switzerland AG 2020
A. Arampatzis et al. (Eds.): CLEF 2020, LNCS 12260, pp. 28–42, 2020.
https://doi.org/10.1007/978-3-030-58219-7_3

is such a context where information should be consumed and processed with respect to its relevance regardless of language. Yearly, millions of potentially relevant technical and scientific publications are published [5], many of them in languages unfamiliar to other researchers. English may become the lingua franca for research publications in certain disciplines such as the natural sciences [10], but a monolingual system of knowledge production systematically disadvantages non-native English speakers and excludes non-English research publications [1].

Providing multilingual access to documents means to overcome the language barrier between the document language and the searcher language. While searchers should not be expected to change their search language, authors should also not be expected to change their document language. Multilingual access therefore requires a translation bridge between searchers and documents [11].

In production systems for academic search, hardly any digital library or search engine offers such a functionality. Usually, there are three reasons provided: (1) machine translation (MT) is a resource-intensive functionality; (2) the sparse queries or text documents (bibliographic references) in most digital libraries decrease translation quality to an unacceptable degree; and (3) translating highly complex technical or scholarly terms is a hard translation problem, which also decreases translation quality [21] and therefore retrieval performance.

In light of recent advances in multilingual MT, it is time to put these arguments to a test. This paper describes a study on improving multilingual information retrieval (MLIR) in the scientific domain of psychology. PubPsych[1], a web-based portal for academic search in the field of psychology, will be used as a case study. With over 1M documents, the size of the test collection makes this one of the largest MLIR evaluation studies to date.

This study does not only evaluate whether multilingual access has a positive effect on retrieval performance in general, it also assesses another long-standing question in multilingual information retrieval: whether to translate queries or documents when providing the translation bridge between searchers and documents to yield better results. While it has long been assumed that document translation is more effective than query translation, translating documents is a much more resource-intensive endeavor, which precluded large-scale document vs. query translation comparisons until recently [27]. Now, large-scale translation is possible, but query translation might have also achieved such a degree of quality so that document translation is not needed anymore. In this paper, we therefore address the following research questions:

1. Does translation improve the retrieval performance in academic search?
2. How do document and query translation compare to each other with respect to their impact on retrieval performance?

The paper is organized as follows: Sect. 2 provides a review of query vs. document translation in MLIR. Section 3 describes PubPsych and its documents. Section 4 provides a description of the MT approaches. Section 5 describes the

---

[1] https://www.pubpsych.eu.

design for evaluating the retrieval performance of the translation approaches, while Sect. 6 discusses the results and Sect. 7 concludes.

2   Query vs. Document Translation in Academic Search

Studies on academic search found significant differences compared to other search environments. Bibliographic metadata records are sparse-text documents compared to full-text search spaces such as the web, but have a particular document structure that allows for structured or field-based retrieval, e.g., for authors or keywords [19]. Search behavior can differ by discipline [43]. Queries are typically longer [29] and contain more technical vocabulary [22].

Studies on multilingual access to academic search environments show that searchers need to be supported in bridging the language gap [11,25,39]. Multilingual knowledge organization systems like MeSH (Medical Subject Headings) can help bridge the multilingual language barrier [35,38] and are also used in this study. Some authors distinguish free-text vs. approaches with knowledge organization systems in MLIR [26], but usually translation approaches are categorized by what is translated: queries, documents or both [31].

It is generally acknowledged that the translation of documents should introduce more multilingual text material to the search space and is less errorprone and noisy than query translation, which would lead to improved performance [44]. Earlier experiments with small document collections confirmed this hypothesis [6,8,23,27,28]. Nevertheless, most MLIR research in the last two decades focused on query translation approaches, because document translation was too resource-intensive. Good overviews are provided in [34,36].

Not many query translation approaches were implemented in production systems and most were only short-lived [3,9,20,24]. Aside from commercial applications, we are not aware of another MLIR case study which studies the effect of translation on multilingual retrieval performance with as large a document collection for document translation as this one.

3   PubPsych – An Academic Search Portal for Psychology

The PubPsych academic search portal for psychology literature, tests, treatment schemes and research data provides metadata from nine source information systems from institutions in six countries [42]. It was released in 2013 and has gone through several updates since then. Over half of the metadata documents come from the PSYNDEX[2] and MEDLINE[3] databases.

The metadata (i.e., publication titles, source information, controlled keywords, abstracts) are provided in several languages, making the portal a multilingual information source. Because search is only based on the metadata, the

---

[2]   https://www.psyndex.de.
[3]   https://www.nlm.nih.gov/pubs/factsheets/medline.html.

metadata language determines whether a document is findable in a given language. Most metadata information in PubPsych is provided in at least one of the four languages English, Spanish, French or German. However, none of the datasets is available in all of these languages. Most of the content providers offer titles, abstract and keywords in English even for metadata records in other languages, making English the dominant language of the document collection (see Sect. 5.2). Nevertheless, about 20% of the content cannot be accessed with an English query and 25% of the content only has a German abstract.

Missing information can lead to duplicate research efforts. In psychology, basing research on partial information bears the risk of drawing conclusions on narrow subpopulations [16] or of testing humans without need. The wish for multilingual access to research publications was confirmed by a survey in 2008 in which psychology researchers considered native language information helpful for access to documents and research findings [37]. PubPsych users stated in 2015 that multilingual access would improve the search engine and their experience with it [41]. This study evaluates the effect of translation of queries or metadata in documents for multilingual access.

4 Machine Translation for Documents and Queries in PubPsych

For this study, titles and abstracts in documents were translated using an in-house neural MT (NMT) system. We built a domain-specific multilingual lexicon to translate controlled keywords and queries.

4.1 Document Translation

The engine for translating titles and abstracts was built on top of a multilingual [17] *transformer big* architecture [40]. We gathered a corpus with 96M parallel sentences from general, medicine-related as well as domain-specific documents from PubPsych as explained in [13] to train the engine. From PubPsych, records with titles or abstracts in more than one language were extracted and aligned to have parallel training sentences and titles. The amount of extracted data depends on the language pair. For example, we obtained 240k parallel sentences for EN–DE, but no parallel records were found for DE–FR. We used a balanced in-domain corpus for transfer learning by back-translating monolingual data until 2,5M parallel sentences were obtained in total. For several pairs, especially those not involving English, most of the data were in fact back-translations. Table 1 reports the BLEU [30] and TER [2] scores on a test with 1000 sentences extracted from the PubPsych data for our NMT system, Google Translate and DeepL. Our multilingual model trained with Marian NMT [18] is freely available [15].

Table 1. Automatic evaluation of the PubPsych NMT system for document translation compared to Google and DeepL. Higher BLEU is better; lower TER is better.

		DE2EN		EN2DE		ES2EN		EN2ES		FR2EN		EN2FR	
		BLEU	TER	BLEU	TER	BLEU	TER	BLEU	TER	BLEU	TER	BLEU	TER
Title	Google	40.9	43.0	31.0	56.3	43.0	41.7	49.9	39.2	**47.3**	39.7	42.6	42.9
	DeepL	40.9	43.6	30.4	57.2	45.1	40.0	50.6	37.2	45.6	41.3	**45.9**	42.1
	PubPsych	**45.8**	**40.0**	**36.4**	**49.1**	**48.6**	**36.7**	**56.3**	**32.0**	47.2	**39.2**	45.3	**41.2**
Abstract	Google	18.7	79.2	13.3	86.1	34.4	53.1	37.9	50.8	29.3	61.0	26.4	62.9
	DeepL	**19.0**	79.5	**14.2**	85.6	**34.8**	52.8	**39.7**	49.6	**29.7**	60.0	**27.9**	61.7
	PubPsych	**19.0**	**74.1**	14.1	**80.1**	34.3	**52.6**	38.2	**48.8**	27.1	61.1	24.5	63.5

4.2 Controlled Keywords and Query Translation

Query translation and keyword translation relies on a quad-lingual lexicon that covers the domain vocabulary. For building the lexicon, five sources, including the multilingual MeSH thesaurus, Wikipedia, Wikidata and the dictionaries within the Apertium translator were used [12]. Additionally, we used DeepL to translate a set of 4,000 frequent tokens within our controlled terms not covered by the previous resources and post-edited them with the help of the APA thesaurus. As a result, we obtained a quad-lingual lexicon with more than 5M entries (*QuadLex*) for each language in the form:

```
Wahrnehmung|||en:Perception|||es:Percepción|||fr:Perception
Echoisches Gedächtnis|||en:Echoic memory|||es:Memoria ecoica|||fr:Mémoire auditive
```

This lexicon was used to translate the controlled vocabulary in the PubPsych documents metadata. QuadLex covers between 25% and 87% of all controlled vocabulary depending on the sub-database and language. When also using word-level mappings, these numbers improved and we could reach almost 100% in all cases. For query translation, we used a language-independent version of QuadLex that joined the 4 dictionaries and eliminated duplicates, established language priorities according to PubPsych users, and removed terms that could be confused with stopwords in any of the languages. A comprehensive description of the structure of the query translator can be found in [14] together with a preliminary manual evaluation of the results. In our logs of 2M queries, 85% of tokens could be translated by this system.

Table 2. Retrieval runs per configuration

Run	Run explanation
Base-X	Baseline run with either DE, EN, ES or FR queries (4 runs)
QT-X	DE, EN, ES or FR queries translated into the requisite other languages and combined for retrieval (4 runs)
DT-X	Either DE, EN, ES or FR queries run against the translated document corpus (4 runs)

5   Experimental Design and Setup

The research questions go beyond the intrinsic translation quality in studying whether the translation of documents or queries will improve retrieval performance. Therefore, the research design builds on retrieval tests with effectiveness evaluation [33] comparing a predominantly monolingual baseline to both translation approaches.

5.1   Research Design

The study compares three configurations (see Fig. 1 for the schematic view):

1. Baseline (no translation): Original language queries were searched against the original corpus.
2. Query translation (QT): Queries were translated into the four languages under study and searched simultaneously against the original corpus (i.e., combined via a Boolean "OR" search).
3. Document translation (DT): The original language documents (titles, abstracts and keywords) were translated into all four languages and provided as a parallel multilingual document corpus. The original language queries were searched against this multilingual corpus.

In all three configurations, we compared the individual retrieval performance of each source-language set of queries separately as translation quality and therefore retrieval performance may differ based on the source language. Table 2 shows the experimental runs. We only considered the first 10 retrieved results for each experimental run, assuming a realistic search scenario where users do not move beyond the first results page[4].

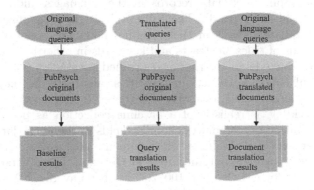

Fig. 1. Different configurations for multilingual retrieval

---

[4] A reviewer of this paper pointed out that recall-oriented searches for systematic reviews are another important use case for academic search portals. This use case was not addressed in this study.

In the QT configuration, the query is expanded to include all four language versions. This configuration simulates a search scenario where a searcher simultaneously translates a query into all languages of interest, thereby trying to achieve maximum recall in the multilingual document collection. If query terms remain untranslated or are translated to the same term, this impacts query term frequency (the same term appears several times) and thus retrieval outcome. We did not exclude redundant query terms, because this reflects a realistic use case as homographical technical terms can appear in several languages.

Conversely, in the DT configuration the document is expanded to include the title, abstract and keywords in four languages. These fields were used for retrieval. Equivalent to the QT configuration, document terms can remain untranslated or appear as the same term in different languages. We also did not control for redundant document terms in the translated document collection.

Table 3. Number of records per language in the PubPsych original document collection

Records with	DE	EN	ES	FR	Total
At least one field	585,273	994,374	256,391	453,765	1,021,327
Title field	265,964	958,758	52,501	42,497	1,004,973
Abstract field	254,870	562,119	35,815	33,210	820,069
Keyword field	582,770	938,538	254,222	453,170	987,812

5.2 The PubPsych Document Collections

All retrieval experiments were performed on a document collection containing 1,021,327 bibliographic metadata records in the languages under study from a total of 1,037,536 (see Sect. 3). The PubPsych original document collection contains the metadata records in their original language, some of them with human translations of titles, abstracts and keywords in other languages. Not all metadata records include an abstract or controlled vocabulary. For experiments with the original language collection, the titles, abstracts and keyword fields including the manual translations were considered for retrieval purposes with the goal of providing as realistic of a baseline collection as possible. Table 3 shows the distribution of metadata document fields in the study languages.

The overview shows that almost all documents contain at least some text in English, more than half contained text in German. The abstract field contains the most text for retrieval (ca. 100–200 words on average). More than half the documents contain an English abstract, about a quarter contain a German abstract. There are far fewer documents in French and Spanish with even fewer abstracts (ca. 3.5%). Spanish is the least represented language in the original search space.

The PubPsych translated document collection contains the same number of metadata records as the original document collection with each selected field (title, keyword, abstract) translated automatically into English, French, German and Spanish, if applicable. The original language fields (including the already existing manual translations) were kept in the document corpus, while the additional language fields were added to the metadata record. In contrast to the original document collection, all fields with relevant information were now considered for retrieval—i.e., original language metadata and both the automatically translated fields and those translated by humans.

5.3 The PubPsych Parallel-Language Topic Sets

We manually selected 50 real English-language queries, which were submitted to the PubPsych portal in the period from 2014–2016. Within that time span, 553,799 queries were submitted to the portal; 378,500 queries were unique. The informational type queries [7] used for evaluation were chosen based on the range of topics they represent and their likelihood of retrieving results in the PubPsych portal based on a previously performed log file study [14]. The 50 English queries were manually translated into French, German and Spanish, and domain experts in psychology created topic descriptions by determining the information need expressed in each of these queries.[5]

5.4 Relevance Assessments

It is important to note that some queries did not retrieve any or fewer than 10 results in some configurations. Only 5022 out of 6000 possible results (50 queries $\times$ 10 results $\times$ 12 runs) were retrieved. These documents were pooled by primary language of their metadata and shown to an appropriate human assessor (six students with psychological background, two for French, German and Spanish documents, respectively; all assessors judged English documents as well). Relevance judgements were done on a three-point scale: highly, partially or non relevant. The assessors were given specific guidelines on how to judge the relevance of a document for a given topic.

In total, 2436 documents pooled out of the 5022 retrieved documents were judged for relevance. This implies a considerable overlap in the result sets between the different configurations. Relevance assessments were conducted using *CLUBS Compa*[6], a web-based tool specifically developed for this purpose.

We calculated the inter-annotator agreement between the six assessors using 100 relevance-assessed documents for the comparison. Some assessors achieved a moderate agreement (Cohen's kappa 0.41–0.60), most agreements were only fair (Cohen's kappa 0.21–0.40), demonstrating the difficulty of judging the relevance of bibliographic metadata records. One of the assessors had rather bad agreements with the others. This may indicate a systematic error that was introduced into the experiment.

---

[5] This dataset is available at https://github.com/clubs-project/documentation/.
[6] https://github.com/alueschow/clubs-compa.

6   Evaluating Query and Document Translation in PubPsych

6.1   Retrieved Documents and Distribution of Languages

In Table 4, the mean number of results retrieved per query and the number of queries which did not retrieve any results are shown for each of the 12 runs.

The effect of translation is visible by looking at the number of queries that result in zero results. For every source query language except for English (where every query retrieves results), translation improves the likelihood of finding documents. This is not surprising as the translation step increases the search space by allowing for more matches. Document translation is even more successful than query translation. While QT retrieves more results per query overall, DT appears to be more effective in finding heretofore unfindable documents.

The number of zero result queries in the DT configurations drops more drastically than in the QT configuration, and more for French and Spanish than for German. Translating to French and Spanish increases the available document space much more because the original document collection did not contain many metadata documents in French and Spanish so that a query in these languages would be more likely to be unsuccessful. For Spanish queries, the effect is the strongest as the original document collection contained the fewest documents in Spanish.

In the baseline configuration, German and French queries retrieve nearly the same number of documents and result in nearly the same number of zero results queries, although the available search space is much larger for German. However, the number of documents with controlled keywords is very similar. This result may be an indicator for the impact of controlled keywords on recall. DT increases the result numbers for French more than for German, indicating that translating the titles and abstracts does contribute to retrieval performance as well.

Both QT and DT retrieve more documents than the baseline with QT retrieving an astonishingly large number compared to even DT. Since the QT configuration searches the documents with a combined multilingual query (all four languages in parallel), the likelihood of finding a match with any of the query terms is higher than for the DT configuration. However, the large result numbers in the QT configuration are not a sign of more effective retrieval. They are probably due to incorrect query translations that contain very generic words and thus find many documents. Because the QT mechanism separates a query phrase into a token-by-token translation if a phrase translation could not be found, the individual tokens introduce a lot of noise. This hypothesis is confirmed by the effectiveness analysis in the following section, which shows that the DT configurations are significantly more precise in the top 10 results.

Table 4. Mean number of results per query (*Mean*) and queries with zero results (*Zero*) in the three configurations per query language. The set includes 50 queries.

	Baseline		Query translation		Document translation	
	Mean	Zero	Mean	Zero	Mean	Zero
DE	474	7	5304	4	1277	3
EN	1399	0	8554	0	2841	0
ES	76	9	1759	7	1608	2
FR	430	8	3682	4	2002	0

6.2   Retrieval Effectiveness of Query and Document Translation Approaches

Table 5 shows the retrieval effectiveness for each query language and translation configuration by reporting both precision (P) and normalized discounted cumulative gain (nDCG) at rank 10. For statistical significance testing, we ran two-tailed paired t-tests with $\alpha = 0.05$. We also report differences to the Wilcoxon signed rank test when they occurred (for most cases, both tests had the same outcome).

Compared to the baseline, both QT and DT improve the retrieval effectiveness for most combinations. This shows that translation does not only find more documents, it provides access to more *relevant* documents in the top 10 results. The impact of the translation for both QT and DT seems to correlate with the available original language search space for the documents. It is not surprising, but good to confirm nevertheless, that translation improves retrieval performance particular for those languages where the original search space was sparse: French and Spanish.

QT is not as effective in finding more relevant documents in another language as DT. While the retrieval performance increases for French, German and Spanish, the absolute numbers show that German queries are still more successful in the QT configuration. This supports the hypothesis that QT also introduces a lot of noise in the translation, i.e., that translations from French and Spanish could be incorrect more often, leading to irrelevant results. The DT configuration balances the likelihood of retrieval success for all languages because all available text is translated into all languages.

The significant exception to this pattern is English, where QT actually decreases the retrieval performance and DT does not significantly increase the effectiveness beyond the baseline results. QT and DT find more documents when starting with an English query (Table 4), but since almost the entire document collection had already available English search text, the translations of the remaining fields did not improve the document relevance in the top 10. This may be different if we had considered a longer ranked list, where a higher recall is important. This effect is also observable for German, where DT does not improve as much over the baseline as it does for French and Spanish.

Table 5. Retrieval effectiveness per query language in the three configurations. We indicate a significant difference to the baseline (†) and to the QT run (‡) according to a two-tailed paired t-test.

	Baseline		Query translation		Document translation	
	P@10	nDCG@10	P@10	nDCG@10	P@10	nDCG@10
DE	0.658	0.596	0.726†	0.638[a]	0.802†‡	0.696†‡
EN	0.892	0.762	0.874	0.733	0.912‡	0.780‡[b]
ES	0.478	0.428	0.590†	0.510†	0.764†‡	0.632†‡
FR	0.574	0.483	0.664†	0.541[a]	0.842†‡	0.698†‡

[a] The Wilcoxon signed rank test found the difference to the baseline to be also significant
[b] The Wilcoxon signed rank test found the difference between QT and DT not to be significant

The document translation effect is particularly strong for French. The retrieval effectiveness in the baseline condition is closer to Spanish—accounting for the fact that the original language search space in these languages is sparse— but in the DT condition it slightly surpasses even the German results. One could argue that more relevant documents are found due to a higher intrinsic translation quality for French. While this is true for the comparison between French and German, it is not true between French and Spanish, where the intrinsic translation quality is actually better for Spanish (see Table 1). Consequently, intrinsic translation quality is not the sole predictor for retrieval effectiveness.

In other MLIR studies, it was already found that translation can introduce terminology that increases retrieval success even beyond the monolingual baseline [32]. The success of the runs with French queries may be due to this effect. The exact analysis of the differences in impact of intrinsic translation quality and other information retrieval effects (such as variant terminology) will be subject to future research.

7   Conclusion

This study demonstrates the effect of query and document translation in academic search. For the research design, we attempted to incorporate as many realistic elements as possible: (1) real-life queries, (2) a real-life document collection of not only realistic size (ca. 1M documents), but also an uneven language distribution of the document languages, (3) retrieval configurations that would be implemented in a production system, e.g., combination of parallel language queries or a merged document collection with all metadata languages.

We found that both query and document translation will not only increase the number of documents retrieved, but also the retrieval effectiveness overall. The sparser the search space in the original language condition is, the stronger this effect gets. Conversely, if this search space already contains a sufficient number of documents in the query language, neither query nor document translation lead to improvements. A very interesting research question is at what point translation will introduce more relevant documents: German language text was available in more than half of the documents and in about a quarter of the abstracts (the field with the most term material)—and translation improved retrieval. English language text was available in almost all of the documents and for about half of the abstracts—and translation did not improve retrieval. How much text (and in which quality) needs to be available in a language for successful retrieval? An answer to this question could also provide minimum thresholds for multilingual access to other languages as the ones we have studied here.

Another question for future study is the effect that parallel translation can have on retrieval performance. In this study, redundant query or document terms introduced through the translation (either because of missing translation or because the term appears in several languages) were not removed and their effect on retrieval performance not analyzed. However, with term frequency as a ranking signal, the potential risk of interference of parallel language versions needs to be analyzed.

The source language of the query and documents is a significant indicator for retrieval success; not only because of the available search space, but also because of the translation quality from a source language to a target language. We found some evidence that intrinsic translation quality (which in turn depends on sufficient training material) is a good indicator, albeit not the only one, for retrieval success. Another interesting research question is the necessary quality that document translation needs to achieve for retrieval.

With powerful neural MT architectures in place, document translation—which was shown to be the better translation option also in this large-scale study—has now become a realistic functionality for academic search portals which provide metadata search. However, a number of open questions still need to be answered.

Acknowledgments. This research was supported by the Leibniz-Gemeinschaft under grant SAW-2016-ZPID-2.

References

1. Ammon, U.: Global scientific communication: open questions and policy suggestions. AILA Rev. **20**, 123–133 (2007)
2. Banerjee, S., Lavie, A.: METEOR: an automatic metric for MT evaluation with improved correlation with human judgments. In: Proceedings of Workshop on Intrinsic and Extrinsic Evaluation Measures for MT and/or Summarization at the 43rd Annual Meeting of the Association of Computational Linguistics (ACL-2005), Ann Arbor, Michigan, June 2005
3. Bernardi, R., et al.: Multilingual search in libraries. The case-study of the Free University of Bozen-Bolzano. In: LREC, pp. 2287–2290 (2006)
4. Biswas, S.C.: Multilingual access to information in a networked environment character encoding & unicode standard. In: INFLIBNET 3rd Convention Planner, Assam University, Silchar, 10–11 November 2005, pp. 176–186. INFLIBNET Centre (2005). http://hdl.handle.net/1944/1391

5. Bornmann, L., Mutz, R.: Growth rates of modern science: a bibliometric analysis based on the number of publications and cited references. J. Am. Soc. Inf. Sci. Technol. **66**(11), 2215–2222 (2015)
6. Braschler, M., Scháuble, P.: Experiments with the eurospider retrieval system for CLEF 2000. In: Peters, C. (ed.) CLEF 2000. LNCS, vol. 2069, pp. 140–148. Springer, Heidelberg (2001). https://doi.org/10.1007/3-540-44645-1_13
7. Broder, A.: A taxonomy of web search. SIGIR Forum **36**(2), 3–10 (2002)
8. Chen, A., Gey, F.C.: Combining query translation and document translation in cross-language retrieval. In: Peters, C., Gonzalo, J., Braschler, M., Kluck, M. (eds.) CLEF 2003. LNCS, vol. 3237, pp. 108–121. Springer, Heidelberg (2004). https://doi.org/10.1007/978-3-540-30222-3_10
9. Clough, P., Sanderson, M.: User experiments with the eurovision cross-language image retrieval system. J. Am. Soc. Inform. Sci. Technol. **57**(5), 697–708 (2006)
10. Di Bitetti, M.S., Ferreras, J.A.: Publish (in English) or perish: the effect on citation rate of using languages other than English in scientific publications. Ambio **46**(1), 121–127 (2017)
11. Diekema, A.R.: Multilinguality in the digital library: a review. Electron. Libr. **30**(2), 165–181 (2012). https://doi.org/10.1108/02640471211221313
12. España-Bonet, C., Ramthun, R.: M3.1—Cross-lingual thesaurus and controlled term translation. Technical report, CLUBS-Project, March 2018. https://doi.org/10.23668/psycharchives.2746
13. España-Bonet, C., Stiller, J., Henning, S.: M1.2—Corpora for the machine translation engines. Technical report, CLUBS-Project, July 2018. https://doi.org/10.23668/psycharchives.2746
14. España-Bonet, C., Stiller, J., Ramthun, R., van Genabith, J., Petras, V.: Query translation for cross-lingual search in the academic search engine PubPsych. In: Garoufallou, E., Sartori, F., Siatri, R., Zervas, M. (eds.) MTSR 2018. CCIS, vol. 846, pp. 37–49. Springer, Cham (2019). https://doi.org/10.1007/978-3-030-14401-2_4
15. España-Bonet, C., Henning, S., Ramthun, R., Stiller, J., van Genabith, J.: MT models for multilingual CLuBS engine (en-de-fr-es), March 2020. https://doi.org/10.5281/zenodo.3709164
16. Henrich, J., Heine, S.J., Norenzayan, A.: Most people are not WEIRD. Nature **466**, 29 (2010)
17. Johnson, M., et al.: Google's multilingual neural machine translation system: enabling zero-shot translation. Trans. Assoc. Comput. Linguist. **5**, 339–351 (2017). https://doi.org/10.1162/tacl_a_00065. https://www.aclweb.org/anthology/Q17-1024
18. Junczys-Dowmunt, M., et al.: Marian: fast neural machine translation in C++. In: Proceedings of ACL 2018, System Demonstrations, pp. 116–121. Association for Computational Linguistics, Melbourne, Australia, July 2018. http://www.aclweb.org/anthology/P18-4020
19. Khabsa, M., Wu, Z., Giles, C.L.: Towards better understanding of academic search. In: JCDL 2016, pp. 111–114. ACM (2016)
20. Király, P.: Query translation in Europeana. Code4Lib J. **27** (2015)
21. Kornadt, H.J., Trommsdorff, G., Kobayashi, R.B.: "Mein Hund hat mich bestorben": sprachlicher Ausdruck von Gefühlen im deutsch-japanischen Vergleich. In: Kornadt, H.J. (ed.) Sprache und Kognition: Perspektiven moderner Sprachpsychologie, pp. 233–250. Spektrum Akad. Verl., Heidelberg (1994)
22. Li, X., Schijvenaars, B.J., de Rijke, M.: Investigating queries and search failures in academic search. Inf. Process. Manag. **53**(3), 666–683 (2017)

23. McCarley, J.S.: Should we translate the documents or the queries in cross-language information retrieval? In: Proceedings of the 37th Annual Meeting of the Association for Computational Linguistics on Computational Linguistics, ACL 1999, USA, pp. 208–299 (1999). https://doi.org/10.3115/1034678.1034716
24. Nikoulina, V., Kovachev, B., Lagos, N., Monz, C.: Adaptation of statistical machine translation model for cross-lingual information retrieval in a service context. In: Proceedings of the 13th Conference of the European Chapter of the Association for Computational Linguistics, pp. 109–119 (2012)
25. Nzomo, P., Ajiferuke, I., Vaughan, L., McKenzie, P.: Multilingual information retrieval & use: perceptions and practices amongst bi/multilingual academic users. J. Acad. Librariansh. **42**(5), 495–502 (2016)
26. Oard, D.W.: Serving users in many languages: cross-language information retrieval for digital libraries. D-Lib Mag. (1997)
27. Oard, D.W.: A comparative study of query and document translation for cross-language information retrieval. In: Farwell, D., Gerber, L., Hovy, E. (eds.) AMTA 1998. LNCS (LNAI), vol. 1529, pp. 472–483. Springer, Heidelberg (1998). https://doi.org/10.1007/3-540-49478-2_42
28. Oard, D.W., Hackett, P.G.: Document translation for cross-language text retrieval at the University of Maryland. In: Proceedings of the Sixth Text REtrieval Conference (TREC-6), pp. 687–696 (1997)
29. Palotti, J.A., Hanbury, A., Müller, H., Kahn Jr., C.E.: How users search and what they search for in the medical domain. Inf. Retrieval **19**(1–2), 189–224 (2016)
30. Papineni, K., Roukos, S., Ward, T., Zhu, W.J.: BLEU: a method for automatic evaluation of machine translation. In: Proceedings of the Association of Computational Linguistics, pp. 311–318 (2002)
31. Peters, C., Braschler, M., Clough, P.: Cross-language information retrieval. In: Peters, C., Braschler, M., Clough, P. (eds.) Multilingual Information Retrieval, pp. 57–84. Springer, Heidelberg (2012). https://doi.org/10.1007/978-3-642-23008-0_3
32. Petras, V., Perelman, N., Gey, F.: UC Berkeley at CLEF-2003 – Russian language experiments and domain-specific retrieval. In: Peters, C., Gonzalo, J., Braschler, M., Kluck, M. (eds.) CLEF 2003. LNCS, vol. 3237, pp. 401–411. Springer, Heidelberg (2004). https://doi.org/10.1007/978-3-540-30222-3_39
33. Sanderson, M., et al.: Test collection based evaluation of information retrieval systems. Found. Trends® Inform. Retrieval **4**(4), 247 375 (2010)
34. Savoy, J., Braschler, M.: Lessons learnt from experiments on the ad hoc multilingual test collections at CLEF. In: Ferro, N., Peters, C. (eds.) Information Retrieval Evaluation in a Changing World. TIRS, vol. 41, pp. 177–200. Springer, Cham (2019). https://doi.org/10.1007/978-3-030-22948-1_7
35. Schuers, M., et al.: Lost in translation? A multilingual query builder improves the quality of pubmed queries: a randomised controlled trial. BMC Med. Inform. Decis. Mak. **17**(1), 94 (2017)
36. Türe, F., Boschee, E.: Learning to translate: a query-specific combination approach for cross-lingual information retrieval. In: Proceedings of the 2014 Conference on Empirical Methods in Natural Language Processing (EMNLP), pp. 589–599 (2014)
37. Uhl, M.: Survey on European psychology publication issues. Psychol. Sci. Q. **51**(1), 19–26 (2009)
38. Vanopstal, K., Buysschaert, J., Laureys, G., Stichele, R.V.: Lost in PubMed. Factors influencing the success of medical information retrieval. Expert Syst. Appl. **40**(10), 4106–4114 (2013)

39. Vassilakaki, E., Garoufallou, E., Johnson, F., Hartley, R.J.: An exploration of users' needs for multilingual information retrieval and access. In: Garoufallou, E., Hartley, R.J., Gaitanou, P. (eds.) MTSR 2015. CCIS, vol. 544, pp. 249–258. Springer, Cham (2015). https://doi.org/10.1007/978-3-319-24129-6_22

40. Vaswani, A., Shazeer, N., Parmar, N., Uszkoreit, J., Jones, L., Gomez, A.N., Kaiser, L., Polosukhin, I.: Attention is all you need. In: Advances in Neural Information Processing Systems, vol. 30. pp. 5998–6008. Curran Associates, Inc. (2017)

41. Waeldin, S.: Results from the PubPsych launch survey: short report. ZPID Sci. Inf. Online **15**(2), 3 (2015). https://www.zpid.de/pub/research/2015_Waeldin_PubPsych-launch.pdf

42. Weichselgartner, E., Baier, C., Ramthun, R.: Pubpsych: a powerful research tool providing access to a broad supranational body of psychological knowledge. Datenbank-Spektrum **17**(1), 35–39 (2017)

43. Yi, K., Beheshti, J., Cole, C., Leide, J.E., Large, A.: User search behavior of domain-specific information retrieval systems: an analysis of the query logs from PsycINFO and ABC-Clio's historical abstracts-America: history and life: research articles. J. Am. Soc. Inf. Sci. Technol. **57**(9), 1208–1220 (2006)

44. Zhang, Y.: Improved cross-language information retrieval via disambiguation and vocabulary discovery. Ph.D. thesis, School of Computer Science and Information Technology RMIT University, Melbourne, Victoria, Australia (2006)

Question Answering When Knowledge Bases are Incomplete

Camille Pradel[1]([⊠]) [iD], Damien Sileo[1] [iD], Álvaro Rodrigo[2] [iD], Anselmo Peñas[2] [iD], and Eneko Agirre[3] [iD]

[1] Synapse Développement, Toulouse, France
camillepradel@gmail.com, damien.sileo@gmail.com
[2] Universidad Nacional de Educación a Distanca, Madrid, Spain
{alvarory,anselmo}@lsi.uned.es
[3] Ixa NLP Group, University of the Basque Country UPV/EHU, Leioa, Spain
e.agirre@ehu.eus

Abstract. While systems for question answering over knowledge bases (KB) continue to progress, real world usage requires systems that are robust to incomplete KBs. Dependence on the closed world assumption is highly problematic, as in many practical cases the information is constantly evolving and KBs cannot keep up. In this paper we formalize a typology of missing information in knowledge bases, and present a dataset based on the Spider KB question answering dataset, where we deliberately remove information from several knowledge bases, in this case implemented as relational databases (The dataset and the code to reproduce experiments are available at https://github.com/camillepradel/IDK.). Our dataset, called IDK (Incomplete Data in Knowledge base question answering), allows to perform studies on how to detect and recover from such cases. The analysis shows that simple baselines fail to detect most of the unanswerable questions.

Keywords: Question answering · Knowledge bases · Unanswerable questions · Text-to-SQL · Lifelong learning

1 Introduction

Structured knowledge has become ubiquitous, abundant and involved in numerous applications. General knowledge bases like DBpedia, Wikidata or business specific databases encode human knowledge that can be queried efficiently with SPARQL or SQL queries. Meanwhile, end users tend to expect less and less friction in user experience. This requires systems to have a form of natural language understanding and to derive formally the intent of a natural language question.

This work has been supported by ERA-Net CHIST-ERA LIHLITH Project funded by the Agencia Estatal de Investigación (AEI, Spain) projects PCIN-2017-118/AEI and PCIN-2017-085/AEI, the Agence Nationale pour la Recherche (ANR, France) projects ANR-17-CHR2-0001-03 and ANR-17-CHR2-0001-04, and the Swiss National Science Foundation (SNF, Switzerland) project 20CH21 174237.

© Springer Nature Switzerland AG 2020
A. Arampatzis et al. (Eds.): CLEF 2020, LNCS 12260, pp. 43–54, 2020.
https://doi.org/10.1007/978-3-030-58219-7_4

Question answering over knowledge graphs has made unusual progress over the last few years, with the introduction of more and more realistic datasets [19]. Even though these datasets are much harder, better models stemming from the recent progress of NLP [5] allowed current systems to push the evaluation metrics further [3,6].

However, most works assume that all user questions have an answer in the knowledge base (closed world assumption). This is highly problematic in practical uses where knowledge is incomplete and evolving. Users could be asked to review whether a knowledge base can provide an answer to their question, but the need to delve into the knowledge base content defeats the whole purpose of the natural language interface.

As an example, consider the following natural language question: *Which cars have more than 4 cylinders?*

Current question answering systems will systematically provide an answer whether or not the database associated with the question contains information about cylinders. For instance, a system relying on word embeddings will use the closest column available according to vector space similarity, e.g. HORSEPOWER, and produce the following SQL query which is a valid query but will return misleading results:

```
SELECT car_name FROM cars_data WHERE horsepower > 4
```

As such, if a KB question answering system yields satisfactory results with the current evaluation frameworks, this doesn't ensure usability in cases where knowledge is missing, since current datasets are designed to work at a closed world setup.

In this work, we make the following contributions to question answering on knowledge bases:

- A general formalization and typology of missing knowledge.
- A KB alteration method which produces a derived dataset with an incomplete KB, natural language questions, SQL queries and corresponding answers.
- A case study on the multi-domain Spider dataset, containing dozens of relational databases, natural language questions, SQL queries and answers.
- An evaluation of whether baselines can detect missing knowledge and thus refrain from answering certain questions.

2 Related Work

The derivation of formal knowledge base queries from natural language, also called semantic parsing, has leveraged annotated pairs of questions and formal language queries in numerous works [1,2,21]. The success of data-driven approaches has led to the construction of many datasets for question answering over structured data [11,14,21]. In particular, the Question Answering Linked Data (QALD) series of evaluation campaign [9] has led to 10 different shared tasks leveraging RDF knowledge graphs.

Several resources focus on SQL relational knowledge instead; these include WikiSQL [22]. Spider [19] was also proposed to provide a more realistic setup (i.e more databases and harder, more natural questions).

However, all these datasets assume a closed world assumption. Since we focus on missing knowledge, our work is also related to the work of [13] who study the problem of QA over KBs in Lifelong Learning scenarios. In such scenarios, as a system evolves over time, it is likely to receive questions that cannot be answered using the initial KB. The authors formalize a task for this problem, where a system must detect if a question is unanswerable and determine the missing knowledge. While the authors restricted themselves to the definition of the task, we continue their work and develop a benchmark dataset for such task.

In the context of how to deal with unanswered questions over KBs, [7] propose a system able to acquire knowledge from users using dialogs and expand the content of the KB to solve the question. Then, this new knowledge can be used for future questions. The main objective of the paper is how to expand KBs using dialogues, while we create a dataset focused on detecting unanswered questions and the corresponding missing knowledge.

[20] presents a cross-domain text-to-sql dataset called SParC, which has been built on top of Spider databases. The dataset differs from Spider on the fact that the authors include questions related to a given context, including follow-up questions depending on the answers from previous questions. Our work differs from theirs on the fact that we do not include context, but we include unanswered questions, while all the questions in SParC are answerable.

In contemporary work, [18] presents a conversational text-to-sql dataset. They do include questions which cannot be answered by a human volunteer, but there is no analysis or formalization of the causes of the failure to answer, which can be due to missing knowledge but also due to nonsensical questions. In contrast, we include a formalization of missing knowledge and a use case showing the effect of deliberately erasing certain kind of information. In addition, we can artificially create many unanswerable examples, while their dataset contains a smaller amount of manual questions which are not answerable.

Finally, datasets for extractive question answering and reading comprehension like SQuad [16] have been criticized for the lack of questions which are not answerable, leading to an overestimate of the performance of systems [15]. This lead to the creation of SQuad 2.0 and TriviaQA [8], which do include a large portion of unanswerable questions. Our work is complementary, in that we address QA systems on KBs.

3   Formalizing Missing Knowledge

In this section we first formalize knowledge graphs, and then draw a typology of missing knowledge cases.

3.1　Knowledge Representation

To define a typology of missing knowledge, we use the Knowledge Graph (KG) formalism as used in the broadly deployed semantic web framework[1]. KGs can be mapped to other knowledge representation formalisms, like relational databases (aka SQL databases).

A KG consists in a taxonomy of classes and properties, instances of classes, literals and relations expressed between these entities in the form of triples. It is formally defined below:

A *knowledge base* KB is a tuple (V, P, E) where

- V is a finite set of vertices. V is conceived as the disjoint union $\mathcal{C} \uplus \mathcal{I} \uplus \mathcal{L}$, where $\mathcal{C}$ is the set of classes, $\mathcal{I}$ is the set of instances and $\mathcal{L}$ is the set of literal values. A literal value can be specified of some type; ℓ is the set of literal types; a function $type : \mathcal{L} \to \ell \cup None$ associates its type to each literal[2].
- P is a finite set of properties, subdivided by $P = \mathcal{R}_o \uplus \mathcal{R}_d \uplus \{instanceOf, subclassOf, subpropertyOf\}$, where $\mathcal{R}_o$ is the set of object properties, $\mathcal{R}_d$ is the set of datatype properties, *instanceOf* expresses the class membership of an entity, and *subclassOf* (resp. *subpropertyOf*) is the taxonomic relation between classes (resp. properties). $\mathcal{R}_d$ contains amongst other properties *"label"* which captures the terminological expression of an entity.
- E is a finite set of edges of the form $p(v_1, v_2)$ fulfilling one of the following conditions:
  1. $p \in \mathcal{R}_o$ and $v_1, v_2 \in \mathcal{I}$,
  2. $p \in \mathcal{R}_d$ and $v_1 \in \mathcal{I}$ and $v_2 \in \mathcal{L}$,
  3. $p = instanceOf$, $v_1 \in \mathcal{I}$ and $v_2 \in \mathcal{C}$,
  4. $p = subclassOf$ and $v_1, v_2 \in \mathcal{C}$,
  5. $p = subpropertyOf$ and $v_1, v_2 \in P$,

$\mathcal{E} = \mathcal{C} \cup \mathcal{I} \cup \ell \cup \mathcal{L} \cup \mathcal{R}_o \cup \mathcal{R}_d \cup E$ is the set of all KB elements.

Figure 1 illustrates under the form of a labeled graph a subset of a possible knowledge base on the cinema domain, stating pieces of knowledge such as "Movie is a class", "Actor is a type of Person", and facts such as "JeanDujardin is an Actor" and "JeanDujardin plays in TheArtist". Note that, to make the graph more understandable, this representation shows properties ranges and domains although they do not appear in our definition. Its translation using previously introduced notation is showed in the following listing:

$\mathcal{C} = \{Movie, Person, Actor\}$
$\mathcal{I} = \{TheArtist, JeanDujardin\}$
$\mathcal{L} = \{2011, "film", "movie", \dots\}$
　　　$type(2011) = integer,$
　　　$type("film") = None, \dots$

---

[1] https://www.w3.org/standards/semanticweb/.
[2] *None* type corresponds to RDF plain literals: https://www.w3.org/TR/rdf-concepts/#dfn-plain-literal.

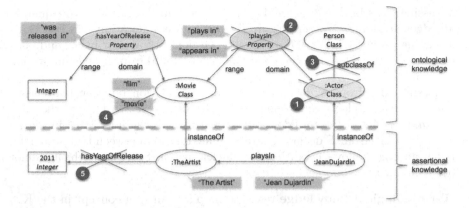

Fig. 1. Graph illustrating a subset of a knowledge base on the cinema domain and some kinds of possible missing knowledge. Red annotations describe examples of missing knowledge pieces; numbers refer to cases described in Sect. 3.2 (Color figure online)

$R_o = \{playsIn\}$

$R_d = \{label, hasYearOfRelease\}$

$E = \{instanceOf(TheArtist, Movie), instanceOf(JeanDujardin, Actor),$
$\quad\quad playsIn(JeanDujardin, TheArtist), hasYearOfRelease(TheArtist,$
$\quad\quad 2011), subclassOf(Actor, Person), label(Movie, "movie"),$
$\quad\quad label(Movie, "film"), \dots \}$

As we have said above, this definition is inspired by the knowledge representation formalisms defined for the semantic web, RDF, RDFS and OWL. These formalisms allow to model more expressive axioms but in practice popular KGs are limited to the tuple (V, P, E) defined above[3].

3.2 Typology of Missing Knowledge Cases

We identify several types of knowledge pieces which, when missing, can prevent answering a question. We distribute these cases along two dimensions: abstraction and question-answering.

Abstraction Dimension. The first dimension is related to the abstraction level, which refers to how the knowledge is contained inside the structure of the KB. Here we can find missing knowledge at three different levels: ontological, terminological and assertional.

On one hand, missing knowledge can fall under the ontological view, i.e. the logical representation of the domain. Possible gaps in **ontological knowledge** are one or a combination of the following cases:

---

[3] Plus domain and range properties, and labels language tags we did not include in our definition for the sake of simplicity.

- a missing class in $\mathcal{C}$, e.g. *actor* does not appear in $\mathcal{C}$ and, as a consequence, all edges involving *actor* are removed from E (see annotation 1 in Fig. 1).
- a missing property in $\mathcal{R}_o \uplus \mathcal{R}_d$, e.g. *playsIn* does not appear in $\mathcal{R}_o$ and, as a consequence, all edges involving *playsIn* are removed from E (see annotation 2 in Fig. 1).
- a missing edge from E declaring a taxonomic relation between two classes (such an edge follows condition 4 from the list in Sect. 3.1), e.g. the edge *subclassOf(Actor, Person)* does not appear in E (see annotation 3 in Fig.1).
- a missing edge from E declaring a taxonomic relation between two properties (such an edge follows condition 5 from the list in Sect. 3.1), which cannot occur in our toy example.

Terminological knowledge refers to map a term to a concept in the KB, e.g. mapping the words "movie" and "film" with the class *movie*. That kind of gap has always the same shape: a missing edge from E defining a *label* property between a vertex from $\mathcal{C} \uplus \mathcal{I}$ and a literal from $\mathcal{L}$ (see annotation 4 in Fig.1). Such an edge is a special case from condition 2 from the list in Sect. 3.1.

The lowest level of abstraction concerns **assertional knowledge**, i.e. knowledge asserting facts at the instance level. In that case, we usually prefer to talk in terms of information than knowledge. These pieces of information have the form of edges stating that an object property holds between two instances, a datatype property holds between an instance and literal value or an instance is declared to belong to a given class. These three cases respectively match the conditions 1, 2 and 3 from the list in Sect. 3.1. We obtain an example of such a lack of information by removing the edge *hasYearOfRelease(TheArtist, 2011)* from $\mathcal{L}$ (see annotation 5 in Fig. 1).

Question-Answering Dimension. The second dimension, related to question answering, can be defined as the way the lack of knowledge affects the answering process:

- Some gaps will prevent NL query interpretation or, in other words, the translation of the NL query into a structured query referring to elements of the KB. These gaps can be reduced to a common case: a missing element (a class, a property, an instance or a label) prevents the mapping from one or several elements constituting the NL question to elements of the KB (see annotations 1, 2, 3 and 4 in Fig. 1). For instance, the question *Who plays in the Artist?* cannot be properly interpreted if the property *playsIn* does not exist (2), or if an actor is not known to be a kind of person (3), assuming the considered QA system somehow knows (after a learning process or through explicit rules) that a question starting with "Who" is asking for a list of persons.
- Other gaps will not prevent the construction of a sound query but will alter the response to that query. For instance, the interpretation of the question *Which movies were released in 2011?*, even if it leads to an accurate formal query, will not return *TheArtist* as an answer if the release date of the movie is not explicitly stated in the KB (see annotation 5 in Fig. 1).

4   Generating Datasets with Missing Information

The formalization and typology of missing knowledge above has been done with knowledge graphs in mind. As our goal is to generate a dataset with missing knowledge, we looked for datasets which comprised knowledge graphs, natural language questions, structured queries and the corresponding answers, with the purpose of reusing them. Most of such datasets involving knowledge graphs are limited to single domains and have small amount of question-answer pairs. The small size limits the possibility of applying machine learning methods, which require larger training datasets, and the limitations to a single domain reduces the generalization of the conclusions. We thus turned our attention to question-answering datasets based on relational datasets.

Among SQL question-answering datasets, we chose to derive our dataset from Spider [19], as it contains a large number of domains and question-query-answer triples. Spider is a semantic-parsing dataset that contains 200 databases with multiple tables over different domains, and includes natural language questions, their SQL translation and the correct answer. In Spider, all the questions and corresponding SQL queries can be answered using databases associated with questions. In this work, we reuse Spider databases and SQL queries, modifying the database automatically so that some queries are unanswerable and systems have to detect the missing information.

But first, we need to apply our typology of missing information to database tables. We leverage the fact that any relational database can be mapped to a knowledge graph [4] and vice versa [17]. The content of KBs is given as a set of triples in the form {subject, propertyName, object/value}, which are binary relations. We can see the content of relational databases as binary relations if we take into account the following:

- For each table column containing literal values, we have a binary relations of the form {primary key, tableName+columnName, value}
- For each table column foreign keys, then we have binary relations of the form {primary key, tableName+columnName, object}, where object is a secondary key.

One of the core contributions of this paper is an algorithm altering the knowledge graph in order to delete information, recording which questions become unanswerable. Given that the automatic procedure has access to which information is going to be deleted, it is possible to automatically detect which questions become unanswerable, thus leading to a dataset containing the incomplete knowledge graph and a set of questions and answers, some of them being unanswerable. Here, instead of mapping the database to a knowledge graph, and then applying the automatic procedures, we decided to work directly on top of the SQL databases, as this allows for a head-to-head comparison with the current technology being used in the Spider dataset. Table 1 shows a sample of our derived dataset.

Table 1. Sample questions on our derived IDK dataset, where db_id refers to the database associated with the question, and answerability is 1 if the question can be answered with the altered database, 0 otherwise.

Question	db_id	Deleted columns	Answerability
Find the emails of the user named "Mary"	twitter_1	name, followers,	0
Which year had the most matches?	wta_1	–	1
How many allergy entries are there?	allergy_1	AllergyType, Sex	1
What is the gender of the student Linda Smith?	restaurant_1	LName, Sex, city_code,	0
Count the total number of counties	election	County_name, Party,	1

More specifically, we decided to focus on the case of removing specific properties from a KB, and leave the rest of cases in the typology for the future. This is analogous to removing full columns from the database tables, provided the column does not contain the primary key of the table (see above). In practice, we first choose such columns at random with a specific deletion rate, and then, for each query in the dataset, check whether the query uses the deleted column in a SELECT, HAVING, WHERE or FROM statement. If that is the case, then the query is unanswerable, otherwise it is still answerable. For each database in the Spider dataset, we can thus produce several new databases with different missing information. Algorithm 1 shows this procedure.

Algorithm 1: Algorithm to derive a dataset with missing information.

Data: Databases, queries, column deletion rate r,
Result: Databases with possible missing knowledge
foreach *database* **do**
| randomly delete r non primary key columns;
end
foreach *query q* **do**
| **if** *any deleted column was used in the SELECT, HAVING, WHERE or FROM statement of q* **then**
| | mark query q as unanswerable
| **else**
| | mark query q as answerable
| **end**
end

The algorithm has a parameter controlling the percentage of columns to be deleted. We decided to set the column deletion rate be 0.5 when generating the

IDK dataset, although different versions of the same database can be derived using different rates, and even different random initializations. Figure 2 shows how this parameter affects the percentage of answerable questions. Note that even when all columns are removed, 30% of questions are still answerable, as they include queries like e.g. the number of entities in a table.

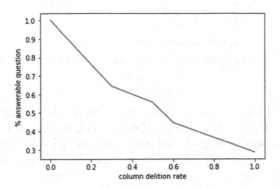

Fig. 2. Relation between column deletion rate r and answerability of questions

This new dataset aims at tackling the task of determining whether or not a NL question can be answered with a given KB. As this task consists in a binary classification, we use accuracy as evaluation measure.

5 Answerability Detection Experiment

In order to ensure that the task we propose is actually challenging for future work, we have conducted some experiments on answerability detection. Given a database and a query in SQL, the task is to detect whether the query can be answered.

We evaluate a few simple baselines in order to check whether simple features allow to determine the answerability of a question in the dataset we propose. Alongside the majority class baseline, we use a logistic regression and evaluate the two following feature sets:

Number of Columns: is the number of columns available in the database associated with the question. This allow us to control for unwantedly easy prediction that does not need the question to determine its answerability.

CBoW: for each question, we represent the associated database columns names and the words in the questions with bag of word embeddings. We use FastText CommonCrawl word embeddings [10][4] and a max pooling to produce the continuous bag of word representations of table columns and the question text. The

---

[4] We used Magnitude [12] in order to query the embeddings in a way that is robust to minor morphological word differences.

column bag of words $h_{columns}$ and question bag of words $h_{question}$ are merged with an element-wise product $h_{columns} \odot h_{question}$.

Table 2. Accuracy of answerability prediction for the proposed baselines.

Model	Accuracy
Majority class	43.5%
Regression on column count	43.5%
Regression on embeddings	**46.3%**

The accuracy of these three baselines on the Spider development set is shown in Table 2. It is worthwhile to note that the column count doesn't affect the accuracy, and that the embeddings-based regression model does not detect unanswerable questions accurately. Our results show that there is ample room for improvement in this area.

6 Conclusion

The goal of this research is to provide a formalization and framework for research in knowledge-base question-answering systems in the face of missing information, with the purpose of moving beyond the unrealistic closed-world assumption. We first presented a thorough typology for numerous types of missing knowledge in knowledge graphs. We then proposed a flexible method to derive evaluation datasets with missing information automatically.

The method takes as input an existing dataset comprising KB, questions, queries and answers, and derives another one with different rates of missing information in the KB, as well as questions, queries and answers, where some of the answers are now unanswerable. The method is demonstrated on Spider, a dataset comprising hundreds of relational databases with their corresponding questions and answers, where we focused on one kind of missing information, that of missing properties. We show empirically that simple baselines fail to detect properly unanswerable questions, calling for further research on this area.

In the future, we would like to extend the dataset generation algorithm with other cases of missing knowledge. Our datasets allow to test how state-of-the-art techniques deal with missing knowledge, and enable research on improving such systems when the closed-world assumption breaks. Beyond that, from a lifelong learning perspective, our dataset is a first step to initiate research on methods to automatically derive knowledge from unstructured documents that could answer currently unanswerable questions, as well as activating conversations with users to try to derive the missing information.

References

1. Artzi, Y., Zettlemoyer, L.: Weakly supervised learning of semantic parsers for mapping instructions to actions. Trans. Assoc. Comput. Linguist. **1**, 49–62 (2013)
2. Berant, J., Chou, A., Frostig, R., Liang, P.: Semantic parsing on Freebase from question-answer pairs. In: Proceedings of the 2013 Conference on Empirical Methods in Natural Language Processing, Seattle, Washington, USA, pp. 1533–1544. Association for Computational Linguistics, October 2013. https://www.aclweb. org/anthology/D13-1160
3. Bogin, B., Gardner, M., Berant, J.: Representing schema structure with graph neural networks for text-to-SQL parsing. In: ACL (2019)
4. Chebotko, A., Lu, S., Fotouhi, F.: Semantics preserving SPARQL-to-SQL translation. Data Knowl. Eng. **68**, 973–1000 (2009)
5. Devlin, J., Chang, M.W., Lee, K., Toutanova, K.: BERT: pre-training of deep bidirectional transformers for language understanding. In: Proceedings of the 2019 Conference of the North American Chapter of the Association for Computational Linguistics: Human Language Technologies, (Long and Short Papers), Minneapolis, Minnesota, vol. 1, pp. 4171–4186. Association for Computational Linguistics, June 2019. https://doi.org/10.18653/v1/N19-1423. https://www.aclweb.org/ anthology/N19-1423
6. Guo, J., et al.: Towards complex text-to-SQL in cross-domain database with intermediate representation. arXiv preprint arXiv:1905.08205 (2019). Version 2
7. Hixon, B., Clark, P., Hajishirzi, H.: Learning knowledge graphs for question answering through conversational dialog. In: Proceedings of the 2015 Conference of the North American Chapter of the Association for Computational Linguistics: Human Language Technologies, Denver, Colorado, pp. 851–861. Association for Computational Linguistics, May–June 2015. https://doi.org/10.3115/v1/N15-1086. https:// www.aclweb.org/anthology/N15-1086
8. Joshi, M., Choi, E., Weld, D.S., Zettlemoyer, L.: Triviaqa: a large scale distantly supervised challenge dataset for reading comprehension. In: Proceedings of the 55th Annual Meeting of the Association for Computational Linguistics, Vancouver, Canada. Association for Computational Linguistics, July 2017
9. Lopez, V., Unger, C., Cimiano, P., Motta, E.: Evaluating question answering over linked data. J. Web Semant. (2013). https://doi.org/10.1016/j.websem.2013.05.006
10. Mikolov, T., Grave, E., Bojanowski, P., Puhrsch, C., Joulin, A.: Advances in pre-training distributed word representations. In: Proceedings of the Eleventh International Conference on Language Resources and Evaluation (LREC 2018), Miyazaki, Japan. European Language Resources Association (ELRA), May 2018. https:// www.aclweb.org/anthology/L18-1008
11. Pasupat, P., Liang, P.: Compositional semantic parsing on semi-structured tables. In: Proceedings of the 53rd Annual Meeting of the Association for Computational Linguistics and the 7th International Joint Conference on Natural Language Processing (Volume 1: Long Papers), Beijing, China, pp. 1470–1480. Association for Computational Linguistics, July 2015. https://doi.org/10.3115/v1/P15-1142. https://www.aclweb.org/anthology/P15-1142
12. Patel, A., Sands, A., Callison-Burch, C., Apidianaki, M.: Magnitude: a fast, efficient universal vector embedding utility package. In: Proceedings of the 2018 Conference on Empirical Methods in Natural Language Processing: System Demonstrations, Brussels, Belgium, pp. 120–126. Association for Computational Linguistics, November 2018. https://doi.org/10.18653/v1/D18-2021. https://www.aclweb.org/ anthology/D18-2021

13. Peñas, A., Veron, M., Pradel, C., Otegi, A., Echegoyen, G., Rodrigo, A.: Continuous learning for question answering. In: Proceedings of the 10th International Workshop on Spoken Dialog Systems (IWSDS 2019) - DSLL Special Session (2019)
14. Price, P.J.: Evaluation of spoken language systems: the ATIS domain. In: Speech and Natural Language: Proceedings of a Workshop Held at Hidden Valley, Pennsylvania, 24–27 June 1990 (1990). https://www.aclweb.org/anthology/H90-1020
15. Rajpurkar, P., Jia, R., Liang, P.: Know what you don't know: unanswerable questions for SQuAD. In: Proceedings of the 56th Annual Meeting of the Association for Computational Linguistics (Volume 2: Short Papers), Melbourne, Australia, pp. 784–789. Association for Computational Linguistics, July 2018. https://doi.org/10.18653/v1/P18-2124. https://www.aclweb.org/anthology/P18-2124
16. Rajpurkar, P., Zhang, J., Lopyrev, K., Liang, P.: SQuAD: 100,000+ questions for machine comprehension of text. In: Proceedings of the 2016 Conference on Empirical Methods in Natural Language Processing, Austin, Texas, pp. 2383–2392. Association for Computational Linguistics, November 2016. https://doi.org/10.18653/v1/D16-1264. https://www.aclweb.org/anthology/D16-1264
17. Soussi, N., Bahaj, M.: Semantics preserving SQL-to-SPARQL query translation for nested right and left outer join. J. Appl. Res. Technol. 15(5), 504–512 (2017)
18. Yu, T., et al.: CoSQL: a conversational text-to-SQL challenge towards cross-domain natural language interfaces to databases. In: Proceedings of EMNLP 2019 (2019)
19. Yu, T., et al.: Spider: a large-scale human-labeled dataset for complex and cross-domain semantic parsing and text-to-SQL task. In: Proceedings of the 2018 Conference on Empirical Methods in Natural Language Processing, Brussels, Belgium, pp. 3911–3921. Association for Computational Linguistics, October–November 2018. https://doi.org/10.18653/v1/D18-1425. https://www.aclweb.org/anthology/D18-1425
20. Yu, T., et al.: SParC: cross-domain semantic parsing in context. In: Proceedings of the 57th Annual Meeting of the Association for Computational Linguistics, Florence, Italy. Association for Computational Linguistics (2019)
21. Zelle, J.M., Mooney, R.J.: Learning to parse database queries using inductive logic programming. In: Proceedings of the Thirteenth National Conference on Artificial Intelligence, AAAI 1996, vol. 2, pp. 1050–1055. AAAI Press (1996). http://dl.acm.org/citation.cfm?id=1864519.1864543
22. Zhong, V., Xiong, C., Socher, R.: Seq2SQL: generating structured queries from natural language using reinforcement learning. arXiv preprint arXiv:1709.00103 (2017)

2AIRTC: The Amharic Adhoc Information Retrieval Test Collection

Tilahun Yeshambel[1][(✉)], Josiane Mothe[2], and Yaregal Assabie[3]

[1] IT PhD Program, Addis Ababa University, Addis Ababa, Ethiopia
tilahun.yeshambel@uog.edu.et
[2] INSPE, Univ. de Toulouse, IRIT, UMR5505 CNRS, Toulouse, France
josiane.mothe@irit.fr
[3] Department of Computer Science, Addis Ababa University, Addis Ababa, Ethiopia
yaregal.assabie@aau.edu.et

Abstract. Evaluation is highly important for designing, developing, and maintaining information retrieval (IR) systems. The IR community has developed shared tasks where evaluation framework, evaluation measures and test collections have been developed for different languages. Although Amharic is the official language of Ethiopia currently having an estimated population of over 110 million, it is one of the under-resourced languages and there is no Amharic adhoc IR test collection to date. In this paper, we promote the monolingual Amharic IR test collection that we build for the IR community. Following the framework of Cranfield project and TREC, the collection that we named 2AIRTC consists of 12,583 documents, 240 topics and the corresponding relevance judgments.

Keywords: Information retrieval · Amharic test collection · Adhoc retrieval · Evaluation · Data collection · Corpus · Under-resourced language

1 Introduction

With the growth of online text information and globalization, information retrieval (IR) has gained more attention especially in commonly used languages. Both the research community and industry have been very active in this field for more than 50 years (Sanderson and Croft 2012). IR also has an old history of evaluation. After the early framework in the Crandfield project, TREC has standardized adhoc retrieval evaluation (Buckley and Voorhees 2005). Performance evaluation of a system is indeed very crucial for scientific progress (Ferro 2014). There are many system evaluation criteria such as effectiveness, efficiency, usability, accessibility, utility, portability, and maintainability. One of the major focuses of IR research evaluation is to measure the IR system effectiveness. In adhoc retrieval, where the task for the system is to retrieve relevant documents for a given query, effectiveness looks at the ability of the system to retrieve only the relevant documents for a given user's query. This implies an evaluation framework consisting of a test collection as well as metrics. The standard adhoc retrieval test collection consists of three components: a corpus of documents to be searched in, a set of users'

© Springer Nature Switzerland AG 2020
A. Arampatzis et al. (Eds.): CLEF 2020, LNCS 12260, pp. 55–66, 2020.
https://doi.org/10.1007/978-3-030-58219-7_5

information needs or topics, and the associated relevance judgments indicating which documents are relevant for which topics. Test collections facilitate reproducibility of results and meaningful effectiveness comparison among different retrieval techniques.

In adhoc retrieval evaluation, a corpus is usually a systematic collection of naturally occurring fixed size documents in machine readable form. Building text collections for adhoc IR is a common task although it is resource demanding. A large number of shared tasks rely on such collections. Some of the well known text collections are Cranfield project (Cleverdon 1959), Text Retrievals Conference[1] (TREC) and more specifically TREC adhoc (Harman 1995), Cross-Language Evaluation Forum[2] (CLEF) datasets (Ferro 2014), and NACSIS Test Collection for Information Retrieval[3] (NTCIR) (Kando et al. 1999). Indeed, the IR international conferences such as TREC, CLEF, NTCIR, INEX[4], and FIRE[5] are held based on their own test collections.

One of the common techniques to build a test collection for adhoc retrieval is pooling, where the document pool to be judged by humans is built by putting together the top N retrieved results from a set of systems (Soboroff 2007). In this technique, documents outside the pool are considered as non-relevant. Pooling is a standard technique to create relevance judgment in TREC, CLEF, and NTCIR test collections. The second technique is exhaustive relevance judgment where every and each document in a dataset is judged according to each query (Kagolovsky and Moehr 2003). Cranfield and CACM test collections are built using exhaustive relevance judgment. A third way of preparing relevance judgment is crowdsourcing in which huge and heterogeneous mass of potential workers are assigned to a relevance task in the form of an open call through the Internet (Samimi and Ravana 2014). Whatever the way they are built, test collections are one of the pillars for testing and comparison of retrieval system performance.

While there are a lot of existing collections in different languages such as English, French, Arabic, and Asian languages, to our best knowledge, there is no test collection for Amharic IR. The lack of reference collection is a major impediment to the development of Amharic IR as well as natural language processing (NLP) tools. Indeed, Amharic is one of the under-resourced languages as computational resources such as training and test data, electronic bilingual dictionary, stemmer, tagger, morphological analyzer, etc. do not exist or the existing ones are not fully functional and the number of studies reported on Amharic is considerably limited compared to what is done for other languages such as English. Tools and resources that have been developed for other languages cannot be directly applied to Amharic because of its very specificities. We do believe that an Amharic reference collection would help to carry out more research and development works on Amharic IR and NLP. This paper describes the construction process and characteristics of the resulting Amharic IR test collection we deliver to the IR community.

---

[1] Text REtrieval Conference http://trec.nist.gov.

[2] Cross Language Evaluation Forum http://www.clef-initiative.eu.

[3] NII Test Collection for Information Retrieval http://research.nii.ac.jp/ntcir.

[4] Initiative for the Evaluation of XML Retrieval http://inex.mmci.uni-saarland.de.

[5] Forum for Information Retrieval Evaluation http://fire.irsi.res.in.

2 Amharic Language

Amharic is an Afro-Asiatic language belonging to the Southwest Semitic group (Hetzron 1972; Argaw *et al.* 2005). It is an official language of the government of Ethiopia currently having an estimated population of over 110 million (countrymeters 2020). It is the second-most commonly spoken Semitic language in the world next to Arabic (Abate and Assabie 2014). Although many languages are spoken in Ethiopia, Amharic is the lingua franca and the most literary language serving as a medium of instruction in the education system of the country for a long period. It uses Ethiopic alphabet for writing and has 34 base characters along with modifications on the respective base characters. The alphabet is conveniently written in a tabular format of seven columns. The first column represents the basic form with vowel ኧ/ä/ and the other six orders represent modifications with vowels in the order of ኡ/u/, ኢ/i/, ኣ/a/, ኤ/e/, እ/ə/, and ኦ/o/. For example, the base character መ/mä/ has the following modifications: ሙ/mu/, ሚ/mi/, ማ/ma/, ሜ/me/, ም/mə/, and ሞ/mo/. The language also uses punctuation marks such as ።(full stop), ፣(comma), ፤(semicolon), ፥(colon), etc. It also adopts some other punctuation marks such as question and exclamation marks from English.

Amharic is known to have a complex morphology. A large number of words can be formed from a base form and word formation is complex involving affixation, reduplication, and Semitic stem inter digitation. Thousands of surface words can be generated from an Amharic root and its stems by changing the shape of alphabets in a stem or root, and by adding affixes on stems (Abate and Assabie 2014). For example, the verb ኣሰበረ/*ässäbbärä*/is derived from the verbal stem ሰበር-/*säbbär-*/ which is itself derived from the verbal root ስ-በ-ር/*s-b-r*/. Furthermore, a verb can be marked for a combination of person, case, gender, number, tense, aspect, and mood. Accordingly, the following verbs can be generated from the verbal stem ሰበር-/*säbbär-*/: ሰበርኩ/*säbbärku* 'I broke'/, ሰበርኩህ/*säbbärkuh* 'I broke you'/, ሰበርን/*säbbärn* 'we broke'/, ተሰበርኩ/*täsäbbärku* 'I was broken'/, ሰበራች/*säbbäräc* 'she broke'/, ኣይሰበርም /*ʔäysäbbäräm* 'he will not be broken'/, etc. Thousands of words can be generated from a single verbal root making analysis, annotation and tagging of Amharic text a non-trivial task. This level of morphological complexity has significantly contributed to the difficulty of producing linguistic resources for Amharic.

3 Related Work

3.1 Test Collections and Evaluation Standards

To investigate the performance of a given retrieval technique, IR research community uses reference collections that have been built for different languages and many of them are publicly available and freely accessible. They are now commonly used in IR studies and helped in promoting research in IR. In this section, we present some of the text test collections.

Cranfield test collection is the first IR test collection that also grounded the evaluation framework used nowadays in IR. It was created in late 1960's and contains the abstract of 1,400 documents, 225 queries and the corresponding relevance judgment (Cleverdon 1967; Harman 1995). The Cranfield test collection is the base for the success of different conferences like Text Retrieval Conference (TREC). However, in the 1990s, the size of the Cranfield collection was considered as too small to generalize a given finding on it.

TREC was established in 1992 in order to support IR researches, to provide larger and more realistic collections, as well as to promote a standard for IR evaluation (Harman 1995). Since then, the TREC conference creates series of evaluation resources specifically for adhoc retrieval. What is now considered as a standard adhoc IR TREC collection consists of documents, topics that correspond to users' needs and that can be structured in various fields, and relevance judgment. While TREC initially focused on English, it had also considered other languages as Spanish, Chinese and Arabic that went later to other conferences.

The Cross-Language Evaluation Forum (CLEF) conference is one of the known conferences that have their own large-scale evaluation test collection for European languages. With the initiative of CLEF, large test collections for languages such as English, French, German, Bulgarian, and Hungarian are now available (Peter 2001; Ferro 2014). One of the CLEF aims was to evaluate both monolingual IR and cross-lingual IR systems while it is now oriented more to other tasks such as image retrieval, health systems, etc.

NII-NACSIS Test Collection for Information Retrieval (NTCIR) focuses on cross-language search for Asian languages such as Japanese, Chinese, and Korean (Kando et al. 1999). Since 1997, it promotes researches in IR, text summarization, information extraction, and question answering with the aims of offering research infrastructure, forming research community and developing evaluation methodology.

3.2 Amharic Corpora, Resources and Tools

The growth of Amharic digital data accelerates the demand for technologies and NLP tools for online data processing. Nonetheless, very few corpora and resources have been built for experimental evaluation of applications and tools. Some of the Amharic text corpora which are available digitally and utilized for the development of Amharic NLP tools, IR or other text-centered tasks are presented in what follows.

Corpora

Walta Information Center (WIC) Corpus: This corpus has been built by linguists from Addis Ababa University and it is available both in Amharic characters and Romanized form. The corpus contains 1,065 Amharic news articles with 4,035 sentences. The domain of the corpus is much diversified including topics like politics, economics, science, sport, religion, business, etc. (Demeke and Getachew 2006).

Ethiopian Language Research Center (ELRC) Corpus: This is the annotated version of WIC corpus. It has been annotated with part-of-speech (POS) tags manually by ELRC at Addis Ababa University. The corpus is tagged with 30 different POS tags (Demeke and Getachew 2006).

Addis Ababa University NLP Task Force Corpus: This corpus is prepared by Language Technology staff members from IT Doctoral Program at Addis Ababa University. The corpus is prepared to create parallel corpus for computational linguistics and includes Amharic, Afaan Oromo, Tigrigna, and English languages with diverse content from historical documents and newspapers. The project is still on-going and the corpus is continuously being updated (Abate et al. 2018).

Amharic Corpus for Machine Learning (ACML): This corpus has been prepared by Gamback (Gamback 2012). The data set consists of free texts collected from Ethiopian News Headlines (ENH), WIC and Amharic fiction "Fikir Iske Meqabir" (FIM). It is a set of 10,000 ENH articles with a total of 3.1 million words, 1,503 words from the WIC corpus, and 470 words from FIM book.

These corpora are simply collections of documents and as such are not appropriate to evaluate adhoc retrieval since there is no query set nor the associated relevance judgment. They are mainly collections of documents from which formatting tags are removed and additional semantic annotations are provided. Moreover, most of the corpora are not publicly accessible.

It is also worth to mention the non-European languages multi-lingual IR track at CLEF where queries in Amharic language were used although document collections were in European languages (Di Nunzio *et al.* 2005; Di Nunzio *et al.* 2007). For Amharic-French IR, one of the most successful approaches was a dictionary-based one Argaw *et al.* (2005).

Resources

Amharic Machine Readable Dictionaries: Some of the commonly used dictionaries involving Amharic are Amharic-English dictionary containing 15,000 Amharic words (Amsalu 1987), Amharic-French dictionary containing 12,000 Amharic entries (Berhanu 2004), and Amharic-Amharic dictionary containing 56,000 entries (Kesatie 1993). Entries of the Amharic machine-readable dictionaries are represented by their citation forms.

Stopword lists: Few researches were conducted on building Amharic stopword list. Researchers who conduct studies on Amharic IR usually build their own list of stopwords. For example, Mindaye *et al.* (2010) built the stopword list with 77 entries while Eyassu and Gambäck (2005) created the stopword list with 745 entries. They collected stopwords from different sources but these lists have not been evaluated by linguists. Recently, Yeshambel *et al.* (2020) built morpheme-based stopword list by systematically analyzing the morphology of the language and their distribution in the corpus. The list consists of 222 stopwords.

Tools

Amharic faces challenges in the development of NLP tools and applications. The major obstacles that hinder the progress on the development of Amharic NLP applications are complex morphology of the language, lack of sufficient corpora, and lack of standards in resource construction and application development. As a result, only few Amharic NLP tools have been developed thus far using rule-based and machine learning approaches. Among the available tools are morphological analyzers (Argaw and Asker 2006; Gasser 2011; Abate and Assabie 2014), stemmer (Alemayehu and Willett 2003), and parser (Argaw and Asker 2006; Tachbelie *et al.* 2011). However, the development of these tools is at prototype stages. They are also limited in scope.

4 Amharic IR Test Collection

4.1 Methodology to Build the 2AIRTC Collection

The document collection creation has been carried out in two steps: we initially collected documents from various sources that produce documents in Amharic without considering any specific topics. We then complement this collection with web documents retrieved considering our target topics. To do this, we run the query part of our topics on a Web search engine and gather the retrieved documents. The topic set was created by considering both current issues but also considering the topics that were likely to be treated in our initial sources. The document relevance judgments were manually done using a precise guideline. For each topic, we run Lemur (http://www.lemurproject.org.) on the initial document set and fuse these results with the ones from the web search engine. The fused lists were then manually assessed with binary relevance for each topic. These steps are described in more details in the next sub-sections.

4.2 Document Set

Since we wanted documents to be diverse enough, we initially collected documents from different sources. More precisely, we collected 777 documents from news agencies sites and social media (Walta Media and Communication Corporate[6], Fana Broadcasting Corporate[7], Amhara Mass Media Agency[8] and Facebook), 701 historical documents from blogger (Daniel Kibret[9]), and 15,000 documents from Amharic Wikipedia[10]. In addition, 8,522 news articles were collected from Walta Information Center and we also collected 1,189 religious documents, 1,773 news articles, and 772 documents (letters, opinions and reports) from various sources. Accordingly, the total number of documents collected is 28,734. The document collection represents various topics about business, sport, entertainment, education, religion, politics, technology, health and culture.

After the topics were created, to select the documents to be assessed, we ran the title fields of these topics on our initial corpus using Lemur toolkit. We also ran the same queries (topic title) using Google on the Web. Here our idea was to use not only the documents from our initial collection but also to enrich the collection with documents that were retrieved on the Web. Our aim was to complement the document collection and to avoid topics with either no or very few relevant documents. For documents collected from the search engine, we considered a maximum of 50 documents per topic and we collected 2,880 documents in that way on the Web. For relevance assessment, we fused both retrieved document list (Lemur on our initial collection and Web documents for the complementary documents). Each document from the fused list was then judged for relevance. Finally, the document collection consists in two sub-collections: documents that have been assessed for at least one topic (either relevant or non-relevant) and the entire document collection.

---

[6] http://www.waltainfo.com.

[7] https://www.fanabc.com.

[8] https://www.facebook.com/AmharaMassMediaAgencyAMMA.

[9] http://www.danielkibret.com.

[10] https://am.wikipedia.org/wiki.

Assessed Document Sub-collection: This collection is created only from the judged documents in the initial corpus and Web documents. The top retrieved documents from both Lemur and Google of each query are fused and organized in separate files and then assessed independently. This sub-collection consists of 12,583 assessed documents though the collected documents were more than this. Out of these, 6,960 documents have been assessed as relevant for at least one topic and the remaining 5,623 documents have been judged as non-relevant. These documents are full length, processed to remove unnecessary parts such as tags and English alphabets, and plain text form. All documents are stored in a single text file using TREC-like format. Each document has a unique document identification number. The content of each document is enclosed with <TEXT> and </TEXT> tags. One document is delimited from the other by "DOC" and "</DOC>" tags. As shown in Table 1, the relevant document set contains various document lengths from small to very large. The same holds for documents that have been judged as non-relevant.

Table 1. Statistics of the 2AIRTC relevant judged document corpus

Parameter	Size
Number of documents	6,960
Number of sentences	63,081
Total number of words in the documents	2,243,372
Number of unique words	6,446
Minimum number of words per document	43
Average number of words per document	1,357
Median of words per document	219
Maximum number of words per document	74,804
Size of the relevant judged document	28.8 MB

Entire Document Collection: While the previous sub-collection contains documents that have been assessed for at least one topic, the entire collection consists of our initial documents plus the ones retrieved from the Web making a total of 31,614 documents. Documents from this collection are not formatted.

4.3 Topic Set

We created the topic set using Amharic language statements from our search experience. The topics were built in such a way to reflect real word information need and cover diverse issues. The assumption considered during topic creation was that words in the topic titles are expected in document collection. The 2AIRTC contains a set of topics which prescribe information needs to be met. We manually created 240 topics for the adhoc IR task where the topics are about specific entities (e.g., people, places or events). Many of these topics were created by skimming some documents in the initial corpus, few of them were created by considering current issues, and the other were simply made up. The topic set is written both in Amharic and its translated version of English. Both the corpus and topic set are coded in UTF-8 (see Fig. 1). Each topic has a unique identification integer number. The title field contains fewer search words which describe a topic and could be a typical query to be submitted to a retrieval system. Topic titles include short topics, medium topics, and collocation which vary in terms of length and types. Since Amharic is a morphologically complex language, topic titles were designed to reflect real operational environment. The base of Amharic words might be stem or root. For Amharic retrieval, on top of stems, the roots of words which are derived from verbs are important rather than stems. Therefore, various types of words are included in the titles. Some of them consist of primary words and others are from derived words.

```
<top>
<num>2</num>
<title_A> የኢትዮጵያዊያን የዘመን አቆጣጠር </title_A>
<title_E> Ethiopian calendar  </title_E>
<desc_A> ስለኢትዮጵያ ዘመን አቆጣጠር ሥርአት የሚያትቱ ሰነዶችን መለየት:: </desc_A>
<desc_E> Identifying documents discussing on Ethiopian calendar system. </desc_E>
<narr_A> ስለ ኢትዮጵያ የዘመን አቆጣጠር ታሪክና አመሰራረት የሚያትቱ ሰነዶች ጥሩ የመረጃ ምንጮች
ናቸው:: ከዚህ በተጨማሪ   የበዓላት ቀናት  እና የአቆጣጠር ስሌት የሚያትቱ ሰነዶች ጠቃሚ የመረጃ ምንጮች
ናቸው:: ይሁን እንጂ ስለአውሮጳውያን የዘመን አቆጣጠር ወይም ስለሌሎች ሀገሮች የቀን አቆጣጠር የሚገልጹ
ሰነዶች ጠቃሚዎች አይደሉም:: እንዲሁም ስለአዲስ አመት የሚያትቱ ሰነዶች ጠቃሚ የመረጃ ምንጮች
አይደሉም::</narr_A>
<narr_E> Documents discussing the origin and history of Ethiopian calendar are good
sources of information. In addition, documents explaining about holidays and methods for
finding the dates and day in each year are relevant. However, documents discussing on
Gregorian calendar or other calendars are not relevant. Moreover, documents discussing
on new year are not relevant.</narr_E>
</top>
```

Fig. 1. 2AIRTC topic number 2

The description field contains description of the topic area in one or two sentences. It is the description of the user's information need. Conceptually, it is consistent with the topic title and states its purpose in a sentence form. The narrative field provides further explanation about each title to decide which types of documents are relevant and which are not. It consists of more than two sentences. Assessors judge document relevance based on this field. Table 2 presents detailed information on the topic set.

4.4 Relevance Judgment

Relevance judgment is the third element of an adhoc IR test collection. It indicates the set of relevant documents to each topic. With regard to the document list to be reviewed by assessors, as mentioned previously, we ran the title field of the topics on our initial corpus using Lemur toolkit to get the first top 50 retrieved documents list per topic.

Table 2. Statistics of the topic set

Parameter	Size
Number of topics	240
Minimum number of words per topic title	1
Average number of topic title's words per topic	4
Median of topic title's words per topic	3
Maximum number of topic title's words per topic	7

We also ran the same topic using Google and considered a maximum of 50 documents. The topics and the associated retrieved results of both were distributed to assessors who judged them. Duplicated documents were removed. The relevant assessment was made manually by reading documents and using the narrative part of each topic. In addition, exhaustive relevance judgment was used on some topics in the initial document collection to get a larger number of relevant documents.

A document is marked as relevant based on the narrative information in the topic; thus it should not simply contain words from the query but rather fulfill the information need. Document relevance assessment has been done by students taking IR course at Addis Ababa University. The students formed groups in which each group consisting of five students was given 20 topics and top 50 retrieved documents for each topic by Google and Lemur. The students judged the relevance of each document for the given topic based on its narrative information and their satisfaction as users. There was one assessor group per topic. However, all students in the group needed to agree to decide the relevance of each document. Therefore, a judgment represents the shared information needs of a group of students. While assessing top 50 documents retrieved by Lemur, sometimes, we could not get any relevant document from our initial corpus of 28,734 documents. Therefore, some documents which were not retrieved for any of the topics using Lemur were assessed carefully in exhaustive relevance judgment during the second phase. For those documents, students had read each of them and judged as relevant or non-relevant to each topic.

As a result of manual relevant assessment, some topics have many relevant documents, while other topics have fewer relevant documents. Each topic has at least 10 relevant documents. This indicates that for some topics it will not be possible to measure effectiveness above rank ten; this is also the case in TREC or alike test collections.

Finally, the 2AIRTC relevance file was produced using TREC format containing *topic ID*, *0*, *document ID* and *relevance* fields. Topic and document IDs are unique identification numbers of topics and documents, respectively. The number zero (0) is common to all topics and documents. The relevance indicates the relevance value of the considered document/topic pair and is 1 if the document is relevant to a topic, 0 otherwise.

Table 3. 2AIRTC relevance judgment statistics

Parameter	Size
Total number of topics	240
Average number of relevant documents per topic	22
Minimum number of relevant documents per topic	10
Maximum number of relevant documents per topic	172

5 Conclusion

Using standard test collections in IR is a common experimental practice. Various test collections for different languages have been built and are used by many research groups. Amharic IR test collection is an under explored research area. In comparison with other resourceful languages, few resources and tools have been built for Amharic. Even the existing Amharic corpora do not have any associated Amharic topics and relevance judgments. Furthermore, most of the existing corpora and resources are small in size and not publicly accessible. However, the importance of building and sharing test collections is well acknowledged. We built the first reusable test collection for IR system benchmarking[11]. Our Amharic test collection is reproducible and contains representative documents and topics. This collection, named 2AIRTC, can serve as a reliable resource for the evaluation and comparison of various Amharic IR systems. We do believe this collection will help to enhance new research on Amharic IR.

Acknowledgement. We would like to thank students who participated in the creation of the test collection. We also thank the owners and sources of documents (Walta Media and Communication Corporate, Fana Broadcasting Corporate, Amhara Mass Media Agency and Daniel Kibret) who provide and permit their documents to carryout academic research experiments and annotate, use and share them for research community.

References

Abate, M., Assabie, Y.: Development of Amharic morphological analyzer using memory-based learning. In: Przepiórkowski, A., Ogrodniczuk, M. (eds.) NLP 2014. LNCS (LNAI), vol. 8686, pp. 1-13. Springer, Cham (2014). https://doi.org/10.1007/978-3-319-10888-9_1

Abate, S.T., et al.: Parallel corpora for Bi-Lingual English-Ethiopian languages statistical machine translation. In: Proceedings of the 27th International Conference on Computational Linguistics, New Mexico, USA, pp. 3102-3111, (2018)

Alemayehu, N., Willett, P.: The effectiveness of stemming for information retrieval in Amharic. Program: Electron. libr. Inf. Syst. **37**(4), 254-259 (2003)

Amsalu, A.: Amharic-English Dictionary. Kuraz Printing Press, Addis Ababa (1987)

---

[11] This collection is accessible by contacting the corresponding author at: tilahun.yeshambel@uog.edu.et

Argaw, A.A., Asker, L.: Amharic-English information retrieval. In: Peters, Carol, Clough, P., et al. (eds.) CLEF 2006. LNCS, vol. 4730, pp. 43-50. Springer, Heidelberg (2007). https://doi.org/10.1007/978-3-540-74999-8_5

Argaw, A.A., Asker, L., Cöster, R., Karlgren, J., Sahlgren, M.: Dictionary-based Amharic-French information retrieval. In: Peters, C., et al. (eds.) CLEF 2005. LNCS, vol. 4022, pp. 83-92. Springer, Heidelberg (2006). https://doi.org/10.1007/11878773_9

Berhanu, A.: Amharic-Français Dictionnaire. Shama Books, Addis Ababa (2004)

Buckley, C., Voorhees, E.: Retrieval system evaluation. In TREC: Experiment and Evaluation in Information Retrieval, 3rd edn, pp. 53-75. MIT Press, Cambridge (2005)

Cleverdon, C.W.: The evaluation of systems used in information retrieval. In: Proceeding of the International Conference on Scientific Information, Washington, DC, pp. 687-698 (1959)

Cleverdon, C.: The Cranfield tests on index language devices. In: Aslib Proceedings, MCB UP Ltd (1967)

Countrymeters. Ethiopian Population (2020). http://countrymeters.info/en/ethiopia. Accessed 05 May 2020

Di Nunzio, G.M., Ferro, N., Jones, G.J.F., Peters, C.: CLEF 2005: Ad Hoc track overview. In: Peters, C., et al. (eds.) CLEF 2005. LNCS, vol. 4022, pp. 11-36. Springer, Heidelberg (2006). https://doi.org/10.1007/11878773_2

Di Nunzio, G.M., Ferro, N., Mandl, T., Peters, C.: CLEF 2007: Ad Hoc track overview. In: Peters, C., et al. (eds.) CLEF 2007. LNCS, vol. 5152, pp. 13-32. Springer, Heidelberg (2008). https://doi.org/10.1007/978-3-540-85760-0_2

Demeke, G.A., Getachew, M.: Manual annotation of Amharic news items with part-of-speech tags and its challenges. Ethiop. Lang. Res. Cent. 2, 1-16 (2006)

Eyassu, S., Gambäck, B.: Classifying Amharic news text using self-organizing maps. 71 (2005). https://doi.org/10.3115/1621787.1621801

Harman, D.: Overview of the second text retrieval conference (TREC-2). Inf. Process. Manage. 31(3), 271-289 (1995)

Ferro, N.: CLEF 15th birthday: past, present, and future. ACM SIGIR Forum 48(2), 31-55 (2014)

Gamback, B.: Tagging and verifying an amharic news corpus. In: Proceedings of the Eighth International Conference on Language Resources and Evaluation, pp. 79-84 (2012)

Gasser, M.: HornMorpho: a system for morphological processing of Amharic, Oromo, and Tigrinya. In: Conference on Human Language Technology for Development, pp. 94-99 (2011)

Hetzron, R.: Ethiopian Semitic: Studies in Classification. Manchester Univesity Press, Manchester (1972)

Kagolovsky, Y., Moehr, J.: Current status of the evaluation of information retrieval. J. Med. Syst. 27(5), 409-424 (2003)

Kando, N., Kuriyama, K., Nozue, T., Eguchi, K., Kato, H., Adachi, J.: The NTCIR workshop the first evaluation workshop on Japanese text retrieval and cross-lingual information retrieval. In: 4th International Workshop on Information Retrieval with Asian Languages (1), INV-1-INV-7 (1999)

Kesatie B.: YeAmarinja Mezgebe Qalat. Ethiopian Languages Research Center, Artistic Publisher, Addis Abeba, Ethiopia (1993)

Mindaye, T., Atnafu, S.: Design and implementation of Amharic search engine. In: Proceeding of the 5th International Conference on Signal Image Technology and Internet Based Systems, pp. 318-325 (2009)

Peters, C., Braschler, M.: European research letter: cross-language system evaluation: The CLEF campaigns. J. Am. Soc. Inf. Sci. Technol. 52(12), 1067-1072 (2001)

Samimi, P., Ravana, S.: Creation of reliable relevance judgments in information retrieval systems evaluation experimentation through crowdsourcing a review. Sci. World J. 2014 (2014)

Sanderson, M., Croft, W.: The history of information retrieval research. Proc. IEEE Spec. Centennial Issue 100, 1444-1451 (2001)

Soboroff, I.: A comparasion of pooled and sampled relevance judgments. In: The TREC 2006 Terabyte Track. The First International Workshop on Evaluation Information Access, Tokyo, Japan (2007)

Tachbelie, M.Y., Abate, S.T., Besacier, L.: Part-of-speech tagging for under resourced and morphologically rich languages the case of Amharic. HLTD **2011**, 50-55 (2011)

Yeshambel, T., Josiane, M., Assabie, Y.: Construction of Morpheme-based Amharic stopword list for information retrieval system. accepted. In: The 8th EAI International Conference on Advancements of Science and Technology, Bahir Dar, Ethiopia (2020)

Short Papers

Short Papers

The Curious Case of Session Identification

Florian Dietz[(✉)]

Berlin School of Library and Information Science, Humboldt-Universität zu Berlin,
Dorotheenstr. 26, 10117 Berlin, Germany
florian.dietz@alumni.hu-berlin.de

Abstract. Dividing interaction logs into meaningful segments has been a core problem in supporting users in search tasks for over 20 years. Research has brought up many different definitions: from simplistic mechanical sessions to complex search missions spanning multiple days. Having meaningful segments is essential for many tasks depending on context, yet many research projects over the last years still rely on early proposals. This position paper gives a quick overview of session identification development and questions the widespread use of the industry standard.

Keywords: Session identification · Task extraction · Interactive information retrieval

1 Introduction

Web usage mining has been around for quite some time now. Since the late 1990s and early 2000s, researchers have contributed dozens of studies about handling interaction logs and how to utilize them in their field of research. These early studies focus on search behaviour, interpreting how users interact with search systems and what is actually searched for [5,34]. Initial findings gave insight about average query length, amount of queries and reformulations or the number of visited result pages.

However, the actual identification of sessions in the interaction logs received a growing interest. Identifying patterns and segmenting logs into user sessions has grown to be a focal point, being the foundation for any further analysis or research [13]. Various methods were tested for finding reasonable session bound aries, often applying mechanical cuts like time outs. The most common inactivity time out of 30 min, most likely evolved from the 25.5 min proposed by [5], is still used today. Later, research interest went from mechanical sessions to a more intent-oriented approach, acknowledging that finding suitable user context is easier when sessions are logically segmented rather than mechanically. Therefore, definitions vary from mechanical [5] to logical [17].

Today, most related publications still apply the 30 min inactivity cut as a foundation. From user modelling to recommendation to personalisation - the 30 min rule seems to be omnipresent. This position paper is part of a dissertation project researching the impact of different session modelling concepts. A quick

© Springer Nature Switzerland AG 2020
A. Arampatzis et al. (Eds.): CLEF 2020, LNCS 12260, pp. 69–74, 2020.
https://doi.org/10.1007/978-3-030-58219-7_6

timeline on the development of session concepts is presented and the solitary use of a temporal constraint discussed.

2 Literature Review

Session Identification. Early studies identifying sessions as the basic unit of measurement in interaction logs mostly relied on time gaps to decide if two consecutive queries belong to the same session, resulting in mechanically segmented sessions. [5] were among the first to introduce a temporal constraint. They report an average time of 9.3 min between interactions, adding 1.5 standard deviations to propose a temporal inactivity limit of 25.5 min. Other temporal cuts are also reported: 5 min [33], 15 min [14,15] or even 60 min and longer [3].

Over the years, these time constraints have evolved into a 30 min inactivity time out. Many works rely exclusively on this arbitrarily set time limit [4,8,21, 24,37], others recognized a need for more evidence, using stopping patterns [39] or dynamic time thresholds based on visited pages [7,41] and users [27]. After [35] reported multitasking during search sessions, even identifying interleaving intents, growing interest was directed to the identification of tasks rather than mechanical sessions.

Task Identification. Tasks may be similar to sessions, but they move away from purely mechanical thresholds to logical boundaries. Simple approaches use lexical similarity between adjacent queries [11] to identify topically related segments, assuming that queries that do not share any terms with previous ones indicate a new session [17] (although the sessions are identified with a temporal constraint in the first place). A prime example of the combination of lexical similarity and temporal relationship is [9], who use a geometric approach to calculate similarity between query pairs based on a 24 h temporal limit. Most approaches still use (mechanical) session-based features to calculate similarity between queries. Some use sequential patterns [28,30], others employ external sources to create a richer semantic context like thesauri [16] or pre-trained embeddings [10].

Even more advanced is the identification of cross-session tasks, recognizing the importance of interleaving and multiple tasks throughout the boundaries of mechanical sessions. [19] identified tasks as just another level of measurement. They define search sessions as user activity within a fixed time window, search goals as the atomic information need producing one or more queries and search missions as the overarching concept, connecting various search goals and therefore possibly spanning multiple sessions. This hierarchical point of view works well for describing user behaviour: visiting an information system in a session, searching for several goals belonging to one search mission. In [22], this concept is exploited via hierarchical clustering algorithms based on multiple query features. [12] and [13] propose a cascading method for connecting related adjacent queries by consecutively using lexical and semantic similarity, temporal proximity, search results and context comparison to find logically coherent search missions. Other studies compare adjacent queries with binary classifiers [1,20], use latent structural Support Vector Machines [38] or utilize term and context embeddings [25,32].

3   Discussion

[40] qualitatively analysed real web sessions, identifying multiple factors as potential indicators for session boundaries: changing topics or tasks related to the topic, switching to a different phase of a mission, different environmental context (i.e. being among people) and the time gap as the traditional measure. Acknowledging the potential co-existence of these measures strongly supports a development from mechanical sessions to logically connected segments, possibly connecting multiple mechanical sessions and tasks. These concepts build upon each other and should be applied accordingly.

However, sessions identified with temporal boundaries are still widely used. 30 min of inactivity is the industry standard [2], despite clear indicators that solitary use of time gaps is not reliable [6,10,26]. Many applications using interaction logs still exclusively apply the 30 min inactivity time out rule as a foundation for algorithms or analysis. Receiving much attention lately is sequential user or topic modeling with recurrent neural networks. From predictions about sequences or session outcomes [36] to session-based or session-aware recommendation [23,29,31], either the 30 min or a slightly changed temporal constraint is used to detect sessions.

[12] criticized that published studies often do not state how sessions are built. But what is actually worse is that often mechanical sessions are used even when the aim of the study strongly suggests logical sessions [12]. Little thought is put into segmentation. Depending on the application, there are multiple possible definitions on how to structure a user's history [18] and the potential impact of different session models should be more present in research.

4   Conclusion

Algorithms need input data. In Information Retrieval, this input data comes excessively often in the form of interaction logs. Besides laboratory studies, interaction logs represent the main source of information regarding the understanding of users, their information needs and how they interact with search engines or information systems.

Although much effort has been put into segmenting logs in a meaningful way, and although task- and mission-based approaches have received much attention, many recent studies still apply only temporal constraints. They use mechanical sessions to model user context in many different ways (i.e. compare the recent wave of studies using recurrent neural networks). The actual basis for these algorithms are still sessions identified with a 30 min inactivity time out.

This position paper questions the lack of effort put into the pre-processing of interaction logs. A significant amount of thought should be put into the input for any algorithm. The 30 min inactivity time out might be perfectly fine for most applications - but arbitrarily and unquestioningly applying it as the basis for any and all algorithms may lead to wrong conclusions, no matter the algorithm quality.

References

1. Agichtein, E., White, R.W., Dumais, S.T., Bennet, P.N.: Search, interrupted: understanding and predicting search task continuation. In: Proceedings of the 35th International ACM SIGIR Conference on Research and Development in Information Retrieval, SIGIR 2012, pp. 315–324 (2012). https://doi.org/10.1145/2348283.2348328
2. Bigon, L., et al.: Prediction is very hard, especially about conversion. Predicting user purchases from clickstream data in fashion e-commerce. CoRR abs/1907.00400 (2019). http://arxiv.org/abs/1907.00400
3. Buzikashvili, N., Jansen, B.J.: Limits of the web log analysis artifacts. In: WWW 2006 Logging Traces of Web Activity Workshop (2006)
4. Cao, H., et al.: Context-aware query suggestion by mining click-through and session data. In: Proceedings of the 14th ACM SIGKDD International Conference on Knowledge Discovery and Data Mining, KDD 2008, pp. 875–883 (2008). https://doi.org/10.1145/1401890.1401995
5. Catledge, L.D., Pitkow, J.E.: Characterizing browsing strategies in the worldwide web. Comput. Netw. ISDN Syst. **27**(6), 1065–1073 (1995). https://doi.org/10.1016/0169-7552(95)00043-7
6. Chitraa, V., Thanamani, D.A.S.: A novel technique for sessions identification in web usage mining preprocessing. Int. J. Comput. Appl. **34**(9), 23–27 (2011)
7. Dinuca, C., Ciobanu, D.: Improving the session identification using the mean time. Int. J. Math. Models Methods Appl. Sci. **6**, 265–272 (2012)
8. Downey, D., Dumais, S., Horvitz, E.: Models of searching and browsing: languages, studies, and applications. In: Proceedings of IJCAI 2007, IJCAI 2007, pp. 2740–2747 (2007)
9. Gayo-Avello, D.: A survey on session detection methods in query logs and a proposal for future evaluation. Inf. Sci. **179**(12), 1822–1843 (2009). https://doi.org/10.1016/j.ins.2009.01.026
10. Gomes, P., Martins, B., Cruz, L.: Segmenting user sessions in search engine query logs leveraging word embeddings. In: Doucet, A., Isaac, A., Golub, K., Aalberg, T., Jatowt, A. (eds.) TPDL 2019. LNCS, vol. 11799, pp. 185–199. Springer, Cham (2019). https://doi.org/10.1007/978-3-030-30760-8_17
11. Guan, D., Zhang, S., Yang, H.: Utilizing query change for session search. In: Proceedings of the 36th International ACM SIGIR Conference on Research and Development in Information Retrieval, SIGIR 2013, pp. 453–462 (2013). https://doi.org/10.1145/2484028.2484055
12. Hagen, M., Gomoll, J., Beyer, A., Stein, B.: From search session detection to search mission detection. In: Proceedings of the 10th Conference on Open Research Areas in Information Retrieval, OAIR 2013, pp. 85–92 (2013)
13. Hagen, M., Stein, B., Rüb, T.: Query session detection as a cascade. In: Proceedings of the 20th ACM International Conference on Information and Knowledge Management, CIKM 2011, pp. 147–152 (2011). https://doi.org/10.1145/2063576.2063602

14. He, D., Göker, A.: Detecting session boundaries from Web user logs. In: Proceedings of of the BCS-IRSG 22nd Annual Colloquium on Information Retrieval Research, pp. 57–66 (2000)

15. He, D., Göker, A., Harper, D.J.: Combining evidence for automatic Web session identification. Inf. Process. Manag. **38**(5), 727–742 (2002). https://doi.org/10.1016/S0306-4573(01)00060-7

16. Hienert, D., Kern, D.: Recognizing topic change in search sessions of digital libraries based on thesaurus and classification system. In: Proceedings of the 18th Joint Conference on Digital Libraries, JCDL 2019, pp. 297–300 (2019). https://doi.org/10.1109/JCDL.2019.00049

17. Jansen, B.J., Spink, A., Blakely, C., Koshman, S.: Defining a session on web search engines: research articles. J. Am. Soc. Inf. Sci. Technol. **58**(6), 862–871 (2007)

18. Jiang, D., Pei, J., Li, H.: Mining search and browse logs for web search: a survey. ACM Trans. Intell. Syst. Technol. **4**(4) (2013). https://doi.org/10.1145/2508037.2508038

19. Jones, R., Klinkner, K.L.: Beyond the session timeout: automatic hierarchical segmentation of search topics in query logs. In: Proceedings of the 17th ACM Conference on Information and Knowledge Management, CIKM 2008, pp. 699–708 (2008). https://doi.org/10.1145/1458082.1458176

20. Kotov, A., Bennett, P.N., White, R.W., Dumais, S.T., Teevan, J.: Modeling and analysis of cross-session search tasks. In: Proceedings of the 34th International ACM SIGIR Conference on Research and Development in Information Retrieval, SIGIR 2011, pp. 5–14 (2011). https://doi.org/10.1145/2009916.2009922

21. Liao, Z., et al.: A vlHMM approach to context-aware search. ACM Trans. Web **7**(4) (2013). https://doi.org/10.1145/2490255

22. Lucchese, C., Orlando, S., Perego, R., Silvestri, F., Tolomei, G.: Identifying task-based sessions in search engine query logs. In: Proceedings of the Fourth ACM International Conference on Web Search and Data Mining, WSDM 2011, pp. 277–286 (2011). https://doi.org/10.1145/1935826.1935875

23. Lv, Y., Zhuang, L., Luo, P.: Neighborhood-enhanced and time-aware model for session-based recommendation. arXiv abs/1909.11252 (2019)

24. Mehrotra, R.: Inferring User Needs & Tasks from User Interactions. Dissertation, University College London, London (2018)

25. Mehrotra, R., Yilmaz, E.: Task embeddings: learning query embeddings using task context. In: Proceedings of the 2017 ACM on Conference on Information and Knowledge Management, CIKM 2017, pp. 2199–2202 (2017). https://doi.org/10.1145/3132847.3133098

26. Montgomery, A., Faloutsos, C.: Identifying Web browsing trends and patterns. Computer **34**(7), 94–95 (2001). https://doi.org/10.1109/2.933515

27. Murray, G.C., Lin, J., Chowdhury, A.: Identification of user sessions with hierarchical agglomerative clustering. Proc. Am. Soc. Inf. Sci. Technol. **43**, 1–9 (2007). https://doi.org/10.1002/meet.14504301312

28. Piwowarski, B., Dupret, G., Jones, R.: Mining user web search activity with layered Bayesian networks or how to capture a click in its context. In: Proceedings of the Second ACM International Conference on Web Search and Data Mining, WSDM 2009, pp. 162–171 (2009). https://doi.org/10.1145/1498759.1498823

29. Quadrana, M., Karatzoglou, A., Hidasi, B., Cremonesi, P.: Personalizing session-based recommendations with hierarchical recurrent neural networks. In: Proceedings of the Eleventh ACM Conference on Recommender Systems, RecSys 2017, pp. 130–137 (2017). https://doi.org/10.1145/3109859.3109896

30. Radlinski, F., Joachims, T.: Query chains: learning to rank from implicit feedback. In: Proceedings of the Eleventh ACM SIGKDD International Conference on Knowledge Discovery in Data Mining, KDD 2005, pp. 239–248 (2005). https://doi.org/10.1145/1081870.1081899

31. Ruocco, M., Skrede, O.S.L., Langseth, H.: Inter-session modeling for session-based recommendation. In: Proceedings of the 2nd Workshop on Deep Learning for Recommender Systems, DLRS 2017, pp. 24–31 (2017). https://doi.org/10.1145/3125486.3125491

32. Sen, P., Ganguly, D., Jones, G.J.: Tempo-lexical context driven word embedding for cross-session search task extraction. In: Proceedings of the 2018 Conference of the North American Chapter of the Association for Computational Linguistics: Human Language Technologies, (Long Papers), vol. 1, pp. 283–292 (2018). https://doi.org/10.18653/v1/N18-1026

33. Silverstein, C., Marais, H., Henzinger, M., Moricz, M.: Analysis of a very large web search engine query log. SIGIR Forum **33**(1), 6–12 (1999). https://doi.org/10.1145/331403.331405

34. Spink, A., Jansen, B.J., Wolfram, D., Saracevic, T.: From e-sex to e-commerce: Web search changes. Computer **35**(3), 107–109 (2002). https://doi.org/10.1109/2.989940

35. Spink, A., Park, M., Jansen, B.J., Pedersen, J.: Multitasking during web search sessions. Inf. Process. Manag. **42**, 264–275 (2006). https://doi.org/10.1016/j.ipm.2004.10.004

36. Twardowski, B.: Modelling contextual information in session-aware recommender systems with neural networks. In: Proceedings of the 10th ACM Conference on Recommender Systems, RecSys 2016, pp. 273–276 (2016). https://doi.org/10.1145/2959100.2959162

37. Völske, M.: Retrieval enhancements for task-based web search. Dissertation, Bauhaus-Universität Weimar, Weimar, Germany (2019)

38. Wang, H., Song, Y., Chang, M.W., He, X., White, R.W., Chu, W.: Learning to extract cross-session search tasks. In: Proceedings of the 22nd International Conference on World Wide Web, WWW 2013, pp. 1353–1364 (2013). https://doi.org/10.1145/2488388.2488507

39. White, R.W., Drucker, S.M.: Investigating behavioral variability in web search. In: Proceedings of the 16th International Conference on World Wide Web, WWW 2007, pp. 21–30 (2007). https://doi.org/10.1145/1242572.1242576

40. Ye, C., Wilson, M.L.: A user defined taxonomy of factors that divide online information retrieval sessions. In: Proceedings of the 5th Information Interaction in Context Symposium, IIiX 2014, pp. 48–57 (2014). https://doi.org/10.1145/2637002.2637010

41. Yuankang, F., Zhiqiu, H.: A session identification algorithm based on frame page and pagethreshold. In: 2010 3rd International Conference on Computer Science and Information Technology, vol. 6, pp. 645–647 (2010)

Argument Retrieval from Web

Mahsa S. Shahshahani[(⊠)] and Jaap Kamps

University of Amsterdam, Amsterdam, The Netherlands
{m.shahshahani,kamps}@uva.nl

Abstract. We are well beyond the days of expecting search engines to help us find documents containing the answer to a question or information about a query. We expect a search engine to help us in the decision-making process. Argument retrieval task in Touché Track at CLEF2020 has been defined to address this problem. The user is looking for information about several alternatives to make a choice between them. The search engine should retrieve opinionated documents containing comparisons between the alternatives rather than documents about one option or documents including personal opinions or no suggestion at all. In this paper, we discuss argument retrieval from web documents. In order to retrieve argumentative documents from the web, we use three features (PageRank scores, domains, argumentative classifier) and try to strike a balance between them. We evaluate the method based on three dimensions: relevance, argumentativeness, and trustworthiness. Since the labeled data and final results for Toucheé Track have not been out yet, the evaluation has been done by manually labeling documents for 5 queries.

Keywords: Argument retrieval · Web · Touché

1 Introduction

Once search engines were created to help users find to help users find the pieces of information relevant to their needs among a large amount of data. But nowadays search engines are more than that. A newer use-case for search engines is to help users in the decision-making process. In this case, the user is looking for recommendations and personal opinions to choose between some options, for example, different brands of laptops, rather than just official comparisons between their features. So, the goal of the search engine would be to retrieve web documents with an argumentative structure in which there is a discussion or personal view about the options that the user wants to choose from. For example, when the user wants to make a decision to buy a laptop, s/he does not expect to receive a ranked list of documents including comparisons between the specifications of each brand or model. Although these documents are helpful, they do not discuss disadvantages or a trade-off between features. To make the final decision, user needs to see reviews and recommendations like *"If you are a gamer, product A is*

© Springer Nature Switzerland AG 2020
A. Arampatzis et al. (Eds.): CLEF 2020, LNCS 12260, pp. 75–81, 2020.
https://doi.org/10.1007/978-3-030-58219-7_7

not useful for you due to its low GPU, but it is the best if you are a programmer as it has a great CPU".

In this paper, we will study argumentative document retrieval from web pages. In lack of a large labeled corpus, we focus on unsupervised methods. We treat this problem as re-ranking rather than ranking. We assume we have an initial ranked list of documents and we use some features to re-rank these documents to make a better ranked list, putting documents with the argumentative structure on top.

Pagerank scores, sources of web documents, and argumentative classes are three features we use to re-rank the initial ranked lists. We use Clueweb12[1] as our web document source.

The rest of this paper is structured as follows. You are now reading the introduction in Sect. 1. Section 2 details the features we used to distinguish argumentative and non-argumentative documents, along with other features. This is followed by Sect. 3 detailing the experimental setup and summarizing the initial results. Finally, we end with conclusion in Sect. 4.

2   Argument Retrieval

In this section first, the task will be defined as a re-ranking task; and then, we will discuss various features that we considered to be relevant and helpful in re-ranking documents will be discussed.

Task. The goal is to re-rank documents $d_1, d_2, ..., d_n$ in response to query q, considering that these documents have already been ranked with an initial ranking model like BM25. A document should be at a higher rank if it is more relevant, more argumentative, and from a more trustworthy source.

In [6] trustworthiness has been addressed. We treat this aspect as a subjective dimension.

Initial Rank. An initial ranking of documents based on a simple method (we chose BM25) is given and we want to re-rank them. Thus, every document has been associated with an initial rank before we perform the re-ranking. As we take the top 10 documents into account, this initial rank feature can be any number in $\{1, 2, ..., 10\}$.

Argumentative Classifier. We trained a simple SVM classifier based on data from a debate corpus and a web corpus to distinguish between argumentative and non-argumentative documents. We used BERT [4] to represent arguments. As BERT model imposes a limit on the length of documents after tokenization, we use the first 512 tokens in an argument if its length exceeds this limit. In order to train the classifier, we picked a small subset of documents from each corpus. To select the documents, we submitted all 50 comparative queries in the first task of Touché shared-task in CLEF 2020 [2] to both corpora and got up to 100 documents for each query. Then, we manually removed argumentative

---

[1] https://lemurproject.org/clueweb12.

documents from the Clueweb subset and considered the remaining documents as negative examples. All retrieved documents from args.me corpus have been considered as positive examples. The final set includes 3000 positive and 3000 negative examples. We trained the classifier on 80% of the data, and tested it on the remaining 20% of documents. It achieved 87% in terms of accuracy.

Web Domains. Clueweb has been formed by crawling web documents with some post-filters in which pages from inappropriate websites (such as pornographic contents) and 10% of pages with the lowest page-rank scores have been removed. But when the user is looking for argumentative documents, documents from particular domains like Wikipedia will not be relevant since they do not present any personal opinion or advice. On the other hand, discussion forums are very helpful for what the user is looking for. We use this intuition to give a bonus to web pages from discussion forums or blogs. To do this, we define a binary feature that indicates if the source URL for a discussion contains 'forum' or 'blog' terms.

PageRank. Although relevant documents are those from discussion websites they should also be trustworthy. To take this element into account, we used page rank scores to prioritize documents from more reliable sources.

Re-ranking. The main goal is to re-rank documents based on defined features (initial rank, argumentativeness, domain addresses, and PageRank scores).

To generate the final ranked list, we make a heuristic ranking pipeline; First we get the initial ranked list. Second, we re-rank the list based on PageRank scores. This can result in putting a document, initially ranked very low, on top of the list. To avoid this, we limit moving documents in the ranked list to a maximum of 10 positions. Third, we re-rank the new list based on domains. To perform this step, we put the documents with positive domain feature (which means the document is taken from a blog or forum website) on top of the list. We do this for every 10 documents. Fourth, we classify the whole list using the argumentativeness classifier we have trained. We put documents with positive class on top of the list. We do this for every 20 documents and we do not move a document more than 20 positions.

This way, we reassure that we have prioritized relevance in comparison with other dimensions.

3   Experiments

In this section we will first explain experimental setup and corpora, followed by the experiments and results.

3.1   Experimental Setup

Corpora. We used two corpora in our study; one argumentative corpus (args.me) and one web corpus (Clueweb12). Args.me [1] has been created by crawling 387,606 arguments from 4 debate websites to ease research in Argument Retrieval. We used the API of a publicly available search engine[2] based on Elasticsearch to retrieve pro and con arguments from this corpus [7] using BM25 model. We used this corpus for our baseline method.

Clueweb12 is a dataset made by crawling 733,019,372 documents seeded with 2,820,500 urls from Clueweb09[3]. We used a publicly available search engine [5] based on Elasticsearch to retrieve documents from Clueweb12.

All documents have been tokenized by nltk toolkit.

PageRank scores are extracted from chatnoir search engine which has been provided by Carnegie Melon University[3].

We used pre-trained BERT-based model from Huggingface Transformers[4] framework to represent arguments for training the argumentative classifier.

All parameters for the argumentativeness classifier have been set to default values in Scikit-learn[5] library for Python.

Queries. We selected 5 out of 50 comparative topics released for the second shared task in Touché track of CLEF2020 to evaluate our model (Ex. "which is better, a laptop or a desktop?").

Initial Ranked List. We retrieved the top 100 documents from Clueweb for each query using BM25 model.

3.2 Experiments

We evaluated the top 10 documents for each ranked list: initial ranked list, re-ranked by PageRank scores, re-ranked by domains, re-ranked by argumentativeness, and mixed model.

Evaluation results have been reported in Table 1 using NDCG@10 evaluation metric on three criteria: relevance, argumentative structure, and trustworthiness. We labeled documents using three labels: 0 for non-relevant, non-argumentative, or untrustworthy; 1 for relevant, argumentative, or trustworthy, and 2 for highly-relevant, highly-argumentative, or highly trustworthy.[6]

Baseline. We retrieve documents from the argumentative corpus and expand the query with a maximum of 5 terms using the top 1000 retrieved documents. Then we use this expanded query to retrieve documents from ClueWeb.

Initial Ranks. Initial ranks have the most impact on putting relevant documents on top.

---

[2] www.args.me.

[3] boston.lti.cs.cmu.edu/cluew eb09/wiki/tiki-index.php?page=PageRank.

[4] https://github.com/huggingface/transformers.

[5] https://scikit-learn.org/stable/supervised_learning.html#supervised-learning.

[6] Since we did not have official labeled data or labeling guidelines from organizers of Toucheé Track, we labeled documents based on our own guidelines.

Table 1. Results-NDCG@10 metric

Model	Relevance	Argumentativeness	Trustworthiness
Initial	0.87	0.71	0.81
Pagerank	0.89	0.66	0.87
Domain	0.84	0.72	0.80
Argumentative classifier	0.80	0.84	0.79
Mixed	0.84	0.78	0.82
Baseline	0.55	0.64	0.92

Pagerank Score. Pagerank scores impact trustworthiness by putting pages with more in-links on top.

Argumentativeness. We put documents with the positive class for argumentativeness on top of the list.

Domain. Blog and forum domains help to put documents from discussion websites on top. This can balance the impact of PageRank, as it tends to give a higher rank to documents from official websites.

Mixture. Being relevant is the first condition for a desired ranked list. In addition, the second priority for a high-ranked document is having an argumentative structure and including comparisons and user reviews, as well as having a trustworthy source. Thus we need to make sure while mixing all the features in order to re-rank the documents, we do not lose track of relevant documents in the initial ranked list. This is the reason that we started the pipeline by relevance, and limited the changes in document ranks to 10–20 positions while performing re-ranking.

Results. As it has been shown in Table 1, the heuristic mixed model does not achieve the same performance as the initial ranked-list in terms of relevance, the same performance as argumentative classifier model in terms of argumentativeness, and the same performance as PageRank model in terms of trustworthiness. But, it struck a balance between all three dimensions.

4   Conclusion

In this paper, we discussed retrieving argumentative documents from the web to assist users in finding the pros and cons of the desired query. The important point in this task is to notice that the user is not only looking for relevant documents; documents including information about one or more options. We should also take argumentativeness and subjectiveness into account.

In this paper, we formulated the problem as a re-ranking task and as we do not have any training data, we treated it in an unsupervised manner.

We used a couple of simple features to re-rank documents from the web in response to an argumentative query. We showed that using a mixture of page-rank scores, web-domain addresses, and argumentative classifier leads to a better ranked list in terms of argumentativeness, relevance, and trustworthiness over the initial BM25 ranked list. PageRank scores help in the trustworthiness dimension by putting documents with more in-links on top of the ranked list. Domains and the argumentativeness classifier help in putting documents with a more argumentative and discussion-based structure in the higher ranks. After all, relevance remains the main ranking dimension: If a document is not relevant, trustworthiness or argumentativeness does not matter anymore. Thus, in the mixed model, we try to limit documents from moving too much in the ranked-list in comparison with the initial BM25 ranked-list. By forcing these limitations, we get a ranked-list with a balance between three dimensions: relevance, argumentativeness, and trustworthiness. However, we did not have the final judgments from Touché track before submission of this paper, and the evaluations have been performed by manually labeling documents for 5 topics out of 50, and are not official results.

Acknowledgments. This research was supported in part by the Netherlands Organization for Scientific Research (NWO, ACCESS project, grant # CISC.CC.016).

References

1. Ajjour, Y., Wachsmuth, H., Kiesel, J., Potthast, M., Hagen, M., Stein, B.: Data acquisition for argument search: the args.me corpus. In: Benzmüller, C., Stuckenschmidt, H. (eds.) KI 2019. LNCS (LNAI), vol. 11793, pp. 48–59. Springer, Cham (2019). https://doi.org/10.1007/978-3-030-30179-8_4
2. Bondarenko, A., et al.: Touché: first shared task on argument retrieval. In: Jose, J.M., et al. (eds.) ECIR 2020. LNCS, vol. 12036, pp. 517–523. Springer, Cham (2020). https://doi.org/10.1007/978-3-030-45442-5_67
3. Clarke, C.L.A., Craswell, N., Soboroff, I.: Overview of the TREC 2009 web track. In: Voorhees, E.M., Buckland, L.P. (eds.) Proceedings of The Eighteenth Text REtrieval Conference, TREC 2009, Gaithersburg, Maryland, USA, 17–20 November 2009. NIST Special Publication, vol. 500–278. National Institute of Standards and Technology (NIST) (2009). http://trec.nist.gov/pubs/trec18/papers/WEB09.OVERVIEW.pdf
4. Devlin, J., Chang, M., Lee, K., Toutanova, K.: BERT: pre-training of deep bidirectional transformers for language understanding. In: Burstein, J., Doran, C., Solorio, T. (eds.) Proceedings of the 2019 Conference of the North American Chapter of the Association for Computational Linguistics: Human Language Technologies, NAACL-HLT 2019, Minneapolis, MN, USA, 2–7 June 2019, (Long and Short Papers), vol. 1, pp. 4171–4186. Association for Computational Linguistics (2019). https://doi.org/10.18653/v1/n19-1423
5. Potthast, M., et al.: Chatnoir: a search engine for the clueweb09 corpus. In: Hersh, W.R., Callan, J., Maarek, Y., Sanderson, M. (eds.) The 35th International ACM SIGIR Conference on Research and Development in Information Retrieval, SIGIR 2012, Portland, OR, USA, 12–16 August 2012, p. 1004. ACM (2012). https://doi.org/10.1145/2348283.2348429

6. Rafalak, M., Abramczuk, K., Wierzbicki, A.: Incredible: is (almost) all web content trustworthy? Analysis of psychological factors related to website credibility evaluation. In: Chung, C., Broder, A.Z., Shim, K., Suel, T. (eds.) 23rd International World Wide Web Conference, WWW 2014, Seoul, Republic of Korea, 7–11 April 2014, Companion Volume, pp. 1117–1122. ACM (2014). https://doi.org/10.1145/2567948.2578997

7. Wachsmuth, H., et al.: Building an argument search engine for the web. In: Habernal, I., et al. (eds.) Proceedings of the 4th Workshop on Argument Mining, ArgMining@EMNLP 2017, Copenhagen, Denmark, 8 September 2017, pp. 49–59. Association for Computational Linguistics (2017). https://doi.org/10.18653/v1/w17-5106

Best of CLEF 2019 Labs

File Forgery Detection Using a Weighted Rule-Based System

João Rafael Almeida[1,2($\boxtimes$)] , Olga Fajarda[1] , and José Luís Oliveira[1]

[1] DETI/IEETA, University of Aveiro, Aveiro, Portugal
{joao.rafael.almeida,olga.oliveira,jlo}@ua.pt
[2] Department of Information and Communications Technologies,
University of A Coruña, A Coruña, Spain

Abstract. The society is becoming increasingly dependent on digital data sources. However, our trust on the sources and its contents is only ensured if we can also rely on robust methods that prevent fraudulent forgery. As digital forensic experts are continually dealing with the detection of forged data, new fraudulent approaches are emerging, making it difficult to use automated systems. This security breach is also a good challenge that motivates researchers to explore computational solutions to efficiently address the problem. This paper describes a weighted rule-based system for file forgery detection. The system was developed and validated in the several tasks of ImageCLEFsecurity 2019 track challenge, where promising results were obtained.

Keywords: ImageCLEF · Security · File forgery detection · Rule-based models

1 Introduction

Over the last years, with the growth of personal computational devices, criminal activities have improved their techniques to communicate without being detected. A possibility to exchange messages without being exposed is making use of steganography techniques, which consists in hiding a message without encrypting its content. This has been used for centuries, long before the first computer. However, the game changed in terms of complexity when the stego techniques started to make use of computational systems. One common procedure is the use of image or video to insert hidden information [23]. Therefore, with a computer, it is simpler to hide a message undetectable by a human eye. It is important to refer that those techniques do not use cryptography. In cryptography, the message is impossible to understand unless the cryptography key is available. On the other hand, the steganography hides a message in plain sight, but no one understands its existence unless the person is aware of it [13].

Another concerning problem for the digital forensic examiners is the file type forgery. In this case, the goal is not to occult a message but instead hide the file itself. Gopal et al. [10] shown the magnitude of File Type Identification for

© Springer Nature Switzerland AG 2020
A. Arampatzis et al. (Eds.): CLEF 2020, LNCS 12260, pp. 85–96, 2020.
https://doi.org/10.1007/978-3-030-58219-7_8

intrusion detection. This helps in the prevention of malware from entering in the system or the network by analysing suspicious files. Moreover, the methods used to discover the original information in the file can be applied in damage store devices, in order to try to recover the data [8].

Those problems encouraged researchers to improve the digital forensics techniques, focusing on the acquisition, preservation and analysis of digital evidence [14]. One initiative is the ImageCLEF [11] that launched a new security challenge, called ImageCLEFsecurity. This challenge addresses the problem of automatically identifying forged files and stego images [15]. The challenge is divided into three sub-tasks: 1) *forged file discovery*, 2) *stego image discovery* and 3) *secret message discovery*.

The *forged files discovery* sub-task is the first task of the challenge and it is independent from the remaining two tasks. The goal of this task is to automatically detect files whose extension and signature has been altered; more specifically, to identify the files with extension PDF that are, actually, image files (with extension JPG, PNG, and GIF). The file type can be identified by the file's extension and the signature, therefore determining the true type of a file when only the file's extension or the signature has been breached is an easy task. However, this task becomes a difficult one when both the file's extension and the signature are altered [15]. There are different techniques for hiding the file types, depending on the algorithm chosen and the complexity involved in this procedure. Along the years, several attempts have been made to solve this difficult task by analysing the file's content [1,16,21], but none of them has a 100% detection rate.

The objective of the second sub-task is to identify the images that hide steganographic content and the goal of the third task is to retrieve these hidden messages. Steganalysis techniques are used to detect and retrieve embedded messages from stego images. A review of steganalysis techniques for digital images can be found in [6].

In this paper, we present a weight rule-based system that assembles the different approaches used to address this challenge. The main solution is based on an orchestration of specialised rule-based models. For each model, a set of rules was defined with the purpose of identifying a specific file or message. Additionally, when there are insufficient rules to provide a good result, other complementary strategies have been combined, namely a random forest classifier. Our approach is different from the approaches used by the other participants since most of them adopted deep learning techniques to solve the challenges [15].

2   Materials and Methods

For each task, a training set and a test set were provided. The training set of the first task is composed of 2400 files, 1200 of which are PDF files. The remaining files, despite having PDF extension, belong to one of three classes: JPEG, PNG, GIF, each with 400 files. In the second and third tasks, the training sets include 1000 JPEG images, 500 of which are clean images and the others are stego images, altered using the same steganography technique. In the case of the third task, the stego images contain five different text messages. Regarding the test sets, the first task is comprised of 1000 files and the second and third tasks are composed of 500 images.

In this section, we present the five methods that were used to solve each task of the challenge.

2.1   Rule-Based Approach

A typical rule-based system is constructed through a set of if-then rules [20] which help identify conditions and patterns in the problem domain. However, the use of simple conditions may not be enough to obtain the best results. Sometimes, to accomplish a more accurate outcome, those rules need to be balanced, with weights. The subject of rule weights in fuzzy rule-based models for classifications is not new, and its positive effect has already been proven [12].

We propose a weighted rule-based system with a set of models (Fig. 1), which are specialised in classifying a specific entry. Each model generates a confidence score regarding the match of the received input with its conditions. The orchestrator collects all the results and chooses the model that gives the highest confidence score. When more than one model give similar good confidence scores for different classes, the weights of the rules are readjusted and a new classification cycle is performed to help separating the classes' scores. These readjustments will, hopefully, allow the right output to stand out.

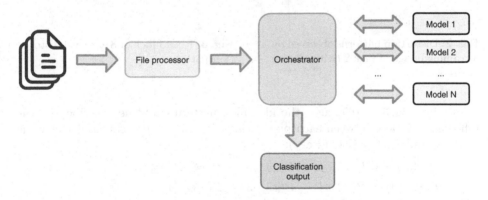

Fig. 1. Proposed rule-based system.

The rules and the weight of the rules are specific to each problem and scenario. Therefore, we used this approach as our base method for all the tasks. The rules and the methods to classify the rules are specified in Sect. 3.

2.2 Image Distortion Pattern Matching

Steganographic techniques permit to hide, within an image, information that should be perceptually and statistically undetectable [3,17]. However, some of these techniques, may not respect these two principles entirely, namely tools like Jsteg, Outguess, F5, JPHide, and Steghide. These tools use the least significant bit (LSB) insertion technique and distort the fidelity of the cover image by choosing the quantized DCT coefficients as their concealment locations [17].

Our approach aims to identify flaws of the used method by searching for a common pattern among all the stego images.

While scanning the training set of the second task for common patterns, it was possible to identify that several stego images had a distortion pattern of 8 × 8 pixels size, that could easily be identified with the naked eye, as described in Fig. 2 and Fig. 3.

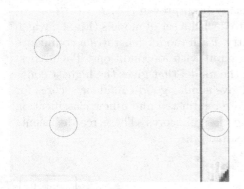 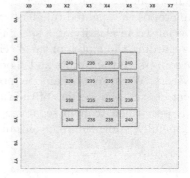

Fig. 2. Distortion patterns observed on a training image of task 2 (with a zoom of 670%).

Fig. 3. Pixel block of 8 × 8 with distortion pattern.

Taking Fig. 3 as reference, the identified pattern could be described by the following relation between each pixel, where P(x, y) represents the mean value of R, G, and B at position (x, y):

$$P(x3, y3) = P(x3, y4) = P(x4, y3) = P(x4, y4)$$
$$P(x2, y3) = P(x2, y4) = P(x5, y3) = P(x5, y4)$$
$$= P(x3, y2) = P(x4, y2) = P(x3, y5) = P(x4, y5)$$
$$P(x2, y2) = P(x2, y5) = P(x5, y2) = P(x5, y5)$$
$$P(x3, y3) > P(x3, y2)$$
$$P(x3, y2) > P(x2, y2)$$

We created a function to scan an image for this pattern and to count the number of occurrences. The function determines that a certain image had a message if the number of patterns found is greater than the specified threshold. Its output was used as a parameter into our weighted rule-base model.

2.3   Image Metadata Pattern Searcher

Another approach used to assist the creation of rules for our rule-based model was a pre-analysis of the file's metadata. This analysis aimed to discover patterns that could be used as rules in the model. For instance, in the JPEG images of the training set of the second task, a set of bits were detected which identified the images with a hidden message.

The pattern search was mainly done with the metadata, ignoring the image bitstream. The rational was that the altered files could be signed in the metadata to quickly identify which files are of interest. This simple signature would go unnoticed and it would increase the decoding procedure.

2.4   Random Forests for Rule Definition

Random forest is a supervised learning algorithm developed by Breiman [4], who was influenced by the work of Amit and Geman [2]. This algorithm constructs a large number of decision trees, considering a random subset of features for each split, and makes a prediction by combining the predictions of the different decision trees. Caruana and Niculescu-Mizil [5] performed an empirical comparison of supervised learning and concluded that random forest was one of the algorithms that gave the best average performance.

The random forest algorithm has several positive characteristics [7] for this challenge, namely it can be used for high-dimensional problems and it gives an estimation of the importance of variables. Moreover, it just needs two parameters: the number of trees in the forest (*ntree*) and the number of features in the random subset used in each split (*mtry*).

To solve the third task we first used the rule-based model to identify the stego images and used the random forest algorithm to retrieve the message of the stego images. The description of our implementation is described in Sect. 3.

2.5   Manual Tuning

In large data sets, manual classification is unrealistic. However, since the training and test set are small, we decide to try a manual validation. This approach consists mainly in a verification of the rule-based output, followed by manual adjustments considered relevant. This method was, essentially, used in the second task.

When analysing the training set, the 8×8 pixel distortion pattern described in Sect. 2.2 was identified. Using the rule-based model in the early stages, made it possible to define rules to reach a precision of 1. However, the recall was low. Therefore, we isolated the images not detected as forged and tried to identify these distortions in the image manually. This procedure increased our recall significantly. However, we did not obtain our best results using this procedure.

3   Results

The described methods were combined and led to several submissions in the different tasks. The performance of the submissions was evaluated using the traditional metrics: precision, recall, and F1, in the first two tasks and edit distance in the third task.

In the first task, the precision was defined as the quotient between the number of altered images correctly detected and the total number of files identified as changed. In its turn, the recall was the quotient between the number of altered images correctly detected and the total number of files modified.

For the second task, the definition of precision and recall was similar. The precision was the quotient between the number of images with hidden messages correctly detected and the total number of images with hidden messages identified. The recall was the quotient between the number of images with hidden messages correctly detected and the total number of images with hidden messages.

Finally, the third task used the edit distance to measure the efficiency into recovering the message. This distance is the minimum-weight count of edit operations that transforms a string in another one.

3.1   Task 1: Identify Forged Images

Detecting the type of file is a process that can be done using three different file characteristics: the file's extension, the magic number, and the file's content [14]. The most straightforward technique to hide a file is changing the file's extension and the magic number, which is a set of standard bytes that signs the file. With this technique, the operation system is unable to open the file. Therefore, four models are built, each one specialised in identifying a file type (PDF, PNG, JPG or GIF). Each model produces a score reflecting the confidence that the analysed file is of the given type. These scores are sent to the orchestrator, who classifies the type of file based on the scores received.

The initial approach considered standard flags in the file structure, such as the last bytes or the number of occurrences of a set of bytes. For instance, a JPEG file has the hexadecimal 0xFFDA at least once in its structure because this is the flag that indicates where the image binary starts. Table 1 presents the flags for the end of file for each file type. For this first task, we used the rule of identifying the end of file flag and obtained an F1 measure of 1.0.

Three more groups submitted to this subtask and two also obtained an F1 measure of 1.0.

3.2   Task 2: Identify Stego Images

In JPEG images there are two different stages of compression: lossy and lossless. Embedding steganographic content inside images that uses lossy compression increases the possibility of that content to be partly lost, which means that, it is not feasible to hide a message on a lossy stage. Therefore, in the case of JPEG

Table 1. The hexadecimal values at the end of each file format. These are the rules used in task one.

File format	Hexadecimal values
GIF	0x3B
JPG	0xFFD9
PNG	0x49454E44AE426082
PDF	0x454F46

files, the steganography should take place on the lossless stage. The DCT and the quantization phase form part of the lossy stage, while the Huffman encoding used to further compress the data is lossless [19].

After scanning the training set of the second task for common parts that distinguishes stego images binary data from non-stego images, it was possible to observe some patterns and specify the weights of the rules that identifies stego images. The patterns and their weights are described on Table 2. We could observe that all the patterns appeared in the Huffman table sequences, i.e. after the marker DHT. The sequences in a JPEG file are identified by a two-byte code described in Table 3.

Table 2. Weighted rules used in Task 2 for the first submission.

Rule N°	Marker	Hexadecimal value	Weight
1	DHT	0x3435363738393a434445464748494a53545556 5758595a636465666768696a737475767778797a	0.35
2	DHT	0x35363738393a434445464748494a535455565 758595a636465666768696a737475767778797a	0.35
3	DHT	0xf2f3f4f5f6f7f8f9fa	0.30

Table 3. Common JPEG file markers [9].

Marker ID	Short values	Description
SOI	0xFFD8	start of image
APPn	0xFFEn	application data
DQT	0xFFDB	quant.tables
DHT	0xFFC4	Huffmantables
SOF	0xFFCn	start of frame
SOS	0xFFDA	start of scan
DRI	0xFFDD	restart interval
RSTn	0xFFDn	restart
COM	0xFFFE	comment
EOI	0xFFD9	end of image

This task was also solved using the rule based-model where the images with a score equal to or greater than 0.70 were considered as altered. However, in this case, strategies and different ways to extract information from the images were combined. Initially, a metadata pattern searcher to compare the metadata fields' content was developed. From this analysis, in all the images with a hidden message, the set of bits represented in the rules displayed in Table 2 were found. However, these rules produced several false positives, achieving, using the training set, a recall of 1.0 and a precision of 0.75.

Due to the lack of precision, we attempt to identify the distortion pattern in the images, the method described in Sect. 2.2. Without the rules used in the first approach and using a threshold of at least one pixel-block with the distortion. The threshold used was obtained by trying different thresholds using the training data set. This method produced a precision of 0.53 and a recall of 0.60 in the training set. It was also the best score obtained from all runs using this approach isolated.

Then, to increase the precision, the decision was made to combine the rules of the first approach with this analyser. The image analyser method was only used when an image was classified through the first approach as having a hidden message. This decreased the recall to 0.604 and the precision remained in the 0.75, the best precision result so far. The decrease of the recall and the bad results in isolated scenarios led to the abandonment of this approach and to focus only on ways to increase the quality of the rules.

At this stage, a submission was made, obtaining an F1 measure of 0.933 and a precision of 0.874.

In the next attempts some manual rectifications were made in the output retrieved from the rule-based system, by observing the images classified as having a message. Some submission were made following only the rule-based approach mixed with the manual validation, and the best result was 0.98, both for F1 and precision.

As a last attempt, the decision was made to re-run the metadata pattern searcher to be more precise. Now, it analysed all the metadata as a binary, ignoring which were the fields or its content. With these changes, the method found a new pattern, which produced a new rule, represented in Table 4, made it possible to achieve a F1 measure of 1 in the training and test sets.

Five more groups submitted to this subtask and the best results obtained by these groups varied between 0.438 and 0.888.

3.3   Task 3: Retrieve the Message

The goal of the third task was to retrieve the hidden text messages from the stego images. To address this task, our first approach was to use freely available steganographic tools, specifically, Hide'N'Send, Image Steganography[1], Quick-

---

[1] https://incoherency.co.uk/image-steganography/.

Table 4. Final weighted rules used in Task 2.

Rule N°	Marker	Hexadecimal value	Weight
1	DHT	0x3435363738393a434445464748494a53545556 5758595a636465666768696a737475767778797a	0.35
2	DHT	0x35363738393a434445464748494a535455565 758595a636465666768696a737475767778797a	0.15
3	DHT	0xf2f3f4f5f6f7f8f9fa	0.15
4	APP0	0x00600060	0.35

Stego, SSuite Picsel[2], Steghide[3], and SteganPEG [22]. However, none of the steganographic tools were able to retrieve the hidden text messages.

In our second approach, the RGB matrix was analyzed. First, each colour component was individually inspected, examining the least and the two least significant bits, in order to detect if they could compose ASCII codes of letters in the alphabet, more precisely, the ASCII character in the range from 65 to 90, and from 97 to 122. As these procedures did not provide a pattern for the stored messages, the decision was made to look to the pixel as a whole, inspecting the three colour component combined. We, also, tried to use the two least significant bits from the four pixels that are in the centre of each 8 × 8 pixel block.

The second approach could not retrieve the hidden messages from the image files and therefore an attempt to find a pattern using the DCT matrix was made, by inspecting the least and the two least significant bits from the value in the first cell of an 8 × 8 block. The change of the least or the two least significant bit of these values would create a small change in the block brightness, which would explain the distortion identified in the 8 × 8 pixel block.

None of the procedures described so far could find a pattern in the images of the training set with the same hidden text message. Therefore, the random forest algorithm, in an attempt to find a pattern in the binary of the image files, was used. The 500 stego images of the training set have, as hidden message, one of five messages. Consequently, the next step was to consider a multiclass classification problem which consists in classifying each stego image into one of the five messages. Initially, for our first model, we used as features the frequency, in percentage, with which each ASCII character appears in the binary of the image files. For the second model, in addition to the features used in the first model, the percentage of 0s and 1s in the binary of the image files were used. To train the models we used the R package *caret* [18] and used cross-validation to chose the optimal value of the parameters *ntree* and *mtry*. In what concerns the performance of the models, this was evaluated using 10-fold cross-validation. Table 5 presents the parameters used and the accuracy of each model.

From the results, the random forest models were unable to find a pattern in the binary of the image files. In the absence of alternatives, the two random

---

[2] https://www.ssuiteoffice.com/software/ssuitepicselsecurity.htm.
[3] http://steghide.sourceforge.net/.

Table 5. Random forest models' parameters (ntree and mtry) and results.

Models	ntree	mtry	Accuracy
First model	247	82	31,57%
Second model	374	59	31,33%

forest models to classify the image files of the test set were used, despite the fact that this task was not a classification problem. The first step was to use the rule based-model defined in the second task to identify the stego images of the test set and, subsequently, the random forest models to classify the images identified as containing a hidden message. For the submissions, all the images in the test set should have a string appointed and therefore, an empty string was assigned to the images identified as having no hidden message. Using the first model an edit distance of 0.588 was obtained and using the second model an edit distance of 0.587. Our best edit distance (0.598) was achieved by assigning the string *"name John Fraud"* to all images we identified as stego images and an empty string to the other images of the test set. These results reflect the fact that we could correctly identify the images with no hidden messages.

One more group submitted to this subtask and the best result they obtained was an edit distance of 0.563.

4   Conclusion

This paper presents the methodologies to identify forged files and stenographic images used in the ImageCLEFsecurity challenge. These methods were developed specifically for the tasks of this challenge. However, the methodology used is extensible and using the same core we can create other processing modules which can be used for other data sets. In the first task, an F1 measure of 1 was obtained. This excellent result was accomplished mainly because the changes done to the files were only the traditional ones, and with simple rules, it was possible to identify each type. The second task also had a submission with a F1 measure of 1. In this case, we could identify a signature in the altered images. On the other hand, in the third task, the best submission had an edit distance of 0.598, mainly due to the success of identifying empty strings, i.e., images without a message. The purposed methodology works if it is possible to define the right rules. The problem in this task was the difficulty to find the stenographic algorithm used.

This challenge allowed for the identification of problems in the developed approach, and most importantly, ways to improve some of these issues. A future work originated from this year's participation could be the creation of a rule generator to fed the rule-based models and more models to be assembled in the system. The message identification task may be improved by creating a database of strategies used by stenographic attackers, mixed with machine learning approach that look into neighbourhood pixel colour.

Acknowledgements. This work was supported by the projects NETDIAMOND (POCI-01-0145-FEDER-016385) and SOCA (CENTRO-01-0145-FEDER-000010), co-funded by Centro 2020 program, Portugal 2020, European Union. JRA is funded by the National Science Foundation (FCT), under the grant SFRH/BD/147837/2019.

References

1. Ahmed, I., Lhee, K., Shin, H., Hong, M.P.: On improving the accuracy and performance of content-based file type identification. In: Boyd, C., González Nieto, J. (eds.) ACISP 2009. LNCS, vol. 5594, pp. 44–59. Springer, Heidelberg (2009). https://doi.org/10.1007/978-3-642-02620-1_4
2. Amit, Y., Geman, D.: Shape quantization and recognition with randomized trees. Neural Comput. **9**(7), 1545–1588 (1997). https://doi.org/10.1162/neco.1997.9.7.1545
3. Attaby, A.A., Ahmed, M.F.M., Alsammak, A.K.: Data hiding inside JPEG images with high resistance to steganalysis using a novel technique: DCT-M3. Ain Shams Eng. J. (2017). https://doi.org/10.1016/j.asej.2017.02.003
4. Breiman, L.: Random forests. Mach. Learn. **45**(1), 5–32 (2001). https://doi.org/10.1023/A:1010933404324
5. Caruana, R., Niculescu-Mizil, A.: An empirical comparison of supervised learning algorithms. In: Proceedings of the 23rd International Conference on Machine Learning, pp. 161–168. ACM (2006). https://doi.org/10.1145/1143844.1143865
6. Chutani, S., Goyal, A.: A review of forensic approaches to digital image Steganalysis. Multimed. Tools Appl. **78**(13), 18169–18204 (2019). https://doi.org/10.1007/s11042-019-7217-0
7. Cutler, A., Cutler, D.R., Stevens, J.R.: Random forests. In: Zhang, C., Ma, Y. (eds.) Ensemble Machine Learning, pp. 157–175. Springer, Boston (2012). https://doi.org/10.1007/978-1-4419-9326-7_5
8. Evensen, J.D., Lindahl, S., Goodwin, M.: File-type detection using naïve Bayes and n-gram analysis. In: Norwegian Information Security Conference, NISK, vol. 7 (2014)
9. Gloe, T.: Forensic analysis of ordered data structures on the example of JPEG files. In: 2012 IEEE International Workshop on Information Forensics and Security (WIFS), pp. 139–144. IEEE (2012). https://doi.org/10.1109/WIFS.2012.6412639
10. Gopal, S., Yang, Y., Salomatin, K., Carbonell, J.: Statistical learning for file-type identification. In: 2011 10th International Conference on Machine Learning and Applications and Workshops, vol. 1, pp. 68–73. IEEE (2011). https://doi.org/10.1109/ICMLA.2011.135
11. Ionescu, B., et al.: ImageCLEF 2019: multimedia retrieval in medicine, lifelogging, security and nature. In: Crestani, F., et al. (eds.) CLEF 2019. LNCS, vol. 11696, pp. 358–386. Springer, Cham (2019). https://doi.org/10.1007/978-3-030-28577-7_28
12. Ishibuchi, H., Nakashima, T.: Effect of rule weights in fuzzy rule-based classification systems. IEEE Trans. Fuzzy Syst. **9**(4), 506–515 (2001). https://doi.org/10.1109/91.940964
13. Karampidis, K., Kavallieratou, E., Papadourakis, G.: A review of image steganalysis techniques for digital forensics. J. Inf. Secur. Appl. **40**, 217–235 (2018). https://doi.org/10.1016/j.jisa.2018.04.005
14. Karampidis, K., Papadourakis, G.: File type identification for digital forensics. In: Krogstie, J., Mouratidis, H., Su, J. (eds.) CAiSE 2016. LNBIP, vol. 249, pp. 266–274. Springer, Cham (2016). https://doi.org/10.1007/978-3-319-39564-7_25

15. Karampidis, K., Vasillopoulos, N., Cuevas Rodríguez, C., del Blanco, C.R., Kavallieratou, E., Garcia, N.: Overview of the ImageCLEFsecurity 2019: fileforgery detection tasks. In: CLEF2019 Working Notes. CEUR Workshop Proceedings, 09–12 September 2019, vol. 2381. CEUR-WS.org, Lugano (2019)
16. Karresand, M., Shahmehri, N.: File type identification of data fragments by their binary structure. In: Proceedings of the IEEE Information Assurance Workshop, pp. 140–147 (2006). https://doi.org/10.1109/IAW.2006.1652088
17. Khalid, S.K.A., Deris, M.M., Mohamad, K.M.: A steganographic technique for highly compressed JPEG images. In: The Second International Conference on Informatics Engineering & Information Science (ICIEIS 2013), pp. 107–118 (2013)
18. Kuhn, M., et al.: Building predictive models in R using the caret package. J. Stat. Softw. 28(5), 1–26 (2008)
19. Kumari, M., Khare, A., Khare, P.: JPEG compression steganography & crypography using image-adaptation technique. J. Adv. Inf. Technol. 1(3), 141–145 (2010). https://doi.org/10.4304/jait.1.3.141-145
20. Liu, H., Gegov, A., Cocea, M.: Rule-based systems: a granular computing perspective. Granular Comput. 1(4), 259–274 (2016). https://doi.org/10.1007/s41066-016-0021-6
21. McDaniel, M., Heydari, M.H.: Content based file type detection algorithms. In: 2003 Proceedings of the 36th Annual Hawaii International Conference on System Sciences, pp. 10–pp. IEEE (2003). https://doi.org/10.1109/HICSS.2003.1174905
22. Reddy, V.L., Subramanyam, A., Reddy, P.C.: Steganpeg steganography + JPEG. In: 2011 International Conference on Ubiquitous Computing and Multimedia Applications, pp. 42–48. IEEE (2011). https://doi.org/10.1109/UCMA.2011.17
23. Singh, M.T.S.A., Sharma, A.: A survey on various techniques of image data cryptography techniques and features. Int. J. Sci. Res. Eng. Trends 5, 192–195 (2019)

Protest Event Detection:
When Task-Specific Models Outperform
an Event-Driven Method

Angelo Basile[1] and Tommaso Caselli[2(✉)]

[1] Symanto Research GmbH & Co., Nürnberg, Germany
angelo.basile@symanto.net
[2] Rijksuniversiteit Groningen, Groningen, The Netherlands
t.caselli@rug.nl
https://www.symanto.net/

Abstract. 2019 has been characterized by worldwide waves of protests. Each country's protests is different but there appear to be common factors. In this paper we present two approaches for identifying protest events in news in English. Our goal is to provide political science and discourse analysis scholars with tools that may facilitate the understanding of this on-going phenomenon. We test our approaches against the ProtestNews Lab 2019 benchmark that challenges systems to perform unsupervised domain adaptation on protest events on three sub-tasks: document classification, sentence classification, and event extraction. Results indicate that developing dedicated architectures and models for each task outperforms simpler solutions based on the propagation of labels from lexical items to documents. Furthermore, we complete the description of our systems with a detailed data analysis to shed light on the limits of the methods.

Keywords: Document classification · Sentence classification · Event extraction · Protest events

1 Introduction

Political unrest has been an essential property of 2019. Countries as diverse as Chile, Spain, Iraq, Lebanon, Sudan, Algeria, Hong Kong, among others, have seen waves of dissent. An analysis in *The Guardian*[1] suggests that all these recent upheavals appear to have as common denominators the following factors: youth, social media connections, and the ubiquity of English.

The combination of the last two factors (i.e., the growth of connectivity among people and the use of English) has increased the availability of data and sources covering such events. This introduces new framings of the protest event narratives but it makes harder for the interested scholars (e.g., political

---

[1] https://bit.ly/31oyS5k - last retrieved May 16th 2020.

© Springer Nature Switzerland AG 2020
A. Arampatzis et al. (Eds.): CLEF 2020, LNCS 12260, pp. 97–111, 2020.
https://doi.org/10.1007/978-3-030-58219-7_9

scientists, sociologists) to obtain a complete coverage of the targeted events, and thus reducing the possible additional bias from their analyses. The use of Natural Language Processing (NLP) tools can be a viable solution to overcome such problems, although imperfect yet. Furthermore, to apply such techniques both to collect and pre-process large quantities of data is necessary to have access to re-usable and generalisable NLP systems.

Following [6], good re-usability of systems would indicate the development of robust NLP technologies, and good generalisability would highlight systems' ability in learning language phenomena rather than datasets. Recent studies [21, 25] in the area of domain adaptation are highlighting that system's performance is affected not only when shifting from one domain (e.g. newspaper articles) to another well-defined target domain (e.g. bio-medical texts) [17], but also when the test data come from a distribution different from the one used for training.

The ProtestNews Lab benchmark [10] targets models' portability and unsupervised domain adaptation in the area of social protest events to support comparative social studies. The lab is organised along three tasks: *a*) document classification (Task 1); *b*) sentence classification (Task 2); and *c*) event trigger and argument extraction (Task 3).

Task 1 and 2 are text classification tasks. The goal is to distinguish between documents and sentences that report on or contain mentions of protest events. Task 3 is an event extraction task where systems have to identify the correct event trigger, a protest event, and its arguments in every sentence of a document.

As described in [8,9], the creation of the datasets followed a detailed procedure to ensure maximal agreement among the annotators. Furthermore, the task is designed as a cascade of sub-tasks: first, identify if a document reports a protest event (Task 1), then identify which sentences are actually describing the protest event in the specific document (Task 2), and, finally, for each protest event sentence, identify the actual event mention(s) and its arguments (Task 3). However, there is no overlap among the training and test data across the three tasks.

The lab's main challenge is unsupervised domain adaptation. The lab organisers made available training and development data for one domain, namely news in English reporting protest events in India, and asked the participants to test their models both on in-domain data and on out-of-domain ones, namely news about protest events in China. In the remainder of the paper, we will refer to these two test distributions as India and China.

For the CLEF 2019 ProtestNews Lab our solution was based on a standard approach that can be summarised as "one system, one task". Besides differences in algorithms and architectures, the core idea is that for each task we trained a dedicated system using the available training material only (closed task). We here challenge this idea with a simpler method based on the use of event information only. We follow a bottom-up approach by adopting a sort of compositional perspective to content identification. In particular, we first detect all protest event mentions (Task 3), and then we propagate this information to coarser-grained levels of analysis, namely at sentence (Task 2) and document levels (Task 1).

Our main contribution is a comparison of these two architectures and tagging philosophies to address the three sub-tasks proposed showing that dedicated systems tend to perform better. We complement this with an in-depth analysis of the data and errors of the systems that help to understand the drops in performance across the test distributions. Our models are publicly available at https:// github.com/anbasile/protest-clef-2020.

2   Data Overview: Training Materials

Table 1, summarises the distributions of the labels of the training and development data for Task 1 and 2, i.e., document and sentence classification, respectively. As the figures show, the positive class, i.e., the protest documents or sentences, is unbalanced with respect to the negative one, i.e., non-protest, ranging between 22.41% for Task 1 to 16.78% for Task 2 in training. This distribution is mirrored in the development data with minor differences for Task 2 where the positive class is slightly larger than the negative one (20.81% *vs.* 16.78%).

Table 1. Distributions of classes for training and development for Task 1 and Task 2. Numbers in parentheses indicate percentages.

Task	Dataset	Protest	Not protest
Task 1 (document classification)	Train	769 (22.41%)	2,661 (77.58%)
	Dev.	102 (22.31%)	355 (77.68%)
Task 2 (sentence classification)	Train	988 (16.78%)	4,897 (83.21%)
	Dev.	138 (20.81%)	525 (79.18%)

Table 2 illustrates the distribution of the annotations for Task 3, i.e., event trigger and argument detection. The data is released in the form of tab-delimited files, with two columns: the first with pre-tokenized tokens and the second with labels for both event triggers and arguments. Overall, seven different argument types were annotated, namely *participant, organiser, target, etime* (event time), *place, fname* (facility name), and *loc* (location). The role set is inspired by the Automatic Content Extraction (ACE) guidelines for event annotation,[2] and especially the event types "Attack" and "Demonstrate". However, the Protest-News benchmark differs from ACE with respect to two aspects. First, there is not a precise overlap between the definitions of the ACE classes "Attack" and "Demonstrate" and that of protest event. Second, ProtestNews adopts a finer-grained representation of event participants than that used in the ACE annotations. For instance, there are dedicated tags for distinguishing among the organisers (**organizer**), the participants (**participant**), and the targets of

---

[2] https://www.ldc.upenn.edu/sites/www.ldc.upenn.edu/files/english-events-guidelines-v5.4.3.pdf.

a protest (`target`). On the other hand, ACE distinguishes only the attacking or instigating agent in "Attack" events and the demonstrating agent(s) in the "Demonstrate" event type. Such differences prevent a direct re-use of the ACE data to extend the training materials. The annotation for events and their participants are encoded in a BIO scheme (Beginning, Inside, Outside), resulting in different alphabets for event triggers (e.g. B-*trigger*, I-*trigger* and O) and each of the arguments (e.g. O, B-*organiser*, I-*organiser*, B-*etime*, I-*etime*, etc.).

Table 2. Distribution of event triggers and arguments for Task 3.

Annotations	Train	Development
Event triggers	844	126
Arguments	1,934	291

The training data contains 250 documents and a total of 594 sentences, while the development set is composed by 36 documents for a total of 93 sentences. The average amount of event trigger per sentence is 1.42 in training and 1.35 in development, indicating that multiple event triggers are available in the same sentence. As for the arguments, the average per event trigger is 2.29 in training and 2.3 in development, indicating both that arguments are shared among different event triggers in the same sentence and that not all arguments are available in every sentence. The development data was used to select the best method(s) rather than fine tuning the models since at test time they have to perform equally well on two different data distributions, in- and out-of-domain (India *vs.* China).

3   Models and Approaches

This section reports on the details of the two systems we want to compare to address the task, focusing on the differences in their architectures and tagging philosophies.

3.1   ProTestA: One System, One Task

ProTestA [2] qualifies as second best system at the CLEF 2019 ProtestNews Lab with an average F1-score on all three tasks of 0.607, only 0.010 points lower than the best system. ProTestA follows a standard approach by developing a dedicated model for each task. In particular, for Task 1 and 2, we opted for a feature-based stacked ensemble model using a set of different Logistic Regression classifiers, while for Task 3, we used a Bi-LSTM architecture optimized for sequence labelling tasks.

Classifying Documents and Sentences (Task 1 and Task2). For Task 1 and Task 2, we have developed a stacked ensemble model of Logistic Regression classifiers [18] using three different sets of features, namely: (i) word embedding representations at document and at sentence levels; (ii) most informative character n-grams and (iii) most informative token unigrams.

Table 3 illustrates the settings of the system for each test distribution and task. The variation in the amount of token and character n-grams has been empirically determined on preliminary results on the test distributions. We observed that the higher the number of tokens and character n-grams is extracted, the better the model performs on the same test data distribution, i.e., India, while downgrading its performances across test distributions, i.e., China.

Table 3. Most important tokens and character n-grams features for Task 1 and Task 2 across the two test distributions, i.e., India and China.

	Feature type	Test set	Amount
TASK 1	Tokens	India	8,000
	Char. n-grams	India	750
	Tokens	China	4,000
	Char. n-grams	China	750
TASK 2	Tokens	India	4,000
	Char. n-grams	India	1,000
	Tokens	China	2,000
	Char. n-grams	China	500

Extracting Events and Their Arguments (Task 3). We framed the event trigger and argument extraction task as a supervised sequence labelling problem [1, 3, 11, 19, 24]. In particular, given a sentence, S, the system is asked to identify all linguistic expressions $w \in S$, where w is a mention of a protest event, ev_w, as well as all linguistic expressions $y \in S$ where y is a mention of an argument, arg_y, associated to a specific event mention ev_w.

We have implemented a two-step approach using a common sequence labelling model based on a publicly available Bi-LSTM network with a CRF classifier as last layer (Bi-LSTM-CRF) [23].[3] In more details, we developed two different models: first, we detect event trigger mentions, and subsequently, the event arguments (and their labels). In Table 4, we report the common hyperparameters of the networks for both tasks. The "LSTM Layers" refers separately to the number of forward and backward layers.

---

[3] https://github.com/UKPLab/emnlp2017-bilstm-cnn-crf.

Table 4. System details

Parameters	Value
LSTM layers	1
Units per layer	100
Optimizer	Nadam
Gradient normalisation	$\tau = 1$
Dropout	Variational, (0.5, 0.5)
Batch size	12

Training is stopped after 5 consecutive epochs with no improvements. Komninos and Manandhar [12] embeddings are used to initialize the ELMo embeddings [20] and fine-tune them with respect to the training data. The ELMo embeddings are used to enhance the network generalisation capabilities for event and argument detection over both test data distributions. As for the event trigger detection sub-task, the embedding representations are further concatenated with character-level embeddings [14], and parts-of-speech (POS) embeddings. POS tags have been obtained from the Stanford CoreNLP toolkit [15].[4] This minimal set of features is further extended with embedding representations for dependency relations and event triggers for the argument detection sub-task. At test time, the protest event triggers are obtained from the event mentions model.

For both the event trigger and argument detection sub-tasks, we have conducted five different runs to better asses the variability of the deep learning models due to random initialisations. At test time, we selected the model that obtained the best F1 scores on the development set out of the five runs.

3.2 BERT-Event: From Tokens to Documents

As an alternative to the "one task, one system" approach of ProTestA, we experimented with a bottom-up approach by starting from the sequence labelling task of event trigger and argument identification (Task 3). Our hypothesis is the following: assuming that we can correctly identify protest event triggers, we can propagate the protest label (i.e., the positive class) first at the sentence level (Task 2) and then at the document one (Task 1). In this way, we address the three tasks in a reverse order from micro- to macro-representation level of information. More formally, a label Y for a sentence is computed as follows:

$$Y = \left\{ \begin{array}{l} 0, \; |T \cap Z| = 0 \\ 1, \; |T \cap Z| > 0 \end{array} \right\}$$

where $T = \{B - trigger, I - trigger\}$ and Z is the vector of predicted tags for a given sentence.

---

[4] We used version 3.9.2.

For classifying a document, we first segment it into a list of sentences,[5] then process each sentence as described above and finally leverage the distribution of predicted labels across sentences to derive a document-level label. If an event trigger T is found in at least n sentences Z of a document, then the document is considered to be about protest events. Based on experiments in the development data, we empirically determined that best results are obtained with n equal to 3.

BERT-Event in Details. The sequence labelling model that we implemented is a fine-tuned BERT [4] model, using a dense softmax activation layer for the prediction of event and argument tags. We have used the English `bert-base-cased` pre-trained network and further fine-tuned it for a maximum of 100 epochs, using early stopping as a form of hyperparameter optimization. We set the maximum sequence length to 512 tokens and we use a static learning rate of 3e−5.

This architecture is similar to the ProTestA Bi-LSTM-CRF tagger when compared to the the input representation, since both leverage contextualized word embeddings. However, the contextualised representations are essentially different. While ELMo embeddings are obtained by jointly optimizing a forward and backward LSTM-based causal language model, BERT embeddings are trained using a Transformer encoder with two learning objectives (a masked language modelling procedure and a next sentence prediction task). Further differences concerns the quantity and the type of data used to generate the two contextualised embeddings.

For BERT-Event, we do not augment such input representation with character embeddings nor with POS embeddings. A further difference concerns the final prediction module which consists of a simple dense layer instead of a CRF.

BERT-Event frames Task 3 as a joined task, attempting to learn event triggers and arguments at the same time. To counteract the limited amount of training data and reduce sparseness of the labels, we experimented with self-training [16]. We extended the original annotated instances with a simple bootstrapping approach. In particular, first we train a sequence labelling model for Task 3 on the manually annotated training data; second, this model is applied to a random portion of the training material from Task 1 obtaining automatically annotated data (i.e., silver data) for event triggers and arguments. Finally, the silver data is concatenated with the gold training data of Task 3, and used to train a new sequence labelling model (BERT-Event Augmented). The silver training data contains 34,593 tokens more than the original, with a total of 1,457 event triggers and 2,586 event participants.

We compared BERT-Event and BERT-Event Augmented on the development data to verify the validity of the self-training hypothesis across all tasks. In our approach, improving the event trigger detection should also lead to improvements in the sentence and document classification tasks. Table 5 illustrates the results (F1-score). We observe an improvement only for Task 3, suggesting that self-training has a positive effect. As for Task 2, the improved version of BERT-Event

---

[5] We use spaCy's English sentence tokenizer module.

does not have any effect, while it seems to harm a bit performance on Task 1. Besides this, we decided to use the augmented version.

Table 5. F1-scores on the development data by BERT-Event (only Task 3 gold training) and BERT-Event augmented (Task 3 gold and silver data).

Task	BERT-Event	BERT-Event augmented
Task 1	0.75	0.73
Task 2	0.78	0.78
Task 3	0.51	0.57

4   Comparing the Approaches: Results and Discussion

Results for the three tasks and the two approaches are reported in Table 6.

Table 6. Results for Task 1, 2, and 3.

Task	System	Dataset	F1 score	Avg. F1
Task 1	ProTestA	India	0.807	**0.702**
		China	0.597	
	BERT-Event	India	0.607	0.462
		China	0.313	
Task 2	ProTestA	India	0.631	0.592
		China	0.553	
	BERT-Event	India	0.606	**0.613**
		China	0.619	
Task 3	ProTestA	India	0.600	**0.528**
		China	0.456	
	BERT-Event	India	0.488	0.417
		China	0.347	

We start our analysis from Task 3. It clearly appears that the ProTestA architecture obtains better results on detecting events and participants than the BERT-Event system. However, the results of BERT-Event on Task 2 signals that the overall picture is more complex than it appears from the raw numbers alone. Disappointingly, but yet inline with the scores on the development set, BERT-Event performs badly also on Task 1, with a delta of 0.24 when compared to ProTestA. Overall, both systems tend to degrade their performances when applied to the China test data. As a general tendency, ProTestA looses ≈0.15

points on China, while BERT-Event limits the losses to ≈0.14 points. Besides the different tagging philosophies, both approaches record their largest drops across test distributions in Task 1, where ProTesTa looses 0.21 points in F1 on China and BERT-Event 0.29. On the other hand, Task 2 appears the one which is less likely to be affected by the differences between the two data distributions, with BERT-Event obtaining better results on China than on India.

Similarities and Differences in the Data Distributions. To better understand these results, we have conducted an analysis of the data to highlight similarities and differences. Following recent work [13,22], we embrace the vision that different corpora belonging to the same domain are not monolithic entities but rather they are regions in a high dimensional space of latent factors that includes topics, genres, writing styles, years of publication, among others. In particular, we have investigated to what extent the test sets of the three tasks occupy a similar (or different) portions of this space with respect to their corresponding training distributions. To do so, we used two metrics, the Jensen-Shannon (J-S) divergence and the out-of-vocabulary rate of tokens (OOV), that previous work in transfer learning [25] has shown to be particularly useful.

The J-S divergence assesses the similarity between two probability distributions and is a smoothed, symmetric variant of the Kullback-Leibler divergence. On the other hand, the OOV rate can be used to assess the differences between data distributions, as it highlights the percentage of unknown tokens. All measures have been computed between the training data and the two test distributions, i.e., India and China. Results are reported on Table 7.

Table 7. J-S (similarity) and OOV (diversity) between train and test distributions for all tasks.

Task	J-S		OOV	
	India	China	India	China
Task 1 (document classification)	0.922	0.822	28.11%	50.25%
Task 2 (sentence classification)	0.822	0.743	29.41%	41.12%
Task 3 (event extraction)	0.703	0.575	44.33%	53.82%
Task 1 BERT-Event augmented training	0.773	0.647	37.28%	42.04%
Task 2 BERT-Event augmented training	0.703	0.654	69.95%	70.80%
Task 3 BERT-Event augmented training	0.677	0.546	84.01%	88.97%

As the figures in Table 7 show, both test distributions can be seen as occupying different portions of this variety of spaces. Not surprisingly, the China data are very different from all the distributions we used to train our models. This variation in similarity, however, also affects the India test distributions, where the highest similarity is observed for Task 1 (0.922 against the corresponding training and 0.773 with BERT-Event augmented training) and the lowest for Task

3, regardless of whether this involves the same training distribution (0.703) or the BERT-Event augmented training (0.677). The J-S scores show that the test distributions for Task 3 and Task 2 are even more distant than those for Task 1, suggesting that the differences in performances across the tasks and tests may also be bigger.

The OOV rates appear to support the observations on the J-S divergence. In general, the OOV rates for India are lower than those of China, clearly signalling that there are strong lexical differences across them. When focusing on the BERT-Event augmented training, we can see that the OOV rates increase mainly on Task 2 and Task 3. In these two latter cases, the OOV rates of India and China are almost equal, indicating that the augmented training set introduces additional variations with respect to the original training distributions. Finally, although the OOV rates of the test data on Task 3 are very close to each other, yet the differences in absolute F1 scores of the systems on these test sets are pretty large, suggesting that large differences in vocabulary across distributions is a major issue that requires either additional training material or the deployment of different models on the line of [7].

Predictions and Errors. A further aspect to account for the behavior of the models concerns the proportion of the predictions and the distributions of errors. We will start this analysis from Task 3, and then move to Task 2 and Task 1.

ProTestA predicts the same proportion of event triggers in both test distributions (0.90 event per sentence on India, and 0.95 event per sentence on China, respectively), although lower than that observed in training. Similarly, BERT-Event predicts almost the same proportion of event triggers per sentence in both test sets (1.26 event on India and 1.24 on China). However, BERT-Event systematically predicts a larger number of event triggers than ProTestA. An error analysis of the two models on the 30% of the gold test sets for India and China has shown that BERT-Event tends to predict less False Negatives than ProTestA on the B labels of the event triggers, while it looses accuracy on I labels (either missed or wrongly predicted as B):

1. they were $protesting_{B-trigger}$ against the University Grants Commission's decision. [India test - Gold]
   Bi-LSTM-CRF: $protesting_O$ *vs.* BERT-Event: $protesting_{B-trigger}$
2. activists staged $road_{B-trigger}$ $blockades_{I-trigger}$. [India test - Gold]
   Bi-LSTM-CRF: $blockades_O$ *vs.* BERT-Event: $blockades_{B-trigger}$

This different behaviour may explain why BERT-Event is actually performing better than ProTestA on Task 2 (sentence level).

Table 8 completes our overview on the performance of the event triggers of the two systems by reporting the results on the protest event trigger identification sub-task only.

In both datasets, ProTestA outperforms BERT-Event, especially for Precision. However, we can observe that BERT-Event is more consistent in maintaining a better balance between Precision and Recall.

Table 8. Results for ProTestA and BERT-Event for protest event trigger identification (P = Precision, R = Recall).

Dataset	ProTestA			BERT-Event		
	P	R	F1	P	R	F1
India	0.861	0.637	0.732	0.609	0.697	0.650
China	0.726	0.534	0.616	0.467	0.493	0.479

The two systems differ mainly when it comes to the participant detection. ProTestA maintains a proportion of predicted arguments that is in line with those in the training on the India test (2.51 *vs.* 2.29 in training, respectively), while they are lower on China (1.94). BERT-Event, on the other hand, under-performs on this task: on India, it predicts only 2.02 participants per event trigger, with a delta of 0.20 when compared to the training data. The drop on China is even more drastic, with only 1.57 participant per event trigger. When comparing the macro-F1 score for participants of the two systems the differences are even more visible. ProTestA achieves a macro-F1 of 0.470 on India while BERT-Event lags behind at 0.307. On China the gap is even larger, with ProTestA obtaining a macro-F1 of 0.336 and BERT-Event only 0.198. Both systems, however, show better results when tested on the same data distribution of the training set, i.e., India.

Reasons for such a different behaviour are multiple, including the use of POS and character embeddings, the presence of a CRF classifier in the last layer, the architectures of the two systems (Bi-LSTM *vs.* Transformer encoder), the definition of the task (two-step *vs.* single step), as well as the contextualized embedding representations they use (ELMo *vs.* BERT). A detailed error analysis[6] has shown, however, some common difficulties of the two systems when it comes to the participant detection. In particular, both systems tend to confuse labels that are semantically close. For instance, ≈22% of the times both of them confuse facility name (**fname**) and location (**loc**) on the India test data. This is partially reflected in the China test, where BERT-Event has a higher proportions of errors on these two labels (≈18.5%) than ProTestA (≈10.5%). Likewise, other affected labels are participant (**participant**) and organisers (**organizers**) (India: 2.3% for the ProTestA *vs.* 4.3% for BERT-Event; China: 14% for the ProTestA *vs.* 10% for BERT-Event), and participant and targets (**target**) (India: 12% for the ProTestA *vs.* 2% for BERT-Event; China: 8.7% for the ProTestA *vs.* 12% for BERT-Event).

As for Task 2 and Task 1, the behaviour of the two systems is the same as for Task 3. ProTestA maintains the proportion of the predictions of the protest documents/sentences of the training sets in the India tests (≈24% *vs.* ≈23% in training) while it drops on the China tests (4.94% for Task 1 and 12.79% for Task 2, respectively). BERT-Event mimics this behaviour only in Task 1, where on China it only predicts 9.21% of the documents as belonging to the positive

---

[6] We used the same 30% of the gold data used for the event triggers.

class. On the contrary, this does not happen in Task 2: both test distributions have an almost identical proportion of predictions of sentences for the positive class (23.93% for India and 22.18% for China, respectively) which is comparable to that of the training data.

As for ProTestA, an error analysis on a random subset of the China test shows an increase in the number of the False Negatives of ≈46% each on Task 1 and Task 2, while False Positives in both tasks are no more than ≈8%, confirming the superiority of ProTesA in Precision. However, this also indicates a strong dependence on the lexical features of the system we have used to address these two initial tasks. The embedding representations do contribute to the performance of the system but not enough to overcome the differences between training and test distributions that we have highlighted by means of the J-S scores and OOV rates.

BERT-Event performs very well on Task 2, while it drastically underperforms on Task 1. This difference provides additional feedback on the quality of BERT-Event on the event trigger detection sub-task, further supporting the observations of the error analysis. Indeed, BERT-Event detects potentially more event triggers but it fails to correctly label event boundaries (i.e., the distinction between B and I components of the tag). An error analysis on the data of Task 1 has revealed that the low performances are strictly related to the proposed bottom-up approach rather than low performances of the event trigger model. Although a document may contain multiple sentences reporting a protest event (Task 2), its core story could be on a different topic (e.g., a trial). In this case, the protest event sentences in the document contribute only to setting the background of the story.

5   Conclusion and Future Work

Our contribution focused on the following aspects: *a*.) compare two different architectures to address the identification of protest events in news articles at varying granularity of semantic representations (i.e., document, sentence, and token levels) and distributions; *b*.) explain the limits of the trained models in terms of similarities and differences across training and test distributions; *c*.) accompany the description of the systems with an in-depth error analysis to better understand their limitations rather than just reporting on their technical aspects.

We have shown that a system like ProTestA, that combines models trained on specific tasks, obtains very good performances when compared to an event-driven bottom-up approach like BERT-Event. We attempted to improve the robustness of BERT-Event using self-supervision. The lower performances of BERT-Event are due to different factors: on the one hand, the system is less robust than ProTestA at labelling opening and closing tags for event triggers, although it predicts a higher proportion of likely correct event triggers. On the other hand, the propagation of label information from tokens to higher semantic levels (i.e., sentences and documents) is not optimal and it fails on more complex units of analysis. The BERT-Event approach presents margins of improvement: i.) use prediction probabilities to improve the quality of the data obtained from self-supervision; ii) use a normalised score of the event sentences to classify documents as protest news; and iii.) add a CRF layer on top of BERT to improve the extraction of events and arguments.

As for ProTestA, Task 1 and Task 2 have shown that a simple system can obtain competitive results in an unsupervised domain adaptation setting. We also believe that the lack of any material for the out-of-domain distributions is a further challenge to take into account, as no fine tuning of the models on the target domain was actually possible. As far as we can put efforts into the development of maximally generalisable systems, the dependence of the models on the training materials remains high, thus posing the problem if we are not just modelling datasets rather than linguistic phenomena.

Task 3 has actually highlighted the contribution of both more complex architectures, such as a Bi-LSTM-CRF network, and contextualised embedding representations, such as ELMo. In this specific case, the trained model is able to predict a comparable amount of event triggers between the two test distributions, although it suffers on the argument sub-task, where less arguments are predicted and confused when semantically close.

Finally, the similarity and diversity measures (i.e., J-S divergence and OOV rates) resulted in useful tools to better understand the different behaviors of the systems on both test distributions. As recent work has shown [5], it would be useful to use this kind of information to predict, or quantify, a margin loss of systems before applying them to out-of-domain test distributions and, consequently, take actions to minimize the losses either by annotating more data or by investigating new approaches based on zero-shot transfer learning [7].

References

1. Ahn, D.: The stages of event extraction. In: Proceedings of the Workshop on Annotating and Reasoning About Time and Events, pp. 1–8. Association for Computational Linguistics (2006)
2. Basile, A., Caselli, T.: ProTestA: identifying and extracting protest events in news notebook for ProtestNews lab at CLEF 2019. In: Working Notes of CLEF 2019 - Conference and Labs of the Evaluation Forum (2019)
3. Bethard, S.: ClearTK-TimeML: a minimalist approach to TempEval 2013. In: Second Joint Conference on Lexical and Computational Semantics (* SEM), vol. 2, pp. 10–14 (2013)
4. Devlin, J., Chang, M.W., Lee, K., Toutanova, K.: BERT: pre-training of deep bidirectional transformers for language understandin. In: Proceedings of the 2019 Conference of the North American Chapter of the Association for Computational Linguistics: Human Language Technologies, vol. 1, pp. 4171–4186. Association for Computational Linguistics, Minneapolis, Minnesota, June 2019. https://doi.org/10.18653/v1/N19-1423

5. Elsahar, H., Gallé, M.: To annotate or not? Predicting performance drop under domain shift. In: Proceedings of the 2019 Conference on Empirical Methods in Natural Language Processing and the 9th International Joint Conference on Natural Language Processing (EMNLP-IJCNLP), pp. 2163–2173. Association for Computational Linguistics, Hong Kong, China, November 2019. https://doi.org/10.18653/v1/D19-1222, https://www.aclweb.org/anthology/D19-1222

6. Ettinger, A., Rao, S., Daumé III, H., Bender, E.M.: Towards linguistically generalizable NLP systems: a workshop and shared task. In: Proceedings of the First Workshop on Building Linguistically Generalizable NLP Systems, pp. 1–10 (2017)

7. Huang, L., Ji, H., Cho, K., Dagan, I., Riedel, S., Voss, C.: Zero-shot transfer learning for event extraction. In: Proceedings of the 56th Annual Meeting of the Association for Computational Linguistics (Volume 1: Long Papers), pp. 2160–2170. Association for Computational Linguistics, Melbourne, July 2018. https://doi.org/10.18653/v1/P18-1201, https://www.aclweb.org/anthology/P18-1201

8. Hürriyetoğlu, A., et al.: Cross-context news corpus for protest events related knowledge base construction. In: Automated Knowledge Base Construction (2020). https://openreview.net/forum?id=7NZkNhLCjp

9. Hürriyetoğlu, A., et al.: A task set proposal for automatic protest information collection across multiple countries. In: Azzopardi, L., Stein, B., Fuhr, N., Mayr, P., Hauff, C., Hiemstra, D. (eds.) ECIR 2019. LNCS, vol. 11438, pp. 316–323. Springer, Cham (2019). https://doi.org/10.1007/978-3-030-15719-7_42

10. Hürriyetoğlu, A., et al.: Overview of CLEF 2019 lab ProtestNews: extracting protests from news in a cross-context setting. In: Crestani, F., et al. (eds.) CLEF 2019. LNCS, vol. 11696, pp. 425–432. Springer, Cham (2019). https://doi.org/10.1007/978-3-030-28577-7_32

11. Ji, H., Grishman, R.: Refining event extraction through cross-document inference. In: Proceedings of ACL-2008: HLT, pp. 254–262 (2008)

12. Komninos, A., Manandhar, S.: Dependency based embeddings for sentence classification tasks. In: Proceedings of the 2016 Conference of the North American Chapter of the Association for Computational Linguistics: Human Language Technologies, pp. 1490–1500 (2016)

13. Liakata, M., Saha, S., Dobnik, S., Batchelor, C., Rebholz-Schuhmann, D.: Automatic recognition of conceptualization zones in scientific articles and two life science applications. Bioinformatics 28(7), 991–1000 (2012). https://doi.org/10.1093/bioinformatics/bts071

14. Ma, X., Hovy, E.: End-to-end sequence labeling via bi-directional LSTM-CNNs-CRF. In: Proceedings of the 54th Annual Meeting of the Association for Computational Linguistics, vol. 1, pp. 1064–1074. Association for Computational Linguistics, Berlin, August 2016. https://doi.org/10.18653/v1/P16-1101

15. Manning, C., Surdeanu, M., Bauer, J., Finkel, J., Bethard, S., McClosky, D.: The stanford CoreNLP natural language processing toolkit. In: Proceedings of the 52nd Annual Meeting of the Association for Computational Linguistics. System Demonstrations, pp. 55–60 (2014)

16. McClosky, D., Charniak, E., Johnson, M.: Effective self-training for parsing. In: Proceedings of the Human Language Technology Conference of the North American Chapter of the ACL, pp. 152–159. Association for Computational Linguistics (2006). https://dl.acm.org/doi/pdf/10.3115/1220835.1220855

17. Miwa, M., Thompson, P., Korkontzelos, I., Ananiadou, S.: Comparable study of event extraction in newswire and biomedical domains. In: Proceedings of COLING 2014, the 25th International Conference on Computational Linguistics: Technical Papers, pp. 2270–2279. Dublin City University and Association for Computational Linguistics, Dublin, August 2014. https://www.aclweb.org/anthology/C14-1214

18. Montani, J.P.: Tuwienkbs at germeval 2018: German abusive tweet detection. In: 14th Conference on Natural Language Processing KONVENS 2018, p. 45 (2018)

19. Nguyen, T.H., Grishman, R.: Event detection and domain adaptation with convolutional neural networks. In: Proceedings of the 53rd Annual Meeting of the Association for Computational Linguistics and the 7th International Joint Conference on Natural Language Processing (Volume 2: Short Papers), vol. 2, pp. 365–371 (2015)

20. Peters, M.E., et al.: Deep contextualized word representations. In: Proceedings of NAACL (2018)

21. Plank, B.: What to do about non-standard (or non-canonical) language in NLP. arXiv preprint arXiv:1608.07836 (2016)

22. Plank, B., Van Noord, G.: Effective measures of domain similarity for parsing. In: Proceedings of the 49th Annual Meeting of the Association for Computational Linguistics: Human Language Technologies, vol. 1, pp. 1566–1576. Association for Computational Linguistics (2011)

23. Reimers, N., Gurevych, I.: Reporting score distributions makes a difference: performance study of LSTM-networks for sequence tagging. In: Proceedings of the 2017 Conference on Empirical Methods in Natural Language Processing, pp. 338–348. Association for Computational Linguistics, Copenhagen, September 2017. https://www.aclweb.org/anthology/D17-1035

24. Ritter, A., Etzioni, O., Clark, S., et al.: Open domain event extraction from Twitter. In: Proceedings of the 18th ACM SIGKDD International Conference on Knowledge Discovery and Data Mining, pp. 1104–1112. ACM (2012)

25. Ruder, S., Plank, B.: Learning to select data for transfer learning with Bayesian optimization. In: Proceedings of the 2017 Conference on Empirical Methods in Natural Language Processing, pp. 372–382. Association for Computational Linguistics, Copenhagen, September 2017. https://www.aclweb.org/anthology/D17-1038

A Study on a Stopping Strategy for Systematic Reviews Based on a Distributed Effort Approach

Giorgio Maria Di Nunzio[1,2(✉)]

[1] Department of Information Engineering, University of Padua, Padua, Italy
giorgiomaria.dinunzio@unipd.it
[2] Department of Mathematics, University of Padua, Padua, Italy

Abstract. Systematic reviews are scientific investigations that use strategies to include a comprehensive search of all potentially relevant articles and the use of explicit, reproducible criteria in the selection of articles for review. As time and resources are limited for compiling a systematic review, limits to the search are needed. In this paper, we describe the stopping strategy that we have been designed and refined over three years of participation to the CLEF eHealth Technology Assisted Review Task. In particular, we present a comparison of a Continuous Active Learning approach that uses either a fixed amount or a variable amount of resources according to the size of the pool. The results show that our approach performs on average much better than any other participant in the CLEF 2019 eHealth TAR task. Nevertheless, a failure analysis allows to understand the weak points of this approach and possible future directions.

1   Background

In the last decades, healthcare and health systems have become increasingly complex ecosystems that require a lot of qualitative and quantitative analysis of the generated data in order to produce informed decisions. In such situations where massive amount of data is produced, the problem of finding the right information in order to take the right decision in a timely fashion has become an important issue, especially in periods of health crisis [25]. In this context, evidence-based healthcare is a fundamental approach that integrates the best research evidence with clinical expertise in order to make decisions based on the best and most consistent practices [4]. Simply knowing 'what works' is not enough as we also want to know why something may not work [24]; therefore, researchers use systematic reviews in order to conduct a proper research and collect enough medical evidence about a topic. Systematic reviews are scientific investigations in themselves, with pre-planned methods and an assembly of original studies as their "subjects" [1]. These kinds of reviews use strategies to include a comprehensive search of all potentially relevant articles and the use of explicit and reproducible criteria in the selection of articles for review.

© Springer Nature Switzerland AG 2020
A. Arampatzis et al. (Eds.): CLEF 2020, LNCS 12260, pp. 112–123, 2020.
https://doi.org/10.1007/978-3-030-58219-7_10

As time and resources are limited for compiling a systematic review, limits to the search are needed: for example, one may want to estimate how far the horizon of the search should be (i.e. all possible cases that could exist in the literature) in order to stop before the resources are finished [11]. As an example, the Cochrane handbook for Systematic Reviews [6, chapter 4] examines how difficult it is to decide in a scientific or objective way when a search is complete and search strategy development can stop. The ability to decide when to stop typically develops through experience of developing many strategies.

Related Works. International evaluation campaigns have recently organized labs in order to study this problem in terms of the evaluation, through controlled simulation, of methods designed to achieve very high recall [5,22] and, in particular, for technology assisted reviews in empirical medicine [3,8]. The CLEF initiative[1] has promoted the eHealth track since 2013 and, from 2017 to 2019 [7,9,10], the Technology Assisted Review (TAR) task was organized with the aim to sharing resources and methodologies as well as evaluating and comparing different related solutions about the aforementioned problem. Many important works about Continuous Active Learning strategies for eHealth have been studied by Cormack and others [2]. Kanoulas and others, apart from being the organizers of the CLEF eHealth track, have been studying the problem of estimating the true recall with different sampling approaches [27]. The work carried out by Zuccon and others is also important from a different perspective with a focus on the Boolean Search [23].

Research Proposal. In this paper, we describe the stopping strategy that we have been designing and refining over three years of participation to the CLEF eHealth [12] TAR task [10]. The objective of our study is to propose and analyze an interactive search strategy that starts from one simple initial question: how many documents is the expert who is compiling the review willing to read? Given this context, we want to tackle the problem with a mixed approach of retrieval and classification to collect as much relevant documents as possible given a fixed amount of resources, by taking advantage of the explicit relevance feedback interaction with the expert.

The paper is organized as follows: Sect. 2 defines the problem, the model and the approach we propose to tackle the problem of the stopping strategy; in Sect. 3, we describe the experimental settings for the analysis of the results that are described in Sect. 4. We conclude with Sect. 5 and we give our future directions.

2   Problem Definition

The objective of our study is to propose and analyze an interactive search strategy that starts from one simple initial question: how many documents is the

---

[1] http://www.clef-initiative.eu.

expert who is compiling the review willing to read? Despite being somewhat naïve, this question allows us to decompose the problem in two parts. On the one hand, if we had an researcher with an "infinite" patience, the problem could be tackled as a traditional Information Retrieval (IR) system where the measure of interest would be more towards recall rather than precision (we still want to finish the work as soon as possible rather than having a good proportion of relevant documents in the top ten ranked documents). On the other hand, since the resources are limited, we might want to change the search strategy during the search process: first we use a traditional ranker, then we switch to a classification problem when the system collects enough relevant documents to train a classifier. Moreover, in those cases where researchers need to compile more than one systematic review, we imagined two different situations regarding the management of the resources: 1) distribute the resources (or the effort) evenly across the different reviews [16]; or 2) distribute the resources proportionally to the size of the documents pooled for the review (see the details in Sect. 3.1).

2.1   Interactive Retrieval and Classification

Systematic reviews are one of the high-recall IR tasks where human interaction is required to find most of (if not all) relevant documents [26]. In particular, Continuous Active Learning (CAL) can be used to engage the user in the search by allowing them to interactively search for relevant documents [2]. The idea of CAL is that we can update the estimates of the parameters of the model iteratively and for each document given to the user. In general, this approach is computationally intensive for large collections and may not be used for applications that require an almost immediate response, such as Web search engines. However, since the temporal horizon of the task of systematic reviews is within days or weeks of work, we do have enough time 1) to give to the user a document to read, 2) to update the estimates of the model based on the last feedback while the user is reviewing the current document, and 3) to present the next most relevant document when the user finishes to read the previous document.

We want to tackle the first part of the problem, that is the use of a mixed approach of retrieval and classification to collect as much relevant documents as possible given a fixed amount of resources, by analyzing the explicit relevance feedback interaction with the two-dimensional interpretation of the probabilistic retrieval models [14,16–20]. This interpretation maps the probability ranking principle [21] onto a two-dimensional space in the following way: given the classes of relevant $\mathcal{R}$ and non-relevant $\mathcal{NR}$ documents, a document d is relevant given a query q if the following inequality holds:

$$\underbrace{a \log \left(P(d|\mathcal{R}, q) \right)}_{x} + \underbrace{b \log \left(P(d|\mathcal{NR}, q) \right)}_{y} + c > 0 \tag{1}$$

where x and y are the log-likelihoods of the document d, while a, b, and c are parameters that can be optimized to compensate for either the unbalanced class issues or different misclassification costs. In Fig. 1, we show an example of the

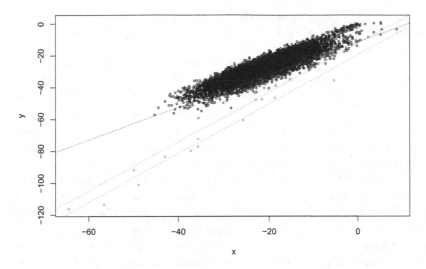

Fig. 1. An example of the two-dimensional representation of the BM25.

two-dimensional representation produced by the BM25 model. The green dots are the documents that were judged relevant, the red dots those judged non relevant, black dots are documents that are still to be judged. An advantage of the two-dimensional visualization is that we have a visual feedback about the distribution of relevant and non relevant documents; consequently, it is easier to take decisions about where and how to stop the search for relevant documents [15,16,20]. For example, in Fig. 1 three decision lines are drawn, they identify three areas where the next relevant document may be found with the highest probability based on the current knowledge.

In this paper, we follow the procedure suggested in [17] to rank and classify documents: we use half of the documents that the user is willing to read to rank documents using explicit relevance feedback, then we use a classifier trained on the first half of the documents and continue to use a CAL approach to update the classifier for the remaining documents.

In particular, given a topic for a systematic review:

- we set a number n of documents that the physician is willing to read;
- for the fist half, $n/2$, we run a BM25 retrieval model and we continuously update the relevance weights of the terms according to the explicit relevance feedback given by the user for each document; in addition we use query expansion to add a number of terms to the original query proportional to the current iteration (at iteration 1 we will add 1 term, at iteration 10 we will add 10 terms);
- for the second half of the documents, we use a Naïve Bayes classifier trained on the first $n/2$ documents to suggest new documents, and we continue to update the parameters of the classifier with the explicit relevance feedback [16].

Table 1. For each topic, we show the number of documents of the pool, the true number of relevant documents, and the the two best runs (see Sect. 4).

	topic	num docs	num rels (k)	equal-t1000 shown	recall@k	recall	abs-hh-ratio shown	recall@k	recall
1	CD000996	281	9	281	0.00	1.00	142	0.67	1.00
2	CD001261	571	72	571	0.40	1.00	250	0.51	0.92
3	CD004414	336	16	336	0.19	1.00	154	0.25	0.88
4	CD006468	3874	52	1243	0.29	0.96	1065	0.29	1.00
5	CD007867	943	17	943	0.12	1.00	319	0.53	0.76
6	CD008874	2382	118	1010	0.62	0.97	879	0.82	1.00
7	CD009044	3169	11	1000	0.00	1.00	2435	0.00	0.64
8	CD009069	1757	78	1006	0.24	0.97	898	0.26	0.79
9	CD009642	1922	62	1033	0.63	1.00	435	0.85	1.00
10	CD010038	8867	23	1006	0.09	0.91	4199	0.35	1.00
11	CD010239	224	12	224	0.83	1.00	95	0.83	1.00
12	CD010558	2815	37	1094	0.14	0.97	1698	0.24	0.81
13	CD010753	2539	29	1000	0.00	0.90	575	0.45	0.86
14	CD011140	289	4	289	0.25	1.00	234	0.00	1.00
15	CD011558	2168	2	1000	0.00	0.00	1739	0.00	1.00
16	CD011571	146	15	146	0.67	1.00	112	0.73	1.00
17	CD011686	9729	64	1206	0.27	0.95	904	0.36	0.81
18	CD011768	9160	54	1243	0.35	0.96	812	0.44	0.93
19	CD011787	4369	111	1445	0.32	0.95	753	0.37	0.84
20	CD011977	195	49	195	0.61	1.00	143	0.76	1.00
21	CD012069	3479	320	1385	0.31	0.70	1903	0.63	0.91
22	CD012080	6643	77	1084	0.13	0.84	2349	0.84	1.00
23	CD012164	61	7	62	0.29	1.00	55	0.71	1.00
24	CD012233	472	43	472	0.37	1.00	219	0.30	0.56
25	CD012342	2353	6	1000	0.00	1.00	1886	0.00	0.67
26	CD012455	1593	7	1000	0.29	1.00	204	0.71	1.00
27	CD012551	591	68	591	0.25	1.00	267	0.43	0.76
28	CD012567	6735	11	1000	0.00	1.00	1682	0.36	0.73
29	CD012661	3367	192	1015	0.35	0.90	1220	0.58	0.95
30	CD012669	1260	71	1004	0.34	1.00	474	0.39	0.94
31	CD012768	131	45	131	0.42	1.00	101	0.47	0.84
	Total	82421	1682	25015	0.282	0.935	28201	0.457	0.890

For the second part of the problem, that is having multiple systematic reviews to compile, since the task we are studying (see next section) uses pools of documents of different sizes for each systematic review, we want to evaluate two approaches: given a set of T topics, where a topic corresponds to a systematic review, and N documents that the user is willing to read, one approach equally distributes

N across topics in order to have $n = N/T$ documents to read per topic; the other approach distributes the effort in order to have an amount of documents per topic proportional to the size of the pool.

In Table 1, we show, for each topic, the number of documents in the pool, the true number of relevant documents, and some results of the best performing runs that will be discussed in Sect. 4.

3   Experiments

In this Section, we describe the dataset used in the CLEF 2019 eHealth task on Technology Assisted Reviews in Empirical Medicine [12] and the experimental settings of our model.

3.1   Dataset

Before giving the details about the dataset used in this task, we first present the process of searching for scientific publications in order to understand which data are available and which data were used in our experiments. In the overview of the CLEF eHealth 2019 task [12], the typical process of searching for scientific publications to conduct a systematic review is described by the following steps:

1. specifying a number of inclusion criteria that characterize the articles relevant to the review,
2. constructing a complex Boolean Query to express them,
3. screening the abstracts and titles that result from the Boolean query, and
4. reading and screening the full documents that passed the abstract and title screening.

The CLEF 2019 TAR task has two subtasks: one with the whole PubMed[2] collection, and the other one with pools of documents given the results of the Boolean Search from step 2) as the starting point. The latter is the subtask we are using in the experimental study of this paper.

For subtask 2, the PubMed Document Identifiers (PMIDs) of potentially relevant PubMed Document abstracts were provided for each topic. The PMIDs were collected by the task coordinators by re-running the Boolean query used in the original systematic reviews conducted by Cochrane to search PubMed.

Topics consisted of the Boolean Search from step 2) of the systematic review process. In addition to a Topic identifier, a title of the review, written by Cochrane experts were given together with the Boolean query, manually constructed by Cochrane experts.

Relevance of the documents in the pool was assessed at two levels, at abstract level (to decide whether to include the article in the list of paper to read) and at full content level (to decide whether to include the article in the review).

---

[2] https://www.ncbi.nlm.nih.gov/pubmed/.

3.2   Model Settings

For all the experiments, we use a BM25 model as the main retrieval model, and we set the values of the BM25 hyper-parameters in the same way we did in [17]. Since we do not have access to the full content of all the documents of each pool, we use only the abstracts both for the retrieval and the evaluation of the model. For the topics, we used only the 'title' of the review and not the boolean search. In order to evaluate the model in terms of the total number of documents N that the user is willing to read, we decided to vary the number of documents per topic n with the following values: 200, 400, 600, 800, 1000, 2000, and then compute $N = n * T$ for each n obtaining the following values for $N = 6200, 12400, 18600, 24800, 31000, 62000$. Finally, in order to evaluate the approach that distributes the effort unevenly across topics, we multiplied N by the proportion of documents shown in Table 1.

3.3   Evaluation Measures

In order to evaluate the performance of the systems, we chose the number of documents shown to the user as one of the performance measures since, in our case, it is also the point where we stop retrieving documents. In addition, we use recall and recall at k, where k is the true number of relevant documents, to measure the accuracy of the retrieval.

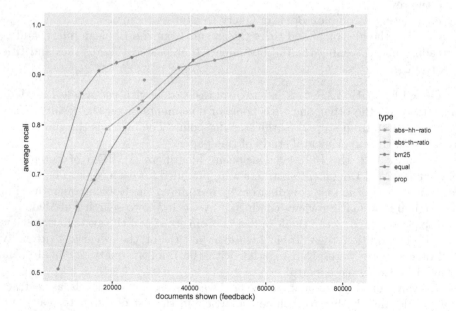

Fig. 2. Average recall vs total number of documents shown to the user

4   Results

In Fig. 2, we show the performance of the three groups of runs in terms of average recall (across topics) given the number of documents shown to the user. The three groups are: *bm25* for the baseline, *equal* for the even distribution of effort, *prop* for the distributed proportional effort. By increasing the number of documents (from left to right), all the three approaches achieve an average recall greater than 80% even when only 25% of the documents of the collection are shown. The equal distribution of effort is without doubt the best approach with a huge margin of improvement over the baseline (BM25) and the distributed effort approach. In the same Figure, we also added the best system that performed the best together with ours designed and implemented by the Information and Language Processing System (ILPS) group at the University of Amsterdam [13]. The two runs use a similar approach under the Continuous Active Learning framework by jointly training a ranking model to rank documents, and conducting a "greedy" sampling to estimate the real number of relevant documents in the collection. The two runs, abs-hh-ratio and abs-th-ratio, differ from the estimator of the number of relevant documents, Hansen-Hurwitz estimator for the former, Horvitz-Thompson estimator for the latter. The first run is below our best evenly distributed effort approach, while the second run is between our distributed effort approach and the baseline. Despite being two very good runs, the difference in terms of number of documents to get the same average recall is almost reduced by fifty percent by our approach. See Table 2 for a comparison between our run equal-t600 (equal effort with 600 documents per topic) and abs-hh-ratio.

Table 2. Best performing runs. Averaged recall at k and recall are shown together with the total number of documents shown (for relevance feedback). The two runs by [13], abs-hh-ratio and abs-hh-ratio, are reported for comparison.

run	recall_at_k	recall	doc shown
equal-t1000	0.28	**0.94**	25015
equal-t600	0.28	0.91	**16529**
abs-hh-ratio	**0.46**	0.89	28201
prop-t600	0.28	0.85	27791
abs-th-ratio	0.43	0.83	26708
bm25-t1000	0.18	0.79	23241

4.1   Failure Analysis

Our system resulted one of the best approaches for the third year in a row in the CLEF eHealth TAR task. However, there are still some parts that can be improved when compared to other systems. For example, one issue that is present in almost every experiment we have carried out in these years is that our approach starts 'slow' in terms of number of relevant documents, then it catches the momentum and rapidly increases the recall. This problem is evident in Table 2, where the runs by the ILPS have an average recall at k which is almost twice as great as the value achieved by our runs. In Fig. 3, we display two examples where our approach clearly shows a sort of slowness to pick up relevant documents at the beginning of the search process. For a detailed comparison topic by topic, we summarize in Table 1 the results for the best runs of the two systems. Once again, for all the topics the recall at k is much better for the ILPS system, on the other hand the overall recall is 16 times out of 31 better with our approach with 10 ties. It is also interesting to note that in 22 cases, our approach shows more documents per topic compared to the abs-hh-ratio run; nevertheless, at the end our run shows to the user about 3,000 documents less. A Wilcoxon signed-rank paired test[3] confirms that we reject the hypothesis that the abs-hh-ratio run is better than our best run ($\alpha = 0.5$, p-value $= 0.02003$).

Moreover, as reported in the overview of the task [12], there are particular subsets of the topics where our approach is extremely slow in retrieving the first relevant documents. This suggests that a mixed approach that uses the

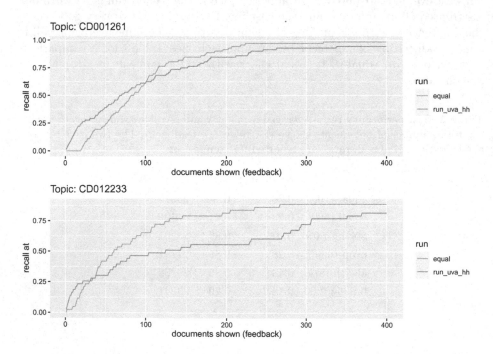

Fig. 3. Recall at k vs number of documents (k) shown to the user.

---

[3] We used the non-exact version given the ties. https://www.rdocumentation.org/packages/stats/versions/3.6.2/topics/wilcox.test.

technique used by ILPS at the beginning and then our approach for ranking and classification may be a killer application in this task.

5   Conclusions

In this work, we presented a variation of the continuous active learning approach used in [17] that uses a fixed stopping strategy to simulate the maximum amount of documents that a user is willing to review. For the third year in a row, our CAL approach performed very well despite being a simple model. The result of the distributed effort approach were worse than expected, compared to the original approach presented in 2017 and 2018. The performance of the system with a fixed effort per topic is still remarkable since it achieves an average recall of 90% by using less than 25% of the documents in the collection. Moreover, we have the advantage to know the exact effort we will spend to achieve that accuracy. The failure analysis and the comparison with the approach of the second best participant in the task has shown the limits of our strategy: it is slow in gathering the first relevant documents. This suggests that a mixed system, one that uses a different ranking model such as a logistic regression model with TF-IDF [13] to get the first relevant documents, and then our model to accurately retrieve the remaining relevant documents could be a successful mix for this task.

References

1. Cook, D.J., Mulrow, C.D., Haynes, R.B.: Systematic reviews: synthesis of best evidence for clinical decisions. Ann. Intern. Med. **126**(5), 376–380 (1997)
2. Cormack, G.V., Grossman, M.R.: Evaluation of machine-learning protocols for technology-assisted review in electronic discovery. In: Geva, S., Trotman, A., Bruza, P., Clarke, C.L., Järvelin, K. (eds.) The 37th International ACM SIGIR Conference on Research and Development in Information Retrieval, SIGIR 2014, Gold Coast , QLD, Australia, 06–11 July 2014, pp. 153–162. ACM (2014)
3. Goeuriot, L., et al.: CLEF 2017 eHealth evaluation lab overview. In: Jones, G.J.F., et al. (eds.) CLEF 2017. LNCS, vol. 10456, pp. 291–303. Springer, Cham (2017). https://doi.org/10.1007/978-3-319-65813-1_26
4. Gopalakrishnan, S., Ganeshkumar, P.: Systematic reviews and meta-analysis: understanding the best evidence in primary healthcare. J. Fam. Med. Primary Care **2**(1), 9–14 (2013)
5. Grossman, M.R., Cormack, G.V , Roegiest, A.: TREC 2016 total recall track overview. In: Proceedings of The Twenty-Fifth TREC 2016, Gaithersburg, Maryland, USA, 15–18 November 2016 (2016)
6. Higgins, J.P.T. (eds.): Cochrane Handbook for Systematic Reviews of Interventions, version 6.9 edn., Cochrane, July 2019. www.training.cochrane.org/handbook
7. Kanoulas, E., Li, D., Azzopardi, L., Spijker, R.: CLEF 2017 technologically assisted reviews in empirical medicine overview. In: Cappellato, L., Ferro, N., Goeuriot, L., Mandl, T. (eds.) CEUR Workshop Proceedings of Working Notes of CLEF 2017 - Conference and Labs of the Evaluation Forum, vol. 1866, Dublin, Ireland, 11–14 September 2017. CEUR-WS.org (2017)

8. Kanoulas, E., Li, D., Azzopardi, L., Spijker, R.: CLEF 2017 technologically assisted reviews in empirical medicine overview. In: CEUR Workshop Proceedings of Working Notes of CLEF 2017 - Conference and Labs of the Evaluation Forum, Dublin, Ireland, 11–14 September 2017. CEUR-WS.org (2017)
9. Kanoulas, E., Li, D., Azzopardi, L., Spijker, R.: CLEF 2018 technologically assisted reviews in empirical medicine overview. In: Cappellato, L., Ferro, N., Nie, J.-Y., Soulier, L., eds. CEUR Workshop Proceedings of Working Notes of CLEF 2018 - Conference and Labs of the Evaluation Forum, Avignon, France, 10–14 September 2018, vol. 2125. CEUR-WS.org (2018)
10. Kanoulas, E., Li, D., Azzopardi, L., Spijker, R.: CLEF 2019 technology assisted reviews in empirical medicine overview. In: CEUR Workshop Proceedings of CLEF 2019 Evaluation Labs and Workshop: Online Working Notes. CEUR-WS.org (2019)
11. Kastner, M., Straus, S., Goldsmith, C.H.: Estimating the horizon of articles to decide when to stop searching in systematic reviews: an example using a systematic review of RCTS evaluating osteoporosis clinical decision support tools. In: Proceedings of AMIA Annual Symposium. AMIA Symposium, vol. 2007, no. 10, pp. 389–393 (2007)
12. Kelly, L., et al.: Overview of the CLEF eHealth evaluation lab 2019. In: Crestani, F., et al. (eds.) CLEF 2019. LNCS, vol. 11696, pp. 322–339. Springer, Cham (2019). https://doi.org/10.1007/978-3-030-28577-7_26
13. Li, D., Kanoulas, E.: Automatic thresholding by sampling documents and estimating recall. In: Cappellato, L., Ferro, N., Losada, D.E., Müller, H. (eds.) CEUR Workshop Proceedings of Working Notes of CLEF 2019 - Conference and Labs of the Evaluation Forum, Lugano, Switzerland, 9–12 September 2019, vol. 2380. CEUR-WS.org (2019)
14. Nunzio, G.M.D.: A new decision to take for cost-sensitive Naïve Bayes classifiers. Inf. Process. Manag. **50**(5), 653–674 (2014)
15. Nunzio, G.M.D.: Interactive text categorisation: the geometry of likelihood spaces. Stud. Comput. Intell. **668**, 13–34 (2017)
16. Di Nunzio, G.M.: A study of an automatic stopping strategy for technologically assisted medical reviews. In: Proceedings of Advances in Information Retrieval - 40th European Conference on IR Research, ECIR 2018, Grenoble, France , 26–29 March 2018, pp. 672–677 (2018)
17. Di Nunzio, G.M., Ciuffreda, G., Vezzani, F.: Interactive sampling for systematic reviews. IMS Unipd at CLEF 2018 ehealth task 2. In: Working Notes of CLEF 2018 - Conference and Labs of the Evaluation Forum, Avignon, France, 10–14 September 2018 (2018)
18. Di Nunzio, G.M., Maistro, M., Vezzani, F.: A gamified approach to Naïve Bayes classification: a case study for newswires and systematic medical reviews. In: Companion of the Web Conference 2018 on the Web Conference 2018, WWW 2018, Lyon, France, 23–27 April 2018, pp. 1139–1146 (2018)
19. Di Nunzio, G.M., Maistro, M., Zilio, D.: Gamification for machine learning: the classification game. In: Proceedings of the Third International Workshop on Gamification for Information Retrieval co-located with 39th International ACM SIGIR Conference on Research and Development in Information Retrieval (SIGIR 2016), pp. 45–52, Pisa, Italy, 21 July 2016 (2016)
20. Di Nunzio, G.M., Maistro, M., Zilio, D.: The University of Padua (IMS) at TREC 2016 total recall track. In: Proceedings of The Twenty-Fifth Text REtrieval Conference, TREC 2016, Gaithersburg, Maryland, USA, 15–18 November 2016 (2016)
21. Robertson, S.E.: The Probability Ranking Principle in IR, pp. 281–286. Morgan Kaufmann Publishers Inc., San Francisco (1997)

22. Roegiest, A., Cormack, G.V., Grossman, M.R., Clarke, C.L.A.: TREC 2015 total recall track overview. In: Proceedings of The Twenty-fourth TREC 2015, Gaithersburg, Maryland, USA, 17–20 November 2015 (2015)
23. Scells, H., Zuccon, G., Koopman, B., Clark, J.: Automatic boolean query formulation for systematic review literature search. In: Huang, Y., King, I., Liu, T.-Y., van Steen, M. (eds.) WWW 2020: The Web Conference 2020, Taipei, Taiwan, 20–24 April 2020, pp. 1071–1081. ACM/IW3C2 (2020)
24. Williams, V., Boylan, A.-M., Nunan, D.: Qualitative research as evidence: expanding the paradigm for evidence-based healthcare. BMJ Evid.-Based Med. **24**(5), 168–169 (2019)
25. Xiang, Y.-T., et al.: Timely research papers about COVID-19 in China. Lancet **395**(10225), 684–685 (2020)
26. Zhang, H., Abualsaud, M., Ghelani, N., Smucker, M.D., Cormack, G.V., Grossman, M.R.: Effective user interaction for high-recall retrieval: less is more. In: Cuzzocrea, A., (eds.) Proceedings of the 27th ACM International Conference on Information and Knowledge Management, CIKM 2018, Torino, Italy, 22–26 October 2018, pp. 187–196. ACM (2018)
27. Zou, J., Li, D., Kanoulas, E.: Technology assisted reviews: Finding the last few relevant documents by asking yes/no questions to reviewers. In: Thompson, K.C., Mei, Q., Brian, D.D., Liu, Y., Yilmaz, E. (eds.) The 41st International ACM SIGIR Conference on Research & Development in Information Retrieval, SIGIR 2018, Ann Arbor, MI, USA, 08–12 July 2018, pp. 949–952. ACM (2018)

Fact Check-Worthiness Detection
with Contrastive Ranking

Casper Hansen[✉], Christian Hansen, Jakob Grue Simonsen,
and Christina Lioma

Department of Computer Science, University of Copenhagen, Copenhagen, Denmark
{c.hansen,chrh,simonsen,c.lioma}@di.ku.dk

Abstract. Check-worthiness detection aims at predicting which sentences should be prioritized for fact-checking. A typical use is to rank sentences in political debates and speeches according to their degree of check-worthiness. We present the first direct optimization of sentence ranking for check-worthiness; in contrast, all previous work has solely used standard classification based loss functions. We present a recurrent neural network model that learns a sentence encoding, from which a check-worthiness score is predicted. The model is trained by jointly optimizing a binary cross entropy loss, as well as a ranking based pairwise hinge loss. We obtain sentence pairs for training through contrastive sampling, where for each sentence we find the top most semantically similar sentences with opposite label. Through a comparison to existing state-of-the-art check-worthiness methods, we find that our approach improves the MAP score by 11%.

Keywords: Check-worthiness · Neural networks · Contrastive ranking

1 Introduction

Automatic fact-checking systems [10] typically consist of three parts: 1) detect sentences that are interesting to fact-check, 2) gather evidence and background knowledge for each sentence, and 3) manually or automatically estimate veracity. This paper is focused on the first step, where the aim is to detect *check-worthy* sentences for further processing in either a manual or automatic pipeline . The detection can be considered a filtering step in order to limit the computational processing needed in total for the later steps. In practice, sentences are ranked according to their check-worthiness such that they can be processed in order of importance. Thus, the ability to correctly rank check-worthy sentences above non-check-worthy is essential for automatic check-worthiness methods to be useful in practice. However, existing check-worthiness methods [3,5,7] do not directly model this aspect, as they are all based on traditional classification based training objectives.

Motivated by the above, we present a recurrent neural model that learns a sentence encoder for predicting the check-worthiness score of a sentence. Our

© Springer Nature Switzerland AG 2020
A. Arampatzis et al. (Eds.): CLEF 2020, LNCS 12260, pp. 124–130, 2020.
https://doi.org/10.1007/978-3-030-58219-7_11

model is optimizing jointly using a cross entropy classification objective, and–more importantly–also a ranking based objective in the form of a hinge loss. We construct ranking pairs through contrastive sampling: For each sentence, we find the top k most semantically similar sentences with the opposite label such that the model more accurately learns to identify the (often) subtle differences between normal and check-worthy sentences. Additionally, we use an existing check-worthiness approach to weakly label a large collection of unlabeled political speeches and debates, which is used for pretraining our model [3]. We experimentally evaluate our model on the CLEF-2019 CheckThat! collection of political speeches and debates [1][1], where our approach outperformed the state of the art by 11% on the MAP metric. In a model ablation, we show that both weak supervision and the ranking component improve the results individually (MAP increases of 25% and 9% respectively), while when used together improve the results even more (39% increase).

2   Related Work

Most existing check-worthiness methods are based on feature engineering to extract meaningful features. Given a sentence, ClaimBuster [7] predicts check-worthiness by extracting a set of features (sentiment, statement length, Part-of-Speech (POS) tags, named entities, and tf-idf weighted bag-of-words), and uses a SVM classifier for the prediction. Patwari et al. [9] presented an approach based on similar features, as well as contextual features based on sentences immediately preceding and succeeding the one being assessed, as well as certain hand-crafted POS patterns. The prediction is made by a multi-classifier system based on a dynamic clustering of the data. In the CLEF 2018 competition on check-worthiness detection, Hansen et al. [5] showed that a recurrent neural network with multiple word representations (word embeddings, part-of-speech tagging, and syntactic dependencies) could obtain state-of-the-art results for check-worthiness prediction. Hansen et al. [3] later extended this work with weak supervision based on a large collection of unlabeled political speeches and showed significant improvements compared to existing state-of-the-art methods. This paper directly improves upon [3] by integrating a ranking component into the model trained via contrastive sampling of semantically similar sentences with opposite labels.

3   Neural Check-Worthiness Model

We now present our *Neural Check-Worthiness Model* (*NCWM*), which employs a dual sentence representation, where each word is represented by both a word embedding and its syntactic dependencies within the sentence. The word embedding is a *word2vec* model [8] that aims at capturing the semantics of the sentence. The syntactic dependencies of a word aim to capture the role of that word in

---

[1] Our approach ranked 1st in the CLEF-2019 CheckThat! competition [6].

modifying the semantics of other words in the sentence. We use a syntactic dependency parser to map each word to its dependency (as a tag) within the sentence, which is then converted to a one-hot encoding. This combination of capturing both semantics and syntactic structure has been shown to work well for predicting check-worthiness [3,5]. For each word in a sentence, the word embedding and one-hot encoding are concatenated and fed to a recurrent neural network with Long Short-Term Memory Units (LSTM) as memory cells:

$$h_i = \text{LSTM}(e_i \oplus o_i) \tag{1}$$

where h_i is the LSTM output for the ith input, e_i is the word embedding of the ith word, o_i is the one-hot syntactic encoding of the ith word, and $\oplus$ is vector concatenation. The output of the LSTM cells are aggregated using an attention weighted sum, where each weight is computed as:

$$\alpha_i = \frac{\exp\left(\text{FF}_{\text{lin}}\left(h_i\right)\right)}{\sum_j \exp\left(\text{FF}_{\text{lin}}\left(h_j\right)\right)} \tag{2}$$

where h_t is the output of the LSTM cell at time t, and FF_{lin} is a feed forward layer with linear activation returning a learned scalar. The final check-worthiness score is produced by transforming the weighted LSTM outputs:

$$s = \text{FF}_\sigma\left(\sum_i h_i \alpha_i\right) \tag{3}$$

where FF_σ is a feed forward layer with a sigmoid activation, such that the score lies between 0 and 1.

Loss functions. The model is jointly optimized using both a classification and ranking loss function. For the classification loss, we use the standard binary cross entropy loss:

$$\text{CE}(y, s) = -y \log(s) - (1 - y) \log(1 - s) \tag{4}$$

where y is the ground truth binary label of a sentence and s is the check-worthiness score computed above. For the ranking loss, we use a hinge loss based on the computed check-worthiness scores of sentence pairs with opposite labels. To obtain these pairs we use *contrastive* sampling, such that for each sentence we sample the top k most semantically similar sentences with the opposite label, i.e., for check-worthy sentences we sample k non-check-worthy sentences. To estimate the semantic similarity we compute an average word2vec [8] embedding vector of all words in a sentence, and then use the cosine similarity to find the top k most semantically similar sentences with the opposite label. The purpose of the contrastive sampling is to enable the model to better learn the subtle differences between check-worthy and non-check-worthy sentences. Specifically, for the ith sentence with score s_i, we denote the check-worthiness score of a contrastive sample as s^c, such that the ranking loss is:

$$\text{hinge}(y, s, s^c) = \max\left(0, 1 - \text{sign}(y)(s - s^c)\right) \tag{5}$$

where sign(y) returns 1 for check-worthy sentences and -1 otherwise. The combination of both the classification and ranking loss enables the model to learn accurate classifications while the predicted scores are sensible for ranking.

4   Experimental Evaluation

We evaluate our approach on the CLEF-2019 CheckThat! dataset [1], which consists of 19 training speeches and debates with a total of 16,421 sentences, where 433 are labeled as being check-worthy (i.e., 2.64% positive samples). The testing set consists of 7 speeches and debates with a total of 7079 sentences, where 110 are labeled as check-worthy (i.e., 1.55% positive samples). We evaluate the performance on the dataset using traditional ranking metrics of MAP and P@k for $k = \{1, 5, 20, 50\}$.

4.1   Tuning

We choose the hyper parameters based on a 19-fold cross validation (1 fold for each training speech and debate). In the following, we list the tuned parameters and underline the optimal values: the LSTM has {50, 100, 150, 200} hidden units, a dropout of {0, 0.1, 0.3, 0.5} was applied to the attention weighted sum, and we used a batch size of {40, 80, 120, 160, 200}. For the contrastive sampling we searched {1, 5, 10, 20} as the number of semantically similar sentences with the opposite label to find for each sentence. For the syntactic dependency parsing we use spaCy[2], and TensorFlow for the neural network implementation.

To train a more generalizable model we employ weak supervision [2,4] by using an online check-worthiness approach[3], to weakly label a large collection of unlabeled political speeches and debates for model pretraining. We obtain 271 political speeches and debates by Hillary Clinton and Donald Trump from the American Presidency Project[4]. Following Hansen et al. [3], we create a domain specific word2vec embedding by crawling documents related to *all* U.S. elections available through the American Presidency Project, e.g., press releases, statements, speeches, and public fundraisers, resulting in 15,059 documents.

4.2   Results

Our Neural Check-Worthiness Model (NCWM) outperformed competitive and state-of-the-art baselines [3,5] with a MAP of 0.1660. To investigate the effect of the ranking component and the weak supervision (see Table 1), we also report the results when these are not part of NCWM. The model without the ranking component is similar to the state-of-the-art work by Hansen et al. [3], and the model without either the ranking component or weak supervision is similar to

---

[2] https://spacy.io/.
[3] https://idir.uta.edu/claimbuster/.
[4] https://web.archive.org/web/20170606011755/http://www.presidency.ucsb.edu/.

earlier work by Hansen et al. [5]. The results show that the ranking component and weak supervision lead to notable improvements, both individually and when combined. The inclusion of weak supervision leads to the largest individual MAP improvement (25% increase), while the individual improvement of the ranking component is smaller (9% increase). We observe that the ranking component's improvement is marginally larger when weak supervision is included (11% increase with weak supervision compared to 9% without), thus showing that even a weakly labeled signal is also beneficial for learning the correct ranking. Combining both the ranking component and weak supervision leads to a MAP increase of 39% compared to a model without either of them, which highlights the benefit of using both for the task of check-worthiness as the combination provides an improvement larger than the individual parts.

Table 1. Test results for the full Neural Check-Worthiness Model (NCWM) and for the model excluding ranking and weak supervision (WS) components.

Test (speeches and debates)	MAP	P@1	P@5	P@20	P@50
NCWM	**0.1660**	**0.2857**	**0.2571**	**0.1571**	**0.1229**
NCWM (w/o. ranking) [3]	0.1496	0.1429	0.2000	0.1429	0.1143
NCWM (w/o. WS)	0.1305	0.1429	0.1714	0.1429	0.1200
NCWM (w/o. ranking and w/o. WS) [5]	0.1195	0.1429	0.1429	0.1143	0.1057
Test (speeches)	MAP	P@1	P@5	P@20	P@50
NCWM	**0.2502**	**0.5000**	**0.3500**	**0.2375**	**0.1800**
NCWM (w/o. ranking) [3]	0.2256	0.2500	0.3000	0.2250	**0.1800**
NCWM (w/o. WS)	0.1937	0.2500	0.3000	0.2000	0.1600
NCWM (w/o. ranking and w/o. WS) [5]	0.1845	0.2500	0.2500	0.1875	0.1450
Test (debates)	MAP	P@1	P@5	P@20	P@50
NCWM	**0.0538**	**0.0000**	**0.1333**	0.0500	0.0467
NCWM (w/o. ranking) [3]	0.0482	**0.0000**	0.0667	0.0333	0.0267
NCWM (w/o. WS)	0.0462	**0.0000**	0.0000	**0.0667**	**0.0667**
NCWM (w/o. ranking and w/o. WS) [5]	0.0329	**0.0000**	0.0000	0.0167	0.0533

To investigate the performance on speeches and debates individually, we split the test data and report the performance metrics on each of the sets. In both of them we observe a similar trend as for the full dataset, i.e., that both the ranking component and weak supervision lead to improvements individually and when combined. However, the MAP on the debates is significantly lower than for the speeches (0.0538 and 0.2502 respectively). We believe the reason for this difference is related to two issues: i) All speeches are by Donald Trump and 15 out of 19 training speeches and debates have Donald Trump as a participant, thus the model is better trained to predict sentences by Donald Trump. ii) Debates are often more varied in content compared to a single speech, and contain participants who are not well represented in the training data. Issue (i) can be alleviated by obtaining larger quantities and more varied training data, while issue (ii) may simply be due to debates being inherently more difficult to predict. Models better equipped to handle the dynamics of debates could be a possible direction to solve this.

5 Conclusion

We presented a recurrent neural model that directly models the ranking of check-worthy sentences, which no previous work has done. This was done through a hinge loss based on contrastive sampling, where the most semantically similar sentences with opposite labels were sampled for each sentence. Additionally, we utilize weak supervision through an existing check-worthiness method to label a large unlabeled dataset of political speeches and debates. We experimentally verified that both the sentence ranking and weak supervision lead to notable performance MAP improvements (increases of 9% and 25% respectively) compared to a model without either of them, while using both lead to an improvement greater than the individual parts (39% increase). In comparison to state-of-the-art check-worthiness models, we found our approach to perform 11% better on the MAP metric.

References

1. Atanasova, P., Nakov, P., Karadzhov, G., Mohtarami, M., Da San Martino, G.: Overview of the CLEF-2019 CheckThat! lab on automatic identification and verification of claims. Task 1: check-worthiness. In: CLEF-2019 CheckThat! Lab (2019)
2. Dehghani, M., Zamani, H., Severyn, A., Kamps, J., Croft, W.B.: Neural ranking models with weak supervision. In: ACM SIGIR Conference on Research and Development in Information Retrieval, pp. 65–74 (2017)
3. Hansen, C., Hansen, C., Alstrup, S., Grue Simonsen, J., Lioma, C.: Neural check-worthiness ranking with weak supervision: finding sentences for fact-checking. In: Companion Proceedings of the World Wide Web Conference (2019)
4. Hansen, C., Hansen, C., Simonsen, J.G., Alstrup, S., Lioma, C.: Unsupervised neural generative semantic hashing. In: ACM SIGIR Conference on Research and Development in Information Retrieval (2019)
5. Hansen, C., Hansen, C., Simonsen, J.G., Lioma, C.: The Copenhagen team participation in the check-worthiness task of the competition of automatic identification and verification of claims in political debates of the CLEF-2018 fact checking lab. In: CLEF-2018 CheckThat! Lab (2018)
6. Hansen, C., Hansen, C., Simonsen, J.G., Lioma, C.: Neural weakly supervised fact check-worthiness detection with contrastive sampling-based ranking loss. In: CLEF-2019 CheckThat! Lab (2019)
7. Hassan, N., Arslan, F., Li, C., Tremayne, M.: Toward automated fact-checking: detecting check-worthy factual claims by claimbuster. In: KDD, pp. 1803–1812 (2017)

8. Mikolov, T., Sutskever, I., Chen, K., Corrado, G.S., Dean, J.: Distributed representations of words and phrases and their compositionality. In: NeurIPS, pp. 3111–3119 (2013)
9. Patwari, A., Goldwasser, D., Bagchi, S.: Tathya: a multi-classifier system for detecting check-worthy statements in political debates. In: CIKM, pp. 2259–2262 (2017)
10. Thorne, J., Vlachos, A.: Automated fact checking: task formulations, methods and future directions. In: ACL, pp. 3346–3359 (2018)

Tuberculosis CT Image Analysis Using Image Features Extracted by 3D Autoencoder

Siarhei Kazlouski[✉]

United Institute of Informatics Problems, Minsk, Belarus
kozlovski.serge@gmail.com

Abstract. This paper presents an approach for the automated analysis of 3D Computed Tomography (CT) images based on the utilization of descriptors extracted using 3D deep convolutional autoencoder (AEC [8]) networks. Both the common flow of AEC model application and a set of techniques for overcoming the lack of training samples are presented in this work. The described approach was used for accomplishing the two subtasks of the ImageCLEF 2019: Tuberculosis competition [2,5] and allowed to achieve the 2nd best performance in the TB Severity Scoring subtask and the 6th best performance in the TB CT Report subtask.

Keywords: Computed tomography · Tuberculosis · Deep learning · Feature extraction · Autoencoder · CNN

1 Introduction

This study was motivated by the author's participation in the Tuberculosis task [2] of the ImageCLEF 2019 Challenge [5]. This task may be relevant for the development of computer-assisted diagnosis systems which may be used for the early detection of pathology. While promising results have been shown in automated analysis of medical images of some modalities [1,4,9–11], the task of CT image analysis remains challenging due to the complexity and scarcity of data. A CT image is 3D data which can be represented as a set of 2D slices with the inter-slice distance usually varying between 0.5 and 5 mm. Variability in the sizes and shapes of CT image voxels implies difficulties in the application of many traditional image analysis algorithms, while low availability of CT imaging data makes it difficult to use data-greedy approaches like deep learning (DL).

Despite the lack of data available, the approach for the analysis of 3D CT images proposed with this study employs the idea of trying to get 3D image descriptors by utilizing 3D CNNs. The motivation for using 3D neural networks is the potential of maximum information usage as soon as the 3D network works with the entire 3D image instead of a subset of some kind of 2D projections, random slices, or other reduced versions of original CT.

At least two different techniques can be used for DL-based descriptor extraction. It is possible either to use the AEC network [7] to get vectors of latent image

© Springer Nature Switzerland AG 2020
A. Arampatzis et al. (Eds.): CLEF 2020, LNCS 12260, pp. 131–140, 2020.
https://doi.org/10.1007/978-3-030-58219-7_12

features directly or to train a classification network for some random reasonable label prediction and retrieve feature vectors from tail layers of the network.

In this study, it was decided to focus on the AEC-based approach because of its generality. In contrast to the scenario when the classification model is used for feature extraction, AEC training is labeling-independent. That means one does not require any initial labeling and extracted descriptors can be used for arbitrary target labels. We should note that such label-independency makes it impossible to control how discriminative the extracted features are in terms of any target label during models training, thus it may lead to lower performance in the competition subtasks compared to the straightforward usage of 3D classification networks. Despite this fact, it was concluded to prioritize the generality of the approach over the potential performance gains in the specific task.

Because of the mentioned lack of data, a significant part of the research was dedicated to optimizing model complexity, input sample dimensionality, and techniques for enriching the training dataset. Detailed descriptions of the experimental setup are presented in Sect. 3, and the results are presented in Sect. 4.

2   Challenge Evaluation Summary

Evaluation of the results was performed using the test dataset of the Tuberculosis task and included two subtasks: TB Severity (SVR) and CT Report (CTR). The same CT imaging data was used in both subtasks and included 218 images in the training dataset and 117 in the test dataset. CT images in both sets vary in the number of slices and have a median size of (512, 512, 128) voxels.

ROC-AUC metric was used for binary classification in the SVR subtask; minimum and mean ROC-AUC metrics were used for multi-binary classification in the CTR subtask.

A detailed description of subtasks, metrics, metadata, target labels, and their distribution can be found in [2, 6].

3   Methods

This section contains a description of the methods used in the current study. An entire experimental pipeline is divided into four logical steps which are split into separate sections. Description of basic CT images preprocessing can be found in Sect. 3.1; further data transformation and creation of AEC training sets can be found in Sect. 3.2; AEC model creation and training are described in Sect. 3.3; application of extracted descriptors for target label prediction is presented in Sect. 3.4.

3.1   Data Preprocessing

The real-world CT images provided in the competition dataset vary in both image file and image content properties. Image files have a difference in slices count, voxel size, a slight difference in the patient position, and relative size of the lungs area.

To make CT image data uniform, images were normalized by voxel size and cropped using the provided lung masks [3]. Specifically, the following steps were executed:

1) All images provided in the training dataset were analyzed to define the target voxel size for normalization. Median voxel size was selected: (0.705, 0.705, 2.5) mm.
2) Each train and test image-mask pair was interpolated to have the selected voxel size.
3) All lung masks provided in the training dataset were analyzed to define the target crop size. As a result, the size of the minimum box that encloses all lungs bounding boxes was selected.
4) Each train and test image-mask pair was cropped using the selected crop size. The corresponding lungs bounding box center was used as a crop box center.

As a result, the training and test datasets included image-mask pairs with uniform image size and voxel size.

3.2 Data Transformation and Datasets

Since the key idea of the proposed approach is based on using an AEC network, the extremely small amount of data samples becomes the main challenge because of the sample dimensionality to sample count ratio. Another issue is the sample dimensionality itself, it restricts possible model architectures due to GPU memory limitations.

The crucial idea for overcoming the mentioned issues was to switch from CT-wise to lung-wise analysis. That means the AECs were applied not to the whole CT image, but to the left and right lungs separately. This approach simultaneously doubled the training dataset size and decreased the sample dimensionality two times.

To achieve lung-wise processing, each CT image was split into two parts, each containing one lung. The split was performed roughly, into equal parts by splitting on the middle Y (transverse axis) coordinate. The part containing the left lung was used as it is, and the part containing the right lung was reflected through the sagittal plane in order to make the right lung oriented similar to the left one. Reflection of right lungs was intended to allow usage of a single AEC model for all lungs instead of training separate AECs for the left and right lungs. An example of extracted lung images is presented in Fig. 1.

Finally, output images were linearly interpolated to a smaller size and normalized by intensity to 0–1 range. Size decrease was used to fit GPU memory limits and further improve sample dimensionality to sample count ratio. Two output sizes were used - $128 \times 128 \times 128$ voxels and $64 \times 64 \times 64$ voxels.

The corresponding lungs mask for each image was processed together with the image itself in the same way.

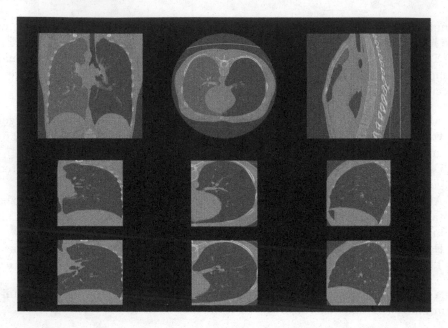

Fig. 1. Example of CT image splitting. First row - center slices of initial CT with lungs mask (red - right, green - left). The second and the third row - center slices of extracted right and left lung. (Color figure online)

As a result, two datasets, 436 images each, were retrieved. Hereinafter these datasets will be referred to as Lungs128 and Lungs64, according to image side size.

Data augmentation was used during AEC models training on both Lungs128 and Lungs64 datasets. For each lung, a random transformation was generated and applied to the lung-mask pair. The mask was binarized after the transformation and applied to the lung image. Image intensity was normalized again.

Transformations included 3D shift, rotation, scale, crop, and shear, which were applied sequentially with a probability of 50% for each transform usage. Because preprocessed images are meaningfully uniform in terms of voxel size and content, relatively small transformation factors were used. The ranges of parameters used for the augmentation are presented in Table 1.

3.3   Autoencoder Model Training

A custom AEC model was used in this study. Conceptually it was a sequential model consisting of symmetrical encoder and decoder units with a latent layer in the middle. The encoder and decoder units were built from a number of [3D Convolution + 3D MaxPooling(3D UpSampling)] blocks. The selection of the number of blocks, convolutional kernel sizes, and filter numbers was made by evaluating AEC validation loss on the Lungs64 dataset. The selected encoder architecture is presented in Table 2. The decoder is symmetric to the encoder

Table 1. Parameters of transformations used for data augmentation.

Transform	Parameter value
Shift, pixels	Up to 5% of each side (X, Y, Z) size
Rotation center	Shifted from image center up to 3% of each side (X, Y, Z) size
Rotation angle	Up to 5°
Scaling	Up to 5%
Shear	Up to 0.01 absolute value, each of six components

but max-pooling layers are replaced with 3D upsampling ones. All convolution layers had kernel size (3, 3, 3) and all 3D MaxPooling (3D UpSampling) had kernel size (2, 2, 2).

Table 2. Autoencoder architecture.

Convolution3D (n_filters = 128) + MaxPooling3D
Convolution3D (n_filters = 64) + MaxPooling3D
Convolution3D (n_filters = 64) + MaxPooling3D
Convolution3D (n_filters = 32) + MaxPooling3D
Convolution3D (n_filters = 32) + MaxPooling3D
Convolution3D (n_filters = 32) + MaxPooling3D

The selected AEC model was trained using Adam optimizer on the Lungs64 and Lungs128 datasets. In both cases, a randomly sampled 90% of training data was used for training and the remaining 10% was used for validation.

The training was performed in the following three stages:

1. *Initial training.*
   The mixture of left and right lung images was used, data augmentation was enabled. At this stage, the main part of model weights optimization was performed. The training was performed until any significant improvements in validation loss were observed (around 70 epochs for both datasets).
2. *Fine-tuning on the left and the right lungs separately.*
   At this stage, the initial model was "forked" into two models with copying retrieved weights. Each of the new models was fine-tuned on the left and right lung images using data augmentation and a 10 times smaller learning rate. The model's weights did not change much at this stage, but a minor improvement of validation loss was observed. At this stage, training was performed for around 20 epochs.
3. *Fine-tuning with disabled augmentation.*
   At this stage, separate tuning for left and right lungs continued, but with disabled augmentation for better fitting to real data. To avoid overfitting, the learning rate was decreased 10 times again and training was performed for just 2 epochs.

So, finally, two AEC models for left and right lung feature extraction were retrieved, each of them trained at around 40k images (assuming random augmentation resulted in a unique image transformation almost always).

At the inference stage both AEC models were used to generate feature vectors for the left and right lung of each CT image. Then feature vectors of lungs were concatenated to get a whole CT descriptor containing 64 and 512 components in total for images from Lungs64 and Lungs128 respectively.

Analysis of encoded vectors showed that around half of the components of the feature vectors for Lungs128 were very close to zero for all images, which probably reflects the non-optimal architecture and/or weights of the model. As soon as no better model was retrieved in experiments, it was decided to drop the "zero" components of the encoded vector, which resulted in the final version of the encoded Lungs128 images descriptors containing 220 components each.

3.4 Prediction of Target Labels

Since the SVR subtask was a binary classification problem and the CTR subtask was a multi-binary classification problem, and subtasks shared the dataset, it was decided to merge subtasks in a single multi-binary classification problem with seven target labels (one from SVR subtask and six from CTR subtask). The same approach was used to predict each target label. The idea of the approach was to use both the encoded image descriptors and the provided CT image meta-information to train an ensemble of independent conventional classification models.

Meta-information feature vectors were used "as is". So were image feature vectors extracted with AEC trained on the Lungs64 dataset. In the case of image features extracted with models trained on Lungs128 dataset, their PCA-transformed versions with 3, 5, 10, 50 components were used together with the original feature vectors. Thus a total of seven descriptors were associated with each CT image: meta-information (META); latent feature vectors extracted from AEC trained on Lungs64 dataset (AEC64); latent feature vectors extracted from AEC trained on Lungs128 dataset (AEC) and PCA-transformed versions of (AEC) descriptors with 3, 5, 10, 50 components (PCA3, PCA5, PCA10, PCA50).

It was decided to restrict available classification models to scikit-learn package implementation of SVM, K-neighbors classifier (kNN), random forest classifier (RF), and AdaBoost classifier. Parameter ranges are presented in Table 3 (only valid parameters combinations were used).

After the sets of classifiers and features were fixed, the performance of all model-descriptor combinations was evaluated on the training dataset as follows:

For each of the seven target labels:
  For each of the descriptors:
    For 1..NUMBER_OF_TRIALS:
      Sample random classifier model and its hyperparameters
      Get the mean AUC-ROC score at 5-fold cross-validation
All model-descriptor pairs were sorted by achieved score, then top-5 models were manually filtered using the following heuristics: a) each model-descriptor

Table 3. Classifier parameters search ranges.

Classifier	Parameters range (format: min .. max .. step)
KNeighborsClassifier	(neighbors number: 1 .. 20 .. 1)
RandomForestClassifier	estimators number: 1 .. 100 .. 5
	max tree depth number: 1 .. 6 .. 1
AdaBoostClassifier	estimators number: 1 .. 200 .. 5
	learning rate : 0.1 .. 1 .. 0.2
SVM	C: 10e−5 .. 10e5 .. by power of 10
	degree : 1 .. 7 .. 1
	kernel: 'linear', 'poly', 'rbf'

combination can be used only once, b) if scores are close, the more simple model-descriptor combination is prioritized (for example, if the kNN model with 11 neighbors scores 0.80 and with 2 neighbors scores 0.78, the second one is used).

The described algorithm resulted in the selection of from 1 to 4 best model-descriptor combinations for each target class prediction, which were later ensembled by the simple averaging of class probabilities. A summary of the selected models and their cross-validation performance is presented in Table 4.

Table 4. Selected classification models.

Label	Classifier	Features	AUC-ROC
LeftLungAffected	RF(E* = 20, D** = 1)	PCA5	0.77
	SVM(linear, C = 10e5)	PCA5	0.81
RightLungAffected	RF(E = 20, D = 1)	PCA5	0.79
	SVM(rbf, C = 10e5)	PCA5	0.77
Calcification	SVM(poly, d = 2, C = 0.01)	META	0.84
	RF(E = 16, D = 1)	PCA10	0.80
	kNN(neighbors = 11)	PCA5	0.82
	SVM(linear, C = 10e3)	AEC	0.90
Caverns	AdaBoost(E = 15, lr = 0.2)	AEC	0.89
Pleurisy	RF(E = 6, D = 2)	META	0.82
	RF(E = 20, D = 1)	AEC	0.89
	RF(E = 10, D = 1)	PCA10	0.90
LungCapacityDecr.	RF(E = 6, D = 2)	META	0.78
	RF(E = 20, D = 1)	AEC	0.83
	SVM(linear, C = 10e3)	PCA5	0.72
Severity	kNN(neighbors = 11)	PCA5	0.71
	RF(E = 8, D = 2)	PCA10	0.82
	RF(E = 30, D = 2)	AEC	0.87

*estimators number
**max depth

Table 5. The best participants' runs submitted for the CTR subtask.

Group name	Mean AUC	Min AUC	Rank
UIIP_BioMed	0.7968	0.6860	1
CompElecEngCU	0.7066	0.5739	2
MedGIFT	0.6795	0.5626	3
San Diego VA HCS/UCSD	0.6631	0.5541	4
HHU	0.6591	0.5159	5
UUIP(SergeKo)	0.6464	0.4099	6
MostaganemFSEI	0.6273	0.4877	7
UniversityAlicante	0.6190	0.5366	8
PwC	0.6002	0.4724	9
LIST	0.5523	0.4317	10

4   Submissions and Results

As a result of this study, the described method was applied to generate predictions for the competition test dataset. Predictions were submitted by the author registered as UUIP(SergeKo[1]) for the CTR and SVR subtasks. The full list of the submitted results for both subtasks is available at the task web page[2].

Before generating the final submission, selected AEC and classifier models were re-trained on the whole available training dataset.

Table 5 shows the best results achieved by the participants in the CTR subtask. The run submitted by the author achieved the 6th best mean AUC, while demonstrating the worst minimum AUC for one of the labels. The contrast of the average mean result and the worst minimum AUC demonstrates that the presented approach works pretty well for some of the target labels in the report while failing for other labels. Since no dramatic difference in performance for different targets was observed on the validation set, one can conclude that approach instability is caused by the overfitting to the validation set. This is quite possible because the uneven distribution of target labels (for some of them just a few positive cases were presented in the training set), implies a high chance of a difference between training and test sets in terms of labels distribution.

Table 6 shows the best results achieved by the participants in the SVR subtask. The run submitted by the author achieved the 2nd highest value for AUC, and shared the 1st best accuracy with UIIP_BioMed participant. Achieved AUC correlates with validation scores and demonstrates the efficiency of the used approach. One should underline that Severity label prediction was made using only autoencoded image features and their PCA-transformed version, without involving meta-information (see Table 4).

---

[1] Participant name was changed during competition.
[2] https://www.imageclef.org/2019/medical/tuberculosis/.

Table 6. The top-5 best participants' runs submitted for the SVR subtask.

Group Name	AUC	Accuracy	Rank
UIIP_BioMed	0.7877	0.7179	1
UUIP(SergeKo)	0.7754	0.7179	2
HHU	0.7695	0.6923	3
CompElecEngCU	0.7629	0.6581	4
San Diego VA HCS/UCSD	0.7214	0.6838	5
MedGIFT	0.7196	0.6410	6

5 Conclusions

The results of this study allow to draw the following conclusions:

- Despite data scarcity, 3D AEC networks may be used for extracting reasonable descriptors from 3D CT data if some tricks for training set extension are used.
- According to experimental results, AEC trained on larger images from the Lungs128 dataset outperformed the one trained on smaller images from the Lungs64 dataset. This means a possible loss of small details caused by sample size reduction may be critical for AEC performance.
- According to experimental results, classifiers trained on meta-information about patients demonstrated good validation scores. Ensembling these models with classifiers trained on the CT image descriptors allowed us to improve test scores for the CTR subtask. This allows us to state that meta-information may be helpful for the more accurate predictions of TB characteristics.
- Although the used approach demonstrated good performance in the SVR subtask, it was not very stable in the generation of the CT report, because of probable overfitting to the validation set.

Acknowledgements. This study was partly supported by the National Institute of Allergy and Infectious Diseases, National Institutes of Health, U.S. Department of Health and Human Services, USA through the CRDF project DAA3–18-64818-1 "Year 7: Belarus TB Database and TB Portals".

References

1. Al-Kofahi, Y., Zaltsman, A., Graves, R., Marshall, W., Rusu, M.: A deeplearning-based algorithm for 2-D cell segmentation in microscopy images. BMC Bioinform. **19**(1), 365 (2018). https://doi.org/10.1186/s12859-018-2375-z
2. Dicente Cid, Y., Liauchuk, V., Klimuk, D., Tarasau, A., Kovalev, V., Müller, H.: Overview of ImageCLEFtuberculosis 2019 - automatic CT-based report generation and tuberculosis severity assessment. In: CLEF2019 Working Notes. CEUR Workshop Proceedings, Lugano, Switzerland, 9–12 September 2019. CEUR-WS.org, <http://ceur-ws.org> (2019)

3. Dicente Cid, Y., Jiménez del Toro, O.A., Depeursinge, A., Müller, H.: Efficient and fully automatic segmentation of the lungs in CT volumes. In: Goksel, O., Jiménez del Toro, O.A., Foncubierta-Rodríguez, A., Müller, H. (eds.) Proceedings of the VISCERAL Anatomy Grand Challenge at the 2015 IEEE ISBI. CEUR Workshop Proceedings, CEUR-WS, pp. 31–35, May 2015

4. Ehteshami Bejnordi, B., et al.: The CAMELYON16 Consortium: diagnostic assessment of deep learning algorithms for detection of lymph node metastases in women with breast cancer. JAMA **318**(22), 2199–2210 (2017). https://doi.org/10.1001/jama.2017.14585

5. Ionescu, B., et al.: ImageCLEF 2019: multimedia retrieval in medicine, lifelogging, security and nature. In: Crestani, F., et al. (eds.) CLEF 2019. LNCS, vol. 11696, pp. 358–386. Springer, Cham (2019). https://doi.org/10.1007/978-3-030-28577-7_28

6. Kazlouski, S.: Imageclef 2019: CT image analysis for TB severity scoring and CT report generationusing autoencoded image features. In: CLEF2019 Working Notes. CEUR Workshop Proceedings, Lugano, Switzerland, 9–12 September 2019. CEUR-WS.org <http://ceur-ws.org> (2019)

7. Krizhevsky, A., Hinton, G.E.: Using very deep autoencoders for content-based image retrieval. In: 19th European Symposium on Artificial Neural Networks, Bruges, Belgium, January 2011

8. Lange, S., Riedmiller, M.: Deep auto-encoder neural networks in reinforcement learning. In: The 2010 International Joint Conference on Neural Networks (IJCNN), pp. 1–8 (2010)

9. Liauchuk, V., Kovalev, V.: Detection of lung pathologies using deep convolutional networks trained on large X-ray chest screening database. In: Proceedings of the 14th international conference on Pattern Recognition and Information Processing (PRIP 2019), Minsk, Belarus, 21–23 May 2019 (2019)

10. Veta, M., et al.: Predicting breast tumor proliferation from whole-slide images: the TUPAC16 challenge. Med. Image Anal. **54**, 111–121 (2019). https://doi.org/10.1016/j.media.2019.02.012, http://www.sciencedirect.com/science/article/pii/S1361841518305231

11. Zaidi, S.M.A., et al.: Evaluation of the diagnostic accuracy of computer-aided detection of tuberculosis on chest radiography among private sector patients in Pakistan. Sci. Rep. **8**(1), 12339 (2018). https://doi.org/10.1038/s41598-018-30810-1

Twitter User Profiling: Bot and Gender Identification
Notebook for PAN at CLEF 2019

Dijana Kosmajac[(✉)] and Vlado Keselj

Faculty of Computer Science, Dalhousie University, Halifax, NS, Canada
dijana.kosmajac@dal.ca, vlado@dnlp.ca

Abstract. Social bots are automated programs that generate a significant amount of social media content. This content can be harmful, as it may target a certain audience to influence opinions, often politically motivated, or to promote individuals to appear more popular than they really are. We proposed a set of feature extraction and transformation methods in conjunction with ensemble classifiers for the PAN 2019 Author Profiling task. For the bot identification subtask we used user behaviour fingerprint and statistical diversity measures, while for the gender identification subtask we used a set of text statistics, as well as syntactic information and raw words.

1 Introduction

Automated user (bot) is a program that mimics a real person's behavior on social media. A bot can operate based on a simple set of behavioral instructions, such as tweeting, retweeting, "liking" posts, or following other users. In general, there are two types of bots based on their purpose: non-malicious and malicious. The non-malicious bots are transparent, with no intent of mimicking real Twitter users. Often, they share motivational quotes or images, tweet news headlines and other useful information, or help companies to respond to users. On the other hand, malicious ones may generate spam, try to access private account information, trick users into following them or subscribing to scams, suppress or enhance political opinions, create trending hashtags for financial gain, support political candidates during elections [2], or create offensive material to troll users. Additionally, some influencers may use bots to boost their audience size.

We explore bot and gender identification techniques on PAN 2019 [5] Author Profiling task [19]. We apply a set of feature extraction methods to describe how diverse the user behaviour is over extended period of time and if the style of writing is different between two genders. The systems were hosted and evaluated on TIRA [18], a web service that aims to facilitate software submissions and evaluations for shared tasks.

The rest of the paper is organized as follows. Related work is discussed in Sect. refsec:rw. Section 3 briefly shows insights into the datasets. In Sects. 4 and 5 we describe a set of features used for user profiling, for both gender and bot identification tasks. Subsect. 4.1 focuses on the method we used to extract and

© Springer Nature Switzerland AG 2020
A. Arampatzis et al. (Eds.): CLEF 2020, LNCS 12260, pp. 141–153, 2020.
https://doi.org/10.1007/978-3-030-58219-7_13

encode features in a form of digital fingerprint. Section 6 is dedicated to experiments and results. Finally, in Sect. 8 we give the conclusions and briefly discuss about future work.

2   Related Work

One of the most prominent tasks in recent social media analysis is detection of automated user accounts (bots). Research on this topic is very active [10,16,28], because bots pose a big threat if they're intentionally steered to target important events across the globe, such as political elections [2,12–14,23,27]. Paper by [16] explore strategies how bot can interact with real users to increase their influence. They show that a simple strategy can trick influence scoring systems. BotOrNot [6] is openly accessible solution available as API for the machine learning system for bot detection. Authors [6,27] show that the system is accurate in detecting social bots. Authors [21] explore methods for fake news detection on social media, which is closely related to the problem of automated accounts. They state that the performance of detecting fake news only from content in general doesn't show good results, and they suggest to use user social interactions as auxiliary information to improve the detection. Ferrara et al. [8] use extensive set of features (tweet timing, tweet interaction network, content, language, sentiment) to detect the online campaigning as early as possible. Another recent work on bot detection by Cresci et al. [3] is based on DNA inspired fingerprinting of temporal user behaviour. They define a vocabulary B^n, where n is the dimension. An element represents a label for a tweet. User activity is represented as a sequence of tweets labels. They found that bots share longer common substrings (LCSs) than regular users. The point where LCS has the biggest difference is used as a cut-off value to separate bots from genuine users. Framework by Ahmed et al. [1] for bot detection uses the Euclidean distance between feature vectors to build a similarity graph of the accounts. After the graph is built, they perform clustering and community detection algorithms to identify groups of similar accounts in the graph.

Bot problem on social media platforms inspired many competitions and evaluation campaigns such as DARPA [24] and PAN[1].

When it comes to gender and age user profiling, advances in natural language processing technology have facilitated the prediction in several text genres using automatic analysis of the variation of linguistic characteristics. However, in social media texts, there are a couple of limitations. First, small amount of meta information about the users' gender, age, social class, race, geographical location, etc., is available to researchers. Second, communication in online social networks typically occurs in a form of very short messages, often containing non-standard language usage, which makes this type of text a challenging text genre for natural language processing. Finally, given the speed at which chat language has originated globally and continues to develop, especially among young people, a third challenge in automatically detecting false profiles on social networks will

---

[1] https://pan.webis.de/publications.html.

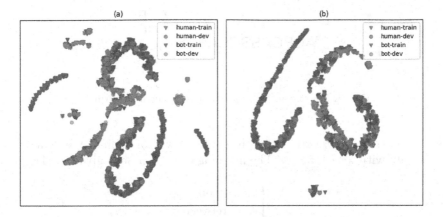

Fig. 1. t-SNE visualization of the bot dataset. (a) English, (b) Spanish

be the constant retraining of the machine learning algorithms in order to learn new variations of chat language. Many researchers have tried to solve some of these challenges [4, 11, 17, 17, 20, 25].

3   Dataset

The dataset provided by the organizers is divided into two parts: English and Spanish. The English dataset consists of training and development subsets, with 2,880 and 1,240 samples, respectively. The Spanish dataset is slightly smaller and consists of training and development subsets, with 2,080 and 920 samples, respectively. Each sample is a user timeline in chronological order, with 100 messages per user. Figure 1 show the datasets using t-SNE [15], an enhanced method based on stochastic neighbour embedding. The features used for both visualizations are the ones used for the classifiers in the final submitted run (Experiments 2 and 4 for bots, and Experiment 5 for gender).

4   Feature Construction for Bot Identification Sub-task

The following sections describe a methodology for feature construction used in the bot identification sub-task. The approach consists of two steps: generation of user behaviour fingerprint and calculation of statistical measures of the fingerprint. Different experimental setups are described later in Sect. 6.

4.1   User Behaviour Fingerprint

DNA sequences have been exploited in different areas such as forensics, anthropology, bio-medical science and similar. Cresci [3] used the idea of DNA coding to describe social media user behaviour in temporal dimension. The same idea

Fig. 2. 3-g extraction example from user fingerprint.

was used in this study, with a slightly modified way of coding. We define a set of codes A_n with length $n = 6$. The meaning of each code is given in (1).

$$
A_n = \begin{cases}
0, & \text{plain} \\
8, & \text{retweet} \\
16, & \text{reply} \\
1, & \text{has hastags} \\
2, & \text{has mentions} \\
4, & \text{has URLs}
\end{cases} \tag{1}
$$

Vocabulary, given the code set A, consists of $3 * 2^3 = 24$ unique characters. Each character, which describes a tweet is constructed by adding up codes for tweet features. First three codes describe the type of the tweet (retweet, reply, or plain) and the rest describe the content of the tweet. For example, if a tweet is neither retweet nor reply, it is plain (with the $code = 0$). If the tweet contains hashtags, then $code = code + 1$, If the same tweet contains URLs, then $code = code + 4$. The final tweet code is 5. We transform it to a character label by using ASCII table character indexes: $ASCII\_tbl[65 + 5] = F$. The number of tweets with attributes encoded with characters determines the length of the sequence. The sequence, in our case, is simply the length of a user timeline, that is, actions in chronological order with the appropriate character encoding.

An example of a user fingerprint generated from their timeline can look like the following:
$$fp_{user} = (ACBCASSCCAFFADADFAFASCB...)$$

Fingerprint Segmentation Using N-Gram Technique. To calculate data statistics, we extracted n-grams of different length (1–3 length appeared to work the best). Figure 2 shows the example on 3-g extraction of sample user fingerprint.

N-gram segments are used to calculate richness and diversity measures, which seem to unveil the difference between genuine user and bot online behaviour.

4.2 Statistical Measures for Text Richness and Diversity

Statistical measures for diversity have long history and wide area of application [26]. A constancy measure for a natural language text is defined, in this article, as a computational measure that converges to a value for a certain amount of text and remains invariant for any larger size. Because such a measure exhibits the same value for any size of text larger than a certain amount, its value could be considered as a text characteristic. Common labels used are: N is the total number of words in a text, $V(N)$ is the number of distinct words, $V(m, N)$ is the number of words appearing m times in the text, and m_{max} is the largest frequency of a word.

Yule's K Index. Yule's original intention for K use is for the author attribution task, assuming that it would differ for texts written by different authors.

$$K = C\frac{S_2 - S_1}{S_1^2} = C\left[-\frac{1}{N} + \sum_{m=1}^{m_{max}} V(m, N)(\frac{m}{N})^2\right]$$

To simplify, $S_1 = N = \sum_m V(m, N)$, and $S_2 = \sum_m m^2 V(m, N)$. C is a constant originally determined by Yule, and it is 10^4.

Shannon's H Index. The Shannon's diversity index (H) is a measure that is commonly used to characterize species diversity in a community. Shannon's index accounts for both abundance and evenness of the species present. The proportion of species i relative to the total number of species (p_i) is calculated, and then multiplied by the natural logarithm of this proportion $(ln(p_i))$. The resulting product is summed across species, and multiplied by -1.

$$H = -\sum_{i=1}^{V(N)} p_i ln(p_i)$$

$V(N)$ is the number of distinct species.

Simpson's D Index. Simpson's diversity index (D) is a mathematical measure that characterizes species diversity in a community. The proportion of species i relative to the total number of species (p_i) is calculated and squared. The squared proportions for all the species are summed, and the reciprocal is taken.

$$D = \frac{1}{\sum_{i=1}^{V(N)} p_i^2}$$

Honoré's R Statistic. Honoré (1979) proposed a measure which assumes that the ratio of hapax legomena $(1, N)$ is constant with respect to the logarithm of the text size:

$$R = 100\frac{log(N)}{1 - \frac{V(1,N)}{V(N)}}$$

Sichel's S Statistic. Sichel [22] observed that the ratio of hapax dis legomena $V(2, N)$ to the vocabulary size is roughly constant across a wide range of sample sizes.

$$S = \frac{V(2, N)}{N}$$

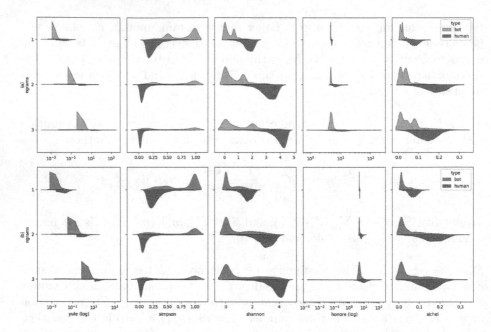

Fig. 3. Diversity measures density per dataset, per user type. (a) English – top row, (b) Spanish – bottom row

We use this measure to express the constancy of n-gram *hapax dis legomena* (number of n-grams that occur two times) which we show to be distinct for genuine and bot accounts.

In Fig. 3 we show the comparison of density plots of all measures of bot accounts versus genuine users. We can see that the diversity measures are different for bots and genuine users. We exploit this characteristic to build a good classifier with as few features as possible.

5 Feature Construction for Gender Identification Sub-task

Features used for the gender identification task can be split into four categories:

Character and Word Features. We used simple text metrics, such as total number of characters, total number of words, number of characters/words per message, number of special characters, number of digits.

PoS Tags Features. Using spacy[2] python library we extracted word unigrams and bigrams, as well as PoS tag bigrams.

---

[2] https://spacy.io/.

Emoji Features. We counted the number of emojis, as well as fine-grained distinction between different types of emojis. To distinguish categories of emojis we used the latest standard at the time of experiments[3].

Text Readability Measures. In 1948, Flesch [9] developed a formula that is considered as one of the oldest and most accurate text readability formulas.

$$R_{Flesch} = 206.835 - 84.6 \cdot \frac{n_{syllables}}{n_{words}} - 1.015 \cdot \frac{n_{words}}{n_{sentences}}$$

The equivalent for Spanish language was developed a few years later by Huerta [7].

$$R_{Huerta} = 206.84 - 60 \cdot \frac{n_{syllables}}{n_{words}} - 102 \cdot \frac{n_{sentences}}{n_{words}}$$

6 Experiments and Results

In the following sections we describe experimental design and results for bot and gender identification sub-tasks, respectively.

6.1 Bot Identification

For bot identification sub-task we conducted four experiments with five different classifiers (Gradient Boosting, Random Forest, SVM, Logistic Regression, K Nearest Neighbours). The differences between the experiments are more focused on testing the improvement with training data increase, as well as feature set generalization using raw fingerprint n-grams versus statistical diversity measures.

Experiment 1. In the Experiment 1 we used character n-grams of user fingerprint described in Sect. 4.1. The length of n-grams used is a combination of 2, 3 and 4. We can see that some classifiers have fairly similar results (Table 1, column E1). The best classifier is Random Forest for both languages. In this experiment we used the training subsets for English and Spanish separately.

Experiment 2. In the Experiment 2 we used the diversity measures calculated on character n-grams of user fingerprint described in Sect. 4.2. The length of n-grams used is a combination of 1, 2 and 3. The best classifier is Random Forest for both languages. In this experiment we used the training subsets for English and Spanish separately.

---

[3] https://unicode.org/Public/emoji/12.0/emoji-test.txt.

Table 1. Bot classification results. The models are tested on the development dataset. The models are developed on language-specific training datasets.

Dataset	Classifier	E1			E2		
		Precision	Recall	F1	Precision	Recall	F1
English	**GB**	0.9197	0.9153	0.9151	0.9263	0.9234	0.9233
	SVM	0.9174	0.9161	0.9161	0.9253	0.9242	0.9241
	LR	0.8840	0.8750	0.8743	0.9261	0.9242	0.9241
	KNN	−*	−*	−*	0.9284	0.9258	0.9257
	RF	0.9284	0.9218	**0.9215**	0.9293	0.9266	**0.9265**
Spanish	**GB**	0.8666	0.8663	0.8663	0.8429	0.8391	0.8387
	SVM	0.8602	0.8598	0.8597	0.8164	0.8163	0.8163
	LR	0.8663	0.8663	0.8663	0.8510	0.8478	0.8475
	KNN	−*	−*	−*	0.8617	0.8587	0.8584
	RF	0.9115	0.9033	**0.9028**	0.8503	0.8489	**0.8488**

*Not available due to memory restrictions.

Table 2. Bot classification results. The models are tested on the development dataset. The models are developed on combined language training datasets.

Dataset	Classifier	E3			E4		
		Precision	Recall	F1	Precision	Recall	F1
English	**GB**[†]	0.9252	0.9242	**0.9241**	0.9330	0.9306	**0.9305**
	SVM	0.9094	0.9081	0.9080	0.9199	0.9177	0.9176
	LR	0.9121	0.9113	0.9112	0.9214	0.9202	0.9201
	KNN	−*	−*	−*	0.9256	0.9242	0.9241
	RF	0.9189	0.9153	0.9151	0.9256	0.9242	0.9241
Spanish	**GB**[†]	0.8896	0.8880	**0.8879**	0.8512	0.8424	0.8414
	SVM	0.8588	0.8587	0.8587	0.8490	0.8435	0.8429
	LR	0.8478	0.8478	0.8478	0.8473	0.8446	0.8443
	KNN	−*	−*	−*	0.8586	0.8543	**0.8539**
	RF	0.8764	0.8696	0.8690	0.8498	0.8435	0.8428

[†]Final classifier (E4 for official ranking).
*Not available due to memory restrictions.

Experiment 3. In the Experiment 3 (Table 2, column E3) we used the same features as in the Experiment 1. The best classifier is Gradient Boosting ensemble for both languages. In this experiment we used the training subsets for the English and Spanish combined. Because the features are language independent, we combined the training datasets into one, and tested it on both languages. The final model is the same for both subsets.

Table 3. Gender classification results. The models are tested on the development dataset.

Dataset	Classifier	Precision	Recall	F1
English	**GB**[†]	0.8167	0.8129	**0.8123**
	SVM	0.7782	0.7774	0.7773
	LR	0.7630	0.7629	0.7629
	KNN	0.6054	0.6048	0.6043
	RF	0.7926	0.7919	0.7918
Spanish	**GB**[‡]	0.7062	0.7000	**0.6977**
	SVM	0.6592	0.6587	0.6584
	LR	0.6418	0.6413	0.6410
	KNN	0.5851	0.5848	0.5845
	RF	0.6568	0.6543	0.6530

[†,‡] Final classifiers.

Table 4. Final results on test dataset. Averaged per language.

Dataset	Bot	Gender
English	0.9216	0.7928
Spanish	0.8956	0.7494
Average	0.9086	0.7711

Experiment 4. In the Experiment 4 (Table 2, column E4) we used the same features as in the Experiment 2. The best classifier for the English is Gradient Boosting ensemble and K Nearest Neighbours for the Spanish. Similar to the Experiment 3, we combined the training datasets into one, and tested it on both languages.

Although a better performance was obtained on separately trained models for two languages (Random Forest, Table 1) with raw features, we opted for Gradient Boosting ensemble which was trained on combined dataset (Spanish portion slightly dropped in performance). The classifier from Experiment 4 was used for the official ranking.

6.2 Gender Identification

For the gender identification sub-task we used the same set of classifiers as for bot detection. The results in Table 3 show that Gradient Boosting classifier performed the best for both languages. This task was language dependent, which means that each language has its own model.

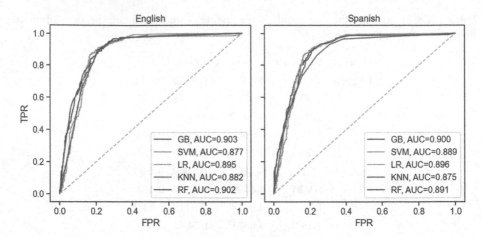

Fig. 4. ROC curves for the classifiers in the Experiment 2.

6.3 Results on the Official Test Dataset

The official results are shown in Table 4. Bot detection for the English performed with the similar results as in our experiments with the development set, while for the Spanish it performed better. Similar improvement was obtained with the Spanish dataset for gender identification. The models for the final evaluation are trained on both, training and development sets.

7 Discussion

In this section we primarily focus on the discussion of the bot identification results. Figure 4 shows the Receiver Operating Characteristic (ROC) curve. The curve is evidently much better than the random classifier model. However, it does not seem that there is significant difference between the tested classifiers.

To analyse mis-classified samples in the bot identification task, we used a multivariate distribution visualisation (Fig. 5). Comparing the distributions of the training subset and mis-classified samples, there are a few interesting observations. For example, in the Shannon-Simpson space (calculated over 3-g) it can be seen that the distribution of "false human" samples are more aligned with the distribution of the training "true human". This means that these samples showed higher diversity in the message usage than the actual "bot" class. However, for the "false bot" samples most of them seem to follow "true human" distribution, although slightly shifted. If we take a look into Honore-Sichel space, we can see that the situation is the opposite. "False bot" samples are more aligned with the "true bot" distribution. This means that some bots do express higher diversity that the average bot, and some genuine users tend to use less diverse types of messages than the average human. This is one of the main drawbacks of our method - it captures only surface behaviour without analysing used language and profile metadata.

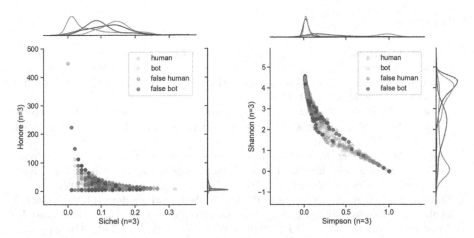

Fig. 5. Plots of the wrongly classified samples relative to variable distributions in the training set for the Spanish language. Honore-Sichel variables (left) and Shannon-Simpson variables calculated on 3-g.

8 Conclusion

We conducted a set of experiments to find a simple, yet effective bot detection method on the Twitter social media platform. We show that it is possible to detect automated users by using a fingerprint of user behaviour and a set of statistical measures that describe different aspects of that behaviour. The measures describe "constancy" or "diversity" of the pattern. The hypothesis was that the automated users show lower diversity, and tend to use a smaller set of types of messages over an extended period of time. Through visual analysis, discussion and classification results we showed that assumption did hold under our experimental setup. For the gender identification task we used a standard set of features usually used in stylometry analysis, with the addition of emoji features on a more granular level. The main drawback of our approach is that a classifier needs at least 20 tweets per user to generate a fingerprint. The number 20 was empirically identified based on the observations during the experiments (keeping the fingerprints shorter than 20 worsened the results of all classifiers). Another point is that social bots evolve over time, and they tend to be more difficult to identify with established machine learning methods. Bot creators can take advantage of the present ML knowledge and enhance their algorithms, so they stay undetected longer. And last, to further verify our results and perform more thorough study, we plan to apply our approach to more datasets. Additionally, we plan to develop an unsupervised method for bot detection on the same set of features using clustering techniques.

References

1. Ahmed, F., Abulaish, M.: A generic statistical approach for spam detection in online social networks. Comput. Commun. **36**(10–11), 1120–1129 (2013)
2. Bessi, A., Ferrara, E.: Social bots distort the 2016 US presidential election online discussion. First Monday **21**(11), 14 (2016)
3. Cresci, S., Di Pietro, R., Petrocchi, M., Spognardi, A., Tesconi, M.: DNA-inspired online behavioral modeling and its application to spambot detection. IEEE Intell. Syst. **31**(5), 58–64 (2016)
4. Dadvar, M., de Jong, F., Ordelman, R., Trieschnigg, D.: Improved cyberbullying detection using gender information. In: Proceedings of the Twelfth Dutch-Belgian Information Retrieval Workshop (DIR 2012). University of Ghent (2012)
5. Daelemans, W., et al.: Overview of PAN 2019: bots and gender profiling, celebrity profiling, cross-domain authorship attribution and style change detection. In: Crestani, F., et al. (eds.) CLEF 2019. LNCS, vol. 11696, pp. 402–416. Springer, Cham (2019). https://doi.org/10.1007/978-3-030-28577-7_30
6. Davis, C.A., Varol, O., Ferrara, E., Flammini, A., Menczer, F.: BotOrNot: a system to evaluate social bots. In: Proceedings of the 25th International Conference Companion on World Wide Web, pp. 273–274. International World Wide Web Conferences Steering Committee (2016)
7. Fernández Huerta, J.: Medidas sencillas de lecturabilidad. Consigna **214**, 29–32 (1959)
8. Ferrara, E., Varol, O., Menczer, F., Flammini, A.: Detection of promoted social media campaigns. In: Tenth International AAAI Conference on Web and Social Media (2016)
9. Flesch, R., Gould, A.J.: The Art of Readable Writing, vol. 8. Harper, New York (1949)
10. Gilani, Z., Wang, L., Crowcroft, J., Almeida, M., Farahbakhsh, R.: Stweeler: a framework for Twitter bot analysis. In: Proceedings of the 25th International Conference Companion on World Wide Web, pp. 37–38. International World Wide Web Conferences Steering Committee (2016)
11. Goswami, S., Sarkar, S., Rustagi, M.: Stylometric analysis of Bloggers' age and gender. In: Third International AAAI Conference on Weblogs and Social Media (2009)
12. Guess, A., Nagler, J., Tucker, J.: Less than you think: prevalence and predictors of fake news dissemination on Facebook. Sci. Adv. **5**(1), eaau4586 (2019)
13. Hjouji el, Z., Hunter, D.S., des Mesnards, N.G., Zaman, T.: The impact of bots on opinions in social networks. arXiv preprint arXiv:1810.12398 (2018)
14. Howard, P.N., Woolley, S., Calo, R.: Algorithms, bots, and political communication in the US 2016 election: the challenge of automated political communication for election law and administration. J. Inf. Technol. Politics **15**(2), 81–93 (2018). https://doi.org/10.1080/19331681.2018.1448735
15. van der Maaten, L., Hinton, G.: Visualizing data using t-SNE. J. Mach. Learn. Res. **9**(Nov), 2579–2605 (2008)
16. Messias, J., Schmidt, L., Oliveira, R., Benevenuto, F.: You followed my bot! transforming robots into influential users in Twitter. First Monday **18**(7) (2013)
17. Peersman, C., Daelemans, W., Van Vaerenbergh, L.: Predicting age and gender in online social networks. In: Proceedings of the 3rd International Workshop on Search and Mining User-Generated Contents, pp. 37–44. ACM (2011)

18. Potthast, M., Gollub, T., Wiegmann, M., Stein, B.: TIRA integrated research architecture. Information Retrieval Evaluation in a Changing World. TIRS, vol. 41, pp. 123–160. Springer, Cham (2019). https://doi.org/10.1007/978-3-030-22948-1_5
19. Rangel, F., Rosso, P.: Overview of the 7th author profiling task at PAN 2019: bots and gender profiling. In: Cappellato, L., Ferro, N., Losada, D., Müller, H. (eds.) CLEF 2019 Labs and Workshops, Notebook Papers. CEUR-WS.org, September 2019
20. Sarawgi, R., Gajulapalli, K., Choi, Y.: Gender attribution: tracing stylometric evidence beyond topic and genre. In: Proceedings of the Fifteenth Conference on Computational Natural Language Learning, pp. 78–86. Association for Computational Linguistics (2011)
21. Shu, K., Wang, S., Liu, H.: Understanding user profiles on social media for fake news detection. In: 2018 IEEE Conference on Multimedia Information Processing and Retrieval (MIPR), pp. 430–435. IEEE (2018)
22. Sichel, H.S.: On a distribution law for word frequencies. J. Am. Stat. Associ. **70**(351a), 542–547 (1975). https://doi.org/10.1080/01621459.1975.10482469
23. Stella, M., Ferrara, E., De Domenico, M.: Bots increase exposure to negative and inflammatory content in online social systems. Proc. Natl. Acad. Sci. **115**(49), 12435–12440 (2018)
24. Subrahmanian, V., et al.: The DARPA Twitter bot challenge. Computer **49**(6), 38–46 (2016)
25. Thelwall, M., Wilkinson, D., Uppal, S.: Data mining emotion in social network communication: gender differences in MySpace. J. Am. Soc. Inf. Sci. Technol. **61**(1), 190–199 (2010)
26. Tweedie, F.J., Baayen, R.H.: How variable may a constant be? Measures of lexical richness in perspective. Comput. Humanit. **32**(5), 323–352 (1998)
27. Varol, O., Ferrara, E., Davis, C.A., Menczer, F., Flammini, A.: Online human-bot interactions: detection, estimation, and characterization. In: Eleventh International AAAI Conference on Web and Social Media (2017)
28. Yang, Z., Wilson, C., Wang, X., Gao, T., Zhao, B.Y., Dai, Y.: Uncovering social network sybils in the wild. ACM Trans. Knowl. Discov. Data (TKDD) **8**(1), 2 (2014)

Medical Image Tagging by Deep Learning and Retrieval

Vasiliki Kougia[1,2], John Pavlopoulos[1,2(✉)], and Ion Androutsopoulos[1]

[1] Department of Informatics, Athens University of Economics and Business, Athens, Greece
{kouyiav,annis,ion}@aueb.gr
[2] Department of Computer and Systems Sciences, Stockholm University, Stockholm, Sweden

Abstract. Radiologists and other qualified physicians need to examine and interpret large numbers of medical images daily. Systems that would help them spot and report abnormalities in medical images could speed up diagnostic workflows. Systems that would help exploit past diagnoses made by highly skilled physicians could also benefit their more junior colleagues. A task that systems can perform towards this end is medical image classification, which assigns medical concepts to images. This task, called Concept Detection, was part of the ImageCLEF 2019 competition. We describe the methods we implemented and submitted to the Concept Detection 2019 task, where we achieved the best performance with a deep learning method we call ConceptCXN. We also show that retrieval-based methods can perform very well in this task, when combined with deep learning image encoders. Finally, we report additional post-competition experiments we performed to shed more light on the performance of our best systems. Our systems can be installed through PyPI as part of the BioCaption package.

Keywords: Medical images · Concept detection · Image retrieval · Multi-label classification · Image captioning · Machine learning · Deep learning

1 Introduction

Medical imaging examinations like radiographs (X-rays) are crucial for the diagnosis of many serious diseases. However, the diagnostic process of these examinations is demanding and time-consuming, while the workload rises and in some cases there are not enough and experienced medical professionals [26,27]. This can lead to medical errors, with negative consequences on healthcare workflows and the treatment of patients [1,3]. Computer-assisted diagnostic systems are being developed to speed up the diagnostic process and help less experienced physicians, for example by retrieving similar past cases for which diagnoses by expert clinicians are available. Towards this end, the ImageCLEFmed Caption

© Springer Nature Switzerland AG 2020
A. Arampatzis et al. (Eds.): CLEF 2020, LNCS 12260, pp. 154–166, 2020.
https://doi.org/10.1007/978-3-030-58219-7_14

task [20], part of ImageCLEF 2019 [11], ran for the 3rd year in 2019.[1] It included a Concept Detection sub-task, where the goal was to perform multi-label classification of medical images by automatically selecting medical concepts (which can also be thought of as medical terms or tags) that should be assigned to each image (see Fig. 1).

This paper presents the four Concept Detection systems that AUEB's NLP Group[2] developed and used to participate in ImageCLEFmed Caption 2019. We include some additional experiments we performed after ImageCLEFmed Caption 2019, using our two best performing systems. Our first system, called Mean@k-NN, is retrieval-based. It consists of a DenseNet-121 [10] Convolutional Neural Network (CNN) image encoder and a k-Nearest Neighbors (k-NN) retrieval component. We also present results of several variants of Mean@k-NN, which include more extensive tuning of k and different concept assignment methods. Our second system, dubbed ConceptCXN, is based on the CheXNet classifier [25], which uses the DenseNet-121 image encoder [10] combined with a feed-forward neural network (FFNN). We found that tuning the probability threshold that is used to decide when to assign each concept (label) to an image had a significant effect. Ablation tests also showed that image augmentation and learning rate decay significantly improve the F1 score of this model. As a third system, we implemented an ensemble that combines concept probability scores obtained from ConceptCXN and image similarity scores produced by Mean@k-NN. The fourth system we implemented, VGGnet@concepts, uses the VGG-19 image encoder [29], which was also used by Jing et al. [14], combined with a FFNN for multi-label classification. ConceptCXN had the best results among all participants in the Concept Detection sub-task of ImageCLEFmed Caption 2019. The results of Mean@k-NN were also very promising, and that system ranked third in the competition. An ensemble that combined the scores of ConceptCXN and Mean@k-NN performed better than Mean@k-NN, ranking second, but did not outperform ConceptCXN. Our VGGnet@concepts classifier was the worst of the four we submitted, but nonetheless ranked fifth.

Section 2 below discusses related work on medical image classification. Section 3 then describes the ImageCLEFmed Caption 2019 dataset that we used for our experiments. Section 4 describes in detail the systems we developed. Section 5 presents the official results of the systems we submitted. Section 6 reports the results of the additional experiments we conducted after the Image-CLEFmed Caption 2019 competition. Section 7 concludes and suggests directions for future work.

2   Related Work

Recent increased interest in automatic and computer-assisted medical image diagnosis has led to a significant body of work on image classification for different types of medical images (radiographs, CTs, MRIs, etc.) and different

---

[1] https://www.imageclef.org/2019/medical/caption/.

[2] http://nlp.cs.aueb.gr/.

classification schemes, including binary classification (normal or abnormal) and multi-label classification (e.g., separate labels per disease) [2,13,25]. Some publicly available datasets of medical images provide only gold diagnostic labels [12,23,32], while others also include full diagnostic reports [15,28]. Recently, large medical image datasets have been released, which can help diagnostic systems achieve better performance [12,15].

A popular approach for image classification that has also been applied to medical images is deep learning, especially Convolutional Neural Networks (CNNs) [2,6,13,24,25]. CNNs pre-trained on ImageNet [4] are known to help systems achieve high performance in image classification tasks. ImageNet, however, contains photographs of general content that are very different from medical images. One way to address this limitation is to pre-train the image encoders on ImageNet, and then fine-tune them on (typically much smaller) datasets of medical images, a form of transfer learning. Esteva et al. [6], for example, achieved high performance on identifying malignant skin lesions by fine-tuning an Inception v3 CNN model that had been pretrained on ImageNet. Following the same approach, CheXNet [25] uses DenseNet-121 pre-trained on ImageNet and fine-tuned on the ChestX-ray 14 dataset [32] to classify the X-rays to 14 disease labels. Islam et al. [13] experimented with several CNN architectures to perform binary classification of chest X-rays. Different architectures performed differently on different diseases, while an ensemble of CNN architectures achieved better overall results.

The ImageCLEFmed Concept Detection tasks require multi-label classification of radiology images. In the tasks of 2017, 2018, and 2019 [5,9,20] both deep learning classifiers and retrieval-based systems were used. In 2017, Valavanis et al. [31] used retrieval-based methods that were ranked at the top 10 positions. They employed a k-NN classifier to retrieve training images similar to each test image, experimenting with several image representations (localized compact features, bag of visual words, bag of colors). On the other hand, in 2018 the best performing systems were deep learning classifiers, while retrieval methods had lower results. The best systems employed an adversarial auto-encoder for unsupervised feature learning [22], and the Inception v3 CNN [34] for multi-label classification. In 2019, we participated in the Concept Detection sub-task [18] with four systems using deep learning classifiers and retrieval approaches, as already noted. Our k-NN system, which was the only retrieval-based method in the competition, achieved the second best performance, surpassed only by our own ConceptCXN (CheXNet-based) deep learning classifier. This shows that the jury is still out on the comparison between retrieval-based and deep learning classifiers. We also note that some retrieval-based methods, like our Mean@k-NN, use pre-trained deep learning image encoders to represent images when retrieving similar past cases.

3   Data

The ImageCLEFmed Caption 2019 dataset is a subset of the Radiology Objects in COntext (ROCO) dataset [21]. It consists of medical images extracted from

Image: ROCO_CLEF_00055

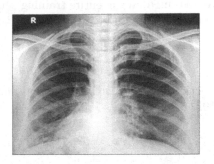

Image: ROCO_CLEF_00051

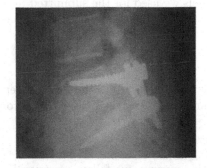

<table>
<tr><td colspan="2" align="center">Concepts</td><td colspan="2" align="center">Concepts</td></tr>
<tr><td>CUI</td><td>UMLS Term</td><td>CUI</td><td>UMLS Term</td></tr>
<tr><td>C0043299</td><td>x-ray procedure</td><td>C0267716</td><td>hernia</td></tr>
<tr><td>C1548003</td><td>radiograph</td><td>C0520904</td><td>postop nausea</td></tr>
<tr><td>C0817096</td><td>thoracics</td><td>C0867390</td><td>postoperative stroke</td></tr>
<tr><td>C1962945</td><td>radiogr</td><td>C0032786</td><td>care postop</td></tr>
<tr><td></td><td></td><td>C0241311</td><td>after surgery</td></tr>
</table>

Fig. 1. Two images from ImageCLEFmed Caption 2019, with their gold CUIs and UMLS terms.

open access biomedical journal articles of PubMed Central.[3] Each image was extracted along with its caption. The caption was processed using QuickUMLS [30] to produce the gold UMLS concept unique identifiers (CUIs).[4] An image can be associated with multiple CUIs (Fig. 1). Each CUI is accompanied by its corresponding UMLS term.

In ImageCLEFmed Caption 2017 [5] and 2018 [9], the datasets were noisy. They included generic and compound images, covering a wide diversity of medical images. There was also a large total number of concepts (111,155) and some of them were too generic and did not appropriately describe the images [34]. In the ROCO dataset, compound and non-radiology images were filtered out using a CNN model. This led to 80,786 radiology images in total, of which 56,629 images were provided as the training set, 14,157 as the validation set, and the remaining 10,000 images were used for testing. In ImageCLEFmed Caption 2019, the total number of UMLS concepts was reduced to 5,528, with 6 concepts assigned to each training image on average. The minimum number of concepts per training image is 1, and the maximum is 72. We note that 312 of the 5,528 total concepts are not assigned to any training image; and 1,530 concepts are assigned to only one training image. We randomly selected 20% of the training images and used

---

[3] https://www.ncbi.nlm.nih.gov/pmc/.
[4] https://www.nlm.nih.gov/research/umls/.

them as our development set (11,326 images along with their gold concepts). The models we used for the submitted results were trained on the entire training set. The validation set was used for hyper-parameter tuning and early stopping.

4   Methods

This section describes the four Concept Detection methods we implemented and submitted to ImageCLEFmed Caption 2019.

4.1   Mean@k-NN

In this system, we follow a retrieval approach, extending the 1-NN baseline of our previous work on biomedical image captioning [17]. Given a test image, the previous 1-NN baseline returned the caption of the most similar training image, using a CNN encoder to map each image to a dense vector. For ImageCLEFmed Caption 2019, we retrieve the k-most similar training images and used their concepts, as described below (Called 'System 1: DenseNet-121 Encoder + k-NN Image Retrieval' in [18].).

We use the DenseNet-121 [10] image encoder, a CNN with 121 layers, where all layers are directly connected to each other improving information flow and avoiding vanishing gradients. We started with DenseNet-121 pre-trained on ImageNet [4] and fine-tuned it on ImageCLEFmed Caption 2019 training images.[5] The fine-tuning was performed as when training DenseNet-121 in ConceptCXN, including data augmentation (see Sect. 4.2 below). Without fine-tuning, the performance of the pre-trained encoder was worse. ImageCLEFmed Caption 2019 images were rescaled to 224×224 and normalized with the mean and standard deviation of ImageNet to match the requirements of DenseNet-121 and how it was pre-trained on ImageNet. Having fine-tuned DenseNet-121, we use it to obtain dense vector encodings, called *image embeddings*, of all training images. The image embeddings are extracted from the last average pooling layer of DenseNet-121. Given a test image (Fig. 2), we again use the fine-tuned DensNet-121 to obtain the image's embedding. We then retrieve the k training images with the highest cosine similarity (computed on image embeddings) to the test image, and return the r concepts that are most frequent among the concepts of the k images. We set r to the mean number of concepts per image of the particular k retrieved images. We tuned the value of k in the range from 1 to 200 using the validation set, which led to $k = 199$. In post-competition experiments, we tried a more extensive tuning in the range from 1 to 300, which offered only a slight improvement (see Sect. 6.2).

4.2   ConceptCXN

This system, which is based on CheXNet [25], achieved the best Concept Detection results in ImageCLEFmed Caption 2019. In its original form, CheXNet

---

[5] We used the implementation of https://keras.io/applications/#densenet.

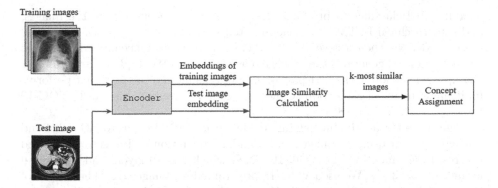

Fig. 2. Illustration of how Mean@k-NN works at test time.

maps X-rays of the ChestX-ray 14 dataset [32] to 14 labels. It uses DenseNet-121 [10] to encode images, adding a FFNN to assign one or more of the 14 labels (classes) to each image (Called 'System 2: CheXNet-based, DenseNet-121 Encoder + FFNN' in [18].).

We re-implemented CheXNet in Keras[6] and extended it for the many more labels (5,528 vs. 14) of ImageCLEFmed Caption 2019. We used DenseNet-121 pre-trained on ImageNet. The images of ImageCLEFmed Caption 2019 were again rescaled to 224×224 and normalized using the mean and standard deviation values of ImageNet. The training images of ImageCLEFmed Caption 2019 were also augmented by horizontal flips; for each training image, we randomly decide whether to apply a horizontal flip (and create an additional image) or not. Image embeddings are again extracted from the last average pooling layer of DenseNet-121. In this system, however, the image embeddings are then passed through a dense layer with 5,528 outputs and sigmoid activations to produce a probability per label. We trained the model by minimizing binary cross entropy loss. We used Adam [16] with its default hyper-parameters, early stopping on the validation set, and patience of 3 epochs. We also decayed the learning rate by a factor of 10 when the validation loss stopped improving.

At test time, we predict the concepts for each test image using their probabilities, as estimated by the trained model. For each concept (label), we assign it to the test image if the corresponding predicted probability exceeds a threshold t. We use the same t value for all 5,528 concepts. We tuned t on the validation set, which led to $t = 0.16$.

4.3   VGGnet@concepts

This system is based on the work of Jing et al. [14], who presented an encoder-decoder model to generate tags and medical reports from medical images. Roughly speaking, the full model of Jing et al. uses a VGG-19 [29] image encoder,

---

[6] https://keras.io/.

a multi-label classifier to produce tags (describing concepts) from the images, and a hierarchical LSTM that generates texts by attending on both image and tag embeddings; the top level of the LSTM generates sentence embeddings, and the bottom level generates the words of each sentence. We implemented in Keras a simplified version of the first part of Jing et al.'s model, the part that performs multi-label image classification (Called 'System 3: Based on Jing et al., VGG-19 Encoder + FFNN' in [18].).

Again, we rescale the ImageCLEFmed Caption 2019 images to 224 × 224 and normalize them using the mean and standard deviation of ImageNet. We feed the resulting images to the VGG-19 CNN, which has 19 layers and uses small kernels of size 3 × 3. We used VGG-19 pre-trained on ImageNet.[7] The output of the last fully connected layer of VGG-19 is then given as input to a dense layer with a softmax activation to obtain a probability distribution over the concepts. The model is trained using categorical cross entropy, which is calculated as:

$$E = - \sum_{i=1}^{|C|} y_{true,i} \log_2(y_{pred,i}) \tag{1}$$

where C is the set of $|C| = 5,528$ concepts, y_{true} is the ground truth binary vector of a training image, and y_{pred} is the predicted softmax probability distribution over the concepts C for the training image. Categorical cross entropy sums loss terms only for the gold concepts of the image, which have a value of 1 in y_{true}. When using softmax and categorical cross-entropy, usually y_{true} is a one-hot vector and the classes are mutually exclusive (single-label classification). To use softmax with categorical cross entropy for multi-label classification, where y_{true} is binary but not necessarily one-hot, the loss is divided by the number of gold labels (true concepts) [8,19]. Jing et al. [14] achieve this by dividing the ground truth binary vector y_{true} by its L1 norm, which equals the number of gold labels. Hence, the categorical cross-entropy loss becomes:

$$E = - \sum_{i=1}^{|C|} \frac{y_{true,i}}{\| y_{true} \|_1} \log_2(y_{pred,i}) = -\frac{1}{M} \sum_{j=1}^{M} \log_2(y_{pred,j}) \tag{2}$$

where M is the number of gold labels (true concepts) of the training image, which is different per training image. In this model, the loss of Eq. 2 achieved better results on the development set, compared to binary cross entropy with a sigmoid activation per concept. We used the Adam optimizer with initial learning rate 1e-5 and early stopping on the validation set with patience 3 epochs. Given a test image, we return the six concepts with the highest probability scores, since the average number of gold concepts per training image is 6.

4.4   ConceptCXN + Mean@k-NN

This method is an ensemble of ConceptCXN and Mean@k-NN, where Mean@k-NN is modified to produce a score for each returned concept. Given a test image

---

[7] https://keras.io/applications/#vgg19.

g, we use Mean@k-NN (Fig. 2) to retrieve the k most similar training images $g_1, \ldots, g_k$, their gold concepts, and the cosine similarities $s(g, g_1), \ldots, s(g, g_k)$ between the test image g and each one of the k retrieved images. Let C be again the set of $|C| = 5,528$ concepts. For each concept $c_j \in C$, the modified Mean@k-NN assigns to c_i the following score (Called 'System 4: Ensemble, k-NN Image Retrieval + CheXNet' in [18].):

$$v_1(c_j, g) = \sum_{i=1}^{k} s(g, g_i)\, \delta(c_j, g_i) \tag{3}$$

where $\delta(c_j, g_i) = 1$ if c_j is a gold concept of the retrieved training image g_i, and $\delta(c_j, g_i) = 0$ otherwise. In other words, the score of each concept c_j is the sum of the cosine similarities of the retrieved documents where c_j is a gold concept.

For the same test image g, we also obtain concept probabilities from ConceptCXN, i.e., a vector of 5,528 probabilities. Let $v_2(c_j, g)$ be the probability of concept c_j being correct for test image g according to ConceptCXN. For each $c_j \in C$, the ensemble's score $v(c_j, g)$ of c_j is simply the average of $v_1(c_j, g)$ and $v_2(c_j, g)$. The ensemble returns the six concepts with the highest $v(c_j, g)$ scores, as in VGGnet@concepts, on the grounds that the average number of gold concepts per training image is 6.

5   Official Experimental Results

The systems submitted to the Concept Detection sub-task of ImageCLEFmed Caption 2019 were evaluated by computing their F1 scores on each test image (in effect comparing the binary ground truth vector to the predicted concepts) and then averaging over all test images [11]. Table 1 reports the results of our four systems on the development and test data. The ConceptCXN + Mean@k-NN ensemble had the best results on the development data, but ConceptCXN had the best results on the test set. The tuning of the probability threshold was essential for the performance of ConceptCXN (see Sect. 4.2). The large number of concepts caused the probabilities of that classifier to be very low, so trying different thresholds helped the model achieve a high F1 score. The retrieval-based Mean@k-NN system achieved high results, close to the ones of the deep learning ConceptCXN classifier, showing that retrieval is also a good approach for this task. Surprisingly, in all systems the results on the test set are higher than the ones on the development set, which suggests that the test set may be easier.[8] This is also an indication that hyper-parameter tuning did not cause over-fitting on the development set. ConceptCXN, Mean@k-NN, and their ensemble were the three best performing systems among all the submitted systems in the 2019 Concept Detection task.

---

[8] A similar observation was made in [7].

Table 1. Results of the Concept Detection systems we submitted to ImageCLEFmed Caption 2019. Our systems were ranked at the top 5 positions among approx. 60 systems that participated.

System	Description	F1 score		Ranking
		Dev	Test	
Mean@k-NN	DenseNet [10] + k-NN	0.2575	0.2740	3
ConceptCXN	DenseNet [10] + FFNN	0.2600	**0.2823**	1
VGGnet@concepts	VGG-19 [29] + FFNN	0.2498	0.2640	5
ConceptCXN + Mean@k-NN	Ensemble	**0.2644**	0.2793	2

6   Post-competition Experiments

After the ImageCLEFmed Caption 2019 competition was over, we performed additional experiments to shed more light on the performance of our two best single (non-ensemble) systems, ConceptCXN and Mean@k-NN.

6.1   Ablation Tests with ConceptCXN

Two important mechanisms in ConceptCXN are the image augmentation of the training set, and learning rate decay when the validation loss does not improve for one epoch (Sect. 4.2). To investigate how these two mechanisms affect the performance of ConceptCXN, we trained it two more times, each time removing one of the two mechanisms. Table 2 shows the results of these ablation tests. Removing any of the two mechanisms leads to inferior F1. We also observed that without the learning rate decay, training takes longer, i.e., convergence is slower. One epoch takes approx. 15 min for the full model, but approx. 21 min without learning decay.

Table 2. F1 scores of ConceptCXN on the test data, when no learning rate reduction mechanism is used (w/o LR reduction) or when no image augmentation is applied to the training set (w/o image augmentation). Each experiment was repeated three times with different random seeds, and we report the mean scores and the standard error of mean. This is also why the score of the full system is slightly different than the corresponding one (ConceptCXN, Test) in Table 1.

Full system	w/o LR reduction	w/o image augmentation
0.2800 ± 0.0015	0.2677 ± 0.0023	0.2681 ± 0.0012

6.2   Further Tuning of Mean@k-NN

Two important hyper-parameters of Mean@k-NN are k and r, i.e., the number of neighbours and the number of concepts to assign to the test image, respectively

(Sect. 4.1). In these additional experiments we performed a more extensive tuning of k, along with different strategies to select k. These experiments did not lead to any substantial improvement in the F1 score of Mean@k-NN, but we report them for completeness.

In particular, a more extensive tuning of k on the development set with values ranging from 1 to 300 (instead of stopping at 200) led to a k value of 262 and just a minor improvement in F1 (see Table 3, row Mean@k-NN + tuning300). We then tried three alternative mechanisms to select the value of r, instead of setting r to the mean number of concepts of the k retrieved images (cf. Sect. 4.1). The first alternative (Distance@k-NN in Table 3) uses the cosine similarities $s(g, g_i)$ between the test images g and each neighbour image g_i, assigning a weight w_i to each neighbour image g_i as follows:

$$w_i = \frac{s(g, g_i)}{\sum_{j=1}^{k} s(g, g_i))}, \ i \in \{1, \ldots, k\} \tag{4}$$

The second mechanism (Rank@k-NN in Table 3) ranks the retrieved images g_i by increasing cosine similarity $s(g, g_i)$ to the test image g, and uses the ranks of the retrieved images to assign weights w_i to them:

$$w_i = \frac{\mathrm{rank}(g_i)}{\sum_{j=1}^{k} \mathrm{rank}(g_j)}, \ i \in \{1, \ldots, k\} \tag{5}$$

The third mechanism (R&D@k-NN) to select the value of r combines the previous two:

$$w_i = \frac{s(g, g_i) \cdot \mathrm{rank}(g_i)}{\sum_{j=1}^{k} s(g, g_j) \cdot \mathrm{rank}(g_j)}, \ i \in \{1, \ldots, k\} \tag{6}$$

In all three cases, having computed the weights w_i of the retrieved images, we compute the value of r (number of concepts to assign to the test image g) as follows:

$$r = \sum_{i=1}^{k} c_i \cdot w_i \tag{7}$$

where c_i is the number of concepts of the i-th retrieved image g_i. We then assign to the image g being classified the r concepts that are most frequent among the concepts of the k retrieved images $g_1, \ldots, g_k$, as in the original Mean@k-NN. These alternative mechanisms to select r, however, did not lead to any improvements (Table 3).

Table 3. Test results of the post-competition tuning experiments with Mean@k-NN.

Method	F1 score
Mean@k-NN	0.2740
Mean@k-NN + tuning300	**0.2745**
Distance@k-NN	0.2741
Rank@k-NN	0.2741
R& D@k-NN	0.2740

7 Conclusions

We described the four systems that AUEB's NLP Group used to participate in the Concept Detection task of ImageCLEFmed 2019 Caption, along with post-competition experiments to further explore the behaviour of our best systems. Our top-ranked system, ConceptCXN, was based on the CheXNet classifier [25], which uses the DenseNet-121 image encoder [10] combined with a feed-forward neural network (FFNN). We modified CheXNet to handle the much larger label set of the Concept Detection task. We also found that tuning the classification threshold, applying data augmentation to the training set, and employing learning rate decay were all important factors in the performance of ConceptCXN. The learning rate decay mechanism was also found to help the model converge faster. Our second-best non-ensemble system, Mean@k-NN, ranked third in the competition. This is a retrieval-based system that also uses the DenseNet-121 image encoder, but then a k-NN classifier to return the most frequent concepts of the most similar training images (neighbours). We considered several alternative mechanisms to select the number of concepts to return per test image (among the most frequent concepts of the neighbours), but all led to very similar results. A more extensive post-competition tuning of k (number of neighbours) also led to only a minor improvement. An ensemble of the previous two systems, ConceptCXN and Mean@k-NN, ranked second in the competition, while our weakest system VGGnet@concepts was ranked 5th.

In future work, we plan to experiment more with ensembles of our Image-CLEFmed Caption 2019 methods, and to pre-train their image encoders on large collections of medical images. We also aim to extend our systems to generate draft medical reports, as in the work of Jing et al. [14] and other more recent work [33].

Acknowledgements. We thank Vasilis Karatzas for his assistance with the post-competition experiments.

References

1. Berlin, L.: Accuracy of diagnostic procedures: has it improved over the past five decades? Am. J. Roentgenol. **188**(5), 1173–1178 (2007)

2. Bien, N., et al.: Deep-learning-assisted diagnosis for knee magnetic resonance imaging: development and retrospective validation of MRNet. PLoS Med. 15(11), 1–19 (2018)
3. Chokshi, F.H., Hughes, D.R., Wang, J.M., Mullins, M.E., Hawkins Jr., C.M., Duszak, R.: Diagnostic radiology resident and fellow workloads: a 12-year longitudinal trend analysis using national medicare aggregate claims data. J. Am. Coll. Radiol. 12(7), 664–669 (2015)
4. Deng, J., Dong, W., Socher, R., Li, L.J., Li, K., Fei-Fei, L.: ImageNet: a large-scale hierarchical image database. In: IEEE Conference on Computer Vision and Pattern Recognition, Miami Beach, FL, USA, pp. 248–255 (2009)
5. Eickhoff, C., Schwall, I., de Herrera, A.G.S., Müller, H.: Overview of ImageCLE-Fcaption 2017 - the image caption prediction and concept extraction tasks to understand biomedical images. In: CLEF2017 Working Notes. CEUR Workshop Proceedings. CEUR-WS.org, Dublin (2017). http://ceur-ws.org
6. Esteva, A., et al.: Dermatologist-level classification of skin cancer with deep neural networks. Nature 542(7639), 115–118 (2017)
7. Gonçalves, A.J., Pinho, E., Costa, C.: Informative and intriguing visual features: UA.PT Bioinformatics in ImageCLEF Caption 2019. In: CLEF2019 Working Notes. CEUR Workshop Proceedings, Lugano, Switzerland (2019)
8. Gong, Y., Jia, Y., Leung, T., Toshev, A., Ioffe, S.: Deep convolutional ranking for multilabel image annotation. In: International Conference on Learning Representations (2014)
9. de Herrera, A.G.S., Eickhoff, C., Andrearczyk, V., Müller, H.: Overview of the ImageCLEF 2018 caption prediction tasks. In: CLEF2018 Working Notes. CEUR Workshop Proceedings, CEUR-WS.org, Avignon (2018). http://ceur-ws.org
10. Huang, G., Liu, Z., van der Maaten, L., Weinberger, K.Q.: Densely connected convolutional networks. In: Proceedings of the IEEE Conference on Computer Vision and Pattern Recognition, Honolulu, HI, USA, pp. 4700–4708 (2017)
11. Ionescu, B., et al.: ImageCLEF 2019: multimedia retrieval in medicine, lifelogging, security and nature. In: Crestani, F., et al. (eds.) CLEF 2019. LNCS, vol. 11696, pp. 358–386. Springer, Cham (2019). https://doi.org/10.1007/978-3-030-28577-7_28
12. Irvin, J., et al.: CheXpert: a large chest radiograph dataset with uncertainty labels and expert comparison. arXiv:1901.07031 (2019)
13. Islam, M.T., Aowal, M.A., Minhaz, A.T., Ashraf, K.: Abnormality detection and localization in chest x-rays using deep convolutional neural networks. arXiv:1705.09850 (2017)
14. Jing, B., Xie, P., Xing, E.: On the automatic generation of medical imaging reports. In: Proceedings of the 56th Annual Meeting of the Association for Computational Linguistics (Long Papers), Melbourne, Australia, pp. 2577–2586 (2018)
15. Johnson, A.E., et al.: MIMIC-CXR: a large publicly available database of labeled chest radiographs. arXiv:1901.07042 (2019)
16. Kingma, D.P., Ba, J.: Adam: a method for stochastic optimization. arXiv:1412.6980 (2014)
17. Kougia, V., Pavlopoulos, J., Androutsopoulos, I.: A survey on biomedical image captioning. In: Workshop on Shortcomings in Vision and Language of the Annual Conference of the North American Chapter of the Association for Computational Linguistics, Minneapolis, MN, USA, pp. 26–36 (2019)
18. Kougia, V., Pavlopoulos, J., Androutsopoulos, I.: AUEB NLP group at ImageCLEFmed caption 2019. In: CLEF2019 Working Notes. CEUR Workshop Proceedings, Lugano, Switzerland (2019)

19. Mahajan, D., et al.: Exploring the limits of weakly supervised pretraining. In: Ferrari, V., Hebert, M., Sminchisescu, C., Weiss, Y. (eds.) ECCV 2018. LNCS, vol. 11206, pp. 185–201. Springer, Cham (2018). https://doi.org/10.1007/978-3-030-01216-8_12

20. Pelka, O., Friedrich, C.M., de Herrera, A.G.S., Müller, H.: Overview of the Image-CLEFmed 2019 concept prediction task. In: CLEF2019 Working Notes. CEUR Workshop Proceedings, vol. ISSN 1613–0073. CEUR-WS.org, Lugano (2019). http://ceur-ws.org/Vol-2380/

21. Pelka, O., Koitka, S., Rückert, J., Nensa, F., Friedrich, C.M.: Radiology objects in COntext (ROCO): a multimodal image dataset. In: Stoyanov, D., et al. (eds.) LABELS/CVII/STENT -2018. LNCS, vol. 11043, pp. 180–189. Springer, Cham (2018). https://doi.org/10.1007/978-3-030-01364-6_20

22. Pinho, E., Costa, C.: Feature learning with adversarial networks for concept detection in medical images: UA.PT bioinformatics at ImageCLEF 2018. In: CLEF2018 Working Notes. CEUR Workshop Proceedings, Avignon, France (2018)

23. Rajpurkar, P., et al.: MURA: large dataset for abnormality detection in musculoskeletal radiographs. arXiv:1712.06957 (2017)

24. Rajpurkar, P., Irvin, J., Ball, R.L., Zhu, K., Yang, B., Mehta, H., et al.: Deep learning for chest radiograph diagnosis: a retrospective comparison of the CheXNeXt algorithm to practicing radiologists. PLOS Med. **15**(11), 1–17 (2018)

25. Rajpurkar, P., Irvin, J., Zhu, K., Yang, B., Mehta, H., et al.: CheXNet: radiologist-level pneumonia detection on chest x-rays with deep learning. arXiv:1711.05225 (2017)

26. Rimmer, A.: Radiologist shortage leaves patient care at risk, warns royal college. Br. Med. J. **359** (2017)

27. Rosman, D.A., et al.: Imaging in the land of 1000 hills: Rwanda radiology country report. J. Glob. Radiol. **1**(1), 5 (2015)

28. Shin, H.C., Roberts, K., Lu, L., Demner-Fushman, D., Yao, J., Summers, R.M.: Learning to read chest x-rays: recurrent neural cascade model for automated image annotation. In: IEEE Conference on Computer Vision and Pattern Recognition, Las Vegas, NV, USA, pp. 2497–2506 (2016)

29. Simonyan, K., Zisserman, A.: Very deep convolutional networks for large-scale image recognition. arXiv:1409.1556 (2014)

30. Soldaini, L., Goharian, N.: QuickUMLS: a fast, unsupervised approach for medical concept extraction. In: MedIR Workshop (2016)

31. Valavanis, L., Stathopoulos, S.: IPL at ImageCLEF 2017 concept detection task. In: CLEF CEUR Workshop, Dublin, Ireland (2017)

32. Wang, X., Peng, Y., Lu, L., Lu, Z., Bagheri, M., Summers, R.M.: ChestX-ray8: hospital-scale chest x-ray database and benchmarks on weakly-supervised classification and localization of common thorax diseases. In: Proceedings of the IEEE Conference on Computer Vision and Pattern Recognition, Honolulu, HI, USA, pp. 2097–2106 (2017)

33. Yin, C., et al.: Automatic generation of medical imaging diagnostic report with hierarchical recurrent neural network. In: IEEE International Conference on Data Mining (ICDM), Beijing, China, pp. 728–737 (2019)

34. Zhang, Y., Wang, X., Guo, Z., Li, J.: ImageSem at ImageCLEF 2018 caption task: image retrieval and transfer learning. In: CLEF2018 Working Notes. CEUR Workshop Proceedings, Avignon, France (2018)

CLEF 2020 Lab Overviews

Overview of ARQMath 2020: CLEF Lab on Answer Retrieval for Questions on Math

Richard Zanibbi[1(✉)], Douglas W. Oard[2(✉)], Anurag Agarwal[1], and Behrooz Mansouri[1]

[1] Rochester Institute of Technology, Rochester, NY, USA
{rxzvcs,axasma,bm3302}@rit.edu
[2] University of Maryland, College Park, USA
oard@umd.edu

Abstract. The ARQMath Lab at CLEF considers finding answers to new mathematical questions among posted answers on a community question answering site (Math Stack Exchange). Queries are question posts held out from the searched collection, each containing both text and at least one formula. This is a challenging task, as both math and text may be needed to find relevant answer posts. ARQMath also includes a formula retrieval sub-task: individual formulas from question posts are used to locate formulae in earlier question and answer posts, with relevance determined considering the context of the post from which a query formula is taken, and the posts in which retrieved formulae appear.

Keywords: Community Question Answering (CQA) · Mathematical Information Retrieval · Math-aware search · Math formula search

1 Introduction

In a recent study, Mansouri et al. found that 20% of mathematical queries in a general-purpose search engine were expressed as well-formed questions, a rate ten times higher than that for all queries submitted [14]. Results such as these and the presence of Community Question Answering (CQA) sites such as Math Stack Exchange[1] suggest there is interest in finding answers to mathematical questions posed in natural language, using both text and mathematical notation. Related to this, there has also been increasing work on math-aware information retrieval and math question answering in both the Information Retrieval (IR) and Natural Language Processing (NLP) communities.

In light of this growing interest, we organized this new lab at the Conference and Labs of the Evaluation Forum (CLEF) on Answer Retrieval for Questions about Math (ARQMath).[2] Using the formulae and text in posts from Math

---

[1] https://math.stackexchange.com.
[2] https://www.cs.rit.edu/~dprl/ARQMath.

© Springer Nature Switzerland AG 2020
A. Arampatzis et al. (Eds.): CLEF 2020, LNCS 12260, pp. 169–193, 2020.
https://doi.org/10.1007/978-3-030-58219-7_15

Table 1. Examples of relevant and not-relevant results for tasks 1 and 2 [12]. For Task 2, formulas are associated with posts, indicated with ellipses at right (see Fig. 1 for more details). Query formulae are from question posts (here, the question at left), and retrieved formulae are from either an answer or a question post.

TASK 1: QUESTION ANSWERING	TASK 2: FORMULA RETRIEVAL
QUESTION I have spent the better part of this day trying to show from first principles that this sequence tends to 1. Could anyone give me an idea of how I can approach this problem? $$\lim_{n \to +\infty} n^{\frac{1}{n}}$$	QUERY FORMULA $$\ldots \ \lim_{n \to +\infty} n^{\frac{1}{n}} \ \ldots$$
RELEVANT You can use AM $\geq$ GM. $$\frac{1 + 1 + \cdots + 1 + \sqrt{n} + \sqrt{n}}{n} \geq n^{1/n} \geq 1$$ $$1 - \frac{2}{n} + \frac{2}{\sqrt{n}} \geq n^{1/n} \geq 1$$	RELEVANT $$\ldots \ \lim_{n \to \infty} \sqrt[n]{n} \ \ldots$$
NOT RELEVANT If you just want to show it converges, then the partial sums are increasing but the whole series is bounded above by $$1 + \int_1^\infty \frac{1}{x^2}\,dx = 2$$	NOT RELEVANT $$\ldots \ \sum_{k=1}^\infty \frac{1}{k^2} = \frac{\pi^2}{6} \ \ldots$$

Stack Exchange, participating systems are given a question, and asked to return a ranked list of potential answers. Relevance is determined by how well each returned post answers the provided question. Through this task we explore leveraging math notation together with text to improve the quality of retrieval results. This is one case of what we generically call math retrieval, in which the focus is on leveraging the ability to process mathematical notation to enhance, rather than to replace, other information retrieval techniques. We also included a formula retrieval task, in which relevance is determined by how useful a retrieved formula is for the searcher's intended purpose, as best could be determined from the query formula's associated question post. Table 1 illustrates these two tasks, and Fig. 1 shows the topic format for each task.

For the CQA task, 70,342 questions from 2019 that contained some text and at least one formula were considered as search topics, from which 77 were selected as test topics. Participants had the option to run queries using only the text or math portions of each question, or to use both math and text. One challenge inherent in this design is that the expressive power of text and formulae are sometimes complementary; so although all topics will include both text and formula(s), some may be better suited to text-based or math-based retrieval.

For the formula search task, an individual formula is used as the query, and systems return a ranked list of other potentially useful instances of formulae found in the collection. Each of the 45 queries is a single formula extracted from a question used in the CQA task.

TASK 1: QUESTION ANSWERING

```
<Topics>
  ...
  <Topic number="A.9">
    <Title>Simplifying this series</Title>
    <Question>
      I need to write the series
      <span class=``math-container'' id=``q_52''>
        $$\sum_{n=0}^N nx^n$$
      </span>
      in a form that does not involve the summation
      notation, for example
      <span class=``math-container'' id=``q_53''>
        $\sum_{i=0}^n i^2 = \frac{(n^2+n)(2n+1)}{6}$
      </span>
      Does anyone have any idea how to do this?
      I have attempted multiple ways including using
      generating functions however no luck.
    </Question>
    <Tags>sequences-and-series</Tags>
  </Topic>
  ...
</Topics>
```

TASK 2: FORMULA RETRIEVAL

```
<Topics>
  ...
  <Topic number="B.9">
    <Formula_Id>q_52</Formula_Id>
    <Latex>\sum_{n=0}^N nx^n</Latex>
    <Title>Simplifying this series</Title>
    <Question>
      ...
    </Question>
    <Tags>sequences-and-series</Tags>
  </Topic>
  ...
</Topics>
```

Fig. 1. XML Topic File Formats for Tasks 1 and 2. Formula queries in Task 2 are taken from questions in Task 1. Here, formula topic B.9 is a copy of question topic A.9 with two additional tags for the query formula identifier and LATEX before the question post.

Mathematical problem solving was amongst the earliest applications of Artificial Intelligence, such as Newell and Simon's work on automatic theorem proving [15]. More recent work in math problem solving includes systems that solve algebraic word problems while providing a description of the solution method [11], and that solve algebra word problems expressed in text and math [10]. The focus of ARQMath is different, rather than prove or solve concrete mathematical problems, we instead look to find answers to informal, and potentially open-ended and incomplete questions posted naturally in a CQA setting.

The ARQMath lab provides an opportunity to push mathematical question answering in a new direction, where answers provided by a community are selected and ranked rather than generated. We aim to produce test collections, drive innovation in evaluation methods, and drive innovation in the development of math-aware information retrieval systems. An additional goal is welcoming new researchers to work together on these challenging problems.

2   Related Work

The Mathematical Knowledge Management (MKM) research community is concerned with the representation, application, and search of mathematical information. Among other accomplishments, their activities informed the development of MathML[3] for math on the Web, and novel techniques for math representation, search, and applications such as theorem proving. This community continues to meet annually at the CICM conferences [8].

Math-aware search (sometimes called *Mathematical Information Retrieval*) has seen growing interest over the past decade. Math formula search has been studied since the mid-1990's for use in solving integrals, and publicly available math+text search engines have been around since the DLMF[4] system in the early 2000's [6,21]. The most widely used evaluation resources for math-aware information retrieval were initially developed over a five-year period at the National Institute of Informatics (NII) Testbeds and Community for Information access Research (at NTCIR-10 [1], NTCIR-11 [2] and NTCIR-12 [20]). NTCIR-12 used two collections, one a set of arXiv papers from physics that is split into paragraph-sized documents, and the other a set of articles from English Wikipedia. The NTCIR Mathematical Information Retrieval (MathIR) tasks developed evaluation methods and allowed participating teams to establish baselines for both "text + math" queries (i.e., keywords and formulas) and isolated formula queries.

A recent math question answering task was held for SemEval 2019 [7]. Question sets from MathSAT (Scholastic Achievement Test) practice exams in three categories were used: Closed Algebra, Open Algebra and Geometry. A majority of the questions were multiple choice, with some having numeric answers. This is a valuable parallel development; the questions considered in the CQA task of ARQMath are more informal and open-ended, and selected from actual MSE user posts (a larger and less constrained set).

At NTCIR-11 and NTCIR-12, formula retrieval was considered in a variety of settings, including the use of wildcards and constraints on symbols or subexpressions (e.g., requiring matched argument symbols to be variables or constants). Our Task 2, Formula Retrieval, has similarities in design to the NTCIR-12 Wikipedia Formula Browsing task, but differs in how queries are defined and how evaluation is performed. In particular, for evaluation ARQMath uses the *visually distinct* formulas in a run, rather than all (possibly identical) formula instances, as had been done in NTCIR-12. The NTCIR-12 formula retrieval test collection also had a smaller number of queries, with 20 fully specified formula queries (plus 20 variants of those same queries with subexpressions replaced by wildcard characters). NTCIR-11 also had a formula retrieval task, with 100 queries, but in that case systems searched only for exact matches [19].

Over the years, the size of the NTCIR-12 formula browsing task topic set has limited the diversity of examples that can be studied, and made it difficult to

---

[3] https://www.w3.org/Math.
[4] https://dlmf.nist.gov.

measure statistically significant differences in formula retrieval effectiveness. To support research that is specifically focused on formula similarity measures, we have create a formula search test collection that is considerably larger, and in which the definition of relevance derives from the specific task for which retrieval is being performed, rather than isolated formula queries.

3   The ARQMath 2020 Math Stack Exchange Collection

In this section we describe the raw data from which we started, collection processing, and the resulting test that was used in both tasks. Topic development for each task is described in the two subsequent sections.

3.1   MSE Internet Archive Snapshot

We chose Math Stack Exchange (MSE), a popular community question answering site as the collection to be searched. The Internet Archive provides free public access to MSE snapshots.[5] We processed the 01-March-2020 snapshot, which in its original form contained the following in separate XML files:

- **Posts**: Each MSE post has a unique identifier, and can be a question or an answer, identified by 'post type id' of 1 and 2 respectively. Each question has a title and a body (content of the question) while answers only have a body. Each answer has a 'parent id' that associates it with the question it is an answer is for. There is other information available for each post, including its score, the post owner id and creation date.
- **Comments**: MSE users can comment on posts. Each comment has a unique identifier and a 'post id' indicating which post the comment is written for.
- **Post links**: Moderators sometimes identify duplicate or related questions that have been previously asked. A 'post link type id' of value 1 indicates related posts, while value 3 indicates duplicates.
- **Tags**: Questions can have one or more tags describing the subject matter of the question.
- **Votes**: While the post score shows the difference between up and down votes, there are other vote types such as 'offensive' or 'spam.' Each vote has a 'vote type id' for the vote type and a 'post id' for the associated post.
- **Users**: Registered MSE users have a unique id, and they can provide additional information such as their website. Each user has a reputation score, which may be increased through activities such as posting a high quality answer, or posting a question that receives up votes.
- **Badges**: Registered MSE users can also receive three badge types: bronze, silver and gold. The 'class' attribute shows the type of the badge, value 3 indicating bronze, 2 silver and 1 gold.

The edit history for posts and comments is also available, but for this edition of the ARQMath lab, edit history information has not been used.

---

[5] https://archive.org/download/stackexchange.

3.2   The ARQMath 2020 Test Collection

Because search topics are built from questions asked in 2019, all training and retrieval is performed on content from 2018 and earlier. We removed any data from the collection generated after the year 2018, using the 'creation date' available for each item. The final collection contains roughly 1 million questions and 28 million formulae.

Formulae. While MSE provides a `<math-container>` HTML tag for some mathematical formulae, many are only present as a LaTeX string located between single or double '$' signs. Using the math-container tags and dollar sign delimiters we identified formulae in question posts, answer posts, and comments. Every identified instance of a formula was assigned a unique identifier, and then placed in a `<math-container>` HTML tag using the form:

<span id=FID class="math-container">... </span>

where FID is the formula id. Overall, 28,320,920 formulae were detected and annotated in this way.

Additional Formula Representations. Rather than use raw LaTeX, it is common for math-aware information retrieval systems to represent formulas as one or both of two types of rooted trees. Appearance is represented by the spatial arrangement of symbols on writing lines (in Symbol Layout Trees (SLTs)), and mathematical syntax (sometimes referred to as (shallow) semantics) is represented using a hierarchy of operators and arguments (in Operator Trees (OPTs)) [5,13,23]. The standard representations for these are Presentation MathML (SLT) and Content MathML (OPT). To simplify the processing required of participants, and to maximize comparability across submitted runs, we used LaTeXML[6] to generate Presentation MathML and Content MathML from LaTeX for each formula in the ARQMath collection. Some LaTeX formulas were malformed and LaTeXML has some processing limitations, resulting in conversion failures for 8% of SLTs, and 10% of OPTs. Participants could elect to do their own formula extraction and conversions, although the formulae that could be submitted in system runs for Task 2 were limited to those with identifiers in the LaTeX TSV file.

ARQMath formulae are provided in LaTeX, SLT, and OPT representations, as Tab Separated Value (TSV) index files. Each line of a TSV file represents a single instance of a formula, containing the formula id, the id of the post in which the formula instance appeared, the id of the thread in which the post is located, a post type (title, question, answer or comment), and the formula representation in either LaTeX, SLT (Presentation MathML), or OPT (Content MathML). There are two sets of formula index files: one set is for the collection (i.e., the posts from 2018 and before), and the second set is for the search topics (see below), which are from 2019.

HTML Question Threads. HTML views of threads, similar to those on the MSE web site (a question, along with answers and other related information)

---

[6] https://dlmf.nist.gov/LaTeXML.

are also included in the ARQMath test collection. The threads are constructed automatically from the MSE snapshot XML files described above. The threads are intended for use by teams who performed manual runs, or who wished to examine search results (on queries other than evaluation queries) for formative evaluation purposes. These threads were also used by assessors during evaluation. The HTML thread files were intended only for viewing threads; participants were asked to use the provided XML and formula index files (described above) to train their models.

Distribution. The MSE test collection was distributed to participants as XML files on Google drive.[7] To facilitate local processing, the organizers provided python code on GitHub[8] for reading and iterating over the XML data, and generating the HTML question threads.

4   Task 1: Answer Retrieval

The primary task for ARQMath 2020 was the answer retrieval task, in which participants were presented with a question that had actually been asked on MSE in 2019, and were asked to return a ranked list of up to 1,000 answers from prior years (2010-2018). System results ('runs') were evaluated using rank quality measures (e.g., nDCG'), so this is a ranking task rather than a set retrieval task, and participating teams were not asked to say where the searcher should stop reading. This section describes for Task 1 the search topics (i.e., the questions), the submissions and baseline systems, the process used for creating relevance judgments, the evaluation measures, and the results.

4.1   Topics

In Task 1 participants were given 101 questions as search topics, of which 3 were training examples. These questions are selected from questions asked on MSE in 2019. Because we wished to support experimentation with retrieval systems that use text, math, or both, we chose from only the 2019 questions that contain some text and at least one formula. Because ranking quality measures can distinguish between systems only on topics for which relevant documents exist, we calculated the number of duplicate and related posts for each question and chose only from those that had at least one duplicate or related post.[9] Because we were interested in a diverse range of search tasks, we also calculated the number of formulae and Flesch's Reading Ease score [9] for each question. Finally, we noted the asker's reputation and the tags assigned for each question. We then manually drew a sample of 101 questions that was stratified along those dimensions. In the end, 77 of these questions were evaluated and included in the test collection.

---

[7] https://drive.google.com/drive/folders/1ZPKIWDnhMGRaPNVLi1reQxZWTfH2 R4u3.

[8] https://github.com/ARQMath/ARQMathCode.

[9] Note that participating systems did not have access to this information.

The topics were selected from various domains (real analysis, calculus, linear algebra, discrete mathematics, set theory, number theory, etc.) that represent a broad spectrum of areas in mathematics that might be of interest to expert or non-expert users. The difficulty level of the topics spanned from easy problems that a beginning undergraduate student might be interested in to difficult problems that would be of interest to more advanced users. The bulk of the topics were aimed at the level of undergraduate math majors (in their 3rd or 4th year) or engineering majors fulfilling their math requirements.

Some topics had simple formulae; others had fairly complicated formulae with subscripts, superscripts, and special symbols like the double integral $\iint_V f(x, y)dx \, dy$ or binomial coefficients such as $\binom{n}{r}$. Some topics were primarily based on computational steps, and some asked about proof techniques (making extensive use of text). Some topics had named theorems or concepts (e.g. Cesàro-Stolz theorem, Axiom of choice).

As organizers, we labeled each question with one of three broad categories, *computation*, *concept* or *proof*. Out the 77 assessed questions, 26 were categorized as *computation*, 10 as *concept*, and 41 as *proof*. We also categorized the questions based on their perceived difficulty level, with 32 categorized as easy, 21 as medium, and 24 as hard.

The topics were published as an XML file with the format shown in Fig. 1, where the topic number is an attribute of the Topic tag, and the Title, Question and asker-provided Tags are from the MSE question post. To facilitate system development, we provided python code that participants could use to load the topics. As in the collection, the formulae in the topic file are placed in 'math-container' tags, with each formula instance being represented by a unique identifier and its LATEX representation. And, as with the collection, we provided three TSV files, one each for the LATEX, OPT and SLT representations of the formulae, in the same format as the collection's TSV files.

4.2 Runs Submitted by Participating Teams

Participating teams submitted runs using Google Drive. A total of 18 runs were received from a total of 5 teams. Of these, 17 runs were declared as automatic (meaning that queries were automatically processed from the topic file, that no changes to the system had been made after seeing the queries, and that ranked lists for each query were produced with no human intervention). One run was declared as manual, meaning that there was some type of human involvement in generating the ranked list for each query. Manual runs can contribute diversity to the pool of documents that are judged for relevance, since their error characteristics typically differ from those of automatic runs. All submitted runs used both text and formulae. The teams and submissions are shown in Table 2. Please see the participant papers in the working notes for descriptions of the systems that generated these runs.

Table 2. Submitted Runs for Task 1 (18 runs) and Task 2 (11 runs). Additional baselines for Task 1 (5 runs) and Task 2 (1 run) were also generated by the organizers.

	Automatic Runs		Manual Runs
	Primary	Alternate	Alternate
TASK 1: QUESTION ANSWERING			
Baselines	4		1
DPRL	1	3	
MathDowsers	1	3	1
MIRMU	3	2	
PSU	1	2	
ZBMath			1
TASK 2: FORMULA RETRIEVAL			
Baseline	1		
DPRL	1	3	
MIRMU	2	3	
NLP-NIST	1		
ZBMath			1

4.3 Baseline Runs

As organizers, we ran five baseline systems for Task 1. The first baseline is a TF-IDF (term frequency–inverse document frequency) model using the Terrier system [17]. In the TF-IDF baseline, formulae are represented using their LATEX string. The second baseline is Tangent-S, a formula search engine using SLT and OPT formula representations [5]. One formula was selected from each Task 1 question title if possible; if there was no formula in the title, then one formula was instead chosen from the question's body. If there were multiple formulae in the selected field, the formula with the largest number of nodes in its SLT representation was chosen. Finally, if there were multiple formulae with the highest number of nodes, one of these was chosen randomly. The third baseline is a linear combination of TF-IDF and Tangent-S results. To create this combination, first the relevance scores from both systems were normalized between 0 and 1 using min-max normalization, and then the two normalized scores were combined using an unweighted average.

The TF-IDF baseline used default parameters in Terrier. The second baseline (Tangent-S) retrieves formulae independently for each representation, and then linearly combines SLT and OPT scoring vectors for retrieved formulae [5]. For ARQMath, we used the average weight vector from cross validation results obtained on the NTCIR-12 formula retrieval task.

The fourth baseline was the ECIR 2020 version of the Approach0 text + math search engine [22], using queries manually created by the third and fourth authors. This baseline was not available in time to contribute to the judgment pools and thus was scored post hoc.

The final baseline was built from duplicate post links from 2019 in the MSE collection (which were not available to participants). This baseline returns *all* answer posts from 2018 or earlier that were in threads from 2019 or earlier that MSE moderators had marked as duplicating the question post in a topic. The posts are sorted in descending order by their vote scores.

4.4   Assessment

Pooling. Participants were asked to rank 1,000 (or fewer) answer posts for each Task 1 topic. Top-k pooling was then performed to create pools of answer posts to be judged for relevance to each topic. The top 50 results were combined from all 7 primary runs, 4 baselines, and 1 manual run. To this, we added the top 20 results from each of the 10 automatic alternate runs. Duplicates were then deleted, and the resulting pool was sorted in random order for display to assessors. The pooling process is illustrated in Figure 2. This process was designed to identify as many relevant answer posts as possible given the available assessment resources. On average, pools contained about 500 answers per topic.

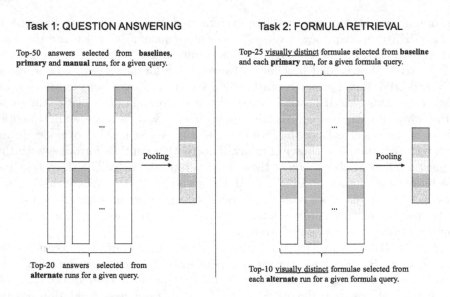

Fig. 2. Pooling Procedures. For Task 1, the pool depth for baselines, primary, and manual runs is 50, and for alternate runs 20. For Task 2 pool depth is the rank at which k visually distinct formulae are observed (25 for primary/baseline, 10 for alternate).

Relevance Definition. Some questions might offer clues as to the level of mathematical knowledge on the part of the person posing the question; others might not. To avoid the need for the assessor to guess about the level of mathematical knowledge available to the person interpreting the answer, we asked assessors to base their judgments on degree of usefulness for an expert (modeled in this case as a math professor) who might then try to use that answer to help the person who had asked the original question. We defined four levels of relevance, as shown in Table 3.

Table 3. Relevance Scores, Ratings, and Definitions for Tasks 1 and 2

		TASK 1: QUESTION ANSWERING
SCORE	RATING	DEFINITION
3	High	Sufficient to answer the complete question on its own
2	Medium	Provides some path towards the solution. This path might come from clarifying the question, or identifying steps towards a solution
1	Low	Provides information that could be useful for finding or interpreting an answer, or interpreting the question
0	Not Relevant	Provides no information pertinent to the question or its answers. A post that restates the question without providing any new information is considered non-relevant

		TASK 2: FORMULA RETRIEVAL
SCORE	RATING	DEFINITION
3	High	Just as good as finding an exact match to the query formula would be
2	Medium	Useful but not as good as the original formula would be
1	Low	There is some chance of finding something useful
0	Not Relevant	Not expected to be useful

Assessors were allowed to consult external sources on their own in order to familiarize themselves with the topic of a question, but the relevance judgments for each answer post were performed using only information available within the collection. For example, if an answer contained an MSE link such as https://math.stackexchange.com/questions/163309/pythagorean-theorem, they could follow that link to better understand the intent of the person writing the answer, but an external link to the Wikipedia page https://en.wikipedia.org/wiki/Pythagorean_theorem would not be followed.

Training Set. The fourth author created a small set of relevance judgment files for three topics. We used duplicate question links to find possibly relevant answers, and then performed relevance judgments on the same 0, 1, 2 and 3 scale that was later used by the assessors. We referred to this as a 'training set,' although in practice such a small collection is at best a sanity check to see if systems were producing reasonable results. Moreover, these relevance judgments were performed before assessor training had been conducted, and thus the definition of relevance used by the fourth author may have differed in subtle ways from the definitions on which the assessors later settled.

Assessment System. Assessments were performed using Turkle[10], a locally installed system with functionality similar to Amazon Mechanical Turk. Turkle uses an HTML task template file, plus a Comma Separate Value (CSV) file to fill HTML templates for each topic. Each row in the CSV file contains the question title, body, and the retrieved answer to be judged. Judgments are exported as CSV files.

As Fig. 4 (at the end of this document) illustrates, there were two panels in the Turkle user interface. The question was shown on the left panel, with the Title on top (in a grey bar); below that was the question body. There was also a Thread link, on which assessors could click to look at the MSE post in context, with the question and all of the answers that were actually given for this question (in 2019). This could help the assessor to better understand the question. In the right panel, the answer to be judged was shown at the top. As with the question, there was a thread link where the assessors could click to see the original thread in which the answer post being judged had been present in MSE. This could be handy when the assessors wanted to see details such as the question that had been answered at the time. Finally, the bottom of the right panel (below the answer) was where assessors selected relevance ratings. In addition to four levels of relevance, two additional choices were available. 'System failure' indicated system issues such as unintelligible rendering of formulae, or the thread link not working (when it was essential for interpretation). If after viewing the threads, the assessors were still not able to decide the relevance degree, they were asked to choose 'Do not know'. The organizers asked the assessors to leave a comment in the event of a system failure or a 'Do no know' selection.

Assessor Training. Eight paid undergraduate mathematics students (or, in three cases, recent graduates with an undergraduate mathematics degree) were paid to perform relevance judgments. Four rounds of training were performed before submissions from participating teams had been received. In the first round, assessors met online using Zoom with the organizers, one of whom (the third author) is an expert MSE user and a Professor of mathematics. The task was explained, making reference to specific examples from the small training set. For each subsequent round, a small additional training set was created using a similar approach (pooling only answers to duplicate questions) with 8 actual Task 1 topics (for which the actual relevance judgments were not then known). The same 8 topics were assigned to every assessor and the assessors worked independently, thus permitting inter-annotator agreement measures to be computed. Each training round was followed by an online meeting with the organizers using Zoom at which assessors were shown cases in which one or more assessor pairs disagreed. They discussed the reasoning for their choices, with the third author offering reactions and their own assessment. These training judgments were not used in the final collection, but the same topic could later be reassigned to one of the assessors to perform judgments on a full pool.

---

[10] https://github.com/hltcoe/turkle.

Some of the question topics would not be typically covered in regular undergraduate courses, so that was a challenge that required the assessors to get a basic understanding of those topics before they could do the assessment. The assessors found the questions threads made available in the Turkle interface helpful in this regard (see Fig. 4).

Through this process the formal definition of each relevance level in Table 3 was sharpened, and we sought to help assessors internalize a repeatable way of making self-consistent judgments that were reasonable in the view of the organizers. Judging relevance is a task that calls for interpretation and formation of a personal opinion, so it was not our goal to achieve identical decisions. We did, however, compute Cohen's Kappa for the three independently conducted rounds of training to check whether reasonable levels of agreement were being achieved. As Fig. 3 shows, kappa of 0.34 was achieved by the end of training on the four-way assessment task. Collapsing relevance to be binary by considering high and medium as relevant and low and not-relevant as a not-relevant (henceforth "H+M binarization") yielded similar results.[11]

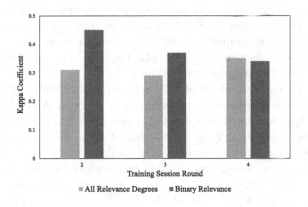

Fig. 3. Inter-annotator agreement (kappa) over 8 assessors during Task 1 training (8 topics per round); four-way classification (gray) and two-way (H+M binarized) classification (black).

Assessment. A total of 80 questions were assessed for Task 1. Three judgment pools (for topics A2, A22, and A70) had zero or one posts with relevance ratings of high or medium; these 3 topics were removed from the collection because

---

[11] H+M binarization corresponds to the definition of relevance usually used in the Text Retrieval Conference (TREC). The TREC definition is "If you were writing a report on the subject of the topic and would use the information contained in the document in the report, then the document is relevant. Only binary judgments ("relevant" or "not relevant") are made, and a document is judged relevant if any piece of it is relevant (regardless of how small the piece is in relation to the rest of the document)." (source: https://trec.nist.gov/data/reljudge_eng.html).

topics with no relevant posts can not be used to distinguish between ranked retrieval systems, and topics with only a single relevant post result in coarsely quantized values for H+M binarized evaluation measures, and that degree of quantization can adversely affect the ability to measure statistically significant differences. For the remaining 77 questions, an average of 508.5 answers were assessed for each question, with an average assessment time of 63.1 seconds per answer post. The average number of answers labeled with any degree of relevance (high, medium, or low; henceforth "H+M+L binarization") was 52.9 per question, with the highest number of relevant answers being 188 (for topic A.38) and the lowest being 2 (for topic A.96).

4.5 Evaluation Measures

One risk when performing a new task for which rich training data is not yet available is that a larger than typical number of relevant answers may be missed. Measures which treat unjudged documents as not relevant can be used when directly comparing systems that contributed to the judgment pools, but subsequent use of such a first-year test collection (e.g., to train new systems for the second year of the lab) can be disadvantaged by treating unjudged documents (which as systems improve might actually be relevant) as not relevant. We therefore chose the nDCG' measure (read as "nDCG-prime") introduced by Sakai and Kando [18] as the primary measure for the task.

The nDCG measure on which nDCG' is based is a widely used measure when graded relevance judgments are available, as we have in ARQMath, that produced a single figure of merit over a set of ranked lists. Each retrieved document earns a gain value of (0, 1, 2, or 3) discounted by a slowly decaying function of the rank position of each document. The resulting discounted gain values are accumulated and then normalized to [0,1] by dividing by the maximum possible Discounted Cumulative Gain (i.e., from all identified relevant documents, sorted by decreasing order of gain value). This results in normalized Discounted Cumulative Gain (nDCG). The only difference when computing nDCG' is that unjudged documents are removed from the ranked list before performing the computation. It has been shown that nDCG' has somewhat better discriminative power and somewhat better system ranking stability (with judgement ablation) than the bpref measure [4] used recently for formula search (e.g., [13]). Moreover, nDCG' yields a single-valued measure with graded relevance, whereas bpref, Precision@k, and Mean Average Precision (MAP) all require binarized relevance judgments. In addition to nDCG', we also compute Mean Average Precision (MAP) with unjudged posts removed (thus MAP'), and Precision at 10 posts (P@10).[12] For MAP' and P@10 we used H+M binarization. We removed

---

[12] Pooling to at least depth 20 ensures that there are no unjudged posts above rank 10 for any primary or secondary submission, and for four of the five baselines. Note, however, that P@10 can not achieve a value of 1 because some topics have fewer than 10 relevant posts.

unjudged posts as a preprocessing step where required, and then computed the evaluation measures using trec_eval.[13]

4.6 Results

Table 4 in the appendix shows the results, with baselines shown first, and then teams and their systems ranked by nDCG$'$. nDCG$'$ values can be interpreted as the average (over topics) of the fraction of the score for the best possible that was actually achieved. As can be seen, the best nDCG$'$ value that was achieved was 0.345, by the MathDowsers team. For measures computed using H+M binarization we can see that MAP$'$ and P@10 generally show system comparison patterns similar to those of nDCG$'$, although with some differences in detail.

5 Task 2: Formula Retrieval

In the formula retrieval task, participants were presented with one formula from a 2019 question used in Task 1, and asked to return a ranked list of up to 1,000 formula instances from questions or answers from the evaluation epoch (2018 or earlier). Formulae were returned by their identifiers in `math-container` tags and the companion TSV LaTeX formula index file, along with their associated post identifiers.

This task is challenging because someone searching for math formulae may have goals not evident from the formula itself. For example:

– They may be looking to learn what is known, to form connections between disciplines, or to discover solutions that they can apply to a specific problem.
– They may want to find formulae of a specific form, including details such as specific symbols that have significance in a certain context, or they may wish to find related work in which similar ideas are expressed using different notation. For example, the Schrödinger equation is written both as a wave equation and as a probability current (the former is used in Physics, whereas the latter is used in the study of fluid flow).
– They may be happy to find formulae that contain only part of their formula query, or they may want only complete matches. For example, searching for $\sum_{i=1}^{n} u_i v_i$ could bring up the Cauchy-Schwarz inequality $\sum_{i=1}^{n} u_i v_i \leq \left(\sum_{i=1}^{n} u_i^2\right)^{\frac{1}{2}} \left(\sum_{i=1}^{n} v_i^2\right)^{\frac{1}{2}}$.

For these reasons (among others), it is difficult to formulate relevance judgments for retrieved formulae without access to the context in which the formula query was posed, and to the context in which each formula instance returned as a potentially useful search result was expressed.

Three key details differentiate Task 2 from Task 1. First, in Task 1 only answer posts were returned, but for Task 2 the formulae may appear in answer posts or in question posts. Second, for Task 2 we distinguish visually distinct formulae from instances of those formulae, and evaluate systems based on the

---

[13] https://github.com/usnistgov/trec_eval.

ranking of the visually distinct formulae that they return. We call formulae appearing in posts *formula instances*, and of course the same formula may appear in more than one post. By *formula,* we mean a set of formula instances that are visually identical when viewed in isolation. For example, x^2 is a formula, $x * x$ is a different formula, and each time x^2 appears is a distinct instance of the formula x^2. Systems in Task 2 rank formula instances in order to support the relevance judgment process, but the evaluation measure for Task 2 is based on the ranking of visually distinct formulae. The third difference between Task 1 and Task 2 is that in Task 2 the goal is not answering questions, but rather, to show the searcher formulae that might be useful to them as they seek to satisfy their information need. Task 2 is thus still grounded in the question, but the relevance of a retrieved formula is defined by the formula's expected utility, not just the post in which that one formula instance was found.

As with Task 1, ranked lists were evaluated using rank quality measures, making this a ranking task rather than a set retrieval task. Unlike Task 1, the design of which was novel, a pre-existing training set for a similar task (the NTCIR-12 Wikipedia Formula Browsing task test collection [20]) was available to participants. However, we note that the definition of relevance used in Task 2 differs from the definition of relevance in the NTCIR-12 task. This section describes for Task 2 the search topics, the submissions and baselines, the process used for creating relevance judgments, the evaluation measures, and the results.

5.1 Topics

In Task 2, participating teams were given 87 mathematical formulae, each found in a different question from Task 1 from 2019, and they were asked to find relevant formulae instances from either question or answer posts in the test collection (from 2018 and earlier). The topics for Task 2 were provided in an XML file similar to those of Task 1, in the format shown in Fig. 1. Task 2 topics differ from their corresponding Task 1 topics in three ways:

1. **Topic number**: For Task 2, topic ids are in form "B.x" where x is the topic number. There is a correspondence between topic id in tasks 1 and 2. For instance, topic id "B.9" indicates the formula is selected from topic "A.9" in Task 1, and both topics include the same question post (see Fig. 1).
2. **Formula_Id**: This added field specifies the unique identifier for the query formula instance. There may be other formulae in the Title or Body of the question post, but the query is only the formula instance specified by this Formula_Id.
3. **LaTeX**: This added field is the LaTeX representation of the query formula instance as found in the question post.

Because query formulae are drawn form Task 1 question posts, the same LaTeX, SLT and OPT TSV files that were provided for the Task 1 topics can be consulted when SLT or OPT representations for a query formula are needed.

Formulae for Task 2 were manually selected using a heuristic approach to stratified sampling over three criteria: complexity, elements, and text dependence. Formulae complexity was labeled low, medium or high by the fourth author. For example, $\frac{df}{dx} = f(x+1)$ is low complexity, $\sum_{k=0}^{n} \binom{n}{k} k$ is medium complexity, and $x - \frac{x^3}{3 \times 3!} + \frac{x^5}{5 \times 5!} - \frac{x^7}{7 \times 7!} + \cdots = \sum_{n=0}^{\infty} (-1)^n \frac{x^{(2n+1)}}{(2n+1) \times (2n+1)!}$ is high complexity. Mathematical elements such as limit, integral, fraction or matrix were manually noted by the fourth author when present. Text dependence reflected the fourth author's opinion of the degree to which text in the Title and Question fields were likely to yield related search results. For instance, for one Task 2 topic, the query formula is $\frac{df}{dx} = f(x + 1)$ whereas the complete question is: "How to solve differential equations of the following form: $\frac{df}{dx} = f(x + 1)$." When searching for this formula, perhaps the surrounding text could safely be ignored. At most one formula was selected from each Task 1 question topic to produce Task 2 topics. In 12 cases, it was decided that no formula in a question post would be a useful query for Task 2, and thus 12 Task 1 queries have no corresponding Task 2 query.

5.2 Runs Submitted by Participating Teams

A total of 11 runs were received for Task 2 from a total of 4 teams, as shown in Table 2. All were automatic runs. Each run contains at most 1,000 formula instances for each query formula, ranked in decreasing order of system-estimated relevance to that query. For each formula instance in a ranked list, participating teams provided the formula_id and the associated post_id for that formula. Please see the participant papers in the working notes for descriptions of the systems that generated these runs.

5.3 Baseline Runs

We again used Tangent-S [5] as our baseline. Unlike Task 1, a single formula is specified for each Task 2 query, so no formula selection step was needed. This Tangent-S baseline makes no use of the question text.

5.4 Assessment

Pooling. The retrieved items for Task 2 are formula instances, but pooling was done based on visually distinct formulae, not formula instances (see Fig. 2). This was done by first clustering all formula instances from all submitted runs to identify visually distinct formulae, and then proceeding down each list until at least one instance of some number of different formulae had been seen. For primary runs and for the baseline run, the pool depth was the rank of the first instance of the 25th visually distinct formula; for secondary runs the pool depth was the rank of the first instance of the 10th visually distinct formulae. Additionally, a pool depth of 1,000 (i.e., all available formulae) was used for any formula for which the associated answer post had been marked as relevant for Task 1.[14] This was the only way in which the post ids for answer posts was used.

Clustering visually distinct formulae instances was performed using the SLT representation when possible, and the LaTeX representation otherwise. We first converted the Presentation MathML representation to a string representation using Tangent-S, which performed a depth-first traversal of the SLT, with each SLT node generating a single character of the SLT string. Formula instances with identical SLT strings were considered to be the same formula; note that this ignores differences in font. For formula instances with no Tangent-S SLT string available, we removed the white space from their LaTeX strings and grouped formula instances with identical strings. This process is simple and appears to have been reasonably robust for our purposes, but it is possible that some visually identical formula instances were not captured due to LaTeXML conversion failures, or where different LaTeX string produce the same formula (e.g., if subscripts and superscripts appear in a different order).

Assessment was done on formula instances, so for each formula we selected at most five instances to assess. We selected the 5 instances that were contributed to the pools by the largest number of runs, breaking ties randomly. Out of 5,843 visually distinct formulae that were assessed, 93 (1.6%) had instances in more than 5 pooled posts.

Relevance Definition. The relevance judgment task was defined for assessors as follows: for a formula query, if a search engine retrieved one or more instances of this retrieved formula, would that have been expected to be useful for the task that the searcher was attempting to accomplish?

Assessors were presented with formula instances, and asked to decide their relevance by considering whether retrieving either that instance or some other instance of that formula would have been useful, assigning each formula instance in the judgment pool one of four scores as defined in Table 3.

For example, if the formula query was $\sum \frac{1}{n^{2+\cos n}}$, and the formula instance to be judged is $\sum_{n-1}^{\infty} \frac{1}{n^2}$, the assessors would decide whether finding the second formula rather than the first would be expected to yield good results. To do this, they would consider the content of the question post containing the query (and, optionally, the thread containing that question post) in order to understand the searcher's actual information need. Thus the question post fills a role akin to Borlund's simulated work task [3], although in this case the title, body and tags from the question post are included in the topic and thus can optionally be used by the retrieval system. The assessor can also consult the post containing a retrieved formula instance (which may be another question post or an answer post), along with the associated thread, to see if in that case the formula instance would indeed have been a useful basis for a search. Note, however, that the assessment task is not to determine whether the specific post containing the retrieved formula instance is useful, but rather to use that context as a basis for

---

[14] One team submitted incorrect post id's for retrieved formulae; those post id's were not used for pooling.

estimating the degree to which useful content would likely be found if this or other instances of the retrieved formula were returned by a search engine.

We then defined the relevance score for a formula to be the maximum relevance score for any judged instance of that formula. This relevance definition essentially asks "if instances of this formula were returned, would we reasonably expect some of those instances to be useful?" This definition of relevance might be used by system developers in several ways. One possibility is using Task 2 relevance judgments to train a formula matching component for use in a Task 1 system. A second possibility is using these relevance judgments to train and evaluate a system for interactively suggesting alternative formulae to users.[15]

Assessment System. As in Task 1, we used Turkle to build the assessment system. As shown in Fig. 4 (at the end of this document), there are two main panels. In the left panel, the question is shown as in Task 1, but now with the formula query highlighted in yellow. In the right panel, up to five retrieval posts (question posts or answer posts) containing instances of the same retrieved formula are displayed, with the retrieved formula instance highlighted in each case. For example, the formula $\sum_{n=1}^{\infty} a_n$ shown in Fig. 4 was retrieved both in an answer post (shown first) and in a question post (shown second). As in Task 1, buttons are provided for the assessor to record their judgment; unlike Task 1, judgments for each instance of the same retrieved formula (up to 5) are recorded separately, and later used to produce a *single* (max) score for each visually distinct formula.

Assessor Training. After some initial work on assessment for Task 1, 3 assessors were reassigned to perform relevance judgements for Task 2, with the remaining 5 continuing to do relevance judgments for Task 1. Two rounds of training were performed.

In the first training round, the assessors were familiarized with the task. To illustrate how formula search might be used, we interactively demonstrated formula suggestion in MathDeck [16] and the formula search capability of Approach0 [23]. Then the task was defined using examples, showing a formula query with some retrieved results, talking through the relevance definitions and how to apply those definitions in specific cases. During the training session, the assessors saw different example results for topics and discussed their relevance based on criteria defined for them with the organizers. They also received feedback from the third author, an expert MSE user. To prepare the judgment pools used for this purpose, we pooled actual submissions from participating teams, but only to depth 10 (i.e., 10 different formulae) for primary runs and the baseline run, and 5 different formulae for alternate runs. The queries used for this initial assessor training were omitted from the final Task 2 query set on which systems were evaluated because they were not judged on full-sized pools.

All three assessors were then assigned two complete Task 2 pools (for topics B.46 and B.98) to independently assess; these topics were not removed from

---

[15] See, for example, MathDeck [16], in which candidate formulae are suggested to the users during formula editing.

the collection. After creating relevance judgments for these full-sized pools, the assessors and organizers met by Zoom to discuss and resolve disagreements. The assessors used this opportunity to refine their understanding of the relevance criteria, and the application of those criteria to specific cases. Annotator agreement was found to be fairly good (kappa = 0.83). An adjudicated judgment was recorded for each disagreement, and used in the final relevance judgment sets for these two topics.

The assessors were then each assigned complete pools to judge for four topics, one of which was also assessed independently by a second assessor. The average kappa on the three dual-assessed topics was 0.47. After discussion between the organizers and the assessors, adjudicated disagreements were recorded and used in the final relevance judgments. The assessors then performed the remaining assessments for Task 2 independently.

Assessment. A total of 47 topics were assessed for Task 2. Two queries (B.58 and B.65) had fewer than two relevant answers after H+M binarization and were removed. Of the remaining 45 queries, an average of 125.0 formulae were assessed per topic, with an average assessment time of 38.1 seconds per formulae. The average number of formulae instances labeled as relevant after H+M+L binarization was 43.1 per topic, with the highest being 115 for topic B.60 and the lowest being 7 for topics B.56 and B.32.

5.5   Evaluation Measures

As for Task 1, the primary evaluation measure for Task 2 is nDCG$'$, and MAP$'$ and P@10 were also computed. Participants submitted ranked lists of formula instances, but we computed these measures over visually distinct formulae. To do this, we replaced each formula instance with its associated visually distinct formula, then deduplicated from the top of the list downward to obtain a ranked list of visually distinct formulae, and then computed the evaluation measures. As explained above, the relevance score for each visually distinct formula was computed as the maximum score over each assessed instance of that formula.

5.6   Results

Table 5 in the appendix shows the results, with the baseline run shown first, and then teams and their systems ranked by nDCG$'$. No team did better than the baseline system as measured by nDCG$'$ or MAP$'$, although the DPRL team did achieve the highest score for P@10.

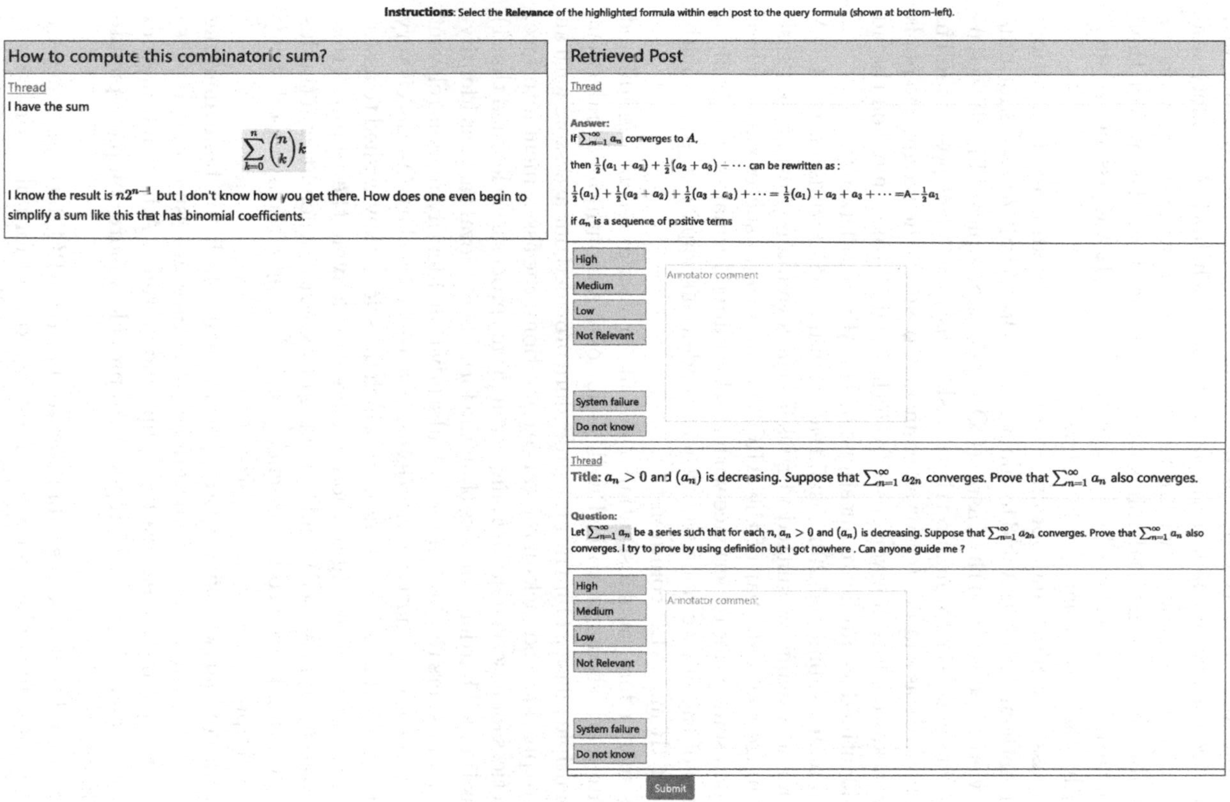

Instructions: Select the **Relevance** of the highlighted formula within each post to the query formula (shown at bottom-left).

How to compute this combinatoric sum?

Thread
I have the sum

$$\sum_{k=0}^{n} \binom{n}{k} k$$

I know the result is $n2^{n-1}$ but I don't know how you get there. How does one even begin to simplify a sum like this that has binomial coefficients.

Retrieved Post

Thread

Answer:
If $\sum_{n=1}^{\infty} a_n$ converges to A,

then $\frac{1}{2}(a_1 + a_2) + \frac{1}{4}(a_3 + a_4) \cdots$ can be rewritten as :

$\frac{1}{2}(a_1) + \frac{1}{2}(a_2 + a_3) + \frac{1}{2}(a_4 + a_5) + \cdots = \frac{1}{2}(a_1) + a_2 + a_4 + \cdots = A - \frac{1}{2}a_1$

If a_n is a sequence of positive terms

- High
- Medium
- Low
- Not Relevant

Annotator comment

- System failure
- Do not know

Thread
Title: $a_n > 0$ and (a_n) is decreasing. Suppose that $\sum_{n=1}^{\infty} a_{2n}$ converges. Prove that $\sum_{n=1}^{\infty} a_n$ also converges.

Question:
Let $\sum_{n=1}^{\infty} a_n$ be a series such that for each n, $a_n > 0$ and (a_n) is decreasing. Suppose that $\sum_{n=1}^{\infty} a_{2n}$ converges. Prove that $\sum_{n=1}^{\infty} a_n$ also converges. I try to prove by using definition but I got nowhere. Can anyone guide me ?

- High
- Medium
- Low
- Not Relevant

Annotator comment

- System failure
- Do not know

Submit

Fig. 4. Turkle Assessment Interface. Shown are hits for Formula Retrieval (Task 2). In the right panel, the formula query is highlighted. In the left panel, one answer post and one question post containing the same retrieved formula are shown. For Task 1, a similar interface was used, but without formula highlighting, and just one returned answer post viewed at a time.

6 Conclusion

The ARQMath lab is the first shared-task evaluation exercise to explore Community Question Answering (CQA) for mathematical questions. Additionally, the lab introduced a new formula retrieval task in which both the query and retrieved formulae are considered within the context of their question or answer posts, and evaluation is performed using visually distinct formulas, rather than all formulas returned in a run. For both tasks, we used posts and associated data from the Math Stack Exchange (MSE) CQA forum.

To reduce assessor effort and obtain a better understanding of the relationship between mathematical CQA and formula search, the formulae used as formula search topics were selected from the Task 1 (CQA) question topics. This allowed us to increase coverage for the formula retrieval task by using relevant posts found in the CQA evaluations as candidates for assessment. To enrich the judgments pools for the CQA task, we added answer posts from the original topic question thread and threads identified as duplicate questions by the MSE moderators.

In total, 6 teams submitted 29 runs: 5 teams submitted 18 runs for the CQA task (Task 1), and 4 teams submitted 11 runs for the formula retrieval task (Task 2). We thus judge the first year of the ARQMath lab to be successful. Each of these teams had some prior experience with math-aware information retrieval; in future editions of the lab we hope to further broaden participation, particularly from the larger IR and NLP communities.

Our assessment effort was substantial: 8 paid upper-year or recently graduated undergraduate math students worked with us for over a month, and underwent training in multiple phases. Our training procedure provided our assessors with an opportunity to provide feedback on relevance definitions, the assessment interface, and best practices for assessment. In going through this process, we learned that 1) the CQA task is much harder to assess than the formula retrieval task, as identifying non-relevant answers requires more careful study than identifying non-relevant formulae, 2) the breadth of mathematical expertise needed for the CQA task is very high; this led us to having assessors indicate which questions they wished to assess and us assigning topics according to those preferences (leaving the 10 topics that no assessor requested unassessed), and 3) having an expert mathematician (in this case, a math Professor) involved was essential for task design, clarifying relevance definitions, and improving assessor consistency.

To facilitate comparison with systems using ARQMath for benchmarking in the future, and to make use of our graded relevance assessments, we chose nDCG' [18] as the primary measure for comparing systems. Additional metrics (MAP' and Precision at 10) are also reported to provide a more complete picture of system differences.

Overall, we found that systems submitted to the first ARQMath lab generally approached the task in similar ways, using both text and formulae for Task 1, and (with two exceptions) operating fully automatically. In future editions of the task, we hope to see a greater diversity of goals, with, for example, systems optimized for specific types of formulae, or systems pushing the state of the art for the use of text queries to find math. We might also consider supporting a broad range of more specialized investigations by, for example, creating subsets of the collection that are designed specifically to formula variants such as simplified forms or forms using notation conventions from different disciplines. Our present collection includes user-generated tags, but we might also consider defining a well-defined tag set to indicate which of these types of results are desired.

Acknowledgements. Wei Zhong suggested using Math Stack Exchange for benchmarking, made Approach0 available for participants, and provided helpful feedback. Kenny Davila helped with the Tangent-S formula search results. We also thank our student assessors from RIT: Josh Anglum, Wiley Dole, Kiera Gross, Justin Haverlick, Riley Kieffer, Minyao Li, Ken Shultes, and Gabriella Wolf. This material is based upon work supported by the National Science Foundation (USA) under Grant No. IIS-1717997 and the Alfred P. Sloan Foundation under Grant No. G-2017-9827.

A   Appendix: Evaluation Results

Table 4. Task 1 (CQA) results, averaged over 77 topics. **P** indicates a primary run, **M** indicates a manual run, and ($\checkmark$) indicates a baseline pooled at the primary run depth. For Precision@10 and MAP, H+M binarization was used. The best baseline results are in parentheses. * indicates that one baseline did not contribute to judgment pools.

Run	Data	Run Type		Evaluation Measures		
		P	M	NDCG$'$	MAP$'$	P@10
Baselines						
Linked MSE posts	n/a	($\checkmark$)		(0.279)	(0.194)	(0.384)
Approach0 *	Both		$\checkmark$	0.250	0.099	0.062
TF-IDF + Tangent-S	Both	($\checkmark$)		0.248	0.047	0.073
TF-IDF	Text	($\checkmark$)		0.204	0.049	0.073
Tangent-S	Math	($\checkmark$)		0.158	0.033	0.051
MathDowsers						
alpha05noReRank	Both			**0.345**	**0.139**	**0.161**
alpha02	Both			0.301	0.069	0.075
alpha05translated	Both		$\checkmark$	0.298	0.074	0.079
alpha05	Both	$\checkmark$		0.278	0.063	0.073
alpha10	Both			0.267	0.063	0.079
PSU						
PSU1	Both			0.263	0.082	0.116
PSU2	Both	$\checkmark$		0.228	0.054	0.055
PSU3	Both			0.211	0.046	0.026
MIRMU						
Ensemble	Both			0.238	0.064	0.135
SCM	Both	$\checkmark$		0.224	0.066	0.110
MIaS	Both	$\checkmark$		0.155	0.039	0.052
Formula2Vec	Both			0.050	0.007	0.020
CompuBERT	Both	$\checkmark$		0.009	0.000	0.001
DPRL						
DPRL4	Both			0.060	0.015	0.020
DPRL2	Both			0.054	0.015	0.029
DPRL1	Both	$\checkmark$		0.051	0.015	0.026
DPRL3	Both			0.036	0.007	0.016
zbMATH						
zbMATH	Both	$\checkmark$	$\checkmark$	0.042	0.022	0.027

Table 5. Task 2 (Formula Retrieval) results, averaged over 45 topics and computed over deduplicated ranked lists of visually distinct formulae. **P** indicates a primary run, and (✓) shows the baseline pooled at the primary run depth. For MAP and P@10, relevance was thresholded H+M binarization. All runs were automatic. Baseline results are in parentheses.

RUN	DATA	P	EVALUATION MEASURES		
			NDCG′	MAP′	P@10
Baseline					
Tangent-S	Math	(✓)	**(0.506)**	**(0.288)**	**(0.478)**
DPRL					
TangentCFTED	Math	✓	**0.420**	**0.258**	**0.502**
TangentCFT	Math		0.392	0.219	0.396
TangentCFT+	Both		0.135	0.047	0.207
MIRMU					
SCM	Math		0.119	0.056	0.058
Formula2Vec	Math	✓	0.108	0.047	0.076
Ensemble	Math		0.100	0.033	0.051
Formula2Vec	Math		0.077	0.028	0.044
SCM	Math	✓	0.059	0.018	0.049
NLP_NITS					
formulaembedding	Math	✓	0.026	0.005	0.042

References

1. Aizawa, A., Kohlhase, M., Ounis, I.: NTCIR-10 math pilot task overview. In: NTCIR (2013)
2. Aizawa, A., Kohlhase, M., Ounis, I., Schubotz, M.: NTCIR-11 Math-2 task overview. In: NTCIR, vol. 11, pp. 88–98 (2014)
3. Borlund, P.: The IIR evaluation model: a framework for evaluation of interactive information retrieval systems. Inf. Res. **8**(3) (2003)
4. Buckley, C., Voorhees, E.M.: Retrieval evaluation with incomplete information. In: Proceedings of the 27th Annual International ACM SIGIR Conference on Research and Development in Information Retrieval, pp. 25–32 (2004)
5. Davila, K., Zanibbi, R.: Layout and semantics: combining representations for mathematical formula search. In: Proceedings of the 40th International ACM SIGIR Conference on Research and Development in Information Retrieval, pp. 1165–1168 (2017)
6. Guidi, F., Sacerdoti Coen, C.: A survey on retrieval of mathematical knowledge. In: Kerber, M., Carette, J., Kaliszyk, C., Rabe, F., Sorge, V. (eds.) CICM 2015. LNCS (LNAI), vol. 9150, pp. 296–315. Springer, Cham (2015). https://doi.org/10.1007/978-3-319-20615-8_20
7. Hopkins, M., Le Bras, R., Petrescu-Prahova, C., Stanovsky, G., Hajishirzi, H., Koncel-Kedziorski, R.: SemEval-2019 task 10: math question answering. In: Proceedings of the 13th International Workshop on Semantic Evaluation (2019)

8. Kaliszyk, C., Brady, E., Kohlhase, A., Sacerdoti Coen, C. (eds.): CICM 2019. LNCS (LNAI), vol. 11617. Springer, Cham (2019). https://doi.org/10.1007/978-3-030-23250-4

9. Kincaid, J.P., Fishburne Jr., R.P., Rogers, R.L., Chissom, B.S.: Derivation of new readability formulas (automated readability index, fog count and Flesch reading ease formula) for Navy enlisted personnel. Technical report, Naval Technical Training Command Millington TN Research Branch (1975)

10. Kushman, N., Artzi, Y., Zettlemoyer, L., Barzilay, R.: Learning to automatically solve algebra word problems. In: Proceedings of the 52nd Annual Meeting of the Association for Computational Linguistics (2014)

11. Ling, W., Yogatama, D., Dyer, C., Blunsom, P.: Program induction by rationale generation: learning to solve and explain algebraic word problems. In: Proceedings of the 55th Annual Meeting of the Association for Computational Linguistics (2017)

12. Mansouri, B., Agarwal, A., Oard, D., Zanibbi, R.: Finding old answers to new math questions: the ARQMath lab at CLEF 2020. In: Jose, J.M., et al. (eds.) ECIR 2020. LNCS, vol. 12036, pp. 564–571. Springer, Cham (2020). https://doi.org/10.1007/978-3-030-45442-5_73

13. Mansouri, B., Rohatgi, S., Oard, D.W., Wu, J., Giles, C.L., Zanibbi, R.: Tangent-CFT: an embedding model for mathematical formulas. In: Proceedings of the 2019 ACM SIGIR International Conference on Theory of Information Retrieval (ICTIR), pp. 11–18 (2019)

14. Mansouri, B., Zanibbi, R., Oard, D.W.: Characterizing searches for mathematical concepts. In: Joint Conference on Digital Libraries (2019)

15. Newell, A., Simon, H.: The logic theory machine-a complex information processing system. IRE Trans. Inf. Theory 2, 61–79 (1956)

16. Nishizawa, G., Liu, J., Diaz, Y., Dmello, A., Zhong, W., Zanibbi, R.: MathSeer: a math-aware search interface with intuitive formula editing, reuse, and lookup. In: Jose, J.M., et al. (eds.) ECIR 2020. LNCS, vol. 12036, pp. 470–475. Springer, Cham (2020). https://doi.org/10.1007/978-3-030-45442-5_60

17. Ounis, I., Amati, G., Plachouras, V., He, B., Macdonald, C., Johnson, D.: Terrier information retrieval platform. In: Losada, D.E., Fernández-Luna, J.M. (eds.) ECIR 2005. LNCS, vol. 3408, pp. 517–519. Springer, Heidelberg (2005). https://doi.org/10.1007/978-3-540-31865-1_37

18. Sakai, T., Kando, N.: On information retrieval metrics designed for evaluation with incomplete relevance assessments. Inf. Retrieval 11(5), 447–470 (2008). https://doi.org/10.1007/s10791-008-9059-7

19. Schubotz, M., Youssef, A., Markl, V., Cohl, H.S.: Challenges of mathematical information retrieval in the NTCIR-11 Math Wikipedia Task. In: SIGIR, pp. 951–954. ACM (2015)

20. Zanibbi, R., Aizawa, A., Kohlhase, M., Ounis, I., Topic, G., Davila, K.: NTCIR-12 MathIR task overview. In: NTCIR (2016)

21. Zanibbi, R., Blostein, D.: Recognition and retrieval of mathematical expressions. Int. J. Doc. Anal. Recognit. (IJDAR) 15(4), 331–357 (2012). https://doi.org/10.1007/s10032-011-0174-4

22. Zhong, W., Rohatgi, S., Wu, J., Giles, C.L., Zanibbi, R.: Accelerating substructure similarity search for formula retrieval. In: Jose, J.M., et al. (eds.) ECIR 2020. LNCS, vol. 12035, pp. 714–727. Springer, Cham (2020). https://doi.org/10.1007/978-3-030-45439-5_47

23. Zhong, W., Zanibbi, R.: Structural similarity search for formulas using leaf-root paths in operator subtrees. In: Azzopardi, L., Stein, B., Fuhr, N., Mayr, P., Hauff, C., Hiemstra, D. (eds.) ECIR 2019. LNCS, vol. 11437, pp. 116–129. Springer, Cham (2019). https://doi.org/10.1007/978-3-030-15712-8_8

Overview of BioASQ 2020: The Eighth BioASQ Challenge on Large-Scale Biomedical Semantic Indexing and Question Answering

Anastasios Nentidis[1,2]([✉]), Anastasia Krithara[1], Konstantinos Bougiatiotis[1,3], Martin Krallinger[4], Carlos Rodriguez-Penagos[4], Marta Villegas[4], and Georgios Paliouras[1]

[1] National Center for Scientific Research "Demokritos", Athens, Greece
{tasosnent,akrithara,bogas.ko,paliourg}@iit.demokritos.gr
[2] Aristotle University of Thessaloniki, Thessaloniki, Greece
[3] National and Kapodistrian University of Athens, Athens, Greece
[4] Barcelona Supercomputing Center, Barcelona, Spain
{martin.krallinger,carlos.rodriguez1,marta.villegas}@bsc.es

Abstract. In this paper, we present an overview of the eighth edition of the BioASQ challenge, which ran as a lab in the Conference and Labs of the Evaluation Forum (CLEF) 2020. BioASQ is a series of challenges aiming at the promotion of systems and methodologies for large-scale biomedical semantic indexing and question answering. To this end, shared tasks are organized yearly since 2012, where different teams develop systems that compete on the same demanding benchmark datasets that represent the real information needs of experts in the biomedical domain. This year, the challenge has been extended with the introduction of a new task on medical semantic indexing in Spanish. In total, 34 teams with more than 100 systems participated in the three tasks of the challenge. As in previous years, the results of the evaluation reveal that the top-performing systems managed to outperform the strong baselines, which suggests that state-of-the-art systems keep pushing the frontier of research through continuous improvements.

Keywords: Biomedical knowledge · Semantic indexing · Question answering

1 Introduction

This paper aims at presenting the shared tasks and the datasets of the eighth BioASQ challenge in 2020, as well as at providing an overview of the participating systems and their performance. Towards this direction, in Sect. 2 we provide an overview of the shared tasks, that took place from February to May 2020, and the corresponding datasets developed for the challenge. In Sect. 3, we present

© Springer Nature Switzerland AG 2020
A. Arampatzis et al. (Eds.): CLEF 2020, LNCS 12260, pp. 194–214, 2020.
https://doi.org/10.1007/978-3-030-58219-7_16

a brief overview of the systems developed by the participating teams for the different tasks. Detailed descriptions for some of the systems are available in the proceedings of the lab. In Sect. 4, we focus on evaluating the performance of the systems for each task and sub-task, using state-of-the-art evaluation measures or manual assessment. Finally, in Sect. 5, we sum up this version of the BioASQ challenge.

2 Overview of the Tasks

This year, the eighth version of the BioASQ challenge comprised three tasks: (1) a large-scale biomedical semantic indexing task (task 8a) (2) a biomedical question answering task (task 8b), both considering documents in English, and (3) a new task on medical semantic indexing in Spanish (task MESINESP). In this section we provide a brief description of the two established tasks with focus on differences from previous versions of the challenge [30]. A detailed overview of these tasks and the general structure of BioASQ are available in [43]. In addition, we describe the new MESINESP task on semantic indexing of medical content written in Spanish (medical literature abstracts, clinical trial summaries and health-related project descriptions), which was introduced this year [21], providing statistics about the dataset developed for it.

2.1 Large-Scale Semantic Indexing - Task 8a

In Task 8a the aim is to classify articles from the PubMed/MedLine[1] digital library into concepts of the MeSH hierarchy. In particular, new PubMed articles that are not yet annotated by the indexers in NLM are gathered to form the test sets for the evaluation of the participating systems. Some basic details about each test set and batch are provided in Table 1. As done in previous versions of the task, the task is divided into three independent batches of 5 weekly test sets each, providing an on-line and large-scale scenario, and the test sets consist of new articles without any restriction on the journal published. The performance of the participating systems is calculated using standard flat information retrieval measures, as well as, hierarchical ones, when the annotations from the NLM indexers become available. As usual, participants have 21 h to provide their answers for each test set. However, as it has been observed that new MeSH annotations are released in PubMed earlier that in previous years, we shifted the submission period accordingly to avoid having some annotations available from NLM while the task is still running. For training, a dataset of 14,913,939 articles with 12.68 labels per article, on average, was provided to the participants.

---

[1] https://pubmed.ncbi.nlm.nih.gov/.

Table 1. Statistics on test datasets for Task 8a.

Batch	Articles	Annotated articles	Labels per article
1	6510	6487	12.49
	7126	7074	12.27
	10891	10789	12.55
	6225	6182	12.28
	6953	6887	12.75
Total	37705	37419	0.99
2	6815	6787	12.49
	6485	6414	12.52
	7014	6975	11.92
	6726	6647	12.90
	6379	6246	12.45
Total	33419	33069	0.99
3	6842	6601	12.70
	7212	6456	12.37
	5430	4764	12.59
	6022	4858	12.33
	5936	3999	12.21
Total	31442	26678	0.85

2.2 Biomedical Semantic QA - Task 8b

Task 8b aims at providing a realistic large-scale question answering challenge offering to the participating teams the opportunity to develop systems for all the stages of question answering in the biomedical domain. Four types of questions are considered in the task: "yes/no", "factoid", "list" and "summary" questions [4]. A training dataset of 3,243 questions annotated with golden relevant elements and answers is provided for the participants to develop their systems. Table 2 presents some statistics about the training dataset as well as the five test sets.

Table 2. Statistics on the training and test datasets of Task 8b. The numbers for the documents and snippets refer to averages per question.

Batch	Size	Yes/No	List	Factoid	Summary	Documents	Snippets
Train	3,243	881	644	941	777	10.15	12.92
Test 1	100	25	20	32	23	3.45	4.51
Test 2	100	36	14	25	25	3.86	5.05
Test 3	100	31	12	28	29	3.35	4.71
Test 4	100	26	17	34	23	3.23	4.38
Test 5	100	34	12	32	22	2.57	3.20
Total	3,743	1033	719	1092	899	9.23	11.78

As in previous versions of the challenge, the task is structured into two phases that focus on the retrieval of the required information (phase A) and answering the question (phase B). In addition, the task is split into five independent bi-weekly batches and the two phases for each batch run during two consecutive days. In each phase, the participants receive the corresponding test set and have 24 h to submit the answers of their systems. In particular, in phase A, a test set of 100 questions written in English is released and the participants are expected to identify and submit relevant elements from designated resources, including PubMed/MedLine articles, snippets extracted from these articles, concepts and RDF triples. In phase B, the manually selected relevant articles and snippets for these 100 questions are also released and the participating systems are asked to respond with *exact answers*, that is entity names or short phrases, and *ideal answers*, that is natural language summaries of the requested information.

2.3   Medical Semantic Indexing in Spanish - MESINESP8

There is a pressing need to improve the access to information comprised in health and biomedicine related documents, not only by professional medical users buy also by researches, public healthcare decision makers, pharma industry and particularly by patients. Currently, most of the Biomedical NLP and IR research is being done on content in English, despite the fact that a large volume of medical documents is published in other languages including Spanish. Key resources like PubMed focus primarily on data in English, but it provides outlinks also to articles originally published in Spanish. MESINESP attempts to promote the development of systems for automatic indexing with structured medical vocabularies (DeCS terms) of healthcare content in Spanish: IBECS[2], LILACS[3], REEC[4] and FIS-ISCIII[5]. The main aim of MESINESP is to promote the development of semantic indexing tools of practical relevance of non-English content, determining the current-state-of-the art, identifying challenges and comparing the strategies and results to those published for English data. This task was organized within the framework of the Spanish Government's Plan for Promoting Language Technologies (Plan TL), that aims to promote the development of natural language processing, machine translation and conversational systems in Spanish and co-official languages.

---

[2] IBECS includes bibliographic references from scientific articles in health sciences published in Spanish journals. http://ibecs.isciii.es.

[3] LILACS is the most important and comprehensive index of scientific and technical literature of Latin America and the Caribbean. It includes 26 countries, 882 journals and 878,285 records, 464,451 of which are full texts https://lilacs.bvsalud.org.

[4] Registro Español de Estudios Clínicos, a database containing summaries of clinical trials https://reec.aemps.es/reec/public/web.html.

[5] Public healthcare project proposal summaries (Proyectos de Investigación en Salud, diseñado por el Instituto de Salud Carlos III, ISCIII) https://portalfis.isciii.es/es/Paginas/inicio.aspx.

A training dataset with 369,368 articles manually annotated with DeCS codes (*Descriptores en Ciencias de la Salud*, derived and extended from MeSH terms)[6] was released. 1,500 articles were manually annotated and verified at least by two human experts (from a pool of 7 annotators), and from them a development and gold standard for evaluation were generated. A further background dataset was produced from diverse sources, including machine-translated text. Consistently, the different collections averaged, per document, around 10 sentences, 13 DeCS codes, and 300 words, of which between 130 and 140 were unique ones.

In order to explore the diversity of content from this dataset, we generated clusters of semantically similar records from the training dataset's titles by, first, creating a Doc2Vec model with the gensim library,[7] and then using that similarity matrix to feed an unsupervised DBScan algorithm from the sklearn python package,[8] that basically creates clusters from high density samples. The resulting 27 clusters were visualized with the libraries from the Carrot Workbench project.[9] (Fig. 1).

Fig. 1. Content visualization of MESINESP training dataset using clustering techniques. Among subjects shown: clinical cases, non-Spanish languages, medication and device reviews, health care management etc. This reflects DeCS extension from MeSH terms to other subjects, such as Public Health issues.

---

[6] 29,716 come directly from MeSH and 4,402 are exclusive to DeCS.
[7] https://radimrehurek.com/gensim/.
[8] https://scikit-learn.org/.
[9] https://project.carrot2.org/.

3   Overview of Participation

3.1   Task 8a

This year, 7 teams participated in the eighth edition of task a, submitting predictions from 16 different systems in total. Here, we provide a brief overview of those systems for which a description was available, stressing their key characteristics. A summing-up of the participating systems and corresponding approaches is presented in Table 3.

Table 3. Systems and approaches for Task 8a. Systems for which no description was available at the time of writing are omitted.

System	Approach
X-BERT BioASQ	X-BERT, Transformers ELMo, MER
NLM CNN	SentencePiece, CNN, embeddings, ensembles
dmiip_fdu	d2v, tf-idf, SVM, KNN, LTR, DeepMeSH, AttentionXML, BERT, PLT
Iria	Luchene Index, k-NN, stem bigrams, ensembles, UIMA ConceptMapper

This year, the LASIGE team from the University of Lisboa, in its "X-BERT BioASQ" system propose a novel approach for biomedical semantic indexing combining a solution based on Extreme Multi-Label Classification (XMLC) with a Named-Entity-Recognition (NER) tool. In particular, their system is based on X-BERT [7], an approach to scale BERT [12] to XMLC, combined with the use of the MER [10] tool to recognize MeSH terms in the abstracts of the articles. The system is structured into three steps. The first step is the semantic indexing of the labels into clusters using ELMo [36]; then a second step matches the indices using a Transformer architecture; and finally, the third step focuses on ranking the labels retrieved from the previous indices.

Other teams, improved upon existing systems already participating in previous versions of the task. Namely, the National Library of Medicine (NLM) team, in its "NLM CNN" system enhance the previous version of their "ceb" systems [37], based on an end-to-end Deep Learning (DL) architecture with Convolutional Neural Networks (CNN), with SentencePiece tokenization [22]. The Fudan University team also builds upon their previous "AttentionXML" [50] and "DeepMeSH" [35] systems as well their new "BERTMeSH" system, which are based on document to vector (d2v) and tf-idf feature embeddings, learning to rank (LTR) and DL-based extreme multi-label text classification, Attention

Mechanisms and Probabilistic Label Trees (PLT) [16]. Finally, this years versions of the *"Iria"* systems [40] are also based on the same techniques used by the systems in previous versions of the challenge which are summarized in Table 3.

Similarly to the previous versions of the challenge, two systems developed by NLM to facilitate the annotation of articles by indexers in MedLine/PubMed, where available as baselines for the semantic indexing task. MTI [29] as enhanced in [51] and an extension based on features suggested by the winners of the first version of the task [44].

3.2 Task 8b

This version of Task b was tackled by 94 different systems in total, developed by 23 teams. In particular, 8 teams participated in the first phase, on the retrieval of relevant material required for answering the questions, submitting results from 30 systems. In the second phase, on providing the exact and ideal answers for the questions, participated 18 teams with 72 distinct systems. Three of the teams participated in both phases. An overview of the technologies employed by the teams is provided in Table 4 for the systems for which a description were available. Detailed descriptions for some of the systems are available at the proceedings of the workshop.

The *"ITMO"* team participated in both phases of the task experimenting in its "pa" systems with differing solutions across the batches. In general, for document retrieval the systems follow an approach with two stages. First, they identify initial candidate articles based on BM25, and then they re-rank them using variations of BERT [12], fine-tuned for the binary classification task with the BioASQ dataset and pseudo-negative documents. They extract snippets from the top documents and rerank them using biomedical Word2Vec based on cosine similarity with the question. To extract exact answers they use BERT fine-tuned on SQUAD [38] and BioASQ datasets and employ a post-processing to split the answer for list questions and additional fine-tuning on PubMedQA [17] for yes/no questions. Finally, for ideal answers they generate some candidates from the snippets and their sentences and rerank them using the model used for phase A. In the last batch, they also experiment with generative summarization, developing a model based on BioMed-RoBERTa [15] to improve the readability and consistency of the produced ideal answers.

Another team participating in both phases of the task is the *"UCSD"* team with its "bio-answerfinder" system. In particular, for phase A they rely on previously developed Bio-AnswerFinder system [32], which is also used as a first step in phase B, for re-ranking the sentences of the snippets provided in the test set. For identifying the exact answers for factoid and list questions they experimented on fine-tuning Electra [8] and BioBERT [23] on SQuAD and BioASQ datasets combined. The answer candidates are then scored considering classification probability, the top ranking of corresponding snippets and number of occurrences. Finally a normalization and filtering step is performed and, for list questions, and enrichment step based on coordinated phrase detection. For

Table 4. Systems and approaches for Task8b. Systems for which no information was available at the time of writing are omitted.

Systems	Phase	Approach
pa	A, B	BM25, BERT, Word2Vec, SQuAD, PubMedQA, BioMed-RoBERTa
bio-answerfinder	A, B	Bio-AnswerFinder, LSTM, ElasticSearch, BERT, Electra, BioBERT, SQuAD, wRWMD
Google	A	BM25, BioBERT, Synthetic Query Generation, BERT, reranking
bioinfo	A	BM25, ElasticSearch, distant learning, DeepRank
KU-DMIS	B	BioBERT, NLI, MultiNLI, SQuAD, BART, beam search, BERN, language_check
NCU-IISR	B	BioBERT, logistic regression, LTR
UoT	B	BioBERT, multi-task learning, BC2GM
BioNLPer	B	BioBERT, multi-task learning, NLTK, ScispaCy
LabZhu	B	BERT, BoiBERT, XLNet, SpanBERT, transfer learning, SQuAD, ensembling
MQ	B	Word2Vec, BERT, LSTM, Reinforcement Learning (PPO)
DAIICT	B	textrank, lexrank, UMLS
sbert	B	Sentence-BERT, BioBERT, SNLI, MutiNLI, multi-task learning, MQU

yes/no questions they fine-tune BioBERT on the BioASQ dataset and use majority voting. For summary questions, they employ hierarchical clustering, based on weighted relaxed word mover's distance (wRWMD) similarity [32] to group the top sentences, and select the sentence ranked highest by Bio-AnswerFinder to be concatenated to form the summary.

In phase A, the *"Google"* team participated with four distinct systems based on different approaches. In particular, they used a BM25 retrieval model, a neural retrieval model, initialized with BioBERT and trained on a large set of questions developed through Synthetic Query Generation (QGen), and a hybrid retrieval model[10] based on a linear blend of BM25 and the neural model [26]. In addition, they also used a reranking model, rescoring the results of the hybrid model with a cross-attention BERT rescorer [34]. The team from the University of Aveiro, also participated in phase A with its "bioinfo" systems, which consists of a fine-tuned BM25 retrieval model based on ElasticSearch [14], followed by a neural reranking step. For the latter, they use an interaction-based model inspired on the DeepRank [33] architecture building upon previous versions of their sys-

---

[10] https://ai.googleblog.com/2020/05/an-nlu-powered-tool-to-explore-covid-19.html.

tem [2]. The focus of the improvements was on the sentence splitting strategy, on extracting of multiple relevance signals, and the independent contribution of each sentence for the final score.

In phase B, this year the "*KU-DMIS*" team participated on both exact and ideal answers. For exact answers, they build upon their previous BioBERT-based systems [49] and try to adapt the sequential transfer learning of Natural Language Inference (NLI) to biomedical question answering. In particular, they investigate whether learning knowledge of entailment between two sentence pairs can improve exact answer generation, enhancing their BioBERT-based models with alternative fine-tuning configurations based on the MultiNLI dataset [46]. For ideal answer generation, they develop a deep neural abstractive summarization model based on BART [24] and beam search, with particular focus on pre-processing and post-processing steps. In particular, alternative systems were developed either considering the answers predicted by the exact answer prediction system in their input or not. In the post-processing step, the generated candidate ideal answers for each question where scored using the predicted exact answers and some grammar scores provided by the language-check tool[11]. For factoid and list questions in particular, the BERN [19] tool was also employed to recognize named entities in the candidate ideal answers for the scoring step.

The "*NCU-IISR*" team also participated in both parts of phase B, constructing two BioBERT-based models for extracting the exact answer and ranking the ideal answers respectively. The first model is fine-tuned on the BioASQ dataset formulated as a SQuAD-type QA task that extracts the answer span. For the second model, they regard the sentences of the provided snippets as candidate ideal answers and build a ranking model with two parts. First, a BioBERT-based model takes as input the question and one of the snippet sentences and provides their representation. Then, a logistic regressor, trained on predicting the similarity between a question and each snippet sentence, takes this representation and outputs a score, which is used for selecting the final ideal answer.

The "*UoT*" team participated with three different DL approaches for generating exact answers. In their first approach, they fine-tune separately two distinct BioBERT-based models extended with an additional neural layer depending on the question type, one for yes/no and one for factoid and list questions together. In their second system, they use a joint-learning setting, where the same BioBERT layer is connected with both the additional layers and jointly trained for all types of questions. Finally, in their third system they propose a multi-task model to learn recognizing biomedical entities and answers to questions simultaneously, aiming at transferring knowledge from the biomedical entity recognition task to question answering. In particular, they extend their joint BioBERT-based model with simultaneous training on the BC2GM dataset [42] for recognizing gene and protein entities.

---

[11] https://pypi.org/project/language-check/.

The "*BioNLPer*" team also participated in the exact answers part of phase B, focusing on factoids. They proposed 5 BioBERT-based systems, using external feature enhancement and auxiliary task methodologies. In particular, in their "factoid qa model" and "Parameters retrained" systems they consider the prediction of answer boundaries (start and end positions) as the main task and the whole answer content prediction as an auxiliary task. In their "Features Fusion" system they leveraged external features including NER and part-of-speach (POS) extracted by NLTK [25] and ScispaCy [31] tools as additional textual information and fused them with the pre-trained language model representations, to improve answer boundary prediction. Then, in their "BioFusion" system they combine the two methodologies together. Finally, their "BioLabel" system employed the general and biomedical domain corpus classification as the auxiliary task to help answer boundary prediction.

The "LabZhu" systems also participated in phase B, with focus on exact answers for the factoid and list questions. They treat answer generation as an extractive machine comprehension task and explore several different pretrained language models, including BERT, BioBERT, XLNet [47] and SpanBERT [18]. They also follow a transfer learning approach, training the models on the SQuAD dataset, and then fine-tuning them on the BioASQ datasets. Finally, they also rely on voting to integrate the results of multiple models.

The "*MQ*" team, as in past years, focused on ideal answers, approaching the task as query-based summarisation. In some of their systems the retrain their previous classification and regression approaches [28] in the new training dataset. In addition, they also employ reinforcement learning with Proximal Policy Optimization (PPO) [41] and two variants to represent the input features, namely Word2Vec-based and BERT-based embeddings. The "*DAIICT*" team also participated in ideal answer generation, using the standard extractive summarization techniques textrank [27] and lexrank [13] as well as sentence selection techniques based on their similarity with the query. They also modified these techniques investigating the effect of query expansion based on UMLS [5] for sentence selection and summarization.

Finally, the "*sbert*" team, also focused on ideal answers. They experimented with different embedding models and multi-task learning in their systems, using parts from previous "*MQU*" systems for the pre-processing of data and the prediction step based on classification and regression [28]. In particular, they used a Universal Sentence Embedding Model [9] (BioBERT-NLI[12]) based on a version of BioBERT fine-tuned on the SNLI [6] and the MultiNLI datasets as in Sentence-BERT [39]. The features were fed to either a single logistic regression or classification model to derive the ideal answers. Additionally, in a multi-task setting, they trained the model on both the classification and regression tasks, selecting for the final prediction one of them.

---

[12] https://huggingface.co/gsarti/biobert-nli.

Table 5. Systems and approaches for Task MESINESP8. Systems for which no description was available at the time of writing are omitted.

System	Approach
Iria	bigrams, Luchene Index, k-NN, ensembles, UIMA ConceptMapper
Fudan University	AttentionXML with multilingual-BERT
Alara (UNED)	Frequency graph matching
Priberam	BERT based classifier, and SVM-rank ensemble
LASIGE	X-BERT, Transformers ELMo, MER

In this challenge too, the open source OAQA system proposed by [48] served as baseline for phase B exact answers. The system which achieved among the highest performances in previous versions of the challenge remains a strong baseline for the exact answer generation task. The system is developed based on the UIMA framework. ClearNLP is employed for question and snippet parsing. MetaMap, TmTool [45], C-Value and LingPipe [3] are used for concept identification and UMLS Terminology Services (UTS) for concept retrieval. The final steps include identification of concept, document and snippet relevance based on classifier components and scoring and finally ranking techniques.

3.3   Task MESINESP8

For the newly introduced MESINESP8 task, 6 teams from China, India, Portugal and Spain participated and results from 24 different systems were submitted. The approaches were similar to the comparable English task, and included KNN and Support Vector Machine classifiers, as well as deep learning frameworks like X-BERT and multilingual-BERT, already described in Subsect. 3.1 (Table 5). A simple lookup system was provided as a baseline for the MESINESP task. This system extracts information from an annotated list. Then checks whether, in a set of text documents, the annotation are present. It basically gets the intersection between tokens in annotations and tokens in words. This simple approach obtains a MiF of 0.2695.

4   Results

4.1   Task 8a

In Task 8a, each of the three batches were independently evaluated as presented in Table 6. Standard flat and hierarchical evaluation measures [4] were used for measuring the classification performance of the systems. In particular, the micro F-measure (MiF) and the Lowest Common Ancestor F-measure (LCA-F) were used to identify the winners for each batch [20]. As suggested by Demar [11], the appropriate way to compare multiple classification systems over multiple datasets is based on their average rank across all the datasets. In this task, the system with the best performance in a test set gets rank 1.0 for this test set, the second best rank 2.0 and so on. In case two or more systems tie, they all receive the average rank. Then, according to the rules of the challenge, the average rank of each system for a batch is calculated based on the four best ranks of the system in the five test sets of the batch. The average rank of each system, based on both the flat MiF and the hierarchical LCA-F scores, for the three batches of the task are presented in Table 6.

Table 6. Average system ranks across the batches of the task 8a. A hyphenation symbol (-) is used whenever the system participated in fewer than 4 test sets in the batch. Systems participating in fewer than 4 test sets in all three batches are omitted.

System	Batch 1		Batch 2		Batch 3	
	MiF	LCA-F	MiF	LCA-F	MiF	LCA-F
deepmesh_dmiip_fdu	**1.25**	**2.25**	1.875	3.25	2.25	2.25
deepmesh_dmiip_fdu_	2.375	3.625	**1.25**	**1.25**	1.75	2
attention_dmiip_fdu	3	**2.25**	3.5	3.125	3	3.25
Default MTI	4.75	3.75	6	5.25	6	5.5
MTI First Line Index	5.5	4.5	6.75	5.875	5.75	5.25
dmiip_fdu	–	–	2.375	1.625	**1.5**	**1.25**
NLM CNN	–	–	5	6.75	5.5	7
iria-mix	–	–	–	–	8.25	8.25
iria-1	–	–	–	–	9.25	9.25
X-BERT BioASQ	–	–	–	–	10.75	10.75

The results in Task 8a show that in all test batches and for both flat and hierarchical measures, the best systems outperform the strong baselines. In particular, the *"dmiip_fdu"* systems from the Fudan University team achieve the best performance in all three batches of the task. More detailed results can be found in the online results page[13]. Comparing these results with the corresponding results from previous versions of the task, suggests that both the MTI baseline and the top performing systems keep improving through the years of the challenge, as shown in Fig. 2.

---

[13] http://participants-area.bioasq.org/results/8a/.

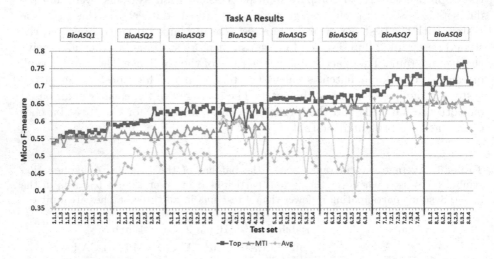

Fig. 2. The micro f-measure (MiF) achieved by systems across different years of the BioASQ challenge. For each test set the MiF score is presented for the best performing system (Top) and the MTI, as well as the average micro f-measure of all the participating systems (Avg).

Table 7. Results for document retrieval in batch 2 of phase A of Task 8b. Only the top-15 systems are presented.

System	Mean precision	Mean recall	Mean F-measure	MAP	GMAP
pa	**0.1934**	0.4501	**0.2300**	**0.3304**	0.0185
AUEB-System1	0.1688	**0.4967**	0.2205	0.3181	0.0165
bioinfo-3	0.1500	0.4880	0.2027	0.3168	**0.0223**
bioinfo-1	0.1480	0.4755	0.1994	0.3149	0.0186
bioinfo-4	0.1500	0.4787	0.2002	0.3120	0.0161
AUEB-System2	0.1618	0.4864	0.2126	0.3103	0.0149
bioinfo-2	0.1420	0.4648	0.1914	0.3084	0.0152
bioinfo-0	0.1380	0.4341	0.1830	0.2910	0.0117
AUEB-System5	0.1588	0.4549	0.2057	0.2843	0.0116
Ir_sys4	0.1190	0.4179	0.1639	0.2807	0.0056
Google-AdHoc-MAGLEV	0.1310	0.4364	0.1770	0.2806	0.0109
Ir_sys2	0.1190	0.4179	0.1639	0.2760	0.0055
Google-AdHoc-BM25	0.1324	0.4222	0.1758	0.2718	0.0088
AUEB-System3	0.1688	**0.4967**	0.2205	0.2702	0.0146
Ir_sys3	0.1325	0.3887	0.1730	0.2678	0.0045

Table 8. Results for snippet retrieval in batch 2 of phase A of Task 8b.

System	Mean precision	Mean recall	Mean F-measure	MAP	GMAP
AUEB-System1	**0.1545**	0.2531	**0.1773**	**0.6821**	0.0015
AUEB-System2	0.1386	0.2260	0.1609	0.6549	0.0011
pa	0.1348	**0.2578**	0.1627	0.3374	**0.0047**
bioinfo-4	0.1308	0.2009	0.1413	0.2767	0.0016
bioinfo-1	0.1373	0.2103	0.1461	0.2721	0.0016
bioinfo-2	0.1299	0.2018	0.1408	0.2637	0.0011
bioinfo-3	0.1321	0.2004	0.1404	0.2607	0.0014
MindLab QA System	0.0811	0.1454	0.0916	0.2449	0.0005
MindLab Red Lions++	0.0830	0.1469	0.0932	0.2394	0.0005
AUEB-System5	0.0943	0.1191	0.0892	0.2217	0.0011
MindLab QA Reloaded	0.0605	0.1103	0.0691	0.2106	0.0002
Deep ML methods for	0.0815	0.0931	0.0811	0.2051	0.0001
bioinfo-0	0.1138	0.1617	0.1175	0.1884	0.0009
MindLab QA System ++	0.0639	0.0990	0.0690	0.1874	0.0001
AUEB-System3	0.0966	0.1285	0.0935	0.1556	0.0011
bio-answerfinder	0.0910	0.1617	0.1004	0.1418	0.0008
AUEB-System4	0.0080	0.0082	0.0077	0.0328	0.0000

4.2   Task 8b

Phase A: In the first phase of Task 8b, the systems are ranked according to the Mean Average Precision (MAP) measure for each of the four types of annotations, namely documents, snippets, concepts and RDF triples. This year, the calculation of Average Precision (AP) in MAP for phase A was reconsidered as described in the official description of the evaluation measures for Task 8b[14]. In brief, since BioASQ3, the participant systems are allowed to return up to 10 relevant items (e.g. documents), and the calculation of AP was modified to reflect this change. However, the number of golden relevant items in the last years have been observed to be lower than 10 in some cases, resulting to relatively small AP values even for submissions with all the golden elements. For this reason, this year, we modified the MAP calculation to consider both the limit of 10 elements and the actual number of golden elements. In Tables 7 and 8 some indicative preliminary results from batch 2 are presented. The full results are available in the online results page of Task 8b, phase A[15]. The results presented here are preliminary, as the final results for the task 8b will be available after the manual assessment of the system responses by the BioASQ team of biomedical experts.

Phase B: In the second phase of task 8b, the participating systems were expected to provide both exact and ideal answers. Regarding the ideal answers,

---

[14] http://participants-area.bioasq.org/Tasks/b/eval_meas_2020/.
[15] http://participants-area.bioasq.org/results/8b/phaseA/.

Table 9. Results for batch 3 for exact answers in phase B of Task 8b. Only the performance of the top-20 systems and the BioASQ Baseline are presented.

System	Yes/No		Factoid			List		
	Acc.	F1	Str. Acc.	Len. Acc.	MRR	Prec.	Rec.	F1
Umass_czi_5	**0.9032**	0.8995	0.2500	0.4286	0.3030	**0.7361**	0.4833	**0.5229**
Umass_czi_1	0.8065	0.8046	0.2500	0.3571	0.2869	0.6806	0.4444	0.4683
Umass_czi_2	0.8387	0.8324	0.2500	0.3571	0.2869	0.6806	0.4444	0.4683
pa-base	**0.9032**	0.8995	0.2500	0.4643	0.3137	0.5278	0.4778	0.4585
pa	**0.9032**	0.8995	0.2500	0.4643	0.3137	0.5278	0.4778	0.4585
Umass_czi_4	**0.9032**	0.9016	**0.3214**	0.4643	0.3810	0.6111	0.4361	0.4522
KU-DMIS-1	**0.9032**	**0.9028**	**0.3214**	0.4286	0.3601	0.6583	0.4444	0.4520
KU-DMIS-4	0.8387	0.8360	0.2857	0.4286	0.3357	0.6167	0.4444	0.4490
KU-DMIS-5	**0.9032**	**0.9028**	**0.3214**	0.4643	0.3565	0.6167	0.4444	0.4490
KU-DMIS-2	0.8710	0.8697	**0.3214**	0.4286	0.3446	0.6028	0.4444	0.4467
KU-DMIS-3	0.8387	0.8360	0.2500	0.4643	0.3357	0.6111	0.4444	0.4431
UoT_allquestions	0.5806	0.3673	**0.3214**	0.3929	0.3423	0.5972	0.4111	0.4290
UoT_baseline	0.5806	0.3673	**0.3214**	0.3929	0.3512	0.4861	0.4056	0.4214
Best factoid	0.5806	0.4732	0.2857	0.3929	0.3333	0.5208	0.4056	0.4107
bio-answerfinder	0.8710	0.8640	**0.3214**	0.4286	0.3494	0.3884	**0.5083**	0.4078
FudanLabZhu2	0.7419	0.6869	**0.3214**	0.5357	**0.3970**	0.5694	0.3583	0.3988
FudanLabZhu3	0.7419	0.6869	**0.3214**	0.4643	0.3655	0.5583	0.3472	0.3777
FudanLabZhu4	0.7419	0.6869	0.2857	**0.5714**	0.3821	0.5583	0.3472	0.3777
FudanLabZhu5	0.7419	0.6869	**0.3214**	0.4286	0.3690	0.5583	0.3472	0.3777
UoT_multitask_1	0.5161	0.3404	**0.3214**	0.4286	0.3643	0.5139	0.3556	0.3721
BioASQ_Baseline	0.5161	0.5079	0.0714	0.2143	0.1220	0.2052	0.4833	0.2562

the systems will be ranked according to manual scores assigned to them by the BioASQ experts during the assessment of systems responses [4]. For the exact answers, which are required for all questions except the summary ones, the measure considered for ranking the participating systems depends on the question type. For the yes/no questions, the systems were ranked according to the macro-averaged F1-measure on prediction of no and yes answer. For factoid questions, the ranking was based on mean reciprocal rank (MRR) and for list questions on mean F1-measure. Some indicative results for exact answers for the third batch of Task 8b are presented in Table 9. The full results of phase B of Task 8b are available online[16]. These results are preliminary, as the final results for Task 8b will be available after the manual assessment of the system responses by the BioASQ team of biomedical experts.

Figure 3 presents the performance of the top systems for each question type in exact answers during the eight years of the BioASQ challenge. The diagram reveals that this year the performance of systems in the yes/no questions keeps

---

[16] http://participants-area.bioasq.org/results/8b/phaseB/.

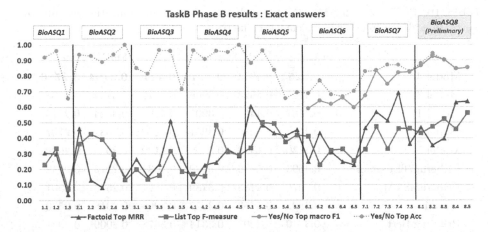

Fig. 3. The official evaluation scores of the best performing systems in Task B, Phase B, exact answer generation, across the eight years of the BioASQ challenge. Since BioASQ6 the official measure for Yes/No questions is the macro-averaged F1 score (macro F1), but accuracy (Acc) is also presented as the former official measure. The results for BioASQ8 are preliminary, as the final results for Task 8b will be available after the manual assessment of the system responses.

improving. For instance, in batch 3 presented in Table 9, various systems manage to outperform by far the strong baseline, which is based on a version of the OAQA system that achieved top performance in previous years. Improvements are also observed in the preliminary results for list questions, whereas the top system performance in factoid questions is fluctuating in the same range as done last year. In general, Fig. 3 suggests that for the latter types of question there is still more room for improvement.

4.3 Task MESINESP8

The task proved to be a challenging one, but overall we believe the results were pretty good. Compared to the setting for English, the overall dataset was significantly smaller, and also the track evaluation contained not only medical literature, but also clinical trial summaries and healthcare project summaries. Moreover, in case of the provided training data, two different indexing approaches were used by the literature databases. IBECS has a more centralized manual indexing contracting system, while in case of LILACS a number of records were indexed in a sort of distributed community human indexer effort. The training set contained 23,423 unique codes, while the 911 articles in the evaluation set contained almost 4,000 correct DeCS codes. The best predictions, by Fudan University, scored a MIF (micro F-measure) of 0.4254 MiF using their AttentionXML with multilingual-BERT system, compared to the baseline score of 0.2695. Table 10 shows the results of the runs for this task. As a matter of fact, the five best scores were from them.

Table 10. Final scores for MESINESP task submissions, including the official MiF metric in addition to other complementary metrics.

System	MiF	MiP	MiR	EBF	MaF	Acc
Model 4	**0.4254**	0.4374	**0.4140**	**0.4240**	**0.3194**	**0.2786**
Model 3	0.4227	0.4523	0.3966	0.4217	0.3122	0.2768
Model 1	0.4167	0.4466	0.3906	0.4160	0.3024	0.2715
Model 2	0.4165	0.4286	0.4051	0.4150	0.3082	0.2707
Model 5	0.4130	0.4416	0.3879	0.4122	0.3039	0.2690
PriberamTEnsemble	0.4093	0.5336	0.3320	0.4031	0.2115	0.2642
PriberamSVM	0.3976	0.4183	0.3789	0.3871	0.2543	0.2501
iria-mix	0.3892	0.5353	0.3057	0.3906	0.2318	0.2530
PriberamBert	0.3740	0.4293	0.3314	0.3678	0.2009	0.2361
iria-1	0.3630	0.5024	0.2842	0.3643	0.1957	0.2326
iria-3	0.3460	0.5375	0.2551	0.3467	0.1690	0.2193
iria-2	0.3423	0.4590	0.2729	0.3408	0.1719	0.2145
PriberamSearch	0.3395	0.4571	0.2700	0.3393	0.1776	0.2146
iria-4	0.2743	0.3068	0.2481	0.2760	0.2619	0.1662
BioASQ_Baseline	0.2695	0.2337	0.3182	0.2754	0.2816	0.1659
graph matching	0.2664	0.3501	0.2150	0.2642	0.1422	0.1594
exact matching	0.2589	0.2915	0.2328	0.2561	0.0575	0.1533
LasigeBioTM TXMC F1	0.2507	0.3559	0.1936	0.2380	0.0858	0.1440
Anuj_Ensemble	0.2163	0.2291	0.2049	0.2155	0.1746	0.1270
Anuj_NLP	0.2054	0.2196	0.1930	0.2044	0.1744	0.1198
NLPUnique	0.2054	0.2196	0.1930	0.2044	0.1744	0.1198
X-BERT BioASQ F1	0.1430	0.4577	0.0847	0.1397	0.0220	0.0787
LasigeBioTM TXMC P	0.1271	0.6864	0.0701	0.1261	0.0104	0.0708
Anuj_ml	0.1149	**0.7557**	0.0621	0.1164	0.0006	0.0636
X-BERT BioASQ	0.0909	0.5449	0.0496	0.0916	0.0045	0.0503

Although MiF represent the official competition metric, other metrics are provided for completeness. It is noteworthy that another team (Anuj-ml, from India) that was not among the highest scoring on MiF, nevertheless scored considerably higher than other teams with Precision metrics such as EBP (Example Based Precision), MaP (Macro Precision) and MiP (Micro Precision). Unfortunately, at this time we have not received details on their system implementation. One problem with the medical semantic concept indexing in Spanish, at least for diagnosis or disease related terms, is the uneven distribution and high variability [1].

5   Conclusions

This paper provides an overview of the eighth BioASQ challenge. This year, the challenge consisted of three tasks: The two tasks on biomedical semantic indexing and question answering in English, already established through the previous seven years of the challenge, and the new MESINESP task on semantic indexing of medical content in Spanish, which ran for the first time. The addition of the new challenging task on medical semantic indexing in Spanish, revealed that in a context beyond the English language, there is even more room for improvement, highlighting the importance of the availability of adequate resources for the development and evaluation of systems to effectively help biomedical experts dealing with non-English resources.

The overall shift of participant systems towards deep neural approaches, already noticed in the previous years, is even more apparent this year. State-of-the-art methodologies have been successfully adapted to biomedical question answering and novel ideas have been investigated. In particular, most of the systems adopted on neural embedding approaches, notably based on BERT and BioBERT models, for all tasks of the challenge. In the QA task in particular, different teams attempted transferring knowledge from general domain QA datasets, notably SQuAD, or from other NLP tasks such as NER and NLI, also experimenting with multi-task learning settings. In addition, recent advancements in NLP, such as XLNet [47], BART [24] and SpanBERT [18] have also been tested for the tasks of the challenge.

Overall, as in previous versions of the challenge, the top preforming systems were able to advance over the state of the art, outperforming the strong baselines on the challenging shared tasks offered by the organizers. Therefore, we consider that the challenge keeps meeting its goal to push the research frontier in biomedical semantic indexing and question answering. The future plans for the challenge include the extension of the benchmark data though a community-driven acquisition process.

Acknowledgments. Google was a proud sponsor of the BioASQ Challenge in 2019. The eighth edition of BioASQ is also sponsored by the Atypon Systems inc. BioASQ is grateful to NLM for providing the baselines for task 8a and to the CMU team for providing the baselines for task 8b. The MESINESP task is sponsored by the Spanish Plan for advancement of Language Technologies (Plan TL) and the Secretaría de Estado para el Avance Digital (SEAD). BioASQ is also grateful to LILACS, SCIELO and Biblioteca virtual en salud and Instituto de salud Carlos III for providing data for the BioASQ MESINESP task.

References

1. Almagro, M., Unanue, R.M., Fresno, V., Montalvo, S.: ICD-10 coding of Spanish electronic discharge summaries: an extreme classification problem. IEEE Access **8**, 100073–100083 (2020)

2. Almeida, T., Matos, S.: Calling attention to passages for biomedical question answering. In: Jose, J.M., et al. (eds.) ECIR 2020. LNCS, vol. 12036, pp. 69–77. Springer, Cham (2020). https://doi.org/10.1007/978-3-030-45442-5_9

3. Baldwin, B., Carpenter, B.: Lingpipe. Available from World Wide Web (2033). http://alias-i.com/lingpipe

4. Balikas, G., et al.: Evaluation framework specifications. Project deliverable D4.1, UPMC (05/2013 2013)

5. Bodenreider, O.: The unified medical language system (UMLS): integrating biomedical terminology. Nucleic Acids Res. **32**(suppl_1), D267–D270 (2004)

6. Bowman, S.R., Angeli, G., Potts, C., Manning, C.D.: A large annotated corpus for learning natural language inference. arXiv preprint arXiv:1508.05326 (2015)

7. Chang, W.C., Yu, H.F., Zhong, K., Yang, Y., Dhillon, I.: X-BERT: eXtreme multi-label text classification with using bidirectional encoder representations from transformers. arXiv preprint arXiv:1905.02331 (2019)

8. Clark, K., Luong, M.T., Le, Q.V., Manning, C.D.: Electra: pre-training text encoders as discriminators rather than generators. arXiv preprint arXiv:2003.10555 (2020)

9. Conneau, A., Kiela, D., Schwenk, H., Barrault, L., Bordes, A.: Supervised learning of universal sentence representations from natural language inference data. arXiv preprint arXiv:1705.02364 (2017)

10. Couto, F.M., Lamurias, A.: MER: a shell script and annotation server for minimal named entity recognition and linking. J. Cheminform. **10**(1), 1–10 (2018). https://doi.org/10.1186/s13321-018-0312-9

11. Demsar, J.: Statistical comparisons of classifiers over multiple data sets. J. Mach. Learn. Res. **7**, 1–30 (2006)

12. Devlin, J., Chang, M.W., Lee, K., Toutanova, K.: BERT: pre-training of deep bidirectional transformers for language understanding. In: NAACL HLT 2019–2019 Conference of the North American Chapter of the Association for Computational Linguistics: Human Language Technologies - Proceedings of the Conference 1(Mlm), pp. 4171–4186, October 2018. http://arxiv.org/abs/1810.04805

13. Erkan, G., Radev, D.R.: Lexrank: graph-based lexical centrality as salience in text summarization. J. Artif. Intell. Res. **22**, 457–479 (2004)

14. Gormley, C., Tong, Z.: Elasticsearch: The Definitive Guide: A Distributed Real-time Search and Analytics Engine. O'Reilly Media Inc., Sebastopol (2015)

15. Gururangan, S., et al.: Don't stop pretraining: adapt language models to domains and tasks. arXiv preprint arXiv:2004.10964 (2020)

16. Jain, H., Prabhu, Y., Varma, M.: Extreme multi-label loss functions for recommendation, tagging, ranking & other missing label applications. In: Proceedings of the 22nd ACM SIGKDD International Conference on Knowledge Discovery and Data Mining - KDD 2016, pp. 935–944. ACM Press, New York (2016). https://doi.org/10.1145/2939672.2939756

17. Jin, Q., Dhingra, B., Liu, Z., Cohen, W.W., Lu, X.: PubMedQA: a dataset for biomedical research question answering. arXiv preprint arXiv:1909.06146 (2019)

18. Joshi, M., Chen, D., Liu, Y., Weld, D.S., Zettlemoyer, L., Levy, O.: Spanbert: improving pre-training by representing and predicting spans. Trans. Assoc. Comput. Linguist. **8**, 64–77 (2020)

19. Kim, D., et al.: A neural named entity recognition and multi-type normalization tool for biomedical text mining. IEEE Access **7**, 73729–73740 (2019)

20. Kosmopoulos, A., Partalas, I., Gaussier, E., Paliouras, G., Androutsopoulos, I.: Evaluation measures for hierarchical classification: a unified view and novel approaches. Data Min. Knowl. Disc. **29**(3), 820–865 (2014). https://doi.org/10.1007/s10618-014-0382-x

21. Krallinger, M., Krithara, A., Nentidis, A., Paliouras, G., Villegas, M.: BioASQ at CLEF2020: large-scale biomedical semantic indexing and question answering. In: Jose, J.M., et al. (eds.) ECIR 2020. LNCS, vol. 12036, pp. 550–556. Springer, Cham (2020). https://doi.org/10.1007/978-3-030-45442-5_71

22. Kudo, T., Richardson, J.: SentencePiece: a simple and language independent subword tokenizer and detokenizer for neural text processing. In: Proceedings of the 2018 Conference on Empirical Methods in Natural Language Processing: System Demonstrations, pp. 66–71. Association for Computational Linguistics, Stroudsburg (2018). https://doi.org/10.18653/v1/D18-2012

23. Lee, J., et al.: BIOBERT: pre-trained biomedical language representation model for biomedical text mining. arXiv preprint arXiv:1901.08746 (2019)

24. Lewis, M., et al.: Bart: denoising sequence-to-sequence pre-training for natural language generation, translation, and comprehension. arXiv preprint arXiv:1910.13461 (2019)

25. Loper, E., Bird, S.: NLTK: the natural language toolkit. arXiv preprint arXiv:cs/0205028 (2002)

26. Ma, J., Korotkov, I., Yang, Y., Hall, K., McDonald, R.: Zero-shot neural retrieval via domain-targeted synthetic query generation. arXiv preprint arXiv:2004.14503 (2020)

27. Mihalcea, R., Tarau, P.: TextRank: bringing order into text. In: Proceedings of the 2004 Conference on Empirical Methods in Natural Language Processing, pp. 404–411 (2004)

28. Mollá, D., Jones, C.: Classification betters regression in query-based multidocument summarisation techniques for question answering. In: Cellier, P., Driessens, K. (eds.) ECML PKDD 2019. CCIS, vol. 1168, pp. 624–635. Springer, Cham (2020). https://doi.org/10.1007/978-3-030-43887-6_56

29. Mork, J.G., Demner-Fushman, D., Schmidt, S.C., Aronson, A.R.: Recent enhancements to the NLM medical text indexer. In: Proceedings of Question Answering Lab at CLEF (2014)

30. Nentidis, A., Bougiatiotis, K., Krithara, A., Paliouras, G.: Results of the seventh edition of the BioASQ challenge. In: Cellier, P., Driessens, K. (eds.) ECML PKDD 2019. CCIS, vol. 1168, pp. 553–568. Springer, Cham (2020). https://doi.org/10.1007/978-3-030-43887-6_51

31. Neumann, M., King, D., Beltagy, I., Ammar, W.: ScispaCy: fast and robust models for biomedical natural language processing. arXiv preprint arXiv:1902.07669 (2019)

32. Ozyurt, I.B., Bandrowski, A., Grethe, J.S.: Bio-AnswerFinder: a system to find answers to questions from biomedical texts. Database **2020**, 1–12 (2020)

33. Pang, L., Lan, Y., Guo, J., Xu, J., Xu, J., Cheng, X.: DeepRank: a new deep architecture for relevance ranking in information retrieval. In: Proceedings of the 2017 ACM on Conference on Information and Knowledge Management, pp. 257–266 (2017)

34. Pappas, D., McDonald, R., Brokos, G.I., Androutsopoulos, I.: AUEB at BioASQ 7: document and snippet retrieval. In: Seventh BioASQ Workshop: A Challenge on Large-scale Biomedical Semantic Indexing and Question Answering (2019)

35. Peng, S., You, R., Wang, H., Zhai, C., Mamitsuka, H., Zhu, S.: DeepMeSH: deep semantic representation for improving large-scale mesh indexing. Bioinformatics **32**(12), i70–i79 (2016)

36. Peters, M.E., et al.: Deep contextualized word representations. In: Proceedings of the Conference on Empirical Methods in Natural Language Processing, pp. 31–40, February 2018. http://arxiv.org/abs/1802.05365

37. Rae, A., Mork, J., Demner-Fushman, D.: Convolutional neural network for automatic MeSH indexing. In: Seventh BioASQ Workshop: A Challenge on Large-scale Biomedical Semantic Indexing and Question Answering (2019)

38. Rajpurkar, P., Zhang, J., Lopyrev, K., Liang, P.: SQuAD: 100,000+ questions for machine comprehension of text. arXiv preprint arXiv:1606.05250 (2016)

39. Reimers, N., Gurevych, I.: Sentence-BERT: sentence embeddings using Siamese BERT-networks. arXiv preprint arXiv:1908.10084 (2019)

40. Ribadas, F.J., De Campos, L.M., Darriba, V.M., Romero, A.E.: CoLe and UTAIat BioASQ 2015: experiments with similarity based descriptor assignment. In: CEUR Workshop Proceedings, vol. 1391 (2015)

41. Schulman, J., Wolski, F., Dhariwal, P., Radford, A., Klimov, O.: Proximal policy optimization algorithms. arXiv preprint arXiv:1707.06347 (2017)

42. Smith, L., et al.: Overview of BioCreative II gene mention recognition. Genome Biol. **9**(S2), S2 (2008). https://doi.org/10.1186/gb-2008-9-s2-s2

43. Tsatsaronis, G., et al.: An overview of the BIOASQ large-scale biomedical semantic indexing and question answering competition. BMC Bioinform. **16**, 138 (2015). https://doi.org/10.1186/s12859-015-0564-6

44. Tsoumakas, G., Laliotis, M., Markontanatos, N., Vlahavas, I.: Large-scale semantic indexing of biomedical publications. In: 1st BioASQ Workshop: A Challenge on Large-Scale Biomedical Semantic Indexing and Question Answering (2013)

45. Wei, C.H., Leaman, R., Lu, Z.: Beyond accuracy: creating interoperable and scalable text-mining web services. Bioinformatics (Oxford, England) **32**(12), 1907–10 (2016). https://doi.org/10.1093/bioinformatics/btv760

46. Williams, A., Nangia, N., Bowman, S.R.: A broad-coverage challenge corpus for sentence understanding through inference. arXiv preprint arXiv:1704.05426 (2017)

47. Yang, Z., Dai, Z., Yang, Y., Carbonell, J.G., Salakhutdinov, R., Le, Q.V.: XLNet: Generalized autoregressive pretraining for language understanding. CoRR abs/1906.08237 (2019). http://arxiv.org/abs/1906.08237

48. Yang, Z., Zhou, Y., Eric, N.: Learning to answer biomedical questions: OAQA at BioASQ 4B. In: ACL 2016, p. 23 (2016)

49. Yoon, W., Lee, J., Kim, D., Jeong, M., Kang, J.: Pre-trained language model for biomedical question answering. In: Seventh BioASQ Workshop: A Challenge on Large-Scale Biomedical Semantic Indexing and Question Answering (2019)

50. You, R., Zhang, Z., Wang, Z., Dai, S., Mamitsuka, H., Zhu, S.: AttentionXML: Label tree-based attention-aware deep model for high-performance extreme multi-label text classification. arXiv preprint arXiv:1811.01727 (2018)

51. Zavorin, I., Mork, J.G., Demner-Fushman, D.: Using learning-to-rank to enhance NLM medical text indexer results. In: ACL 2016, p. 8 (2016)

Overview of CheckThat! 2020: Automatic Identification and Verification of Claims in Social Media

Alberto Barrón-Cedeño[1]([✉]), Tamer Elsayed[2], Preslav Nakov[3],
Giovanni Da San Martino[3], Maram Hasanain[2], Reem Suwaileh[2],
Fatima Haouari[2], Nikolay Babulkov[4], Bayan Hamdan[5], Alex Nikolov[4],
Shaden Shaar[3], and Zien Sheikh Ali[2]

[1] DIT, Università di Bologna, Forlì, Italy
`a.barron@unibo.it`
[2] Computer Science and Engineering Department, Qatar University, Doha, Qatar
`{telsayed,maram.hasanain,rs081123,200159617,zs1407404}@qu.edu.qa`
[3] Qatar Computing Research Institute, HBKU, Doha, Qatar
`{pnakov,gmartino,sshaar}@hbku.edu.qa`
[4] FMI, Sofia University "St Kliment Ohridski", Sofia, Bulgaria
`nbabulkov@gmail.com,alexnickolow@gmail.com`
[5] Amman, Jordan
`bayan.hamdan995@gmail.com`

Abstract. We present an overview of the third edition of the `CheckThat!` Lab at CLEF 2020. The lab featured five tasks in two different languages: English and Arabic. The first four tasks compose the full pipeline of claim verification in social media: Task 1 on check-worthiness estimation, Task 2 on retrieving previously fact-checked claims, Task 3 on evidence retrieval, and Task 4 on claim verification. The lab is completed with Task 5 on check-worthiness estimation in political debates and speeches. A total of 67 teams registered to participate in the lab (up from 47 at CLEF 2019), and 23 of them actually submitted runs (compared to 14 at CLEF 2019). Most teams used deep neural networks based on BERT, LSTMs, or CNNs, and achieved sizable improvements over the baselines on all tasks. Here we describe the tasks setup, the evaluation results, and a summary of the approaches used by the participants, and we discuss some lessons learned. Last but not least, we release to the research community all datasets from the lab as well as the evaluation scripts, which should enable further research in the important tasks of check-worthiness estimation and automatic claim verification.

Keywords: Check-worthiness estimation · Fact-checking · Veracity · Evidence-based verification · Detecting previously fact-checked claims · Social media verification · Computational journalism

---

B. Hamdan—Independent Researcher.

© Springer Nature Switzerland AG 2020
A. Arampatzis et al. (Eds.): CLEF 2020, LNCS 12260, pp. 215–236, 2020.
https://doi.org/10.1007/978-3-030-58219-7_17

1   Introduction

The CheckThat! lab[1] was run for the third time in the framework of CLEF 2020. The purpose of the 2020 edition was to foster the development of technology that would enable the (semi-)automatic verification of claims posted in social media, in particular *Twitter*.[2] We turn our attention to Twitter because information posted on that platform is not checked by an authoritative entity before publication and such information tends to disseminate very quickly.[3] Moreover, social media posts lack context due to their short length and conversational nature; thus, identifying a claim's context is sometimes key for enabling effective fact-checking [13].

The full identification and verification pipeline is displayed in Fig. 1. The four tasks are defined as follows:

Task 1. Check-worthiness estimation for tweets. Predict which tweet from a stream of tweets on a topic should be prioritized for fact-checking.

Task 2. Verified claim retrieval: Given a check-worthy tweet, and a set of claims previously checked, determine whether the claim in the tweet has been fact-checked already.

Task 3. Evidence retrieval. Given a check-worthy claim in a tweet on a specific topic and a set of text snippets extracted from potentially-relevant Web pages, return a ranked list of evidence snippets for the claim.

Task 4. Claim verification. Given a check-worthy claim in a tweet and a set of potentially-relevant Web pages, estimate the veracity of the claim.

Task 5. complements the lab. It is as Task 1, but on political debates ad speeches rather than on tweets: given a debate segmented into sentences, together with speaker information, prioritize sentences for fact-checking.

Figure 1 shows how the different tasks relate to each other. The first step is to detect tweets that contain check-worthy claims (Task 1; also, Task 5, which is on debates and speeches). The next step is to check whether a target check-worthy claim has been previously fact-checked (Task 2). If not, then there is a need for fact-checking, which involves supporting evidence retrieval (Task 3), followed by actual fact-checking based on that evidence (Task 4). Tasks 1, 3, and 4 were run for Arabic, while Tasks 1, 2 and 5 were offered for English.

The rest of the paper is organized as follows. Sect. 2 discusses related work. Sect. 3 describes the tasks that were run in Arabic (Tasks 1, 3 and 4). Section 4 presents the tasks that were run in English (Tasks 1, 2, and 5). Note that Sects. 3 and 4 are not exhaustive; the reader should refer to [27] and [46], respectively, for further details. Finally, Sect. 5 concludes with final remarks.

---

[1] https://sites.google.com/view/clef2020-checkthat/.

[2] The 2018 edition [41] focused on the identification and verification of claims in political debates. Beside political debates, the 2019 edition [15,16] also focused on isolated claims in conjunction with a closed set of Web documents to retrieve evidence from.

[3] Recently, Twitter started flagging some tweets that violate its policy.

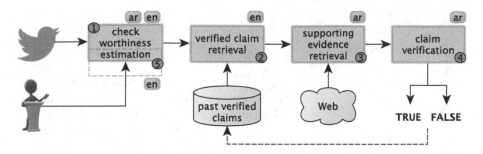

Fig. 1. The `CheckThat!` claim verification pipeline. Our tasks cover all four steps of the pipeline in Arabic or English. Tasks 1–4 focus on Twitter, while task 5 is run on political debates and speeches.

2 Related Work

Both the information retrieval and the natural language processing communities have invested significant efforts in the development of systems to deal with disinformation, misinformation, factuality, and credibility. There has been work on checking the factuality/credibility of a claim, of a news article, or of an information source [5–7,33,36,40,44,54]. Claims can come from different sources, but special attention has been paid to those originating in social media [22,39,47,53]. Check-worthiness estimation is still a relatively under-explored problem, and has been previously addressed primarily in political debates and speeches [19,29–31,51], and only recently in social media [1]. Similarly, severely under-explored is the task of detecting previously fact-checked claims [45].

This is the third edition of the `CheckThat!` lab, and it represents a clear evolution from the tasks that were featured in the previous two editions. Figure 2 shows the evolution of the `CheckThat!` tasks over these three years. The lab started in 2018 with only two tasks: check-worthiness estimation and factuality (fact-checking), with focus on political debates, speeches, and claims. In that first edition, the English language was leading and the Arabic datasets were produced by translation (manual or automatic with post-editing). The `CheckThat!` 2019 lab offered a continuity in the check-worthiness task. The Arabic task —still under the factuality umbrella— started to unfold into four subtasks in order to boost the development of models specialized in each of the stages of verification, from the ranking of relevant Websites to the final claim verification. Regarding data, transcriptions of press conferences were added, as well as news to be used to verify the claims. In 2020, we unfolded the claim verification pipeline into four differentiated tasks. Regarding data, all tasks in 2020 turned to micro-blogging with focus on Twitter, with the exception of legacy task 5 on check-worthiness, which focused on political debates and speeches.

Below, we present a brief overview of the tasks and of the most successful approaches in the 2019 and the 2018 editions of the lab. We refer the reader to [16] and to [41] for more detailed overviews of these earlier editions.

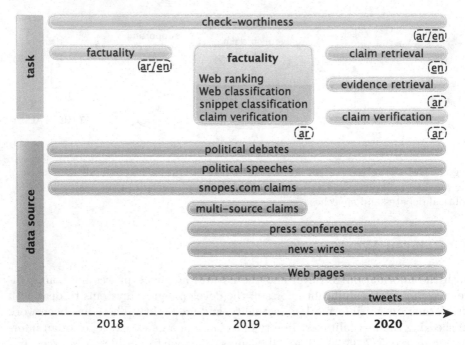

Fig. 2. The evolution of the tasks at the `CheckThat!` lab over its three editions. Top: the unfolding of the tasks that compose a full fact-checking pipeline. Bottom: the source texts and the genres included in the datasets used by these tasks.

2.1   CheckThat! 2019

The 2019 edition of the `CheckThat!` lab featured two tasks [16]:

Task 1₂₀₁₉. Given a political debate, an interview, or a speech, transcribed and segmented into sentences, rank the sentences by the priority with which they should be fact-checked.

The most successful approaches used by the participating teams relied on neural networks for the classification of the instances. For example, Hansen et al. [24] learned domain-specific word embeddings and syntactic dependencies and applied an LSTM classifier. They pre-trained the network with previous Trump and Clinton debates, supervised weakly with the ClaimBuster system. Some efforts were carried out in order to consider context. Favano et al. [17] trained a feed-forward neural network, including the two previous sentences as a context. While many approaches relied on embedding representations, feature engineering was also popular [18]. We refer the interested reader to [4] for further details.

Task 2₂₀₁₉. Given a claim and a set of potentially-relevant Web pages, identify which of the pages (and passages thereof) are useful for assisting a human in fact-checking the claim. Finally, determine the factuality of the claim.

The systems for evidence passage identification followed two approaches. BERT was trained and used to predict whether an input passage is useful to fact-check a claim [17]. Other participating systems used classifiers (e.g., SVM) with a variety of features including the similarity between the claim and a passage, bag of words, and named entities [25]. As for predicting claim veracity, the most effective approach used a textual entailment model. The input was represented using word embeddings and external data was also used in training [20]. See [28] for further details.

Note that Task 5 of the 2020 edition of the CheckThat! lab is a follow-up of Task 1_{2019}, while Task 1 of the 2020 edition is a reformulation that focuses on tweets. In contrast, Task 2_{2019} was decomposed into two tasks in 2020: Tasks 3 and 4.

2.2 CheckThat! 2018

The 2018 edition featured two tasks:

Task 1$_{2018}$ was identical to Task 1_{2019}.

The most successful approaches used either a multilayer perceptron or an SVM. Zuo et al. [55] enriched the dataset by producing *pseudo-speeches* as a concatenation of all interventions by a debater. They used averaged word embeddings and bag of words as representations. Hansen et al. [23] represented the entries with embeddings, part of speech tags, and syntactic dependencies, and used a GRU neural network with attention as a learning model. More details can be found in the task overview paper [3].

Task 2$_{2018}$. *Given a check-worthy claim in the form of a (transcribed) sentence, determine whether the claim is likely to be true, half-true, or false.*

The best way to address this task was to retrieve relevant information from the Web, followed by a comparison against the claim in order to assess its factuality. After retrieving such *evidence*, it is fed into the supervised model, together with the claim in order to assess its veracity. In the case of Hansen et al. [23], they fed the claim and the most similar Web-retrieved text to convolutional neural networks and SVMs. Meanwhile, Ghanem et al. [21] computed features, such as the similarity between the claim and the Web text, and the Alexa rank for the website. Once again, this year a similar procedure had to be carried out, but this time explicitly decomposed into tasks 3 and 4. We refer the interested reader to [8] for further details.

3 Overview of the Arabic Tasks

In order to enable research on Arabic claim verification, we ran three tasks from the verification pipeline (see Fig. 1) over Arabic tweets. These tasks are check-worthiness on tweets (Task 1), evidence retrieval (Task 3), and claim verification (Task 4). They attracted nine teams. Below, we describe the evaluation dataset created to support each of these tasks. We also present a summary of the approaches used by the participating systems, and we discuss the evaluation results. Further details can be found in our extended overview paper [27].

Table 1. Summary of the best approaches for Task 1 Arabic for the participating teams. Shown is information about the learning models (including Transformers), about the main representations, whether the participants used external data, and whether they used machine translation to be able to use additional data from English (MT).

Team		Models					Distrib.					Represent.						Other	
		BERT	Bi-LSTM	NN	SVM	SGD	Laser	FastText	GloVe	word2vec	PCA	One-hot	Morphology	Syntax	Sentiment	Dependencies	NER	External data	MT
Accenture	[52]	●																●	●
bigIR	[26]	●																●	
Check_square	[14]				●					●	●	●			●				
DamascusTeam	[32]		●									●						●	
EvolutionTeam	[50]															●	●	●	
NLP&IR@UNED	[37]			●					●										
TOBB ETU	[34]	●							●										
WSSC_UPF	–					●	●					●	●					●	

3.1 Task 1$_{ar}$. Check-Worthiness on Tweets

Since check-worthiness estimation for tweets in general, and for *Arabic* tweets in particular, is a relatively new task, we constructed a new dataset specifically designed for training and evaluating systems for this task. We identified the need for a "context" that affects check-worthiness of tweets and we used "topics" to represent that context. Given a topic, we define a check-worthy tweet as a tweet that is relevant to the topic, contains one main claim that can be fact-checked by consulting reliable sources, and is important enough to be worthy of verification. More on the annotation criteria is presented later in this section.

Dataset. To construct the dataset for this task, we first manually created 15 topics over the period of several months. The topics were selected based on trending topics at the time among Arab social media users. Each topic was represented using a title and a description. Some example topic titles include: "Coronavirus in the Arab World", "Sudan and normalization", and "Deal of the century". Additionally, we augmented the topic by a set of keywords, hashtags and usernames to track in Twitter. Once we created a topic, we immediately crawled a 1-week stream using the constructed search terms, where we searched Twitter (via Twitter search API) using each term by the end of each day. We limited the search to original Arabic tweets (i.e., we excluded retweets). We de-duplicated the tweets and we dropped tweets matching our qualification filter that excludes tweets containing terms from a blacklist of explicit terms and tweets that contain more than four hashtags or more than two URLs. Afterwards, we ranked the tweets by popularity (defined by the sum of their retweets and likes) and selected the top 500 to be annotated.

The annotation process was performed in two steps; we first identified the tweets that are relevant to the topic and contain factual claims, then identified the check-worthy tweets among those relevant tweets.

We first recruited one annotator to annotate each tweet for its relevance to the target topic. In this step, we labeled each tweet as one of three categories:

- Non-relevant tweet for the target topic.
- Relevant tweet but *with no factual claims*, such as tweets expressing opinions about the topic, references, or speculations about the future, etc.
- Relevant tweet that contains a factual claim that can be fact-checked by consulting reliable sources.

Relevant tweets with factual claims were then labelled for check-worthiness. Two annotators initially annotated the relevant tweets. A third *expert* annotator performed disagreement resolution whenever needed. Due to the subjective nature of check-worthiness, we chose to represent the check-worthiness criteria by several questions, to help annotators think about different aspects of check-worthiness. Annotators were asked to answer the following three questions for each tweet (using a scale of 1–5):

- Do you think the claim in the tweet is of interest to the public?
- To what extent do you think the claim can negatively affect the reputation of an entity, country, etc.?
- Do you think journalists will be interested in covering the spread of the claim or the information discussed by the claim?

Once an annotator answers the above questions, she/he is required to answer the following fourth question considering all the ratings given previously: "Do you think the claim in the tweet is check-worthy?". This question is a yes/no question, and the resulting answer is the label we use to represent check-worthiness in this dataset.

For the final set, all tweets but those labelled as check-worthy were considered not check-worthy. Given 500 tweets annotated for each of the fifteen topics, the annotated set contained 2,062 check-worthy claims (27.5%). Three topics constituted the training set and the remaining twelve topics were used to later evaluate the participating systems.

Overview of the Approaches. Eight teams participated in this task submitting a total of 28 runs. Table 1 shows an overview of the approaches. The most successful runs adopted fine-tuning existing pre-trained models, namely AraBERT and multilingual BERT models. Other approaches relied on pre-trained models such as Glove, Word2vec, and Language-Agnostic SEntence Representations (LASER) to obtain embeddings for the tweets, which were fed either to neural network models or to traditional machine learning models such as SVMs. In addition to text representations, some teams included other features to their models, namely morphological and syntactic features, part-of-speech (POS) tags, named entities, and sentiment features.

Evaluation. We treated Task 1 as a ranking problem where we expected check-worthy tweets to be ranked at the top. We evaluated the runs using precision at k ($P@k$) and Mean Average Precision (MAP). We considered $P@30$ as the

Table 2. Performance of the best run per team for Arabic Task 1.

RunID	P@10	P@20	P@30	MAP
Accenture-AraBERT	0.7167	0.6875	0.7000	0.6232
TOBB-ETU-AF	0.7000	0.6625	0.6444	0.5816
bigIR-bert	0.6417	0.6333	0.6417	0.5511
Check_square-w2vposRun2	0.6083	0.6000	0.5778	0.4949
DamascusTeam-Run03	0.5833	0.5750	0.5472	0.4539
NLP& IR@UNED-run4	0.6083	0.5625	0.5333	0.4614
baseline2	0.3500	0.3625	0.3472	0.3149
baseline1	0.3250	0.3333	0.3417	0.3244
EvolutionTeam-Run1	0.2500	0.2667	0.2833	0.2675
WSSC_UPF-RF01	0.1917	0.1667	0.2028	0.2542

official measure, as we anticipated the user would check maximum of 30 claims per week. We also developed two simple baselines: *baseline 1*, which ranks tweets in descending order based on their popularity score (sum of likes and retweets a tweet has received) and *baseline 2*, which ranks tweets in reverse chronological order, i.e. most-recent first. Table 2 shows the performance of the best run per team in addition to the two baselines, ranked by the official measure. We can see that most teams managed to improve over the two baselines by a large margin.

3.2 Task 3_{ar}. Evidence Retrieval

Dataset. For this task, we needed a set of claims and a set of potentially-relevant Web pages from which evidence snippets will be extracted by a system.

We first collected the set of Web pages using the topics we developed for Task 1. While developing the topics, we represented each one by a set of search phrases. We used these phrases in Google Web search daily as we crawled tweets for the topic. By the end of a week, we collected a set of Web pages that was ready to be used for constructing a dataset to evaluate evidence retrieval systems.

As for the set of claims, we draw a random sample from the check-worthy tweets identified for each topic for Task 1. Since data from Task 2, Subtask C in the last year's edition of the lab could be used for training [28], we only released test claims and Web pages from the twelve test topics used in Task 1. The dataset for this task contains a total of 200 claims and 14,742 corresponding Web pages.

Since we seek a controlled method to allow systems to return snippets, which in turn would allow us to label a consistent set of potential evidence snippets, we automatically pre-split these pages into snippets that we eventually released per page. To extract snippets from the Web pages, we first de-duplicated the crawled Web pages using the page URL. Then, we extracted the textual content from the

HTML document for each page after removing any markup and scripts. Finally, we detected Arabic text and split it into snippets, where full-stops, question marks, or exclamation marks delimit the snippets. Overall, we extracted 169,902 snippets from the Web pages.

Due to the large number of snippets collected for the claims, annotating all pairs of claims and snippets was not feasible given the limited time. Therefore, we followed a *pooling* method; we annotate pooled evidence snippets returned from submitted runs by the participating systems. Since the official evaluation measure for the task was set to be $P@10$, we first extracted the top 10 evidence snippets returned by each run for each claim. We then created a pool of unique snippets per claim (considering both snippet IDs and content for de-duplication). Finally, a single annotator annotated each snippet for a claim. The annotators were asked to decide whether a snippet contains evidence useful to verify the given claim. An evidence can be statistics, quotes, facts extracted from verified sources, etc.

Overall, we annotated 3,380 snippets. After label propagation, we had 3,720 annotated snippets of which only 95 are evidence snippets. Our annotation volume was limited due to the very small number of runs participating in the task (2 runs submitted by one team).

Overview of the Approaches. One team, EvolutionTeam, submitted two runs for this task [50]. They used machine learning models with two different types of features in each of the runs. In one run, they exploited the similarity feature by computing the cosine similarity between the claim and the snippets to rank them accordingly. They also explored the effectiveness of using linguistic features to rank snippets for usefulness in the second run for which they reported use of external data.

Evaluation. This task is modeled as a ranking problem where the system is expected to return evidence at the top of the list of returned snippets. In order to evaluate the submitted runs, we computed $P@k$ at different cutoff ($k = 1, 5, 10$). The official measure was $P@10$. The team's best-performing run achieved an average $P@10$ of 0.0456 over the claims.

3.3   Task 4_{ar}. Claim Verification

Starting with the same 200 claims used in Task 3, one expert fact-checker verified each claim's veracity. We limited the annotation categories to two, true and false, excluding partially-true claims. A true claim is a claim that is supported by a reliable source that confirms the authenticity of the information published in the tweet. A false claim can be a claim that mentions information contradicting that in a reliable source or has been explicitly refuted by a reliable source.

Dataset. The claims in the tweets were annotated considering two main factors; the content of the tweet (claim) and the date of the tweet publication. For the annotation, we considered supporting or refuting information that was reported before, on, or few days after the time of the claim. We consulted several reliable sources to verify the claims. The sources that were used differed according to the topic of the claim. For example, for health-related claims, we consulted refereed studies or articles published in reliable medical journals or websites such as APA.[4]

Out of the initial 200 claims, we ended up with 165 claims for which we managed to find a definite label. Six claims among these 165 were found to be False. Since data from Task 2, Subtask D in the last year's edition of the lab can be used for training [28], the final set of 165 annotated claims was used to evaluate the submitted runs.

Evaluation. For this task, there were a total of two runs submitted by the same team, EvolutionTeam. The models relied on linguistic features, and they used external data in one of the runs. We treated the task as a classification problem and we used typical evaluation measures for such tasks in the case of class imbalance: Precision, Recall, and F_1 score. The latter was the official evaluation measure. The best-performing run achieved a macro-averaged F_1 score of 0.5524.

4 Overview of the English Tasks

This year we proposed three of the tasks of the verification pipeline in English: check-worthiness estimation over tweets, verified claim retrieval, and check-worthiness estimation in political debates and speeches (cf. Fig. 1). A total of 18 teams participated in the English tasks.

4.1 Task 1$_{en}$. Check-Worthiness on Tweets

Task 1 (English). *Given a topic and a stream of potentially-related tweets, rank the tweets according to their check-worthiness for the topic.*

Previous work on check-worthiness focused primarily on political debates and speeches, while here we focus on tweets instead.

Dataset. We focused on a single topic, namely *COVID-19*, and we collected tweets that matched one of the following keywords and hashtags: *#covid19, #CoronavirusOutbreak, #Coronavirus, #Corona, #CoronaAlert, #CoronaOutbreak, Corona*, and *covid-19*. We ran all the data collection in March 2020, and we selected the most retweeted tweets for manual annotation.

For the annotation, we considered a number of factors. These include tweet popularity in terms of retweets, which is already taken into account as part of the data collection process. We further asked the annotators to answer the following five questions:[5]

– **Q1: Does the tweet contain a verifiable factual claim?** This is an objective question. Positive examples include[6] tweets that state a definition,

---

[4] https://www.apa.org/.

[5] We used the following MicroMappers setup for the annotations: http://micromappers.qcri.org/project/covid19-tweet-labelling/.

[6] This is influenced by [35].

mention a quantity in the present or the past, make a verifiable prediction about the future, reference laws, procedures, and rules of operation, discuss images or videos, and state correlation or causation, among others.

- **Q2: To what extent does the tweet appear to contain false information?** This question asks for a subjective judgment; it does not ask for annotating the actual factuality of the claim in the tweet, but rather whether the claim appears to be false.
- **Q3: Will the tweet have an effect on or be of interest to the general public?** This question asks for an objective judgment. Generally, claims that contain information related to potential cures, updates on number of cases, on measures taken by governments, or discussing rumors and spreading conspiracy theories should be of general public interest.
- **Q4: To what extent is the tweet harmful to the society, person(s), company(s) or product(s)?** This question also asks for an objective judgment: to identify tweets that can negatively affect society as a whole, but also specific person(s), company(s), product(s).
- **Q5: Do you think that a professional fact-checker should verify the claim in the tweet?** This question asks for a subjective judgment. Yet, its answer should be informed by the answer to questions Q2, Q3 and Q4, as a check-worthy factual claim is probably one that is likely to be false, is of public interest, and/or appears to be harmful.

For the purpose of the task, we consider as worth fact-checking the tweets that received a positive answer both to Q1 and to Q5; if there was a negative answer for either Q1 or Q5, the tweet was considered not worth fact-checking. The answers to Q2, Q3, and Q4 were not considered directly, but they helped the annotators make a better decision for Q5.

The annotations were performed by 2–5 annotators independently, and then consolidated after a discussion for the cases of disagreement. The annotation setup was part of a broader COVID-19 annotation initiative; see [1] for more details about the annotation instructions and setup.

Table 3 shows statistics about the data, which is split into training, development, and testing. We can see that the data is fairly balanced with the check-worthy claims making 34–43% of the examples across the datasets.

Table 3. Task 1, English: Statistics about the tweets in the dataset

Partition	Total	Check-worthy
Train	672	231
Dev	150	59
Test	140	60

Evaluation. This is a ranking task, where a tweet has to be ranked according to its check-worthiness. Therefore, we consider mean average precision (MAP)

as the official evaluation measure, which we complement with reciprocal rank (RR), R-precision (R-P), and P@k for $k \in \{1, 3, 5, 10, 20, 30\}$. The data and the evaluation scripts are available online.[7]

Overview of the Approaches. A total of 12 teams took part in Task 1. The submitted models range from state-of-the-art Transformers such as BERT and RoBERTa to more traditional machine learning models such as SVM and Logistic Regression. Table 4 shows a summary of the approaches used by the primary submissions of the participating teams. The highest overall score was achieved using a RoBERTa model.

The top-ranked team **Accenture** used RoBERTa with mean pooling and dropout.

The second-best **Team_Alex** trained a logistic regression classifier using as features the RoBERTa's cross-validation predictions on the data and metadata from the provided JSON file as features.

Team **Check_square** used BERT embeddings along with syntactic features with SVM/PCA and ensembles.

Team **QMUL-SDS** fine-tuned the uncased COVID-Twitter-BERT architecture, which was pre-trained on COVID-19 Twitter stream data.

Team **TOBB ETU** used BERT and word embeddings as features in a logistic regression model, adding POS tags and important hand-crafted word features.

Team **SSN_NLP** also used a RoBERTa classifier.

Team **Factify** submitted a BERT-based classifier.

Table 4. Task 1, English: Summary of the approaches used in the primary system submissions. Shown is which systems used transformers, learning models, distributional features, standard features, and other.

Team		BERT	RoBERTa	Huggingface	BiLSTM	CNN	Rnd forest	Linear reg	Logistic reg	SVM	FastText	GloVe	PCA	Topic models	tf-idf	Dependencies	POS	NEs	Ext. data	Graph relations
		Transf			Models						Distrib.				Features					Other
Accenture	[52]		●																	
BustingMisinformation	–					●			●		●		●	●	●					
Check_square	[14]	●								●			●			●	●	●		
Factify	–	●																	●	
NLP&IR@UNED	[37]				●									●						●
QMUL-SDS	[2]	●				●														
Team_Alex	[42]		●																	
TheUofSheffield	[38]								●								●			
TOBB ETU	[34]	●							●								●			
UAICS	–			●	●															
SSN_NLP	–		●																	
ZHAW	–						●										●	●		

Table 5. Task 1, English: Evaluation results for the primary submissions.

Team	MAP	RR	R-P	P@1	P@3	P@5	P@10	P@20	P@30
Accenture	**0.806**	**1.000**	**0.717**	**1.000**	**1.000**	**1.000**	**1.000**	**0.950**	**0.740**
Team_Alex	0.803	**1.000**	0.650	**1.000**	**1.000**	**1.000**	**1.000**	**0.950**	**0.740**
Check_square	0.722	**1.000**	0.667	**1.000**	0.667	0.800	0.800	0.800	0.700
QMUL-SDS	0.714	**1.000**	0.633	**1.000**	**1.000**	**1.000**	0.900	0.800	0.640
TOBB ETU	0.706	**1.000**	0.600	**1.000**	**1.000**	**1.000**	0.900	0.800	0.660
SSN_NLP	0.674	**1.000**	0.600	**1.000**	**1.000**	0.800	0.800	0.800	0.620
Factify	0.656	0.500	0.683	0.000	0.333	0.600	0.700	0.750	0.700
BustingMisinformation	0.617	**1.000**	0.583	**1.000**	**1.000**	0.800	0.700	0.600	0.600
NLP& IR@UNED	0.607	**1.000**	0.567	**1.000**	**1.000**	**1.000**	0.700	0.600	0.580
Baseline (n-gram)	0.579	1.000	0.500	1.000	0.667	0.800	0.800	0.700	0.600
ZHAW	0.505	0.333	0.533	0.000	0.333	0.400	0.600	0.500	0.520
UAICS	0.495	**1.000**	0.467	**1.000**	0.333	0.400	0.600	0.600	0.460
TheUofSheffield	0.475	0.250	0.533	0.000	0.000	0.400	0.200	0.350	0.480

Team **BustingMisinformation** used an SVM with TF-IDF features and GloVe embeddings, along with topic modelling using NMF.

Team **NLP&IR@UNED** trained a bidirectional LSTM on top of GloVe embeddings. They increased the number of inputs with a graph generated from the additional information provided for each tweet.

Team **ZHAW** used a logistic regression with POS tags and named entities along with additional features about the location of posting, its time, etc.

Team **UAICS** submitted predictions from a fine-tuned custom BERT large model.

Team **TheUofSheffield** trained a custom 4-gram FastText model. Their pre-processing includes lowercasing, lemmatization, as well as URL, emoji, stop words, and punctuation removal.

Table 5 shows the performance of the primary submissions to Task 1 in English. We can see that Accenture and Team_Alex achieved very high scores on all evaluation measures and outperformed the remaining teams by a wide margin, e.g., by about eight points absolute in terms of MAP. We can further see that most systems managed to outperform an n-gram baseline by a very sizeable margin.

4.2   Task 2_{en}. Verified Claim Retrieval

Task 2 (English). *Given a check-worthy input claim and a set of verified claims, rank those verified claims, so that the claims that can help verify the input claim, or a sub-claim in it, are ranked above any claim that is not helpful to verify the input claim.*

Unlike the other tasks of the CheckThat! lab, Task 2 is a new one. Table 6 shows an example of a tweet by Donald Trump claiming that a video footage

Table 6. Task 2, English: example input. A subset of verified claims ordered by relevance with respect to the input claim according to our baseline system.

Input tweet:	A big scandal at @ABC News. They got caught using really gruesome FAKE footage of the Turks bombing in Syria. A real disgrace. Tomorrow they will ask softball questions to Sleepy Joe Biden's son, Hunter, like why did Ukraine & China pay you millions when you knew nothing? Payoff? — Donald J. Trump (@realDonaldTrump) October 15, 2019
Verified claims:	**(1)** ABC News mistakenly aired a video from a Kentucky gun range during its coverage of Turkey's attack on northern Syria in October 2019
	(2) In a speech to U.S. military personnel, President Trump said if soldiers were real patriots, they wouldn't take a pay raise
	(3) Former President Barack Obama tweeted: "Ask Ukraine if they found my birth certificate."

about Syria aired by BBC is fake (input claim), and it further shows some already verified claims ranked by their relevance with respect to the input claim.

Note that the input claim and the most relevant verified claim, while expressing the same concept, are phrased quite differently. A good system for ranking the verified claims might greatly reduce the time that a fact-checkers or a journalist would need to check whether a given input claim has already been fact-checked.

Each input claim was retrieved from the fact-checking website Snopes,[8] which dedicates an article to assessing the truthfulness of each claim they have analyzed. In that article, there might be listed different tweets that contain (a paraphrase of) the target claim. Together with the title of the article page and the rating of the claim, as assigned by Snopes, we collect all those tweets and we use them as input claims. Then, the task is, given such a tweet, to find the corresponding claim. The set of target claims consists of the claims that correspond to the tweets we collected, augmented with all Snopes claims collected by ClaimsKG [48]. Note that we have just one list of verified claims, which is used for matching by all input tweets.

Our data consists of 1,197 input tweets, which we split into training (800 input tweets), development (197 tweets), and test set (200 tweets). These input tweets are to be matched against a set of 10,375 verified claims.

Overview of the Approaches. A total of eight teams participated in Task 2. A variety of scoring functions have been tested, based on supervised learning such as BERT and its variants and SVM, to unsupervised approaches such as simple cosine similarity and scores produced by Terrier and Elastic Search. Two teams focused also on data cleaning by removing URLs, hashtags, usernames

---

[8] www.snopes.com.

Table 7. Task 2, English: summary of the approaches used by the primary system submissions. We report which systems used search engines scores, scoring functions (supervised or not), representations (other than Transformers), and the removal of tokens. We further indicate whether external data was used.

Team		Engine		Scoring							Repr.			Removal					External data
		Terrier	ElasticSearch	LambdaMART	BERT	RoBERTa	Unspecified Transf.	KD search	SVM	Cosine	tf-idf	BM25	Term dependencies	URL removal	Emoji removal	Time removal	Username removal	Hashtag removal	
Buster.AI	[9]					●													●
Check_square	[14]						●	●											
elec-dlnlp	–				●						●								
iit	–				●					●				●	●	●			
TheUofSheffield	[38]								●		●	●		●			●	●	
trueman	–							●											
UB_ET	[49]	●		●										●	●	●			
UNIPI-NLE	[43]		●		●					●									

and emojis from the tweets. Table 7 shows a summary of the approaches used by the primary submissions of the participating teams.

The winning team, **Buster.AI**, cleaned the tweets from non-readable input and used a pre-trained and fine-tuned version of RoBERTa to build their system.

Team **UNIPI-NLE** performed two cascade fine-tuning of a sentence-BERT model. Initially, they fine-tuned on the task of predicting the cosine similarity for tweet–claim. For each tweet, they trained on 20 random negative verified claims and the gold verified claim. The second fine-tuning step fine-tuned the model as a classification task for which sentence-BERT has to output 1 if the pair is correct, and 0 otherwise. They selected randomly two negative examples and used them with the gold to fine-tune the model. Before inference, they pruned the verified claim list, top-2500 using Elastic Search and simple word matching techniques.

Team **UB_ET** trained their model on a limited number of tweet–claim pairs per tweet. They retrieved the top-1000 tweet–claim pairs for each tweet using the DPH information retrieval weighing model and computed several query-related features and then built a LambdaMart model on top of them.

Team **NLP&IR@UNED** used the Universal Sentence Encoder to obtain embeddings for the tweets and for the verified claims. They then trained a feed-forward neural network using the cosine similarity between a tweet and a verified claim, and statistics about the use of words from different parts of speech.

Team **TheUniversityofSheffield** pre-processed the input tweets in order to eliminate hashtags, and then trained a Linear SVM using as features TF.IDF-weighted cosine similarity and BM25 matching scores between the tweets and the verified claims.

Table 8. Task 2, English: performance for the primary submissions and for an Elastic Search (ES) baseline.

Team	MAP				Precision			RR		
	@1	@3	@5	–	@1	@3	@5	@1	@3	@5
Buster.AI	0.897	0.926	0.929	0.929	0.895	0.320	0.195	0.895	0.923	0.927
UNIPI-NLE	0.877	0.907	0.912	0.913	0.875	0.315	0.193	0.875	0.904	0.909
UB_ET	0.818	0.862	0.864	0.867	0.815	0.307	0.186	0.815	0.859	0.862
NLP& IR@UNED	0.807	0.851	0.856	0.861	0.805	0.300	0.185	0.805	0.848	0.854
TheUofSheffield	0.807	0.807	0.807	0.807	0.805	0.270	0.162	0.805	0.805	0.805
trueman	0.743	0.768	0.773	0.782	0.740	0.267	0.164	0.740	0.766	0.771
elec-dlnlp	0.723	0.749	0.760	0.767	0.720	0.262	0.166	0.720	0.747	0.757
Check_square	0.652	0.690	0.695	0.706	0.650	0.247	0.152	0.650	0.688	0.692
baseline (ES)	0.470	0.601	0.609	0.619	0.472	0.249	0.156	0.472	0.603	0.611
iit	0.263	0.293	0.298	0.311	0.260	0.112	0.071	0.260	0.291	0.295

Teams **trueman** and **elec-dlnlp** prepared the input tweets to eliminate hashtags and then used Transformer-based similarity along with Elastic Search scores.

Team **Check_square** fine-tuned sentence-BERT with mined triplets and KD-search.

Team **iit** used cosine similarity using a pre-trained BERT model between the embeddings of the tweet and of the verified claim.

Evaluation. The official evaluation measure for Task 2 is MAP@k for $k = 5$. However, we further report MAP for $k \in \{1, 3, 10, 20\}$, overall MAP, R-Precision, Average Precision, Reciprocal Rank, and Precision@k. Table 8 shows the evaluation results in terms of some of the performance measures for the primary submissions to Task 2. We can see that the winner Buster.AI and the second-best UNIPI-NLE are well ahead of the remaining teams by several points absolute on all evaluation measures. We can further see that most systems managed to outperform an Elastic Search (ES) baseline by a huge margin. The data and the evaluation scripts are available online.[9]

4.3   Task 5$_{en}$. Check-Worthiness on Debates

Task 5 is a legacy task that has evolved from the first edition of `CheckThat`! In each edition, more data from more diverse sources have been added, always with focus on politics. The task focuses on mimicking the selection strategy that fact-checkers, e.g., in PolitiFact, use to select the sentences and the claims to fact-check. The task is defined as follows:

Task 5 (English). *Given a transcript, rank the sentences in the transcript according to the priority to fact-check them.*

---

[9] https://github.com/sshaar/clef2020-factchecking-task2/.

Table 9. Task 5, English: total number of sentences and number of sentences containing claims that are worth fact-checking —organized by type.

Type	Partition	Transcripts	Sentences	Check-worthy
Debates	Train	18	25,688	254
	Test	7	11,218	56
Speeches	Train	18	7,402	163
	Test	8	7,759	50
Interviews	Train	11	7,044	62
	Test	4	2,220	23
Town-halls	Train	3	2,642	8
	Test	1	317	7
Total	**Train**	**50**	**42,776**	**487**
	Test	**20**	**21,514**	**136**

We used *PolitiFact* as the main fact-checking source. On *PolitiFact*, often after a major political event such as a public debate or a speech by a government official, a journalist would go through the transcript of the event and would select few claims that would then be fact-checked. These claims would then be discussed in an article about the debate, published on the same site. We collected all such articles, we further obtained the official transcripts of the event from ABCNews, Washington Post, CSPAN, etc. Since sometimes the claims published in the articles are paraphrased, we double-checked and we manually matched them to the transcripts.

We collected a total of 70 transcripts, and we annotated them based on overview articles from *PolitiFact*. The transcripts belonged to one of four types of political events: Debates, Speeches, Interviews, and Town-halls. We used 50 transcripts for training and 20 for testing. We used the older transcripts for training and the more recent ones for testing. Table 9 shows the total number of sentences of the transcripts and the number of sentences that were fact-checked by *PolitiFact*.

Overview of the Approaches. Three teams participated in this task submitting a total of eight runs. Each of the teams used different text embedding models for the transcripts. The best results were obtained using GloVe's embeddings.

Team **NLP&IR@UNED** used 6B-100D GloVe embeddings as an input to a bidirectional LSTM. They further tried sampling techniques but without success.

Team **UAICS** used the TF.IDF representations using sentences unigrams. They then trained different binary classifiers, such as Logistic regression, Decision Trees, and Naïve Bayes, and they found the latter to perform best.

Team **TOBB ETU** tried fine-tuning BERT and modeling the task as a classification task, but ultimately used part-of-speech (POS) tags with logistic regression and a handcrafted word list from the dataset as their official submission.

Evaluation. As this task was very similar to Task 1, but on a different genre, we used the same evaluation measures: MAP as the official measure, and we also report P@k for various values of k. Table 10 shows the performance of the primary submissions of the participating teams. The overall results are quite low, and only one team managed to beat the n-gram baseline. Once again, the data and the evaluation scripts are available online.[10]

Table 10. Performance of the primary submissions to Task 5 English.

Team	MAP	RR	R-P	P@1	P@3	P@5	P@10	P@20	P@30
NLP&IR@UNED	**0.087**	**0.277**	**0.093**	**0.150**	**0.117**	**0.130**	**0.095**	**0.073**	**0.039**
Baseline (n-gram)	0.053	0.151	0.053	0.050	0.033	0.040	0.055	0.043	0.038
UAICS	0.052	0.225	0.053	**0.150**	0.100	0.070	0.050	0.038	0.027
TOBB ETU P	0.018	0.033	0.014	0.000	0.017	0.020	0.010	0.010	0.006

5 Conclusion and Future Work

We have described the 2020 edition of the `CheckThat!` lab, intended to foster the creation of technology for the (semi-)automatic identification and verification of claims in social media. The task attracted submissions from 23 teams (up from 14 at CLEF 2019): 18 made submissions for English, and 8 for Arabic. We believe that the technology developed to address the five tasks we have proposed will be useful not only as a supportive technology for investigative journalism, but also for the lay citizen, which today needs to be aware of the factuality of the information available online.

Acknowledgments. This work was made possible in part by NPRP grant# NPRP11S-1204-170060 from the Qatar National Research Fund (a member of Qatar Foundation). The statements made herein are solely the responsibility of the authors. The work of Reem Suwaileh was supported by GSRA grant# GSRA5-1-0527-18082 from the Qatar National Research Fund and the work of Fatima Haouari was supported by GSRA grant# GSRA6-1-0611-19074 from the Qatar National Research Fund. This research is also part of the Tanbih project, which aims to limit the effect of disinformation, "fake news", propaganda, and media bias.

References

1. Alam, F., et al.: Fighting the COVID-19 infodemic: modeling the perspective of journalists, fact-checkers, social media platforms, policy makers, and the society. ArXiv:2005.00033 (2020)
2. Alkhalifa, R., Yoong, T., Kochkina, E., Zubiaga, A., Liakata, M.: QMUL-SDS at CheckThat! 2020: determining COVID-19 tweet check-worthiness using an enhanced CT-BERT with numeric expressions. In: Cappellato et al. [10]

---

[10] https://github.com/sshaar/clef2020-factchecking-task5/.

3. Atanasova, P., et al.: Overview of the CLEF-2018 CheckThat! lab on automatic identification and verification of political claims. Task 1: check-worthiness. In: Cappellato et al. [12]

4. Atanasova, P., Nakov, P., Karadzhov, G., Mohtarami, M., Da San Martino, G.: Overview of the CLEF-2019 CheckThat! lab on automatic identification and verification of claims. Task 1: Check-worthiness. In: Cappellato et al. [11]

5. Ba, M.L., Berti-Equille, L., Shah, K., Hammady, H.M.: VERA: a platform for veracity estimation over web data. In: Proceedings of the 25th International Conference Companion on World Wide Web WWW 2016 Companion, pp. 159–162 (2016)

6. Baly, R., et al.: What was written vs. who read it: news media profiling using text analysis and social media context. In: Proceedings of the 58th Annual Meeting of the Association for Computational Linguistics ACL 220, pp. 3364–3374, Seattle, WA, USA (2020)

7. Baly, R., Karadzhov, G., Saleh, A., Glass, J., Nakov, P.: Multi-task ordinal regression for jointly predicting the trustworthiness and the leading political ideology of news media. In: Proceedings of the 17th Annual Conference of the North American Chapter of the Association for Computational Linguistics: Human Language Technologies NAACL-HLT 2019, pp. 2109–2116, Minneapolis, MN, USA (2019)

8. Barrón-Cedeño, A., et al.: Overview of the CLEF-2018 CheckThat! lab on automatic identification and verification of political claims. Task 2: Factuality. In: Cappellato et al. [12]

9. Bouziane, M., Perrin, H., Cluzeau, A., Mardas, J., Sadeq, A.: Buster.AI at CheckThat! 2020: insights and recommendations to improve fact-checking. In: Cappellato et al. [10]

10. Cappellato, L., Eickhoff, C., Ferro, N., Névéol, A. (eds.): Working Notes of CLEF 2020–Conference and Labs of the Evaluation Forum (2020)

11. Cappellato, L., Ferro, N., Losada, D., Müller, H. (eds.): Working Notes of CLEF 2019 Conference and Labs of the Evaluation Forum. In: CEUR Workshop Proceedings, CEUR-WS.org (2019)

12. Cappellato, L., Ferro, N., Nie, J.Y., Soulier, L. (eds.): Working Notes of CLEF 2018-Conference and Labs of the Evaluation Forum. In: CEUR Workshop Proceedings, CEUR-WS.org (2018)

13. Cazalens, S., Lamarre, P., Leblay, J., Manolescu, I., Tannier, X.: A content management perspective on fact-checking. In: 2018 Proceedings of the Web Conference WWW 2018, pp. 565–574 (2018)

14. Cheema, G.S., Hakimov, S., Ewerth, R.: Check_square at CheckThat! 2020: claim detection in social media via fusion of transformer and syntactic features. In: Cappellato et al. [10]

15. Elsayed, T., et al.: CheckThat! at CLEF 2019: automatic identification and verification of claims. In: Azzopardi, L., Stein, B., Fuhr, N., Mayr, P., Hauff, C., Hiemstra, D. (eds.) ECIR 2019. LNCS, vol. 11438, pp. 309–315. Springer, Cham (2019). https://doi.org/10.1007/978-3-030-15719-7_41

16. Elsayed, T., Nakov, P., Barrón-Cedeño, A., Hasanain, M., Suwaileh, R., Da San Martino, G., Atanasova, P.: Overview of the CLEF-2019 CheckThat! lab: automatic identification and verification of claims. In: Crestani, F., Braschler, M., Savoy, J., Rauber, A., Müller, H., Losada, D.E., Heinatz Bürki, G., Cappellato, L., Ferro, N. (eds.) CLEF 2019. LNCS, vol. 11696, pp. 301–321. Springer, Cham (2019). https://doi.org/10.1007/978-3-030-28577-7_25

17. Favano, L., Carman, M., Lanzi, P.: TheEarthIsFlat's submission to CLEF 2019 CheckThat! challenge. In: Cappellato et al. [11]

18. Gasior, J., Przybyła, P.: The IPIPAN team participation in the check-worthiness task of the CLEF2019 CheckThat! lab. In: Cappellato et al. [11]

19. Gencheva, P., Nakov, P., Màrquez, L., Barrón-Cedeño, A., Koychev, I.: A context-aware approach for detecting worth-checking claims in political debates. In: Proceedings of the International Conference Recent Advances in Natural Language Processing RANLP 2017, pp. 267–276 (2017)

20. Ghanem, B., Glavaš, G., Giachanou, A., Ponzetto, S., Rosso, P., Rangel, F.: UPV-UMA at CheckThat! lab: verifying arabic claims using cross lingual approach. In: Cappellato et al. [11]

21. Ghanem, B., Montes-y Gómez, M., Rangel, F., Rosso, P.: UPV-INAOE-Autoritas - check that: preliminary approach for checking worthiness of claims. In: Cappellato et al. [12]

22. Gupta, A., Kumaraguru, P., Castillo, C., Meier, P.: TweetCred: real-time credibility assessment of content on twitter. In: Aiello, L.M., McFarland, D. (eds.) SocInfo 2014. LNCS, vol. 8851, pp. 228–243. Springer, Cham (2014). https://doi.org/10.1007/978-3-319-13734-6_16

23. Hansen, C., Hansen, C., Simonsen, J., Lioma, C.: The Copenhagen team participation in the check-worthiness task of the competition of automatic identification and verification of claims in political debates of the CLEF-2018 fact checking lab. In: Cappellato et al. [12]

24. Hansen, C., Hansen, C., Simonsen, J., Lioma, C.: Neural weakly supervised fact check-worthiness detection with contrastive sampling-based ranking loss. In: Cappellato et al. [11]

25. Haouari, F., Ali, Z., Elsayed, T.: bigIR at CLEF 2019: Automatic verification of Arabic claims over the web. In: Cappellato et al. [11]

26. Hasanain, M., Elsayed, T.: bigIR at CheckThat! 2020: multilingual BERT for ranking Arabic tweets by check-worthiness. In: Cappellato et al. [10]

27. Hasanain, M., et al.: Overview of CheckThat! 2020 Arabic: automatic identification and verification of claims in social media. In: Cappellato et al. [10]

28. Hasanain, M., Suwaileh, R., Elsayed, T., Barrón-Cedeño, A., Nakov, P.: Overview of the CLEF-2019 CheckThat! lab on automatic identification and verification of claims. Task 2: Evidence and factuality. In: Cappellato et al. [11]

29. Hassan, N., Li, C., Tremayne, M.: Detecting check-worthy factual claims in presidential debates. In: Proceedings of the 24th ACM International Conference on Information and Knowledge Management CIKM 2015, pp. 1835–1838 (2015)

30. Hassan, N., Tremayne, M., Arslan, F., Li, C.: Comparing automated factual claim detection against judgments of journalism organizations. In: Computation+Journalism Symposium (2016)

31. Hassan, N., et al.: Claimbuster: the first-ever end-to-end fact-checking system. Proc. VLDB Endowment 10(12), 1945–1948 (2017)

32. Hussein, A., Hussein, A., Ghneim, N., Joukhadar, A.: DamascusTeam at CheckThat! 2020: check worthiness on twitter with hybrid CNN and RNN models. In: Cappellato et al. [10]

33. Karadzhov, G., Nakov, P., Màrquez, L., Barrón-Cedeño, A., Koychev, I.: Fully automated fact checking using external sources. In: Proceedings of the International Conference Recent Advances in Natural Language Processing RANLP 2017, pp. 344–353 (2017)

34. Kartal, Y.S., Kutlu, M.: TOBB ETU at CheckThat! 2020: Prioritizing English and Arabic claims based on check-worthiness. In: Cappellato et al. [10]

35. Konstantinovskiy, L., Price, O., Babakar, M., Zubiaga, A.: Towards automated factchecking: developing an annotation schema and benchmark for consistent automated claim detection (2018). arXiv:1809.08193
36. Ma, J., et al.: Detecting rumors from microblogs with recurrent neural networks. In: Proceedings of the International Joint Conference on Artificial Intelligence IJCAI 2016, pp. 3818–3824 (2016)
37. Martinez-Rico, J., Araujo, L., Martinez-Romo, J.: NLP&IR@UNED at CheckThat! 2020: a preliminary approach for check-worthiness and claim retrieval tasks using neural networks and graphs. In: Cappellato et al. [10]
38. McDonald, T., et al.: The University of Sheffield at CheckThat! 2020: Claim identification and verification on Twitter. In: Cappellato et al. [10]
39. Mitra, T., Gilbert, E.: Credbank: A large-scale social media corpus with associated credibility annotations. In: Proceedings of the Ninth International AAAI Conference on Web and Social Media ICWSM 2015, pp. 258–267 (2015)
40. Mukherjee, S., Weikum, G.: Leveraging joint interactions for credibility analysis in news communities. In: Proceedings of the 24th ACM International Conference on Information and Knowledge Management CIKM 2015, pp. 353–362 (2015)
41. Nakov, P., et al.: Overview of the CLEF-2018 lab on automatic identification and verification of claims in political debates. In: Working Notes of CLEF 2018 - Conference and Labs of the Evaluation Forum CLEF 2018, Avignon, France (2018)
42. Nikolov, A., Da San Martino, G., Koychev, I., Nakov, P.: Team_Alex at CheckThat! 2020: identifying check-worthy tweets with transformer models. In: Cappellato et al. [10]
43. Passaro, L., Bondielli, A., Lenci, A., Marcelloni, F.: UNIPI-NLE at CheckThat! 2020: approaching fact checking from a sentence similarity perspective through the lens of transformers. In: Cappellato et al. [10]
44. Popat, K., Mukherjee, S., Strötgen, J., Weikum, G.: Credibility assessment of textual claims on the web. In: Proceedings of the 25th ACM International Conference on Information and Knowledge Management CIKM 2016, pp. 2173–2178 (2016)
45. Shaar, S., Babulkov, N., Da San Martino, G., Nakov, P.: That is a known lie: Detecting previously fact-checked claims. In: Proceedings of the 58th Annual Meeting of the Association for Computational Linguistics ACL 2020, pp. 3607–3618 (2020)
46. Shaar, S., et al.: Overview of CheckThat! 2020 English: automatic identification and verification of claims in social media. In: Cappellato et al. [10]
47. Shu, K., Sliva, A., Wang, S., Tang, J., Liu, H.: Fake news detection on social media: a data mining perspective. SIGKDD Explor. Newsl. 19(1), 22–36 (2017)
48. Tchechmedjiev, A., et al.: ClaimsKG: a knowledge graph of fact-checked claims. In: Proceedings of the 18th International Semantic Web Conference ISWC 2019, pp. 309–324, Auckland, New Zealand (2019)
49. Thuma, E., Motlogelwa, N.P., Leburu-Dingalo, T., Mudongo, M.: UB_ET at CheckThat! 2020: exploring ad hoc retrieval approaches in verified claims retrieval. In: Cappellato et al. [10]
50. Touahri, I., Mazroui, A.: EvolutionTeam at CheckThat! 2020: integration of linguistic and sentimental features in a fake news detection approach. In: Cappellato et al. [10]
51. Vasileva, S., Atanasova, P., Màrquez, L., Barrón-Cedeño, A., Nakov, P.: It takes nine to smell a rat: neural multi-task learning for check-worthiness prediction. In: Proceedings of the International Conference on Recent Advances in Natural Language Processing RANLP 2019, pp. 1229–1239 (2019)

52. Williams, E., Rodrigues, P., Novak, V.: Accenture at CheckThat! 2020: if you say so: post-hoc fact-checking of claims using transformer-based models. In: Cappellato et al. [10]
53. Zhao, Z., Resnick, P., Mei, Q.: Enquiring minds: early detection of rumors in social media from enquiry posts. In: Proceedings of the 24th International Conference on World Wide Web WWW 2015, pp. 1395–1405 (2015)
54. Zubiaga, A., Liakata, M., Procter, R., Hoi, G.W.S., Tolmie, P.: Analysing how people orient to and spread rumours in social media by looking at conversational threads. PLoS ONE **11**(3), e0150989 (2016)
55. Zuo, C., Karakas, A., Banerjee, R.: A hybrid recognition system for check-worthy claims using heuristics and supervised learning. In: Cappellato et al. [12]

Overview of ChEMU 2020: Named Entity Recognition and Event Extraction of Chemical Reactions from Patents

Jiayuan He[1], Dat Quoc Nguyen[1,4], Saber A. Akhondi[7],
Christian Druckenbrodt[6], Camilo Thorne[6], Ralph Hoessel[2], Zubair Afzal[7],
Zenan Zhai[1], Biaoyan Fang[1], Hiyori Yoshikawa[1,5], Ameer Albahem[3],
Lawrence Cavedon[3], Trevor Cohn[1], Timothy Baldwin[1],
and Karin Verspoor[1(✉)]

[1] The University of Melbourne, Melbourne, Australia
{estrid.he,hiyori.yoshikawa,trevor.cohn,
tbaldwin,karin.verspoor}@unimelb.edu.au
{zenan.zhai,biaoyanf}@student.unimelb.edu.au
[2] Elsevier, Amsterdam, The Netherlands
r.hoessel@elsevier.com
[3] RMIT University, Melbourne, Australia
{ameer.albahem,lawrence.cavedon}@rmit.edu.au
[4] VinAI Research, Hanoi, Vietnam
v.datnq9@vinai.io
[5] Fujitsu Laboratories Ltd., Kawasaki, Japan
[6] Elsevier Information Systems GmbH, Frankfurt, Germany
{c.druckenbrodt,c.thorne.1}@elsevier.com
[7] Elsevier BV, Amsterdam, The Netherlands
{s.akhondi,m.afzal.1}@elsevier.com

Abstract. In this paper, we provide an overview of the Cheminformatics Elsevier Melbourne University (ChEMU) evaluation lab 2020, part of the Conference and Labs of the Evaluation Forum 2020 (CLEF2020). The ChEMU evaluation lab focuses on information extraction over chemical reactions from patent texts. Using the ChEMU corpus of 1500 "snippets" (text segments) sampled from 170 patent documents and annotated by chemical experts, we defined two key information extraction tasks. Task 1 addresses chemical named entity recognition, the identification of chemical compounds and their specific roles in chemical reactions. Task 2 focuses on event extraction, the identification of reaction steps, relating the chemical compounds involved in a chemical reaction. Herein, we describe the resources created for these tasks and the evaluation methodology adopted. We also provide a brief summary of the participants of this lab and the results obtained across 46 runs from 11 teams, finding that several submissions achieve substantially better results than our baseline methods.

Keywords: Named entity recognition · Event extraction · Information extraction · Chemical reactions · Patent text mining

© Springer Nature Switzerland AG 2020
A. Arampatzis et al. (Eds.): CLEF 2020, LNCS 12260, pp. 237–254, 2020.
https://doi.org/10.1007/978-3-030-58219-7_18

1   Introduction

The discovery of new chemical compounds and their synthesis processes is of great importance to the chemical industry. Patent documents contain critical and timely information about newly discovered chemical compounds, providing a rich resource for chemical research in both academia and industry. Chemical patents are often the initial venues where a new chemical compound is disclosed. Only a small proportion of chemical compounds are ever published in journals and these publications can be delayed by up to 3 years after the patent disclosure [5,15]. In addition, chemical patent documents usually contain unique information, such as reaction steps and experimental conditions for compound synthesis and mode of action. These details are crucial for the understanding of compound prior art, and provide a means for novelty checking and validation [3,4]. Due to the high volume of chemical patents [11], approaches that enable automatic information extraction from these patents are in demand. Natural language processing methods are core to meeting the need for large-scale mining of chemical information from patent texts.

The ChEMU (Cheminformatics Elsevier Melbourne University) lab provides participants with opportunities to develop automated approaches for information extraction from chemical reactions in chemical patents. The ChEMU 2020 lab, first introduced in Nguyen et al. (2020) [12], was the first running of ChEMU. Specifically, we provided two information extraction tasks. The first task, named entity recognition, requires identification of essential elements of a chemical reaction, including compounds, conditions and yields, and their specific roles in the reaction. The second task, event extraction, requires the identification of specific event steps that are involved in a chemical reaction. In collaboration with chemical domain experts, we have prepared a high-quality annotated data set of 1,500 segments of chemical patent texts specifically targeting these two tasks.

The rest of the paper is structured as follows. We first introduce the corpus we created for use in the lab in Sect. 2. Then we give an overview of the tasks in Sect. 3 and detail the evaluation framework of ChEMU in Sect. 4 including the evaluation methods and baseline models for each task. We present the evaluation results in Sect. 5 and finally conclude this paper in Sect. 6.

2   The ChEMU Chemical Reaction Corpus

The annotated corpus prepared for the ChEMU shared task consists of 1,500 patent snippets that were sampled from 170 English document patents from the European Patent Office and the United States Patent and Trademark Office. Each snippet contains a meaningful description of a chemical reaction [18].

The corpus was based on information captured in the Reaxys® database.[1] This resource contains details of chemical reactions identified through a mostly manual process of extracting key reaction details from sources including patents and scientific publications, dubbed "excerption" [9].

---

[1] https://www.reaxys.com Reaxys® Copyright ©2020 Elsevier Limited except certain content provided by third parties. Reaxys is a trademark of Elsevier Limited.

2.1 Annotation Process

To prepare the gold-standard annotations for the extracted patent snippets, multiple domain experts with rich expert knowledge in chemistry were invited to assist with corpus annotation. A silver-standard annotation set was first derived by mapping details from records in the Reaxys database to the source patents from which the information was originally extracted, by scanning the texts for mentions of relevant entities. Since the original records refer only to the patent IDs of source texts and do not provide the precise locations of excerpted entities or event steps, these annotations needed to be manually reviewed to produce higher quality annotations. Two domain experts manually annotated all patent snippets independently by correcting location information and adding more annotations. Their annotations were then evaluated by measuring their inter-annotator agreement (IAA) [6], and thereafter merged by a third domain expert who acted as an adjudicator, to resolve differences. More details about the quality evaluation over the annotations and the harmonization process will be provided in a more in-depth paper to follow.

An example snippet

[Step 4] Synthesis of N-((5-(hydrazinecarbonyl)pyridin-2-yl)methyl)-1-methyl-N-phenylpiperidine-4-carboxamide Methyl 6-((1-methyl-N-phenylpiperidine-4-carboxamido)methyl)nicotinate (0.120 g, 0.327 mmol), synthesized in step 3, and hydrazine monohydrate (0.079 mL, 1.633 mmol) were dissolved in ethanol (10 mL) at room temperature, and the solution was heated under reflux for 12 hours, and then cooled to room temperature to terminate the reaction. The reaction mixture was concentrated under reduced pressure to remove the solvent, and the concentrate was purified by column chromatography (SiO2, 4 g cartridge; methanol/dichloromethane = from 5% to 30%) and concentrated to give the title compound (0.115 g, 95.8%) as a foam solid.

Fig. 1. An example snippet with key focus text highlighted.

We present an example of a patent snippet in Fig. 1. This snippet describes the synthesis of a particular chemical compound, named *N-((5-(hydrazinecarbonyl) pyridin-2-yl)methyl)-1-methyl-N-phenylpiperidine-4-carboxamide.* The synthesis process consists of an ordered sequence of reaction steps: (1) dissolving the chemical compound synthesized in step 3 and hydrazine monohydrate in ethanol; (2) heating the solution under reflux; (3) cooling the solution to room temperature; (4) concentrating the cooled mixture under reduced pressure; (5) purification of the concentrate by column chromatography; and (6) concentration of the purified product to get the title compound. We aim to extract the synthesis process from the patent snippet. To achieve this, it is crucial for us to first identify the entities that are involved in these reaction steps (e.g., hydrazine monohydrate and ethanol) and then determine the relations between the involved entities (e.g., hydrazine monohydrate is dissolved in ethanol). Thus, our annotation process consists of two steps: named entity annotations and relation annotations. Next, we describe the two steps of annotations in Sect. 2.2 and Sect. 2.3, respectively.

2.2   Named Entity Annotations

Four categories of entities are annotated over the corpus: (1) chemical compounds that are involved in a chemical reaction; (2) conditions under which a chemical reaction is carried out; (3) yields obtained for the final chemical product; and (4) example labels that are associated with reaction specifications.

Ten labels are further defined under the four categories. We define five different roles that a chemical compound can play within a chemical reaction, corresponding to five labels under this category: STARTING_MATERIAL, REAGENT_CATALYST, REACTION_PRODUCT, SOLVENT, and OTHER_COMPOUND. For example, the chemical compound "ethanol" in Fig. 1 must be annotated with the label "SOLVENT".

We also define two labels under the category of conditions, TIME and TEMPERATURE, and two labels under the category of yields, YIELD_PERCENT and YIELD_OTHER. The definitions of all labels are summarized in Table 1. Interested readers may find more information about the labels in [12] and examples of named entity annotations in the Task 1—NER annotation guidelines [17].

2.3   Relation Annotations

A reaction step usually involves an action (i.e., a trigger word) and chemical compound(s) on which the action takes effect. To fully quantify a reaction step, it is also crucial for us to link an action to the conditions under which the action is carried out, and resultant yields from the action. Thus, annotations in this step are performed to identify the relations between actions (trigger words) and other arguments that are involved in the reaction steps, e.g., chemical compounds and conditions.

We define two types of trigger words: **WORKUP** which refers to an event step where a chemical compound is isolated/purified, and **REACTION_STEP** which refers to an event step that is involved in the conversion from a starting material to an end product. When labelling event arguments, we adapt semantic argument role labels **Arg1** and **ArgM** from the Proposition Bank [13] to label the relations between the trigger words and other arguments. Specifically, the label Arg1 refers to the relation between an event trigger word and a chemical compound. Here, Arg1 represents argument roles of being causally affected by another participant in the event [7]. ArgM represents adjunct roles with respect to an event, used to label the relation between a trigger word and a temperature, time or yield entity. The definitions of trigger word types and relation types are summarized in Table 1. Detailed annotation guidelines for relation annotation are available online [17].

Table 1. Definitions of entity and relation types, i.e., labels, in Task 1 and Task 2.

Label	Definition
Entity annotations	
STARTING_MATERIAL	A substance that is consumed in the course of a chemical reaction providing atoms to products is considered as starting material
REAGENT_CATALYST	A reagent is a compound added to a system to cause or help with a chemical reaction
REACTION_PRODUCT	A product is a substance that is formed during a chemical reaction
SOLVENT	A solvent is a chemical entity that dissolves a solute resulting in a solution
OTHER_COMPOUND	Other chemical compounds that are not the products, starting materials, reagents, catalysts and solvents
TIME	The reaction time of the reaction
TEMPERATURE	The temperature at which the reaction was carried out
YIELD_PERCENT	Yield given in percent values
YIELD_OTHER	Yields provided in other units than %
EXAMPLE_LABEL	A label associated with a reaction specification
Relation annotations	
WORKUP	An event step which is a manipulation required to isolate and purify the product of a chemical reaction
REACTION_STEP	An event within which starting materials are converted into the product
Arg1	The relation between an event trigger word and a chemical compound
ArgM	The relation between an event trigger word and a temperature, time, or yield entity

2.4   Snippet Annotation Format

The gold standard annotations for the data set were delivered in the BRAT standoff format [16]. Two files were delivered for each snippet: a text file (.txt) containing the original texts in the snippet, and a paired annotation file (.ann) containing all the annotations that have been made for that text, including entities, trigger words, and event steps. Continuing with the above snippet example, we show the formatted annotations for the highlighted sentence in Tables 2 and 3. For ease of presentation, we illustrate the format of the annotated named entities and trigger words in Table 2 and the format of the annotated event steps in Table 3 separately. We can see that two entities (i.e., T1 and T2) and one trigger word are included in Table 2. Two event steps are included in Table 3.

Table 2. The annotated entities and trigger words of the snippet example in BRAT standoff format [16].

ID	Entity type	Offsets	Text span
T1	TEMPERATURE	313 329	Room temperature
T2	REAGENT_CATALYST	231 252	Hydrazine monohydrate
T3	REACTION_STEP	281 290	Dissolved

Table 3. The annotated relations of the snippet example in BRAT standoff format [16]. Building on the annotations in Table 2, we see that R6 expresses the relation between a compound participating as a reagent (T2) in the T3 "dissolved" reaction step, and R8 captures the temperature (T1) at which that step occurred.

ID	Event type	Entity 1	Entity 2
R6	Arg1	T3	T2
R8	ArgM	T3	T1

2.5   Data Partitions

We randomly partitioned the whole data set into three splits for training, development and test purposes, with a ratio of 0.6/0.15/0.25. The training and development sets were released to participants for model development. Note that participants are allowed to use the combination of training and development sets and to use their own partitions to build models. The test set is withheld for use in the formal evaluation. The statistics of the three splits including their number of snippets, total number of sentences, and number of words per snippet, are summarized in Table 4.

To ensure the snippets included in the training, development, and test splits have similar distributions over labels, we compare the distributions of entity labels (ten classes of entities in Task 1 and two classes of trigger words in Task 2) of the three splits and summarize the results in Table 5. In Table 5, each cell represents the proportion (e.g., 0.038) of an entity label (e.g., EXAMPLE_LABEL) in the gold annotations of a data split (e.g., Train). The results in Table 5 confirm that the label distributions in the three splits are similar. Only some slight fluctuations (≤ 0.004) across the three splits are observed for each label.

We further compare the International Patent Classification (IPC) [2] distributions of the training, development and test sets. The IPC information of each patent snippet reflects the application category of the original patent, e.g., "A61K" represents the category of patents that are preparations for medical, dental, or toilet purposes. Patents with different IPCs may be written in different ways and may differ in the vocabulary. Thus, they may differ in their linguistic characteristics. For each data split, we extract the primary IPC of each patent snippet included in the data split, and summarize the IPC distributions of the three splits in Table 6.

Table 4. Summary of data set statistics.

Data split	# snippets	#sentences	# words per snippet
Train	900	5,911	112.16
Dev	225	1,402	104.00
Test	375	2,363	108.63

Table 5. Distributions of entity labels in the training, development, and test sets.

Entity label	Train	Dev.	Test
EXAMPLE_LABEL	0.038	0.040	0.037
OTHER_COMPOUND	0.200	0.198	0.205
REACTION_PRODUCT	0.088	0.093	0.091
REAGENT_CATALYST	0.055	0.053	0.053
SOLVENT	0.049	0.046	0.045
STARTING_MATERIAL	0.076	0.076	0.075
TEMPERATURE	0.065	0.064	0.065
TIME	0.046	0.046	0.048
YIELD_OTHER	0.046	0.048	0.047
YIELD_PERCENT	0.041	0.042	0.041
REACTION_STEP	0.164	0.163	0.160
WORKUP	0.132	0.132	0.133

Table 6. Distributions of International Patent Classifications (IPCs) in the training, development, and test sets. Only dominating IPC groups that take up more than 1% of a data split are included in this table.

IPC	Train	Dev.	Test
A61K	0.277	0.278	0.295
A61P	0.129	0.134	0.113
C07C	0.063	0.045	0.060
C07D	0.439	0.444	0.437
C07F	0.011	0.009	0.010
C07K	0.013	0.012	0.008
C09K	0.012	0.021	0.011
G03F	0.012	0.019	0.014
H01L	0.019	0.021	0.019

3   Overview of Tasks

We provide two tasks in ChEMU lab: Task 1—Named Entity Recognition (NER), and Task 2—Event Extraction (EE). We also host a third track where participants can work on building end-to-end systems addressing both tasks jointly.

3.1   Task 1: Named Entity Recognition

In order to understand and extract a chemical reaction from natural language texts, the first essential step is to identify the entities that are involved in the chemical reaction. The first task aims to accomplish this step by identifying the ten types of entities described in Sect. 2.2. The task requires the detection of the entity names in patent snippets and the assignment of correct labels to the detected entities (see Table 1). For example, given a detected chemical compound, the task requires the identification of both its text span and its specific type according to the role in which it plays within a chemical reaction description.

Participants in this track were provided with the patent snippets in the training and development sets and the gold standard entities of these snippets. In the evaluation phase, their models were evaluated using the snippets in the test set.

3.2   Task 2: Event Extraction

A chemical reaction usually consists of an ordered sequence of event steps that transforms a starting product to an end product, such as the five reaction steps in the synthesis process of the chemical compound described in the example in Fig. 1. The event extraction task (Task 2) targets identifying these event steps.

Similarly to conventional event extraction problems [8], Task 2 involves three subtasks: event trigger word detection, event typing and argument prediction. First, it requires the detection of event trigger words and assignment of correct labels for the trigger words. Second, it requires the determination of argument entities that are associated with the trigger words, i.e., which entities identified in Task 1 participate in event or reaction steps. This is done by labelling the connections between event trigger words and their arguments. Given an event trigger word e and a set S of arguments that participate in e, Task 2 requires the creation of $|S|$ relation entries connecting e to an argument entity in S. Here, $|S|$ represents the cardinality of the set S. Finally, Task 2 requires the assignment of correct relation type labels (Arg1 or ArgM) to each of the detected relations.

Participants in the track for Task 2 were provided with the patent snippets in the training and development sets, along with the gold standard entity and event annotations in these snippets. In the evaluation phase, they were provided with the patent snippets in the test set as well as the gold standard entities in these snippets. Their models were evaluated against the ground truth events annotated in the test snippets. While in a real-world use of an event extraction system, gold standard entities would not typically be available, this framework allowed participants to focus on event extraction in isolation of the NER task.

This track was delayed until after both Task 1 and the end-to-end track (described below) were complete, in order to prevent any leakage of the information about gold standard entities from this track to the others.

3.3   End-to-End Systems

We also hosted a third track which allows participants to develop end-to-end systems that address both tasks simultaneously, i.e., the extraction of reaction events including their constituent entities directly from chemical patent snippets. This is a more realistic scenario for an event extraction system to be applied for large-scale annotation of events.

In the evaluation phase, participants in this track were provided only with the text of a patent, and were required to identify the named entities defined in Table 1, the trigger words defined in Sect. 3.2, and the event steps involving the entities, that is, the reaction steps. Proposed models in this track were evaluated against the events that they predict for the test snippets, which is the same as in Task 2. However, a major difference between this track and Task 2 is that the gold named entities were not provided but rather had to be predicted by the systems.

3.4   Track Overview

We illustrate the workflows of the three tracks in Fig. 2 using as example the sentence highlighted in Fig. 1. In Task 1—NER—, participants need to identify entities that defined in Table 1, e.g., the text span "ethanol" is identified as "SOLVENT". In Task 2—EE—, participants are provided with the three gold standard entities in the sentence. They are required to firstly identify the trigger

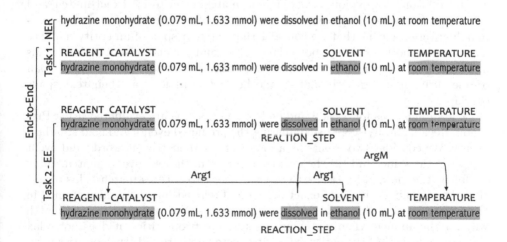

Fig. 2. Illustration of the three tasks. Shaded text spans represents annotated entities or trigger words. Arrows represent relations between entities.

words and their types (e.g., the text span "dissolved" is identified as "REAC-TION_STEP") and then identify the relations between the trigger words and the provided entities (e.g., a directed link from "dissolved" to "ethanol" is added and labeled as "ARG1"). In the track of end-to-end systems, participants are only provided with the original text. They are required to identify both the entities and the trigger words, and predict the event steps directly from the text.

4   Evaluation Framework

In this section, we describe the evaluation framework of the ChEMU lab. We introduce three baseline algorithms for Task 1, Task 2, and end-to-end systems, respectively.

4.1   Evaluation Methods

The evaluation process consists of two phases. In phase one, the text files of the snippets in the test set are provided to all teams participating in Task 1 and the track for end-to-end systems. Once phase one is completed, the gold standard entities of the snippets in the test set are provided to all teams participating in Task 2. For each track, each participating team is allowed to select up to 3 rounds of results (runs) as their final submissions.

We use BRATEval [1] to evaluate all the runs that we receive. Three metrics are used to evaluate the performance of all the submissions for Task 1: Precision, Recall, and F_1-score. Specifically, given a predicted entity and a ground-truth entity, we treat the two entities as a match if (1) the types associated with the two entities match; and (2) their text spans match. The overall Precision, Recall, and F_1-score are computed by micro-averaging all instances (entities).

In addition, we exploit two different matching criteria, exact-match and relaxed-match, when comparing the texts spans of two entities. Here, the exact-match criterion means that we consider that the text span of an entity matches with that of another entity if both the starting and the end offsets of their spans match. The relaxed-match criterion means that we consider that the text span of one entity matches with that of another entity as long as their text spans overlap.

The submissions for Task 2 and end-to-end systems are evaluated using Precision, Recall, and F_1-score by comparing the predicted events and gold standard events. We consider two events as a match if (1) their trigger words and event types are the same; and (2) the entities involved in the two events match. Here, we follow the method in Task 1 to test whether two entities match. This means that the matching criteria of exact-match and relaxed-match are also applied in the evaluation of Task 2 and of end-to-end systems. Note that the relaxed-match will only be applied when matching the spans of two entities; it does not relax the requirement that the entity type of predicted and ground truth entities must agree. Since Task 2 provides gold entities but not event triggers with their ground truth spans, the relaxed-match only reflects the accuracy of spans of predicted trigger words.

To somewhat accommodate a relaxed form of entity type matching, we also evaluate submissions in Task 1—NER using a set of high-level labels shown in the hierarchical structure of entity classes in Fig. 3. The higher-level labels used are highlighted in grey. In this set of evaluations, given a predicted entity and a ground-truth entity, we consider that their labels match as long as their corresponding high-level labels match. For example, suppose we get as predicted entity "STARTING_MATERIAL, [335, 351), boron tribromide" while the (correct) ground-truth entity instead reads "REAGENT_CATALYST, [335, 351), boron tribromide", where each entity is presented in the form of "TYPE, SPAN, TEXT". In the evaluation framework described earlier this example will be counted as a mismatch. However, in this additional set of entity type relaxed evaluations we consider the two entities as a match, since both labels "START-ING_MATERIAL" and "REAGENT_CATALYST" specialize their parent label "COMPOUND".

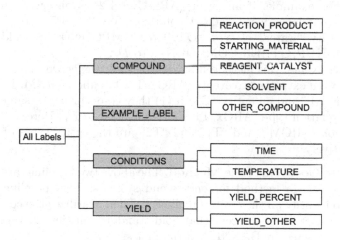

Fig. 3. Illustration of the hierarchical NER class structure used in evaluation.

4.2   Baselines

We released one baseline method for each task as a benchmark method. Specifically, the baseline for Task 1 is based on retraining **BANNER** [10] on the training and development data; the baseline for Task 2 is a co-occurrence method; and the baseline for end-to-end systems is a two-stage algorithm that first uses BANNER to identify entities in the input and then uses the co-occurrence method to extract events.

BANNER. BANNER is a named entity recognition tool for bio-medical data. In this baseline, we first use the GENIA Sentence Splitter (GeniaSS) [14] to split input texts into separate sentences. The resulting sentences are then fed into BANNER, which predicts the named entities using three steps, namely tokenization, feature generation, and entity labelling. A simple tokenizer is used to break sentences into either a contiguous block of letters and/or digits or a single punctuation mark. BANNER uses a conditional random field (CRF) implementation derived from the MALLET toolkit[2] for feature generation and token labelling. The set of machine learning features used consist primarily of orthographic, morphological and shallow syntax features.

Co-occurrence Method. This method first creates a dictionary D_e for the observed trigger words and their corresponding types from the training and development sets. For example, if a word "added" is annotated as a trigger word with the label of "WORKUP" in the training set, we add an entry $\langle$added, WORKUP$\rangle$ to D_e. In the case where the same word has been observed to appear as both types of "WORKUP" and "REACTION_STEP", we only keep as entry in D its most frequent label. The method also creates an event dictionary D_r for the observed event types in the training and development sets. For example, if an event $\langle$ARG1, E1, E2$\rangle$ is observed where "E1" corresponds to trigger word "added" of type "WORKUP" and "E2" corresponds to entity "water" of type "OTHER_COMPOUND", we add an entry $\langle$ARG1, WORKUP, OTHER_COMPOUND$\rangle$ to D_r.

To predict events, this method first identifies all trigger words in the test set using D_e. It then extracts two events $\langle$ARG1, T1, T2$\rangle$ and $\langle$ARGM, T1, T2$\rangle$ for a trigger word "E1" and an entity "E2" if (1) they co-occur in the same sentence; and (2) the relation type $\langle$ARGx, T1, T2$\rangle$ is included in D_r. Here, "ARGx" can be "ARG1" or "ARGM", and "T1" and "T2" are the entity types of "E1" and "E2" respectively.

BANNER + Co-occurrence Method. The above two baselines are combined to form a two-stage method for end-to-end systems. This baseline first uses BANNER to identify all the entities in Task 1. Then it utilizes the co-occurrence method to predict events, except that gold standard entities are replaced with the entities predicted by BANNER in the first stage.

4.3 Submission Website

We developed a submission website which allows participants to submit their predictions for each task during the evaluation phase.[3] In addition, the website offers several important functions to facilitate organizing the lab.

First, it hosts the download links for the training, development, and test data sets so that participants can access the data sets conveniently. Second, it allows participants to test the performance (against the development set) of their models before the evaluation phase starts, which also offers a chance for participants to familiarize themselves with the evaluation tool BRATEval [1].

---

[2] http://mallet.cs.umass.edu/.
[3] http://chemu.eng.unimelb.edu.au/.

The website also hosts a private leaderboard for each team that ranks all runs submitted by each team, and a public leaderboard that ranks all runs that have been made public by teams.

5 Results and Discussions

A total of 39 teams registered for the ChEMU shared task. Among them, 36 teams registered for Task 1, 31 teams registered for Task 2, and 28 teams registered for both tasks. The 39 teams are spread across 13 different countries, from both the academic and industry research communities. In this section, we report the results of all the runs that we received for each task.

5.1   Task 1—Named Entity Recognition

Task 1 received considerable interest with the submission of 25 runs from 11 teams. The 11 teams include 1 team from Germany (OntoChem), 3 teams from India (AUKBC, SSN_NLP and JU_INDIA), 1 team from Switzerland (BiTeM), 1 team from Portugal (Lasige_BioTM), 1 team from Russia (KFU_NLP), 1 team from the United Kingdom (NextMove Software/Minesoft), 2 teams from the United States of America (Melaxtech and NLP@VCU), and 1 team from Vietnam (VinAI). We evaluate the performance of all 25 runs, comparing their predicted entities with the ground-truth entities of the patent snippets in the test set. We report the performances of all runs under both matching criteria in terms of three metrics, namely Precision, Recall, and F_1-score.

We report the overall performance of all runs in Table 7. The baseline of Task 1 achieves 0.8893 in F_1-score under exact match. Nine runs outperform the baseline in terms of F_1-score under exact match. The best run was submitted by team Melaxtech, achieving a high F_1-score of 0.9570. There were sixteen runs with an F_1-score greater than 0.90 under relaxed-match. However, under exact-match, only seven runs surpassed 0.90 in F_1-score. This difference between exact-match and relaxed-match may be related to the long text spans of chemical compounds, which is one of the main challenges in NER tasks in the domain of chemical documents.

Next, we evaluate the performance of all 25 runs using the high-level labels in Fig. 3 (highlighted in grey). We report the performances of all runs in terms of Precision, Recall, and F_1-score in Table 8.

5.2   Task 2—Event Extraction

We received 10 runs from five teams. Specifically, the five teams include 1 team from Portugal (Lasige_BioTM), 1 team from Turkey (BOUN_REX), 1 team from the United Kingdom (NextMove Software/Minesoft) and 2 teams from the United States of America (Melaxtech and NLP@VCU). We evaluate all runs using the metrics Precision, Recall, and F_1-score. Again, we utilize the

Table 7. Overall performance of all runs in Task 1—Named Entity Recognition. Here, P, R, and F represents the Precision, Recall, and F_1-score, respectively. For each metric, we highlight the best result in **bold** and the second best result in *italic*. The results are ordered by their performance in terms of F_1-score under exact-match.

Run	Exact-Match			Relaxed-Match		
	P	R	F	P	R	F
Melaxtech-run1	0.9571	**0.9570**	**0.9570**	0.9690	**0.9687**	**0.9688**
Melaxtech-run2	**0.9587**	*0.9529*	*0.9558*	0.9697	0.9637	0.9667
Melaxtech-run3	*0.9572*	0.9510	0.9541	0.9688	0.9624	0.9656
VinAI-run1	0.9462	0.9405	0.9433	**0.9707**	0.9661	*0.9684*
Lasige_BioTM-run1	0.9327	0.9457	0.9392	0.9590	0.9671	0.9630
BiTeM-run1	0.9378	0.9087	0.9230	0.9692	0.9558	0.9624
BiTeM-run2	0.9083	0.9114	0.9098	0.9510	*0.9684*	0.9596
NextMove/Minesoft-run1	0.9042	0.8924	0.8983	0.9301	0.9181	0.9240
NextMove/Minesoft-run2	0.9037	0.8918	0.8977	0.9294	0.9178	0.9236
Baseline	0.9071	0.8723	0.8893	0.9219	0.8893	0.9053
NLP@VCU-run1	0.8747	0.8570	0.8658	0.9524	0.9513	0.9518
KFU_NLP-run1	0.8930	0.8386	0.8649	*0.9701*	0.9255	0.9473
NLP@VCU-run2	0.8705	0.8502	0.8602	0.9490	0.9446	0.9468
NLP@VCU-run3	0.8665	0.8514	0.8589	0.9486	0.9528	0.9507
KFU_NLP-run2	0.8579	0.8329	0.8452	0.9690	0.9395	0.9540
NextMove/Minesoft-run3	0.8281	0.8083	0.8181	0.8543	0.8350	0.8445
KFU_NLP-run3	0.8197	0.8027	0.8111	0.9579	0.9350	0.9463
BiTeM-run3	0.8330	0.7799	0.8056	0.8882	0.8492	0.8683
OntoChem-run1	0.7927	0.5983	0.6819	0.8441	0.6364	0.7257
AUKBC-run1	0.6763	0.4074	0.5085	0.8793	0.5334	0.6640
AUKBC-run2	0.4895	0.1913	0.2751	0.6686	0.2619	0.3764
SSN_NLP-run1	0.2923	0.1911	0.2311	0.8633	0.4930	0.6276
SSN_NLP-run2	0.2908	0.1911	0.2307	0.8595	0.4932	0.6267
JU_INDIA-run1	0.1411	0.0824	0.1041	0.2522	0.1470	0.1857
JU_INDIA-run2	0.0322	0.0151	0.0206	0.1513	0.0710	0.0966
JU_INDIA-run3	0.0322	0.0151	0.0206	0.1513	0.0710	0.0966

two matching criteria, namely exact-match and relaxed-match, when comparing the trigger words in the submitted runs and ground-truth data.

The overall performance of each run is summarized in Table 9.[4] The baseline (co-occurrence method) scored relatively high in Recall, i.e, 0.8861. This was expected, since the co-occurrence method aggressively extracts all possible events

---

[4] The run that we received from team Lasige_BioTM is not included in the table due to a technical issue found in this run.

within a sentence. However, the F_1-score was low due to its low Precision score. Here, all runs outperform the baseline in terms of F_1-score under exact-match. Melaxtech ranks first among all official runs in this task, with an F_1-score of 0.9536.

Table 8. Overall performance of all runs in Task 1—Named Entity Recognition where the set of high-level labels in Fig. 3 is used. Here, P, R, and F represents the Precision, Recall, and F_1-score, respectively. For each metric, we highlight the best result in **bold** and the second best result in *italic*. The results are ordered by their performance in terms of F_1-score under exact-match.

Run	Exact-Match			Relaxed-Match		
	P	R	F	P	R	F
Melaxtech-run1	*0.9774*	**0.9774**	**0.9774**	0.9906	0.9901	*0.9903*
Melaxtech-run2	**0.9789**	*0.9732*	*0.9760*	*0.9910*	0.9849	0.9879
Melaxtech-run3	0.9775	0.9714	0.9744	0.9905	0.9838	0.9871
Lasige_BioTM-run1	0.9571	0.9706	0.9638	0.9886	*0.9943*	**0.9915**
VinAI-run1	0.9635	0.9579	0.9607	0.9899	0.9854	0.9877
Baseline	0.9657	0.9288	0.9469	0.9861	0.9519	0.9687
BiTeM-run1	0.9573	0.9277	0.9423	0.9907	0.9770	0.9838
NextMove/Minesoft-run2	0.9460	0.9330	0.9394	0.9773	0.9611	0.9691
NextMove/Minesoft-run1	0.9458	0.9330	0.9393	0.9773	0.9610	0.9691
BiTeM-run2	0.9323	0.9357	0.9340	0.9845	**0.9962**	*0.9903*
NextMove/Minesoft-run3	0.9201	0.8970	0.9084	0.9571	0.9308	0.9438
NLP@VCU-run1	0.9016	0.8835	0.8925	0.9855	0.9814	0.9834
NLP@VCU-run2	0.9007	0.8799	0.8902	0.9882	0.9798	0.9840
NLP@VCU-run3	0.8960	0.8805	0.8882	0.9858	0.9869	0.9863
KFU_NLP-run1	0.9125	0.8570	0.8839	**0.9911**	0.9465	0.9683
BiTeM-run3	0.9073	0.8496	0.8775	0.9894	0.9355	0.9617
KFU_NLP-run2	0.8735	0.8481	0.8606	0.988	0.9569	0.9722
KFU_NLP-run3	0.8332	0.8160	0.8245	0.9789	0.9516	0.9651
OntoChem-run1	0.9029	0.6796	0.7755	0.9611	0.7226	0.8249
AUKBC-run1	0.7542	0.4544	0.5671	0.9833	0.5977	0.7435
AUKBC-run2	0.6605	0.2581	0.3712	0.9290	0.3612	0.5201
SSN_NLP-run2	0.3174	0.2084	0.2516	0.9491	0.5324	0.6822
SSN_NLP-run1	0.3179	0.2076	0.2512	0.9505	0.5304	0.6808
JU_INDIA-run1	0.2019	0.1180	0.1489	0.5790	0.3228	0.4145
JU_INDIA-run2	0.0557	0.0262	0.0357	0.4780	0.2149	0.2965
JU_INDIA-run3	0.0557	0.0262	0.0357	0.4780	0.2149	0.2965

5.3   End-to-end Systems

We received 10 end-to-end system runs from four teams. The four teams include 1 team from Turkey (BOUN_REX), 1 team from the United Kingdom (NextMove Software/Minesoft) and 2 teams from the United States of America (Melaxtech and NLP@VCU).

Table 9. Overall performance of all runs in Task 2—Event Extraction. Here, P, R, and F represent the Precision, Recall, and F_1-score, respectively. For each metric, we highlight the best result in **bold** and the second best result in *italics*. The results are ordered by their performance in terms of F_1-score under exact-match.

Run	Exact-Match			Relaxed-Match		
	P	R	F	P	R	F
Melaxtech-run1	*0.9568*	**0.9504**	**0.9536**	*0.9580*	**0.9516**	**0.9548**
Melaxtech-run2	**0.9619**	0.9402	*0.9509*	**0.9632**	0.9414	*0.9522*
Melaxtech-run3	0.9522	*0.9437*	0.9479	0.9534	*0.9449*	0.9491
NextMove/Minesoft-run1	0.9441	0.8556	0.8977	0.9441	0.8556	0.8977
NextMove/Minesoft-run2	0.8746	0.7816	0.8255	0.8909	0.7983	0.8420
BOUN_REX-run1	0.7610	0.6893	0.7234	0.7610	0.6893	0.7234
NLP@VCU-run1	0.8056	0.5449	0.6501	0.8059	0.5451	0.6503
NLP@VCU-run2	0.5120	0.7153	0.5968	0.5125	0.7160	0.5974
NLP@VCU-run3	0.5085	0.7126	0.5935	0.5090	0.7133	0.5941
Baseline	0.2431	0.8861	0.3815	0.2431	0.8863	0.3816

Table 10. Overall performance of all runs in end-to-end systems. Here, P, R, and F represent the Precision, Recall, and F_1-score, respectively. For each metric, we highlight the best result in **bold** and the second best result in *italics*. The results are ordered by their performance in terms of F_1-score under exact-match.

Run	Exact-Match			Relaxed-Match		
	P	R	F	P	R	F
Melaxtech-run1	**0.9201**	**0.9147**	**0.9174**	**0.9319**	**0.9261**	**0.929**
NextMove/Minesoft-run1	*0.8492*	*0.7609*	*0.8026*	*0.8663*	*0.7777*	*0.8196*
NextMove/Minesoft-run2	0.8486	0.7602	0.8020	0.8653	0.7771	0.8188
NextMove/Minesoft-run3	0.8061	0.7207	0.7610	0.8228	0.7371	0.7776
OntoChem-run1	0.7971	0.3777	0.5126	0.8407	0.3984	0.5406
OntoChem-run2	0.7971	0.3777	0.5126	0.8407	0.3984	0.5406
OntoChem-run3	0.7971	0.3777	0.5126	0.8407	0.3984	0.5406
Baseline	0.2104	0.7329	0.3270	0.2135	0.7445	0.3319
Melaxtech-run2	0.2394	0.2647	0.2514	0.2429	0.2687	0.2552
Melaxtech-run3	0.2383	0.2642	0.2506	0.2421	0.2684	0.2545

The overall performance of all runs is summarized in Table 10 in terms of Precision, Recall, and F_1-score under both exact-match and relaxed-match.[5] Since gold entities are not provided in this task, the average performance of the runs in this task are slightly lower than those in Task 2. Note that the Recall scores of most runs are substantially lower than their Precision scores. This may reveal that the task of identifying a relation from a chemical patent is harder than the task of typing an identified relation. The first run from Melaxtech team ranks best among all runs received for this task.

6 Conclusions

This paper presents a general overview of the activities and outcomes of the ChEMU 2020 evaluation lab. The ChEMU lab targets two important information extraction tasks applied to chemical patents: (1) named entity recognition, which aims to identify chemical compounds and their specific roles in chemical reactions; and (2) event extraction, which aims to identify the single event steps that form a chemical reaction.

We received registrations from 39 teams and 46 runs from 11 teams across all tasks and tracks. The evaluation results show that many effective solutions have been proposed, achieving high accuracy on each task. We look forward to fruitful discussions and exploring the methodological details of these submissions at the workshop.

Acknowledgements. We are grateful for the detailed excerption and annotation work of the domain experts that support Reaxys, and the support of Ivan Krstic, Director of Chemistry Solutions at Elsevier. Funding for the ChEMU project is provided by an Australian Research Council Linkage Project, project number LP160101469, and Elsevier.

References

1. BRATEval evaluation tool. https://bitbucket.org/nicta_biomed/brateval/src/master/. Accessed 23 June 2020
2. International Patent Classification. https://www.wipo.int/classifications/ipc/en/. Accessed 23 June 2020
3. Akhondi, S.A., et al.: Annotated chemical patent corpus: a gold standard for text mining. PLoS ONE **9**(9), e107477 (2014)
4. Akhondi, S.A., et al.: Automatic identification of relevant chemical compounds from patents. Database **2019** (2019)
5. Bregonje, M.: Patents: a unique source for scientific technical information in chemistry related industry? World Patent Inf. **27**(4), 309–315 (2005)

---

[5] The run that we received from the Lasige_BioTM team is not included in the table as there was a technical issue in this run. Two runs from Melaxtech, Melaxtech-run2 and Melaxtech-run3, had very low performance, due to an error in their data pre-processing step.

6. Carletta, J.: Assessing agreement on classification tasks: the Kappa statistic. Comput. Linguist. **22**(2), 249–254 (1996). https://www.aclweb.org/anthology/J96-2004

7. Jurafsky, D., Martin, J.H.: Semantic role labeling and argument structure. In: Speech & Language Processing, 3rd edn. Pearson Education India (2009)

8. Kim, J.D., Ohta, T., Pyysalo, S., Kano, Y., Tsujii, J.: Overview of BioNLP 2009 shared task on event extraction. In: Proceedings of the BioNLP 2009 Workshop Companion Volume for Shared Task, pp. 1–9 (2009)

9. Lawson, A.J., Roller, S., Grotz, H., Wisniewski, J.L., Goebels, L.: Method and software for extracting chemical data. German patent no. DE102005020083A1 (2011)

10. Leaman, R., Gonzalez, G.: BANNER: an executable survey of advances in biomedical named entity recognition. In: Pacific Symposium on Biocomputing 2008, pp. 652–663. World Scientific (2008)

11. Muresan, S., et al.: Making every SAR point count: the development of Chemistry Connect for the large-scale integration of structure and bioactivity data. Drug Discov. Today **16**(23–24), 1019–1030 (2011)

12. Nguyen, D.Q., et al.: ChEMU: named entity recognition and event extraction of chemical reactions from patents. In: Jose, J.M., et al. (eds.) ECIR 2020. LNCS, vol. 12036, pp. 572–579. Springer, Cham (2020). https://doi.org/10.1007/978-3-030-45442-5_74

13. Palmer, M., Gildea, D., Kingsbury, P.: The proposition bank: an annotated corpus of semantic roles. Comput. Linguist. **31**(1), 71–106 (2005)

14. Sætre, R., Yoshida, K., Yakushiji, A., Miyao, Y., Matsubayashi, Y., Ohta, T.: AKANE system: protein-protein interaction pairs in BioCreAtIvE2 challenge, PPI-IPS subtask. In: Proceedings of the second BioCreative challenge workshop, Madrid, vol. 209, p. 212 (2007)

15. Senger, S., Bartek, L., Papadatos, G., Gaulton, A.: Managing expectations: assessment of chemistry databases generated by automated extraction of chemical structures from patents. J. Cheminform. **7**(1), 1–12 (2015). https://doi.org/10.1186/s13321-015-0097-z

16. Stenetorp, P., Pyysalo, S., Topić, G., Ohta, T., Ananiadou, S., Tsujii, J.: BRAT: a web-based tool for NLP-assisted text annotation. In: Proceedings of the Demonstrations at the 13th Conference of the European Chapter of the Association for Computational Linguistics, pp. 102–107 (2012)

17. Verspoor, K., et al.: ChEMU dataset for information extraction from chemical patents. https://doi.org/10.17632/wy6745bjfj.1

18. Yoshikawa, H., et al.: Detecting chemical reactions in patents. In: Proceedings of the 17th Annual Workshop of the Australasian Language Technology Association, pp. 100–110 (2019)

Overview of the CLEF eHealth
Evaluation Lab 2020

Lorraine Goeuriot[1]([✉])[iD], Hanna Suominen[2,3,4][iD], Liadh Kelly[5][iD],
Antonio Miranda-Escalada[6][iD], Martin Krallinger[6][iD], Zhengyang Liu[2],
Gabriella Pasi[7][iD], Gabriela Gonzalez Saez[1][iD], Marco Viviani[7][iD],
and Chenchen Xu[2,3]

[1] Univ. Grenoble Alpes, CNRS, Grenoble INP, LIG, 38000 Grenoble, France
`Lorraine.Goeuriot@imag.fr,`
`gabriela-nicole.gonzalez-saez@univ-grenoble-alpes.fr`
[2] The Australian National University,
Canberra, ACT, Australia
`{hanna.suominen,zhengyang.liu,chenchen.xu}@anu.edu.au`
[3] Data61/Commonwealth Scientific and Industrial Research Organisation,
Canberra, ACT, Australia
[4] University of Turku, Turku, Finland
[5] Maynooth University, Maynooth, Ireland
`liadh.kelly@mu.ie`
[6] Barcelona Supercomputing Center (BSC), Barcelona, Spain
`{antonio.miranda,martin.krallinger}@bsc.es`
[7] Department of Informatics, Systems, and Communication,
University of Milano-Bicocca, Milan, Italy
`{gabriella.pasi,marco.viviani}@unimib.it`

Abstract. In this paper, we provide an overview of the eight annual
edition of the Conference and Labs of the Evaluation Forum (CLEF)
eHealth evaluation lab. The Conference and Labs of the Evaluation
Forum (CLEF) eHealth 2020 continues our development of evaluation
tasks and resources since 2012 to address laypeople's difficulties to
retrieve and digest valid and relevant information in their preferred language to make health-centred decisions. This year's lab advertised two
tasks. Task 1 on Information Extraction (IE) was new and focused on
automatic clinical coding of diagnosis and procedure the tenth revision of
the International Statistical Classification of Diseases and Related Health
Problems (ICD10) codes as well as finding the corresponding evidence
text snippets for clinical case documents in Spanish. Task 2 on Information Retrieval (IR) was a novel extension of the most popular and
established task in the Conference and Labs of the Evaluation Forum
(CLEF) eHealth on Consumer Health Search (CHS). In total 55 submissions were made to these tasks. Herein, we describe the resources created

With equal contribution, LG, HS & LK co-chaired the lab. The leaders of Task 1 were
AM-E and MK. The leaders of Task 2 were LG and HS, with LK, ZL, GP, GGS, MV,
and CX as co-organizers and contributors to the evaluation conceptualization, dataset
creation, assessments, and measurements.

© Springer Nature Switzerland AG 2020
A. Arampatzis et al. (Eds.): CLEF 2020, LNCS 12260, pp. 255–271, 2020.
https://doi.org/10.1007/978-3-030-58219-7_19

for the two tasks and evaluation methodology adopted. We also summarize lab submissions and results. As in previous years, the organizers have made data and tools associated with the lab tasks available for future research and development. The ongoing substantial community interest in the tasks and their resources has led to the Conference and Labs of the Evaluation Forum (CLEF) eHealth maturing as a primary venue for all interdisciplinary actors of the ecosystem for producing, processing, and consuming electronic health information.

Keywords: eHealth · Evaluation · Health records · Medical informatics · Information extraction · Information storage and retrieval · Speech recognition · Test-set generation

1 Introduction

Easy-to-understand *Electronic Health Records* (EHRs) can contribute to patients' right—and, if applicable, also their home-based carers or other next-of-kins' right—to be informed about their health and health care. The requirement to ensure that patients can understand their official, privacy-sensitive health information in their own EHR is stipulated by policies and laws [21]. Improving patients' ability to access and digest this content could mean paraphrasing the EHR-text, enriching it with hyperlinks to term definitions, care guidelines, and further supportive information on patient-friendly and reliable websites, helping them to discover good search queries to retrieve more contents, allowing not only text but also speech as a query modality, enabling search in multiple languages, and developing methods for such reading aids to release health care workers' time from EHR-writing to, for example, longer patient-education discussions [39,41].

The *Conference and Labs of the Evaluation Forum* (CLEF) and other information access conferences have organized evaluation labs on related *Electronic Health* (eHealth) *Information Extraction* (IE), *Information Management* (IM), and *Information Retrieval* (IR) tasks for approximately 20 years. Yet they have predominantly targeted the health care experts' information needs only [2,3,12]. A rare exception is the annual *CLEF eHealth Evaluation-lab and Lab-workshop Series* from 2012 to 2020 [9,10,15–17,38,42,44]. In 2012, the first scientific CLEF workshop took place, with an aim of establishing an evaluation campaign, and from 2013 to 2020, this annual workshop has been supplemented with a lead-up evaluation lab, consisting of up to three shared tasks each year. Although the tasks have been centered around the patients and their families' needs in accessing and understanding eHealth information, additional use cases were also addressed in 2015–2019, for example, *Automatic Speech Recognition* (ASR) and IE to aid clinicians in IM.

In 2020, CLEF eHealth advertised two tasks. Task 1 on IE was new and focused on clinical coding of terms or evidence for assigning diagnosis or procedure codes to clinical textual data in Spanish. Task 2 on IR included a traditional adhoc task, as well as a novel extension of the adhoc task with spoken queries on

Consumer Health Search (CHS). Further details on the previous task/problem specifications and data and methods releases of these tasks are available in [39] and [17].

The remainder of this overview paper is structured as follows: First, in Sect. 2, we detail for each task its text documents; human annotations, queries, and relevance assessments; and evaluation methods. After this, in Sect. 3, we describe the task submissions and results of the CLEF eHealth 2020 evaluation lab. Finally, we compare with prior editions of CLEF eHealth and conclude the paper.

2   Materials and Methods

In this section, we describe the materials and methods used in the two tasks of the CLEF eHealth evaluation lab 2020. After specifying our text documents to process in Sect. 2.1, we address their human annotations, queries, and relevance assessments in Sect. 2.2. Finally, in Sect. 2.3, we introduce our evaluation methods.

2.1   Text Documents

Task 1. For the 2020 Task 1 (abbreviated as CodiEsp; promoted by the Plan de Impulso de las Tecnologías del Lenguaje - Plan TL, https://www.plantl.gob. es) we used the SPACCC corpus of Spanish clinical case documents [1,13], a collection of 1,000 carefully selected clinical cases resembling EHRs classified manually using the MyMiner File Labelling tool [35] by a practicing physician with assistance of a clinical documentalist. This dataset was already exploited previously for other shared tasks related to the automatic detection of drugs, chemical compounds and genes (PharmaCoNER Track, [1]) and partially for the detection and resolution of medical abbreviations (BARR2, [13]). Overall, this corpus contains a total of 16,504 sentences and 396,988 tokens, with an average of 396.99 tokens per clinical case, thus these records are considerably longer than the data used by past CLEF clinical coding tasks employing death certificates [24–26] and non-technical summaries of animal experimentation [27].[1]

As this corpus includes records from a variety of clinical disciplines, such as oncology, cardiology, ophthalmology, urology or infectious diseases it covers a great diversity of clinical fields, increasing the complexity for natural language processing tasks.

Mentions of diagnostics and medical procedures evidence text snippets were annotated manually and mapped to the *tenth revision of the International Statistical Classification of Diseases and Related Health Problems* (ICD10) codes by experts in clinical coding to generate a Gold Standard corpus (annotation information is depicted in Sect. 2.2). Thereafter, we randomly generated three

---

[1] The CodiEsp corpus, together with the other generated resources are available at the *Medical Natural Language Processing* (NLP) Zenodo community, https://zenodo. org/communities/medicalnlp/ and at the shared task webpage, https://temu.bsc.es/ codiesp/.

non-overlapping subsets: training set (500 documents), development and test set (250 documents each).

To facilitate comparison to systems working with data in English, and explore the use of machine translation technologies to extend or complement traditional corpus construction approaches, we also provided participants an automatically translated version of our corpus into English (CodiEsp *Machine Translation* (MT) corpus). Therefore we constructed a machine translation approach (English-Spanish) adapted to the language characteristics of the medical domain [37].

To use this task setting to extend the initial CodiEsp corpus (Gold Standard manual annotations) by generating a silver standard consisting of automatic annotations generated by participating teams, similar to the CALBC initiative [33], we added to the test set an additional collection of 2,751 documents [22].

It is noteworthy to point out that a corpus of only 1,000 documents for a complex clinical coding task with thousands of possible codes or class labels is rather small to fully exploit the predictive power of more advanced machine learning approaches.

To overcome this issue, we generated two additional data collections, exploiting existing mappings between clinical coding terms from the *tenth revision of the International Statistical Classification of Diseases and Related Health Problems* (ICD10) to *Medical Subject Headings* (MeSH) terms using the *Unified Medical Language System* (UMLS) Metathesaurus. Moreover, in turn most *Medical Subject Headings* (MeSH) terms do have a corresponding DeCS code. Thus by using the mapping chain [DeCS →*Medical Subject Headings* (MeSH) → *Unified Medical Language System* (UMLS) →the *tenth revision of the International Statistical Classification of Diseases and Related Health Problems* (ICD10)] we could generate a collection of medical literature manually indexed with either DeCS or *Medical Subject Headings* (MeSH) and index them with their corresponding the *tenth revision of the International Statistical Classification of Diseases and Related Health Problems* (ICD10) codes resulting in the CodiEsp-abstracts corpus. It is composed of 176,294 Spanish medical abstracts indexed with the *tenth revision of the International Statistical Classification of Diseases and Related Health Problems* (ICD10) codes.

Task 2. The 2018 CLEF eHealth Consumer Health Search document collection was used in this year's IR challenge. As detailed in [14], this collection consists of web pages acquired from the CommonCrawl. An initial list of websites was identified for acquisition. The list was built by submitting queries on the 2018/2020 topics to the Microsoft Bing APIs (through the Azure Cognitive Services) repeatedly over a period of a few weeks, and acquiring the URLs of the retrieved results. The domains of the URLs were then included in the list, except some domains that were excluded for decency reasons. The list was further augmented by including a number of known reliable health websites and other known unreliable health websites, from lists previously compiled by health institutions and agencies. See [11] for full details on the Task 2 dataset.

2.2   Human Annotations, Queries, and Relevance Assessments

Task 1. Due to the complexity and practical importance of clinical coding the CodiEsp corpus was generated by a team of professional clinical coding experts. In addition to assigning clinical codes they also had to label the textual evidence supporting the code assignment.

To assure quality and to determine the difficulty of this task, the annotation process followed an iterative annotation team training exercise until a satisfactory *Inter-Annotator Agreement* (IAA) was reached. Finally, a set of 50 records were double annotated (blinded) by two different expert annotators, reaching a pairwise agreement of 80.5% on the annotations of the evidence text spans and of 88.6% for the assignment of documents to diagnostic codes and 88.9% for procedure codes.

We released the plain text documents together with a tab-separated file with the annotation information similar to the format employed in past CLEF clinical coding tasks [27].

The CodiEsp corpus covers 3,427 unique ICD-10 codes corresponding to a total of 18,435 manual document-code annotations. The most common code is r52, corresponding to "unspecified pain"; which is repeated 361 times across the entire corpus. 1,830 codes appear more than once, among which 346 codes appear more than 10 times. A large amount of infrequent codes poses an extra challenge for CodiEsp participants, which some of them have surpassed using the additional corpus, CodiEsp-abstracts.

Task 2. Historically the CLEF eHealth IR task has released text queries representative of layperson medical information needs in various scenarios. In recent years query variations issued by multiple laypeople for the same information need have been offered. In this year's task, we extended this to spoken queries. These spoken queries were generated by 6 individuals using the information needs derived for the 2018 challenge. We also provided textual transcripts of these spoken queries and automatic speech-to-text translations. The topics for the adhoc subtask were similar to 2018 CHS task topics: 50 queries, which were issued by the general public to the HON (*Health on the Net*) search service. These queries were manually selected by a domain expert from a sample of raw queries collected over a period of 6 months to be representative of the type of queries posed to the search engine. Queries were not preprocessed, for example any spelling mistakes that may be present have not been removed. All the queries from the adhoc task have been recorded with several users for the subtask on Spoken queries retrieval. A transcription of these audio files was also provided, using ESPNET, Librispeech, CommonVoice and Google API (with three models). Spoken queries could be downloaded from a secured server, with an agreement signed by the participating team.

The relevance assessment has been conducted on three relevance dimensions: topicality, understandability and credibility. Topicality is a classical relevance dimension ensuring that the document and the query are on the same topic and the document answers the query. Understandability is an estimation of whether the document is understandable by a patient. Topicality and understandability have been used as relevance dimensions in the CHS task of CLEF eHealth for several years. This year, we introduced a novel dimension, i.e., *credibility*, which is as a perceived quality of the information receiver. It is composed of *multiple dimensions* that have to be considered and evaluated together in the process of information credibility assessment [4, 36]. In the health-related context, the multiple dimensions that have to be considered when evaluating information credibility are related to the *source* that disseminate a content, the characteristics related to the *message* diffused, and *social aspects* if the information is disseminated through virtual communities [45]. Therefore, the assessors were asked to evaluate the above-mentioned multiple aspects by considering, at the same time, any information available about the trustworthiness of the source of the health-related information [20] (the fact that information comes from a Web site with a good or bad *reputation*, or the level of *expertise* of an individual answering on a blog or a question-answering system, etc.), the *syntactic/semantic characteristics* of the content [5] (in terms of completeness, language register, style, etc.), and any information emerging from social interactions [32] (the fact circle of social relationships of the author of a content is reliable or not, the fact that the author is involved in many discussions, etc.). All the dimensions were considered on a 3-levels scale:

- *not relevant/understandable/credible*
- *somewhat relevant/understandable/credible*
- *highly relevant/understandable/credible*
- We added a 4th option for credibility for assessors uncertainty: *I am not able to judge.*

Relevance assessments are currently in progress.

Similar to the 2016, 2017 and 2018 pools, we created the pool using the RBP-based Method A (Summing contributions) by Moffat et al. [23], in which documents are weighted according to their overall contribution to the effectiveness evaluation as provided by the RBP formula (with p=0.8, following Park and Zhang [31]). This strategy, named RBPA, was chosen because it was shown that it should be preferred over traditional fixed-depth or stratified pooling when deciding upon the pooling strategy to be used to evaluate systems under fixed assessment budget constraints [19], as it is the case for this task. As the topics were similar, the pool is an extension of 2018's pool.

2.3   Evaluation Methods

Task 1. Task 1 was composed of three distinct subtasks: CodiEsp-Diagnostic, CodiEsp-Procedure, and CodiEsp-Explainability. Participants of the CodiEsp-Diagnostic and CodiEsp-Procedure tracks predicted the ICD-10 codes for the 250 documents contained in the test set. Predictions were compared or assessed against manually assigned annotations. CodiEsp-Explainability participants had to predict not only the codes but also the corresponding textual evidence snippets to enable human interpretation or validation of automatic assignments. For the

CodiEsp-Diagnostic and CodiEsp-Procedure subtasks, the codes assigned to each document had to be ranked, providing high confidence codes on the top of the list. Thus more relevance was given to predictions for which the system was more confident. The main metric for these two subtasks was Mean Average Precision (MAP). MAP is a widely established metric in ranking problems and was used by other challenges like TREC. It stands for Mean Average Precision, where the Average Precision represents the average precision of a document at every position in the ranked codes. That is, precision is computed considering only the first ranked code; then, it is computed considering the first two codes, and so on. Finally, precision values are averaged over the number of codes in the gold standard (the relevant number of codes).

For completeness, error analysis, and comparison reasons, other metrics are computed for these two subtasks: MAP@k (MAP taking into account just the first k results), f-score, precision, and recall.

Since the scope of the explainability subtask is different and more challenging, participants were evaluated with f-score, precision, and recall.

Task 2. For Subtasks 1 and 2, participants could submit up to 4 runs in TREC format. Evaluation measures are NDCG@10, BPref and RBP. Metrics such as uRBP will be used to capture various relevance dimensions.

3   Results

CLEF eHealth tasks offered every year in 2013–2020 have brought together researchers working on health information access topics. It has provided them with data and computational resources to work with and validate their outcomes. These contributions of the lab have accelerated pathways from scientific ideas through influencing research and development to societal impact. Targeted use scenarios for the designed, developed, and evaluated technologies have included easing patients, their families, clinical staff, health scientists, and health care policy makers in accessing and understanding health information. Its niche is addressing health information needs of laypeople (including, but not limited to, patients, their families, clinical staff, health scientists, and health care policy makers)—and not health care experts only—in a range of languages—in retrieving and digesting valid and relevant eHealth information to make health-centered decisions [2,3,12,39,40].

By 2020, the CLEF cHealth evaluation lab has matured as a popular primary venue for all interdisciplinary actors of the ecosystem for producing, processing, and consuming eHealth information. In 2013, 2014, 2015, 2016, 2017, 2018, 2019, and 2020 as many as 170, 220, 100, 116, 67, 70, 67, and 57 teams have registered their expression of interest in the CLEF eHealth tasks, respectively, and the number of teams proceeding to the task submission stage has been 53, 24, 20,

20, 32, 28, 9, and 55 respectively [9,10,15–17,42,44].[2] In 2020, 51 and 24 teams registered to CLEF eHealth Task 1 and Task 2, respectively; 18 teams expressed their interest in this way to both offered tasks. Of the 55 CLEF eHealth submissions in 2020, 22 targeted the CodiEspD Diagnostic subtask of Task 1, 17 the CodiEspP Procedure subtask of Task 1, and 8 the CodiEspX Explainability subtask of Task 1. Among five submission to the 2020 CLEF eHealth Task 2, the ad hoc IR subtask was the most popular with its three submissions; the subtasks that used transcriptions of the spoken queries and the original audio files received one submission each.

Next, more details about the task outcomes are presented. See [22] and [11] for further details.

3.1 Task 1

51 teams registered for Task 1 (CodiEsp), out of which 22 submitted predictions for at least one of the three subtracks. We allowed a total of 5 runs for each sub-track, so that teams could explore different approaches. 47 submissions were made in total, 22 for subtask CodiEsp-Diagnostic, 17 for CodiEsp-Procedure, and 8 for CodiEsp-Explainability. The number of submitted runs were: 78 for CodiEsp-Diagnostic, 64 for CodiEsp-Procedure, and 25 for CodiEsp-Explainability. In total, 167 clinical coding systems were created in the context of Task 1.

From the 22 participant teams, 3 reported being a commercial organization. Despite the fact that the used data was in Spanish, the participation was global covering teams not only from Spanish-speaking countries (Spain and Argentina) but also from India, Italy, Germany, United States, Japan, France, Belgium, Turkey, and the UK.

All best-performing teams obtained higher results than the baseline. In CodiEsp-Diagnostic, the best Mean Average Precision result has been 0.593, obtained by the team IXA-AAA. In the CodiEsp-Procedure subtask, team IAM obtained 0.493 MAP, the best result. For comparison purposes with past clinical coding shared tasks, we also provide the best results in terms of f1-score, precision, and recall. In CodiEsp-Diagnostic, the highest achieved f1-score was 0.687; the highest precision was 0.866, and the highest recall was 0.897. In CodiEsp-Procedure, they were 0.522, 0.833, and 0.825, respectively. Finally, in CodiEsp-Explainability, two teams (FLE and IAM) achieved 0.611 f1-score, 0.75 was the top precision, and 0.562 the top recall. In the three subtasks, teams that developed the highest-performing systems were closely followed by others.

3.2 Task 2

The 2020 CLEF eHealth Task 2 attracted five submissions (Table 1). Its ad hoc IR subtask was the most popular (three submissions). Two of these teams also

---

[2] "Expressing an interest" for a CLEF task consists of filling in a form on the CLEF conference website with contact information, and tick boxes corresponding to the labs of interest.

submitted to the subtasks based on spoken queries. Specifically, the subtask that used transcriptions of the spoken queries had one submission and the subtask where the original audio files were processed had one submission. The submitting teams were from Australia, France, and Italy and had 4, 1, and 6 team members, respectively. They were all from academia and each team had members from a single organization.

Although these submission numbers were considerably smaller than in the seven previous years of running the CHS task [39–41], the organizers were pleased with this newly introduced task, with its novel spoken queries element attracting interest and submissions.

Table 1. Descriptive statistics about teams that submitted to the CLEF eHealth 2020 Task 2

Subtasks	No. of coauthors	Authors' affliction	Affiliation country
Ad Hoc search & spoken queries using transcriptions	1	1 university	Italy
Ad Hoc search & spoken queries using audio files	6	1 university	France
Ad Hoc search	4	1 university	Australia

The Italian submission to the Ad Hoc Search and Spoken Queries Using Transcription subtasks was by Associate Professor Giorgio Maria Di Nunzio from the Information Management System (IMS) Group of the University of Padua. His submission to the former task included BM25 of the original query; Reciprocal Rank fusion with BM25, *Query Language Model* (QLM), and *Divergence from Randomness* (DFR) approaches. Reciprocal Rank fusion with BM25, QLM, and DFR approaches using pseudo relevance feedback with 10 documents and 10 terms (the query weight of 0.5); and Reciprocal rank fusion with BM25 run on manual variants of the query. His submission to the latter task included the Reciprocal Rank fusion with BM25; Reciprocal Rank fusion with BM25 using pseudo relevance feedback with 10 documents and 10 terms (the query weight of 0.5); Reciprocal Rank fusion of BM25 with all transcriptions; and Reciprocal Rank fusion of BM25 with all transcripts using pseudo relevance feedback with 10 documents and 10 terms (the query weight of 0.5).

The French team was formed by Dr Philippe Mulhem, Aidan Mannion, Gabriela Gonzalez Saez, Associate Professor Didier Schwab, and Jibril Frej from the Laboratoire d'Informatique de Grenoble of the Univ. Grenoble Alpes. Their team name was LIG-Health. To the Ad Hoc Search task, they submitted runs using Terrier BM25 as a baseline, and explored various expansion methods using UMLS, using the Consumer Health Vocabulary, expansion using Fast Text; and Terrier BM25 with RF (bose-Einstein) weighted expansion. For the

Spoken Queries they used various transcriptions on the same models, opting for the best performing ones based on 2018 qrels. They submitted merged runs for each query.

The Australian team—called SandiDoc from the Our Health In Our Hands (OHIOH) Big Data program, Research School of Computer Science, College of Engineering and Computer Science, The Australian National University had Sandaru Seneviratne, Dr Eleni Daskalaki, Dr Artem Lenskiy, and Dr Zakir Hossain as its members—took part in the Ad Hoc Search task with a method founded on $TF \times IDF$ scoring. First, they pre-processed both the queries and the dataset. Then, they obtained TF×ID scores for the queries and used these TF × ID scores to obtain the most similar documents for the queries. Finally, they supplemented this method by working on the clefehealth2018_B dataset using the medical skip-gram word embeddings (vectors_medtrack_skipgram_s500_w5_neg20_hs0_sam1e-4_iter5) provided. To represent the documents and queries, they used the average word vector representations as well as the average of minimum and maximum vector representations of the document or query. In documents, these representations were obtained using the 100 most frequent words in a document. For each of these two representations, they calculated the similarity among documents and queries using the cosine measure to obtain the final results for the task. The aim was to experiment with different vector representations for text.

In addition to these participants' methods, we as the organizers developed baseline methods that were based on the renown OKapi BM25 but now with REINFORCE based query expansion. This baseline method had the following two phases: First, the initial query was enriched with a query expansion model, which was pre-trained on general corpora and then used to retrieve documents by reusing the commonly-used BM25 algorithm [34]. Second, in the query expansion phase, the system was optimized in an reinforcement learning paradigm as proposed in [28]. Given an original query, the system performed trials of generating new queries and rewarded them by matching the documents retrieved from these queries against the ground truth ranking. The context words in the newly retrieved documents also contributed to the construction of queries for the next iteration in order to ensure enough data sources for the learning process. This baseline adopted the pre-trained model optimized on the TREC-CAR, Jeopardy, and MSA datasets [28]. Once the query was expanded to a few related candidates, they were fed to a general implementation of BM25 algorithm to retrieve the final set of documents.

The intuition behind this query expansion was that a layperson may lack the professional knowledge to accurately describe medical terms; differently to the rigorous wording in the medical documents to be retrieved, a layperson's input query usually contains inexact and long descriptions. Thus, query expansion was applied to automatically rewrite the query in a way that increases the probability of matching more candidates. In this baseline method, we employed the REINFORCE algorithm introduced in [46]. Given an original query q_0, it retrieved some ranked documents D_0 and from where new candidate query q_0' was constructed. The new query q_0' was fed back into the retrieval system to produce ranked documents D'_0. This process of documents retrieval and construction of new query was iterated to create training examples $\{(q'_0, D'_0), (q'_1, D'_1), \ldots\}$. At each step, the operations adopted to reformulate the new query were recorded as the actions. The retrieved documents D'_k were then compared against the ground truth ranking result to calculate the reward for this new query and so were the actions to generate it. The process was optimized in a reinforcement learning paradigm to learn a system that could generate a series of candidate queries from an input one. In particular, the stochastic objective to optimize was:

$$C_a = (R - \bar{R}) \sum_{t \in T} - \log P(t \mid q_0),$$

where R and $\bar{R}$ are the reward from the new query and baseline reward, and $t \in T$ are words from the new query.

The relevance assessments are being collected at the time of writing of this paper. See the Task 2 overview paper for further details and the results of the evaluation [11].

4   Comparison with Prior CLEF eHealth Work

Since its inception the CLEF eHealth lab series has offered IE and IR shared challenges. In particular, IE challenges related to ICD-10 coding started in 2016, and query driven IR challenges started in 2013 with the commencement of the lab.

4.1   Information Extraction

CLEF eHealth 2016 evaluation lab [24] challenged participants to assign ICD-10 codes to death certificates in French. The corpus contained a collection of sentences extracted from 27,850 death certificates. The coding of these documents is relevant to guide public health policies. There were 5 participant teams, teams achieved 0.719 f1-score on average and the best run reached 0.848 f1-score. In terms of precision, the best run reached 0.813 and in terms of recall, 0.890.

On CLEF eHealth 2017 Multilingual Information Extraction task [25], participants again had to assign ICD-10 codes to sentences extracted from death certificates. In this case, both in English and French. The corpus contained a collection of sentences extracted from 31,690 French death certificates and 6,665 English death certificates. There were 10 competing systems for the English subtask and 9 for the French one. The highest performance in French was 0.867 f1-score. The highest precision was 0.881 and highest recall 0.875.

The same setting was replicated on CLEF eHealth 2018 Multilingual Information Extraction task [26]. However, death certificates in Hungarian and Italian are added in this edition. There was higher participation, with 14 teams working on French death certificates, 5 on Hungarian, and 6 on Italian. The best systems achieved 0.838 f1-score on French, 0.963 on Hungarian, and 0.952 on Italian.

The best precision scores were 0.835, 0.955 and 0.945. Finally, best recalls were 0.846, 0.97 and 0.96.

CLEF eHealth 2019 Multilingual Information Extraction [27] proposed a novel type of document to code, non-technical summaries of animal experimentation. Coding them is relevant to support the analysis of animal experimentation data. In addition, this year's evaluation lab provided the documents in German language and the goal of the edition was to assign ICD-10 codes to the complete document, not to individual sentences. There were 6 competing teams and the top-performing team achieved an f1-score of 0.80. The best recall was 0.86 and the best precision 0.98.

This year's CLEF eHealth Multilingual Information Extraction task (CodiEsp) introduced a clinical coding challenge in a new language, Spanish; on a new kind of document, clinical case reports; and with a different evaluation metric, Mean Average Precision. It has attracted a higher interest within the community since the number of participants has increased to 22 (Fig. 1).

The CodiEsp corpus was more complex (longer documents covering heterogeneous clinical specialties) than in the shared tasks from 2016, 2017 and 2018; since death certificates are much shorter narratives than clinical case records [18]. In addition, these past shared tasks involved clinical coding of diagnostics; while this year's shared task included a subtask on clinical coding of procedures. Finally, the dataset employed in 2016, 2017 and 2018 was more extensive: for 3,457 unique codes, there were 377,677 code assignments; while our contains 18,435 annotations for 3427 unique codes.

The CodiEsp corpus was also more complex than the corpus of 2019's shared task. Both had a similar number of code assignments, but the latter included 233 distinct codes, while our corpus had 3,427 unique codes. However, the CodiEsp corpus provided the textual evidence supporting the coding decision, which has helped teams building systems not based on document or sentence classification and partially bridges the complexity gap between both datasets.

This increase in complexity may have been one of the reasons for the differences in team performance (see Sect. 3 on results). However, it is noteworthy that team IAM, which employed a similar method in 2018's and in this year's shared tasks obtained comparable f1-scores: 0.666 in the French raw clinical coding and 0.687 in CodiEsp-Diagnostic.

4.2 Information Retrieval

In 2013 and 2014 the focus of the IR task was on evaluating the effectiveness of search engines to support people when searching for information about known conditions, for example, to answer queries like "thrombocytopenia treatment corticosteroids length", with multilingual queries added in the 2014 challenge [6–8]. This task aimed to model the scenario of a patient being discharged from hospital and wanting to seek more information about diagnosed conditions or prescribed treatments.

In 2015 the IR task changed to focus on studying the effectiveness of search engines to support individuals' queries issued for self-diagnosis purposes, and

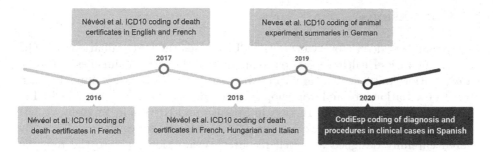

Fig. 1. Clinical coding CLEF eHealth shared tasks.

again offered a multilingual queries challenge [29]. In addition, we began adding personalization elements to the challenge on an incremental basis by assessing the readability of information and taking this into account in the evaluation framework.

This individualized IR approach was continued in the 2016 and 2017 labs [30,47] and we also introduced gradual shifts from an ad-hoc search paradigm (that of a single query and a single document ranking) to a session based search paradigm. Along these lines we also revised how relevance is measured for evaluation purposes, taking into account instead whole-of-session usefulness.

In 2018 [14] we continued this evolution, and introduced query intent elements. 7 teams participated in this challenge. The IR task did not run in 2019.

This year's challenge built on the 2018 challenge by introducing a new spoken query element, whereby participants had the additional optional challenge of retrieving using speech-to-text translations of the queries. This challenge used the same document collection as that used in 2018 and also the same topics, for which new spoken queries were generated by 6 individuals accounting for 6 query variants. Text transcripts of the queries were also available. The primary new element then of this year's challenge was the provision of spoken queries and speech-to-text translations of these queries.

The CHS task has been exploring for several years health documents relevance and its dimensions. This has been a great success and has led to the creation of systems better suited to the patients. The introduction of the credibility in the dimension this year is another step towards better and safer health information online.

Given 5 teams participated in this year's challenge relative to the 7 in the 2018 IR challenge, one might conjecture that the optional use of spoken queries was off putting for potential teams. However, both 2018 and 2020 participant figures are down on the earlier years of the IR challenge, where in excess of 10 teams participated each year. Earlier cycles of the IR challenge adopted a simpler ad-hoc IR challenge approach and used simpler IR metrics. We have found that as the task increased in complexity and further options for participation in the form of subtasks have been added that the number of participating teams has decreased. That being said, we find much use of the datasets post CLEF [39].

5 Conclusions

This paper provided an overview of the CLEF eHealth 2020 evaluation lab. The inaugural CLEF eHealth workshop took place in 2012 with an aim of establishing an evaluation lab [38]. This ambition was realised in 2013, with annual CLEF eHealth evaluation labs and workshops organized every year since 2013 [9,10,15–17,43,44]. In 2020, it ran an IE task in Spanish and IR task in English.

During these past nine years, the CLEF eHealth series has continuously offered carefully designed and well resourced evaluation tasks to the research and development community. This contribution includes, but is not limited to, the creation and dissemination of speech and text analytics resources such as problem/task specifications, test collections, annotations, assessments, annotation/assessment methods, processing methods, evaluation methods, and evaluation benchmarks in understanding, accessing, and authoring health information in a multilingual setting.

Given the significance of the CLEF eHealth community, tasks, and resources over the years, our aim is to keep the tasks going in years to come. Our releases so far can be found on our CLEF eHealth website[3].

Acknowledgements. We gratefully acknowledge the contribution of the people and organizations involved in CLEF eHealth in 2012–2020 as participants or organizers. We thank the CLEF Initiative, Benjamin Lecouteux (Université Grenoble Alpes), João Palotti (Qatar Computing Research Institute), and Guido Zuccon (University of Queensland). We also thank the individuals who generated spoken queries for the IR challenge. We are very grateful to our assessors that helped despite the COVID-19 crisis: Paola Alberti, Vincent Arnone, Nathan Baran, Pierre Barbe, Francesco Bartoli, Nicola Brew-Sam, Angela Calabrese, Sabrina Caldwell, Daniele Cavalieri, Madhur Chhabra, Luca Cuffaro, Yerbolat Dalabayev, Emine Darici, Marco Di Sarno, Mauro Guglielmo, Weiwei Hou, Yidong Huang, Zhengyang Liu, Federico Moretti, Marie Revet, Paritosh Sharma, Haozhan Sun, Christophe Zeinaty. The lab has been supported in part by (in alphabetical order) The Australian National University, College of Engineering and Computer Science, Research School of Computer Science; and the CLEF Initiative. We acknowledge the Encargo of Plan TL (SEAD) to CNIO and BSC for funding, and the scientific committee for their valuable comments and guidance.

References

1. Agirre, A.G., Marimon, M., Intxaurrondo, A., Rabal, O., Villegas, M., Krallinger, M.: Pharmaconer: pharmacological substances, compounds and proteins named entity recognition track. In: Proceedings of The 5th Workshop on BioNLP Open Shared Tasks, pp. 1–10 (2019)
2. Demner-Fushman, D., Elhadad, N.: Aspiring to unintended consequences of natural language processing: a review of recent developments in clinical and consumer-generated text processing. Yearb. Med. Inform. **1**, 224–233 (2016)

---

[3] https://clefehealth.imag.fr/ (last accessed on 19 June 2020).

3. Filannino, M., Uzuner, Ö.: Advancing the state of the art in clinical natural language processing through shared tasks. Yearb. Med. Inform. **27**(01), 184–192 (2018)

4. Fogg, B.J., Tseng, H.: The elements of computer credibility. In: Proceedings of SIGCHI (1999)

5. Fontanarava, J., Pasi, G., Viviani, M.: Feature analysis for fake review detection through supervised classification. In: 2017 IEEE International Conference on Data Science and Advanced Analytics (DSAA), pp. 658–666. IEEE (2017)

6. Goeuriot, L., et al.: ShARe/CLEF eHealth Evaluation Lab 2013, Task 3: Information retrieval to address patients' questions when reading clinical reports. CLEF 2013 Online Working Notes 8138 (2013)

7. Goeuriot, L., et al.: An analysis of evaluation campaigns in ad-hoc medical information retrieval: CLEF eHealth 2013 and 2014. Inf. Retriev. J. **21**(6), 507–540 (2018). https://doi.org/10.1007/s10791-018-9331-4

8. Goeuriot, L., et al.: ShARe/CLEF eHealth evaluation lab 2014, task 3: user-centred health information retrieval. In: CLEF 2014 Evaluation Labs and Workshop: Online Working Notes. Sheffield, England (2014)

9. Goeuriot, L., et al.: Overview of the CLEF eHealth evaluation lab 2015. In: Mothe, J., et al. (eds.) CLEF 2015. LNCS, vol. 9283, pp. 429–443. Springer, Cham (2015). https://doi.org/10.1007/978-3-319-24027-5_44

10. Goeuriot, L., et al.: CLEF 2017 eHealth evaluation lab overview. In: Jones, G.J.F., et al. (eds.) CLEF 2017. LNCS, vol. 10456, pp. 291–303. Springer, Cham (2017). https://doi.org/10.1007/978-3-319-65813-1_26

11. Goeuriot, L., et al.: Overview of the CLEF eHealth 2020 task 2: consumer health search with ad hoc and spoken queries. In: Working Notes of Conference and Labs of the Evaluation (CLEF) Forum. CEUR Workshop Proceedings (2020)

12. Huang, C.C., Lu, Z.: Community challenges in biomedical text mining over 10 years: Success, failure and the future. Briefings Bioinform. **17**(1), 132–144 (2016)

13. Intxaurrondo, A., et al.: Finding mentions of abbreviations and their definitions in spanish clinical cases: the barr2 shared task evaluation results. In: IberEval@ SEPLN, pp. 280–289 (2018)

14. Jimmy, J., Zuccon, G., Palotti, J., Goeuriot, L., Kelly, L.: Overview of the CLEF 2018 consumer health search task. In: Working Notes of Conference and Labs of the Evaluation (CLEF) Forum. CEUR Workshop Proceedings (2018)

15. Kelly, L., Goeuriot, L., Suominen, H., Névéol, A., Palotti, J., Zuccon, G.: Overview of the CLEF eHealth evaluation lab 2016. In: Fuhr, N., Quaresma, P., Gonçalves, T., Larsen, B., Balog, K., Macdonald, C., Cappellato, L., Ferro, N. (eds.) CLEF 2016. LNCS, vol. 9822, pp. 255–266. Springer, Cham (2016). https://doi.org/10.1007/978-3-319-44564-9_24

16. Kelly, L., et al.: Overview of the ShARe/CLEF eHealth evaluation lab 2014. In: Kanoulas, E., et al. (eds.) CLEF 2014. LNCS, vol. 8685, pp. 172–191. Springer, Cham (2014). https://doi.org/10.1007/978-3-319-11382-1_17

17. Kelly, L., et al.: Overview of the CLEF eHealth evaluation lab 2019. In: Crestani, F., et al. (eds.) CLEF 2019. LNCS, vol. 11696, pp. 322–339. Springer, Cham (2019). https://doi.org/10.1007/978-3-030-28577-7_26

18. Lavergne, T., Névéol, A., Robert, A., Grouin, C., Rey, G., Zweigenbaum, P.: A dataset for ICD-10 coding of death certificates: creation and usage. In: Proceedings of the Fifth Workshop on Building and Evaluating Resources for Biomedical Text Mining (BioTxtM2016), pp. 60–69. The COLING 2016 Organizing Committee, Osaka, Japan, December 2016. https://www.aclweb.org/anthology/W16-5107

19. Lipani, A., Palotti, J., Lupu, M., Piroi, F., Zuccon, G., Hanbury, A.: Fixed-cost pooling strategies based on IR evaluation measures. In: Jose, J.M., et al. (eds.) ECIR 2017. LNCS, vol. 10193, pp. 357–368. Springer, Cham (2017). https://doi.org/10.1007/978-3-319-56608-5_28
20. Livraga, G., Viviani, M.: Data confidentiality and information credibility in on-line ecosystems. In: Proceedings of the 11th International Conference on Management of Digital EcoSystems, pp. 191–198 (2019)
21. McAllister, M., Dunn, G., Payne, K., Davies, L., Todd, C.: Patient empowerment: the need to consider it as a measurable patient-reported outcome for chronic conditions. BMC Health Serv. Res. **12**, 157 (2012)
22. Miranda-Escalada, A., Gonzalez-Agirre, A., Armengol-Estapé, J., Krallinger, M.: Overview of automatic clinical coding: annotations, guidelines, and solutions for non-English clinical cases at codiesp track of CLEF eHealth 2020. In: Working Notes of Conference and Labs of the Evaluation (CLEF) Forum. CEUR Workshop Proceedings (2020)
23. Moffat, A., Zobel, J.: Rank-biased precision for measurement of retrieval effectiveness. ACM Trans. Inf. Syst. **27**(1), 2:1–2:27 (2008). https://doi.org/10.1145/1416950.1416952
24. Névéol, A., et al.: Clinical information extraction at the CLEF eHealth evaluation lab 2016. In: Balog, K., Cappellato, L., Ferro, N., Macdonald, C. (eds.) CLEF 2016 Working Notes. CEUR Workshop Proceedings (CEUR-WS.org) (2016). ISSN 1613–0073, http://ceur-ws.org/Vol-1609/
25. Névéol, A., et al.: CLEF eHealth 2017 multilingual information extraction task overview: Icd10 coding of death certificates in English and french. In: CLEF 2017 Online Working Notes. CEUR-WS (2017)
26. Névéol, A., et al.: CLEF eHealth 2018 multilingual information extraction task overview: Icd10 coding of death certificates in French, Hungarian and Italian. In: CLEF 2018 Online Working Notes. CEUR-WS (2018)
27. Neves, M., et al.: Overview of task 1 in CLEF eHealth 2019: indexing German non-technical summaries of animal experiments. In: CLEF 2019 Online Working Notes. CEUR-WS (2019)
28. Nogueira, R., Cho, K.: Task-oriented query reformulation with reinforcement learning. In: Proceedings of the 2017 Conference on Empirical Methods in Natural Language Processing. Association for Computational Linguistics (2017). https://doi.org/10.18653/v1/d17-1061
29. Palotti, J., et al.: CLEF eHealth evaluation lab 2015, task 2: retrieving information about medical symptoms. In: CLEF 2015 Online Working Notes. CEUR-WS (2015)
30. Palotti, J., et al.: CLEF 2017 task overview: the IR task at the eHealth evaluation lab. In: Working Notes of Conference and Labs of the Evaluation (CLEF) Forum. CEUR Workshop Proceedings (2017)
31. Park, L.A., Zhang, Y.: On the distribution of user persistence for rank-biased precision. In: Proceedings of the 12th Australasian Document Computing Symposium, pp. 17–24 (2007)
32. Pasi, G., Viviani, M.: Information credibility in the social web: Contexts, approaches, and open issues. arXiv preprint arXiv:2001.09473 (2020)
33. Rebholz-Schuhmann, D., et al.: CALBC silver standard corpus. J. bioinform. Comput. Biol. **8**(01), 163–179 (2010)
34. Robertson, S.: The probabilistic relevance framework: BM25 and beyond. Found. Trends® Inf. Retriev. **3**(4), 333–389 (2010). https://doi.org/10.1561/1500000019
35. Salgado, D., et al.: MyMiner: a web application for computer-assisted biocuration and text annotation. Bioinformatics **28**(17), 2285–2287 (2012)

36. Self, C.C.: Credibility. In: An Integrated Approach to Communication Theory and Research, pp. 449–470. Routledge (2014)
37. Soares, F., Krallinger, M.: BSC participation in the WMT translation of biomedical abstracts. In: Proceedings of the Fourth Conference on Machine Translation (Volume 3: Shared Task Papers, Day 2), pp. 175–178 (2019)
38. Suominen, H.: CLEFeHealth2012 – The CLEF 2012 workshop on cross-language evaluation of methods, applications, and resources for eHealth document analysis. In: Forner, P., Karlgren, J., Womser-Hacker, C., Ferro, N. (eds.) CLEF 2012 Working Notes. CEUR Workshop Proceedings (CEUR-WS.org) (2012). ISSN 1613–0073, http://ceur-ws.org/Vol-1178/
39. Suominen, H., Kelly, L., Goeuriot, L.: Scholarly influence of the conference and labs of the evaluation forum eHealth Initiative: review and bibliometric study of the 2012 to 2017 outcomes. JMIR Res. Protoc. **7**(7), e10961 (2018). https://doi.org/10.2196/10961
40. Suominen, H., Kelly, L., Goeuriot, L.: The scholarly impact and strategic intent of CLEF eHealth labs from 2012 to 2017. Information Retrieval Evaluation in a Changing World. TIRS, vol. 41, pp. 333–363. Springer, Cham (2019). https://doi.org/10.1007/978-3-030-22948-1_14
41. Suominen, H., Kelly, L., Goeuriot, L., Krallinger, M.: CLEF ehealth evaluation lab 2020. In: Jose, J.M., Yilmaz, E., Magalhães, J., Castells, P., Ferro, N., Silva, M.J., Martins, F. (eds.) Advances in Information Retrieval, pp. 587–594. Springer International Publishing, Cham (2020)
42. Suominen, H., et al.: Overview of the CLEF eHealth evaluation lab 2018. In: Bellot, P., et al. (eds.) Experimental IR Meets Multilinguality, Multimodality, and Interaction, pp. 286–301. Springer, Cham (2018). https://doi.org/10.1007/978-3-319-98932-7_26
43. Suominen, H., et al.: Overview of the CLEF ehealth evaluation lab 2018. In: International Conference of the Cross-Language Evaluation Forum for European Languages, pp. 286–301. Springer, Heidelberg (2018)
44. Suominen, H., et al.: Overview of the ShARe/CLEF eHealth evaluation lab 2013. In: Forner, P., Müller, H., Paredes, R., Rosso, P., Stein, B. (eds.) CLEF 2013. LNCS, vol. 8138, pp. 212–231. Springer, Heidelberg (2013). https://doi.org/10.1007/978-3-642-40802-1_24
45. Viviani, M., Pasi, G.: Credibility in social media: opinions, news, and health information–a survey. Wiley Interdisc. Rev.: Data Mining Knowl. Disc. **7**(5), e1209 (2017)
46. Williams, R.J.: Simple statistical gradient-following algorithms for connectionist reinforcement learning. In: Reinforcement Learning, pp. 5–32. Springer, US (1992). https://doi.org/10.1007/978-1-4615-3618-5_2
47. Zuccon, G., et al.: The IR Task at the CLEF eHealth evaluation lab 2016: user-centred Health information retrieval. In: CLEF 2016 Evaluation Labs and Workshop: Online Working Notes, CEUR-WS, September 2016

Overview of eRisk 2020: Early Risk Prediction on the Internet

David E. Losada[1]([✉]), Fabio Crestani[2], and Javier Parapar[3]

[1] Centro Singular de Investigación en Tecnoloxías Intelixentes (CiTIUS),
Universidade de Santiago de Compostela, Santiago de Compostela, Spain
david.losada@usc.es
[2] Faculty of Informatics, Università della Svizzera italiana (USI),
Lugano, Switzerland
fabio.crestani@usi.ch
[3] Information Retrieval Lab, Centro de Investigación en Tecnologías de la
Información y las Comunicaciones, Universidade da Coruña, A Coruña, Spain
javierparapar@udc.es

Abstract. This paper provides an overview of eRisk 2020, the fourth edition of this lab under the CLEF conference. The main purpose of eRisk is to explore issues of evaluation methodology, effectiveness metrics and other processes related to early risk detection. Early detection technologies can be employed in different areas, particularly those related to health and safety. This edition of eRisk had two tasks. The first task focused on early detecting signs of self-harm. The second task challenged the participants to automatically filling a depression questionnaire based on user interactions in social media.

1 Introduction

The main purpose of eRisk is to explore issues of evaluation methodologies, performance metrics and other aspects related to building test collections and defining challenges for early risk detection. Early detection technologies are potentially useful in different areas, particularly those related to safety and health. For example, early alerts could be sent when a person starts showing signs of a mental disorder, when a sexual predator starts interacting with a child, or when a potential offender starts publishing antisocial threats on the Internet.

Although the evaluation methodology (strategies to build new test collections, novel evaluation metrics, etc) can be applied on multiple domains, eRisk has so far focused on psychological problems (essentially, depression, self-harm and eating disorders). In 2017 [3,4], we ran an exploratory task on early detection of depression. This pilot task was based on the evaluation methodology and test collection presented in [2]. In 2018 [5,6], we ran a continuation of the task on early detection of signs of depression together with a new task on early detection of signs of anorexia. In 2019 [7,8], we had a continuation of the task on early detection of signs of anorexia, a new task on early detection of signs of

© Springer Nature Switzerland AG 2020
A. Arampatzis et al. (Eds.): CLEF 2020, LNCS 12260, pp. 272–287, 2020.
https://doi.org/10.1007/978-3-030-58219-7_20

self-harm and a third task oriented to estimate a user's answers to a depression questionnaire based on his interactions on social media.

Over these years, we have been able to compare a number of solutions that employ multiple technologies and models (e.g. Natural Language Processing, Machine Learning, or Information Retrieval). We learned that the interaction between psychological problems and language use is challenging and, in general, the effectiveness of most contributing systems is modest. For example, most challenges had levels of performance (e.g. in terms of F1) below 70%. This suggests that this kind of early prediction tasks require further research and the solutions proposed so far still have much room from improvement.

In 2020, the lab had two campaign-style tasks. The first task had the same orientation of previous early detection tasks. It focused on early detection of signs of self-harm. The second task was a continuation of 2019's third task. It was oriented to analyzing a user's history of posts and extracting useful evidence for estimating the user's depression level. More specifically, the participants had to process the user's posts and, next, estimate the user's answers to a standard depression questionnaire. These tasks are described in the next sections of this overview paper.

2   Task 1: Early Detection of Signs of Self-Harm

This is the continuation of eRisk 2019's T2 task. The challenge consists of sequentially processing pieces of evidence and detect early traces of self-harm as soon as possible. The task is mainly concerned about evaluating Text Mining solutions and, thus, it concentrates on texts written in Social Media. Texts had to be processed in the order they were posted. In this way, systems that effectively perform this task could be applied to sequentially monitor user interactions in blogs, social networks, or other types of online media.

The test collection for this task had the same format as the collection described in [2]. The source of data is also the same used for previous eRisks. It is a collection of writings (posts or comments) from a set of Social Media users. There are two categories of users, self-harm and non-self harm, and, for each user, the collection contains a sequence of writings (in chronological order).

In 2019, we moved from a chunk-based release of data (used in 2017 and 2018) to a item-by-item release of data. We set up a server that iteratively gave user writings to the participating teams. In 2020, the same server was used to provide the users' writings during the test stage. More information about the server can be found at the lab website[1].

The 2020 task was organized into two different stages:

- Training stage. Initially, the teams that participated in this task had access to a training stage where we released the whole history of writings for a set of training users (we provided all writings of all training users), and we indicated what users had explicitly mentioned that they have done self-harm.

---

[1] http://early.irlab.org/server.html.

Table 1. Task1 (self-harm). Main statistics of the train and test collections

	Train		Test	
	Self-harm	Control	Self-harm	Control
Num. subjects	41	299	104	319
Num. submissions (posts & comments)	6,927	163,506	11,691	91,136
Avg num. of submissions per subject	169.0	546.8	112.4	285.6
Avg num. of days from first to last submission	≈495	≈500	≈270	≈426
Avg num. words per submission	24.8	18.8	21.4	11.9

The participants could therefore tune their systems with the training data. In 2020, the training data for Task 1 was composed of all 2019's T2 users.

- Test stage. The test stage consisted of a period of time where the participants had to connect to our server and iteratively got user writings and sent responses. Each participant had the opportunity to stop and make an alert at any point of the user chronology. After reading each user post, the teams had to choose between: i) emitting an alert on the user, or ii) making no alert on the user. Alerts were considered as final (i.e. further decisions about this individual were ignored), while *no alerts* were considered as non-final (i.e. the participants could later submit an alert for this user if they detected the appearance of risk signs). This choice had to be made for each user in the test split. The systems were evaluated based on the accuracy of the decisions and the number of user writings required to take the decisions (see below). A REST server was built to support the test stage. The server iteratively gave user writings to the participants and waited for their responses (no new user data provided until the system said alert/no alert). This server was running from March 2nd, 2020 to May 24th, 2020[2].

Table 1 reports the main statistics of the train and test collections used for T1. Evaluation measures are discussed in the next section.

2.1 Decision-Based Evaluation

This form of evaluation revolves around the (binary) decisions taken for each user by the participating systems. Besides standard classification measures (Precision, Recall and F1[3]), we computed $ERDE$, the early risk detection error used in the previous editions of the lab. A full description of $ERDE$ can be found in [2].

---

[2] In the initial configuration, the test period was shorter but, because of the COVID-19 situation, we decided to extend the test stage in order to facilitate participation.

[3] Computed with respect to the positive class.

Essentially, $ERDE$ is an error measure that introduces a penalty for late correct alerts (true positives). The penalty grows with the delay in emitting the alert, and the delay is measured here as the number of user posts that had to be processed before making the alert.

Since 2019, we complemented the evaluation report with additional decision-based metrics that try to capture additional aspects of the problem. These metrics try to overcome some limitations of $ERDE$, namely:

- the penalty associated to true positives goes quickly to 1. This is due to the functional form of the cost function (sigmoid).
- a perfect system, which detects the true positive case right after the first round of messages (first chunk), does not get error equal to 0.
- with a method based on releasing data in a chunk-based way (as it was done in 2017 and 2018) the contribution of each user to the performance evaluation has a large variance (different for users with few writings per chunk vs users with many writings per chunk).
- $ERDE$ is not interpretable.

Some research teams have analysed these issues and proposed alternative ways for evaluation. Trotzek and colleagues [10] proposed $ERDE_o^\%$. This is a variant of ERDE that does not depend on the number of user writings seen before the alert but, instead, it depends on the *percentage* of user writings seen before the alert. In this way, user's contributions to the evaluation are normalized (currently, all users weight the same). However, there is an important limitation of $ERDE_o^\%$. In real life applications, the overall number of user writings is not known in advance. Social Media users post contents online and screening tools have to make predictions with the evidence seen. In practice, you do not know when (and if) a user's thread of message is exhausted. Thus, the performance metric should not depend on such lack of knowledge about the total number of user writings.

Another proposal of an alternative evaluation metric for early risk prediction was done by Sadeque and colleagues [9]. They proposed $F_{latency}$, which fits better with our purposes. This measure is described next.

Imagine a user $u \in U$ and an early risk detection system that iteratively analyzes u's writings (e.g. in chronological order, as they appear in Social Media) and, after analyzing k_u user writings ($k_u \geq 1$), takes a binary decision $d_u \in \{0, 1\}$, which represents the decision of the system about the user being a risk case. By $g_u \in \{0, 1\}$, we refer to the user's golden truth label. A key component of an early risk evaluation should be the delay on detecting true positives (we do not want systems to detect these cases too late). Therefore, a first and intuitive measure of delay can be defined as follows[4]:

---

[4] Observe that Sadeque et al. (see [9], p. 497) computed the latency for all users such that $g_u = 1$. We argue that latency should be computed only for the true positives. The false negatives ($g_u = 1$, $d_u = 0$) are not detected by the system and, therefore, they would not generate an alert.

$$\text{latency}_{TP} = \text{median}\{k_u : u \in U, d_u = g_u = 1\} \tag{1}$$

This measure of latency goes over the true positives detected by the system and assesses the system's delay based on the median number of writings that the system had to process to detect such positive cases. This measure can be included in the experimental report together with standard measures such as Precision (P), Recall (R) and the F-measure (F):

$$P = \frac{|u \in U : d_u = g_u = 1|}{|u \in U : d_u = 1|} \tag{2}$$

$$R = \frac{|u \in U : d_u = g_u = 1|}{|u \in U : g_u = 1|} \tag{3}$$

$$F = \frac{2 \cdot P \cdot R}{P + R} \tag{4}$$

Furthermore, Sadeque et al. proposed a measure, $F_{latency}$, which combines the effectiveness of the decision (estimated with the F measure) and the delay[5]. This is based on multiplying F by a penalty factor based on the median delay. More specifically, each individual (true positive) decision, taken after reading k_u writings, is assigned the following penalty:

$$penalty(k_u) = -1 + \frac{2}{1 + \exp^{-p \cdot (k_u - 1)}} \tag{5}$$

where p is a parameter that determines how quickly the penalty should increase. In [9], p was set such that the penalty equals 0.5 at the median number of posts of a user[6]. Observe that a decision right after the first writing has no penalty ($penalty(1) = 0$). Figure 1 plots how the latency penalty increases with the number of observed writings.

The system's overall speed factor is computed as:

$$speed = (1 - \text{median}\{penalty(k_u) : u \in U, d_u = g_u = 1\}) \tag{6}$$

speed equals 1 for a system whose true positives are detected right at the first writing. A slow system, which detects true positives after hundreds of writings, will be assigned a speed score near 0.

Finally, the *latency-weighted* F score is simply:

$$F_{latency} = F \cdot speed \tag{7}$$

---

[5] Again, we adopt Sadeque et al.'s proposal but we estimate latency only over the true positives.

[6] In the evaluation we set p to 0.0078, a setting obtained from the eRisk 2017 collection.

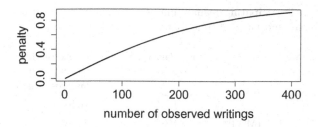

Fig. 1. Latency penalty increases with the number of observed writings (k_u)

Since 2019 user's data was processed by the participants in a post by post basis (i.e. we avoided a chunk-based release of data). Under these conditions, the evaluation approach has the following properties:

- smooth grow of penalties.
- a perfect system gets $F_{latency} = 1$.
- for each user u the system can opt to stop at any point k_u and, therefore, now we do not have the effect of an imbalanced importance of users.
- $F_{latency}$ is more interpretable than $ERDE$.

2.2   Ranking-Based Evaluation

This section discusses an alternative form of evaluation, which was used as a complement of the evaluation described above. After each release of data (new user writing) the participants had to send back the following information (for each user in the collection): i) a decision for the user (alert/no alert), which was used to compute the decision-based metrics discussed above, and ii) a score that represents the user's level of risk (estimated from the evidence seen so far). We used these scores to build a ranking of users in decreasing estimation of risk. For each participating system, we have one ranking at each point (i.e., ranking after 1 writing, ranking after 2 writings, etc.). This simulates a continuous re-ranking approach based on the evidence seen so far. In a real life application, this ranking would be presented to an expert user who could take decisions (e.g. by inspecting the rankings).

Each ranking can be scored with standard IR metrics, such as P@10 or NDCG. We therefore report the ranking-based performance of the systems after seeing k writings (with varying k).

2.3   Task 1: Results

Table 2 shows the participating teams, the number of runs submitted and the approximate lapse of time from the first response to the last response. This lapse of time is indicative of the degree of automation of each team's algorithms.

Table 2. Task 1. Participating teams: number of runs, number of user writings processed by the team, and lapse of time taken for the whole process.

Team	#runs	#user writings processed	Lapse of time (from 1st to last response)
UNSL	5	1990	10 h
INAOE-CIMAT	5	1989	7 days + 7 h
BiTeM	5	1	1 min
EFE	3	1991	12 h
NLP-UNED	5	554	1 day
BioInfo@UAVR	3	565	2 days + 21 h
SSN_NLP	5	222	3 h
Anji	5	1990	1 day + 3 h
hildesheim	5	522	72 days + 20 h
RELAI	5	1990	2 days + 8 h
prhlt-upv	5	627	1 day + 8 h
iLab	5	954	20 h

A few of the submitted runs processed the entire thread of messages (nearly 2000), but many variants opted for stopping earlier. Six teams processed the thread of messages in a reasonably fast way (less than a day or so for processing the entire history of user messages). The rest of the teams took several days to run the whole process. Some teams took even more than a week. This suggests that they incorporated some form of offline processing.

Table 3 reports the decision-based performance achieved by the participating teams.

In terms of Precision, $F1$, ERDE measures and latency-weighted $F1$, the best performing runs were submitted by the iLab team. The first two iLab runs had extremely high precision (.833 and .913, respectively) and the first one (run #0) had the highest latency-weighted F1 (.658). These runs had low levels of recall (.577 and .404) and they only analyzed a median of 10 user writings. This suggests that you can get to a reasonably high level of precision based on a few user writings. The main limitation of these best performing runs is the low levels of recall achieved. In terms of $ERDE$, the best performing runs show low levels of error (.134 and .071). ERDE measures set a strong penalty on late decisions and the two best runs show a good balance between the accuracy of the decisions and the delays (latency of the true positives was 2 and 45, respectively, for the two runs that achieved the lowest $ERDE_5$ and $ERDE_{50}$).

Other teams submitted high recall runs but their precision was very low and, thus, these automatic methods are hardly usable to filter out non-risk cases.

Most teams submitted quick decisions. Only iLab and prhlt-upv have some runs that analysed more than a hundred submissions before emitting the alerts (mean latencies higher than 100).

Overall, these results suggest that with a few dozen user writings some systems led to reasonably high effectiveness. The best predictive algorithms could be used to support expert humans in early detecting signs of self-harm.

Table 4 reports the ranking-based performance achieved by the participating teams. Some teams only processed a few dozens of user writings and, thus, we could only compute their rankings of users for the initial points.

Some teams (e.g., INAOE-CIMAT or BioInfo@UAVR) have the same levels of ranking-based effectiveness over multiple points (after 1 writing, after 100 writings, and so forth). This suggests that these teams did not change the risk scores estimated from the initial stages (or their algorithms were not able to enhance their estimations as more evidence was seen).

Other participants (e.g., EFE, iLab or hildesheim) behave as expected: the rankings of estimated risk get better as they are built from more user evidence. Notably, some iLab variants led to almost perfect $P@10$ and $NDCG@10$ performance after analyzing more than 100 writings. The $NDCG@100$ scores achieved by this team after 100 or 500 writings were also quite effective (above .81 for all variants). This suggests that, with enough pieces of evidence, the methods implemented by this team are highly effective at prioritizing at risk users.

3   Task 2: Measuring the Severity of the Signs of Depression

This task is a continuation of 2019's T3 task. The task consists of estimating the level of depression from a thread of user submissions. For each user, the participants were given the user's full history of postings (in a single release of data) and the participants had to fill a standard depression questionnaire based on the evidence found in the history of postings. In 2020, the participants had the opportunity to use 2019's data as training data (filled questionnaires and SM submissions from the 2019 users, i.e. a training set composed of 20 users).

The questionnaires are derived from the Beck's Depression Inventory (BDI) [1], which assesses the presence of feelings like sadness, pessimism, loss of energy, etc, for the detection of depression. The questionnaire contains 21 questions (see Figs. 2 and 3).

The task aims at exploring the viability of automatically estimating the severity of the multiple symptoms associated with depression. Given the user's history of writings, the algorithms had to estimate the user's response to each individual question. We collected questionnaires filled by Social Media users together with their history of writings (we extracted each history of writings right after the user provided us with the filled questionnaire). The questionnaires filled by the users (ground truth) were used to assess the quality of the responses provided by the participating systems.

The participants were given a dataset with 70 users and they were asked to produce a file with the following structure:

Table 3. Task 1. Decision-based evaluation

team name	run id	P	R	F1	$ERDE_5$	$ERDE_{50}$	$latency_{TP}$	speed	latency-weighted F1
hildesheim	0	.248	1	.397	.292	.196	1	1	.397
hildesheim	1	.246	1	.395	.304	.185	5	.984	.389
hildesheim	2	.297	.740	.424	.237	.226	1	1	.424
hildesheim	3	.270	.942	.420	.400	.251	33.5	.874	.367
hildesheim	4	.256	.990	.406	.409	.210	12	.957	.389
UNSL	0	.657	.423	.515	.191	.155	2	.996	.513
UNSL	1	.618	.606	.612	.172	.124	2	.996	.609
UNSL	2	.606	.548	.576	.267	.142	11	.961	.553
UNSL	3	.598	.529	.561	.267	.149	12	.957	.537
UNSL	4	.545	.519	.532	.271	.151	12	.957	.509
EFE	0	.730	.519	.607	.257	.142	11	.961	.583
EFE	1	.625	.625	.625	.268	.117	11	.961	.601
EFE	2	.496	.615	.549	.283	.140	11	.961	.528
iLab	0	.833	.577	.682	.252	.111	10	.965	**.658**
iLab	1	**.913**	.404	.560	.248	.149	10	.965	.540
iLab	2	.544	.654	.594	**.134**	.118	2	.996	.592
iLab	3	.564	.885	.689	.287	**.071**	45	.830	.572
iLab	4	.828	.692	**.754**	.255	.255	100	.632	.476
prhlt-upv	0	.469	.654	.546	.291	.154	41	.845	.462
prhlt-upv	1	.710	.212	.326	.251	.235	133	.526	.172
prhlt-upv	2	.271	.577	.369	.339	.269	51.5	.806	.298
prhlt-upv	3	.846	.212	.338	.248	.232	133	.526	.178
prhlt-upv	4	.765	.375	.503	.253	.194	42	.841	.423
INAOE-CIMAT	0	.488	.567	.524	.203	.145	4	.988	.518
INAOE-CIMAT	1	.500	.548	.523	.193	.144	4	.988	.517
INAOE-CIMAT	2	.848	.375	.520	.207	.160	5	.984	.512
INAOE-CIMAT	3	.525	.702	.601	.174	.119	3	.992	.596
INAOE-CIMAT	4	.788	.394	.526	.198	.160	4	.988	.519
BioInfo@UAVR	0	.609	.375	.464	.260	.178	14	.949	.441
BioInfo@UAVR	1	.591	.654	.621	.273	.120	11	.961	.597
BioInfo@UAVR	2	.629	.375	.470	.259	.177	13	.953	.448
RELAI	0	.341	.865	.489	.188	.136	2	.996	.487
RELAI	1	.350	.885	.501	.190	.130	2	.996	.499
RELAI	2	.438	.740	.550	.245	.132	8	.973	.535
RELAI	3	.291	.894	.439	.306	.168	7	.977	.428
RELAI	4	.381	.846	.525	.260	.141	7	.977	.513
SSN_NLP	0	.264	1	.419	.206	.170	1	1.0	.419
SSN_NLP	1	.283	1	.442	.205	.158	1	1.0	.442
SSN_NLP	2	.287	.990	.445	.228	.159	2	.996	.443
SSN_NLP	3	.688	.423	.524	.233	.171	15.5	.944	.494
SSN_NLP	4	.287	.952	.441	.263	.214	4	.988	.436
BiTeM	0	.333	.01	.02	.245	.245	1	1.0	.019
BiTeM	1	0	0	0					
BiTeM	2	0	0	0					
BiTeM	3	0	0	0					
BiTeM	4	0	0	0					
NLP-UNED	0	.237	.913	.376	.423	.199	11	.961	.362
NLP-UNED	1	.246	1	.395	.210	.185	1	1.0	.395
NLP-UNED	2	.246	1	.395	.210	.185	1	1.0	.395
NLP-UNED	3	.246	1	.395	.210	.185	1	1.0	.395
NLP-UNED	4	.246	1	.395	.210	.185	1	1.0	.395
Anji	0	.266	1	.420	.205	.167	1	1.0	.420
Anji	1	.266	1	.420	.211	.167	1	1.0	.420
Anji	2	.269	1	.424	.213	.164	1	1.0	.424
Anji	3	.333	.038	.069	.248	.243	7	.977	.067
Anji	4	.258	.990	.410	.208	.174	1	1.0	.410

Table 4. Task 1. Ranking-based evaluation

team	run	1 writing			100 writings			500 writings			1000 writings		
		P	NDCG	NDCG	P	NDCG	NDCG	P	NDCG	NDCG	P	NDCG	NDCG
		@10	@10	@100	@10	@10	@100	@10	@10	@100	@10	@10	@100
hildesheim	0	.1	.10	.26	.4	.43	.42	.5	.53	.42			
hildesheim	1	.4	.44	.30	.5	.48	.49	.5	.54	.57			
hildesheim	2	.2	.15	.24	1	1	.69	1	1	.68			
hildesheim	3	.2	.14	.20	.1	.07	.13	.1	.06	.11			
hildesheim	4	.2	.16	.18	1	1	.62	1	1	.69			
UNSL	0	.9	.92	.47	1	1	.60	1	1	.60	1	1	.60
UNSL	1	.8	.87	.55	1	1	.76	1	1	.75	1	1	.75
UNSL	2	.7	.80	.42	.8	.84	.70	.8	.87	.74	.9	.94	.73
UNSL	3	.7	.79	.43	.8	.84	.70	.8	.87	.74	.9	.94	.73
UNSL	4	.5	.63	.36	.8	.86	.62	.8	.86	.62	.8	.86	.62
EFE	0	.7	.65	.59	1	1	.78	1	1	.79	1	1	.79
EFE	1	.6	.54	.58	1	1	.78	1	1	.80	1	1	**.80**
EFE	2	.6	.64	.55	.9	.92	.71	.9	.92	.73	.9	.92	.72
iLab	0	.8	.88	.63	1	1	.82	1	1	.83			
iLab	1	.7	.69	.60	1	1	.82	.9	.94	.81			
iLab	2	.7	.69	.60	1	1	.82	.9	.94	.81			
iLab	3	.9	.94	**.66**	1	1	**.83**	1	1	**.84**			
iLab	4	.8	.88	.63	1	1	.82	1	1	.83			
prhlt-upv	0	.2	.13	.30	.9	.93	.68	1	1	.68			
prhlt-upv	1	.9	.90	.63	.9	.92	.70	.9	.81	.75			
prhlt-upv	2	.5	.41	.42	.6	.69	.48	.6	.69	48			
prhlt-upv	3	.9	.90	63	.9	.92	.70	.9	.81	.75			
prhlt-upv	4	.8	.75	.49	1	1	70	.9	.90	.69			
INAOE-CIMAT	0	.3	.25	.30	.3	.26	.24	.3	.26	.24	.3	.26	.24
INAOE-CIMAT	1	.3	.25	.30	.3	.26	.24	.3	.26	.24	.3	.26	.24
INAOE-CIMAT	2	.3	.25	.30	.3	.26	.24	.3	.26	.24	.3	.26	.24
INAOE-CIMAT	3	.3	.25	.30	.3	.26	.24	.3	.26	.24	.3	.26	.24
INAOE-CIMAT	4	.3	.25	.30	.3	.26	.24	.3	.26	.24	.3	.26	.24
BioInfo@UAVR	0	.6	.62	.33	.6	.62	.31	.6	.62	.31			
BioInfo@UAVR	1	.6	.62	.33	0	0	.07	0	0	.04			
BioInfo@UAVR	2	.6	.62	.33	.6	.62	.31	.6	.62	.31			
RELAI	0	.7	.80	.52	.8	.87	.52	.8	.87	.52	.8	.87	.50
RELAI	1	.3	.28	.43	.6	.69	.47	.6	.69	.47	.7	.75	.47
RELAI	2	.2	.20	.27	.7	.81	.63	.8	.87	.70	.8	.87	.72
RELAI	3	.2	.20	.27	.9	.94	.51	1	1	.59	1	1	.60
RELAI	4	.2	.20	.27	.7	.68	.59	1	1	.71	.9	.81	.66
SSN_NLP	0	.7	.68	.50	.5	.38	.43						
SSN_NLP	1	.7	.68	.50	.5	.38	.43						
SSN_NLP	2	.7	.68	.50	.5	.38	.43						
SSN_NLP	3	0	0	.22	.1	.12	.16						
SSN_NLP	4	.7	.68	.50	.5	.38	.43						
BiTeM	0												
BiTeM	1												
BiTeM	2												
BiTeM	3												
BiTeM	4												
NLP-UNED	0	.7	.69	.49	.6	.73	.26	.6	.73	.24			
NLP-UNED	1	.6	.62	.27	.2	27	.18	.2	.27	.16			
NLP-UNED	2	.6	.62	.27	.2	.27	.18	.2	.27	.16			
NLP-UNED	3	.6	.62	.27	.2	.27	.18	.2	.27	.16			
NLP-UNED	4	.6	.62	.27	.2	.27	.18	.2	.27	.16			
Anji	0	.7	.73	.58	.6	.57	.46	.4	.32	.36	.4	.32	.36
Anji	1	.9	.81	.54	.8	.62	.69	.8	.62	.70	.8	.62	.69
Anji	2	.8	.88	.51	.7	.76	.58	.5	.34	.47	.6	.48	.50
Anji	3	.3	.25	.31	.3	.28	.27	.3	.26	.27	.3	.26	.27
Anji	4	.3	.22	.25	.6	.44	.59	.6	.44	.61	.6	.44	.60

Instructions:

This questionnaire consists of 21 groups of statements. Please read each group of statements
carefully, and then pick out the one statement in each group that best describes the way you feel.
If several statements in the group seem to apply equally well, choose the highest
number for that group.

1. Sadness
0. I do not feel sad.
1. I feel sad much of the time.
2. I am sad all the time.
3. I am so sad or unhappy that I can't stand it.

2. Pessimism
0. I am not discouraged about my future.
1. I feel more discouraged about my future than I used to be.
2. I do not expect things to work out for me.
3. I feel my future is hopeless and will only get worse.

3. Past Failure
0. I do not feel like a failure.
1. I have failed more than I should have.
2. As I look back, I see a lot of failures.
3. I feel I am a total failure as a person.

4. Loss of Pleasure
0. I get as much pleasure as I ever did from the things I enjoy.
1. I don't enjoy things as much as I used to.
2. I get very little pleasure from the things I used to enjoy.
3. I can't get any pleasure from the things I used to enjoy.

5. Guilty Feelings
0. I don't feel particularly guilty.
1. I feel guilty over many things I have done or should have done.
2. I feel quite guilty most of the time.
3. I feel guilty all of the time.

6. Punishment Feelings
0. I don't feel I am being punished.
1. I feel I may be punished.
2. I expect to be punished.
3. I feel I am being punished.

7. Self-Dislike
0. I feel the same about myself as ever.
1. I have lost confidence in myself.
2. I am disappointed in myself.
3. I dislike myself.

8. Self-Criticalness
0. I don't criticize or blame myself more than usual.
1. I am more critical of myself than I used to be.
2. I criticize myself for all of my faults.
3. I blame myself for everything bad that happens.

9. Suicidal Thoughts or Wishes
0. I don't have any thoughts of killing myself.
1. I have thoughts of killing myself, but I would not carry them out.
2. I would like to kill myself.
3. I would kill myself if I had the chance.

10. Crying
0. I don't cry anymore than I used to.
1. I cry more than I used to.
2. I cry over every little thing.
3. I feel like crying, but I can't.

11. Agitation
0. I am no more restless or wound up than usual.
1. I feel more restless or wound up than usual.
2. I am so restless or agitated that it's hard to stay still.
3. I am so restless or agitated that I have to keep moving or doing something.

12. Loss of Interest
0. I have not lost interest in other people or activities.
1. I am less interested in other people or things than before.
2. I have lost most of my interest in other people or things.
3. It's hard to get interested in anything.

13. Indecisiveness
0. I make decisions about as well as ever.
1. I find it more difficult to make decisions than usual.
2. I have much greater difficulty in making decisions than I used to.
3. I have trouble making any decisions.

14. Worthlessness
0. I do not feel I am worthless.
1. I don't consider myself as worthwhile and useful as I used to.
2. I feel more worthless as compared to other people.
3. I feel utterly worthless.

15. Loss of Energy
0. I have as much energy as ever.
1. I have less energy than I used to have.
2. I don't have enough energy to do very much.
3. I don't have enough energy to do anything.

Fig. 2. Beck's Depression Inventory (part 1)

```
16. Changes in Sleeping Pattern
0. I have not experienced any change in my sleeping pattern.
1a. I sleep somewhat more than usual.
1b. I sleep somewhat less than usual.
2a. I sleep a lot more than usual.
2b. I sleep a Iot less than usual.
3a. I sleep most of the day.
3b. I wake up 1-2 hours early and can't get back to sleep.

17. Irritability
0. I am no more irritable than usual.
1. I am more irritable than usual.
2. I am much more irritable than usual.
3. I am irritable all the time.

18. Changes in Appetite
0. I have not experienced any change in my appetite.
1a. My appetite is somewhat less than usual.
1b. My appetite is somewhat greater than usual.
2a. My appetite is much less than before.
2b. My appetite is much greater than usual.
3a. I have no appetite at all.
3b. I crave food all the time.

19. Concentration Difficulty
0. I can concentrate as well as ever.
1. I can't concentrate as well as usual.
2. It's hard to keep my mind on anything for very long.
3. I find I can't concentrate on anything.

20. Tiredness or Fatigue
0. I am no more tired or fatigued than usual.
1. I get more tired or fatigued more easily than usual.
2. I am too tired or fatigued to do a lot of the things I used to do.
3. I am too tired or fatigued to do most of the things I used to do.

21. Loss of Interest in Sex
0. I have not noticed any recent change in my interest in sex.
1. I am less interested in sex than I used to be.
2. I am much less interested in sex now.
3. I have lost interest in sex completely
```

Fig. 3. Beck's Depression Inventory (part 2)

```
username1 answer1 answer2 .... answer21
username2 ....
....
```

Each line has a user identifier and 21 values. These values correspond to the responses to the questions of the depression questionnaire (the possible values are 0, 1a, 1b, 2a, 2b, 3a, 3b -for questions 16 and 18- and 0, 1, 2, 3 -for the rest of the questions-).

3.1 Task 2: Evaluation Metrics

For consistency purposes, we employed the same evaluation metrics utilised in 2019. These metrics assess the quality of a questionnaire filled by a system in comparison with the real questionnaire filled by the actual Social Media user:

- **Average Hit Rate** (AHR): Hit Rate (HR) averaged over all users. HR is a stringent measure that computes the ratio of cases where the automatic questionnaire has exactly the same answer as the real questionnaire. For example, an automatic questionnaire with 5 matches gets HR equal to 5/21 (because there are 21 questions in the form).
- **Average Closeness Rate** (ACR): Closeness Rate (CR) averaged over all users. CR takes into account that the answers of the depression questionnaire represent an ordinal scale. For example, consider the #17 question:

```
17. Irritability
0. I am no more irritable than usual.
1. I am more irritable than usual.
2. I am much more irritable than usual.
3. I am irritable all the time.
```

Imagine that the real user answered "0". A system S1 whose answer is "3" should be penalised more than a system S2 whose answer is "1".

For each question, CR computes the absolute difference (ad) between the real and the automated answer (e.g. ad $= 3$ and ad $= 1$ for S1 and S2, respectively) and, next, this absolute difference is transformed into an effectiveness score as follows: $CR = (mad - ad)/mad$, where mad is the maximum absolute difference, which is equal to the number of possible answers minus one.

NOTE: in the two questions (#16 and #18) that have seven possible answers $\{0, 1a, 1b, 2a, 2b, 3a, 3b\}$ the pairs $(1a, 1b)$, $(2a, 2b)$, $(3a, 3b)$ are considered equivalent because they reflect the same depression level. As a consequence, the difference between $3b$ and 0 is equal to 3 (and the difference between $1a$ and $1b$ is equal to 0).

– **Average DODL (ADODL):** Difference between overall depression levels (DODL) averaged over all users. The previous measures assess the systems' ability to answer each question in the form. DODL, instead, does not look at question-level hits or differences but computes the overall depression level (sum of all the answers) for the real and automated questionnaire and, next, the absolute difference ($ad\_overall$) between the real and the automated score is computed.

Depression levels are integers between 0 and 63 and, thus, DODL is normalised into [0,1] as follows: $DODL = (63 - ad\_overall)/63$.

– **Depression Category Hit Rate (DCHR).** In the psychological domain, it is customary to associate depression levels with the following categories:

```
minimal depression (depression levels 0--9)
mild depression (depression levels 10--18)
moderate depression (depression levels 19--29)
severe depression (depression levels 30--63)
```

The last effectiveness measure consists of computing the fraction of cases where the automated questionnaire led to a depression category that is equivalent to the depression category obtained from the real questionnaire.

3.2   Task 2: Results

Table 5 presents the results achieved by the participants in this task. Although the teams could use training data from 2019 (while 2019's participants had no training data), the performance scores tend to be lower than 2019's performance scores (only ADODL had higher performance). This could be due to various reasons, including the intrinsic difficulty of the task and the lack of discussion on SM of psychological concerns by 2020 users.

In terms of AHR, the best performing run (BioInfo@UAVR) only got 38.30% of the answers right. The scores of the distance-based measure (ACR) are below 70%. Most of the questions have four possible answers and, thus, a random algorithm would get AHR near 25%[7]. This suggests that the analysis of the user posts was useful at extracting some signals or symptoms related to depression. However, ADODL and, particularly, DCHR show that the participants, although effective at answering some depression-related questions, do not fare well at estimating the overall level of depression of the individuals. For example, the best performing run gets the depression category right for only 35.71% of the individuals.

Overall, these experiments indicate that we are still far from a really effective depression screening tool. In the near future, it will be interesting to further analyze the participants' estimations in order to investigate which particular BDI questions are easier or harder to automatically answer based on Social Media activity.

Table 5. Task 2. Performance results

Run	AHR	ACR	ADODL	DCHR
BioInfo@UAVR	**38.30%**	69.21%	76.01%	30.00%
iLab run1	36.73%	68.68%	81.07%	27.14%
iLab run2	37.07%	**69.41%**	81.70%	27.14%
iLab run3	35.99%	69.14%	82.93%	34.29%
prhlt_logreg_features	34.01%	67.07%	80.05%	**35.71%**
prhlt_svm_use	36.94%	69.02%	81.72%	31.43%
prhlt_svm_features	34.56%	67.44%	80.63%	**35.71%**
svm_features	34.56%	67.44%	80.63%	**35.71%**
relai_context_paral_user	36.80%	68.37%	80.84%	22.86%
relai_context_sim_answer	21.16%	55.40%	73.76%	27.14%
relai_lda_answer	28.50%	60.79%	79.07%	30.00%
relai_lda_user	36.39%	68.32%	**83.15%**	34.29%
relai_sylo_user	37.28%	68.37%	80.70%	20.00%
Run1_resultat_CNN_Methode_max	34.97%	67.19%	76.85%	25.71%
Run2_resultat_CNN_Methode_suite	32.79%	66.08%	76.33%	17.14%
Run3_resultat_BILSTM_Methode_max	34.01%	67.78%	79.30%	22.86%
Run4_resultat_BILSTM_Methode_suit	33.54%	67.26%	78.91%	20.00%

---

[7] Actually, slightly less than 25% because a couple of questions have more than four possible answers.

4 Conclusions

This paper provided an overview of eRisk 2020. This was the fourth edition of this lab and the lab's activities concentrated on two different types of tasks: early detection of signs of self-harm (T1), where the participants had a sequential access to the user's social media posts and they had to send alerts about at-risk individuals, and measuring the severity of the signs of depression (T2), where the participants were given the full user history and their systems had to automatically estimate the user's responses to a standard depression questionnaire.

Overall, the proposed tasks received 73 variants or runs from 12 teams. Although the effectiveness of the proposed solutions is still modest, the experiments suggest that evidence extracted from Social Media is valuable and automatic or semi-automatic screening tools could be designed to detect at-risk individuals. This promising result encourages us to further explore the creation of benchmarks for text-based screening of signs of risk.

Acknowledgements. We thank the support obtained from the Swiss National Science Foundation (SNSF) under the project "Early risk prediction on the Internet: an evaluation corpus", 2015. This work was funded by FEDER/Ministerio de Ciencia, Innovación y Universidades - Agencia Estatal de Investigación/Project (RTI2018-093336-B-C21).

This work has also received financial support from the Consellería de Educación, Universidade e Formación Profesional (accreditation 2019–2022 ED431G-2019/04, ED431C 2018/29) and the European Regional Development Fund (ERDF), which acknowledges the CiTIUS-Research Center in Intelligent Technologies of the University of Santiago de Compostela as a Research Center of the Galician University System.

References

1. Beck, A.T., Ward, C.H., Mendelson, M., Mock, J., Erbaugh, J.: An inventory for measuring depression. JAMA Psychiatry **4**(6), 561–571 (1961)
2. Losada, D.E., Crestani, F.: A test collection for research on depression and language use. In: Fuhr, N., et al. (eds.) CLEF 2016. LNCS, vol. 9822, pp. 28–39. Springer, Cham (2016). https://doi.org/10.1007/978-3-319-44564-9_3
3. Losada, D.E., Crestani, F., Parapar, J.: eRISK 2017: CLEF lab on early risk prediction on the internet: experimental foundations. In: Jones, G., et al. (eds.) CLEF 2017. LNCS, vol. 10456, pp. 346–360. Springer, Cham (2017). https://doi.org/10.1007/978-3-319-65813-1_30
4. Losada, D.E., Crestani, F., Parapar, J.: eRISK 2017: CLEF lab on early risk prediction on the internet: experimental foundations. In: CEUR Proceedings of the Conference and Labs of the Evaluation Forum, CLEF 2017, Dublin, Ireland (2017)
5. Losada, D.E., Crestani, F., Parapar, J.: Overview of eRISK 2018: early risk prediction on the internet (extended lab overview). In: CEUR Proceedings of the Conference and Labs of the Evaluation Forum, CLEF 2018, Avignon, France (2018)
6. Losada, D.E., Crestani, F., Parapar, J.: Overview of eRisk: early risk prediction on the Internet. In: Bellot, P., et al. (eds.) CLEF 2018. LNCS, vol. 11018, pp. 343–361. Springer, Cham (2018). https://doi.org/10.1007/978-3-319-98932-7_30

7. Losada, D.E., Crestani, F., Parapar, J.: Overview of eRisk 2019 early risk prediction on the Internet. In: Crestani, F., et al. (eds.) CLEF 2019. LNCS, vol. 11696, pp. 340–357. Springer, Cham (2019). https://doi.org/10.1007/978-3-030-28577-7_27

8. Losada, D.E., Crestani, F., Parapar, J.: Overview of eRisk at CLEF 2019: early risk prediction on the Internet (extended overview). In: CEUR Proceedings of the Conference and Labs of the Evaluation Forum, CLEF 2019, Lugano, Switzerland (2019)

9. Sadeque, F., Xu, D., Bethard, S.: Measuring the latency of depression detection in social media. In: WSDM, pp. 495–503. ACM (2018)

10. Trotzek, M., Koitka, S., Friedrich, C.: Utilizing neural networks and linguistic metadata for early detection of depression indications in text sequences. IEEE Trans. Knowl. Data Eng. **32**(3), 588–601 (2018)

Overview of CLEF HIPE 2020: Named Entity Recognition and Linking on Historical Newspapers

Maud Ehrmann[1]([✉])(iD), Matteo Romanello[1](iD), Alex Flückiger[2], and Simon Clematide[2](iD)

[1] Ecole Polytechnique Fédérale de Lausanne, Lausanne, Switzerland
{maud.ehrmann,matteo.romanello}@epfl.ch
[2] University of Zurich, Zurich, Switzerland
{alex.flueckiger,simon.clematide}@uzh.ch

Abstract. This paper presents an overview of the first edition of HIPE (Identifying Historical People, Places and other Entities), a pioneering shared task dedicated to the evaluation of named entity processing on historical newspapers in French, German and English. Since its introduction some twenty years ago, named entity (NE) processing has become an essential component of virtually any text mining application and has undergone major changes. Recently, two main trends characterise its developments: the adoption of deep learning architectures and the consideration of textual material originating from historical and cultural heritage collections. While the former opens up new opportunities, the latter introduces new challenges with heterogeneous, historical and noisy inputs. In this context, the objective of HIPE, run as part of the CLEF 2020 conference, is threefold: strengthening the robustness of existing approaches on non-standard inputs, enabling performance comparison of NE processing on historical texts, and, in the long run, fostering efficient semantic indexing of historical documents. Tasks, corpora, and results of 13 participating teams are presented.

Keywords: Named entity recognition and classification · Entity linking · Historical texts · Information extraction · Digitized newspapers · Digital humanities

1 Introduction

Recognition and identification of real-world entities is at the core of virtually any text mining application. As a matter of fact, referential units such as names of persons, locations and organizations underlie the semantics of texts and guide their interpretation. Around since the seminal Message Understanding Conference (MUC) evaluation cycle in the 1990s [18], named entity-related tasks have undergone major evolutions until now, from entity recognition and classification to entity disambiguation and linking [33,43].

© Springer Nature Switzerland AG 2020
A. Arampatzis et al. (Eds.): CLEF 2020, LNCS 12260, pp. 288–310, 2020.
https://doi.org/10.1007/978-3-030-58219-7_21

Context. Recently, two main trends characterise developments in NE process-ing. First, at the technical level, the adoption of deep learning architectures and the usage of embedded language representations greatly reshapes the field and opens up new research directions [2,26,27]. Second, with respect to application domain and language spectrum, NE processing has been called upon to con-tribute to the field of Digital Humanities (DH), where massive digitization of historical documents is producing huge amounts of texts [50]. Thanks to large-scale digitization projects driven by cultural institutions, millions of images are being acquired and, when it comes to text, their content is transcribed, either manually via dedicated interfaces, or automatically via Optical Character Recog-nition (OCR). Beyond this great achievement in terms of document preservation and accessibility, the next crucial step is to adapt and develop appropriate lan-guage technologies to search and retrieve the contents of this 'Big Data from the Past' [22]. In this regard, information extraction techniques, and particularly NE recognition and linking, can certainly be regarded among the first and most crucial processing steps.

Motivation. Admittedly, NE processing tools are increasingly being used in the context of historical documents. Research activities in this domain target texts of different nature (e.g., museum records, state-related documents, genealogical data, historical newspapers) and different tasks (NE recognition and classifica-tion, entity linking, or both). Experiments involve different time periods, focus on different domains, and use different typologies. This great diversity demon-strates how many and varied the needs—and the challenges—are, but also makes performance comparison difficult, if not impossible.

Furthermore, it appears that historical texts poses new challenges to the application of NE processing [11,41], as it does for language technologies in gen-eral [47]. First, inputs can be extremely noisy, with errors which do not resem-ble tweet misspellings or speech transcription hesitations, for which adapted approaches have already been devised [7,29,46]. Second, the language under study is mostly of earlier stage(s), which renders usual external and internal evi-dences less effective (e.g., the usage of different naming conventions and presence of historical spelling variations) [4,5]. Further, beside historical VIP's, texts from the past contain rare entities which have undergone significant changes (esp. locations) or do no longer exist, and for which adequate linguistic resources and knowledge bases are missing [20]. Finally, archives and texts from the past are not as anglophone as in today's information society, making multilingual resources and processing capacities even more essential [34].

Overall, and as demonstrated by Vilain et al. [52], the transfer of NE tools from one domain to another is not straightforward, and the performance of NE tools initially developed for homogeneous texts of the immediate past are affected when applied on historical materials [48]. This echoes the proposition of Plank [42], according to whom what is considered as standard data (i.e. contemporary news genre) is more a historical coincidence than a reality: in NLP non-canonical, heterogeneous, biased and noisy data is rather the norm than the exception.

Objectives. In this context of new needs and materials emerging from the humanities, the HIPE shared task[1] puts forward for the first time the systematic evaluation of NE recognition and linking on diachronic historical newspaper material in French, German and English. In addition to the release of a multilingual, historical NE-annotated corpus, the objective of this shared task is threefold:

1. strengthening the robustness of existing approaches on non-standard inputs;
2. enabling performance comparison of NE processing on historical texts;
3. fostering efficient semantic indexing of historical documents in order to support scholarship on digital cultural heritage collections.

Even though many evaluation campaigns on NE were organized over the last decades[2], only one considered French historical texts [16]. To the best of our knowledge, no NE evaluation campaign ever addressed multilingual, diachronic historical material. The present shared task is organized as part of *"impresso - Media Monitoring of the Past"*, a project which tackles information extraction and exploration of large-scale historical newspapers.[3]

The remainder of this paper is organized as follows. Sects. 2 and 3 present the tasks and the material used for the evaluation. Section 4 details the evaluation metrics and the organisation of system submissions. Section 5 introduces the 13 participating systems while Sect. 6 presents and discusses their results. Finally, Sect. 7 summarizes the benefits of the task and concludes.[4]

2   Task Description

The HIPE shared task includes two NE processing tasks with sub-tasks of increasing level of difficulty.

Task 1: Named Entity Recognition and Classification (NERC)

– **Subtask 1.1 - NERC coarse-grained** (NERC-Coarse): this task includes the recognition and classification of entity mentions according to high-level entity types.
– **Subtask 1.2 - NERC fine-grained** (NERC-Fine): this task includes the recognition and classification of mentions according to finer-grained entity types, as well as of nested entities and entity mention components (e.g. function, title, name).

Task 2: Named Entity Linking (EL).
This task requires the linking of named entity mentions to a unique referent in a knowledge base – here Wikidata – or to a NIL node if the mention's referent is not present in the base. The entity linking task includes two settings: without and with prior knowledge of mention types and boundaries, referred to as end-to-end EL and EL only respectively.

---

[1] https://impresso.github.io/CLEF-HIPE-2020/.

[2] MUC, ACE, CONLL, KBP, ESTER, HAREM, QUAERO, GERMEVAL, etc.

[3] https://impresso-project.ch/.

[4] For space reasons, the discussion of related work is included in the extended version of this overview [12].

Table 1. Entity types used for NERC tasks.

Types	Sub-types	
pers	pers.ind pers.coll	pers.ind.articleauthor
org	org.ent org.adm	org.ent.pressagency
prod	prod.media prod.doctr	
date	time.date.abs	
loc	loc.adm	loc.adm.town loc.adm.reg loc.adm.nat loc.adm.sup
	loc.phys	loc.geo loc.hydro loc.astro
	loc.oro loc.fac	
	loc.add	loc.add.phys loc.add.elec

3 Data

3.1 Corpus

The shared task corpus is composed of digitized and OCRized articles originating from Swiss, Luxembourgish and American historical newspaper collections and selected on a diachronic basis.[5]

Corpus Selection. The corpus was compiled based on systematic and purposive sampling. For each newspaper and language, articles were randomly sampled among articles that a) belong to the first years of a set of predefined decades covering the life-span of the newspaper (longest duration spans ca. 200 years), and b) have a title, have more than 50 characters, and belong to any page. For each decade, the set of selected articles was additionally manually triaged in order to keep journalistic content only. Items corresponding to feuilleton, tabular data, cross-words, weather forecasts, time-schedules, obituaries, and those with contents

---

[5] From the Swiss National Library, the Luxembourgish National Library, and the Library of Congress (Chronicling America project), respectively. Original collections correspond to 4 Swiss and Luxembourgish titles, and a dozen for English. More details on original sources can be found in [12].

that a human could not even read because of extreme OCR noise were therefore removed. Different OCR versions of same texts are not provided, and the OCR quality of the corpus therefore corresponds to real-life setting, with variations according to digitization time and preservation state of original documents. The corpus features an overall time span of ca. 200 years, from 1798 to 2018.

Corpus Annotation. The corpus was manually annotated according to the HIPE annotation guidelines [14]. Those guidelines were derived from the Quaero annotation guide, originally designed for the annotation of named entities in French speech transcriptions and already used on historical press corpora [44,45]. HIPE slightly recast and simplified this guide, considering only a subset of entity types and components, as well as of linguistic units eligible as named entities. HIPE guidelines were iteratively consolidated via the annotation of a "mini-reference" corpus – consisting of 10 content items per language –, where annotation decisions were tested and difficult cases discussed. Despite these adaptations, the HIPE corpus mostly remain compatible with Quaero-annotated data, as well as with the NewsEye project's NE data sets[6], annotated with guidelines derived from HIPE.

Table 1 presents the entity types and sub-types used for annotation, which participant systems had to recognize for NERC-Coarse (types) and NERC-Fine (most fine-grained sub-types). Named entity components, annotated for the type `Person` only, correspond to `name`, `title`, `function`, `qualifier` and `demonym`. Nested entities were annotated for `Person`, `Organization` and `Location` (a depth of 1 was considered during the evaluation), as well as metonymic senses, producing double tags for those entities referring to something intimately associated (metonymic sense) to the concept usually associated with their name (literal sense). As per entity linking, links correspond to Wikidata QID[7].

The annotation campaign was carried out by the task organizers with the contribution of trilingual collaborators. We used the INCEpTION annotation tool [23], which allows the visualisation of image segments alongside OCR transcriptions. Before starting annotating, each annotator was first trained on the mini-reference corpus in order to ensure a good understanding of the guidelines. The inter-annotator agreement rates between 2 annotators was computed on a selection of documents (test set) using Krippendorf's α [25]. Scores correspond to, for Fr, De and En respectively: .81, .79 and .80 for NERC, .73, .69 and .78 for linking towards a QID, and .95, .94 and .90 for linking towards NIL. NERC and linking towards NIL show a good agreement between annotators. The lower scores on entity linking confirm the difficulty of the task, especially in the context of historical documents where, almost as a detective, one has to research the correct entities. The low score observed on German (.69) is due to annotation discrepancies with respect to the linking of metonymic entities. The historical normalization of the fuzzy evaluation regime for EL (see Sect. 4.1) helps mitigate these flaws.

---

[6] https://www.newseye.eu/.

[7] The November 2019 dump used for annotation is available at https://files.ifi.uzh.ch/cl/impresso/clef-hipe.

Table 2. Overview of corpus statistics (v1.3).

	Lang.	docs	tokens	mentions	nested	comp.	% meto.	% NIL	% noisy
Train	Fr	158	129,925	7885	480	3091	12.10	22.04	–
	De	103	71,507	3988	160	1494	16.75	13.67	–
	All	261	201,432	11,873	640	4585	13.66	19.23	–
Dev	Fr	43	29,571	1938	98	743	11.76	17.75	–
	De	33	27,032	1403	65	489	13.68	16.25	–
	En	80	24,266	1032	–	–	4.26	40.79	–
	All	156	80,869	4373	163	1232	10.61	22.71	–
Test	Fr	43	32,035	1802	83	732	13.32	17.70	12.15
	De	48	24,771	1317	64	431	18.45	14.35	13.74
	En	46	13,925	483	–	–	10.77	36.02	6.21
	All	137	70,731	3602	147	1163	14.85	18.93	11.10
All	Fr	244	191,531	11,625	661	4566	13.39	18.87	–
	De	184	123,310	6708	289	2414	16.44	14.34	–
	En	126	38,191	1515	–	–	11.17	24.82	–
	All	554	353,032	19,848	950	6980	13.38	19.67	–

Corpus Characteristics. For each task and language—with the exception of English—the HIPE corpus was divided into training, dev and test data sets (70/15/15). English was included later in the shared task and only dev and test sets were released for this language. The overall corpus consists of 554 annotated documents, for a total of 353,032 tokens and 19,848 (linked) mentions (see Table 2 for detailed overview statistics). With 11,625 and 6,708 mentions, French and German corpora are larger than the English one (1,515). Despite our efforts to devise a balanced sampling strategy, the diachronic distribution of mentions is not entirely uniform across languages (see Fig. 1). This is mainly due to the following factors: the temporal boundaries of data to sample from (the German corpus stops at 1950, and the English one shortly afterwards); the varying content of newspaper articles; and, finally, the difficulty of sampling enough materials for certain decades due to OCR noise, such is the case with years 1850–1879 in the English corpus.

An important aspect of the HIPE corpus, and of historical newspaper data in general, is the noise generated by OCR. Annotators were asked to transcribe the surface form of noisy mentions so as to enable studying the impact of noisy mentions on NERC and EL tasks. In the test set—where we manually verified the consistency of annotators' transcriptions—about 11% of all mentions contain OCR mistakes.

Together with OCR, the limited coverage of knowledge bases such as Wikidata tends to have an impact on historical NE processing, and especially on linking. In our corpus, entities that cannot be linked to a Wikidata entry (NIL entities) constitute 30% of the total. Interestingly, and contrary to our initial assumption, NIL entities are uniformly distributed across time periods (see

Table 3. Statistics per coarse entity type (all data sets).

	Lang.	mentions	% nested	% meto.	% NIL
Person	Fr	3745	1.04	0.40	44.49
	De	1867	1.39	0.27	29.24
	En	558	–	0.18	72.40
	All	6170	1.05	0.34	42.40
Location	Fr	5278	10.27	13.02	4.53
	De	3148	6.26	17.15	3.91
	En	599	–	6.01	13.69
	All	9025	8.19	13.99	4.92
Organisation	Fr	1873	3.74	0.16	19.54
	De	1213	4.29	0.25	17.07
	En	241	–	5.81	31.95
	All	3327	3.67	0.60	19.54
Date	Fr	399	0.00	0.00	–
	De	241	2.49	0.00	–
	En	46	–	0.00	–
	All	686	0.87	0.00	–
Media	Fr	313	0.96	0.32	24.92
	De	227	1.32	0.88	31.28
	En	52	–	0.00	61.54
	All	592	1.01	0.51	30.57

Fig 2). The NIL ratio is higher for Person, Media and Organisation entities, whereas for geographic places (Location) Wikidata shows a substantial coverage (see Table 3). Date mentions were not linked as per HIPE annotation guidelines.

Corpus Release. Data sets were released in IOB format with hierarchical information, in a similar fashion to CoNLL-U[8], and consist of UTF-8, tab-separated-values files containing the necessary information for all tasks (NERC-Coarse, NERC-Fine, and EL) [13].

Given the noisy quality of the material at hand, we chose not to apply sentence splitting nor sophisticated tokenization but, instead, to provide all necessary information to rebuild the OCR text. Alongside each article, metadata (journal, date, title, page number, image region coordinates) and IIIF links to original page images are additionally provided when available.

---

[8] https://universaldependencies.org/format.html.

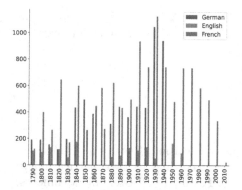

Fig. 1. Diachronic distribution of mentions across languages.

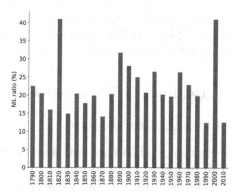

Fig. 2. Diachronic ratio of NIL entities.

The HIPE corpus, comprising several versions of each data set for the 3 languages, is released under a CC BY-NC 4.0 license[9] and is available on Zenodo[10] as well as on the HIPE GitHub repository[11].

3.2 Auxiliary Resources

In order to support participants in their system design and experiments, we provided auxiliary resources in the form of 'in-domain' word and character-level embeddings acquired from the same *impresso* newspapers titles and time periods from which HIPE training and development sets were extracted. Those embeddings correspond to fastText word embeddings [3] and flair contextualized string embeddings [1], both for French, German and English.

More specifically, fastText embeddings came in two versions, with subword 3–6 character n-grams and without, and were computed after a basic pre-processing (i.e., lower-casing, replacement of digits by 0 and deletion of all tokens/punctuation of length 1) that also tried to imitate the tokenization of the shared task data. Flair character embeddings were computed using flair 0.4.5[12] with a context of 250 characters, a batch size of 400–600 (depending on the GPU's memory), 1 hidden layer (size 2048), and a dropout of 0.1. Input was normalized with lower-casing, replacement of digits by 0, and of newlines by spaces; everything else was kept as in the original text (e.g. tokens of length 1). It is to be noted that the amount of training material greatly differed between languages (20G for French and 8.5G for German taken from Swiss and Luxembourgish newspapers; 1.1 G for English taken from Chronicling America material).

---

[9] https://creativecommons.org/licenses/by-nc/4.0/legalcode.
[10] https://zenodo.org/deposit/3706857.
[11] https://github.com/impresso/CLEF-HIPE-2020/tree/master/data.
[12] https://github.com/flairNLP/flair.

These embeddings are released under a CC BY-SA 4.0 license[13] and are available for download.[14] Contextualized character embeddings were also integrated into the flair framework[15].

4   Evaluation Framework

4.1   Evaluation Measures

NERC and EL tasks are evaluated in terms of Precision, Recall and F-measure (F1) [30]. Evaluation is done at entity level according to two metrics: micro average, with the consideration of all TP, FP, and FN[16] over all documents, and macro average, with the average of document's micro figures. Our definition of macro differs from the usual one: averaging is done at document-level and not across entity-types, and allows to account for (historical) variance in document length and entity distribution within documents instead of overall class imbalances.

Both NERC and EL benefit from strict and fuzzy evaluation regimes. For NERC (Coarse and Fine), the strict regime corresponds to exact boundary matching and the fuzzy to overlapping boundaries. It is to be noted that in the strict regime, predicting wrong boundaries leads to a 'double' punishment of one false negative (entity present in the gold standard but not predicted by the system) and one false positive (entity predicted by the system but not present in the gold standard). Although it punishes harshly, we keep this metric to be in line with CoNLL and refer to the fuzzy regime when boundaries are of less importance.

The definition of strict and fuzzy regimes differs for entity linking. In terms of boundaries, EL is always evaluated according to overlapping boundaries in both regimes (what is of interest is the capacity to provide the correct link rather than the correct boundaries). EL strict regime considers only the system's top link prediction (NIL or QID), while the fuzzy regime expands system predictions with a set of historically related entity QIDs. For example, "Germany" QID is complemented with the QID of the more specific "Confederation of the Rhine" entity and both are considered as valid answers. The resource allowing for such historical normalization was compiled by the task organizers for the entities of the test data sets, and is released as part of the HIPE scorer. For this regime, participants were invited to submit more than one link, and F-measure is additionally computed with cut-offs @3 and @5.

The HIPE scorer was provided to the participants early on, and the full evaluation toolkit (including all recipes and resources to replicate the present evaluation) is published under MIT license[17].

---

[13] https://creativecommons.org/licenses/by-sa/4.0/legalcode.
[14] https://files.ifi.uzh.ch/cl/siclemat/impresso/clef-hipe-2020/flair/.
[15] https://github.com/flairNLP/flair.
[16] True positive, False positive, False negative.
[17] https://github.com/impresso/CLEF-HIPE-2020-scorer.

4.2   Task Bundles

In order to allow the greatest flexibility to participating teams as to which tasks to compete for while keeping a manageable evaluation frame, we introduced a system of task bundles offering different task combinations (see Table 4). Teams were allowed to choose only one bundle per language and to submit up to 3 runs per language. Only Bundle 5 (EL only) could be selected in addition to another one; this exception was motivated by the intrinsic difference between end-to-end linking and linking of already extracted entity mentions. Detailed information on system submission can be found in the HIPE Participation Guidelines [13].

Table 4. Task bundles.

Bundle	Tasks	# teams	# runs
1	NERC coarse, NERC fine and EL	2	10
2	NERC coarse and EL	3	10
3	NERC coarse and NERC fine	1	8
4	NERC coarse	7	27
5	EL only	5	20

5   System Descriptions

In this first HIPE edition, 13 participating teams submitted a total of 75 system runs. All teams participated to NERC-Coarse, 3 to NERC-Fine, and 5 to end-to-end EL and EL only. The distribution of runs per language reflects the data, with 35 runs for French (42%), 26 for German (31%), and 22 for English (26%). Besides, six teams worked on all 3 languages. For NERC, all but 2 teams applied neural approaches, and most of them also worked with contextualized embeddings.

5.1   Baselines

As a baseline for NERC-Coarse, we trained a traditional CRF sequence classifier [37] using basic spelling features such as a token's character prefix and suffix, the casing of the initial character, and whether it is a digit. The model, released to participating teams as part of the HIPE scorer, dismisses the segmentation structure and treats any document as a single, long sentence. No baseline is provided for the NERC-Fine sub-task.

The baseline for entity linking (end-to-end EL and EL only) corresponds to AIDA-light [35], which implements the collective mapping algorithm by [19]. The wikimapper[18] tool was used to map Wikipedia URLs onto Wikidata QIDs,

---

[18] https://github.com/jcklie/wikimapper.

and the end-to-end EL baseline run relied on the CRF-based NERC baseline. Given the multilingual nature of the HIPE shared task, it is worth noting that AIDA-light was trained on a 2014 dump of the English Wikipedia, therefore accounting for a generous baseline.

5.2 Participating Systems

The following system descriptions are compiled from information provided by the participants. More accurate implementation details are available in the participants' system papers [6].

CISTERIA, a collaboration of the *Ludwig-Maximilians Universität* and the *Bayerische Staatsbibliothek München* from Germany, focused on NERC-coarse for German. They experimented with external and HIPE character and word embeddings as well as several transformer-based BERT-style language models (e.g., German Europeana BERT[19]), all integrated by the neural flair NER tagging framework [1]. Interestingly, they trained different models with different embeddings for literal and metonymic NERC. No additional training material was used.

EHRMAMA, affiliated with the University of Amsterdam, tackled coarse and fine-graind NERC for all languages. They build on the LSTM-CRF architecture of [27] and introduce a multi-task approach by splitting the top layers for each entity type. Their general embedding layer combines a multitude of embeddings, on the level of characters, sub-words and words; some newly trained by the team, as well as pre-trained BERT and HIPE's in-domain fastText embeddings. No additional training material was applied.

ERTIM, affiliated with *Inalco*, Paris, applied their legacy (2010-13) NER system mXS[20] [36] for contemporary texts on the historical French HIPE data without any adaptation or training. The system uses pattern mining and non-neural machine learning for NERC and their model is based on the QUAERO standard [45], which is the basis for the HIPE annotation guidelines. For EL, only the type Person was considered. The resolution is done in two steps, first an approximate string match retrieves French Wikipedia pages, second the Wikidata item is selected whose Wikipedia article has the highest cosine similarity with the HIPE newspaper article containing the mention.

INRIA, by the *ALMAnaCH* project team affiliated at *Inria*, Paris, used DeLFT (Deep Learning Framework for Text)[21] for NERC tagging of English and French. For English, the pre-trained Ontonotes 5.0 CoNLL-2012 model was used with a BiLSTM-CRF architecture. For EL, the system entity-fishing[22] was used.

IRISA, by a team from *IRISA*, Rennes, France, focused on French NERC and EL. For NERC, they improved the non-neural CRF baseline system with additional features such as context tokens, date regex match, ASCII normalization

---

[19] https://huggingface.co/dbmdz.
[20] https://github.com/eldams/mXS.
[21] https://github.com/kermitt2/delft.
[22] https://github.com/kermitt2/entity-fishing.

of the focus token, and the 100 most similar words from the HIPE fastText word embeddings provided by the organizers. For EL, a knowledge-base driven approach was applied to disambiguate and link the mentions of their NERC systems and the gold oracle NERC mentions [15]. Their experiments with the HIPE data revealed that collective entity linking is also beneficial for this type of texts—in contrast to linking mentions separately.

L3I, affiliated with *La Rochelle University*, France, tackled all prediction tasks of HIPE for all languages and achieved almost everywhere the best results. They used a hierarchical transformer-based model [51] built upon BERT [9] in a multi-task learning setting. On top of the pre-trained BERT blocks (German Europeana BERT, French CamemBERT, Multilingual BERT), several transformer layers were added to alleviate data sparsity issues, out-of-vocabulary words, spelling variations, or OCR errors in the HIPE dataset. A CRF was added on top to model the context dependencies between entity tags. An important pre-processing step for NERC was sentence segmentation and the reconstruction of words with hyphenation. For their EL approach, which is based on [24], the team built a Wikipedia/Wikidata knowledge base per language and trained entity embeddings for the most frequent entries [17]. Based on Wikipedia co-occurrence counts, a probabilistic mapping table was computed for linking mentions with entities—taking several mention variations (e.g. lowercase, Levenshtein distance) into account to improve the matching. The candidates were filtered using DBpedia and Wikidata by prioritizing those that corresponded to the named entity type. For persons, they analysed the date of birth to discard anachronistic entities. Finally, the five best matching candidates were predicted.

LIMSI, affiliated with *LIMSI, CNRS*, Paris, France, focused on coarse NERC for French and achieved second best results there. They submitted runs from 3 model variations: a) A model based on CamemBERT [31] that jointly predicts the literal and metonymic entities by feeding into two different softmax layers. This model performed best on the dev set for metonymic entities. b) The model (a) with a CRF layer on top, which achieved their best results on literal tags (F1=.814 strict). c) A standard CamemBERT model that predicts concatenated literal and metonymic labels directly as a combined tag (resulting in a larger prediction tagset). This model performed best (within LIMSI's runs) on the test set for metonymic entities (F1=.667 strict).

NLP-UQAM, affiliated with *Université du Quebec*, Montréal, Canada, focused on coarse NERC for French. Their architecture involves a BiLSTM layer for word-level feature extraction with a CRF layer on top for capturing label dependencies [27], and an attention layer in between for relating different positions of a sequence [51]. For their rich word representation, they integrate a character-based CNN approach [8] and contextualized character-based flair embeddings [2] as provided by the HIPE organizers.

SBB, affiliated with the Berlin State Library, Berlin, focused on coarse NERC and EL for all languages. For NERC, they applied a model based on multilingual BERT embeddings, which were additionally pre-trained on OCRed historical German documents from the SBB collection and subsequently fine-tuned on various multilingual NER data sets [26]. For EL, they constructed a multilingual knowledge base from Wikipedia (WP) articles roughly resembling the categories Person, Location, and Organization. The title words of these pages were embedded by BERT and stored in a nearest neighbor lookup index. A lookup applied to a mention returns a set of linked entity candidates. The historical text segment containing *the mention* and sentences from WP containing *a candidate* are then scored by a BERT sentence comparison model. This model was trained to predict for arbitrary WP sentence pairs whether they talk about the same entity or not. A random forest classifier finally ranks the candidates based on their BERT sentence comparison scores.

SINNER, affiliated with *INRIA* and Paris-Sorbonne University, Paris, France, focused on coarse literal NERC for French and German. They provided 2 runs based on a BiLSTM-CRF architecture, which combines fastText [3] and contextualized ELMo [40] embeddings[23]. For run 2, which performs better than their run 1 and is the one reported here, they applied propagation of entities at the document level. They optimized hyperparameters by training each variant three times and by selecting on F-score performance on the dev set. For run 3, they retrained SEM[24] with the official HIPE data sets and applied entity propagation. For German, they augmented SEM's gazetteers with location lexicons crawled from Wikipedia. The considerably lower performance of run 3 illustrates the advantage of embedding-based neural NER tagging.

UPB, affiliated with the *Politehnica University of Bucharest*, Bucarest, Bulgaria, focused on coarse literal NERC for all languages. Their BERT-based model centers around the ideas of transfer and multi-task learning as well as multilingual word embeddings. Their best performing runs combine multilingual BERT embeddings with a BiLSTM layer followed by a dense layer with local SoftMax predictions or alternatively, by adding a CRF layer on top of the BiLSTM.

UVA-ILPS, affiliated with the University of Amsterdam, The Netherlands, focused on coarse NERC and end-to-end EL for all languages, and EL-only on English. They fine-tuned BERT models for token-level NERC prediction. Their EL approach was implemented by searching for each entity mention in the English Wikidata dump indexed by ElasticSearch[25]. The main problem there was the lack of German and French entities, although person names still could be found. For run 1 and 2 of EL only on English, they improved the candidate entity ranking by calculating cosine similarities between the contextual embeddings of a sentence containing the target entity mention and a modified sentence where the mention was replaced with a candidate entity description from Wikidata. The semantic similarity scores were multiplied by relative Levenshtein similarity scores between target mention and candidate labels to prefer precise character-level matches. Run 2 added historical spelling variations, however, this resulted in more false positives. Run 3 used REL [21], a completely different neural NERC and EL system. Candidate selection in REL is twofold, 4 candidates are selected

---

[23] [38] for French, [32] for German.
[24] SEM [10] is a CRF-based tool using Wapiti [28] as its linear CRF implementation.
[25] https://www.elastic.co/.

by a probabilistic model predicting entities given a mention, and 3 candidates are proposed by a model predicting entities given the context of the mention. Candidate disambiguation combines local compatibility (prior importance, contextual similarity) and global coherence with other document-level entity linking decisions. Their REL-based run 3 outperformed their runs 1 and 2 clearly.

WEBIS, by the *Webis* group affiliated with the *Bauhaus University Weimar*, Germany, focused on coarse NERC for all languages. For each language, they trained a flair NERC sequence tagger [1] with a CRF layer using a stack of 4 embeddings: Glove embeddings [39], contextual character-based flair embeddings, and the forward and backward HIPE character-based flair embeddings. Their pre-processing included sentence reconstruction (by splitting the token sequence on all periods, except after titles, month abbreviations or numbers), and dehyphenation of tokens at the end of lines. For German, they experimented with data augmentation techniques by duplicating training set sentences and replacing the contained entities by randomly chosen new entities of the same type retrieved from Wikidata. A post-processing step resolved IOB tag sequence inconsistencies and applied a pattern-based tagging for time expressions. Although internal dev set validation F-scores looked promising, their official results on the test set had a bias towards precision. This could be due to format conversion issues.

6   Results and Discussion

We report results for the best run of each team and consider micro Precision, Recall and F1 exclusively. Results for NERC-Coarse and NERC-Fine for the three languages, both evaluation regimes and the literal and metonymic senses are presented in Table 5 and 6 respectively, while results for nested entities and entity components are presented in Table 7. Table 8 reports performances for end-to-end EL and EL only, with a cut-off @1. We refer the reader to the HIPE 2020 website[26] for more detailed results, and to the extended HIPE overview for a more in-depth discussion [12].

General Observations. Neural systems with strong embedding resources clearly prevailed in HIPE NERC, beating symbolic CRF or pattern-matching based approaches by a large margin (e.g., compare baseline performance in Table 5). However, we also notice performance differences between neural systems that rely on BiLSTMs or BERT, the latter generally performing better.

In general and not unexpectedly, we observe that the amount of available training and development data correlates with system performances. French with the largest amount of training data has better results than German, and English is worse than German (see median numbers in Table 5). The one exception is EL only where English, as a well-resourced language, seems to have the necessary tooling to also excel on non-standard, historical text material (cf. INRIA results). NERC-Coarse performances show a great diversity but top results are

---

[26] https://impresso.github.io/CLEF-HIPE-2020/.

Table 5. Results for NERC-Coarse (micro P, R and F-measure). Bold font indicates the highest, and underlined font the second-highest value.

(a) Literal

	French						German						English					
	Strict			Fuzzy			Strict			Fuzzy			Strict			Fuzzy		
	P	R	F	P	R	F	P	R	F	P	R	F	P	R	F	P	R	F
CISTERIA	-	-	-	-	-	-	.745	.578	.651	**.880**	.683	.769	-	-	-	-	-	-
EHRMAMA	.793	.764	.778	.893	.861	.877	.697	.659	.678	.814	.765	.789	.249	.439	.318	.405	.633	.494
ERTIM	.435	.248	.316	.604	.344	.439	-	-	-	-	-	-	-	-	-	-	-	-
INRIA	.605	.675	.638	.755	.842	.796	-	-	-	-	-	-	.461	.606	.524	.568	.746	.645
IRISA	.705	.634	.668	.828	.744	.784	-	-	-	-	-	-	-	-	-	-	-	-
L3I	**.831**	**.849**	**.840**	**.912**	**.931**	**.921**	**.790**	**.805**	**.797**	.870	**.886**	**.878**	**.623**	**.641**	**.632**	.794	**.817**	**.806**
LIMSI	.799	.829	.814	.887	.909	.898	-	-	-	-	-	-	-	-	-	-	-	-
NLP-UQAM	.705	.634	.668	.828	.744	.784	-	-	-	-	-	-	-	-	-	-	-	-
SBB	.530	.477	.502	.765	.689	.725	.499	.484	.491	.730	.708	.719	.347	.310	.327	.642	.572	.605
SINNER	.788	.802	.795	.886	.902	.894	.658	.658	.658	.775	.819	.796	-	-	-	-	-	-
UPB	.693	.686	.689	.825	.817	.821	.677	.575	.621	.788	.740	.763	.522	.416	.463	.743	.592	.659
UVA-ILPS	.656	.719	.686	.794	.869	.830	.499	.556	.526	.689	.768	.726	.443	.508	.473	.635	.728	.678
WEBIS	.731	.228	.347	.876	.273	.416	.695	.337	.454	.833	.405	.545	.476	.067	.117	**.873**	.122	.215
Baseline	.693	.606	.646	.825	.721	.769	.643	.378	.476	.790	.464	.585	.531	.327	.405	.736	.454	.562
Median	.705	.680	.677	.828	.829	.808	.686	.576	.636	.801	.752	.766	.461	.439	.463	.642	.633	.645

(b) Meto.

	Strict			Fuzzy			Strict			Fuzzy			Strict			Fuzzy		
	P	R	F	P	R	F	P	R	F	P	R	F	P	R	F	P	R	F
CISTERIA	-	-	-	-	-	-	.738	.500	.596	.787	.534	.636	-	-	-	-	-	-
EHRMAMA	.697	.554	.617	.708	.562	.627	.696	.542	.610	.707	.551	.619	-	-	-	-	-	-
L3I	**.734**	**.839**	**.783**	**.734**	**.839**	**.783**	.571	**.712**	**.634**	.626	**.780**	**.694**	.667	.080	.143	1.00	.120	.214
LIMSI	.647	.688	.667	.655	.696	.675	-	-	-	-	-	-	-	-	-	-	-	-
NLP-UQAM	.423	.420	.422	.468	.464	.466	-	-	-	-	-	-	-	-	-	-	-	-
Baseline	.541	.179	.268	.541	.179	.268	**.814**	.297	.435	**.814**	.297	.435	1.00	.040	.077	1.00	.040	.077
Median	.647	.554	.617	.655	.562	.627	-	-	-	-	-	-	-	-	-	-	-	-

Table 6. Results for NERC-Fine.

(a) Literal	French						German					
	Strict			Fuzzy			Strict			Fuzzy		
	P	R	F	P	R	F	P	R	F	P	R	F
EHRMAMA	.696	.724	.710	.776	.807	.791	**.650**	.592	.620	**.754**	.687	.719
ERTIM	.418	.238	.303	.568	.324	.412	–	–	–	–	–	–
L3I	**.772**	**.797**	**.784**	**.843**	**.869**	**.856**	.628	**.712**	**.668**	.734	**.813**	**.771**
(b) Metonymic												
EHRMAMA	.667	.554	.605	.667	.554	.605	**.707**	.551	.619	**.717**	.559	.629
L3I	**.718**	**.661**	**.688**	**.738**	**.679**	**.707**	.601	**.703**	**.648**	.659	**.771**	**.711**

Table 7. Results for nested entities and entity components.

(a) Comp.	French						German					
	Strict			Fuzzy			Strict			Fuzzy		
	P	R	F	P	R	F	P	R	F	P	R	F
EHRMAMA	**.695**	.632	**.657**	**.801**	.707	.751	**.681**	.494	.573	**.735**	.534	.618
ERTIM	.042	.045	.043	.074	.080	.077	–	–	–	–	–	–
L3I	.680	**.732**	**.657**	.773	**.832**	**.801**	.595	**.698**	**.642**	.654	**.768**	**.707**
(b) Nested												
EHRMAMA	**.397**	.280	.329	**.448**	.317	.371	–	–	–	–	–	–
L3I	.337	**.402**	**.367**	.357	**.427**	**.389**	.471	.562	.513	.517	.616	.562

better than expected, specifically for French where they are almost on a par with performances on contemporary texts. Here, six teams have fuzzy F1 scores higher than .8, suggesting good prospects for entity extraction systems on historical texts, when trained with appropriate and sufficient data. Fine-grained NERC with more than 12 classes is obviously more difficult than predicting only 5 categories. However, the performance drop of the best performing system L3I is relatively mild for French, 6.5% points on fuzzy F1, and a little stronger for German (10.7). Finally, the recognition of entity components shows reasonable performances and suggests that knowledge base population and/or biography reconstruction from historical texts is feasible. The same cannot be said of nested entities.

System-Based Observations. With L3I, the HIPE 2020 campaign has a clear overall winner on NERC coarse and fine, literal and metonymic entities, components as well as EL. The one exception is EL only for English, where INRIA's entity-fishing system outperforms L3I. L3I is particularly convincing in terms of F1, as it consistently keeps precision and recall in good balance (even trending toward recall many times). Other systems, e.g. INRIA, EHRMAMA, or the baseline, typically suffer from a bias towards precision. We assume that actively tackling the problem of OCR noise and hyphenation issues helps to achieve better recall.

Time-Based Observations. In order to gauge the impact of the article's publication date on system performances, we analyze the variation of F1 scores as a function of time (see Fig. 3). The initial hypothesis here was that the older the article, the more difficult it is to extract and link the mentions it contains. In general, there does not seem to be a strong correlation between the article's publication date and F1 scores. In the specific case of EL, this finding is in line with the uniform distribution of NIL entities across time (see Sect. 3).

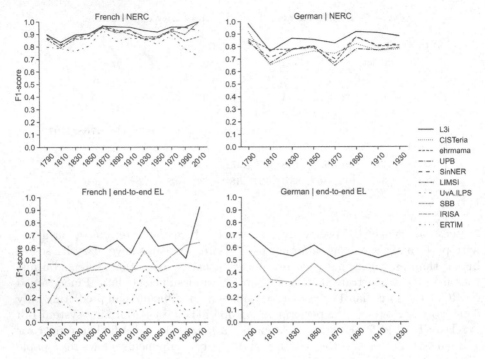

Fig. 3. F1-score as a function of time for the 5 best systems for NERC (top) and end-to-end EL (bottom) for the languages French (left) and German (right). The x-axis shows 20-years time buckets (e.g. 1790 = 1790–1809).

Impact of OCR Noise. To assess the impact of noisy entities on the task of NERC and EL, we evaluated the system performances on various noise levels (see Fig. 4). The level of noise is defined as the length-normalized Levenshtein distance between the surface form of an entity and its human transcription. There is a remarkable difference between the performances for noisy and non-noisy mentions on both NERC and EL. Already as little noise as 0.1 severely hurts the system's ability to predict an entity and may cut its performance by half. Interestingly, EL also suffers badly from little noise (norm. lev. dist. > 0.0 and < 0.1) even when providing the gold annotations of NERC (EL only, not shown in the plot). Slightly and medium noisy mentions (norm. lev. dist. > 0.0 and < 0.3) show a similar impact, while for highly noisy mentions, the performance deteriorates further. We can observe the greatest variation between systems at the medium noise level suggesting that the most robust systems get their competitive advantage when dealing with medium noisiness. On the effect of OCR noise on NERC, [49] claim that OCR errors impact more GPE mentions than persons or dates; in our breakdown of OCR noise impact by type, we can confirm that claim for little noise only (norm. lev. dist. > 0.0 and < 0.1), while this trend turns into the opposite for highly noisy entities.

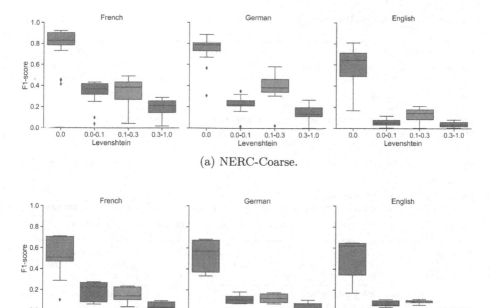

(a) NERC-Coarse.

(b) End-to-end EL with the relaxed evaluation regime and a cutoff @3.

Fig. 4. Impact of OCR noise: distribution of performances across systems on entities with different noise level severity for NERC (a) and end-to-end EL (b).

7   Conclusion and Perspectives

From the perspective of natural language processing, the HIPE evaluation lab provided the opportunity to test the robustness of NERC and EL approaches against challenging historical material and to gain new insights with respect to domain and language adaptation. With regard to NERC, results show that it is possible to design systems capable of dealing with historical and noisy inputs, whose performances compete with those obtained on contemporary texts. Entity linking, as well as the processing of metonymy and nested entities remain challenging aspects of historical NE processing (the latter two probably due to the limited amount of annotated material).

From the perspective of digital humanities, the lab's outcomes will help DH practitioners in mapping state-of-the-art solutions for NE processing on historical texts, and in getting a better understanding of what is already possible as opposed to what is still challenging. Most importantly, digital scholars are in need of support to explore the large quantities of digitized text they currently have at hand, and NE processing is high on the agenda. Such processing can support research questions in various domains (e.g. history, political science, literature, historical linguistics) and knowing about their performance is crucial in order to make an informed use of the processed data.

Table 8. Results for end-to-end EL (top) and EL only (bottom) with P, R and F1 @1.

End-to-end EL	French						German						English					
(a) Literal	Strict			Fuzzy			Strict			Fuzzy			Strict			Fuzzy		
	P	R	F	P	R	F	P	R	F	P	R	F	P	R	F	P	R	F
ERTIM	.150	.084	.108	.150	.084	.108	-	-	-	-	-	-	-	-	-	-	-	-
IRISA	.446	.399	.421	.465	.417	.439	-	-	-	-	-	-	-	-	-	-	-	-
L3I	.594	.602	.598	.613	.622	.617	.531	.538	.534	.553	.561	.557	.523	.539	.531	.523	.539	.531
SBB	.594	.310	.407	.616	.321	.422	.540	.304	.389	.561	.315	.403	.257	.097	.141	.257	.097	.141
UVA-ILPS	.352	.195	.251	.353	.196	.252	.245	.272	.258	.255	.283	.268	.249	.375	.300	.249	.375	.300
Baseline	.206	.342	.257	.257	.358	.270	.173	.187	.180	.188	.203	.195	.220	.263	.239	.220	.263	.239
(b) Meton.																		
IRISA	.023	.295	.043	.041	.527	.076	-	-	-	-	-	-	-	-	-	-	-	-
L3I	.236	.402	.297	.366	.625	.462	.324	.508	.396	.384	.602	.469	.172	.200	.185	.172	.200	.185
Baseline	.002	.027	.004	.008	.098	.015	.025	.136	.042	.026	.144	.044	.004	.040	.007	.004	.040	.007

EL only	French						German						English					
	Strict			Fuzzy			Strict			Fuzzy			Strict			Fuzzy		
(a) Literal	P	R	F	P	R	F	P	R	F	P	R	F	P	R	F	P	R	F
INRIA	.585	.650	.616	.604	.670	.635	-	-	-	-	-	-	.633	.685	.658	.633	.685	.658
IRISA	.475	.473	.474	.492	.491	.492	-	-	-	-	-	-	-	-	-	-	-	-
L3I	.640	.638	.639	.660	.657	.659	.581	.582	.582	.601	.602	.602	.593	.593	.593	.593	.593	.593
SBB	.677	.371	.480	.699	.383	.495	.615	.349	.445	.636	.361	.461	.344	.119	.177	.344	.119	.177
UVA.ILPS	-	-	-	-	-	-	-	-	-	-	-	-	.607	.580	.593	.607	.580	.593
Baseline	.502	.495	.498	.516	.508	.512	.420	.416	.418	.440	.435	.437	.506	.506	.506	.506	.506	.506
(b) Meto.																		
IRISA	.025	.357	.047	.041	.580	.076	-	-	-	-	-	-	-	-	-	-	-	-
L3I	.303	.446	.361	.461	.679	.549	.443	.627	.519	.515	.729	.604	.286	.480	.358	.286	.480	.358
UVA.ILPS	-	-	-	-	-	-	-	-	-	-	-	-	.031	.058	.031	.031	.058	.031
Baseline	.213	.312	.254	.323	.473	.384	.265	.373	.310	.331	.466	.387	.219	.280	.246	.219	.280	.246

Overall, HIPE has contributed to advance the state of the art in semantic indexing of historical newspapers and, more generally, of historical material. As future work, we intend to explore the several directions for a potential second edition of HIPE: expanding the language spectrum, strengthening the already covered languages by providing more training data, considering other types of historical documents, and exploring to what extent the improvements shown in HIPE can be transferred to similar tasks in other domains, or to linking problems that require knowledge bases other than Wikidata.

Acknowledgements. This HIPE evaluation lab would not have been possible without the interest and commitment of many. We express our warmest thanks to: the Swiss newspapers *NZZ* and *Le Temps*, and the Swiss and Luxembourg national libraries for sharing part of their data in the frame of the *impresso* project; Camille Watter and Gerold Schneider for their commitment and hard work with the construction of the data set; the INCEPTION project team for its valuable and efficient support with the annotation tool; Richard Eckart de Castillo, Clemens Neudecker, Sophie Rosset and David Smith for their encouragement and guidance as part of the HIPE advisory board; and, finally, the 13 teams who embarked in this first HIPE edition, for their patience and scientific involvement. HIPE is part of the research activities of the project *"impresso* – Media Monitoring of the Past", for which we also gratefully acknowledge the financial support of the Swiss National Science Foundation under grant number CR-SII5_173719.

References

1. Akbik, A., Bergmann, T., Blythe, D., Rasul, K., Schweter, S., Vollgraf, R.: FLAIR: an easy-to-use framework for state-of-the-art NLP. In: Proceedings of the 2019 Conference of the North American Chapter of the Association for Computational Linguistics (demonstrations), pp. 54–59. Association for Computational Linguistics, Minneapolis, Minnesota, June 2019. https://www.aclweb.org/anthology/N19-4010

2. Akbik, A., Blythe, D., Vollgraf, R.: Contextual string embeddings for sequence labeling. In: Proceedings of the 27th International Conference on Computational Linguistics, pp. 1638–1649. Association for Computational Linguistics, Santa Fe, New Mexico, USA, August 2018. http://www.aclweb.org/anthology/C18-1139

3. Bojanowski, P., Grave, E., Joulin, A., Mikolov, T.: Enriching word vectors with subword information. Trans. Assoc. Comput. Linguist. **5**, 135–146 (2017). https://www.aclweb.org/anthology/Q17-1010

4. Bollmann, M.: A large-scale comparison of historical text normalization systems. In: Proceedings of the 2019 Conference of the North American Chapter of the Association for Computational Linguistics: Human Language Technologies, Volume 1 (Long and Short Papers), pp. 3885–3898. Association for Computational Linguistics, Minneapolis, Minnesota (2019). https://doi.org/10.18653/v1/N19-1389

5. Borin, L., Kokkinakis, D., Olsson, L.J.: Naming the past: named entity and animacy recognition in 19th century Swedish literature. In: Proceedings of the Workshop on Language Technology for Cultural Heritage Data (LaT-eCH 2007), pp. 1–8 (2007)

6. Cappellato, L., Eickhoff, C., Ferro, N., Névéol, A. (eds.): CLEF 2020 Working Notes. In: CEUR Workshop Proceedings Working Notes of CLEF 2020 - Conference and Labs of the Evaluation Forum (2020)

7. Chiron, G., Doucet, A., Coustaty, M., Visani, M., Moreux, J.P.: Impact of OCR errors on the use of digital libraries: towards a better access to information. In: Proceedings of the 17th ACM/IEEE Joint Conference on Digital Libraries JCDL 2017, pp. 249–252. IEEE Press, Piscataway (2017), http://dl.acm.org/citation.cfm?id=3200334.3200364

8. Chiu, J.P., Nichols, E.: Named entity recognition with bidirectional LSTM-CNNs. Trans. Assoc. Comput. Linguist. **4**, 357–370 (2016). https://doi.org/10.1162/tacl_a_00104

9. Devlin, J., Chang, M.W., Lee, K., Toutanova, K.: BERT: pre-training of deep bidirectional transformers for language understanding. CoRR abs/1810.04805 (2018). http://arxiv.org/abs/1810.04805

10. Dupont, Y., Dinarelli, M., Tellier, I., Lautier, C.: Structured named entity recognition by cascading CRFs. In: Intelligent Text Processing and Computational Linguistics (CICling) (2017)

11. Ehrmann, M., Colavizza, G., Rochat, Y., Kaplan, F.: Diachronic evaluation of NER systems on old newspapers. In: Proceedings of the 13th Conference on Natural Language Processing KONVENS 2016, pp. 97–107. Bochumer Linguistische Arbeitsberichte (2016). https://infoscience.epfl.ch/record/221391?ln=en

12. Ehrmann, M., Romanello, M., Flückiger, A., Clematide, S.: Extended overview of CLEF HIPE 2020: named entity processing on historical newspapers. In: Cappellato, L., Eickhoff, C., Ferro, N., Névéol, A. (eds.) CLEF 2020 Working Notes. Working Notes of CLEF 2020 - Conference and Labs of the Evaluation Forum CEUR-WS (2020)

13. Ehrmann, M., Romanello, M., Flückiger, A., Clematide, S.: HIPE - shared task participation guidelines (v1.1) (2020). https://doi.org/10.5281/zenodo.3677171

14. Ehrmann, M., Romanello, M., Flückiger, A., Clematide, S.: Impresso named entity annotation guidelines (2020). https://doi.org/10.5281/zenodo.3604227

15. El Vaigh, C.B., Goasdoué, F., Gravier, G., Sébillot, P.: Using knowledge base semantics in context-aware entity linking. In: 2019 Proceedings of the ACM Symposium on Document Engineering DocEng 2019, pp. 1–10. Association for Computing Machinery, Berlin, Germany, September 2019. https://doi.org/10.1145/3342558.3345393

16. Galibert, O., Rosset, S., Grouin, C., Zweigenbaum, P., Quintard, L.: Extended named entity annotation on OCRed documents : from corpus constitution to evaluation campaign. In: Proceedings of the Eighth conference on International Language Resources and Evaluation, pp. 3126–3131. Istanbul, Turkey (2012)

17. Ganea, O.E., Hofmann, T.: Deep joint entity disambiguation with local neural attention. In: Proceedings of the 2017 Conference on Empirical Methods in Natural Language Processing, pp. 2619–2629 (2017)

18. Grishman, R., Sundheim, B.: Design of the MUC-6 evaluation. In: Proceedings of the Sixth Conference on Message Understanding Conference (MUC-6), Columbia, Maryland (1995)

19. Hoffart, J., et al.: Robust disambiguation of named entities in text. In: EMNLP (2011)

20. Hooland, S.V., Wilde, M.D., Verborgh, R., Steiner, T., Van de Walle, R.: Exploring entity recognition and disambiguation for cultural heritage collections. Digit. Sch. Humanit. 30(2), 262–279 (2015). https://doi.org/10.1093/llc/fqt067

21. van Hulst, J.M., Hasibi, F., Dercksen, K., Balog, K., de Vries, A.P.: REL: an entity linker standing on the shoulders of giants. In: Proceedings of the 43rd International ACM SIGIR Conference on Research and Development in Information Retrieval SIGIR 2020. ACM (2020)

22. Kaplan, F., di Lenardo, I.: Big data of the past. Front. Digit. Humanit. 4 (2017). https://doi.org/10.3389/fdigh.2017.00012

23. Klie, J.C., Bugert, M., Boullosa, B., de Castilho, R.E., Gurevych, I.: The inception platform: machine-assisted and knowledge-oriented interactive annotation. In: Proceedings of the 27th International Conference on Computational Linguistics: System Demonstrations, pp. 5–9 (2018)

24. Kolitsas, N., Ganea, O.E., Hofmann, T.: End-to-end neural entity linking. In: Proceedings of the 22nd Conference on Computational Natural Language Learning, pp. 519–529. Association for Computational Linguistics, Brussels, Belgium, October 2018. https://doi.org/10.18653/v1/K18-1050

25. Krippendorff, K.: Content Analysis: An Introduction to its Methodology. Sage Publications, Thousand Oaks (1980)

26. Labusch, K., Neudecker, C., Zellhöfer, D.: BERT for named entity recognition in contemporary and historic german. In: Preliminary proceedings of the 15th Conference on Natural Language Processing (KONVENS 2019): Long Papers, pp. 1–9. German Society for Computational Linguistics & Language Technology, Erlangen, Germany (2019)
27. Lample, G., Ballesteros, M., Subramanian, S., Kawakami, K., Dyer, C.: Neural architectures for named entity recognition, March 2016. arXiv:1603.01360. http://arxiv.org/abs/1603.01360
28. Lavergne, T., Cappé, O., Yvon, F.: Practical very large scale CRFs. In: Proceedings of the 48th Annual Meeting of the Association for Computational Linguistics, pp. 504–513. Association for Computational Linguistics (2010)
29. Linhares Pontes, E., Hamdi, A., Sidere, N., Doucet, A.: Impact of OCR quality on named entity linking. In: Jatowt, A., Maeda, A., Syn, S.Y. (eds.) ICADL 2019. LNCS, vol. 11853, pp. 102–115. Springer, Cham (2019). https://doi.org/10.1007/978-3-030-34058-2_11
30. Makhoul, J., Kubala, F., Schwartz, R., Weischedel, R.: Performance measures for information extraction. In: Proceedings of DARPA Broadcast News Workshop, pp. 249–252 (1999)
31. Martin, L., et al.: Camembert: a tasty french language model (2019)
32. May, P.: German ELMo model (2019). https://github.com/t-systems-on-site-services-gmbh/german-elmo-model
33. Nadeau, D., Sekine, S.: A survey of named entity recognition and classification. Lingvisticae Investigationes 30(1), 3–26 (2007)
34. Neudecker, C., Antonacopoulos, A.: Making Europe's historical newspapers searchable. In: 2016 12th IAPR Workshop on Document Analysis Systems (DAS), pp. 405–410. IEEE, Santorini, Greece, April 2016. https://doi.org/10.1109/DAS.2016.83
35. Nguyen, D.B., Hoffart, J., Theobald, M., Weikum, G.: Aida-light: high-throughput named-entity disambiguation. In: LDOW (2014)
36. Nouvel, D., Antoine, J.-Y., Friburger, N.: Pattern mining for named entity recognition. In: Vetulani, Z., Mariani, J. (eds.) LTC 2011. LNCS (LNAI), vol. 8387, pp. 226–237. Springer, Cham (2014). https://doi.org/10.1007/978-3-319-08958-4_19
37. Okazaki, N.: CRFsuite: a fast implementation of Conditional Random Fields (CRFs) (2007). http://www.chokkan.org/software/crfsuite/
38. Ortiz Suárez, P.J., Dupont, Y., Muller, B., Romary, L., Sagot, B.: Establishing a new state-of-the-art for French named entity recognition. In: Proceedings of the 12th Language Resources and Evaluation Conference, pp. 4631–4638. European Language Resources Association, Marseille, France, May 2020. https://www.aclweb.org/anthology/2020.lrec-1.569
39. Pennington, J., Socher, R., Manning, C.D.: Glove: global vectors for word representation. EMNLP 14, 1532–43 (2014)
40. Peters, M., et al.: Deep Contextualized Word Representations. In: Proceedings of the 2018 Conference of the North American Chapter of the Association for Computational Linguistics: Human Language Technologies, Volume 1 (Long Papers). pp. 2227–2237. Association for Computational Linguistics, New Orleans, Louisiana (2018). https://doi.org/10.18653/v1/N18-1202
41. Piotrowski, M.: Natural language processing for historical texts. Synth. Lect. Hum. Lang. Technol. 5(2), 1–157 (2012)
42. Plank, B.: What to do about non-standard (or non-canonical) language in NLP. In: Proceedings of the 13th Conference on Natural Language Processing KONVENS 2016. Bochumer Linguistische Arbeitsberichte (2016)

43. Rao, D., McNamee, P., Dredze, M.: Entity linking: finding extracted entities in a knowledge base. In: Poibeau, T., Saggion, H., Piskorski, J., Yangarber, R. (eds.) Multi-source, Multilingual Information Extraction and Summarization, pp. 93–115. Springer, Heidelberg (2013). https://doi.org/10.1007/978-3-642-28569-1_5

44. Rosset, S., Grouin, C., Fort, K., Galibert, O., Kahn, J., Zweigenbaum, P.: Structured named entities in two distinct press corpora: contemporary broadcast news and old newspapers. In: Proceedings of the 6th Linguistic Annotation Workshop, pp. 40–48. Association for Computational Linguistics (2012)

45. Rosset, S., Grouin, C., Zweigenbaum, P.: Entités nommées structurées : guide d'annotation Quaero. NOTES et DOCUMENTS 2011–04, LIMSI-CNRS (2011)

46. Smith, D.A., Cordell, R.: A research agenda for historical and multilingual optical character recognition. Technical report (2018). http://hdl.handle.net/2047/D20297452

47. Sporleder, C.: Natural language processing for cultural heritage domains. Lang. Linguist. Compass **4**(9), 750–768 (2010). https://doi.org/10.1111/j.1749-818X.2010.00230.x

48. van Strien, D., Beelen, K., Ardanuy, M.C., Hosseini, K., McGillivray, B., Colavizza, G.: Assessing the impact of OCR quality on downstream NLP tasks. In: ICAART 2020 - Proceedings of the 12th International Conference on Agents and Artificial Intelligence. SCITEPRESS - Science and Technology Publications, January 2020. https://doi.org/10.17863/CAM.52068

49. van Strien, D., Beelen, K., Ardanuy, M., Hosseini, K., McGillivray, B., Colavizza, G.: Assessing the impact of OCR quality on downstream NLP tasks. In: Proceedings of the 12th International Conference on Agents and Artificial Intelligence, pp. 484–496. SCITEPRESS - Science and Technology Publications, Valletta, Malta (2020). https://doi.org/10.5220/0009169004840496

50. Terras, M.: The rise of digitization. In: Rikowski, R. (ed.) Digitisation Perspectives, pp. 3–20. Sense Publishers, Rotterdam (2011). https://doi.org/10.1007/978-94-6091-299-3_1

51. Vaswani, A., et al.: Attention is all you need. CoRR abs/1706.03762 (2017). http://arxiv.org/abs/1706.03762

52. Vilain, M., Su, J., Lubar, S.: Entity extraction is a boring solved problem: or is it? In: Human Language Technologies 2007: The Conference of the North American Chapter of the Association for Computational Linguistics; Companion Volume, Short Papers, NAACL-Short 2007, Rochester, New York, pp. 181–184. Association for Computational Linguistics (2007). http://dl.acm.org/citation.cfm?id=1614108.1614154

Overview of the ImageCLEF 2020: Multimedia Retrieval in Medical, Lifelogging, Nature, and Internet Applications

Bogdan Ionescu[1(✉)], Henning Müller[2], Renaud Péteri[3], Asma Ben Abacha[4],
Vivek Datla[5], Sadid A. Hasan[6], Dina Demner-Fushman[4], Serge Kozlovski[7],
Vitali Liauchuk[7], Yashin Dicente Cid[8], Vassili Kovalev[7], Obioma Pelka[9],
Christoph M. Friedrich[9], Alba García Seco de Herrera[10], Van-Tu Ninh[11],
Tu-Khiem Le[11], Liting Zhou[11], Luca Piras[12], Michael Riegler[13],
Pål Halvorsen[13], Minh-Triet Tran[14], Mathias Lux[15], Cathal Gurrin[11],
Duc-Tien Dang-Nguyen[16], Jon Chamberlain[10], Adrian Clark[10],
Antonio Campello[17], Dimitri Fichou[18], Raul Berari[18], Paul Brie[18],
Mihai Dogariu[1], Liviu Daniel Ştefan[1], and Mihai Gabriel Constantin[1]

[1] University Politehnica of Bucharest, Bucharest, Romania
bogdan.ionescu@upb.ro
[2] University of Applied Sciences Western Switzerland (IIES-SO),
Sierre, Switzerland
[3] University of La Rochelle, La Rochelle, France
[4] National Library of Medicine, Bethesda, USA
[5] Philips Research Cambridge, Cambridge, USA
[6] CVS Health, Monroeville, USA
[7] United Institute of Informatics Problems, Minsk, Belarus
[8] University of Warwick, Coventry, UK
[9] University of Applied Sciences and Arts Dortmund, Dortmund, Germany
[10] University of Essex, Colchester, UK
[11] Dublin City University, Dublin, Ireland
[12] Pluribus One and University of Cagliari, Cagliari, Italy
[13] University of Oslo, Oslo, Norway
[14] University of Science, Ho Chi Minh City, Vietnam
[15] Klagenfurt University, Klagenfurt, Austria
[16] University of Bergen, Bergen, Norway
[17] Wellcome Trust, London, UK
[18] teleportHQ, Cluj-Napoca, Romania

Abstract. This paper presents an overview of the ImageCLEF 2020 lab
that was organized as part of the Conference and Labs of the Evaluation Forum - CLEF Labs 2020. ImageCLEF is an ongoing evaluation
initiative (first run in 2003) that promotes the evaluation of technologies for annotation, indexing and retrieval of visual data with the aim
of providing information access to large collections of images in various
usage scenarios and domains. In 2020, the 18th edition of ImageCLEF
runs four main tasks: (i) a *medical* task that groups three previous tasks,

© Springer Nature Switzerland AG 2020
A. Arampatzis et al. (Eds.): CLEF 2020, LNCS 12260, pp. 311–341, 2020.
https://doi.org/10.1007/978-3-030-58219-7_22

i.e., caption analysis, tuberculosis prediction, and medical visual question answering and question generation, (ii) a *lifelog* task (videos, images and other sources) about daily activity understanding, retrieval and summarization, (iii) a *coral* task about segmenting and labeling collections of coral reef images, and (iv) a new *Internet* task addressing the problems of identifying hand-drawn user interface components. Despite the current pandemic situation, the benchmark campaign received a strong participation with over 40 groups submitting more than 295 runs.

Keywords: Visual question answering · Visual question generation · Lifelogging retrieval and summarization · Medical image classification · Coral image segmentation and classification · Recognition of hand-drawn website user interface components · ImageCLEF benchmark · Annotated data · Common evaluation framework

1   Introduction

ImageCLEF[1] is the image retrieval and classification lab of the CLEF (Conference and Labs of the Evaluation Forum) conference. ImageCLEF has started in 2003 with only four participants [11]. It increased its impact with the addition of medical tasks in 2004 [10], attracting over 20 participants already in the second year. An overview of ten years of the medical tasks can be found in [31]. It continued the ascending trend, reaching over 200 participants in 2019. The tasks have changed much over the years but the general objective has always been the same, i.e., *to combine text and visual data to retrieve and classify visual information*. Tasks have evolved from more general object classification and retrieval to many specific application domains, e.g., nature, security, medical, Internet. A detailed analysis of several tasks and the creation of the data sets can be found in [37]. ImageCLEF has shown to have an important impact over the years, already detailed in 2010 [53,54].

Since 2018, ImageCLEF uses the crowdAI platform, now migrated to AIcrowd[2] from 2020, to distribute the data and receive the submitted results. The system allows having an online leader board and gives the possibility to keep data sets accessible beyond competition, including a continuous submission of runs and addition to the leader board. Over the years, ImageCLEF and also CLEF have shown a strong scholarly impact that was analyzed in [53,54]. For instance, the term "ImageCLEF" returns on Google Scholar[3] over 5,300 article results (search on July 3rd, 2020). This underlines the importance of evaluation campaigns for disseminating best scientific practices. We introduce here the four tasks that were run in the 2020 edition[4], namely: ImageCLEFmedical, ImageCLEFlifelog, ImageCLEFcoral, and the new ImageCLEFdrawnUI.

---

[1] http://www.imageclef.org/.
[2] https://www.aicrowd.com/.
[3] https://scholar.google.com/.
[4] https://www.imageclef.org/2020/.

2   Overview of Tasks and Participation

ImageCLEF 2020 consists of four main tasks with the objective of covering a *diverse range* of multimedia retrieval applications, namely: *medicine, lifelogging, nature*, and *Internet applications*. It followed the 2019 tradition [30] of diversifying the use cases [2,8,21,33,38,42]. The 2020 tasks are presented as follows:

- **ImageCLEFmedical.** Medical tasks have been part of ImageCLEF every year since 2004. In 2018, all but one task were medical, but little interaction happened between the medical tasks. For this reason, starting with 2019, the medical tasks were focused towards one specific problem but combined as a single task with several subtasks. This allows exploring synergies between the domains:
  - *Visual Question Answering*: This is the third edition of the VQA-Med task. With the increasing interest in artificial intelligence (AI) to support clinical decision making and improve patient engagement, opportunities to generate and leverage algorithms for automated medical image interpretation are currently being explored. The clinicians' confidence in interpreting complex medical images can be enhanced by a "second opinion" provided by an automated system. Since patients may now access structured and unstructured data related to their health via patient portals, such access motivates the need to help them better understand their conditions regarding their available data, including medical images. In view of this and inspired by the success of visual question answering in the general domain[5] and the previous VQA-Med editions [3,25], we propose this year two tasks on visual question answering (VQA) and visual Question Generation (VQG) [2]. For the VQA task, given a radiology image accompanied with a clinically relevant question, participating systems are tasked with answering the question based on the visual content, while for the VQG task, given a radiology image, participating systems are tasked with generating relevant questions based on the visual content;
  - *Tuberculosis*: This is the fourth edition of the task. The main objective is to provide an automatic CT-based evaluation of tuberculosis (TB) patients. This is done by detecting visual TB-related findings and by assessing a TB severity score based on the automatic analysis of lung CT scans and clinically relevant meta-data. Being able to generate this automatic analysis from the image data allows to limit laboratory analyses to determine the TB stage. This can lead to quicker decisions on the best treatment strategy, reduced use of antibiotics and lower impact on the patient. In this year edition, we decided to concentrate on the automated CT lung-based report generation task and labels include presence of TB lesions in general, presence of pleurisy and caverns in particular [33];
  - *Caption*: This is the fourth edition of the task in this format, however, it is based on previous medical tasks. The proposed task is to automatically predict UMLS (Unified Medical Language System®) concepts, which is

---

[5] https://visualqa.org/.

the first step towards automatic medical image semantic tagging. These relevant UMLS® concepts can be further adopted for several medical imaging tasks such as image captioning, multi-modal image classification and image retrieval. There is a considerable need for automatic mapping of visual information to textual content, as the interpretation of knowledge from medical images is time-consuming. In view of better-structured medical reports, the more information and image characteristics known, the more efficient are the radiologist regarding interpretation. Based on the lessons learned in previous years [16,28,29,41], this year [42] the task focuses on detecting UMLS® concepts in radiology images including a more diverse wealth of imaging modality information.

- **ImageCLEFlifelog.** This is the fourth edition of the task. The increasingly wide range of personal devices, such as smartphones, video cameras as well as wearable devices allow capturing pictures, videos, and audio clips for every moment of our lives are becoming available. Considering the huge volume of data created, there is a need for systems that can automatically analyse the data in order to categorize, summarize and also query to retrieve the information the user may need. This year edition of the task comes with new, enriched data, focused on daily living activities and the chronological order of the moments. Two tasks are proposed: lifelog moment retrieval (LMRT) requiring participants to retrieve a number of specific predefined activities in a lifelogger's life, and sport performance lifelog (SPLL) requiring participants to predict the expected performance (e.g., estimated finishing time) for an athlete who trained for a sport event [38].

- **ImageCLEFcoral.** The increasing use of structure-from-motion photogrammetry for modelling large-scale environments from action cameras has driven the next generation of visualization techniques. The task addresses the problem of automatically segmenting and labeling a collection of images that can be used in combination to create 3D models for the monitoring of coral reefs. Last year was the first time a coral annotation task formed part of ImageCLEF [7]. Participants' entries showed that some level of automatically annotating corals and benthic substrates was possible, despite this being a difficult task due to the variation of colour, texture and morphology between and within classification types. This year [8], the volume of training data has been increased and there are four subsets of test data ranging in geographical similarity and ecological connectedness to the training data. The intention is to explore how well systems trained on one area of data will perform on data from other geographical regions.

- **ImageCLEFdrawnUI.** This task is new for 2020. Building websites requires a very specific set of skills. Currently, the two main ways to achieve this is either by using a visual website builder or by programming. Both approaches have a steep learning curve. Enabling people to create websites by drawing them on a whiteboard or on a piece of paper would make the webpage building process more accessible. In this context, the detection and recognition of hand drawn website UIs task addresses the problem of automatically recognizing the hand drawn objects representing website UIs, which are further used to be translated automatically into website code.

Table 1. Key figures regarding participation in Image CLEF 2020.

Task	Completed registrations	Groups thatsubm. results	Submitted runs	Submitted working notes
VQ answering	30	11	62	11
Tuberculosis	21	9	67	9
Caption	23	7	47	7
Lifelog	12	6	48	6
Coral	15	4	53	4
DrawnUI	14	3	18	3
Overall	115	40	295	40

To participate in the evaluation campaign, the research groups had to register by following the instructions on the ImageCLEF 2020 web page(See footnote 4). To ease the overall management of the campaign, in 2020 the challenge was organized through the AIcrowd platform(See footnote 2). To actually get access to the data sets, the participants were required to submit a signed End User Agreement (EUA). Table 1 summarizes the participation in ImageCLEF 2020, including the number of completed registrations, indicated both per task and for the overall lab. The table also shows the number of groups that submitted runs and the ones that submitted a working notes paper describing the techniques used. Teams were allowed to register for participating in several different tasks.

After a decrease in participation in 2016, the participation increased in 2017 and 2018, and increased again in 2019. In 2018, 31 teams completed the tasks and 28 working notes papers were received. In 2019, 63 teams completed the tasks and 50 working notes papers were retrieved. In 2020, 40 teams completed the tasks and submitted working notes papers. Given the previous ascending trend, we estimate that this drop is mostly due to the outbreak of the COVID-19 pandemic and lock-down, started during the registration time and continued till the end of the challenge. This triggered a significant perturbation of the tasks. Although additional time was granted, the final participation is lower. Nevertheless, we see a significant improvement in the involvement of the teams and success ratio, which is more important that the sole high participation. The number of teams registering is less than half of as in 2019, however, the number of groups submitting results was not proportionally reduced, and the success ratio, i.e., the number of teams completing the tasks reported to the number of teams completing the registration, is higher, i.e., 35%, compared to 27% for 2019, and 23% for 2018.

In the following sections, we present the tasks. Only a short overview is reported, including general objectives, description of the tasks and data sets, and a short summary of the results. A detailed review of the received submissions for each task is provided with the task overview working notes: ImageCLEFmedical VQA [2], Tuberculosis [33], and Caption [42], ImageCLEFlifelog [38], Image-CLEFcoral [8], and ImageCLEFdrawnUI [21].

3   The Visual Question Answering Task

Visual Question Answering is an exciting problem that combines natural language processing and computer vision techniques. With the increasing interest in artificial intelligence (AI) technologies to support clinical decision making and improve patient engagement, opportunities to generate and leverage algorithms for automated medical image interpretation are being explored at a faster pace. To offer more training data and evaluation benchmarks, we organized the first visual question answering (VQA) task in the medical domain in 2018 [25], and continued the task in 2019 [3]. Following the strong engagement from the research community in both editions of VQA in the medical domain (VQA-Med) and the ongoing interests from both computer vision and medical informatics communities, we continued the task this year (VQA-Med 2020) [2] with an enhanced focus on answering questions about abnormalities from the visual content of associated radiology images. Furthermore, we introduced an additional task this year, visual question generation (VQG), consisting in generating relevant natural language questions about radiology images based on their visual content.

3.1   Task Setup

For the visual question answering task, similar to 2019, given a radiology medical image accompanied by a clinically relevant question, participating systems in VQA-Med 2020 were tasked with answering the question based on the visual image content. In VQA-Med 2020, we specifically focused on questions about abnormality (e.g., "what is most alarming about this ultrasound image?"), which can be answered from the image content without requiring additional medical knowledge or domain-specific inference. Additionally, the visual question generation (VQG) task was introduced for the first time in this third edition of the VQA-Med challenge. This task required participants to generate relevant natural language questions about radiology images using their visual content.

3.2   Data Set

For the visual question answering task, we automatically constructed the training, validation, and test sets by: (i) applying several filters to select relevant images and associated annotations, and, (ii) creating patterns to generate the questions and their answers. We selected relevant medical images from the Med-Pix[6] database with filters based on their captions, localities, and diagnosis methods. We selected only the cases where the diagnosis was made based on the image. Examples of the selected diagnosis methods include: CT/MRI imaging, angiography, characteristic imaging appearance, radiographs, imaging features, ultrasound, and diagnostic radiology. Finally, we considered the most frequent abnormality question categories to create the data set, which included a training set of 4,000 radiology images with 4,000 Question-Answer (QA) pairs, a

---

[6] https://medpix.nlm.nih.gov/.

validation set of 500 radiology images with 500 QA pairs, and a test set of 500 radiology images with 500 questions. To further ensure the quality of the data, the test set was manually validated by a medical doctor. The participants were also encouraged to utilize VQA-Med-2019 data set as additional training data.

For the visual question generation task, we automatically constructed the training, validation, and test sets in a similar fashion by using a separate collection of radiology images and their associated captions. We semi-automatically generated questions from the image captions first by using a rule-based sentence-to-question generation approach[7], and then, three annotators manually curated the list of question-answer pairs by removing or editing the noises related to grammatical inconsistencies. The final curated corpus for the VQG task was comprised of 780 radiology images with 2,156 associated questions (and answers) for training, 141 radiology images with 164 questions for validation, and 80 radiology images for testing. For more details, please refer to [2].

3.3 Participating Groups and Submitted Runs

Out of 47 online registrations, 30 participants submitted signed end user agreement forms. Finally, 11 groups submitted a total of 49 successful runs for the VQA task, while 3 groups submitted a total of 13 successful runs for the VQG task, indicating a notable interest in the VQA-Med 2020 challenge. Table 2 and Table 3 give an overview of all participants and the number of submitted runs (please note that were allowed only 5 runs per team).

Table 2. Participating groups in the VQA-Med 2020 VQA task.

Team	Institution	# Valid runs
bumjun_jung	Machine Intelligence Lab, University of Tokyo (Japan)	5
dhruv_sharma	Virginia Tech (USA)	1
going	Sun Yat-Sen University (China)	5
harendrakv	Vadict Innovation Solutions (India)	5
kdevqa	Toyohashi University of Technology (Japan)	4
NLM	National Library of Medicine (USA)	5
sheerin	individual participation (India)	5
Shengyan	Yunnan University (China)	5
TheInceptionTeam	Jordan University of Science and Technology (Jordan)	5
umassmednlp	University of Massachusetts Medical School (USA)	4
z_liao	The Australian Institute for Machine Learning, The University of Adelaide (Australia)	5

---

[7] http://www.cs.cmu.edu/~ark/mheilman/questions/.

Table 3. Participating groups in the VQA-Med 2020 VQG task.

Team	Institution	# Valid runs
NLM	National Library of Medicine (USA)	3
TheInceptionTeam	Jordan University of Science and Technology (Jordan)	5
z_liao	The Australian Institute for Machine Learning, The University of Adelaide (Australia)	5

Table 4. Maximum accuracy and maximum BLEU scores for VQA Task (out of each team's submitted runs).

Team	Accuracy	BLEU
z_liao	0.496	0.542
TheInceptionTeam	0.480	0.511
bumjun_jung	0.466	0.502
going	0.426	0.462
NLM	0.400	0.441
harendrakv	0.378	0.439
Shengyan	0.376	0.412
kdevqa	0.314	0.350
sheerin	0.282	0.330
umassmednlp	0.220	0.340
dhruv_sharma	0.142	0.177

3.4 Results

Similar to the evaluation setup of the VQA-Med 2019 challenge [3], the evaluation of the participant systems for the VQA task in the VQA-Med 2020 challenge is also conducted based on two primary metrics: accuracy and BLEU. We used an adapted version of accuracy from the general domain VQA[8] task that strictly considers exact matching of a participant provided answer and the ground truth answer. To compensate for the strictness of the accuracy metric, BLEU [40] is used to capture the word overlap-based similarity between a system-generated answer and the ground truth answer. The overall methodology and resources for the BLEU metric are essentially similar to last year's VQA task [3]. The BLEU metric is also used to evaluate the submissions for the VQG task, where we essentially compute the word overlap-based average similarity score between the system-generated questions and the ground truth question for each given test image. The overall results of the participating systems are presented in Table 4

---

[8] https://visualqa.org/evaluation.html.

Table 5. Maximum average BLEU scores for VQG task (out of each team's submitted runs).

Team	Average BLEU
z_liao	0.348
TheInceptionTeam	0.339
NLM	0.116

and Table 5 in a descending order of the accuracy and average BLEU scores respectively (the higher the better).

3.5   Lessons Learned and Next Steps

Similar to last two years, participants continued to use state-of-the-art deep learning techniques to build their VQA-Med systems for both VQA and VQG tasks [3,25]. In particular, most systems leveraged encoder-decoder architectures with, e.g., deep convolutional neural networks (CNNs) like VGGNet or ResNet. A variety of pooling strategies were explored, e.g., global average pooling to encode image features and transformer-based architectures like BERT or recurrent neural networks (RNN) to extract question features (for the VQA task). Various types of attention mechanisms are also used coupled with different pooling strategies such as multimodal factorized bilinear (MFB) pooling or multi-modal factorized high-order pooling (MFH) in order to combine multimodal features followed by bilinear transformations to finally predict the possible answers in the VQA task and generate possible question words in the VQG task. Additionally, the top performing systems first classified the questions into two types: yes/no, and abnormality, then added another multi-class classification framework for abnormality-related question answering, while using the same backbone architecture along with utilizing additional training data, leading to better results.

Analyses of the results in Table 4 suggest that in general, participating systems performed well for the VQA task and achieved better accuracy results relatively compared to last year's results for answering abnormality-related questions [3]. They obtained slightly lower BLEU scores as we focused on only abnormality questions this year that are generally complex than modality, plane, or organ category questions given in the last year. Overall, the VQA task results obtained this year entail the robustness of the provided data set compared to last year's task due to the enhanced focus on the abnormality-related questions for corpus creation. For the VQG task, results in Table 5 suggest that the task was comparatively challenging than the VQA task as the systems achieved lower BLEU scores. As BLEU is not the ideal metric to semantically compare the generated questions with the ground-truth questions, this could also urge the necessity of an embedding-based similarity metric to be explored in the future edition of this task. We would like to also expand the VQG corpus with more images and questions to enable effective development of learning models.

4   The Tuberculosis Task

Tuberculosis (TB) is a bacterial infection caused by a germ called Mycobacterium tuberculosis. About 130 years after its discovery, the disease remains a persistent threat and one of the top 10 causes of death worldwide according to the WHO [55]. The bacteria usually attack the lungs and generally TB can be cured with antibiotics. However, the different types of TB require different treatments, and therefore detection of the specific case characteristics is important. In particular, detection of the TB type and presence of different lesion types are important real-world tasks.

In the previous editions of this task, setup evolved from year to year. In the first two editions of this task [16,18] participants had to detect Multi-drug resistant patients (MDR subtask) and to classify the TB type (TBT subtask) both based only on the CT image. After 2 editions it was concluded to drop the MDR subtask because it seemed impossible to solve based only on the image, and the TBT subtask was also suspended because of a very little improvement in the results between the 1st and the 2nd editions. At the same time, most of the participants obtained good results in the severity scoring (SVR) subtask introduced in 2018. In the third edition, SVR subtask was included again for the updated data set, and a new subtask based on providing an automatic report (CT Report) for the TB case was added [17].

In this year's edition, we decided to skip the SVR subtask and concentrate on the automated CT report generation task, since it has an important outcome that can have a major impact in the real-world clinical routines. To make the task both more attractive for participants and practically valuable, this year's report generation was lung-based rather than CT-based, which means the labels for left and right lungs were provided independently. The set of target labels in the CT Report was updated in accordance with the opinion of medical experts.

4.1   Task Setup

In this task, participants had to generate automatic lung-wise reports based on the CT image data. Each report should include the probability scores (ranging from 0 to 1) for each of the three labels and for each of the lungs. Two labels indicated the presence of a specific lesion in the lung - caverns and pleurisy, the third label indicated that the lung is affected by any lesion (not limited to the mentioned two).

The resulting list of entries for each CT included six entries: "left lung affected", "right lung affected", "caverns in the left lung", "caverns in the right lung", "pleurisy in the left lung", "pleurisy in the right lung".

4.2   Data Set

In this edition, the data set containing chest CT scans of 403 TB patients was used, divided into 283 patients for training and 120 for testing. For all patients,

Table 6. Results obtained by the participants of the task. Only the best run of each participant is reported here.

Group name	Run ID	Mean AUC	Min AUC	Run rank
SenticLab.UAIC	68148	0.924	0.885	1
SDVA-UCSD	67950	0.875	0.811	6
chejiao	68118	0.791	0.682	16
CompElecEngCU	67732	0.767	0.733	21
KDE-lab	60707	0.753	0.698	28
FAST_NU_DS	67947	0.705	0.644	37
uaic2020	68081	0.659	0.562	40
JBTTM	67681	0.601	0.432	49
sztaki_dsd	68061	0.595	0.546	50

we provided 3D CT images with an image size per slice of 512×512 pixels and a variable number of slices (the median number was 128).

For all patients, we provided two versions of automatically extracted masks of the lungs obtained using methods described in [15, 35]. The first version of segmentation was retrieved using the same technique as the previous years and provides accurate masks, but it tends to miss large abnormal regions of lungs in the most severe TB cases. The second version of segmentation was retrieved using a non-rigid image registration scheme, which on the contrary provides more rough bounds, but behaves more stable in terms of including lesion areas.

4.3 Participating Groups and Submitted Runs

In 2020, 9 groups from 8 countries submitted at least one run. Similar to the previous editions, each group could submit up to 10 runs. 67 runs were submitted in total. The trend toward using convolutional neural networks (CNNs) is stronger again. Last year, 10 out of the 12 groups used CNNs at least in one of their attempts, and this year all groups used CNNs in some way. Several groups tried a few different methods during their experiments, all reported approaches are listed below.

The majority of participants (six groups) used variations of the projection-based approach. These groups extracted axial, coronal, and sagittal projections from the CT image and executed further analysis using 2D CNNs. Different CNN architectures and model training tweaks were used. Two groups also used conventional methods like SVM or handcrafted features in addition to 2D CNNs for projection analysis. Four groups tried 3D CNN for direct analysis of the CT volumetric data. Two groups used per slice analysis, and one of the groups performed additional manual adaptation of lung-based labeling to slice-based labeling. All participants used different techniques for artificial data set enlargement and a few pre-processing steps, such as resizing, normalization, slice filtering or concatenations etc.

4.4   Results

The task was evaluated as a multi-binary classification problem and measured using Area Under the ROC Curve (AUC) metric. AUC was calculated over the 3 target labels ("caverns", "pleurisy", "affected") in a lung-wise manner. The ranking of this task is done first by average AUC and then by min AUC. Table 6 shows the final results for each group's best run and includes the run rank. More detailed results, including other performance measures, are presented in the overview article [33].

4.5   Lessons Learned and Next Steps

The results obtained in the task improved with respect to the similar CTR sub-task presented in the 2019 edition. SenticLab.UAIC group achieved 0.92 mean AUC, which is a significant improvement compared to 0.80 achieved last year by UIIP_BioMed. The group used per-slice analysis, which required some manual pre-processing of training data to utilize per-slice affection labeling. The second-ranked, SDVA-UCSD group, also overcome last year's top result with a score of 0.88 achieved using 3D CNN. Groups that participated in both editions demonstrated improvements over last year results. Only one group applied differing techniques for each finding, the others used a single approach to detect each of the CT-findings in a multi-binary classification setup.

Overall improvement of results, appearing of new more efficient approaches, variability in network architectures and training schemes, suggests that future development and extension of the proposed task is reasonable and may introduce new valuable results. Possible updates for future editions should consider: (i) extending the number of lesion classes; (ii) inclusion of lesion location information, up to switching from binary classification to a detection task.

5   The Caption Task

A large amount of data found in hospital information systems, including radiology reports are stored as free-text. This poses certain problems, as some of these medical narratives are written differently with respect to grammar, acronyms, abbreviations, transcription errors and misspellings. The virtuosity to search through such unstructured database systems and retrieve relevant information is demanding and labour-intensive, hence developing standardized semantic tagging for such stored data is crucial.

The caption task was first proposed as part of the ImageCLEFmedical [29] in 2016. In 2017 and 2018 [16,28] the ImageCLEFcaption task comprised two subtasks: concept detection and caption prediction. In 2019 [41], the task concentrated on extracting Unified Medical Language System® (UMLS) Concept Unique Identifiers (CUIs) [5] from radiology images. These automatically predicted concepts enable perceivable order for unlabeled and unstructured radiology images and for data sets lacking text information, as multi-modal approaches prove to obtain better results regarding image classification [44].

Table 7. Explorative analysis on data distribution ImageCLEFmed 2020 Concept Detection Task [42].

Imaging technique	Train	Validation	Test	Sum
Angiography	4,713	1,132	325	6,170
Combined Modalities	487	73	49	609
Computer Tomography	20,031	4,992	1,140	26,163
Magnetic resonance	11,447	2,848	562	14,857
PET	502	74	38	614
Ultrasound	8629	2,134	502	11,265
X-Ray	18,944	4,717	918	24,579
Sum	65,753	15,970	3534	84,257

In 2020, additional label information is included. For each images in the data set, the imaging modality technique is distributed. This extra information can be adopted for pre-filtering and fine-tuning approaches.

5.1 Task Setup

The ImageCLEFmed Caption 2020 [42] follows the format of the Image-CLEFmed caption 2019 [41], as well as the concept detection subtask running as part of the ImageCLEFcaption task in 2017 [16] and 2018 [28]. As in all three previous editions, participating teams are tasked with predicting Unified Medical Language System® (UMLS) Concept Unique Identifiers (CUIs) [5] based on the visual image representation in a given image.

In 2017 and 2018, all images commonly found in biomedical literature, were distributed. However in 2019, the focus was reduced to solely radiology images, without targeting any specific disease or anatomic structure. This led to more focused semantic scope of UMLS Concepts that were to be predicted. In 2020, the focus is still on radiology images. Additional information regarding the imaging modality was included. This extra label knowledge can be adopted for certain pre-processing steps, as well as for fine-tuning the models.

The performance of the participating teams was evaluated using the balanced precision and recall trade-off in terms of F1-scores, as in the three previous years This was measured per image and averaged across all test images and computed with the default implementation of the Python scikit-learn (v0.17.1-2) library.

5.2 Data Set

The training and validation sets distributed are a extension of the Radiology Objects in COntext (ROCO) data set [43]. The training set include 64,753 images and the validation set has 15,970 images. Both sets are associated with 3,047 concepts. All images distributed originate from biomedical journal articles extracted from the PubMed Central® (PMC)[9] repository [48].

For the concept detection evaluation, the test set containing 3,534 images was distributed. This test set does not originate from the ROCO data set and was created using the same procedures applied for the creation of ROCO. It has images from PubMed Central® articles archived between 02.2019 - 02.2020, hence containing no overlap with previous editions. The maximum number of concepts per image varies between 140, 142 and 95 for the training, validation and training sets, respectively. The original imaging technique used for acquiring each image is added as extra label information and the distribution across the training, validation and test set is displayed in Table 7. All concepts in the ground truth that were used for evaluation, as well as in the validation set, are associated and exist in the training set.

5.3 Participating Groups and Submitted Runs

In the fourth edition of the concept detection task, 23 teams registered and signed the End-User-Agreement license, needed to download the development data. 57 graded runs were submitted for evaluation by 7 teams from the following countries: Germany, Great Britain, India, Greece and United States of America. Each of the group was allowed 10 graded runs and 5 faulty runs altogether. 10 of the submitted runs were faulty and were not used for the official evaluation.

Majority of the participating teams were new to the task. Only one team, the AUEB Natural Language Processing Group, participated for the second time. Similar to 2019 [41], deep learning techniques were broadly adopted for training the concept detection models, as improved accuracy rates have been published in the past year [56]. Many teams incorporated the addition modality information for pre-processing steps, fine-tuning of the models, filtering of concepts and late fusion ensemble approaches. The commonly used approaches adopted by most participating teams are: transfer learning with pre-trained deep learning models such as CheXNet [45] and ImageNet [49] on multi-label classification models, image encoding using convolutional neural networks (CNNs), adversarial auto-encoders and long short-term memory (LSTM) recurrent neural networks (RNNs).

5.4 Results

The binary ground truth vector is compared to the predicted UMLS CUIs. To get a better overview of the submitted runs, the best results for each team are presented in Table 8. An in-depth analysis is presented in [42].

5.5 Lessons Learned and Next Steps

The F1-score improved with respect to the previous three editions, from 0.1583 in ImageCLEF 2017, 0.1108 in ImageCLEF 2018 and 0.2823 in ImageCLEF 2019,

---

[9] https://www.ncbi.nlm.nih.gov/pmc/.

Table 8. Performance of the participating teams in the ImageCLEF 2020 Concept Detection Task. The best run per team is selected. Teams with previous participation in 2019 are marked with an asterix.

Team	Institution	F1 score
AUEB NLP Group*	Department of Informatics, Athens University of Economics and Business	0.3940
PwC_Healthcare	PRICEWATERHOUSECOOPERS Service Delivery Center PVT. LTD. India	0.3924
Essex	School of computer Science and Electronic Engineering, University of Essex, United Kingdom	0.3808
IML	Interactive Machine Learning Group, German Research Center for Artificial Intelligence (DFKI)	0.3745
TUC_MC	Technische Unversität Chemnitz	0.3512
Morgan_CS	Morgan State University	0.1673
CSE_SSN	Department of Computer Science and Engineering, SSN College of Engineering, Chennai, India	0.1347

to 0.3940 this year. The majority of the participating teams this year were new to the task. The AUEB NLP Group [32] from Athens University of Economics and Business, the only teams with previous participation, achieved the highest ranked F1-score.

The decision made for the ImageCLEFmed Caption 2019 to focus on radiology images proved to go into the right direction. By doing so, noisy concepts were removed, as the biomedical content contained a wide diversity scope. This led to the reduction in the number of concepts from 111,155 in the previous editions to 5,528 in ImageCLEF 2019, and to 3,047 this year, making the amount manageable. The inclusion of imaging modality was adopted by all teams at several model creating steps, which shows to be supportive towards improving the prediction models. Challenging for all teams however, is the imbalance in the concept distribution and imaging modality over the images.

For future improvements, as the UMLS CUIs were extracted from the original PubMed figure captions, it is intended to manually evaluate the clinical relevance content. The natural language captions contain some parts that have important context relation to the published article and not necessarily medical semantic information. By manually screening the extracted CUIs, a data set with expressive and suitable content will be generated, leading to robust concept prediction models that can be incorporated in clinical routine.

6 ImageCLEFlifelog

The goal of the ImageCLEFlifelog 2020 is to continue to promote research in lifelogging as an application supporting human memory and well-being. This year, the ImageCLEFlifelog task is again divided into two sub-tasks: Lifelog

Moment Retrieval (LMRT) and Sport Performance Lifelog (SPLL). The core task of Lifelog is LMRT, which has the same format as of previous editions but with a large-scaled data set and different test topics to measure the retrieval performance of participants' system. Again, the LMRT task mainly focuses on images which means that participants need to retrieve photos as the evidence of relevant moments for some predefined queries. The evaluation metrics are unchanged, which use precision, cluster recall and f1-score for top-10 retrieved results. These metrics require participants to diversify their results while still retrieving the correct moments. The data used in LMRT task is the merging version of three previous NTCIR challenges in three years: 2016 [22], 2017 [23], and 2019 [24]. It was collected using many wearable devices to capture daily life activities, moments, well-being status and current locations of the lifelogger passively and continuously for years. The data contains five main types: multimedia contents, biometrics data, location and GPS, visual concepts and annotations, and human activity information.

The Sport Performance Lifelog (SPLL) is a new task in 2020. The data is totally different from and independent of the data used in the LMRT task. The aim of SPLL is to monitor the change of both well-being status and improvement during the training process of 16 people for a sport event. In particular, participants are required to predict the expected performance of these people in different measurements after the training. This yields three subtasks as follows:

- *Subtask 1*: Predict the change in running speed given by the change in seconds used per km (kilometer speed) from the initial run to the run at the end of the reporting period.
- *Subtask 2*: Predict the change in weight since the beginning of the reporting period to the end of the reporting period in kilos.
- *Subtask 3*: Predict the change in weight from the beginning of February to the end of the reporting period in kilos using the images.

6.1   Task Setup

The ImageCLEFlifelog 2020 proposes two tasks which are *Lifelog Moment Retrieval (LMRT)* and *Sport Performance Lifelog (SPLL)*. The LMRT task has the same requirements and evaluation methodology as the ones of three previous editions but with brand-new topics and different data set structure. Particularly, in this task, participants are required to retrieve moments which are relevant to a predefined topic. The moments are defined as "semantic events or activities that happened through out the day" [12]. For instance, participants should find the images of the relevant moments for the topic "Find the moments that the lifelogger was looking at items in a toy shop". To achieve full-score of each query, participants need to pay attention not only on the precision of the top-10 retrieved results but they should also re-arrange them to increase the diversification of the selected moments with respect to the narrative of each topic.

The ground-truth of this task was manually created. The SPLL task is a new task with the aim of predicting the expected performance (weight change,

Table 9. Statistics of the ImageCLEFlifelog 2020 LMRT data

Characters	Size
Number of lifeloggers	1
Number of Days	114 days
Size of the collection	37.1 GB
Number of images	191,439 images
Number of locations	166 semantic locations
Number of LMRT dev queries	10 queries
Number of LMRT test queries	10 queries

running speed improvement) of 16 people who trained for a sport event. For this task, there are two evaluation metrics to rank the submissions of participants which are accuracy of the change (primary score) and absolute difference between the actual change and the predicted one (secondary score). While the primary score is ranked in descending order, the secondary score is arranged in ascending order. If there is a draw in the primary score, the secondary score is considered to rank the teams.

6.2 Data Set

LMRT Task—The data is a large-scaled collection of multimodal lifelog data gathered from 114 days of three different years in one lifelogger's life. It was a merging data from three previous NTCIR challenges: NTCIR-12, NTCIR-13, and NTCIR-14. The statistics of the LMRT 2020 dataset is demonstrated in Table 9. In general, the data can be divided into five main types with some similar features as in previous editions including:

- *Multimedia Content*—Non-annotated egocentric images captured passively from OMG Autographer and Narrative Clip worn by the lifelogger for 16–18 hours a day. The total number of images per day ranges from 1,500 to 2,500.
- *Biometrics Data*—Using the FitBit fitness trackers[10], the lifeloggers gathered 24 × 7 heart rate, calorie burn and steps.
- *Semantic Locations and GPS*—GPS data with 166 semantic locations are captured using Moves app and smartphones. In addition, time zones are inferred using the GPS data, which is essential to convert the time in different wearable devices into the same format and time zone.
- *Human Activity Data*—The daily activities of the lifeloggers were captured in terms of physical activities (e.g., walking, running, transporting) from the Moves app[11].
- *Visual Concepts and Annotations*—The wearable camera images were annotated with the outputs of a visual concept detector, which provided three

---

[10] Fitbit Fitness Tracker (FitBit Versa) - https://www.fitbit.com/.
[11] Moves App for Android and iOS - http://www.moves-app.com/.

Table 10. Official results of the ImageCLEFlifelog 2020 LMRT task.

Team	Run	P@10	CR@10	F1@10	Team	Run	P@10	CR@10	F1@10
Organiser [39]	RUN1*	0.19	0.31	0.21	HCMUS [47]	RUN1	0.79	0.73	0.72
	RUN2*	0.23	**0.44**	0.27		RUN2	0.78	0.73	0.72
	RUN3*	**0.36**	0.38	**0.32**		RUN3	0.79	0.69	0.71
REGIM [52]	RUN1	0.04	0.08	0.05		RUN4	0.80	0.74	0.74
	RUN2	0.16	0.22	0.17		RUN5	0.81	0.77	0.75
	RUN3	0.17	**0.24**	**0.19**		RUN6	0.81	0.79	0.77
	RUN4	0.00	0.00	0.00		RUN7	0.82	**0.81**	0.79
	RUN5	**0.19**	0.16	0.16		RUN8	0.77	0.76	0.74
	RUN6	0.03	0.05	0.04		RUN9	0.85	**0.81**	**0.81**
	RUN7	0.17	**0.24**	**0.19**		RUN10	**0.86**	**0.81**	**0.81**
UATP [13]	RUN1	0.02	0.07	0.03	BIDAL [19]	RUN1	0.69	0.68	0.65
	RUN2	0.02	0.07	0.03		RUN2	0.68	0.63	0.58
	RUN3	**0.50**	**0.58**	**0.52**		RUN3	0.68	0.69	0.65
DCU-DDTeam [34]	RUN1	0.07	0.13	0.09		RUN4	0.70	0.69	0.66
	RUN2	0.22	0.39	0.25		RUN5	0.72	0.69	0.66
	RUN3	0.44	**0.63**	0.41		RUN6	0.73	0.69	0.67
	RUN4	**0.58**	0.53	**0.48**		RUN7	0.75	0.65	0.64
	RUN5	0.16	0.36	0.21		RUN8	0.73	0.69	0.67
						RUN9	0.73	**0.70**	**0.69**
						RUN10	**0.74**	**0.70**	**0.69**

Notes: *submissions from the organizer teams are just for reference.

Table 11. Official results of the ImageCLEFlifelog 2020 SPLL Task.

Team	Run	Primary score	Secondary score
Organiser [39]	RUN1*	0.47	313.30
	RUN2*	0.41	203.10
BIDAL [13]	RUN1	0.77	306.90
	RUN2	0.52	309.10
	RUN3	0.59	254.70
	RUN4	0.59	372.60
	RUN5	0.53	375.20
	RUN6	0.65	319.60
	RUN7	0.71	250.20
	RUN8	**0.82**	245.60
	RUN9	**0.82**	128.00
	RUN10	0.65	**112.00**

Notes: *submissions from the organizer teams are just for reference.

types of outputs (Attributes, Categories and Concepts). Two visual concepts which include attributes and categories of the place in the image are extracted using PlacesCNN [57]. The remaining one is the detected object category and its bounding box extracted by using Mask R-CNN [27] trained on MSCOCO data set [36].

SPLL Task—The data is collected from 16 people during their training for a 5 km run. Fitbit Versa 2 sport watch is used to capture the heart rate and calories information while the PMSYS system is employed to collect information about subjective wellness, training load, and injury data. Moreover, information such as meals, drinks, medication, etc. is also collected via Google Forms. The data contain information about daily sleeping patterns, daily heart rate, sport activities, logs of food consumed during the training period from at least 2 participants and self reported data like mode, stress, fatigue, readiness to train and other measurements also used for professional soccer teams [51]. For this task, we have the data approved by the Norwegian Center for Research Data with proper copyright and ethical approval to release.

6.3 Participating Groups and Submitted Runs

We received in total 48 valid submissions from 6 teams. These include 38 valid submissions for LMRT and 10 valid ones for SPLL. Their submissions and the results are summarised in Tables 10 and 11. A detailed analysis of the results is presented in the task overview paper [38].

6.4 Lessons Learned and Next Steps

For the LMRT task, we learned that most of the approaches are building interactive systems using multi-modal data and extended visual concepts to retrieve the relevant moments. One team tried to implement an automatic retrieval system but the results are not as competitive as the interactive ones. We also confirm that visual concepts extracted automatically from different deep networks are extremely useful when creating the indexing system for retrieval. If visual concepts and annotations of visual images are enriched, the interactive retrieval systems can be improved in precision and diversification, significantly. The ImageCLEFlifelog 2020 results are competitive with great improvements compared to previous systems. In this year's challenge, only 6 teams participated in the LMRT task, including an organizer team. We received 48 run submissions. Each team was allowed to submit up to 10 runs. For the LMRT task, among five teams which participated in ImageCLEFlifelog 2019 (including the organizer team), four teams managed to obtain better results with the highest F1-score up to 0.81. The mean (SD) increase of final F1-score from these five teams is 0.25 (0.18). The new team from Dublin City University also managed to achieve the 4th rank with a 0.48 F1-score. For the SPLL task, as the task is new, only one team from The Big Data Analytics Laboratory submitted 10 runs. Their best submission achieves an accuracy of performance change and the absolute difference between the prediction and actual change are 0.82 and 128 respectively, which is a good result.

For the next edition of the LMRT task, we plan to provide better concepts and descriptions of the egocentric images including activities, locations, and visual objects, while still expanding the data set. This year, the submitted results are better, with competitive scores. For the SPLL task, although the number of non-organizer teams participating in the task is only one, results show that the task has potential and should be improved in the next run.

7 The Coral Task

Coral reefs are some of the most biodiverse regions of the ocean, yet are undergoing unprecedented decline through a combination of factors such as climate change, ocean acidification, fertiliser run-off from land and unsustainable fishing practices [4]. Marine biologists and ecologists want to find ways for those living in the vicinity of reefs to maintain their food supplies [6,50] without destroying the very reefs on which they depend. It is therefore crucial that they are able to monitor the health of reefs and the classes of structure they contain—but currently, they have to do this manually.

The ImageCLEFcoral task organisers have developed a novel multi-camera system that allows large amounts of imagery to be captured by a SCUBA diver or autonomous underwater vehicle in a single dive. These images can be used within a structure-from-motion framework to reconstruct 3D point clouds of large regions of reef; and while these point clouds produce information of interest to marine biologists and ecologists on reef complexity, determining benthic substrate 3D point clouds is a significantly more difficult task than from the 2D images. That is why ImageCLEFcoral task encourages vision researchers to develop automatic ways of performing the annotation, yielding information that helps the marine researchers monitor coral reefs.

7.1 Task Setup

Following the success of the first edition of the ImageCLEFcoral task [7], in 2020 participants were again asked to devise and implement algorithms for automatically annotating regions in a collection of images containing several types of benthic substrate, such as hard coral or sponge. The images were captured using an underwater multi-camera system developed at the Marine Technology Research Unit at the University of Essex (MTRU), UK[12].

The ground truth annotations of the training and test sets were made by a combination of marine biology MSc students at Essex and experienced researchers. All annotations were double checked by an experienced coral reef researcher. The annotations were performed using a web-based tool, initially developed in a collaborative project with London-based company Filament Ltd and subsequently extended by one of the organisers. This tool was designed to be simple to learn, quick to use and, almost uniquely, allowing many people to work concurrently [7].

The overall task comprises two sub-tasks. In the first, the annotation is a bounding box, with sides parallel to the edges of the image, around identified

---

[12] https://essexnlip.uk/marine-technology-research-unit/.

features. In the second, participants submit a series of boundary image coordinates which form a single polygon around each identified feature; this has been dubbed *pixel-wise parsing* (these polygons should not have self-intersections). Participants were invited to make submissions for either or both tasks.

As in the first edition, algorithmic performance is evaluated on the unseen test data using the popular intersection over union metric from the PASCAL VOC[13] exercise. This computes the area of intersection of the output of an algorithm and the corresponding ground truth, normalizing that by the area of their union to ensure its maximum value is bounded.

7.2   Data Set

The images used in both editions of the ImageCLEFcoral task originates from a growing, large-scale collection of images taken from coral reefs around the world as part of a coral reef monitoring project with the Marine Technology Research Unit (MTRU) at the University of Essex.

The data set comprises 440 human-annotated training images, with 12,082 substrates, from the Wakatobi Marine Reserve, Indonesia; this is the complete training and test sets used in the ImageCLEFcoral 2019 task. The test set comprises a further 400 test images, with 8,640 substrates annotated, from four geographical regions, 100 images per subset:

1. Wakatobi Marine Reserve, Indonesia – the same location as the training images;
2. Spermonde archipelago, Indonesia – geographically similar location to the training set with a similar benthic composition;
3. Seychelles, Indian Ocean – geographically distinct but ecologically connected coral reef;
4. Dominica, Caribbean – geographically and ecologically distinct rocky reef.

The images are part of a monitoring collection and therefore many have a tape measure running through a portion of the image. As in 2019, the data set comprises an area of underwater terrain. Many images contain the same ground features captured from different viewpoints. Each image contains some of the same thirteen types of benthic substrates as in 2019, namely hard coral—branching, submassive, boulder, encrusting, table, foliose, mushroom; soft coral—gorgonian; sponge—barrel; fire coral—millepora; algae—macro or leaves.

The test set from the same area as the training set will give an indication as to how well a submitted algorithm can localise and classify marine substrate, i.e., the maximum performance. We hypothesise that performance will deteriorate with other test subsets as the composition, morphology and identifying features of the substrate change and exhibit less similarity with the training data.

---

[13] http://host.robots.ox.ac.uk/pascal/VOC/.

Table 12. Coral reef image annotation and localisation performance in terms of $MAP0.5IoU$, and $MAP0IoU$. The best run per team in terms of $MAP0.5IoU$ is selected.

Run id	Team	$MAP0.5IoU$	$MAP0IoU$
68143	FAV ZČU PiVa	0.582	0.853
67539	FAV ZČU CV	0.49	0.822
68181	FHD	0.457	0.775
68201	HHU	0.392	0.806

Table 13. Pixel-wise coral reef parsing performance in terms of $MAP0.5IoU$, and $MAP0IoU$. The best run per team in terms of $MAP0.5IoU$ is selected.

Run id	Team	$MAP0.5IoU$	$MAP0IoU$
67864	FAV ZČU PiVa	0.678	0.845
68190	FHD	0.474	0.715
67620	FAV ZČU CV	0.304	0.602

7.3 Participating Groups and Submitted Runs

In this second edition of the ImageCLEFcoral task, 15 teams registered, of which 4 teams submitted 53 runs. Teams were limited to submit 10 runs per task. The majority of submissions use deep neural networks, generally convolutional ones. For example, some of the submissions were performed using a R-CNN with ResNet 101 backbone, with 30 epochs of training on the full training data set. Data augmentation (using flips, random crops and contrast, hue, saturation and brightness adjustments) was employed, then averaging over the top five models. Others used different types of networks, so there is a good comparison of different approaches. However, at least one submission is based on k-nearest neighbours, perhaps one of the longest-standing clustering techniques, with statistical features. It is also interesting that most training seemed to use sub-sampled images, though the image size varied from group to group and run to run.

7.4 Results

As in 2019, the task was evaluated using the PASCAL VOC style metric of intersection over union (IoU), as discussed above. The evaluation was carried out using two measures: MAP 0.5 IoU—the localised mean average precision (MAP) for each submitted method for using the performance measure of IoU $>=0.5$ of the ground truth; and MAP 0 IoU—the image annotation average for each method with success if the concept is simply detected in the image without any localisation. Tables 12 and 13 present the best runs per team in terms of $MAP0.5IoU$. The complete overview of the results can be found in [8], including the results on each of the geographical locations in the test set and the accuracy per benthic substrate type.

The $MAP0.5IoU$ score from FAV ZČU PiVa of 0.582 over the entire test set is excellent, bearing in mind both the difficulty of the problem and the number of classes involved. There is a significant margin before the best run from the second-placed team, FAV ZČU CV, and the other teams' best submissions, which are quite closely spaced. FAV ZČU PiVa also made the best-ranked submission for $MAP0IoU$ but the other teams' best-scoring submissions are much closer to this. However, when one compares the accuracy obtained by these runs, the best-scoring one for $MAP0.5IoU$ does not yield the highest accuracy of all the submissions. Clearly then, there is some inconsistency in the evaluation measures employed—and this is perhaps more of an indication that performance evaluation should be revisited.

It is interesting to review the scores obtained from the four categories of test data. For the first three geographic regions, performance is quite similar, which is good, but performance drops off for other geographic regions. Although not at all unexpected, this shows how difficult it will be to develop a system for marine biologists who can take it to any part of the world and preserve its accuracy.

The results of the pixel-wise parsing task, in which teams attempt to identify the boundaries of features rather than their bounding boxes are shown in Table 13. The $MAP0.5IoU$ score of the best-placed team, FAV ZČU PiVa, is actually higher than for the first task, showing that their approach is able to identify the boundaries of the image features somewhat better than those of the other teams. This makes the performance gap between first- and second-placed teams somewhat larger than for the first task. Again, the best-scoring run in terms of $MAP0.5IoU$ is not the best in terms of accuracy.

7.5 Lessons Learned and Next Steps

The results of the 2020 coral exercise are interesting and demonstrate how well modern deep neural networks in particular are at a range of problems. For the coral exercise, the authors regard a performance approaching 70% for a 13-class problem as excellent. The results show that the best pixel-wise parsing technique outperformed the best bounding box one, suggesting that future exercises should concentrate on pixel-wise parsing. There are always difficulties with overlapping bounding boxes and other types of feature in the background of bounding boxes which together reduce the value of that type of annotation.

An in-depth analysis of the test results is not presented here but it is clear that there are genuine performance differences between the four geographical categories of test images described above. This is an immensely important practical problem for coral annotation, and also for vision systems in general. We anticipate future coral annotation tasks will explore ways to overcome this difficulty. Close examination of the ground truth annotations for the pixel-parsing task shows that annotators tend to place the bounding polygons just outside the boundaries of the features being annotated. We are considering producing other annotations that lie within feature boundaries and encourage teams in a future exercise to train the same architecture with both, then see which works best.

That would give us the opportunity to learn something about how annotations should be produced.

The fact that different measures rank-order the different runs differently does not come as a surprise but does show how difficult it is to devise a simple measure that encapsulates performance well. There is clearly research to be done in this regard. Although there are performance differences between the runs, there is no indication as to whether they are statistically significant or not. This analysis can be done however, and we shall explore this as future work. Bearing in mind the point made about performance measures in the previous paragraph, it will be especially interesting to ascertain whether different performance measure yield statistically-significant but inconsistent results.

8   The DrawnUI Task

User interfaces (UIs) represent the medium where interactions between humans and computers occur. The increasing dependence on web and mobile applications has led many enterprises to prioritize the development of UIs in an effort to improve the overall user experience. Currently, the performance of any modern digital product is strongly correlated to the quality and usability of its user interface. However, building one poses a complex problem, requiring the interaction of multiple specialists, each with their own domain-specific knowledge. The process becomes increasingly error prone as the number of workers increases. Moreover, UI experts are in limited supply too, with 22 million developers in the whole world[14], among which only 10 million are estimated to also be JavaScript UI developers[15].

Recently, the use of machine learning to facilitate the creation of UIs has been demonstrated as a viable solution. In 2018, pix2code proposed an open-source, machine-learning based approach to generate low fidelity, domain specific languages from screenshots [1]. In the same year, Chen Chunyang et al. [9] created their own data set based on Android applications, providing 185,277 pairs of UI images and GUI skeletons. The data set and code were open-sourced as well.

8.1   Task Setup

The 2020 ImageCLEF DrawnUI task is at its first edition and consists of a single task. The participants are required to develop a computer vision model to predict the type and position (bounding box) of different UI elements in hand-drawn wireframes. The data set is split approximately 75% for training and 25% for testing. During the competition, the submissions were evaluated using the overall precision. In addition, $MAP0.5IoU$ and $R0.5IoU$ were computed after the competition [20].

---

[14] http://evansdata.com/.
[15] http://appdevelopermagazine.com/.

Table 14. Participation in the DrawUI 2020 task: the best score from all runs for each team.

Team	# Runs	Overall precision	MAP 0.5 IoU	R 0.5 IoU
zip	7	**0.970**	0.755	0.555
CudaMemError1	8	0.950	**0.793**	**0.598**
OG_SouL	3	0.940	0.641	0.501

Table 15. Overall precision, $MAP0.5IoU$, and $R0.5IoU$ for each run. Organizers baseline is marked with an asterix.

Team	Run ID	Method description	Overall precision	MAP 0.5 IoU	R 0.5 IoU
zip	67816	resnet50 Faster R-CNN, full-size, grayscale	**0.970**	0.582	0.445
zip	68014	inception resnet v2 Faster R-CNN, full-size, merging	0.956	0.693	0.519
zip	68003	inception resnet v2 Faster R-CNN, full-size, grayscale	0.956	0.694	0.520
zip	67814	resnet50 Faster R-CNN, 12MP, grayscale	0.955	0.675	0.517
CudaMemError1	67814	fusiont-3	0.950	0.715	0.556
CudaMemError1	67833	obj wise 2	0.950	0.681	0.533
CudaMemError1	67710	resnet101	0.949	0.649	0.505
dimitri.fichou*	67413	baseline: Faster R-CNN, data augmentation	0.947	0.572	0.403
zip	67991	resnet50 Faster R-CNN, full-size, all data	0.944	0.647	0.472
zip	68015	inception resnet v2 Faster R-CNN, full-size, merging	0.941	0.755	0.555
OG_SouL	67391	Transfer Learning using Mask R-CNN pre-trained with COCO	0.940	0.573	0.417
zip	67733	-	0.939	0.687	0.536
CudaMemError1	67722	resnet101	0.934	0.723	0.585
CudaMemError1	67706	-	0.934	**0.793**	**0.598**
CudaMemError1	67829	obj fusion	0.932	0.738	0.556
CudaMemError1	67707	-	0.931	0.792	0.594
CudaMemError1	67831	image wise fusion	0.929	0.791	0.600
OG_SouL	67699	Mask R-CNN, multi-pass inference, grayscale	0.918	0.637	0.501
OG_SouL	67712	Mask R-CNN, multi-pass inference	0.917	0.641	0.496

8.2   Data Set

The task data set consists of 3,000 hand-drawn wireframe images based on 1,000 different templates of mobile and web UIs. Mobile UI templates were manually selected from the RICO data set [14] while web pages UIs were parsed using a custom web parser. Three people were involved in this drawing step, which involved the use of a predefined shape dictionary with 21 different UI elements. This shape dictionary was focused on unambiguous drawing instead of fidelity to the original screenshot in order to facilitate the annotation step. Finally, a last check was performed by a master annotator to ensure consistency.

8.3   Participating Groups and Submitted Runs

14 teams registered and 3 teams from 2 countries submitted 18 runs. Teams were limited to submit 10 runs.

8.4 Results

The $MAP0.5IoU$ and $R0.5IoU$ scores have been compiled using an adapted version of the COCO data set evaluator[16]. All submissions fared better than expected on this challenge, confirming our assumptions regarding the usage of machine learning in streamlining the process of wireframing. While transferring paper information into its digital counterpart is only one part of the design and implementation process, the high accuracy of the results clearly indicates potential for further extending this challenge to other areas, such as predicting directly the nested UI structure.

8.5 Lessons Learned and Next Steps

Each submission used object detection algorithms such as Faster R-CNN [46] or Mask R-CNN [26] with different types of data augmentation and pre-processing. Two teams obtained scores superior to our baseline according to the overall precision. All submissions were superior to our baseline according to the $MAP0.5IoU$ and $R0.5IoU$. Although overall precision is as high as 0.97 and may show the task as more or less solved, this is not the best metric in terms of localization as it does not take into account a high number of false negatives or poor results on the rare classes of the data set. Mean Average Precision and Recall are more appropriate metrics in this case. In this case, best results are significantly lower, e.g., 0.79 for MAP, meaning that there is still room for improvement.

As future challenges, for the next edition of this task, we plan to tackle two different problems: (i) predicting the nested structure of the UI based on either the wireframe or the bounding boxes. The current task was focused on absolute positioning but the final UI is built using relative positioning, to handle responsiveness. This task is particularly challenging and could be solved with a mix of computer vision and natural language processing; (ii) object detection from screenshots instead of drawings. Mockups are often used by designers as a medium to hand off their designs to the developers. It is possible to parse the web to obtain a similar data set to the one from DrawnUI 2020 by analysing the DOM trees and capturing screenshots. However, due to the nature of the world wide web, compiling a clean data set will represent a challenge. Instead, we propose to only manually clean the test set and let the participant train using a large, raw data set. The challenge here will be close to real life data set, where the data contains numerous errors.

9 Conclusions

This paper presents a general overview of the activities and outcomes of the ImageCLEF 2020 evaluation campaign. Four tasks were organised, covering challenges in the medical domain (visual question answering and visual question generation, tuberculosis prediction, and caption analysis), lifelogging (daily activity

---

[16] https://github.com/philferriere/cocoapi/.

understanding, retrieval and summarization), nature (segmenting and labeling collections of coral images), and Internet (identifying hand-drawn website user interface components). Despite the outbreak of the COVID-19 pandemic and lock-down during the benchmark, 115 teams registered, 40 teams completed the tasks and submitted over 295 runs. Although the number of registrations was lower than in 2019, the success rate of the participants increased with over 8% points.

Most of the proposed solutions evolved around state-of-the-art deep neural network architectures, also for the medical domain. For the visual question answering, most systems leveraged encoder-decoder architectures with various pooling strategies and attention mechanisms. There was a visible improvement in performance compared to previous editions. The visual question generation, on the other hand, proved to be more challenging. For the tuberculosis prediction task, results also improved compared to previous editions. Best runners employed per-slice analysis involving some manual pre-processing of the training data. Classification is achieved with deep neural networks. For the caption analysis task, all participants embraced the imaging modality in their prediction deep models. A challenge was posed by the imbalance in the concept distribution. However, results improved compared to last year. For the lifelog task, most approaches built interactive systems using multi-modal information and visual concepts for the retrieval. Automated retrieval systems proved to be less competitive. The most reliable information were the visual concepts extracted automatically from the data. The sport performance subtask, although newly introduced, lead to good results. Overall, results also improved compared to last year. For the coral task, pixel-wise parsing outperformed bounding boxing. Also, geographical position of the corals influenced significantly the results. Finally, for the drawn UI task, even in the first edition, systems were able to achieve very high performance in terms of precision (up to 97%) with variation of R-CNNs. The detection problem seems to be solved, however the precise UI localization is not yet that accurate and leaves room for improvement.

ImageCLEF 2020 brought again together an interesting mix of tasks and approaches and we are looking forward to the fruitful discussions at the CLEF 2020 workshop.

Acknowledgements. Data collection for the Tuberculosis task was supported by the National Institute of Allergy and Infectious Diseases, National Institutes of Health, US Department of Health and Human Services, CRDF project DAA9-19-65087-1.

References

1. Beltramelli, T.: pix2code: generating code from a graphical user interface screenshot. In: Proceedings of the ACM SIGCHI Symposium on Engineering Interactive Computing Systems, pp. 1–9 (2018)
2. Ben Abacha, A., Datla, V.V., Hasan, S.A., Demner-Fushman, D., Müller, H.: Overview of the VQA-med task at imageclef 2020: visual question answering and generation in the medical domain. In: CLEF 2020 Working Notes, CEUR Workshop Proceedings, CEUR-WS.org, Thessaloniki (2020)

3. Ben Abacha, A., Hasan, S.A., Datla, V.V., Liu, J., Demner-Fushman, D., Müller, H.: VQA-Med: overview of the medical visual question answering task at image-clef 2019. In: CLEF2019 Working Notes, CEUR Workshop Proceedings, CEUR-WS.org, Lugano (2019). http://ceur-ws.org

4. Birkeland, C.: Global status of coral reefs: in combination, disturbances and stressors become ratchets. In: World Seas: An Environmental Evaluation, pp. 35–56. Elsevier (2019)

5. Bodenreider, O.: The unified medical language system (UMLS): integrating biomedical terminology. Nucleic Acids Res. **32**(Database–Issue), 267–270 (2004). https://doi.org/10.1093/nar/gkh061

6. Brander, L.M., Rehdanz, K., Tol, R.S., Van Beukering, P.J.: The economic impact of ocean acidification on coral reefs. Clim. Change Econ. **3**(01), 1250002 (2012)

7. Chamberlain, J., Campello, A., Wright, J.P., Clift, L.G., Clark, A., García Seco de Herrera, A.: Overview of ImageCLEFcoral 2019 task. In: CLEF2019 Working Notes, CEUR Workshop Proceedings. CEUR-WS.org (2019)

8. Chamberlain, J., Campello, A., Wright, J.P., Clift, L.G., Clark, A., García Seco de Herrera, A.: Overview of the ImageCLEFcoral 2020 task: automated coral reef image annotation. In: CLEF2020 Working Notes, CEUR Workshop Proceedings. CEUR-WS.org (2020)

9. Chen, C., Su, T., Meng, G., Xing, Z., Liu, Y.: From UI design image to GUI skeleton : a neural machine translator to bootstrap mobile GUI implementation. In: International Conference on Software Engineering, vol. 6 (2018)

10. Clough, P., Müller, H., Sanderson, M.: The CLEF 2004 cross-language image retrieval track. In: Peters, C., Clough, P., Gonzalo, J., Jones, G.J.F., Kluck, M., Magnini, B. (eds.) CLEF 2004. LNCS, vol. 3491, pp. 597–613. Springer, Heidelberg (2005). https://doi.org/10.1007/11519645_59

11. Clough, P., Sanderson, M.: The CLEF 2003 cross language image retrieval track. In: Peters, C., Gonzalo, J., Braschler, M., Kluck, M. (eds.) CLEF 2003. LNCS, vol. 3237, pp. 581–593. Springer, Heidelberg (2004). https://doi.org/10.1007/978-3-540-30222-3_56

12. Dang-Nguyen, D.T., et al.: Overview of ImageCLEFlifelog 2019: solve my life puzzle and lifelog moment retrieval. In: CLEF2019 Working Notes, CEUR Workshop Proceedings. CEUR-WS.org, Lugano (2019)

13. Dao, M.S., Vo, A.K., Phan, T.D., Zettsu, K.: BIDAL@imageCLEFlifelog2019: the role of content and context of daily activities in insights from lifelogs. In: CLEF2019 Working Notes, CEUR Workshop Proceedings. CEUR-WS.org, Lugano (2019). http://ceur-ws.org

14. Deka, B., et al.: Rico: a mobile app dataset for building data-driven design applications. In: UIST 2017 - Proceedings of the 30th Annual ACM Symposium on User Interface Software and Technology, pp. 845–854 (2017). https://doi.org/10.1145/3126594.3126651

15. Dicente Cid, Y., Jimenez-del-Toro, O., Depeursinge, A., Müller, H.: Efficient and fully automatic segmentation of the lungs in CT volumes. In: Goksel, O., Jimenez-del-Toro, O., Foncubierta-Rodriguez, A., Müller, H. (eds.) Proceedings of the VISCERAL Challenge at ISBI, CEUR Workshop Proceedings, pp. 31–35, no. 1390, April 2015

16. Dicente Cid, Y., Kalinovsky, A., Liauchuk, V., Kovalev, V., Müller, H.: Overview of ImageCLEFtuberculosis 2017 - predicting tuberculosis type and drug resistances. In: CLEF2017 Working Notes, CEUR Workshop Proceedings. CEUR-WS.org, Dublin (2017). http://ceur-ws.org

17. Dicente Cid, Y., Liauchuk, V., Klimuk, D., Tarasau, A., Kovalev, V., Müller, H.: Overview of ImageCLEFtuberculosis 2019 - Automatic CT-based Report Generation and Tuberculosis Severity Assessment. In: CLEF2019 Working Notes, CEUR Workshop Proceedings. CEUR-WS.org, Lugano (2019). http://ceur-ws.org
18. Dicente Cid, Y., Liauchuk, V., Kovalev, V., Müller, H.: Overview of ImageCLEFtuberculosis 2018 - detecting multi-drug resistance, classifying tuberculosis type, and assessing severity score. In: CLEF2018 Working Notes, CEUR Workshop Proceedings. CEUR-WS.org, Avignon (2018). http://ceur-ws.org
19. Dogariu, M., Ionescu, B.: Multimedia lab @ ImageCLEF 2019 lifelog moment retrieval task. In: CLEF2019 Working Notes. CEUR Workshop Proceedings. CEUR-WS.org, Lugano (2019). http://ceur-ws.org
20. Everingham, M., Gool, L.V., Williams, C.K.I., Winn, J., Zisserman, A.: The PASCAL visual object classes (VOC) challenge. Int. J. Comput. Vis. **88**, 303–338 (2010). https://doi.org/10.1007/s11263-009-0275-4
21. Fichou, D., et al.: Overview of ImageCLEFdrawnUI 2020: the detection and recognition of hand drawn website UIs task. In: CLEF2020 Working Notes, CEUR Workshop Proceedings. CEUR-WS.org, Thessaloniki (2020). http://ceur-ws.org
22. Gurrin, C., Joho, H., Hopfgartner, F., Zhou, L., Albatal, R.: Overview of NTCIR-12 lifelog task. In: NTCIR (2016)
23. Gurrin, C., et al.: Overview of NTCIR-13 lifelog-2 task (2017)
24. Gurrin, C., et al.: Overview of the NTCIR-14 lifelog-3 task (2019)
25. Hasan, S.A., Ling, Y., Farri, O., Liu, J., Lungren, M., Müller, H.: Overview of the ImageCLEF 2018 medical domain visual question answering task. In: CLEF2018 Working Notes, CEUR Workshop Proceedings. CEUR-WS.org, Avignon (2018). http://ceur-ws.org
26. He, K., Gkioxari, G., Dollár, P., Girshick, R.: Mask R-CNN. IEEE Trans. Pattern Anal. Mach. Intell. **42**(2), 386–397 (2020). https://doi.org/10.1109/TPAMI.2018.2844175
27. He, K., Gkioxari, G., Dollár, P., Girshick, R.B.: Mask R-CNN. In: 2017 IEEE International Conference on Computer Vision (ICCV), pp. 2980–2988 (2017)
28. García Seco de Herrera, A., Eickhoff, C., Andrearczyk, V., Müller, H.: Overview of the ImageCLEF 2018 caption prediction tasks. In: CLEF2018 Working Notes, CEUR Workshop Proceedings. CEUR-WS.org, Avignon (2018). http://ceur-ws.org
29. García Seco de Herrera, A., Schaer, R., Bromuri, S., Müller, H.: Overview of the ImageCLEF 2016 medical task. In: Working Notes of CLEF 2016 (Cross Language Evaluation Forum), September 2016
30. Ionescu, B., et al.: ImageCLEF 2019: multimedia retrieval in medicine, lifelogging, security and nature. In: Crestani, F., et al. (eds.) CLEF 2019. LNCS, vol. 11696, pp. 358–386. Springer, Cham (2019). https://doi.org/10.1007/978-3-030-28577-7_28
31. Kalpathy-Cramer, J., García Seco de Herrera, A., Demner-Fushman, D., Antani, S., Bedrick, S., Müller, H.: Evaluating performance of biomedical image retrieval systems: overview of the medical image retrieval task at ImageCLEF 2004–2014. Comput. Med. Imaging Graph. **39**, 55–61 (2015)
32. Kougia, V., Pavlopoulos, J., Androusopoulos, I.: AUEB NLP group at ImageCLEFMED caption 2019. In: CLEF2019 Working Notes, CEUR Workshop Proceedings. CEUR-WS.org, Lugano (2019). http://ceur-ws.org
33. Kozlovski, S., Liauchuk, V., Dicente Cid, Y., Tarasau, A., Kovalev, V., Müller, H.: Overview of ImageCLEFtuberculosis 2020 - automatic CT-based report generation. In: CLEF2020 Working Notes, CEUR Workshop Proceedings, CEUR-WS.org, Thessaloniki (2020). http://ceur-ws.org

34. Le, N.K., Nguyen, D.H., Nguyen, V.T., Tran, M.T.: Lifelog moment retrieval with advanced semantic extraction and flexible moment visualization for exploration. In: CLEF2019 Working Notes, CEUR Workshop Proceedings, CEUR-WS.org, Lugano (2019). http://ceur-ws.org

35. Liauchuk, V., Kovalev, V.: Imageclef 2017: supervoxels and co-occurrence for tuberculosis CT image classification. In: CLEF2017 Working Notes. CEUR Workshop Proceedings. CEUR-WS.org, Dublin (2017). http://ceur-ws.org

36. Lin, T.-Y., et al.: Microsoft COCO: common objects in context. In: Fleet, D., Pajdla, T., Schiele, B., Tuytelaars, T. (eds.) ECCV 2014. LNCS, vol. 8693, pp. 740–755. Springer, Cham (2014). https://doi.org/10.1007/978-3-319-10602-1_48

37. Müller, H., Clough, P., Deselaers, T., Caputo, B. (eds.): ImageCLEF - Experimental Evaluation in Visual Information Retrieval, The Springer International Series On Information Retrieval, vol. 32. Springer, Heidelberg (2010). https://doi.org/10.1007/978-3-642-15181-1

38. Ninh, V.T., et al.: Overview of ImageCLEF lifelog 2020: lifelog moment retrieval and sport performance lifelog. In: CLEF2020 Working Notes, CEUR Workshop Proceedings. CEUR-WS.org, Thessaloniki (2020). http://ceur-ws.org

39. Ninh, V.T., et al.: LIFER 2.0: discover personal lifelog insight by interactive lifelog retrieval system. In: CLEF2019 Working Notes, CEUR Workshop Proceedings. CEUR-WS.org, Lugano (2019). http://ceur-ws.org

40. Papineni, K., Roukos, S., Ward, T., Zhu, W.J.: BLEU: a method for automatic evaluation of machine translation. In: Proceedings of the 40th Annual Meeting on Association for Computational Linguistics, pp. 311–318. Association for Computational Linguistics (2002)

41. Pelka, O., Friedrich, C.M., García Seco de Herrera, A., Müller, H.: Overview of the ImageCLEFmed 2019 concept prediction task. In: CLEF2019 Working Notes, CEUR Workshop Proceedings. CEUR-WS.org, Lugano (2019). http://ceur-ws.org

42. Pelka, O., Friedrich, C.M., García Seco de Herrera, A., Müller, H.: Overview of the ImageCLEFmed 2020 concept prediction task: medical image understanding. In: CLEF2020 Working Notes, CEUR Workshop Proceedings. CEUR-WS.org, Thessaloniki (2020)

43. Pelka, O., Koitka, S., Rückert, J., Nensa, F., Friedrich, C.M.: Radiology Objects in COntext (ROCO): a multimodal image dataset. In: Stoyanov, D., et al. (eds.) LABELS/CVII/STENT -2018. LNCS, vol. 11043, pp. 180–189. Springer, Cham (2018). https://doi.org/10.1007/978-3-030-01364-6_20

44. Pelka, O., Nensa, F., Friedrich, C.M.: Adopting semantic information of grayscale radiographs for image classification and retrieval. In: Proceedings of the 11th International Joint Conference on Biomedical Engineering Systems and Technologies (BIOSTEC 2018), BIOIMAGING, Funchal, Madeira, Portugal, 19–21 January 2018, vol. 2, pp. 179–187 (2018). https://doi.org/10.5220/0006732301790187

45. Rajpurkar, P., et al.: Chexnet: radiologist-level pneumonia detection on chest x-rays with deep learning. CoRR abs/1711.05225 (2017). http://arxiv.org/abs/1711.05225

46. Ren, S., He, K., Girshick, R., Sun, J.: Faster R-CNN: towards real-time object detection with region proposal networks. IEEE Trans. Pattern Anal. Mach. Intell. **39**(6), 1137–1149 (2017). https://doi.org/10.1109/TPAMI.2016.2577031

47. Ribeiro, R., Neves, A.J.R., Oliveira, J.L.: UAPTBioinformatics working notes at ImageCLEF 2019 lifelog moment retrieval (LMRT) task. In: CLEF2019 Working Notes, CEUR Workshop Proceedings. CEUR-WS.org, Lugano (2019). http://ceur-ws.org

48. Roberts, R.J.: PubMed central: the GenBank of the published literature. Proc. Nat. Acad. Sci. U.S.A. **98**(2), 381–382 (2001). https://doi.org/10.1073/pnas.98.2. 381
49. Russakovsky, O.: Imagenet large scale visual recognition challenge. Int. J. Comput. Vis. **115**(3), 211–252 (2015). https://doi.org/10.1007/s11263-015-0816-y
50. Speers, A.E., Besedin, E.Y., Palardy, J.E., Moore, C.: Impacts of climate change and ocean acidification on coral reef fisheries: an integrated ecological-economic model. Ecol. Econ. **128**, 33–43 (2016)
51. Thambawita, V., et al.: PMData: a sports logging dataset (2020). https://doi.org/ 10.31219/osf.io/k2apb
52. Tournadre, M., Dupont, G., Pauwels, V., Cheikh, B., Lmami, M., Ginsca, A.L.: A multimedia modular approach to lifelog moment retrieval. In: CLEF2019 Working Notes, CEUR Workshop Proceedings. CEUR-WS.org, Lugano (2019). http://ceur-ws.org
53. Tsikrika, T., de Herrera, A.G.S., Müller, H.: Assessing the scholarly impact of ImageCLEF. In: Forner, P., Gonzalo, J., Kekäläinen, J., Lalmas, M., de Rijke, M. (eds.) CLEF 2011. LNCS, vol. 6941, pp. 95–106. Springer, Heidelberg (2011). https://doi.org/10.1007/978-3-642-23708-9_12
54. Tsikrika, T., Larsen, B., Müller, H., Endrullis, S., Rahm, E.: The scholarly impact of CLEF (2000–2009). In: Forner, P., Müller, H., Paredes, R., Rosso, P., Stein, B. (eds.) CLEF 2013. LNCS, vol. 8138, pp. 1–12. Springer, Heidelberg (2013). https://doi.org/10.1007/978-3-642-40802-1_1
55. World Health Organization, et al.: Global tuberculosis report 2019 (2019)
56. Xu, Y., Mo, T., Feng, Q., Zhong, P., Lai, M., Chang, E.I.: Deep learning of feature representation with multiple instance learning for medical image analysis. In: IEEE International Conference on Acoustics, Speech and Signal Processing, ICASSP 2014, Florence, Italy, 4–9 May 2014, pp. 1626–1630 (2014). https://doi.org/10. 1109/ICASSP.2014.6853873
57. Zhou, B., Lapedriza, A., Khosla, A., Oliva, A., Torralba, A.: Places: a 10 million image database for scene recognition. IEEE Trans. Pattern Anal. Mach. Intell. **40**, 1452–1464 (2017)

Overview of LifeCLEF 2020: A System-Oriented Evaluation of Automated Species Identification and Species Distribution Prediction

Alexis Joly[1](✉)[iD], Hervé Goëau[2,3][iD], Stefan Kahl[7], Benjamin Deneu[1][iD],
Maximillien Servajean[8][iD], Elijah Cole[10][iD], Lukáš Picek[11][iD],
Rafael Ruiz de Castañeda[9][iD], Isabelle Bolon[9][iD], Andrew Durso[13][iD],
Titouan Lorieul[1][iD], Christophe Botella[12][iD], Hervé Glotin[4][iD], Julien Champ[1][iD],
Ivan Eggel[6], Willem-Pier Vellinga[5], Pierre Bonnet[2,3][iD], and Henning Müller[6][iD]

[1] Inria, LIRMM, Montpellier, France
alexis.joly@inria.fr
[2] CIRAD, UMR AMAP, 34398 Montpellier, France
[3] AMAP, Univ Montpellier, CIRAD, CNRS, INRAE, IRD, Montpellier, France
[4] Aix Marseille Univ, Université de Toulon, CNRS, LIS, DYNI, Marseille, France
[5] Xeno-canto Foundation, The Hague, The Netherlands
[6] HES-SO, Sierre, Switzerland
[7] Cornell Lab of Ornithology, Cornell University, Ithaca, USA
[8] LIRMM, Université Paul Valéry, University of Montpellier, CNRS,
Montpellier, France
[9] Institute of Global Health, Department of Community Health and Medicine,
Faculty of Medicine, University of Geneva, Geneva, Switzerland
[10] Caltech, Pasadena, USA
[11] Department of Cybernetics, FAV, University of West Bohemia, Pilsen, Czechia
[12] CNRS, LECA, Grenoble, France
[13] Department of Biological Sciences,
Florida Gulf Coast University, Fort Myers, USA

Abstract. Building accurate knowledge of the identity, the geographic distribution and the evolution of species is essential for the sustainable development of humanity, as well as for biodiversity conservation. However, the difficulty of identifying plants and animals in the field is hindering the aggregation of new data and knowledge. Identifying and naming living plants or animals is almost impossible for the general public and is often difficult even for professionals and naturalists. Bridging this gap is a key step towards enabling effective biodiversity monitoring systems. The LifeCLEF campaign, presented in this paper, has been promoting and evaluating advances in this domain since 2011. The 2020 edition proposes four data-oriented challenges related to the identification and prediction of biodiversity: (i) PlantCLEF: cross-domain plant identification based on herbarium sheets (ii) BirdCLEF: bird species recognition in audio soundscapes, (iii) GeoLifeCLEF: location-based prediction of species based on environmental and occurrence data, and (iv) SnakeCLEF: snake identification based on image and geographic location.

© Springer Nature Switzerland AG 2020
A. Arampatzis et al. (Eds.): CLEF 2020, LNCS 12260, pp. 342–363, 2020.
https://doi.org/10.1007/978-3-030-58219-7_23

1   LifeCLEF Lab Overview

Accurately identifying organisms observed in the wild is an essential step in ecological studies. Unfortunately, observing and identifying living organisms requires high levels of expertise. For instance, plants alone account for more than 400,000 different species and the distinctions between them can be quite subtle. Since the Rio Conference of 1992, this *taxonomic gap* has been recognized as one of the major obstacles to the global implementation of the Convention on Biological Diversity[1]. In 2004, Gaston and O'Neill [14] discussed the potential of automated approaches for species identification. They suggested that, if the scientific community were able to (i) produce large training datasets, (ii) precisely evaluate error rates, (iii) scale up automated approaches, and (iv) detect novel species, then it would be possible to develop a generic automated species identification system that would open up new vistas for research in biology and related fields.

Since the publication of [14], automated species identification has been studied in many contexts [5,16,32,42,47,51,52,57]. This area continues to expand rapidly, particularly due to recent advances in deep learning [4,15,43,53,55,56]. In order to measure progress in a sustainable and repeatable way, the LifeCLEF[2] research platform was created in 2014 as a continuation and extension of the plant identification task [27] that had been run within the ImageCLEF lab[3] since 2011 [22–24]. Since 2014, LifeCLEF expanded the challenge by considering animals in addition to plants, and including audio and video content in addition to images [33–38]. Four challenges were evaluated in the context of LifeCLEF 2020 edition:

1. **PlantCLEF 2020:** Identifying plant pictures from herbarium sheets.
2. **BirdCLEF 2020:** Bird species recognition in audio soundscapes.
3. **GeoLifeCLEF 2020:** Species distribution prediction based on occurrence data, environmental data and remote sensing data.
4. **SnakeCLEF 2020:** Automated snake species identification based on images and two level geographic location data - continent and country.

The system used to run the challenges (registration, submission, leaderboard, etc.) was the AICrowd platform[4]. About 172 researchers or students registered to at least one of the four challenges of the lab and 16 of them finally crossed the finish line by completing runs and participating in the collaborative evaluation. In the following sections, we provide a synthesis of the methodology and main results of each of the four challenges of LifeCLEF2020. More details can be found in the overview reports of each challenge and the individual reports of the participants (references provided below).

---

[1]   https://www.cbd.int/.
[2]   http://www.lifeclef.org/.
[3]   http://www.imageclef.org/.
[4]   https://www.aicrowd.com.

2   PlantCLEF Challenge: Identifying Plant Pictures from Herbarium Sheets

A detailed description of the task and a more complete discussion of the results can be found in the dedicated working note [21].

2.1   Objective

Automated identification of plants has recently improved considerably thanks to the progress of deep learning and the availability of training data with more and more photos in the field. For instance, we measured in 2018 a top-1 classification accuracy over 10 K species up to 90% and we showed that automated systems are not so far from human expertise [33]. However, this profusion of field images only concerns a few tens of thousands of species, mostly located in North America and Western Europe, with fewer images from the richest regions in terms of biodiversity such as tropical countries. On the other hand, for several centuries, botanists have collected, catalogued and systematically stored plant specimens in herbaria, particularly in tropical regions. Recent huge efforts by the biodiversity informatics community such as iDigBio[5] or e-ReColNat[6] made it possible to put millions of digitized collections online. In the continuity of the PlantCLEF challenges organized in previous years [17–20, 22–24, 26, 28], this year's challenge was designed to evaluate to what extent automated plant species identification on tropical data deficient regions can be improved by the use of herbarium sheets. Herbaria collections represent potentially a large pool of data to train species prediction models, but they also introduce a difficult and interesting problem of cross domain classification because typically a same plant photographed in the field takes on a different visual appearance when dried and placed on a herbarium sheet as it can be seen in Fig. 1.

2.2   Dataset and Evaluation Protocol

The challenge is based on a dataset of 997 species mainly focused on the South America's Guiana Shield (Fig. 2), an area known to have one of the greatest diversity of plants in the world. The challenge was evaluated as a cross-domain classification task where the training set consist of 321,270 herbarium sheets and 6,316 photos in the field to enable learning a mapping between the two domains. A valuable asset of this training set is that a set of 354 plant observations are provided with both herbarium sheets and field photos to potentially allow a more precise mapping between the two domains.

The test set relied on two highly trusted experts and was composed of 3,186 photos in the field related to 638 plant observations.

Participants were allowed to use complementary training data (e.g. for pre-training purposes) but on the condition that (i) the experiment is entirely reproducible, i.e. that the used external resource is clearly referenced and accessible

---

[5] http://portal.idigbio.org/portal/search.
[6] https://explore.recolnat.org/search/botanique/type=index.

Fig. 1. Field photos and herbarium sheets of the same specimen (*Tapirira guianensis* Aubl.). Despite the very different visual appearances between the two types of images, similar structures and shapes of flowers, fruits and leaves can be observed.

to any other research group in the world, (ii) the use of external training data or not is mentioned for each run, and (iii) the additional resource does not contain any of the test observations. External training data was allowed but participants had to provide at least one submission that used only the training data provided this year.

The main evaluation measure for the challenge was the Mean Reciprocal Rank (MRR), which is defined as

$$\frac{1}{Q} \sum_{q=1}^{Q} \frac{1}{\text{rank}_q}$$

where Q is the number of plant observations and rank_q is the predicted rank of the true label for the qth observation.

A second metric was again the MRR but computed on a subset of observations of species that are rarely photographed in the field. The species were chosen based on the most comprehensive estimates possible from different data sources (IdigBio, GBIF, Encyclopedia of Life, Bing and Google Image search engines, previous datasets related to PlantCLEF and ExpertCLEF challenges). It is therefore a more challenging metric because it focuses on the species which impose a mapping between herbarium and field photos.

2.3   Participants and Results

68 participants registered for the PlantCLEF challenge 2020 (PC20) and downloaded the data set, and 7 research groups succeeded in submitting runs, *i.e.* files containing the predictions of the system(s) they ran. Details of the methods and systems used in the runs are synthesized in the overview working note paper of the task [21] and further developed in the individual working notes of most of the participants (Holmes [7], ITCR PlantNet [54], SSN [46], LU [58]). The remaining teams did not provide an extended description of their systems but sometimes a few informal descriptions were provided in the metadata associated with the submissions and partially contributed to the comments below. We report in Fig. 3 the performance achieved by the 49 collected runs.

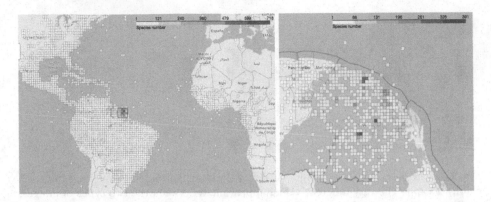

Fig. 2. Density grid maps of the number of species of geolocated plants in Plant-CLEF2020. Many species have also been collected to a lesser extent in other regions outside French Guiana, such as the Americas and Africa.

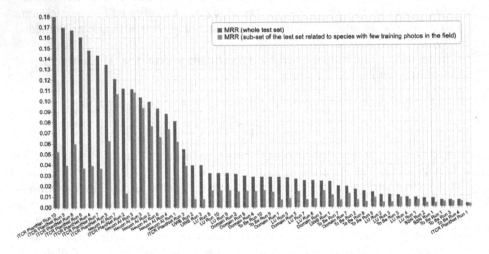

Fig. 3. PlantCLEF 2020 results

The Most Difficult Plant Challenge Ever. This year's challenge is confirmed to be the most difficult of all previous editions, with at best a quite low MRR value of 0.18. As already noticed last year, tropical flora is inherently more difficult than the generalist flora explored during the previous eight years, even for experts [20]. The asymmetry between training data based on herbarium sheets and test data based on field photos did not make the task any easier.

Traditional CNNs Performed Poorly. Figure 3 shows a great disparity between the performance obtained by the different submissions. To explain that we have first to distinguish between approaches based on CNNs alone (typically pretrained on ImageNet and finetuned with the provided training data) and approaches that additionally incorporate an explicit and formal Domain Adaptation (DA) technique between the herbarium and field domains. As expected regarding the low number of field photos in the training set for numerous species, directly finetuned CNNs with the PC20 data obtained the lowest scores (ITCR Run 1, SSN Run 1&2, UWB Run 1).

External Training Data on Traditional CNNs Did Not Really Improve Performances. CNNs can be improved by the use of external data, involving more field photos, as it is demonstrated with the UWB runs 2 & 3 and ITCR Run 2. All these runs extended the training data with the previous year's PC19 training data and the GBIF training data provided by [49]). ITCR Run 2 made a greater improvement on the overall MRR probably by using a two stage training strategy: they first finetuned an ImageNet-pretrained ResNet50 with all the herbarium sheets from PC20, and then finetuned it again with all the field photos extracted from PC20 and the external training data. This two stages strategy can be seen as a naive DA technique because the second stage shifts the learned features in an initial herbarium feature space to a field photo feature space. However, regarding the second MRR metric focusing on the most difficult species with few field photos in the training set, performance for all these runs is still quite low. This means that the performance of a traditional CNN approach (without a more formal adaptation technique) is too dependent from the number of field photos available in the training data, and is not able to efficiently transfer visual knowledge from herbarium domain to field photos domain.

Adversarial DA Techniques Performed the Best. Among other submissions, two participants stood out from the crowd with two quite different DA techniques. ITCR PlantNet team based all its remaining runs on a Few Shot Adversarial Domain Adaptation approach [45] (FSADA), directly applied in the run 3. FSADA approach uses a discriminator that helps the initial encoder trained on herbarium sheets to shift the learned feature representations to a domain agnostic feature space where the discriminator is no longer able to distinguish if a picture comes from the herbarium or the photo domain, while maintaining the discriminative power regarding the final species classification task. The basic FSADA approach (ITCR Run 3) clearly outperformed the traditional CNN approach (run 1), while both approaches are based on the same initial finetuned ResNet50 model on the PC20 training herbarium data. It should be noted that the LU team also used an adversarial approach but with less success.

Mapping DA Technique Reached an Impressive Genericity on Difficult Species. While the adversarial DA technique used by the ITCR PlantNet team obtained the best result on the main MRR metric, the Neuon AI team obtained the best results on the second MRR metric focusing on the most difficult species in the test set. This last team used two encoders, one trained on the herbarium sheets in PC20 and a second one trained on the photos from the PC17 dataset. Then they learned a distance function based on a triplet loss to maximize the embedding distance of different species and at the same time minimize the distance of the same species. Performances measured from the Neuon AI Run 5, which is an ensemble of 3 instances of their initial approach, gave especially impressive results with quite high MRRs and above all similar values between the two MRR metrics. It means that Neuon AI's approach is very robust to the lack of training field photos and able to generalize on rare difficult species in the test set. In other words, their approach is able to transfer knowledge to rare species which was the underlying objective of the challenge.

External Data Improved DA Approaches. ICTR Run 4 shows a significant impact on the main MRR metric from using external training data compared to the same adversarial DA approach (run 3), while maintaining the same level of genericity on rare species with similar MRRs value on the second metric. Unfortunately it is not possible to measure this impact on the Neuon AI method because they did not provide a run using only this year's training data.

Auxiliary tasks have impact, notably by the use of upper taxon level information in a multi classification task way integrated to the FSADA approach (ITCR Run 6 is better than run 4 with a single species classification task). This is the first time over all the years of PlantCLEF challenges that we clearly observe an important impact of the use of genus and family information to improve the species identification. Many species with few training data have apparently been able to benefit indirectly from a "sibling" species with many data related to a same genus or family. The impact is probably enhanced this year because of the lack of visual data on many species. To a lesser extent, self supervision auxiliary task such as jigsaw solving prediction task (ITCR Run 5 improved a little the baseline of this team (run 4), and the best submission over all this year challenge is an ensemble of all FSADA approaches, combining self supervision or not, upper taxons or not.

3   BirdCLEF Challenge: Bird Sound Recognition in Complex Acoustic Environments

A detailed description of the task and a more complete discussion of the results can be found in the dedicated overview paper [39].

3.1   Objective

The *LifeCLEF Bird Recognition Challenge* (BirdCLEF) launched in 2014 and has since become the largest bird sound recognition challenge in terms of dataset size and species diversity with multiple tens of thousands of recordings covering up to 1,500 species [25], [40]. Birds are ideal indicators to identify early warning signs of habitat changes that are likely to affect many other species. They have been shown to respond to various environmental changes over many spatial scales. Large collections of (avian) audio data are an excellent resource to conduct research that can help to deal with environmental challenges of our time. The community platform Xeno-canto[7] launched in 2005 and hosts bird sounds from all continents and daily receives new recordings from some of the remotest places on Earth. The Xeno-canto archive currently consists of more than 550,000 recordings covering over 10,000 species of birds, making it one of the most comprehensive collections of bird sound recordings worldwide, and certainly the most comprehensive collection shared under Creative Commons licenses. Xeno-canto data was used for BirdCLEF in all past editions to provide researchers with large and diverse datasets for training and testing.

The diversity of this data made BirdCLEF a demanding competition and required participating research groups to develop efficient processing and classification pipelines. The large number of recordings often forced participants to reduce the training data and the number of features—strongly implying the deficiencies of low-level audio feature classification for extremely large datasets. In 2016, Sprengel et al. applied the classical scheme of image classification with deep neural networks to the domain of acoustic event recognition and introduced a convolutional neural network (CNN) classifier trained on extracted spectrograms that instantly outperformed all previous systems by a significant margin [12]. The success of deep neural networks in the domain of sound identification led to the disappearance of MFCCs, SVMs and decision trees which dominated previous editions.

Despite their success for bird sound recognition in focal recordings, the classification performance of CNN on continuous, omnidirectional soundscapes remained low. Passive acoustic monitoring can be a valuable sampling tool for habitat assessments and the observation of environmental niches which often are endangered. However, manual processing of large collections of soundscape data is not desirable and automated attempts can help to advance this process. Yet, the lack of suitable validation and test data prevented the development of reliable techniques to solve this task. This changed in 2019 when 350 h of fully annotated soundscapes were introduced as test data. Participants were asked to design a detection system that was trained on focal recordings (provided by the Xeno-canto community) and applied to hour-long soundscapes. Bridging the acoustic gap between high-quality training recordings and soundscapes with high ambient noise levels is one of the most challenging tasks in the domain of audio event recognition.

3.2 Dataset and Evaluation Protocol

Deploying a bird sound recognition system to a new recording and observation site requires classifiers that generalize well across different acoustic domains. Focal recordings of bird species from around the world form an excellent base to develop such a detection system. However, the lack of annotated soundscape data for a new deployment site poses a significant challenge. As in previous

---

[7] https://www.xeno-canto.org/.

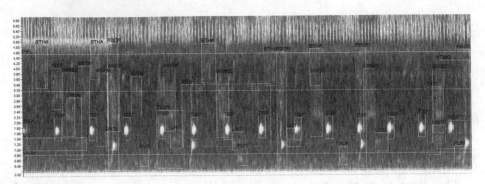

Fig. 4. South American soundscapes often have an extremely high call density. The 2020 BirdCLEF test data contains 48 fully annotated soundscapes recorded in Peru.

editions, training data was provided by the Xeno-canto community and consisted of more than 70,000 recordings covering 960 species from three continents (South and North America and Europe). Participants were allowed to use this and other (meta) data to develop their systems. A representative validation dataset with two hours of soundscape data was also provided, but participants were not allowed to use this data for training—detection systems had to be trained on focal recordings only.

In addition to the 2019 test data, soundscapes from three other recording sites were added in the 2020 edition of BirdCLEF. All audio data were collected with passive acoustic recorders from deployments in Germany (GER), Peru (PER), the High Sierra Nevada (HSN) of California, USA and the Sapsucker Woods area (SSW) in New York, USA. In an attempt to lower the entry level of this challenge, the total amount of soundscape data was reduced to 153 recordings with a duration of ten minutes each. Expert ornithologists provided annotations for often extremely dense acoustic scenes with up to eight species vocalizing at the same time (1.9 on average, see Fig. 4).

The goal of the task was to localize and identify all audible birds within the provided soundscape test set. Each soundscape was divided into segments of 5 seconds, and a list of species associated to probability scores had to be returned for each segment. The used evaluation metric was the classification mean Average Precision ($cmAP$), considering each class c of the ground truth as a query. This means that for each class c, all predictions with $ClassId = c$ are extracted from the run file and ranked by decreasing probability in order to compute the average precision for that class. The mean across all classes is computed as the main evaluation metric. More formally:

$$cmAP = \frac{\sum_{c=1}^{C} AveP(c)}{C}$$

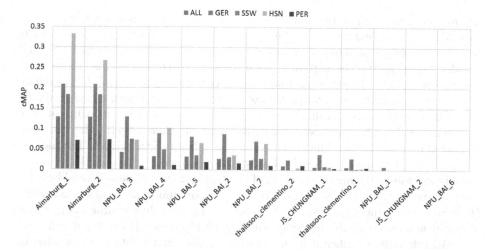

Fig. 5. Scores achieved by all systems evaluated within the bird identification task of LifeCLEF 2020.

where C is the number of classes (species) in the ground truth and $AveP(c)$ is the average precision for a given species c computed as:

$$AveP(c) = \frac{\sum_{k=1}^{n_c} P(k) \times rel(k)}{n_{rel}(c)}.$$

where k is the rank of an item in the list of the predicted segments containing c, n_c is the total number of predicted segments containing c, $P(k)$ is the precision at cut-off k in the list, $rel(k)$ is an indicator function equaling 1 if the segment at rank k is a relevant one (*i.e.* is labeled as containing c in the ground truth) and $n_{rel}(c)$ is the total number of relevant segments for class c.

3.3   Participants and Results

69 participants registered for the BirdCLEF 2020 challenge and downloaded the dataset. Four teams succeeded in submitting runs. Details of the methods and systems used in the runs are synthesized in the overview working notes paper of the task [39] and further developed in the individual working notes of the participants ([1,8]). In Fig. 5 we report the performance achieved by the 13 collected runs.

All submitted runs featured a CNN classifier trained on extracted audio features and all approaches employ current best practices from past editions. Established neural network architectures like VGG, Inception v3, EfficientNet, Xception, or the baseline repository [41] were used in the majority of the submitted runs. Most attempts used log-scale spectrograms as input, only one team used a custom Gabor wavelet layer in their network design. All participants used pre-processed data and distinguished between salient audio chunks and noise (i.e. non-events) to improve the performance of their classifier. Data augmentation is key for generalization and all participating research groups used a set of domain-specific augmentation methods. The results reflect the slight imbalance of the test data in terms of number of soundscapes per recording site and individual vocalization density. The highest scoring team achieved a class-wise mean average precision of 0.128 across all four recording sites (0.148 on validation data). Some of the participating groups did not manage to score above a cmAP of 0.01 which highlights the demanding nature of this task despite the versatility of deep neural networks. This becomes even more apparent when investigating the classification performance for the South American split of the test data. The highest scoring system achieved a cmAP of only 0.07, on average, the cmAP across all submission was 0.017 for this portion of the test set. Participants scored best for soundscapes recorded in North America with a maximum score of 0.333 for the High Sierra Nevada data. Species composition and recording characteristics play a significant role and the detection quality highly depends on avian call density. Additionally, significant improvements of current classifiers are needed to develop a reliable bird sound recognition system for highly endangered habitats in South America. Current training regimes and neural network architectures might not be suited for this task.

4   GeoLifeCLEF Challenge: Species Distribution Prediction Based on Occurrence Data, Environmental Data and Remote Sensing Data

A detailed description of the task and a more complete discussion of the results can be found in the dedicated working note [10].

4.1   Objective

Automatic prediction of the list of species most likely to be observed at a given location is useful for many scenarios related to biodiversity management and conservation. First, it could improve species identification tools (whether automatic, semi-automatic or based on traditional field guides) by reducing the list of candidate species observable at a given site. More generally, it could facilitate biodiversity inventories through the development of location-based recommendation services (*e.g.* on mobile phones), encourage the involvement of citizen scientist observers, and accelerate the annotation and validation of species observations to produce large, high-quality data sets. Last but not least, this could be used for educational purposes through biodiversity discovery applications with features such as contextualized educational pathways.

4.2   Data Set and Evaluation Protocol

Data Collection: A detailed description of the GeoLifeCLEF 2020 dataset is provided in [9]. In a nutshell, it consists of over 1.9 million observations in US and France covering 31, 435 plant and animal species (as illustrated in Figure 7). Each species observation is paired with high-resolution covariates (RGB-IR imagery, land cover and altitude) as illustrated in Fig. 6. These high-resolution covariates are resampled to a spatial resolution of 1 m per pixel and provided as 256×256 images covering a 256 m $\times$ 256 m square centered on each observation. RGB-IR imagery come from the 2009–2011 cycle of the National Agriculture Imagery Program (NAIP) for the U.S.[8], and from the BD-ORTHO® 2.0 and ORTHO-HR® 1.0 databases from the IGN for France[9]. Land cover data originates from the National Land Cover Database (NLCD) [31] for the U.S. and from CESBIO[10] for France. All elevation data comes from the NASA Shuttle Radar Topography Mission (SRTM)[11]. In addition, the dataset also includes traditional coarser resolution covariates: bio-climatic rasters (1 km^2/pixel, from WorldClim [30]) and pedologic rasters (250 m^2/pixel, from SoilGrids [29]).

Train-Test Split: The full set of occurrences was split in a training and testing set using a spatial block holdout procedure (see Fig. 7). This limits the effect of *spatial auto-correlation* in the data as explained in [50]. This means that a model cannot achieve a high performance by simply interpolating between training samples. The split was based on a global grid of 5 km $\times$ 5 km quadrats. 2.5% of the quadrats were randomly sampled for the test set, and the remaining quadrats were assigned to the training set.

Evaluation Metric: For each occurrence in the test set, the goal of the task was to return a candidate set of species with associated confidence scores. The main evaluation criterion is an adaptive variant of the top-K accuracy. Contrary to a classical top-K accuracy, this metric assumes that the number of species K may not be the same at each location. It is computed by thresholding the confidence score of the predictions and keeping only the species above that threshold. The threshold is determined automatically so as to have $K = 30$ results per occurrence on average. See [9] for full details and justification.

4.3 Participants and Results

40 participants registered for the GeoLifeCLEF 2020 challenge and downloaded the dataset. Only two of them succeeded in submitting runs: **Stanford** and **LIRMM**. A major hindrance to participation was the volume of data as well as the computing power needed to train the models (e.g. almost two weeks to train a convolutional neural network on 8 GPUs). Details of the methods and systems used in the runs of both participants are synthesized in the overview working note paper for this task [10]. Runs of the LIRMM team are further developed in

---

[8] National Agriculture Image Program, https://www.fsa.usda.gov.
[9] https://geoservices.ign.fr.
[10] http://osr-cesbio.ups-tlse.fr/~oso/posts/2017-03-30-carte-s2-2016/.
[11] https://lpdaac.usgs.gov/products/srtmgl1v003/.

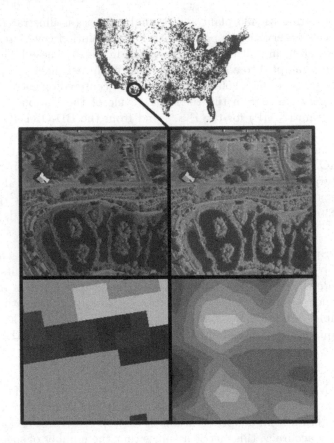

Fig. 6. Each species observation is paired with high-resolution covariates (clockwise from top left: RGB imagery, IR imagery, altitude, land cover).

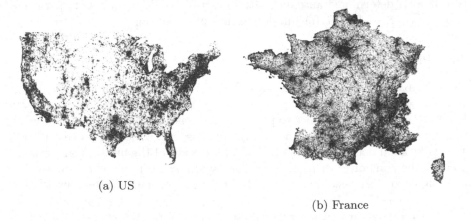

(a) US

(b) France

Fig. 7. Occurrences distribution over the US and France. Blue dots represent training data, red dots represent test data. (Color figure online)

the individual working note [11]. Due to convergence issues for runs of Stanford team, after discussion with the authors, it was mutually agreed that they would not provide additional working notes for their runs.

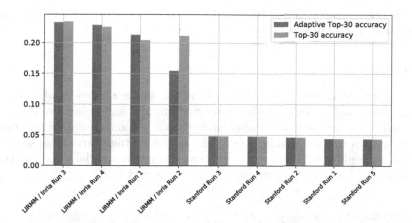

Fig. 8. Adaptive top-30 accuracy and top-30 accuracy per run and participant on GeoLifeCLEF 2020 task.

In Fig. 8 we report the performance achieved by the 9 collected runs[12]. The main outcome of the challenge was that the method achieving the best results (LIRMM/Inria Run 3) was based solely on a convolutional neural network (CNN) trained on the high-resolution covariates (RGB-IR imagery, land cover, and altitude). It did not make use of any bioclimatic variable or soil type variable whereas these variables are often considered as the most informative in the ecological literature. On the contrary, the method used in LIRMM/Inria Run 1 was based solely on the punctual environmental variables using a machine learning method classically used for species distribution models (Random Forest, [13]). This shows two things: (i) important information explaining the species composition is contained in the high-resolution covariates and (ii), convolutional neural networks are able to capture this information. An important following question would be to know whether the information captured by the high-resolution CNN is complementary to the one captured from the bioclimatic and soil variables. This was the purpose of LIRMM/Inria Run 4 that merged the prediction of both models by averaging their outputs Unfortunately, this was not really conclusive. Either the high-resolution CNN already captured most of the information contained in the bioclimatic variables, or the fusion method was not able to take the best of each model.

---

[12] Most of the Stanford team's methods were based on deep neural networks, but the authors informed us that they encounter convergence issues resulting in performance poorer than expected.

5   SnakeCLEF Challenge: Automated Snake Species Identification Based on Images and Two-Level Geographic Location Data (Continent and Country)

A detailed description of the task and a more complete discussion of the results can be found in the dedicated overview paper [48].

5.1   Objective

To create an automatic and robust system for snake species identification is an important goal for biodiversity, conservation, and global health. With over half a million victims of death and disability from venomous snakebite annually, having a system that is capable to recognize or differentiate various snake species from images could significantly improve eco-epidemiological data and treatment outcomes (e.g. based on specific use of antivenoms) [3,6].

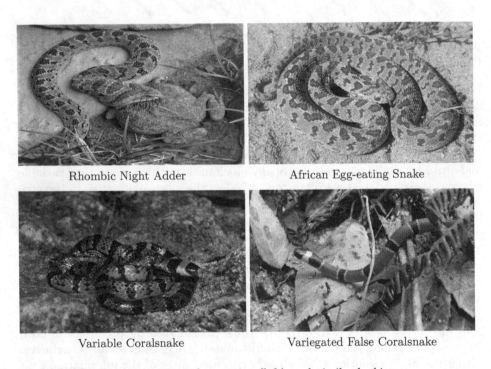

Rhombic Night Adder   African Egg-eating Snake

Variable Coralsnake   Variegated False Coralsnake

Fig. 9. Medically important snake species (left) and similar-looking non-venomous species (right). © Peter Vos, iNaturalist, CC-BY-NC and © Alex Rebelo, iNaturalist, CC-BY-NC and © Peter Vos, iNaturalist, CC-BY-NC and © Iris Melgar, iNaturalist, CC-BY-NC.

Since snake species identification is a fine-grained visual categorization task, the main difficulty of this challenge is the high intra-class and low inter-class

Fig. 10. Two observations of the same snake species (Boomslang, *Dispholidus typus*) with high visual dissimilarity related to sex (female left, male right). © Mark Heystek, iNaturalist, CC-BY-NC and © Daniel Rautenbach, iNaturalist, CC-BY-NC.

variances. In other words, certain classes could be highly variable in appearance depending on geographic location, sex, or age (Fig. 9) and at the same time could be visually similar to other species (e.g. mimicry) (Fig. 10). The goals and usage of image-based snake identification are complementary with those of other challenges: classifying snake species in images and predicting the list of species that are the most likely to be observed at a given location.

5.2   Dataset and Evaluation Protocol

Dataset Overview: For this challenge we have prepared a dataset with 259,214 images belonging to 783 snake species from 145 countries. The dataset has a heavy long-tailed class distribution, where the most frequent species (*Thamnophis sirtalis*) is represented by 12,201 images and the least frequent by just 17 (*Naja pallida*). Such a distribution with small inter-class variance and high intra-class variance creates a challenging task.

Training-Validation Split: To allow participants to easily validate their intermediate results, we have split the full dataset into a training subset with 245,185 images, and validation subset with 14,029 images. Both subsets have similar class distribution, while the minimum number of validation images per class is one.

Testing Dataset: Apart from other LifeCLEF challenges, the final testing set remains undisclosed as it is a composition of private images from individual reporters and natural history museums who have not put those images online in any form. A brief description of this closure method is as follows - twice as big as the validation set, contains all 973 classes, and observations from almost all the countries presented in training and validation sets.

Geographical Information: For approximately 80% of the images we provided a two levels of geographical information - country and continent. We have collected observations across 145 countries and all continents. Such information could be crucial for the AI based recognition as it is useful for human experts.

Fig. 11. Randomly selected images from the SnakeCLEF 2020 training set. © stewartb, iNaturalist, CC-BY-NC and © Jennifer Linde, iNaturalist, CC-BY-NC and © Gilberto Ponce Tejeda, iNaturalist, CC-BY-NC and © Ryan van Huyssteen, iNaturalist, CC-BY-NC and © Jessica Newbern, iNaturalist, CC-BY-NC.

Evaluation: The main goal of this challenge was to build a system that is autonomously able of recognizing 973 snake species based on the given image and geographical location input. Every participant had to submit their whole solution into the GitLab based evaluation system that performed evaluation over the secret testing set. Since data were secret each participated team could submit up to 5 submissions per day. The main evaluation metric for this challenge was the Dice Similarity Coefficient (DSC), also known as F1 score.

$$F_1 = 2 \times \frac{\text{Precision} \times \text{Recall}}{\text{Precision} + \text{Recall}}$$

This score represents the harmonic mean of the Precision and the Recall.

$$Precision = \frac{TP}{TP + FN}; \qquad Recall = \frac{TP}{TP + FN}$$

The secondary metric was calculated as Multi-class Classification Logarithmic Loss e.g. Cross Entropy Loss.

$$LogLoss = -\sum_{c=1}^{M} y_{o,c} \cdot \log(p_{o,c})$$

This metric considers the uncertainty of a given prediction based on how much it differs from the actual label. This gives us a more subtle evaluation of the performance.

5.3 Participants and Results

Out of 8 registered teams in the SnakeCLEF 2020 challenge, only 2 teams managed to submit a working version of their recognition system. Even though participants were able to evaluate their system 5 times a day, we have registered only 27 submissions. Details of the methods and systems used in the runs are synthesized in the overview working note paper of the task [48] and further developed in the individual working notes (FHDO_BCSG [2]], Gokuleloop [44]). In a nutshell, both participants featured deep convolutional neural network architectures (ResNet50 and EfficientNet). They completely avoided CNN ensembles and used geological locations in a test time. The Gokuleloop team approaches were focused on the domain specific fine-tuning where this team tried different pre-trained weights. With the Imagenet-21k weights, ResNet50 architecture, and naive probability weighting approach, Gokuleloop team achieved top F1 score of 0.625 while having a Log Loss of 0.83. The FHDO_BCSG team approaches combined two stages. Firstly, they used a Mask R-CNN instance detection method for snake detection. Secondly, different EfficientNet models were used to classify regions detected by the previous stage. Their best submitted model was an EfficientNet-B4 fine-tuned from the ImageNet pre-trained checkpoint. This model achieves F1 score of 0.404 and a Log-Loss of 6.650. The high Log-Loss was achieved due to the application of softmax normalization after the multiplication of the location data which leads to small differences in the predictions. All submission and their achieved scores are reported in the Fig. 12.

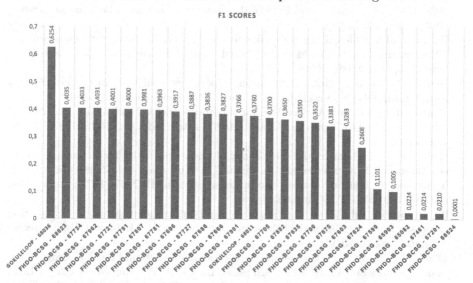

Fig. 12. F1 Scores achieved within the SnakeCLEF 2020.

6   Conclusions and Perspectives

The main outcome of this collaborative evaluation is a new snapshot of the performance of state-of-the-art computer vision, bio-acoustic and machine learning techniques towards building real-world biodiversity monitoring systems. This study shows that recent deep learning techniques still allow some consistent progress for most of the evaluated tasks. The results of the PlantCLEF challenge, in particular, revealed that the last advances in domain adaptation enable the use of herbarium data to facilitate the identification of rare tropical species for which no or very few other training images are available. The results of the GeoLifeCLEF challenge were also highly relevant, revealing that deep convolutional neural networks trained on high-resolution geographic images are able to effectively predict species distribution even without using bioclimatic or soil variables. Furthermore, the results of the SnakeCLEF challenge showed that both traditional approaches and deep convolutional neural networks can benefit from geographical information.

Acknowledgements. This project has received funding from the European Union's Horizon 2020 research and innovation programme under grant agreement No° 863463 (Cos4Cloud project), and the support of #DigitAG.

References

1. Bai, J., Chen, C., Chen, J.: Xception based system for bird sound detection. In: CLEF Working Notes 2020, CLEF: Conference and Labs of the Evaluation Forum, Thessaloniki, Greece, September 2020 (2020)
2. Bloch, L., et al.: Combination of image and location information for snake species identification using object detection and efficientnets. In: CLEF Working Notes 2020, CLEF: Conference and Labs of the Evaluation Forum, Thessaloniki, Greece, September 2020 (2020)
3. Bolon, I., et al.: Identifying the snake: first scoping review on practices of communities and healthcare providers confronted with snakebite across the world. PLoS One **15**(3), e0229989 (2020)
4. Bonnet, P., et al.: Plant identification: experts vs. machines in the era of deep learning. In: Joly, A., Vrochidis, S., Karatzas, K., Karppinen, A., Bonnet, P. (eds.) Multimedia Tools and Applications for Environmental & Biodiversity Informatics. MSA, pp. 131–149. Springer, Cham (2018). https://doi.org/10.1007/978-3-319-76445-0_8
5. Cai, J., Ee, D., Pham, B., Roe, P., Zhang, J.: Sensor network for the monitoring of ecosystem: bird species recognition. In: 2007 3rd International Conference on Intelligent Sensors, Sensor Networks and Information, ISSNIP 2007 (2007). https://doi.org/10.1109/ISSNIP.2007.4496859
6. de Castañeda, R.R., et al.: Snakebite and snake identification: empowering neglected communities and health-care providers with AI. Lancet Digit. Health **1**(5), e202–e203 (2019)
7. Chulif, S., Chang, Y.L.: Cross-domain plant identification on French Guyana Flora: neuon submission to LifeCLEF 2020 plant. In: CLEF Working Notes 2020, CLEF: Conference and Labs of the Evaluation Forum, Thessaloniki, Greece, September 2020 (2020)
8. Clementino, T., Colonna, J.G.: Using triplet loss to bird species recognition on BirdCLEF 2020. In: CLEF Working Notes 2020, CLEF: Conference and Labs of the Evaluation Forum, Thessaloniki, Greece, September 2020 (2020)
9. Cole, E., et al.: The GeoLifeCLEF 2020 dataset. arXiv preprint arXiv:2004.04192 (2020)
10. Deneu, B., et al.: Overview of LifeCLEF location-based species prediction task 2020 (GeoLifeCLEF). In: CLEF task overview 2020, CLEF: Conference and Labs of the Evaluation Forum, Thessaloniki, Greece, September 2020 (2020)
11. Deneu, B., Servajean, M., Joly, A.: Participation of LIRMM/Inria to the GeoLifeCLEF 2020 challenge. In: CLEF Working Notes 2020, CLEF: Conference and Labs of the Evaluation Forum, Thessaloniki, Greece, September 2020 (2020)
12. Sprengel, E., Jaggi, M., Kilcher, Y., Hofmann, T.: Audio based bird species identification using deep learning techniques. In: CLEF Working Notes 2016, CLEF: Conference and Labs of the Evaluation Forum, Évora, Portugal, September 2016 (2016)

13. Evans, J.S., Murphy, M.A., Holden, Z.A., Cushman, S.A.: Modeling species distribution and change using random forest. In: Drew, C., Wiersma, Y., Huettmann, F. (eds.) Predictive Species and Habitat Modeling in Landscape Ecology, pp. 139–159. Springer, New York (2011). https://doi.org/10.1007/978-1-4419-7390-0_8

14. Gaston, K.J., O'Neill, M.A.: Automated species identification: why not? Philos. Trans. Roy. Soc. Lond. B: Biol. Sci. **359**(1444), 655–667 (2004)

15. Ghazi, M.M., Yanikoglu, B., Aptoula, E.: Plant identification using deep neural networks via optimization of transfer learning parameters. Neurocomputing **235**, 228–235 (2017)

16. Glotin, H., Clark, C., LeCun, Y., Dugan, P., Halkias, X., Sueur, J.: Proceedings of 1st Workshop on Machine Learning for Bioacoustics - ICML4B. ICML, Atlanta (2013). http://sabiod.org/ICML4B2013_book.pdf

17. Goëau, H., Bonnet, P., Joly, A.: Plant identification in an open-world (LifeCLEF 2016). In: CLEF Task Overview 2016, CLEF: Conference and Labs of the Evaluation Forum, September 2016, Évora, Portugal (2016)

18. Goëau, H., Bonnet, P., Joly, A.: Plant identification based on noisy web data: the amazing performance of deep learning (LifeCLEF 2017). In: CLEF Task Overview 2017, CLEF: Conference and Labs of the Evaluation Forum, Dublin, Ireland, September 2017 (2017)

19. Goëau, H., Bonnet, P., Joly, A.: Overview of ExpertLifeCLEF 2018: how far automated identification systems are from the best experts? In: CLEF Task Overview 2018, CLEF: Conference and Labs of the Evaluation Forum, Avignon, France, September 2018 (2018)

20. Goëau, H., Bonnet, P., Joly, A.: Overview of LifeCLEF plant identification task 2019: diving into data deficient tropical countries. In: CLEF Task Overview 2019, CLEF: Conference and Labs of the Evaluation Forum, Lugano, Switzerland, September 2019 (2019)

21. Goëau, H., Bonnet, P., Joly, A.: Overview of LifeCLEF plant identification task 2020. In: CLEF Task Overview 2020, CLEF: Conference and Labs of the Evaluation Forum, Thessaloniki, Greece, September 2020 (2020)

22. Goëau, H., et al.: The ImageCLEF 2013 plant identification task. In: CLEF Task Overview 2013, CLEF: Conference and Labs of the Evaluation Forum, Valencia, Spain, September 2013 (2013)

23. Goëau, H., et al.: The ImageCLEF 2011 plant images classification task. In: CLEF Task Overview 2011, CLEF: Conference and Labs of the Evaluation Forum, Amsterdam, Netherlands, September 2011 (2011)

24. Goëau, H., et al.: ImageCLEF 2012 plant images identification task. In: CLEF Task Overview 2012, CLEF: Conference and Labs of the Evaluation Forum, Rome, Italy, September 2012 (2012)

25. Goëau, H., Glotin, H., Planqué, R., Vellinga, W.P., Stefan, Kahl, J.A.: Overview of BirdCLEF 2018: monophone vs. soundscape bird identification. In: CLEF Task Overview 2018, CLEF: Conference and Labs of the Evaluation Forum, Avignon, France, September 2018 (2018)

26. Goëau, H., Joly, A., Bonnet, P.: LifeCLEF plant identification task 2015. In: CLEF Task Overview 2015, CLEF: Conference and Labs of the Evaluation Forum, Toulouse, France, September 2015 (2015)

27. Goëau, H., et al.: The ImageCLEF plant identification task 2013. In: Proceedings of the 2nd ACM International Workshop on Multimedia Analysis for Ecological Data, pp. 23–28. ACM (2013)

28. Goëau, H., et al.: The LifeCLEF 2014 plant images identification task. In: CLEF Task Overview 2014, CLEF: Conference and Labs of the Evaluation Forum, Sheffield, United Kingdom, September 2014 (2014)
29. Hengl, T., et al.: SoilGrids250m: global gridded soil information based on machine learning. PLoS One **12**(2), e0169748 (2017)
30. Hijmans, R.J., Cameron, S.E., Parra, J.L., Jones, P.G., Jarvis, A.: Very high resolution interpolated climate surfaces for global land areas. Int. J. Climatol.: J. Roy. Meteorol. Soc. **25**(15), 1965–1978 (2005)
31. Homer, C., et al.: Completion of the 2011 national land cover database for the conterminous united states - representing a decade of land cover change information. Photogram. Eng. Rem. Sens. **81**(5), 345–354 (2015)
32. Joly, A., et al.: Interactive plant identification based on social image data. Ecol. Inf. **23**, 22–34 (2014)
33. Joly, A., et al.: Overview of LifeCLEF 2018: a large-scale evaluation of species identification and recommendation algorithms in the era of AI. In: Bellot, P., et al. (eds.) CLEF 2018. LNCS, vol. 11018, pp. 247–266. Springer, Cham (2018). https://doi.org/10.1007/978-3-319-98932-7_24
34. Joly, A., et al.: Overview of LifeCLEF 2019: identification of Amazonian plants, South & North American Birds, and Niche prediction. In: Crestani, F., et al. (eds.) CLEF 2019. Lecture Notes in Computer Science, vol. 11696, pp. 387–401. Springer, Cham (2019). https://doi.org/10.1007/978-3-030-28577-7_29. https://hal.umontpellier.fr/hal-02281455
35. Joly, A., et al.: LifeCLEF 2016: multimedia life species identification challenges. In: Fuhr, N., et al. (eds.) CLEF 2016. LNCS, vol. 9822, pp. 286–310. Springer, Cham (2016). https://doi.org/10.1007/978-3-319-44564-9_26. https://hal.archives-ouvertes.fr/hal-01373781
36. Joly, A., et al.: LifeCLEF 2017 lab overview: multimedia species identification challenges. In: Jones, G.J.F., et al. (eds.) CLEF 2017. LNCS, vol. 10456, pp. 255–274. Springer, Cham (2017). https://doi.org/10.1007/978-3-319-65813-1_24. https://hal.archives-ouvertes.fr/hal-01629191
37. Joly, A., et al.: LifeCLEF 2014: multimedia life species identification challenges. In: Kanoulas, E., et al. (eds.) CLEF 2014. LNCS, vol. 8685, pp. 229–249. Springer, Cham (2014). https://doi.org/10.1007/978-3-319-11382-1_20. https://hal.inria.fr/hal-01075770
38. Joly, A., et al.: LifeCLEF 2015: multimedia life species identification challenges. In: Mothe, J., et al. (eds.) CLEF 2015. Lecture Notes in Computer Science, vol. 9283, pp. 462–483. Springer, Cham (2015). https://doi.org/10.1007/978-3-319-24027-5_46
39. Kahl, S., et al.: Overview of BirdCLEF 2020: bird sound recognition in complex acoustic environments. In: CLEF Task Overview 2020, CLEF: Conference and Labs of the Evaluation Forum, Thessaloniki, Greece, September 2020 (2020)
40. Kahl, S., Stöter, F.R., Glotin, H., Planqué, R., Vellinga, W.P., Joly, A.: Overview of BirdCLEF 2019: large-scale bird recognition in soundscapes. In: CLEF Task Overview 2019, CLEF: Conference and Labs of the Evaluation Forum, Lugano, Switzerland, September 2019 (2019)
41. Kahl, S., Wilhelm-Stein, T., Klinck, H., Kowerko, D., Eibl, M.: Recognizing birds from sound - the 2018 BirdCLEF baseline system. arXiv preprint arXiv:1804.07177 (2018)
42. Lee, D.J., Schoenberger, R.B., Shiozawa, D., Xu, X., Zhan, P.: Contour matching for a fish recognition and migration-monitoring system. In: Optics East. pp. 37–48. International Society for Optics and Photonics (2004)

43. Lee, S.H., Chan, C.S., Remagnino, P.: Multi-organ plant classification based on convolutional and recurrent neural networks. IEEE Trans. Image Process. **27**(9), 4287–4301 (2018)
44. Moorthy, G.K.: Impact of pretrained networks for snake species classification. In: CLEF Working Notes 2020, CLEF: Conference and Labs of the Evaluation Forum, Thessaloniki, Greece, September 2020 (2020)
45. Motiian, S., Jones, Q., Iranmanesh, S., Doretto, G.: Few-shot adversarial domain adaptation. In: Advances in Neural Information Processing Systems, pp. 6670–6680 (2017)
46. Krishna, N.H., Ram Kaushik, R., R.M.: Plant species identification using transfer learning - PlantCLEF 2020. In: CLEF Working Notes 2020, CLEF: Conference and Labs of the Evaluation Forum, Thessaloniki, Greece, September 2020 (2020)
47. NIPS International Conference: Proceedings of Neural Information Processing Scaled for Bioacoustics, from Neurons to Big Data (2013). http://sabiod.org/nips4b
48. Picek, L., Ruiz De Castañeda, R., Durso, A.M., Sharada, P.M.: Overview of the SnakeCLEF 2020: automatic snake species identification challenge. In: CLEF Task Overview 2020, CLEF: Conference and Labs of the Evaluation Forum, Thessaloniki, Greece, September 2020 (2020)
49. Picek, L., Sulc, M., Matas, J.: Recognition of the Amazonian flora by inception networks with test-time class prior estimation. In: CLEF Working Notes 2019, CLEF: Conference and Labs of the Evaluation Forum, Lugano, Switzerland, September 2019 (2019)
50. Roberts, D.R., et al.: Cross-validation strategies for data with temporal, spatial, hierarchical, or phylogenetic structure. Ecography **40**(8), 913–929 (2017)
51. Towsey, M., Planitz, B., Nantes, A., Wimmer, J., Roe, P.: A toolbox for animal call recognition. Bioacoustics **21**(2), 107–125 (2012)
52. Trifa, V.M., Kirschel, A.N., Taylor, C.E., Vallejo, E.E.: Automated species recognition of antbirds in a mexican rainforest using hidden markov models. J. Acoust. Soc. Am. **123**, 2424 (2008)
53. Van Horn, G., et al.: The inaturalist species classification and detection dataset. In: CVPR (2018)
54. Villacis, J., Goëau, H., Bonnet, P., Mata-Montero, E., Joly, A.: Domain adaptation in the context of herbarium collections: a submission to PlantCLEF 2020. In: CLEF Working Notes 2020, CLEF: Conference and Labs of the Evaluation Forum, Thessaloniki, Greece, September 2020 (2020)
55. Wäldchen, J., Mäder, P.: Machine learning for image based species identification. Methods Ecol. Evol. **9**(11), 2216–2225 (2018)
56. Wäldchen, J., Rzanny, M., Seeland, M., Mäder, P.: Automated plant species identification–trends and future directions. PLoS Comput. Biol. **14**(4), e1005993 (2018)
57. Yu, X., Wang, J., Kays, R., Jansen, P.A., Wang, T., Huang, T.: Automated identification of animal species in camera trap images. EURASIP J. Image Video Process. **2013**, 52 (2013)
58. Zhang, Y., Davison, B.D.: Adversarial consistent learning on partial domain adaptation of PlantCLEF 2020 challenge. In: CLEF Working Notes 2020, CLEF: Conference and Labs of the Evaluation Forum, Thessaloniki, Greece, September 2020 (2020)

Overview of LiLAS 2020 – Living Labs for Academic Search

Philipp Schaer[1]([✉])(iD), Johann Schaible[2](iD), and Leyla Jael Garcia Castro[3](iD)

[1] TH Köln - University of Applied Sciences, Cologne, Germany
philipp.schaer@th-koeln.de
[2] GESIS - Leibniz Institute for the Social Sciences, Cologne, Germany
johann.schaible@gesis.org
[3] ZB MED - Information Centre for Life Sciences, Cologne, Germany
ljgarcia@zbmed.de

Abstract. Academic Search is a timeless challenge that the field of Information Retrieval has been dealing with for many years. Even today, the search for academic material is a broad field of research that recently started working on problems like the COVID-19 pandemic. However, test collections and specialized data sets like CORD-19 only allow for system-oriented experiments, while the evaluation of algorithms in real-world environments is only available to researchers from industry. In LiLAS, we open up two academic search platforms to allow participating researchers to evaluate their systems in a Docker-based research environment. This overview paper describes the motivation, infrastructure, and two systems LIVIVO and GESIS Search that are part of this CLEF lab.

Keywords: Evaluation · Living labs · Academic search · Reproducibility

1 Introduction

The field of Information Retrieval (IR) originated in the domain of scientific/academic information and documentation. Back in the 1960s, the original Cranfield studies dealt with the indexation and the retrieval of scientific documents. Cleverdon et al. established their whole evaluation methodology around the use-case of scientific and academic retrieval requirements. Today, the search for relevant scientific documents is still an open endeavor, and although retrieval systems show substantial performance gains, it is not a solved problem yet. The current COVID-19 pandemic, for example, showed once again that even old problems like the search for scientific documents are not solved. Therefore, current efforts like the CORD-19 collection[1] and the TREC COVID retrieval campaign[2] gather much attraction and are in the spotlight of the IR community,

---

[1] https://www.semanticscholar.org/cord19.
[2] https://ir.nist.gov/covidSubmit/index.html.

© Springer Nature Switzerland AG 2020
A. Arampatzis et al. (Eds.): CLEF 2020, LNCS 12260, pp. 364–371, 2020.
https://doi.org/10.1007/978-3-030-58219-7_24

even though at their core, they deal with the same – timeless – problem set as Cleverdon more than 50 years ago.

Besides these timeless retrieval issues, the need for innovation in academic search is shown by the stagnating system performance in controlled evaluation campaigns, as demonstrated in TREC and CLEF meta-evaluation studies [1,15]. User studies in real systems of scientific information and digital libraries show similar conditions. Although massive data collections of scientific documents are available in platforms like arXiv, PubMed, or other digital libraries, central user needs and requirements remain unsatisfied. The central mission is to find both relevant and high-quality documents - if possible, directly on the first result page. Besides this ad-hoc retrieval problem, other tasks such as the recommendation of relevant cross-modality content including research data sets or specialized tasks like expert finding are not even considered here. On top of that, relevance in academic search is multi-layered [5] and a topic that drives research communities like the Bibliometrics-enhanced Information Retrieval (BIR) workshops [10].

The Living Labs for Academic Search (LiLAS) workshop fosters the discussion, research, and evaluation of academic search systems, and it employs the concept of living labs to the domain of academic search [13]. The goal is to expand the knowledge on improving the search for academic resources like literature, research data, and the interlinking between these resources. To support this goal, LiLAS introduces an online evaluation infrastructure that directly connects to real-world academic search systems [12]. LiLAS cooperates with two academic search systems providers from Life Sciences and Social Sciences. Both system providers support LiLAS by allowing participants of the lab to employ experimental search components into their production online system. We will have access to the click logs of these systems and use them to employ A/B tests or more complex interleaving experiments. Our living lab platform STELLA makes this possible by bringing platform operators and researchers together and providing a methodological and technical framework for online experiments [3].

2   Related Work from CLEF and TREC

CLEF and TREC hosted the Living Labs for Information Retrieval (LL4IR) and Open Search (TREC-OS) initiatives that are the predecessors to LiLAS. Both initiatives shared a common evaluation infrastructure that was released as an API[3]. This API allows academic researchers to access the search systems of other platforms. Participants of LL4IR and TREC-OS had access to the search systems' head queries and document sets. They had to precompute ranked result lists for a given set of candidate documents for the given head queries. Therefore it was a typical ad-hoc search task. Another task was run during the CLEF NewsReel campaign, where participants had to recommend news articles. This was possible by employing an offline test collection or in real-time via the Open Recommendation Platform (ORP) used by PLISTA.

---

[3] https://bitbucket.org/living-labs/ll-api.

All these labs can be considered living labs and represent a user-centric study methodology for researchers to evaluate retrieval systems' performance within real-world applications. Thus, they aim to offer a more realistic experiment and evaluation environment as offline test collections and therefore, should be further investigated to raise IR-evaluation to a more holistic level.

Within TREC and CLEF, only very few tracks or labs focused on the evaluation of academic search systems. Some used scientific documents or use-cases to generate test collections but did not necessarily focus on the unique requirements of the academic domain. Within CLEF, the Domain-specific track [8] compiled a collection of bibliographic records and research project descriptions from the Social Sciences to test the needs of scientific retrieval tasks. This test collection was created to contrast the then usual "general-purpose news documents" and to employ "different search criteria than those used for reference retrieval in databases of scientific literature items, and also offer no possibility for comparable test runs with domain-specific terminology". More recently, the TREC Precision Medicine/Clinical Decision Support Track released a large test collection in 2016 based on open access full-text documents from PubMedCentral. TREC-COVID is the latest retrieval campaign aiming at academic search with a particular focus on the rapidly growing corpus of scientific work on the current COVID-19 pandemic.

The LiLAS workshop is a blend of the most successful parts of these previous evaluation campaigns. The Domain-specific track had a strong focus on scientific search, thesauri, and multilingual search. NewsREEL had an active technological component, and LL4IR/TREC-OS turned from product search to academic search but was not able to implement the scientific focus into the last iteration. There is much potential that is still not used in the question of how to evaluate academic search platforms online.

3   STELLA – Evaluation Infrastructure for LiLAS

Nowadays, testing approaches are commonly used to try out and evaluate how users interact when presented with some new or modified features on a website. Whenever the new or modified features differ from what has been done before, when multiple features change at once, or when the user interaction is to be gathered in a systematic way, A/B testing comes into place. An A/B testing, a controlled online experiment, allows to expose a percentage of real users and life-test those new or modified features [2,9] offering to website designers and developers a living lab where to assess reactions and usage of new features better, allowing them for more accurate tuning based on data collected from production systems.

For LiLAS, we use STELLA as our living lab evaluation infrastructure. STELLA is aiming to make it easier to evaluate academic retrieval information and recommendation systems [3]. Figure 1 shows an overview of how the steps flow from a researcher's or developer's idea to the evaluation feedback so the changes can be tuned and improved. It all starts with an idea, for instance

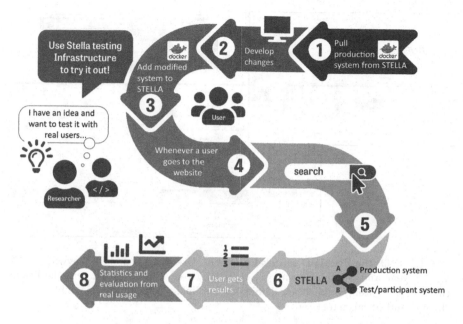

Fig. 1. STELLA workflow, an online living lab supporting testing from ideas to evaluation: Participants package their systems with the help of Docker containers that are deployed in the backend of academic information retrieval and recommendation systems. Users interact directly with the system, with a percentage diverted to the experimental features. Researchers and developers retrieve results and deliver feedback to tune and improve changes.

adding synonyms to the keywords used by an end-user when searching for information. Developers will work on a modified version of the production system, including this change they want to analyze. Whenever an end-user goes to the system, everything will look as usual. Once the search keywords are introduced, STELLA will show end-user some results from the experimental system and some results from the regular production system. End-users will continue their regular interaction with the system. Based on the retrieved documents and the following interaction, STELLA will create an evaluation profile together with some statistics. Researchers and developers will then analyze STELLA's feedback and will react accordingly to get the usage level they are aiming at.

STELLA's infrastructure relies on the container virtualization environment Docker [11], making it easier for STELLA to run multiple experimental systems, i.e., a multi-container environment, and compare them to each other and the production system as well. The core component in STELLA is a central Application Public Interface (API) connecting data and content providers with experimental systems, aka participant systems or participants, encapsulated as

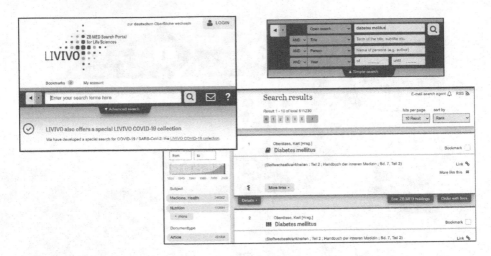

Fig. 2. LIVIVO, the ZB MED retrieval platform. Users can search by keywords, title, author or year and obtain a result set sorted by relevance together with additional features such is filters, publication details, access links, other publications like the one on display and library stock.

Docker containers. Further information can be found at the project website[4], including some technical details via a series of blogs published regularly.

Currently, STELLA supports two main tasks: ad-hoc retrieval and recommendation. In the following subsections, we will introduce two systems used during the STELLA development phase to understand better, learn, and test these two tasks. Although a fully functional version is already available, there is still room for improvement, particularly regarding the events logging, statistics analysis, and overall evaluation. LiLAS will promote an early discussion with future adopters and participants that will benefit not only STELLA but living labs in general.

3.1   LIVIVO

LIVIVO[5] is a retrieval platform provided by ZB MED – Information Centre for Life Sciences. It serves the Life Sciences domain with a focus on medicine, health, nutrition, environment, and agriculture. LIVIVO includes unique features tailored to the German public and the national inter-library loan system, making it easier for researchers, practitioners, students, and the general public to access material licensed and hosted at different German libraries. LIVIVO brings together publication from 30 different sources, e.g., Medline, AGRICOLA, and AGRIS, including more than 58 million publications in different languages including English, German, Spanish, French and Portuguese. It uses automatic

---

[4] https://stella-project.org/.
[5] https://livivo.de.

Fig. 3. GESIS Search, social science information portal. It provides different types of information from the social sciences, like literature, research data, questions and variables, as well as instruments and tools.

and semantic links to well-known vocabularies, for instance the Medical Subheading (MeSH) [14] for medical sciences, UMTHES [6] for environmental sciences, and AGROVOC [4] for agricultural sciences. The resultset ranked by relevance and can be narrowed down using filters such as the ZB MED subject fields. We include a sample query and corresponding results in Fig. 2. From March 2020, there is a dedicated portal serving Covid-19 related information.

Regarding the integration to STELLA, a test instance of LIVIVO has been set up with a twofold purpose: introducing those elements needed in LIVIVO to integrate it to the STELLA framework, e.g., calling the STELLA API whenever a search is triggered in the production system, and evaluating the STELLA framework itself, i.e., how the containerization. Communication via the API and central STELLA server work with real production systems. We are also working on a LIVIVO dataset suitable for participant systems, mainly targeting MEDLINE articles written in English, about 25 million abstracts with their corresponding metadata including title, authors, affiliations, MeSH term among others.

3.2   GESIS Search

The internal GESIS academic search GESIS Search[6] aims to aid their users in finding appropriate scholarly information on the broad topic of social sciences [7]. To this end, it provides different types of information from the social sciences, comprising literature (95k publications), research data (84k), questions and variables (12.7k), as well as instruments and tools (370) as depicted in Fig. 3. The publications are mostly in English and German and are annotated with further textual metadata like title, abstract, topic, persons, and others. With the Social

---

[6] https://search.gesis.org/.

Science Open Access Repository (SSOAR)[7], GESIS Search also provides access to nearly 60k open access publications. Metadata on research data comprises (among others) a title, topics, datatype, abstract, collection method, primary investigators, and contributors in English and/or German.

Regarding STELLA, the amount of different types of data allows not only for typical recommendations, such as from publications to publications but also for *cross-domain recommendations*, i.e., recommendations from different types such as from publications to research data. While this is still work in progress, the GESIS Search data and possible relevance indicators, such as click-paths, can be obtained. The data can be used to train a recommender and report lessons learned, and file issue requests on how to improve the training data.

4   Conclusion and Outlook

We presented the artifacts we would like to use for the actual evaluation tasks at CLEF 2021. These artifacts are: (1) the STELLA living lab evaluation infrastructure, and (2) the two academic search systems LIVIVO and GESIS Search. These systems are from the two disjunct scientific domains life sciences and social sciences and include different metadata on research articles, data sets, and many other entities.

With this at hand, we will derive the CLEF 2020 workshop participants' evaluation tasks for CLEF 2021. Promising task candidates are:

- Ad-hoc retrieval for life Science documents
- Dataset recommendation

These tasks allows us to use the different data types available in the platforms.

Acknowledgements. This work was partially funded by the German Research Foundation (DFG) under the project no. 407518790.

References

1. Armstrong, T.G., Moffat, A., Webber, W., Zobel, J.: Improvements that don't add up: ad-hoc retrieval results since 1998. In: Proceeding of the 18th ACM Conference on Information and Knowledge Management, CIKM 2009, pp. 601–610. ACM, Hong Kong (2009). https://doi.org/10.1145/1645953.1646031
2. Bakshy, E., Eckles, D., Bernstein, M.S.: Designing and deploying online field experiments. In: Proceedings of the 23rd International Conference on World Wide Web, WWW 2014, pp. 283–292. Association for Computing Machinery, Seoul, April 2014. https://doi.org/10.1145/2566486.2567967
3. Breuer, T., Schaer, P., Tavalkolpoursaleh, N., Schaible, J., Wolff, B., Müller, B.: Stella: towards a framework for the reproducibility of online search experiments. In: Proceedings of the the Open-Source IR Replicability Challenge (OSIRRC) @ SIGIR (2019)

---

[7] https://www.gesis.org/en/ssoar/home.

4. Caracciolo, C., et al.: The AGROVOC linked dataset. Seman. Web **4**(3), 341–348 (2013). https://doi.org/10.3233/SW-130106

5. Mayr, P., Scharnhorst, A., Larsen, B., Schaer, P., Mutschke, P.: Bibliometric-enhanced information retrieval. In: de Rijke, M., et al. (eds.) ECIR 2014. LNCS, vol. 8416, pp. 798–801. Springer, Cham (2014). https://doi.org/10.1007/978-3-319-06028-6_99

6. Fock, J.: Environmental Thesaurus UMTHES - environment terminology evolvement for a broad thematic matter and for different use conditions - practicably handling of structural challenges (2009). http://dl.gi.de/handle/20.500.12116/27912

7. Hienert, D., Kern, D., Boland, K., Zapilko, B., Mutschke, P.: A digital library for research data and related information in the social sciences. In: 19th ACM/IEEE Joint Conference on Digital Libraries, JCDL 2019, Champaign, IL, USA, 2–6 June 2019, pp. 148–157. IEEE (2019). https://doi.org/10.1109/JCDL.2019.00030

8. Kluck, M., Gey, F.C.: The domain-specific task of CLEF - specific evaluation strategies in cross-language information retrieval. In: Peters, C. (ed.) CLEF 2000. LNCS, vol. 2069, pp. 48–56. Springer, Heidelberg (2001). https://doi.org/10.1007/3-540-44645-1_5

9. Knijnenburg, B.P.: Conducting user experiments in recommender systems. In: Proceedings of the Sixth ACM Conference on Recommender Systems. RecSys 2012, pp. 3–4. Association for Computing Machinery, Dublin, September 2012. https://doi.org/10.1145/2365952.2365956

10. Mayr, P., Scharnhorst, A., Larsen, B., Schaer, P., Mutschke, P.: Bibliometric-enhanced information retrieval. In: de Rijke, M., et al. (eds.) ECIR 2014. LNCS, vol. 8416, pp. 798–801. Springer, Cham (2014). https://doi.org/10.1007/978-3-319-06028-6_99

11. Merkel, D.: Docker: lightweight Linux containers for consistent development and deployment. Linux J. **2014**(239), 2:2 (2014)

12. Schaer, P., Schaible, J., Müller, B.: Living labs for academic search at CLEF 2020. In: Jose, J.M., et al. (eds.) ECIR 2020. LNCS, vol. 12036, pp. 580–586. Springer, Cham (2020). https://doi.org/10.1007/978-3-030-45442-5_75

13. Schaible, J., Breuer, T., Tavakolpoursaleh, N., Müller, B., Wolff, B., Schaer, P.: Evaluation infrastructures for academic shared tasks. Datenbank-Spektrum **20**(1), 29–36 (2020). https://doi.org/10.1007/s13222-020-00335-x

14. USA National Library of Medicine: Medical Subject Headings - Home Page. Thesaurus (2020). https://www.nlm.nih.gov/mesh/meshhome.html

15. Yang, W., Lu, K., Yang, P., Lin, J.: Critically examining the "neural hype": weak baselines and the additivity of effectiveness gains from neural ranking models. In: Proceedings of the 42nd International ACM SIGIR Conference on Research and Development in Information Retrieval - SIGIR 2019, pp. 1129–1132. ACM Press, Paris (2019). https://doi.org/10.1145/3331184.3331340

Overview of PAN 2020: Authorship Verification, Celebrity Profiling, Profiling Fake News Spreaders on Twitter, and Style Change Detection

Janek Bevendorff[1], Bilal Ghanem[2,3], Anastasia Giachanou[3], Mike Kestemont[4], Enrique Manjavacas[4], Ilia Markov[4], Maximilian Mayerl[6], Martin Potthast[5], Francisco Rangel[2], Paolo Rosso[3], Günther Specht[6], Efstathios Stamatatos[7], Benno Stein[1], Matti Wiegmann[1(✉)], and Eva Zangerle[6]

[1] Bauhaus-Universität Weimar, Weimar, Germany
pan@webis.de, matti.wiegmann@uni-weimar.de
[2] Symanto Research, Nuremberg, Germany
[3] Universitat Politècnica de València, Valencia, Spain
[4] University of Antwerp, Antwerp, Belgium
[5] Leipzig University, Leipzig, Germany
[6] University of Innsbruck, Innsbruck, Austria
[7] University of the Aegean, Samos, Greece
http://pan.webis.de

Abstract. We briefly report on the four shared tasks organized as part of the PAN 2020 evaluation lab on digital text forensics and authorship analysis. Each tasks is introduced, motivated, and the results obtained are presented. Altogether, the four tasks attracted 230 registrations, yielding 83 successful submissions. This, and the fact that we continue to invite the submissions of software rather than its run output using the TIRA experimentation platform, marks for a good start into the second decade of PAN evaluations labs.

1 Introduction

The PAN 2020 evaluation lab organized four shared tasks related to authorship analysis, i.e., the analysis of authors based on their writing style. Two of the tasks addressed the profiling of authors with respect to traditional demographics as well as new ones from two perspectives: whether the authors are inclined to spread fake news, and whether the stylometric properties of demographic are also represented in their followers' text. The third task started a new evaluation cycle on authorship verification as the core authorship analysis discipline, starting with closed-set attribution on a significantly improved dataset. The fourth task addressed the important, yet exceedingly difficult task of handling multi-author documents and the detection of style changes within a given text written by more than one author.

© Springer Nature Switzerland AG 2020
A. Arampatzis et al. (Eds.): CLEF 2020, LNCS 12260, pp. 372–383, 2020.
https://doi.org/10.1007/978-3-030-58219-7_25

In this paper, each of the following sections gives a brief, condensed overview of the four aforementioned tasks, including their motivation and the results obtained.

2   Authorship Verification

From the very beginning onward, authorship analysis tasks have played a key role in the PAN series [1]. Many task variations have been devised over the last decade, including the development of the respective corpora for authorship attribution, authorship clustering, and authorship verification, both within and across genres, and within and across languages. This year we opted for a task in the domain of authorship verification, that fits in a renewed three-year strategy, via which we aim to contribute tasks of an increasing difficulty and realism. In this endeavour, special attention will go out to open challenges in the field, such as topical shifts (author-topic orthogonality), text varieties (cross-genre authorship) and limited text length.

2.1   Dataset

This year, two training datasets of different magnitudes ("small" and "large") are provided with text pairs, crawled from fanfiction.net, a sharing platform for fanfiction that comes from various topical domains (or 'fandoms') and with rich, user-contributed metadata [7]. Participants were allowed to submit systems calibrated on either dataset (or both). All texts were heavily preprocessed to avoid textual artifacts [2] and have a length of $\approx 21,000$ characters. To construct the dataset, we bucketed the texts by author and fandom to ensure a good mix of the two and, despite the very uneven popularity of fandoms and activity of authors, prevent gross overrepresentation of individual fandoms and authors. For the large dataset, 148,000 same-author (SA) and 128,000 different-authors (DA) pairs were drawn from the fan fiction crawl. The SA pairs encompass 41,000 authors of which at least 4 and not more than 400 have written in the same fandom (median: 29). In total, 1,600 fandoms were selected and each single author has written in at least 2, but not more than 6 fandoms (median: 2). The pairs were assembled by building all possible $\binom{n}{2}$ pairings of author texts (n being the actual number of texts from this author) without allowing two pairs with the same author *and* fandom. The small training set is a subset of the large training set with 28,000 same-author and 25,000 different-authors pairs from the same 1,600 fandoms, but with a reduced author number of 6,400 (4–68 per fandom, median: 7) and 48,500 (2–63 per fandom, median: 38), respectively. The test dataset contains 10,000 same-author and 6,900 different-authors pairs from 400 fandoms and 3,500/12,000 authors which are guaranteed to exist in the training sets, but either in a different author-fandom relation or in the same author-fandom relation, but with a previously unseen text. This creates a closed-set authorship identification scenario, a condition which will be broken in the next year with unseen fandoms and authors.

Table 1. Evaluation results for authorship verification at PAN-2020 in terms of area under the curve (AUC) of the receiver operating characteristic (ROC), c@1, F0.5u, F1-score and overall score (sorted by overall score). Large stands for training on the large dataset; small stands for training on the small dataset.

Submission	AUC	c@1	F0.5u	F1-score	Overall
boenninghoff20-large	**0.969**	**0.928**	**0.907**	**0.936**	**0.935**
weerasinghe20-large	0.953	0.880	0.882	0.891	0.902
boenninghoff20-small	0.940	0.889	0.853	0.906	0.897
weerasinghe20-small	0.939	0.833	0.817	0.860	0.862
halvani20b-small	0.878	0.796	0.819	0.807	0.825
kipnis20-small	0.866	0.801	0.815	0.809	0.823
araujo20-small	0.874	0.770	0.762	0.811	0.804
niven20	0.795	0.786	0.842	0.778	0.800
gagala20-small	0.786	0.786	0.809	0.800	0.796
araujo20-large	0.859	0.751	0.745	0.800	0.789
baseline (naive)	0.780	0.723	0.716	0.767	0.747
baseline (compression)	0.778	0.719	0.703	0.770	0.742
ordonez20-large	0.696	0.640	0.655	0.748	0.685
faber20-small	0.293	0.331	0.314	0.262	0.300

2.2 Evaluation

Metrics. Because of the considerable size of the data sets, we opted for a combination of 4 evaluation metrics that each focus on different aspects. For each problem (i.e. individual text pair) in the test set, the participating systems submitted a scalar in the [0, 1] range, indicating the probability of this being a SA pair. For a small number of difficult cases, the systems could submit a score of exactly 0.5, which was equivalent to a non-response [9]. The following metrics were used to score the submissions: (1) **AUC**: the conventional area-under-the-curve score, in a reference implementation [10]; (2) **F1-score**: the well-known performance measure (*not* taking into account non-answers), in a reference implementation [10]; (3) **c@1**: a variant of the conventional F1-score, which rewards systems that leave difficult problems unanswered [9]; (4) **F0.5u**: a newly proposed measure that puts more emphasis on deciding same-author cases correctly [3]. The overall score is the mean of the scores of all the evaluation metrics.

Baselines. We applied two baseline systems (calibrated on the small training set). (1) The first method calculates the cosine similarities between TFIDF-normalized tetragram representations of the texts in a pair. The resulting scores are shifted using a grid search on the calibration data (naive, distance-based baseline). (2) Secondly, we applied a text compression method that, given a pair of texts, calculates the cross-entropy of text2 using the Prediction by Partial

Matching model of text1 and vice-versa. The mean and absolute difference of the two cross-entropies are used by a logistic regression model to estimate a score in $[0, 1]$.

2.3 Results

The authorship verification task received submissions from nine participating teams. A detailed evaluation results can be found in Table 1. A pairwise significance comparison of the F1-scores (according to approximate randomization test [15]) is shown in Table 2. The symbolic notation is based on the following thresholds: '=' (not significantly different: $p > 0.5$), '*' (significantly different: $p < 0.05$), '**' (very significantly different: $p < 0.01$), '***' (highly significantly different: $p < 0.001$). These comparisons highlight how, compared to recent editions, the received submissions used a variety of learning approaches and feature extractors. Consequently, the reported scores lie in a wide range.

Table 2. Significance of pairwise differences in output between submissions (using F1-score as the reference metric).

	boenninghoff20-large	weerasinghe20-large	boenninghoff20-small	weerasinghe20-small	halvani20b-small	kipnis20-small	araujo20-small	niven20	gagala20-small	araujo20-large	baseline (naive)	baseline (compression)	ordonez20-large	faber20-small
boenninghoff20-large		***	***	***	***	***	***	***	***	***	***	***	***	***
weerasinghe20-large			***	***	***	***	***	***	***	***	***	***	***	***
boenninghoff20-small				***	***	***	***	***	***	***	***	***	***	***
weerasinghe20-small					***	***	***	***	***	***	***	***	***	***
halvani20b-small						=	=	***	=	=	***	***	***	***
kipnis20-small							***	***	=	=	***	***	***	***
araujo20-small								***	**	***	***	***	***	***
niven20									***	***	***	***	***	***
gagala20-small										=	***	***	***	***
araujo20-large											***	***	***	***
baseline (naive)												=	=	***
baseline (compression)													=	***
ordonez20-large														***

3 Celebrity Profiling

In 2019, we introduced the task of celebrity profiling [17] and organized the first competition on this task [18] with the goal of predicting the demographics age, gender, fame, and occupation of a celebrity from the matching Twitter timeline. For the continuation of the celebrity profiling task at PAN, we utilize the unique position of celebrities highly influential hubs of their communities to explore the idea of distributional author profiling: If the stylometric features of a demographic are consistent within a community, then we can profile an author from the texts of his followers. For this task, we compiled the Twitter timelines of 10 followers for 2,320 celebrities and asked participants to determine age, gender, and occupation of each celebrity by profiling the Tweets of the followers. We received submissions by 3 teams, all beating the baselines and demonstrating with a healthy margin above random that the task can be solved.

3.1 Dataset

We compiled the dataset based on the PAN19 Celebrity Profiling dataset by extracting all celebrities with an annotated birthyear between 1940 and 1999, a binary gender, and an occupation of either sports, performer, creator, politics. We discarded all celebrities with less than 1,000 followers, which left 10,585 complete celebrity profiles. For this initial set of celebrities, we compiled the follower network and collected the timelines of all followers, discarding all followers with less than 10 English tweets excluding retweets, more than 100,000 or less than 10 followers, and more than 1,000 or less than 10 followees, yielding reasonably active and well-connected followers. From the remaining list of followers, we randomly selected 10 followers for each celebrity.

From the selected timelines, we removed retweets and non-English tweets and sampled a 2,320 celebrity dataset that is balanced by occupation and by gender, leaving 8,265 celebrities for an unbalanced, supplemental dataset. We split the 2,320 celebrity dataset roughly 80:20 into a 1,920 author training dataset and a 400 author test dataset test. We handed out the training and supplemental datasets to the participants and kept the test dataset hidden for evaluation on TIRA.

3.2 Evaluation

As in 2019, the decisive performance metric for this task is the harmonic mean of the minor metrics for each demographic:

$$cRank = \frac{3}{\frac{1}{F_{1,age}} + \frac{1}{F_{1,gender}} + \frac{1}{F_{1,occupation}}} \tag{1}$$

The performances of the gender and occupation predictions are evaluated as micro-averaged, multi-class F_1, which is consistent with the 2019 task on celebrity profiling. Since we commit to precisely predicting age instead of bucketing age-groups, the performance of the age predictions is evaluated with a variable-bucket strategy, where the predicted age of an author is correct if it is within an m-window of the truth. The window size m is between 2 and 9 years, increasing linearly with the true age of the author.

We released the results of three baselines at the beginning of the evaluation cycle: (1) the expected random values, (2) baseline-ngram, a logistic regression

Table 3. Overall results for the celebrity profiling task.

Participant	cRank	Age	Gender	Occupation
hodge20	0.577	0.432	0.681	0.707
koloski20	0.521	0.407	0.616	0.597
tuksa20	0.477	0.315	0.696	0.598
baseline-oracle	0.631	0.500	0.753	0.700
baseline-ngram	0.469	0.362	0.584	0.521
expectation	0.333	0.333	0.500	0.250

classifier using tf-idf weighted word 3-grams on the concatenated follower tweets, and (3) baseline-oracle, which is identical to baseline-ngram but uses the celebrities' timelines instead of the follower timelines.

3.3   Results

Table 3 shows the results of the participants with successful submissions as well as the baseline performance. All participants managed to surpass the random expectation and improve on the baseline by a healthy margin. The peak performance of the submitted solutions already closes in on the oracle-baseline, which shows that the followers' texts contain noticeable hints about the demographics of the followee. The details of the submitted solutions are discussed in the overview paper of this task [16].

4   Profiling Fake News Spreaders on Twitter

Although the detection of fake news, and credibility in general, has received a lot of research attention [6], there are only few studies that have addressed the problem from a user or author profiling perspective. For example, Shu et al. [13] analyzed different features, such as registration time, and found that users that share fake news have more recent accounts than users who share real news. Vo and Lee [14] analyzed the linguistic characteristics (e.g., use of tenses, number of pronouns) of fact-checking tweets and proposed a deep learning framework to generate responses with fact-checking intention. Recently, Giachanou et al. [5] employed a model based on a Convolutional Neural Network that combines word embeddings with features that represent users' personality traits and linguistic patterns, to discriminate between fake news spreaders and fact-checkers.

We believe that fact-checkers are likely to have a set of different characteristics compared to fake news spreaders. For example, fact-checkers may use different linguistic patterns when they share posts compared to fake news spreaders. This is what we aim at investigating in this year's author profiling shared task where we address the problem of fake news detection from the author profiling perspective. The final goal is profiling those authors that have shared some fake news in the past. This will allow for identifying possible fake news spreaders on Twitter as a first step towards preventing fake news from being propagated among social media users. This should help for their early detection and, therefore, for preventing their further dissemination.

4.1 Dataset and Evaluation

We built a dataset of fake and real news spreaders, i.e. discriminating authors that have shared some fake news in the past from those that, to the best of our knowledge, have never done it. Table 4 presents the statistics of the dataset that consists of 500 authors for each of the two languages, English and Spanish. For each author, we retrieved via the Twitter API her last 100 Tweets. The dataset for each language is balanced, with 250 authors for each class (fake and real news spreaders).

Therefore, the performance of the systems has been ranked by accuracy. For each language, we calculated individual accuracy in discriminating between the two classes. Finally, we averaged the accuracy values per language to obtain the final ranking.

Table 4. Number of authors in the PAN-AP-20 dataset created for this task.

Language	Training	Test	Total
English	300	200	500
Spanish	300	200	500

4.2 Results

We represent each author in the dataset by concatenating her tweets into one document and then we feed this document to the models.

In total 66 teams participated in this year's author profiling task on profiling fake news spreaders on Twitter (record in terms of participants at PAN Lab). In Table 5 we present the results in terms of accuracy of the teams that participated in both languages and the results of the teams that addressed the problem only in English.

As baselines to compare the performance of the participants with, we have selected: (1) an LSTM that uses fastText[1] embeddings to represent texts; (2) a Neural Network (NN) with word n-grams (size 1–3) and (3) a Support Vector Machine (SVM) with char n-grams (size 2–6); (4) an SVM with Low Dimensionality Statistical Embeddings (LDSE) [12] to represent texts; (5) the Emotionally-Infused Neural (EIN) network [4] with word embedding and emotional features as the input of an LSTM, and (6) a Random prediction.

The description of the models of the participating teams and the detailed analysis of the results are presented in the shared task overview paper [11].

---

[1] https://fasttext.cc/docs/en/crawl-vectors.html.

Table 5. Overall accuracy of the submission to the task on profiling fake news spreaders on Twitter: The teams that participated in both languages (English and Spanish) are ranked by the average accuracy between both languages, teams that participated only in English (bottom right) are ranked by the accuracy on English. The best results for each language are printed in bold.

	Participant	En	Es	Avg
1	bolonyai20	**0.750**	0.805	0.7775
1	pizarro20	0.735	**0.820**	0.7775
	SYMANTO (LDSE)	*0.745*	*0.790*	*0.7675*
3	koloski20	0.715	0.795	0.7550
3	deborjavalero20	0.730	0.780	0.7550
3	vogel20	0.725	0.785	0.7550
6	higueraporras20	0.725	0.775	0.7500
6	tarela20	0.725	0.775	0.7500
8	babaei20	0.725	0.765	0.7450
9	staykovski20	0.705	0.775	0.7400
9	hashemi20	0.695	0.785	0.7400
11	estevecasademunt20	0.710	0.765	0.7375
	SVM + c nGrams	*0.680*	*0.790*	*0.7350*
12	castellanospellecer20	0.710	0.760	0.7350
13	shrestha20	0.710	0.755	0.7325
13	tommasel20	0.690	0.775	0.7325
15	johansson20	0.720	0.735	0.7275
15	murauer20	0.685	0.770	0.7275
17	espinosagonzales20	0.690	0.760	0.7250
17	ikae20	0.725	0.725	0.7250
19	morenosandoval20	0.715	0.730	0.7225
20	majumder20	0.640	0.800	0.7200
20	sanchezromero20	0.685	0.755	0.7200
22	lopezchilet20	0.680	0.755	0.7175
22	nadalalmela20	0.680	0.755	0.7175
22	carrodve20	0.710	0.725	0.7175
25	gil20	0.695	0.735	0.7150
26	elexpuruortiz20	0.680	0.745	0.7125
26	labadietamayo20	0.705	0.720	0.7125
28	grafiaperez20	0.675	0.745	0.7100
28	jilka20	0.665	0.755	0.7100
28	lopezfernandez20	0.685	0.735	0.7100
31	pinnaparaju20	0.715	0.700	0.7075
31	aguirrezabal20	0.690	0.725	0.7075
33	kengyi20	0.655	0.755	0.7050
33	gowda20	0.675	0.735	0.7050
33	jakers20	0.675	0.735	0.7050
33	cosin20	0.705	0.705	0.7050

	Participant	En	Es	Avg
37	navarromartinez20	0.660	0.745	0.7025
38	heilmann20	0.655	0.745	0.700
39	cardaioli20	0.675	0.715	0.6950
39	females20	0.605	0.785	0.6950
	NN + w nGrams	*0.690*	*0.700*	*0.6950*
41	kaushikamardas20	0.700	0.690	0.6950
42	monteroceballos20	0.630	0.745	0.6875
43	ogaltsov20	0.695	0.665	0.6800
44	botticebria20	0.625	0.720	0.6725
45	lichouri20	0.585	0.760	0.6725
46	manna20	0.595	0.725	0.6600
47	fersini20	0.600	0.715	0.6575
48	jardon20	0.545	0.750	0.6475
	EIN	*0.640*	*0.640*	*0.6400*
49	shashirekha20	0.620	0.645	0.6325
50	datatontos20	0.725	0.530	0.6275
51	soleramo20	0.610	0.615	0.6125
	LSTM	*0.560*	*0.600*	*0.5800*
52	russo20	0.580	0.515	0.5475
53	igualadamoraga20	0.525	0.505	0.5150
	RANDOM	*0.510*	*0.500*	*0.5050*

	Participant	En
54	hoertenhuemer20	0.725
55	duan20	0.720
55	andmangenix20	0.720
57	saeed20	0.700
58	baruah20	0.690
59	anthonio20	0.685
60	zhang20	0.670
61	espinosaruiz20	0.665
62	shen20	0.650
63	suareztrashorras20	0.640
64	niven20	0.610
65	margoes20	0.570
66	wu20	0.560

5   Style Change Detection

In previous editions, the style change detection task aimed at detecting whether a document is single- or multi-authored [20] or predicting the actual number of authors within a document [8]. Considering the promising results achieved in the last years, we steer the task back to its original goal: detecting the exact position of authorship changes. Therefore, the goal is to determine whether the given document contains style changes and if it indeed does, we aim to find the position of the change in the document (between paragraphs). For each pair of consecutive paragraphs of a document, we ask participants to estimate whether there is indeed a style change between those two paragraphs. Consequently, we ask participants to answer the following two questions for a given document:

(1) Task 1: Was the given document written by multiple authors? (2) Task 2: For each pair of consecutive paragraphs in the given document: is there a style change between these paragraphs?

5.1   Dataset

For this year's style change detection task, we prepared two datasets. Both datasets were extracted from the StackExchange network of Q&A sites; nonetheless, they differ in the number and topical variety of sites included in the dataset. The first dataset, *dataset-narrow*, includes texts from StackExchange sites dealing with topics related to computer technology. The second dataset, *dataset-wide*, includes texts from a broader and larger selection of StackExchange sites, and therefore covers a broader range of topics. The goal behind using those two different datasets was to see how the topical range of texts impacts the performance of the submitted approaches.

Aside from the specific sites that were included, both datasets were generated in the same way. We used a dump of questions and answers on the StackExchange network as our data source, which we cleaned by removing questions and answers that contain fewer than 30 characters, or that were edited by a different user than the original author. We also removed images, URLs, code snippets, blockquotes, and bullet lists from all questions and answers. We then took all the questions and answers written by the same user and split them into paragraphs, dropping all paragraphs with fewer than 100 characters. This gave us a list of paragraphs for every user on a single StackExchange site. We constructed documents by drawing paragraphs from those lists. We generated an equal number of single-author and multi-author documents for our datasets. For single-author documents, the paragraphs making up the document are drawn from the paragraph list of a single user of a single StackExchange site. For multi-author documents, we combine paragraphs from the paragraph lists of two or three users, in a way that leads to the author changing between paragraphs between one and ten times for a single document; again, combining only paragraphs of the same StackExchange site. A more detailed description of the dataset generation can be found in the task overview.

Both datasets were then split into training, validation, and test sets, with 50% of the documents going into the training set and 25% each going into the validation and test set. Table 6 summarizes the properties of the documents in our datasets, and the exact composition of both the narrow and the wide dataset, showing the number of documents written by one, two, and three authors in the training, validation, and test sets of both.

Table 6. Left. Properties for the documents in the style change detection datasets. **Right.** Overview of the datasets, listing the number of documents per dataset (narrow and wide) for the training, validation, and test sets split by the number of authors per document.

Parameter	Configurations
Number of collaborators	1–3
Number of style changes	0–10
Document length	1,000–3,000
Change positions	Between paragraphs
Document language	English

Dataset	Training Set			Validation Set			Test Set		
	1	2	3	1	2	3	1	2	3
narrow	1,709	854	855	855	415	443	852	426	423
wide	4,025	1,990	2,015	2,018	969	1032	2,014	987	1,004

5.2   Evaluation

For the comparison of the submitted approaches, we report both the achieved performances for the subtasks in isolation and their combination as a staged task. Furthermore, we evaluate the approaches on both datasets individually.

Submissions are evaluated by the F_α-Measure for each document, where we set α to 1. For task 1, we compute the average F_1 measure across all documents, and for task 2, we use the micro-averaged F_1 measure across all documents. The submissions for the two datasets are evaluated independently and the resulting F_1 measures for the two tasks will be averaged across the two datasets.

5.3   Results

The style change detection task received three software submissions, which were evaluated on the TIRA experimentation platform. Table 7 depicts the results of the individual submissions for both tasks independently and the average of the two task results per participant. We also include a random baseline, which predicts a document being single- vs multi-authored as well as author changes occurring between every two paragraphs at random, with equal probabilities. As can be seen, iyer20 achieved the highest scores in both tasks, whereas the other two participants achieved comparable results in both tasks. Every approach managed to beat the baseline on both tasks, with the differences between the baseline and the participants' approaches being particularly noteworthy for task 2. More details on the approaches taken can be found in the task overview paper [19].

Table 7. Overall results for the style change detection task ranked by average F_1.

Participant	Task1 F_1	Task2 F_1	Avg. F_1
iyer20	0.6401	0.8567	0.7484
castro20	0.5399	0.7579	0.6489
nath20	0.5204	0.7526	0.6365
baseline (random)	0.5007	0.5001	0.5004

6   Summary and Outlook

Despite the generally bleak circumstances, this year's PAN lab has succeeded in both retaining the core community and in expanding beyond it. Although we had far fewer registrations than in 2019, we managed to increase the turnout and thus the number of submissions from 72 last year to 81 in 2020. The increasing participation can mostly be attributed to the tireless effort of PAN's largest task with 64 participants, Profiling Fake News Spreaders on Twitter, while the other recurring tasks addressed their core community and retained consistent participation.

Going into PAN 2020, we continued to tackle long-standing authorship issues and scrutinize societal problems through the lens of stylometry, improved our datasets, and re-invented our task design. As a larger innovation, we experimented with the design of evaluation episodes as multi-year series of shared tasks on difficult problems: At the start of this years' evaluation cycle we announced the future questions for some tasks two years in advance, not only to provide necessary context but to create the stability needed for participants to invest in difficult challenges. Besides positive feedback from the community, we already noticed significant improvements in the quality of the submitted approaches and aim to expand this strategy to our other tasks and nurture the idea of organizing evaluation episodes over mere evaluation cycles.

Acknowledgments. We thank Symanto for sponsoring the ex aequo award for the two best performing systems at the author profiling shared task of this year on Profiling fake news spreaders on Twitter. The work of Paolo Rosso was partially funded by the Spanish MICINN under the research project MISMIS-FAKEnHATE on Misinformation and Miscommunication in social media: FAKE news and HATE speech (PGC2018–096212-B-C31). The work of Anastasia Giachanou is supported by the SNSF Early Postdoc Mobility grant under the project Early Fake News Detection on Social Media, Switzerland (P2TIP2_181441).

References

1. Bevendorff, J., et al.: Shared tasks on authorship analysis at PAN 2020. In: Jose, J.M., et al. (eds.) ECIR 2020. LNCS, vol. 12036, pp. 508–516. Springer, Cham (2020). https://doi.org/10.1007/978-3-030-45442-5_66
2. Bevendorff, J., Stein, B., Hagen, M., Potthast, M.: Bias analysis and mitigation in the evaluation of authorship verification. In: 57th Annual Meeting of the Association for Computational Linguistics (ACL), pp. 6301–6306 (2019)
3. Bevendorff, J., Stein, B., Hagen, M., Potthast, M.: Generalizing unmasking for short texts. In: Proceedings of the 2019 Conference of the North American Chapter of the Association for Computational Linguistics: Human Language Technologies, NAACL-HLT, pp. 654–659 (2019)
4. Ghanem, B., Rosso, P., Rangel, F.: An emotional analysis of false information in social media and news articles. ACM Trans. Internet Technol. (TOIT) **20**(2), 1–18 (2020)

5. Giachanou, A., Ríssola, E.A., Ghanem, B., Crestani, F., Rosso, Paolo: The role of personality and linguistic patterns in discriminating between fake news spreaders and fact checkers. In: Métais, E., Meziane, F., Horacek, H., Cimiano, P. (eds.) NLDB 2020. LNCS, vol. 12089, pp. 181–192. Springer, Cham (2020). https://doi.org/10.1007/978-3-030-51310-8_17

6. Giachanou, A., Rosso, P., Crestani, F.: Leveraging emotional signals for credibility detection. In: Proceedings of the 42nd International ACM SIGIR Conference on Research and Development in Information Retrieval, pp. 877–880 (2019)

7. Kestemont, M., Stamatatos, E., Manjavacas, E., Daelemans, W., Potthast, M., Stein, B.: Overview of the cross-domain authorship attribution task at PAN 2019. In: Working Notes Papers of the CLEF 2019 Evaluation Labs. CEUR Workshop Proceedings (2019)

8. Kestemont, M., et al.: Overview of the author identification task at PAN-2018: cross-domain authorship attribution and style change detection. In: Working Notes Papers of the CLEF 2018 Evaluation Labs. CEUR Workshop Proceedings (2018)

9. Peñas, A., Rodrigo, A.: A simple measure to assess non-response. In: Proceedings of the 49th Annual Meeting of the Association for Computational Linguistics: Human Language Technologies (2011)

10. Pedregosa, F., et al.: Scikit-learn: machine learning in Python. J. Mach. Learn. Res. **12**, 2825–2830 (2011)

11. Rangel, F., Giachanou, A., Ghanem, B., Rosso, P.: Overview of the 8th author profiling task at PAN 2020: profiling fake news spreaders on Twitter. In: CLEF 2020 Labs and Workshops, Notebook Papers (2020)

12. Rangel, F., Franco-Salvador, M., Rosso, P.: A low dimensionality representation for language variety identification. In: Gelbukh, A. (ed.) CICLing 2016. LNCS, vol. 9624, pp. 156–169. Springer, Cham (2018). https://doi.org/10.1007/978-3-319-75487-1_13

13. Shu, K., Wang, S., Liu, H.: Understanding user profiles on social media for fake news detection. In: 2018 IEEE Conference on Multimedia Information Processing and Retrieval (MIPR), pp. 430–435 (2018)

14. Vo, N., Lee, K.: Learning from fact-checkers: analysis and generation of fact-checking language. In: Proceedings of the 42nd International ACM SIGIR Conference on Research and Development in Information Retrieval (2019)

15. Noreen, E.W.: Computer-Intensive Methods for Testing Hypotheses: An Introduction. A Wiley-Interscience Publication, Hoboken (1989)

16. Wiegmann, M., Potthast, M., Stein, B.: Overview of the celebrity profiling task at PAN 2020. In: CLEF 2020 Labs and Workshops, Notebook Papers (2020)

17. Wiegmann, M., Stein, B., Potthast, M.: Celebrity profiling. In: 57th Annual Meeting of the Association for Computational Linguistics (ACL 2019). Association for Computational Linguistics (2019)

18. Wiegmann, M., Stein, B., Potthast, M.: Overview of the celebrity profiling task at PAN 2019. In: CLEF 2019 Labs and Workshops, Notebook Papers (2019)

19. Zangerle, E., Mayerl, M., Specht, G., Potthast, M., Stein, B.: Overview of the style change detection task at PAN 2020. In: CLEF 2020 Labs and Workshops, Notebook Papers (2020)

20. Zangerle, E., Tschuggnall, M., Specht, G., Potthast, M., Stein, B.: Overview of the style change detection task at PAN 2019. In: CLEF 2019 Labs and Workshops, Notebook Papers (2019)

Overview of Touché 2020: Argument Retrieval
Extended Abstract

Alexander Bondarenko[1(✉)], Maik Fröbe[1], Meriem Beloucif[2], Lukas Gienapp[3],
Yamen Ajjour[1], Alexander Panchenko[6], Chris Biemann[2], Benno Stein[4],
Henning Wachsmuth[5], Martin Potthast[3], and Matthias Hagen[1]

[1] Martin-Luther-Universität Halle-Wittenberg, Halle, Germany
`alexander.bondarenko@informatik.uni-halle.de`
[2] Universität Hamburg, Hamburg, Germany
[3] Universität Leipzig, Leipzig, Germany
[4] Bauhaus-Universität Weimar, Weimar, Germany
[5] Paderborn University, Paderborn, Germany
[6] Skolkovo Institute of Science and Technology, Moscow, Russia
`https://touche.webis.de`

Abstract. This paper is a condensed report on Touché: the first shared task on argument retrieval that was held at CLEF 2020. With the goal to create a collaborative platform for research in argument retrieval, we run two tasks: (1) supporting individuals in finding arguments on socially important topics and (2) supporting individuals with arguments on everyday personal decisions.

1 Introduction

Decision making and opinion formation processes are kind of routine tasks for many of us. Often, such opinion formation relates to a decision between two sides based on previous experience and knowledge, but it may also require accumulating new knowledge. With the wide-spread access to any kind of information on the web, everyone theoretically has the chance to acquire new knowledge and to form an informed opinion about any topic. In the process, be it on the level of socially important topics or "just" personal decisions, one of the at least two sides (i.e., decision options) will challenge the other with an appeal to justify its stance. In the simplest form, a justification might be simple facts or opinions, but more complex justifications often are based on argumentation: a complex relational aggregation of evidence and opinions, where one element is supported by the other.

Web resources such as blogs, community question answering websites, or social platforms contain an immense variety of opinions and argumentative

Copyright © 2020 for this paper by its authors. Use permitted under Creative Commons License Attribution 4.0 International (CC BY 4.0). CLEF 2020, 22–25 September 2020, Thessaloniki, Greece.

© Springer Nature Switzerland AG 2020
A. Arampatzis et al. (Eds.): CLEF 2020, LNCS 12260, pp. 384–395, 2020.
https://doi.org/10.1007/978-3-030-58219-7_26

texts—including many of biased, faked, or populist nature—which has motivated research on the development of high-quality argument retrieval. While standard web search engines support the retrieval of factual information fairly well, they hardly address the retrieval of argumentative texts specifically, let alone the retrieval and ranking of individual arguments or opinions. In contrast, the argument search engine args.me [29] was developed to retrieve relevant arguments to a given controversial query. So far, however, it is limited to the document collections crawled from a few debating web portals. Other argument retrieval systems such as ArgumenText [26] and TARGER [8] take advantage of the large web document collection Common Crawl, but their ability to reliably retrieve arguments to support sides in a decision process is limited. The comparative argumentation machine CAM [25], a system for argument retrieval in comparative search, tries to support decision making in comparison scenarios based on billions of sentences from the Common Crawl but still lacks a proper ranking of diverse arguments.

To foster the research on a better support of argument retrieval, we organize the Touché lab at CLEF 2020—the first lab on argument retrieval [7].[1] The lab is a collaborative platform to develop retrieval approaches for decision support on a societal (e.g., "Is climate change real and what to do?") and personal level (e.g., "Should I buy real estate or rent, and why?") featuring two tasks:

1. Argument retrieval from a focused debate collection to support conversations by providing justifications for claims on socially important and controversial topics.
2. Argument retrieval from a generic web crawl to answer comparative questions with argumentative results and to support personal decision making.

Research on argument retrieval approaches will not only allow search engines to deliver more argumentative results for argumentative information needs (e.g., decision making in complex comparative search scenarios), but it will also be an important part of open-domain conversational agents that "discuss" controversial societal topics with humans—as showcased by IBM's Project Debater [3,17].[2]

2 Previous Work

The input for argument retrieval can be a controversial topic, a question that compares two entities, or even a complete argument [31]. In the Touché lab, we address the first two types of information needs in two different shared tasks. Here, we summarize related work for both tasks.

---

[1] The name of the lab is inspired by the usage of the term "touché" as an exclamation "used to admit that someone has made a good point against you in an argument or discussion." [https://dictionary.cambridge.org/dictionary/english/touche].

[2] https://www.research.ibm.com/artificial-intelligence/project-debater/.

2.1 Argument Retrieval

Argument retrieval aims for delivering arguments to support users in taking a decision or persuading an audience with a specific point of view. An argument is usually modeled as a conclusion with supporting or attacking premises [29]. While a conclusion is a statement that can be accepted or rejected, a premise is a more grounded statement, e.g., a statistical evidence. The development of an argument search engine is faced with challenges that range from mining arguments from unstructured text to assessing their relevance and quality [29]. Argument retrieval follows several paradigms that start from different sources and perform argument mining and retrieval tasks in different orders [1]. Wachsmuth et al. [29], e.g., extract arguments offline using heuristics that are tailored for online debate portals. The argument search engine args.me uses BM25F to rank arguments while giving conclusions more weight than premises. Levy et al. [15] uses distant-supervision to mine arguments offline for a set of topics from Wikipedia before ranking them. Stab et al. [26] retrieve documents from the Common Crawl[3] and then use a topic-dependent neural network to extract arguments from the retrieved documents. The two tasks in the Touché lab address the paradigms of Wachsmuth et al. [29] and Stab et al. [26] respectively.

Apart from its relevance to a topic, argument retrieval should rank arguments according to their quality. What makes a good argument has been studied since the time of Aristotle [2]. Recently, Wachsmuth et al. [28] categorized the different aspects of argument quality into a taxonomy that covers three dimensions: logic, rhetoric, and dialectic. Logic concerns the local structure of an argument, i.e, the conclusion and the premises and their relations. Rhetoric covers the effectiveness of the argument in persuading an audience with its conclusion. Dialectic addresses the relations of an argument to other arguments on the topic. For example, many attacking arguments make the argument vulnerable in a debate. The relevance of an argument to an input topic is categorized by Wachsmuth et al. [28] under dialectic quality. Researchers assess argument relevance by measuring its similarity to an input topic or incorporating its support/attack relations to other arguments. Potthast et al. [22] evaluate four standard retrieval models at ranking 437 arguments with regard to their quality. For argument quality, the researchers adopt three dimensions from Wachsmuth et al. [28]: logic, rhetoric, and dialectic. One of the main findings is that DirchletDM is better than BM25, DPH, and TF-IDF at ranking arguments. Gienapp et al. [10] extend this work by crowdsourcing a corpus of 1,271 arguments that are annotated in a pair-wise fashion with the same quality dimensions. The paper proposes a strategy that reduces costs by 93% by annotating only a subset of argument pairs. Wachsmuth et al. [30] create a graph of arguments by connecting two arguments if an argument uses another's conclusion as a premise. Later on, they exploit this structure to rank the arguments in the graph using PageRank [19]. This method is shown to outperform several

---

[3] http://commoncrawl.org.

baselines that utilize the content of the argument and its local structure (conclusion and premises). Dumani et al. [9] introduce a probabilistic framework that operates on semantically similar claims and premises. The framework utilizes the support/attack relations between the premises and claims clusters and the claims clusters and a query. The proposed framework is found to outperform BM25 in ranking arguments.

2.2 Comparative Argument Retrieval

User comparative information need was originally addressed in web search with the proposed simplistic interface, where the two compared objects would be separately typed in the search boxes on the left and right sides of the web interface [18,27]. Additionally, opinion mining research has dealt with the identification of comparative sentences and mining the user opinion (in favor or not) towards one or the other compared object in product reviews using Class Sequential Rule and SVM [12–14]. Recently, identification of the comparison preference ("winning" object) in comparative sentences has been addressed in open domain (not just product reviews) by applying feature-based and neural classifiers [16,21]. This preference classification formed the basis of the comparative argumentation machine CAM [25], which is able to accept two compared objects and a comparison aspect as input, retrieves comparative sentences in favor of one or the other object using BM25, and clusters them in the for/against table to present to the user, but still lacks a proper ranking of diverse arguments.

3   Touché Task 1: Conversational Argument Retrieval

The goal of the Touché lab's first task is to provide assistance to users searching for good and relevant pro and con arguments on various societal topics (climate change, electric cars, etc.) while, for instance, being engaged in an argumentative conversation. A respective retrieval system may aid users in collecting evidence on issues of general societal interest and support them in forming their own opinion.

Several existing community question answering websites like Yahoo! Answers and Quora and also debating portals like debatewise.org or idebate.org are designed to accumulate opinions and arguments and to engage users in dialogues. General web search engines lack an effective solution to retrieve relevant arguments from these and other platforms beyond, for instance, simply returning complete longer threads. One reason probably is that the argumentative nature of the underlying discussions is ignored which results in general web search engines not really offering sufficient support during conversations or debates. This motivates the development of robust and effective approaches specifically focused on conversational argument retrieval.

3.1 Task Definition

The participants of Task 1 were asked to retrieve relevant arguments from a focused crawl of online debate portals for a given query on a controversial topic. Given the amount of argumentative texts readily available on online debate platforms, instead of extracting argumentative passages from unstructured text, the participants should build systems that retrieve items from a provided large collection of arguments covering a wide range of popular debate topics. For easy access to the document collection, we provided the openly accessible and flexible API of args.me,[4] also allowing participants to participate in the lab without having to index the collection on their end.

3.2 Data Description

Retrieval Topics. We have formulated 50 search scenarios on controversial issues in the form of TREC-style topics with a title (the query potentially issued by a user), a description (a short summary of the search context and information need), and a narrative (a definition of what constitutes relevant results for this topic, serving as a guideline for human assessors). An example topic is shown in Table 1. As topics, we selected those issues that have the largest number of user-generated comments on the debate portals, and thus probably having a high societal interest. Further, we ensured that relevant items for each topic are present in the provided document collection.

Table 1. Example topic for task 1: conversational argument retrieval

Number	21
Title	Is human activity primarily responsible for global climate change?
Description	As the evidence that the climate is changing rapidly mounts, a user questions the common belief that climate change is anthropogenic and desires to know whether humans are the primary cause, or whether there are other causes
Narrative	Highly relevant arguments include those that take a stance in favor of or opposed to climate change being anthropogenic and that offer valid reasons for either stance. Relevant arguments talk about human or non-human causes, but not about primary causes. Irrelevant arguments include ones that deny climate change

---

[4] https://www.args.me/api-en.html.

Document Collection. Task 1 is based on the args.me corpus [1] that is freely available for download[5] and also accessible via the mentioned args.me API. The corpus contains about 400,000 arguments crawled from four online debate portals: debatewise.org, idebate.org, debatepedia.org, and debate.org. Each argument in the corpus consists of a conclusion (claim) and one or more premises (reasons) supporting the conclusion.

3.3   Task Evaluation

In the first edition of the lab, we evaluate only the *relevance* of the retrieved documents (not the quality of the comprised arguments), given that the collection of manual judgments is a rather complex and time-consuming task. We collected the participants' results as classical TREC-style runs where, for each topic, the document IDs are returned in a ranked list ordered by descending relevance (i.e., the most relevant document should occur at Rank 1). The document pools for judgments were created with the TrecTools Python library [20][6] using a top-5 pooling strategy that resulted in 5,291 unique retrieval results to be judged.

The relevance judgments were collected on Amazon Mechanical Turk following previously designed annotation guidelines [10,22]. We tasked the crowd workers to decide whether or not a given retrieved text is an argument, and to annotate the relevance of the item on a scale ranging from 1 (low relevance) to 5 (high relevance). Non-arguments were subsequently marked as spam and received a score of −2. Each retrieval result was separately annotated by five crowd workers, using majority vote as a decision rule. To further ensure the annotation quality, we recruited only workers for the task with an approval rate of at least 95%, and checked for occurrences of systematic spam.

We will evaluate the participants' approaches using nDCG [11] on the graded relevance judgments, and we will summarize the submitted approaches and report their results in the forthcoming complete lab overview [6].

4   Touché Task 2: Comparative Argument Retrieval

The goal of the Touché lab's second task is to support individuals' personal decisions in everyday life that can be expressed as a comparative information need ("Is X better than Y with respect to Z?") and that do not have a single "correct" answer. Such questions can, for instance, be found on community question answering (CQA) websites like Yahoo! Answers or Quora, or in discussions on Reddit, but are also submitted as queries to search engines. The search engines then often simply show content from CQA websites or some web document mentioning the query terms as a direct answer above the classic "ten blue links". However, a problem of such attempts at short direct answers is that CQA websites may not always provide a diverse and sufficient overview of all

---

[5] https://webis.de/data/args-me-corpus.html.
[6] https://pypi.org/project/trectools/.

Table 2. Example topic for task 2: comparative argument retrieval

Number	16
Title	Should I buy or rent?
Description	A person is planning to move out from their current small flat to start a family. Hoping that the new family will stay together in the new place for some longer time, the person is considering to even buy a new home and not just to rent it. However, this is kind of an important decision with many different angles to be considered: financial situation, the duties coming with owning a flat/house, potential happiness living in a property owned by someone else without any further (financial) responsibilities when major redos are needed, etc
Narrative	Highly relevant documents contain various pros and cons for buying or renting a home. Particularly interesting could be checklists of what to favor in what situations. Documents containing definitions and "smaller" comparisons of buying or renting a property are relevant. Documents without any personal opinion/recommendation or pros/cons are not relevant

possible options with well-formulated arguments, nor will all underlying textual information be credible—a broader set of such issues recently was named as the dilemma of direct answers [24]. As a first step to work on technology to present several credible arguments and different angles in a search engine's potential direct comparative answers, we propose Task 2 on web-based comparative argument retrieval.

4.1 Task Definition

The participants of Task 2 were asked to retrieve and rank documents from the ClueWeb12[7] that help to answer a comparative question. Ideally, the retrieved documents contain convincing arguments for or against some of the possible options for a given comparison. Similar to Task 1, participation was possible without indexing the document collection on the participants' side since we provide easy access to the document collection through the BM25F-based ChatNoir search engine [4]—via a web-interface[8] and an API.[9] To identify arguments in texts, the participants were not restricted to any system; they could use own technology or any existing argument tagger of their choice. To lower the entry barriers for participants new to argument mining, we offered support for using the neural TARGER argument tagger [8] hosted on our own servers.

---

[7] https://lemurproject.org/clueweb12/.
[8] https://www.chatnoir.eu/.
[9] https://www.chatnoir.eu/doc/.

4.2 Data Description

Retrieval Topics. We selected 50 comparative questions from questions submitted to commercial search engines [5] or asked on question answering platforms, each covering some personal decision from everyday life. For every question, we have formulated a respective TREC-style topic with the question as the title, a description of the searcher's possible context and information need, and a narrative describing what makes a result relevant (i.e., serving as a guideline for human assessors). An example topic is shown in Table 2. For each topic, we ensured that relevant documents are present in the ClueWeb12.

Document Collection. Task 2 is based on the ClueWeb12 document collection (See footnote 7). crawled by the Language Technologies Institute at Carnegie Mellon University between February and May 2012 (733 million English web pages; 27.3 TB uncompressed). Participants of Task 2 could index the ClueWeb12 on their own or could use the Elasticsearch-based ChatNoir API for a BM25F-based baseline retrieval.

4.3 Task Evaluation

Similar to Task 1, in the first edition of the lab, we evaluate only the relevance of the retrieved documents using a top-5 pooling strategy of the submitted participants' runs that resulted in 1,374 unique documents to be judged.

For the relevance judgments, we internally recruited seven grad and undergrad student volunteers, all with computer science background. We used a κ-test of five documents from five topics to "calibrate" the annotators' interpretations of the guidelines (i.e., the topics including the narratives) in follow-up discussions among the annotators. After the κ-test, the annotators judged disjoint subsets of the topics (each topic judged by one annotator only) and assigned one of three labels to a document: 0 (not relevant), 1 (relevant), or 2 (highly relevant).

We will evaluate the participants' approaches using nDCG [11] on the graded relevance judgments, and we will summarize the submitted approaches and report their results in the forthcoming complete lab overview [6].

5 Lab Overview and Statistics

A total of 28 teams registered, with a majority coming from Germany but also teams from the US, Europe, and Asia (17 from Germany, 2 from France, 2 from India, and 1 each from China, Italy, the Netherlands, Pakistan, Russia, Switzerland, and the US). As part of the registration, we asked the participants to choose as their team name a real or fictional fencer or swordsman character (e.g., Zorro)—aligned with the lab's fencing-related title.

From the 28 registered teams, 20 did submit results. To improve the reproducibility of the developed approaches, we asked the participants to use the TIRA platform [23] to also submit running software of their approaches. TIRA is an integrated cloud-based evaluation-as-a-service research architecture in which the participants have full administrative access to a virtual machine. By default, the virtual machines operate Ubuntu 18.04 with one CPU (Intel Xeon E5-2620), 4 GB of RAM, and 16 GB HDD, but we adjusted the resources to the participants' requirements when needed (e.g., one team asked for 24 GB of RAM, 5 CPUs, and 30 GB of HDD). Each virtual machine has standard software preinstalled (e.g., Docker and Python) to simplify the deployment of participants' approaches. After the deployment of an approach, the participants can create result submissions via the web UI of TIRA.

As an alternative to software submissions, we also allowed traditional run submissions but this option was only taken by 2 out of the 20 teams who submitted results. To allow a wide diversity of different approaches, we encouraged the teams to provide multiple solutions—asking the participants to prioritize runs/softwares when more than one was submitted. The runs needed to follow the standard TREC-style format.[10] Upon submission, we checked the validity and asked the participants to re-submit in case of problems, also offering our assistance. This resulted in 42 valid runs from 18 teams. From every team, the 5 runs with the highest priorities were used for the assessment pools.

To increase the reproducibility of participants' software submissions, TIRA follows a standard pipeline. To create a run submission from a participating team's software, the respective virtual machine is shut down, disconnected from the internet, powered on, and the datasets for the respective task are mounted in a sandbox mode. The interruption of the internet connection ensures that the participants' software works without external web services that may disappear or get incompatible in the future, which could reduce the reproducibility. However, we enabled two exceptions from the interruption of the internet connection for all participants: the APIs of ChatNoir and args.me were available, even in the sandbox mode. Additionally, we allowed external web services based on the participants' requirements, but only one team additionally asked to access the web of Trust API.[11] We will archive all the virtual machines that participants have used to make submissions to the Touché lab. This way, all submitted pieces of software can be re-evaluated or applied to new datasets as long as the APIs of the used web services remain available.

6   Summary and Outlook

In this paper, we have briefly reported on the Touché lab at CLEF 2020—the first shared task on argument retrieval. Touché features two tasks: (1) conversational argument retrieval to support argumentation on socially important problems in dialogue or debate scenarios, and (2) comparative argument retrieval to support decision making on a personal level. From 28 registered teams, 18 submitted at least one valid run. The respective evaluation results and an overview of the developed approaches will be part of the forthcoming complete lab overview [6].

---

[10] Also described on the lab website: https://touche.webis.de.
[11] https://www.mywot.com/developers.

For the next iteration of the Touché lab, we plan to have deeper judgment pools and to also evaluate an argument's quality dimensions like logical cogency or strength of support.

Acknowledgments. This work was supported by the DFG through the project "ACQuA: Answering Comparative Questions with Arguments" (grants BI 1544/7-1 and HA 5851/2-1) as part of the priority program "RATIO: Robust Argumentation Machines" (SPP 1999).

References

1. Ajjour, Y., Wachsmuth, H., Kiesel, J., Potthast, M., Hagen, M., Stein, B.: Data acquisition for argument search: the args.me corpus. In: Benzmüller, C., Stuckenschmidt, H. (eds.) KI 2019. LNCS (LNAI), vol. 11793, pp. 48–59. Springer, Cham (2019). https://doi.org/10.1007/978-3-030-30179-8_4
2. Kennedy, G.A.: Aristotle On Rhetoric: A Theory of Civic Discourse. Oxford University Press, Oxford (2006)
3. Bar-Haim, R., et al.: From surrogacy to adoption; from bitcoin to cryptocurrency: debate topic expansion. In: Proceedings of the 57th Conference of the Association for Computational Linguistics, ACL 2019, pp. 977–990. Association for Computational Linguistics (2019). https://doi.org/10.18653/v1/p19-1094
4. Bevendorff, J., Stein, B., Hagen, M., Potthast, M.: Elastic ChatNoir: search engine for the ClueWeb and the common crawl. In: Pasi, G., Piwowarski, B., Azzopardi, L., Hanbury, A. (eds.) ECIR 2018. LNCS, vol. 10772, pp. 820–824. Springer, Cham (2018). https://doi.org/10.1007/978-3-319-76941-7_83
5. Bondarenko, A., et al.: Comparative web search questions. In: Proceedings of the 13th International Conference on Web Search and Data Mining, WSDM 2020, pp. 52–60. ACM (2020). https://doi.org/10.1145/3336191.3371848
6. Bondarenko, A., et al.: Overview of Touché 2020: conversational and comparative argument retrieval. In: Working Notes of CLEF 2020 - Conference and Labs of the Evaluation Forum. CEUR Workshop Proceedings, CLEF and CEUR-WS.org (2020, to appear)
7. Bondarenko, A., et al.: Touché: first shared task on argument retrieval. In: Jose, J.M., et al. (eds.) ECIR 2020. LNCS, vol. 12036, pp. 517–523. Springer, Cham (2020). https://doi.org/10.1007/978-3-030-45442-5_67
8. Chernodub, A.N., et al.: TARGER: neural argument mining at your fingertips. In: Proceedings of the 57th Conference of the Association for Computational Linguistics, ACL 2019, pp. 195–200. Association for Computational Linguistics (2019). https://doi.org/10.18653/v1/p19-3031
9. Dumani, L., Neumann, P.J., Schenkel, R.: A framework for argument retrieval. In: Jose, J., et al. (eds.) ECIR 2020. LNCS, vol. 12035, pp. 431–445. Springer, Cham (2020). https://doi.org/10.1007/978-3-030-45439-5_29
10. Gienapp, L., Stein, B., Hagen, M., Potthast, M.: Efficient pairwise annotation of argument quality. In: Proceedings of the 58th Annual Meeting of the Association for Computational Linguistics, ACL 2020, pp. 5772–5781. Association for Computational Linguistics (2020). https://www.aclweb.org/anthology/2020.acl-main.511/
11. Järvelin, K., Kekäläinen, J.: Cumulated gain-based evaluation of IR techniques. ACM Trans. Inf. Syst. **20**(4), 422–446 (2002). http://doi.acm.org/10.1145/582415.582418

12. Jindal, N., Liu, B.: Identifying comparative sentences in text documents. In: Proceedings of the 29th Annual International Conference on Research and Development in Information Retrieval, SIGIR 2006, pp. 244–251. ACM (2006). https://doi.org/10.1145/1148170.1148215

13. Jindal, N., Liu, B.: Mining comparative sentences and relations. In: Proceedings of the 21st National Conference on Artificial Intelligence and the 18th Innovative Applications of Artificial Intelligence Conference, AAAI 2006, pp. 1331–1336. AAAI Press (2006). http://www.aaai.org/Library/AAAI/2006/aaai06-209.php

14. Kessler, W., Kuhn, J.: A corpus of comparisons in product reviews. In: Proceedings of the 9th International Conference on Language Resources and Evaluation, LREC 2014, pp. 2242–2248. European Language Resources Association (ELRA) (2014). http://www.lrec-conf.org/proceedings/lrec2014/summaries/1001.html

15. Levy, R., Bogin, B., Gretz, S., Aharonov, R., Slonim, N.: Towards an argumentative content search engine using weak supervision. In: Bender, E.M., Derczynski, L., Isabelle, P. (eds.) Proceedings of the 27th International Conference on Computational Linguistics, COLING 2018, pp. 2066–2081. Association for Computational Linguistics (2018). https://www.aclweb.org/anthology/C18-1176/

16. Ma, N., Mazumder, S., Wang, H., Liu, B.: Entity-aware dependency-based deep graph attention network for comparative preference classification. In: Proceedings of the 58th Annual Meeting of the Association for Computational Linguistics, ACL 2020, pp. 5782–5788. Association for Computational Linguistics (2020). https://www.aclweb.org/anthology/2020.acl-main.512/

17. Mass, Y., et al.: Word emphasis prediction for expressive text to speech. In: Proceedings of the 19th Annual Conference of the International Speech Communication Association, Interspeech 2018, pp. 2868–2872. ISCA (2018). https://doi.org/10.21437/Interspeech.2018-1159

18. Nadamoto, A., Tanaka, K.: A Comparative Web Browser (CWB) for browsing and comparing web pages. In: Proceedings of the 12th International World Wide Web Conference, WWW 2003, pp. 727–735. ACM (2003). https://doi.org/10.1145/775152.775254

19. Page, L., Brin, S., Motwani, R., Winograd, T.: The PageRank citation ranking: bringing order to the web (1998)

20. Palotti, J.R.M., Scells, H., Zuccon, G.: TrecTools: an open-source Python library for information retrieval practitioners involved in TREC-like campaigns. In: Proceedings of the 42nd International Conference on Research and Development in Information Retrieval, SIGIR 2019, pp. 1325–1328. ACM (2019). https://doi.org/10.1145/3331184.3331399

21. Panchenko, A., Bondarenko, A., Franzek, M., Hagen, M., Biemann, C.: Categorizing comparative sentences. In: Proceedings of the 6th Workshop on Argument Mining, ArgMining@ACL 2019, pp. 136–145. Association for Computational Linguistics (2019). https://doi.org/10.18653/v1/w19-4516

22. Potthast, M., et al.: Argument search: assessing argument relevance. In: Proceedings of the 42nd International Conference on Research and Development in Information Retrieval, SIGIR 2019, pp. 1117–1120. ACM (2019). https://doi.org/10.1145/3331184.3331327

23. Potthast, M., Gollub, T., Wiegmann, M., Stein, B.: TIRA integrated research architecture. Information Retrieval Evaluation in a Changing World. TIRS, vol. 41, pp. 123–160. Springer, Cham (2019). https://doi.org/10.1007/978-3-030-22948-1_5

24. Potthast, M., Hagen, M., Stein, B.: The dilemma of the direct answer. SIGIR Forum **54**(1) (2020). http://sigir.org/forum/issues/june-2020/

25. Schildwächter, M., Bondarenko, A., Zenker, J., Hagen, M., Biemann, C., Panchenko, A.: Answering comparative questions: better than ten-blue-links? In: Proceedings of the Conference on Human Information Interaction and Retrieval, CHIIR 2019, pp. 361–365. ACM (2019). https://doi.org/10.1145/3295750.3298916
26. Stab, C., et al.: ArgumenText: searching for arguments in heterogeneous sources. In: Proceedings of the Conference of the North American Chapter of the Association for Computational Linguistics, NAACL-HLT 2018, pp. 21–25. Association for Computational Linguistics (2018). https://doi.org/10.18653/v1/n18-5005
27. Sun, J., Wang, X., Shen, D., Zeng, H., Chen, Z.: CWS: a comparative web search system. In: Proceedings of the 15th International Conference on World Wide Web, WWW 2006, pp. 467–476. ACM (2006). https://doi.org/10.1145/1135777.1135846
28. Wachsmuth, H., et al.: Argumentation quality assessment: theory vs. practice. In: Proceedings of the 55th Annual Meeting of the Association for Computational Linguistics, ACL 2017, pp. 250–255. Association for Computational Linguistics (2017). https://doi.org/10.18653/v1/P17-2039
29. Wachsmuth, H., et al.: Building an argument search engine for the web. In: Proceedings of the 4th Workshop on Argument Mining, ArgMining@EMNLP 2017, pp. 49–59. Association for Computational Linguistics (2017). https://doi.org/10.18653/v1/w17-5106
30. Wachsmuth, H., Stein, B., Ajjour, Y.:"PageRank" for argument relevance. In: Proceedings of the 15th Conference of the European Chapter of the Association for Computational Linguistics, EACL 2017, pp. 1117–1127. Association for Computational Linguistics (2017). https://doi.org/10.18653/v1/e17-1105
31. Wachsmuth, H., Syed, S., Stein, B.: Retrieval of the best counterargument without prior topic knowledge. In: Proceedings of the 56th Annual Meeting of the Association for Computational Linguistics, ACL 2018, pp. 241–251. Association for Computational Linguistics (2018). https://www.aclweb.org/anthology/P18-1023/

Author Index

Printed in the United States
By Bookmasters

Printed in the United States
By Bookmasters